CREATED EQUAL

CREATED EQUAL

A SOCIAL AND POLITICAL
HISTORY OF THE UNITED STATES

BRIEF SECOND EDITION
VOLUME I ■ TO 1877

Jacqueline Jones
Brandeis University

Peter H. Wood
Duke University

Thomas Borstelmann
University of Nebraska

Elaine Tyler May
University of Minnesota

Vicki L. Ruiz
University of California, Irvine

PEARSON
Longman

New York San Francisco Boston
London Toronto Sydney Tokyo Singapore Madrid
Mexico City Munich Paris Cape Town Hong Kong Montreal

Executive Editor: Michael Boezi
Development Editor: Marion B. Castellucci
Assistant Development Manager: David Kear
Executive Marketing Manager: Sue Westmoreland
Supplements Editor: Brian Belardi
Production Manager: Ellen MacElree
Project Coordination, Text Design, and Electronic Page Makeup: Electronic Publishing Services Inc., NYC
Cover Design Manager: Wendy Ann Fredericks
Cover Designer: Base Art Co., Ltd.
Cover and frontispiece photos: ©National Archives/Corbis
Photo Researcher: Photosearch, Inc.
Manufacturing Buyer: Lucy Hebard
Printer and Binder: Courier/Kendallville
Cover Printer: Coral Graphics

Credits for literary selections, selected maps and figures, and photos not credited on page appear on pages C-1 to C-2.

Library of Congress Cataloging-in-Publication Data
Created equal : a social and political history of the United States / Jacqueline Jones ...
[et al.]. -- Brief 2nd ed.
    p. cm.
  Includes bibliographical references and index.
  ISBN-13: 978-0-321-42980-3 (Complete Edition)
  ISBN-10:   0-321-42980-X
1. United States--History. 2. United States--Social conditions. 3. United States--
Politics and government. 4. Pluralism (Social sciences)--United States--History. 5.
Minorities--United States--History. 6. Pluralism (Social sciences)--United States--History-
-Sources. 7. Minorities--United States--History--Sources.
E178.C86 2007
973--dc22

                                             200610165

Please visit our website at http://www.ablongman.com

ISBN-13: 978-0-321-42980-3 (Complete Edition)
ISBN-10:   0-321-42980-X

ISBN-13: 978-0-321-42981-0 (Volume I: To 1877)
ISBN-10:   0-321-42981-8

ISBN-13: 978-0-321-42979-7 (Volume II: From 1865)
ISBN-10:   0-321-42979-6

1 2 3 4 5 6 7 8 9 10—CRK—10 09 08 07

To our own teachers, who helped set us on the historian's path, and to our students, who help keep us there. You have touched our intellects, our hearts, and our lives.

A nuestros propios maestros, quienes nos ayudaron a seguir en el sendero de historiador, y a nuestros estudiantes que ayudan a mantenernos alli. Usted ha tocado nuestros intelectos, nuestros corazones, y nuestras vidas.

Brief Contents

Detailed Contents

Maps

Figures and Tables

Figures

Tables

Preface

> *"We hold these truths to be self-evident: That all men are created equal; that they are endowed by their Creator with certain unalienable rights; that among these are life, liberty, and the pursuit of happiness. . . . "*

Ever since the Continental Congress approved the Declaration of Independence on July 4, 1776, the noble sentiments expressed in the document have inspired people in the United States and around the world. The Founding Fathers conceived of the new nation in what we today would consider narrow terms—as a political community of white men of property. Gradually, as the generations unfolded, diverse racial and ethnic groups, as well as women of all backgrounds, cited the Declaration in their struggle to achieve a more inclusive definition of American citizenship. American history is the story of various groups of men and women, all "created equal" in their common humanity, claiming an American identity for themselves.

In fact, American history consists of many stories—the story of territorial growth and expansion, the story of the rise of the middle class, the story of technological innovation and economic development, and the story of U.S. engagement with the wider world. *Created Equal* incorporates these traditional narratives into a new and fresh interpretation of American history, one that includes the stories of diverse groups of people and explores expanding notions of American identity. Not surprisingly, when we first published our overview, it took us more than a thousand pages to tell this dramatic story. But even as the first full-length edition of *Created Equal* rolled off the press, we knew that we wanted to tackle a shorter version. Our aim was not merely to lighten students' backpacks. Instead, we hoped to make this rich saga more accessible to a broad audience, so we published a brief edition several years ago. Since then we have revised the full edition, and we have now taken time to craft a second brief edition as well.

The Second Edition

This second brief edition of *Created Equal* retains and strengthens the basic structure of the original brief text—its organization, themes, and style. This edition covers key events during both administrations of President George W. Bush, adding new material in sections titled "The President and the War on Terrorism," "Security and Politics at Home," "The War in Iraq," and "The Election of 2004 and After." The second edition also includes substantial revisions that reflect the suggestions of the many instructors who used the first edition in their classrooms.

First-time users of the book told us that they appreciated the elements that make *Created Equal* unique. These elements include a strong chronological narrative emphasizing significant political developments throughout American history, the stories of individuals that enliven the narrative, and the intertwining of four themes: our rich social diversity, the changing natural environment, class and power relations, and ongoing globalization: the vital intersection of foreign and domestic affairs. We added new material related to all of these themes.

Several new features enhance the book's accessibility for students. At the request of instructors we have included an "Interpreting History" primary document feature in each chapter, and the new topics covered by these primary materials vary widely. For the eighteenth century, documents include a brochure recruiting German immigrants to Carolina (Chapter 5), a surprising Proclamation of Independence from 1776 (Chapter 7), and a candid discussion of demobilization by a Revolutionary War soldier (Chapter 8). Among the new texts for the nineteenth century are documents describing opportunities for sheep farming in New Mexico (Chapter 11), a Southern labor contract during Reconstruction (Chapter 15), and Congressional testimony regarding conduct of the 1898 War in the Philippines (Chapter 18). The new "Interpreting History" features for the twentieth century include songs of the Great Depression (Chapter 22), a provocative sermon by Martin Luther King Jr. concerning the Vietnam War (Chapter 26), and the views of two ministers on religion and politics in the 1980s (Chapter 28). We have added study questions with each document to encourage students to hone their critical thinking skills. Also, a glossary at the back of the book defines terms that are highlighted in the body of the text, providing a handy reference for students as they read.

Perhaps most important of all—since historical interpretation never stands still, and new research calls for deeper discussion—we have enlivened the narrative with fresh material in many chapters. Chapter 2, for example, concludes with a new section on dramatic changes in the early Chesapeake economy entitled "Tobacco Becomes a Way of Life," and Chapter 10 contains a new section on "The Market Revolution" of the early nineteenth century. The next four chapters (11-14), incorporate new material on such varied topics as the Erie Canal, the treatment of the insane, the role of immigrants in the Confederacy, and General Custer's defeat at the Little Big Horn. New opening vignettes concern industrialist Andrew Carnegie (Chapter 16) and the attacks of September 11, 2001 (Chapter 30).

Four Themes

We have chosen to highlight four significant themes that run throughout American history.

- **Diversity.** In considering the theme of diversity, we acknowledge that the formation of social identity is a central element of the American story. We examine how individual Americans have understood and identified themselves by gender, religion, region, income, race, and ethnicity, among other factors. Native Americans, African Americans, Spanish-speaking inhabitants of the Southwest, Chinese immigrants, members of the laboring classes, women of all groups—all of these people have played a major role in defining what it means to be an American. At the same time, diverse forms of identity are by no means fixed or static. For example, in the early twentieth century, a Russian immigrant garment worker on New York's Lower East Side might think of herself in any number of ways—as a Jew, an employee, a union member, a single woman, a resident of a thriving city—and these forms of identity might change over time, depending on the woman's circumstances.

- **Class and systems of power.** Socioeconomic class and power systems have shaped American society in profound ways, and an understanding of them is fundamental to understanding events in American history. Class and power structures take many forms. The institution of slavery denied people of African descent basic human freedoms. Class differences based on income and formal education mocked broader ideals of social equality. Some groups used the law to deny other groups the right to participate in the political system. Popular ideas related to alleged social differences and innate inferiority served to justify the treatment of certain groups as second-class citizens. U.S. military leaders launched military campaigns against vulnerable peoples within and outside the nation's borders. By the end of the nineteenth century, the United States boasted the largest and most comfortable middle class in the world—and yet the most substantial political and economic power was distributed among a relatively small contingent of white men. During the twentieth century, Americans dismantled the legal system of inequality that reduced blacks, women, and other groups to second-class citizenship. Nevertheless, a growing gap between the rich and poor continued to mock the notion of true equality.

- **Globalization.** The globalization of the United States' economy and society increased in recent decades. But as an immigrant nation and the modern world's superpower,

America has long been engaged with the rest of the world. Since the earliest days of colonial settlement, Americans have traded goods, cultural practices, and ideas with peoples outside their borders. America's foreign and domestic relations have always been intertwined. After World War II, Americans' fears of communism and the Soviet Union exerted a profound effect upon the country's politics and society. In the wake of the terrorist attacks of September 11, 2001, all Americans were forced to confront the role of the United States in the larger world, with all the opportunities and dangers that role entailed.

- **Environment.** The role of the environment in American history has been significant. The physical landscape has profoundly shaped American society, and has in turn been shaped by it. The theme of the environment is key to understanding cultural, political, and economic developments. Many Native American groups shared a sense of oneness with the land; for them, the material and spiritual worlds were intimately related. In contrast, many European Americans saw the land as a means of making a living or making money, or as the source of valuable raw materials—in other words, as a thing to be bought, sold, and used. The vast richness of the American landscape has provoked violent conflict over the years, even as it has formed a key component in American wealth and power. We examine regional differences in all geographical areas—not just the eastern seaboard.

These four themes serve as the lenses through which we view the traditional narrative framework of American history. Readers of *Created Equal* will understand the major political developments that shaped the country's past, as well as the role of diverse groups in initiating and reacting to those developments. Chapter 13, for example, which focuses on the 1850s, includes a detailed account of the effects of the slavery crisis on Congress and the political party system, as well as a discussion of shifting group identities affecting Indians, Latinos, northern women, and enslaved and free blacks. Chapter 18, focusing on the 1890s, covers the rise of the Populist party and stirrings of American imperialism, as well as a discussion of barriers to a U.S. workers' political party and challenges to traditional gender roles. Thus, *Created Equal* builds upon the basic history that forms the foundation of most major textbooks and offers a rich and comprehensive look at the past by including the stories of all Americans.

Chronological Organization

One of the challenges in writing *Created Equal* has been to emphasize the way in which the four major themes come together and influence each other, affecting specific generations of Americans. Thus, the text is organized into ten parts, most of these covering a generation. Many textbooks organize discussions of immigrants, cities, the West, and foreign diplomacy (to name a few topics) into separate chapters that cover large time periods. In contrast, *Created Equal* integrates material related to a variety of topics within individual chapters. Although the text adheres to a chronological organization, it stresses coherent discussions of specific topics within that framework. This provides students with a richer understanding of events. Chapter 15, for example, which covers the dozen or so years after the end of the Civil War, deals with Reconstruction in the South, Indian wars on the High Plains, and the rise of the women's and labor movements, stressing the relationships among all these developments. To cite another example: many texts devote a chapter exclusively to America's post–World War II rise to global power; *Created Equal* integrates material related to that development in a series of six chapters that cover the period of 1945 to 2006. Each of these chapters illustrates the effects of dramatic world developments on American social relations and domestic policy on a decade-by-decade basis. This approach allows readers to appreciate the rich complexity of any particular time period and to understand that major events occur not in a vacuum, but in a larger social context.

Special Features

The book includes a number of features designed to make American history clear and engaging to the reader, and to encourage students to "do" history on their own. These features include:

- **Parts and timelines.** *Created Equal* consists of ten parts covering three chapters each. An opening section that lays out the basic themes of the period introduces each part. Each part opener also includes an illustrated timeline highlighting major events covered in the three chapters that follow.

- **Chapter introductory vignettes and conclusions.** Each chapter begins with a story that introduces the reader to groups and individuals representative of the themes developed in the chapter. Among the chapter introductory vignettes are the stories of a Norwegian immigrant woman in Wisconsin (Chapter 12), a group of runaway slaves accused of treason by Confederate authorities in wartime (Chapter 14), Spanish-speaking inhabitants of northern New Mexico struggling to retain their culture in the face of an onslaught of European American settlers (Chapter 17), and a Sioux Indian boy at a government boarding school (Chapter 18). At the end of each chapter, a concluding section sums up the chapter's themes and points the reader toward the next chapter.

- **Maps, charts, pullout quotes, and artifacts.** Illustrations—photographs, tables, pictures of objects from the time period, and figures—enhance the narrative. Large maps offer geographical detail and invite students to see the relationship between geography and history. Highlighted quotes help the reader grasp the chapter's major themes.

- **"Interpreting History."** Every chapter includes a boxed feature entitled "Interpreting History." Each full-page box consists of an intriguing primary document on a topic relevant to the chapter's themes. Through these documents, we hear the voices of a variety of Americans, such as an eighteenth-century Virginia slave, a council of Cherokee women, industrial titan Andrew Carnegie, and environmental activist Rachel Carson. We have added a brief introduction before each original text, and we have placed several questions at the end of the feature in order to guide study and prompt further discussion.

- **"Sites to Visit" and "For Further Reading."** At the end of each chapter is a list of "Sites to Visit," identifying sites on the World Wide Web relevant to the chapter and occasionally listing the location of important historical sites and landmarks as well. There is also a list of suggested works related to each section of the chapter. These features encourage students to follow up on major topics on their own—either on the computer or in the library.

- *New!* **MyHistoryLab Icons** Icons in the margins throughout the book identify additional materials on **MyHistoryLab.com**, Longman's premium Web site for U.S. history. Each icon indicates the type of resource—document, image, map, video, or audio—and is placed in context to relate directly to the chapter contents and themes.

- **Glossary.** The second edition includes a glossary of terms culled from the text and defined at the back of the book. Sample terms (out of several hundred) include pocket veto, aqueduct, canal locks, sit-down strike, antebellum, carpetbaggers, scalawags, vigilantes, and fatigue work. Glossary terms are highlighted in **boldface type** in the chapter text.

Combining Social and Political History

In designing this book, we have built upon a strong chronological foundation, emphasizing change over time. After all, it is important to understand events in their full contemporary context as they unfold. Within this logical and familiar chronological framework, the text offers a unique combination of social and political perspectives. *Created Equal* introduces students to recent scholarship in social history as well as providing a firm grounding in the traditional political narrative. In each period, from the distant past to the present day, we have interwoven the important political developments with the social and economic changes taking place throughout the country.

Along the way, we incorporate numerous groups and individuals who impelled, and experienced, the nation's most significant changes. Their stories, both familiar and unfamiliar, enliven the narrative and help to provide a more accurate, thorough, and compelling view of the American past. We hope that readers will gain an understanding of our country's social diversity but also learn about the power relations that have shaped our past—which groups have had influence and how they have maintained and wielded that influence. *Created Equal* tells the evolving saga of America in all its complexity. It is the story of a diverse and idealistic people—"created equal," yet struggling through generations to achieve true equality.

The Authors

Supplements For Qualified College Adopters

Instructor Supplements

• *Instructor Resource Center* This instructor-only resource allows you to browse and download book-specific instructor resources (see below) and to receive immediate access and instructions on installing course management content to your campus server. If you already have access to CourseCompass, you can log in to the IRC immediately using your existing login and password. Otherwise, please visit the Instructor Resource Center at **www.ablongman.com/irc** to register for access today.

• *Instructor's Manual* This book-specific supplement offers suggestions on how to generate lively class discussion and involve students in active learning, as well as a file of exam questions and lists of resources, including films, slides, photo collections, records, and audio cassettes. It was prepared by Yvonne Johnson of Central Missouri University and Nancy Zens of Central Oregon Community College. ISBN: 0-205-56251-5.

• *Test Bank* Prepared by David Rice of the University of Florida, this test bank contains more than 3,500 objective, conceptual, and essay questions. All questions are keyed to specific pages in *Created Equal,* Brief Edition. ISBN: 0-205-56248-5.

• *TestGen-EQ Computerized Testing System* This flexible, easy-to-master computerized test bank includes all of the items in the printed test bank. The software allows instructors to edit existing questions and to add their own items. Tests can be printed in several different formats and can include features such as graphs and tables. ISBN: 0-205-53007-9.

• *Text-Specific Transparency Set* A set of full-color transparencies showing maps from the comprehensive edition of *Created Equal.* The transparencies are available for download at **www.ablongman.com/irc**.

• *PowerPoint Presentations* These presentations prepared to accompany the comprehensive version of *Created Equal* may include key points and terms for a lecture on the chapter, as well as full-color slides of selected important maps, graphs, and charts within a particular chapter. The presentations are available for download at **www.ablongman.com/irc**.

• *History Digital Media Archive CD-ROM* This resource contains electronic images, interactive and static maps, and video clips. ISBN: 0-321-14976-9.

• *Visual Archives of American History, Updated Edition* Available on two CD-ROMs, this encyclopedic collection of instructor resources contains dozens of narrated vignettes and videos, as well as hundreds of photos and illustrations. ISBN: 0-321-18694-X.

• *Discovering American History Through Maps and Views Transparencies* This set of 140 full-color acetates contains an introduction to teaching history through maps and a detailed commentary on each transparency. Prepared by Gerald Danzer of the University of Illinois at Chicago, the collection includes pictorial maps, views, photos, urban plans, building diagrams, and works of art. The transparencies are available for download at **www.ablongman.com/irc**.

• *History Video Program* Qualified adopters are granted access to our list of over 250 videos for classroom use. Adopters can choose 1 video per 100 books that are ordered each semester (maximum of 3 for each adopter). Videos are available for virtually every topic of United States history.

• *Readers and Biographies—Available at Half Price!* Qualified adopters can choose from more than 100 half-priced options to supplement *Created Equal*, Brief Second Edition. From comprehensive readers and brief biographies to discounted Penguin books, Longman has a wide selection of products to broaden your students' history experience beyond the textbook. To learn more about this special offer, visit us at **www.ablongman.com/historyvaluepacks**.

Student Supplements

• *Voices of* **Created Equal** This collection of primary sources, tied to the table of contents of *Created Equal,* includes both classic and lesser-known documents describing the rich mosaic of American life from the pre-contact era to the present day. Ranging from letters, diary excerpts, stories, and novels, to speeches, court cases, and government reports, these sources tell the story of American history in the words of those who lived it. These titles are available at no additional cost when bundled with a *Created Equal* text. Volume I ISBN: 0-321-39591-3; Volume II ISBN: 0-321-39599-9.

• *Study Guide* Created by William Pelz of De Paul University, each volume includes chapter outlines, significant themes and highlights, a glossary, learning enrichment ideas, sample test questions, exercises for identification and interpretation, and geography exercises based on maps in the brief version of *Created Equal.* Volume I ISBN: 0-205-56249-3; Volume II ISBN: 0-205-56250-7.

• *Study Card for American History* Students are given a chronological context to understand important political, diplomatic, social, economical, cultural, and technological events in American history on this study card. This study card is available at no additional cost when valuepacked with a new book. ISBN: 0-321-29232-4.

• *Research Navigator™ Guide* This guidebook includes exercises and tips on how to use the Internet to further your study of American history. It also includes an access code for Research Navigator™—the easiest way for students to start a research assignment or research paper. Research Navigator™ is composed of three exclusive databases of credible and reliable source material including EBSCO's ContentSelect™ Academic Journal Database, *New York Times* Search by Subject Archive, and "Best of the Web" Link Library. This comprehensive site also includes a detailed help section. Also Available on MyHistoryLab. ISBN: 0-205-40838-9.

• *Longman American History Atlas* A full-color reference tool and visual guide to American history that includes almost 100 maps and covers the full scope of history. The Atlas is $3.00 when bundled with a new book. ISBN: 0-321-00486-8.

• *Mapping American History,* **Third Edition** This two-volume workbook, written by Sharon Bollinger of El Paso Community College, presents the basic geography of the United States, helping students place the history of the United States into perspective. Available at no additional cost to qualified college adopters when bundled with a new book. Volume I ISBN: 0-321-47559-3; Volume II ISBN: 0-321-47560-7.

Supplements for Students and Instructors

• *MyHistoryLab* MyHistory Lab is a comprehensive collection of Longman's online multimedia resources. Instructive, intuitive, and interactive, MyHistoryLab allows both students and professors to be a few clicks away from a host of materials that support your American history survey course: primary sources; maps and illustrations; quizzes and review materials; and an electronic version of the textbook itself. MyHistoryLab gives students dozens of different avenues in which to learn, explore, and analyze the material outside of the classroom, no matter what type of learner they are. One-Semester Student Access Code Card ISBN: 0-205-53961-0; Two-Semester Student Access Code Card ISBN: 0-205-53956-4; Course Compass Student Access Code Card ISBN: 0-205-53960-2; BlackBoard WEB CT Student Access Code Card ISBN: 0-205-55039-8. Available for purchase at **www.myhistorylab.com**, or packaged at no additional charge with your textbook.

• *MyHistoryKit* MyHistoryKit for American history contains a sampling of Longman's premium history content from MHL. This Web site includes practice tests to challenge students' knowledge, learning objectives and chapter summaries introducing the major American history topics, flashcards for help with studying and remembering terms and events, Web links to assist in the research process, media and primary source activities (documents, maps, video and audio clips, and more), and Research Navigator™. Available for purchase at **www.myhistorykit.com** or packaged at no additional cost with your textbook.

• *American History Study Site* The American History Study Site is an open-access Web site that is designed to support all of Longman's American history survey titles. Organized by topic, this Web site includes practice tests to challenge students' knowledge, flashcards for help with studying and remembering terms and events, and Web links to assist in the research process.

Meet the Authors

Jacqueline Jones teaches American history at Brandeis University, where she is Harry S. Truman Professor. She was born in Christiana, Delaware, a small town of 400 people in the northern part of the state. The local public school was desegregated in 1955, when she was a third grader. That event, combined with the peculiar social etiquette of relations between blacks and whites in the town, sparked her interest in American history. She attended the University of Delaware in nearby Newark and went on to graduate school at the University of Wisconsin, Madison, where she received her Ph.D. in history. Her scholarly interests have evolved over time, focusing on American labor, and women's, African American, and southern history. In 1999 she received a MacArthur Fellowship. One of her biggest challenges has been to balance her responsibilities as teacher, historian, wife, and mother (of two daughters). She is currently working on a history of Savannah, Georgia, during the Civil War era (1854–1872). She is the author of several books, including *Soldiers of Light and Love: Northern Teachers and Georgia Blacks* (1980); *Labor of Love, Labor of Sorrow: Black Women, Work, and Family Since Slavery* (1985), which won the Bancroft Prize and was a finalist for a Pulitzer Prize; *The Dispossessed: America's Underclasses Since the Civil War* (1992); and *American Work: Four Centuries of Black and White Labor* (1998). In 2001 she completed a memoir that recounts her childhood in *Christiana: Creek Walking: Growing Up in Delaware in the 1950s.*

Peter H. Wood was born in St. Louis (before the famous arch was built). He recalls seeing Jackie Robinson play against the Cardinals, visiting the courthouse where the *Dred Scott* case originated, and traveling up the Mississippi to Hannibal, birthplace of Mark Twain. Summer work on the northern Great Lakes aroused his interest in Native American cultures, past and present. He studied at Harvard (B.A., 1964; Ph.D., 1972) and at Oxford, where he was a Rhodes Scholar (1964–1966). His pioneering book *Black Majority* (1974), concerning slavery in colonial South Carolina, won the Beveridge Prize of the American Historical Association. Since 1975 he has taught early American history at Duke University, where he also coached the women's lacrosse club for three years. The topics of his articles range from the French explorer LaSalle to Gerald Ford's pardon of Richard Nixon. In 1989 he coedited *Powhatan's Mantle: Indians in the Colonial Southeast.* His demographic essay in that volume (now in a new edition) provided the first clear picture of population change in the eighteenth-century South. His most recent books are *Strange New Land: Africans in Colonial America* (2003) and *Weathering the Storm: Inside Winslow Homer's "Gulf Stream"* (2004). Dr. Wood has served on the boards of the Highlander Center, Harvard University, Houston's Rothko Chapel, the Menil Foundation, and the Institute of Early American History and Culture in Williamsburg. He is married to colonial historian Elizabeth Fenn; his varied interests include archaeology, documentary film, and growing gourds. He keeps a baseball bat used by Ted Williams beside his desk.

Thomas ("Tim") Borstelmann, the son of a university psychologist, taught and coached at the elementary and high school levels in Washington state and Colorado before returning to graduate school. From 1991 to 2003, he taught American history at Cornell University while living in Syracuse, New York, before becoming the Elwood N. and Katherine Thompson Distinguished Professor of Modern World History at the University of Nebraska–Lincoln. He lives with his wife, a health care administrator, and two sons in Lincoln. An avid bicyclist, runner, swimmer, and cross-country skier, he earned his B.A. from Stanford University in 1980 and Ph.D. from Duke University in 1990. He became a historian to figure out the Cold War and American race relations, in part because he had grown up in the South. His first book, concerning American relations with southern Africa in the mid-twentieth century, won the Stuart L. Bernath Book Prize of the Society for Historians of Foreign Relations. His second book, *The Cold War and the Color Line,* appeared in 2001. His commitment to the classroom earned him a major teaching award at Cornell, the Robert and Helen Appel Fellowship. He found writing *Created Equal* a natural complement to what he does in the classroom, trying to provide both telling details of the American past and the broad picture of how the United States has developed as it has. A specialist in U.S. foreign relations and modern world history, he is equally fascinated with domestic American politics and social change. He is currently working on a book about the United States and the world in the 1970s.

Elaine Tyler May grew up in the shadow of Hollywood, performing in neighborhood circuses with her friends. She went to high school before girls could play on sports teams, so she spent her after-school hours as a cheerleader and her summer days as a bodysurfing beach bum. Her passion for American history developed in college when she spent her junior year in Japan. The year was 1968. The Vietnam War was raging, along with turmoil at home. As an American in Asia, often called on to explain her nation's actions, she yearned for a deeper understanding of America's past and its place in the world. She returned home to study history at UCLA, where she earned her B.A., M.A., and Ph.D. She has taught at Princeton and Harvard Universities and since 1978 at the University of Minnesota. She has written four books examining the relationship between politics, public policy, and private life. Her widely acclaimed *Homeward Bound: American Families in the Cold War Era* was the first study to link the baby boom and suburbia to the politics of the Cold War. The *Chronicle of Higher Education* featured *Barren in the Promised Land: Childless Americans and the Pursuit of Happiness* as a pioneering study of the history of reproduction. *Lingua Franca* named her coedited volume *Here, There, and Everywhere: The Foreign Politics of American Popular Culture* a "Breakthrough Book." She served as president of the American Studies Association in 1996 and as Distinguished Fulbright Professor of American History in Dublin, Ireland, in 1997. She is married to historian Lary May and has three children, who have inherited their parents' passion for history.

Vicki L. Ruiz is a professor of history and Chicano/Latino studies at the University of California, Irvine. She is currently chair of the department of history. For her, history remains a grand adventure, one that she began at the kitchen table, listening to the stories of her mother and grandmother, and continued with the help of the local bookmobile. She read constantly as she sat on the dock, catching small fish ("grunts") to be used as bait on her father's fishing boat. As she grew older, she was promoted to working with her mother, selling tickets for the *Blue Sea II.* The first in her family to receive an advanced degree, she graduated from Gulf Coast Community College and Florida State University, then went on to earn a Ph.D. in history at Stanford in 1982, the fourth Mexican American woman to receive a doctorate in history. Her first book, *Cannery Women, Cannery Lives,* received an award from the National Women's Political Caucus, and her second, *From Out of the Shadows: Mexican Women in 20th-Century America,* was named a *Choice* Outstanding Academic Book of 1998 by the American Library Association. She is coeditor with Ellen Carol Dubois of *Unequal Sisters: A Multicultural Reader in U.S. Women's History.* She and Virginia Sánchez Korrol have also edited the three-volume *Latinas in the United States: A Historical Encyclopedia* and a recent anthology *Latina Legacies.* Ruiz and Sánchez Korrol were recognized by *Latina Magazine* as Latinas of the Year in Education for 2000 and in 2005 they received a "21 Leaders for the 21st Century" award by women's e-news network. In addition, she and Donna Gabaccia have completed the anthology *American Dreaming, Global Realities: Re-Thinking U.S. Immigration History.* Active in student mentorship projects, summer institutes for teachers, and public humanities programs, Dr. Ruiz served as an appointee to the National Council of the Humanities. A fellow in the Society of American Historians, she was elected to the national governing bodies of the American Historical Association, the Organization of American Historians, and the American Studies Association. Currently, she is immediate past president of both the Berkshire Conference of Women Historians and the Organization of American Historians. She is also the president-elect of the American Studies Association. The mother of two grown sons, she is married to Victor Becerra, urban planner and gourmet cook extraordinaire.

Acknowledgments

As authors, we could not have completed this project without the loving support of our families. We wish to thank Jeffrey Abramson, Lil Fenn, Lynn Borstelmann, Lary May, and Victor Becerra for their interest, forbearance, and encouragement over the course of several editions. Our own children have been a source of inspiration, as have our many students, past and present. We are grateful to scores of colleagues and friends who have helped shape this book, both directly and indirectly, in more ways than they know. Along the way, Matt Basso, Chad Cover, Eben Miller, Andrea Sachs, Mary Strunk, and Melissa Williams provided useful research and administrative assistance; their help was invaluable. Louis Balizet provided careful reading of several chapter drafts.

Our friends at Longman have continued their generous support and assistance for our efforts. We thank all the creative people associated with Longman (and there are many) who have had a hand in bringing this book to life. We are especially grateful to Michael Boezi and Marion Castellucci for their care and encouragement in bringing this edition to life. Former Development Manager Betty Slack improved the text in lasting ways; Executive Marketing Manager Sue Westmoreland and her great sales force have embraced the book with enthusiasm. We also acknowledge with gratitude the contributions of Managing Editor Val Zaborski, Production Manager Ellen MacElree, and Production Editor Scott Hitchcock and the staff at Electronic Publishing Services Inc. who put the finishing touches on this brief second edition and deftly guided it through the many phases of production.

Finally, we wish to express our deep gratitude to the following individuals who read and commented on the first brief edition. Their thoughtful criticism, advice, and suggestions have all helped improve the book.

S. Carol Berg
College of St. Benedict

Roger Bromert
Southwestern Oklahoma State University

Charlotte Brooks
State University of New York— Albany

Eduardo Canedo
Columbia University

Nancy Carnevale
Montclair State University

John A. Collins
Freed-Hardeman University

Cole P. Dawson
Warner Pacific College

Barbara C. Fertig
Armstrong Atlantic State University

Van Forsyth
Clark College

Martin Hershock
University of Michigan, Dearborn

Richard Hughes
Eastern Oregon University

Kimberly Jensen
Western Oregon University

Cynthia M. Kennedy
Clarion University of Pennsylvania

Annette Laing
Georgia Southern University

Michael Lansing
Augsburg College

Carolyn J. Lawes
Old Dominion University

Sandy Moats
University of Wisconsin— Parkside

Earl F. Mulderink
Southern Utah University

C. Samuel Nelson II
Ridgewater College

Jason C. Newman
Cosumnes River College

David R. Novak
Purdue University

Melissa Soto-Schwartz
Cuyahoga Community College

Deborah Syrdal
Humboldt State University

Michael M. Topp
University of Texas, El Paso

Sylvia Tyson
Texas Lutheran University

Mark D. Van Ells
Queenborough Community College, CUNY

David Voelker
University of Wisconsin— Green Bay

Charles Westmoreland
University of Mississippi

Julie Winch
University of Massachusetts, Boston

David Wolcott
Miami University

Jason Young
State University of New York, Buffalo

This brief edition owes much to the many conscientious historians who reviewed the full-length edition of the textbook. For their insights and constructive critiques, we are indebted to the following reviewers.

Ken Adderley
Upper Iowa University

Leslie Alexander
Ohio State University

Marynita Anderson
Nassau Community College

John Andrew
Franklin and Marshall College

Abel Bartley
University of Akron

Donald Scott Barton
Central Carolina Technical College

Mia Bay
Rutgers University

Chris Bierwith
Treasure Valley Community College

Charles Bolton
University of Arkansas at Little Rock

Susan Burch
Gallaudet University

Tommy Bynum
Georgia Perimeter College

Robert B. Carey
Empire State College–SUNY

Todd Carney
Southern Oregon University

Kathleen Carter
Highpoint University

Jonathan Chu
University of Massachusetts

Barak Cook
University of Missouri

Amy E. Davis
University of California–Los Angeles

Judy DeMark
Northern Michigan University

James A. Denton
University of Colorado

Joseph A. Devine
Stephen F. Austin University

Margaret Dwight
North Carolina Agricultural and Technical University

Nancy Gabin
Purdue University

Lori Ginzberg
Pennsylvania State University

Gregory Goodwin
Bakersfield College

Amy S. Greenberg
Pennsylvania State University

Charlotte Haller
Worcester State College

Nadine Isitani Hata
El Camino College

James Hedtke
Cabrini College

Traci Hodgson
Chemeketa Community College

Rose Holz
University of Nebraska—Lincoln

Fred Hoxie
University of Illinois

Tera Hunter
Carnegie Mellon University

Creed Hyatt
Lehigh Carbon Community College

David Jaffe
City College of New York

Jeremy Johnson
Northwest College

Yvonne Johnson
Central Missouri State University

Kurt Keichtle
University of Wisconsin

Anne Klejment
University of St. Thomas

Dennis Kortheuer
California State University–Long Beach

Joel Kunze
Upper Iowa University

Joseph Laythe
Edinboro College of Pennsylvania

Chana Kai Lee
Indiana University

Dan Letwin
Pennsylvania State University

Gaylen Lewis
Bakersfield College

Kenneth Lipartito
Florida International University

Kyle Longley
Arizona State University

Edith L. Macdonald
University of Central Florida

Lorie Maltby
Henderson Community College

Sandra Mathews-Lamb
Nebraska Wesleyan University

Constance M. McGovern
Frostburg State University

Henry McKiven
University of South Alabama

James H. Merrell
Vassar College

Carl Moneyhan
University of Arkansas—Little Rock

Earl Mulderink
Southern Utah State University

Jason C. Newman
Consumnes River College

Steven Noll
University of Florida

Jim Norris
North Dakota State University

Elsa Nystrom
Kennesaw State University

Keith Pacholl
California State University–Fullerton

William Pelz
Elgin Community College

Melanie Perrault
University of Central Arkansas

Delores D. Petersen
Foothill College

Robert Pierce
Foothill College

Louis Potts
University of Missouri–Kansas City

Sarah Purcell
Central Michigan University

Niler Pyeatt
Wayland Baptist University

Steven Reschly
Truman State University

Arthur Robinson
Santa Rosa Junior College

Robert E. Rook
Fort Hays State University

Thomas J. Rowland
*University of
Wisconsin–Oshkosh*

Steven Ruggles
University of Minnesota

Leonard J. Sadosky
Iowa State University

Rebecca Shoemaker
Indiana State University

Howard Shore
Columbia River High School

James Sidbury
University of Texas

Arwin D. Smallwood
Bradley University

Margaret Spratt
*California University of
Pennsylvania*

Rachel Standish
Foothill College

Jon Stauff
St. Ambrose University

David Steigerwald
Ohio State University–Marion

Kay Stockbridge
*Central Carolina Technical
College*

Daniel Thorp
Virginia Tech University

Michael M. Topp
University of Texas–El Paso

Clifford Trafzer
*University of
California–Riverside*

Deborah Gray White
Rutgers University

Scott Wong
Williams College

Bill Woodward
Seattle Pacific University

Nancy Zens
*Central Oregon Community
College*

David Zonderman
*North Carolina State
University*

CREATED EQUAL

PART ONE

North American Founders

WE SOMETIMES CALL THE FRAMERS OF THE U.S. CONSTITUTION America's Founding Fathers, using capital letters for emphasis. The men who met in Philadelphia in 1787 were indeed founders in a political sense, having drafted our enduring frame of government. But the 1780s seem recent in relation to most of North America's long human history. We must explore far back in time, long before the eighteenth century, to find the varied men and women who were the continent's first founders.

Two kinds of foundation builders emerge: the distant ancestors of today's Native Americans and newcomers from abroad who colonized North America in the sixteenth and seventeenth centuries.

Our earliest human ancestors evolved in Africa and then spread across the landmass of Eurasia. In the Southern Hemisphere, they managed to cross to Australia some 40,000 years ago, but evidence suggests that they reached the Americas from Asia much later, probably less than 20,000 years ago. These first human arrivals took advantage of the land bridge that joined Siberia to Alaska when Ice Age glaciers prompted a dramatic decline in sea levels. Roughly 14,000 years ago, these hunters apparently bypassed melting glaciers to reach the North American interior. They came on foot, but additional newcomers may have skirted the Pacific coast in small boats or even drifted across the South Pacific.

We still understand very little about these earliest Americans. What we do know is that they spread rapidly across North America over the next thousand years, and they continued to hunt mammoths and other large animals until these ancient species became extinct. Later, their descendants adapted to a wide range of different environments, learning to fish, hunt for smaller game, and gather berries. It has been 10,000 years since the extinction of the mammoths and 3,000 years since the early signs of agriculture in the Americas. By A.D. 500 complex societies were beginning to appear in equatorial America, and a succession of diverse and rich societies had arisen in the Americas by the time a second set of founders appeared around A.D. 1500.

Although Vikings from Scandinavia had preceded Christopher Columbus by five centuries, their small outpost on the coast of Newfoundland lasted only a few years. In contrast, when Columbus reached the West Indies and returned to Spain in 1492, his voyage launched a human and biological exchange between the Eastern and Western Hemispheres that has never ceased. Spanish and Portuguese ships initiated this exchange, but they were soon followed by vessels from England, France, and Holland. Half a century after Columbus's first voyage, Spanish overland expeditions had already pushed from Florida to Arkansas and from Mexico to Kansas. French explorers, hoping to find a Northwest Passage to Asia, had penetrated far up the St. Lawrence River in Canada.

Europeans brought new materials such as iron and new animals such as horses, cattle, and pigs. They also brought deadly diseases previously unknown in the Americas, such as measles and smallpox, which had a catastrophic impact on Native American societies. By 1565 Europeans had established their first lasting outpost in the North American continent, the town of St. Augustine in Spanish Florida. Two decades later the English tried, unsuccessfully, to plant a similar colony at Roanoke Island along the coast of what is now North Carolina.

In the first decades of the seventeenth century, permanent European settlements took hold at Quebec on the St. Lawrence River and at Santa Fe near the Rio Grande. A transatlantic outpost of English society appeared at Jamestown on Chesapeake Bay in 1607. Farther north, behind the sheltering hook of Cape Cod, other settlers formed additional coastal outposts and renamed the region New England.

Numbers were small at first, but these communities and others endured and expanded, often with crucial help from Native Americans who knew the keys to survival in their own domains. The gradual success of these European footholds prompted imitation and competition; colonizers clashed with each other and with longtime Indian inhabitants over control of the land and its resources. Disappointed in their early searches for easy mineral wealth, the new arrivals made do in various ways: cutting timber, catching fish, raising tobacco, or trading for furs. The French in particular, with aid once again from Native Americans, explored the interior of the continent. By 1700 they had laid claim to the entire Mississippi River valley and established a colony on the Gulf of Mexico.

Each new colonizing enterprise in the seventeenth century took on a distinctive life of its own—or, rather, numerous lives. First of all, there was the internal life of the community: who would be allowed to take part, how would participants govern themselves, and how would they subsist? In each instance, relations with the region's native inhabitants constituted a second unfolding story. Complicated ties to Europe—economic, religious, social, and political—made a third crucial narrative. Furthermore, relations between colonies and between the distant European powers that backed them had a determining influence, as when England took over the Dutch colony at New Netherland in the third quarter of the seventeenth century. Finally, there was the compelling drama of the newcomers' relationship to the environment itself. These founding generations labored to understand—or to subdue and exploit without fully understanding—the continent they had started to colonize.

1519 to 1522	Magellan's ship circumnavigates the globe and returns to Spain
1533	Pizarro overthrows Inca Empire in Peru
1534 to 1543	Expeditions of Cartier (Canada), de Soto (Southeast), and Coronado (Southwest) probe North America
1565	Spanish establish St. Augustine
1577 to 1580	Voyage of Drake challenges Spanish dominance in the Pacific
1585 to 1590	English attempt to establish Roanoke colony fails
1588	Spanish Armada fails in effort to invade England
1599	Spanish colonize New Mexico
1607	England's Virginia Company launches colony at Jamestown
1620	*Mayflower* passengers establish Plymouth Colony
1630	English Puritans found Massachusetts Bay Colony
1637	Pequot War in New England
1660	Restoration of monarchy in England under Charles II
1664	Charles II grants charter to his brother James, Duke of York, sanctioning the takeover of the Dutch New Netherland colony and the creation of New York
1675 to 1676	Metacom's War in New England
1676	Bacon's Rebellion in Virginia
1680	Pueblo Revolt in New Mexico
1681	Quaker William Penn receives charter for Pennsylvania
1682	La Salle explores the Mississippi River and claims Louisiana for France
1689	Dutch leader William of Orange and his wife Mary become joint English sovereigns in the Glorious Revolution, replacing King James II
1691	Witchcraft trials in Salem, Massachusetts
1699	Iberville begins colony in French Louisiana
1711 to 1715	Tuscarora Indians in North Carolina, and then the Yamasee in South Carolina, resist English colonial expansion

CHAPTER

1

First Founders

ONE DAY IN 1908, A COWBOY NAMED GEORGE MCJUNKIN WAS CHECKING FENCES ON A CATTLE ranch near Folsom, New Mexico, when something strange caught his eye. McJunkin noticed several large bones protruding from the earth. Dismounting from his horse, he also spotted an old arrowhead, something common in these parts. But it was the bones beside it that seemed unusual. They were larger than cattle bones and buried under layers of dirt, so McJunkin decided to show them to others.

Nearly twenty years later, ancient-bones expert Jesse Figgins came to Folsom after seeing McJunkin's evidence. Soon Figgins unearthed an extensive bone bed containing the remains of twenty-three large Ice Age bison of a species that had been extinct for 10,000 years. He also uncovered a spear point, clearly fashioned by human hands, embedded between two bison ribs. Figgins's finds confirmed McJunkin's earlier discovery. The objects stirred first disbelief and then excitement, for they proved that human hunters had existed in North America 7,000 years earlier than scientists had supposed. The discovery of the thin projectile tips, named Folsom points

■ In 1908 a discovery by African American cowboy George McJunkin started a revolution in American archaeology.

after the site, sparked a revolution in North American archaeology.

In 1908, the year of McJunkin's discovery, the nation still had a great deal to learn about the oldest chapters in American history. The United States had just commemorated the 300th anniversary of England's Jamestown settlement in Virginia, and across the country, U.S. citizens memorialized Anglo-American beginnings. Textbooks of the era paid scant attention to the earlier Spanish and French arrivals in North America and none at all to the Native American inhabitants who had preceded them by thousands of years.

In the century since George McJunkin picked up a prehistoric bison bone, all of that has changed. Scholars who explore and debate the long history of early North America have steadily learned more about the continent's first inhabitants. An expanding American history now stretches back in time far before the Jamestown settlement and reaches broadly from coast to coast. Its earliest roots lie with the indigenous inhabitants of the continent over many millennia. In addition, the foreigners who suddenly intruded into portions of the Native American world in the sixteenth century—speaking Spanish, French, and occasionally English—also represent a significant beginning. All these people now number, in different ways, among America's first founders.

Ancient America

The discoveries at Folsom more than doubled archaeologists' estimates of the time span that humans had lived in North America. Clearly, they had resided on the continent for at least 10,000 years.

After the Folsom find, collectors soon located additional evidence at nearby Clovis, New Mexico, 170 miles south of Folsom and close to the Texas border. In 1929 a teenager reported spotting large, well-chipped spearheads near Clovis. Three years later, amateur collectors located more in the same vicinity, this time beside the tooth of an extinct mammoth. These so-called Clovis points lay beneath a soil layer containing Folsom points, so they were clearly older than McJunkin's and Figgins's finds.

Since then, scientists have unearthed Clovis-like points throughout much of North America. According to the latest calculations, humans started creating these weapons roughly 13,900 years ago and ceased about 12,900 years ago. This means that people were hunting widely on the continent nearly 14,000 years ago. Archaeologists continue to push back and refine the estimated date for the appearance of the first people in the Americas. Recently, they have unearthed evidence suggesting the possible presence of pre-Clovis inhabitants.

The Question of Origins

Like all other peoples, the Native American societies whose ancestors have lived in America for at least 14,000 years retain rich and varied accounts of their own origins. No amount of scientific data can diminish or replace the powerful creation stories, in the Americas or elsewhere throughout the world, that have been passed down from distant ancestors and continue to serve an important cultural purpose. Nevertheless, modern researchers continue to compile evidence about the origin and migrations of the diverse peoples whom explorer Christopher Columbus mistakenly lumped together as "Indians" more than 500 years ago.

DOCUMENT

Iroquois Creation Story

Scientists have determined that it was scarcely 70,000 years ago when the most recent ancestors of modern humans moved from Africa to spread across the Eurasian landmass, the area comprising Europe and Asia. By 40,000 years ago some of these Stone Age hunter-gatherers had already reached Australia. Others lived on the steppes of central Asia and the frozen **tundra** of Siberia. They had perfected the tools they needed to survive in a cold climate: flint spear points for killing mammoths, reindeer, and the woolly rhinoceros; and bone needles to sew warm, waterproof clothes out of animal skin.

Over thousands of years, bands of these northern hunters migrated east across Siberia in search of game. Eventually they arrived at the region where the Bering Strait now separates Russia from Alaska. Between 25,000 and 11,000 years ago, cold conditions expanded arctic ice caps, trapping vast quantities of the earth's water in the form of huge **glaciers**. As a result, ocean levels sank by 300 feet—enough to expose a bridge of land 600 miles wide between Asia and America.

The Bering Land Bridge formed part of a frigid, windswept region known as Beringia. Small groups of people could have subsisted in this cold landscape by hunting mammoths

■ Archaeologists digging at Cactus Hill, Virginia, and several other sites have unearthed artifacts that suggest human habitation before the arrival of hunters using Clovis points. The foreground objects are laid out clockwise by apparent age, with the most recent at the top. Clovis-like spearheads appear in the second group. The third and fourth groups, taken from lower layers of soil, are thought to be older items, some reaching back well beyond 14,000 years. With the most primitive tools, it becomes difficult to separate implements made by humans from natural rock fragments.

and musk oxen until Ice Age glaciers receded about 14,000 years ago. As the climate warmed and the ocean rose again, some might have headed farther east onto higher ground in Alaska. If so, these newcomers would have been cut off permanently from Siberia as water once more submerged the land bridge. But the same warming process also eventually opened a pathway through the glaciers blanketing northern America.

IMAGE

Clovis Points

This ice-free corridor along the eastern slope of the Rocky Mountains could account for the sudden appearance of Clovis hunters across much of North America nearly 14,000 years ago. Small bands of people, armed with razor-sharp Clovis points, spread rapidly across the continent, destroying successive herds of large animals that had never faced human predators before. According to this theory, generations of hunters (known as **Paleo Indians**) could have migrated as far as the tip of South America within several thousand years.

In recent decades, three new developments have complicated the picture. At Cactus Hill, Virginia, and other sites, archaeologists have uncovered artifacts suggesting the presence of immediate predecessors to the Clovis people. In addition, a provocative discovery in South America—a campsite at Monte Verde, Chile, dating back more than 14,000 years—suggests to some that small groups may have used a coastal route around the North Pacific rim to reach the Americas by water. Meanwhile, genetic comparisons of different peoples, present and past, are yielding increasingly specific, if controversial, details about ancient migrations and interactions. Advances in understanding DNA—the genetic material that determines our physical make-up and transmits it to our offspring—may someday sharpen or change our awareness regarding the origins of the earliest Paleo-Indians.

Genetic comparisons of different peoples are yielding increasingly specific, if controversial, details about ancient migrations and interactions.

The Archaic World

Some 10,000 years ago, the Paleo-Indian period in North America gradually gave way to the **Archaic** period, which lasted for roughly 7,000 years. Major changes in wildlife played a large part in the transition. As the continent warmed further and the great glaciers receded north, more than 100 of America's largest species disappeared. These included mammoths, mastodons, horses, camels, and the great long-horned bison. Researchers debate whether these large animals were hunted to extinction, wiped out by disease, or destroyed by climate change.

Human groups had to adapt to the shifting conditions. They developed new methods of survival. Inhabitants turned to the smaller bison, similar to modern-day ones, that had managed to survive and flourish on the northern plains. Archaic-era hunters learned to drive herds over cliffs and use the remains for food, clothing, and tools. A weighted spear-throwing device, called an **atlatl**, let hunters bring down medium-sized game. Archaic peoples also devised nets, hooks, and snares for catching birds, fish, and small animals. By 4,000 years ago, they were even using duck decoys in the Great Basin of Utah and Nevada.

Though genetically similar, these far-flung bands of Archaic Indians developed diverse cultures as they adapted to very different landscapes and environments. Nothing illustrates this diversity more clearly than speech. A few early languages branched into numerous language families, then divided further into hundreds of separate tongues. Similar cultural variations emerged in everything from diet and shelter to folklore and spiritual beliefs.

The Rise of Maize Agriculture

One condition remained common to all the various Archaic American groups, despite their emerging regional differences: they all shared a lack of domesticated animals. Archaic Indians, like their Asian forebears, did possess dogs, and settlers in the Andes domesticated the llama over 5,000 years ago. But no mammal remaining in the Americas could readily be made to provide humans with milk, meat, hides, and hauling power.

Although their prospects for domesticating animals were severely limited, early Americans had many more options when it came to the domestication of plants. Humans managed to domesticate plants independently in five different areas around the world, and three of those regions were located in the Americas. First, across parts of South America, inhabitants learned to cultivate root crops of potatoes and manioc (also known as cassava, which yields a nutritious starch). Second, in **Mesoamerica** (modern-day Mexico and Central America), people gradually brought squash, beans, and maize (corn) under cultivation—three foods that complement one another effectively in dietary terms.

Maize agriculture became a crucial ingredient for the growth of complex societies in the Americas, but its development and diffusion took time. Unlike wheat, the Eurasian cereal crop which offered a high yield from the start, maize took thousands of years of cultivation in the Americas to evolve into an extremely productive food source. The differences between Mesoamerica and North America proved substantial when it came to mastering maize agriculture. Southwestern Indians in North America began growing thumb-sized ears of maize only about 3,000 years ago (at a time of increasing rainfall), well after the crop had taken hold in Mesoamerica. More than a thousand years later, maize reached eastern North America, where it adapted slowly to the cooler climate and shorter growing season.

In the east, a different agriculture had already taken hold, centered on other once-wild plants. This was the third zone where the independent domestication of plants occurred in the Americas. As early as 4,000 years ago, eastern Indians at dozens of Archaic sites were cultivating squash and sunflowers. These domesticated plants provided supplemental food sources for eastern communities that continued to subsist primarily by hunting and gathering until the arrival of maize agriculture in the eastern woodlands during the first millennium A.D.

About 3,000 years ago, as maize cultivation began in the Southwest and gardens of squash and sunflowers appeared in the Northeast, the first of several powerful Mesoamerican cultures—the Olmec—emerged in the lowlands along the southwestern edge of the Gulf of Mexico. Their name meant "those who live in the land of rubber," for they had learned how to turn the milky juice of several plants into an unusual elastic substance. The Olmec grew maize

Southwestern Indians in North America began growing thumb-sized ears of maize only about 3,000 years ago.

and manioc in abundance, and their surplus of food supported a hierarchical society. They built large burial mounds and pyramids, revered the jaguar in their religion, developed a complex calendar, and played a distinctive game with a large ball of solid rubber. Since they traded widely with people across Mesoamerica, they passed on these cultural traits, which reappeared later in other societies in the region.

Olmec traders, traveling by coastal canoe, may even have encountered and influenced the Poverty Point culture that existed in northeast Louisiana 4,200 to 2,700 years ago. The Poverty Point culture, with a trade network on the lower Mississippi River and its tributaries, stands as a mysterious precursor to the mound-building societies of the Mississippi Valley that emerged much later. Remnants of these more extensive Mississippian cultures still existed when newcomers from Europe arrived to stay, around 1500. In many parts of North America, smaller and less stratified Archaic cultures remained intact well into the era of European colonization. To subsist, they combined hunting for a variety of animals with gathering and processing local plant foods.

A Thousand Years of Change: 500 to 1500

The millennium stretching from the fifth century to the explorations of Columbus in the fifteenth century witnessed dramatic and far-reaching changes in the separate world of the Americas. In the warm and temperate regions on both sides of the equator, empires rose and fell as maize agriculture and elaborate irrigation systems provided food surpluses, allowing the creation of cities and the emergence of hierarchical societies.

On the coast of Peru, the expansive Inca empire emerged in the 1400s, building on previous societies. Inca emperors, ruling from the capital at Cuzco, prompted the construction of a vast road system throughout the Peruvian Andes. Stonemasons built large storage facilities at provincial centers to hold food for garrisons of soldiers and to store tribute items such as gold and feathers destined for the capital. Until the empire's fall in the 1530s, officials leading pack trains of llamas ferried goods to and from Cuzco along mountainous roadways.

Similarly, Mesoamerica also saw a series of impressive civilizations—from the Maya to the Aztec—in the millennium spanning 500 to 1500 in the western calendar. Developments in North America in the same millennium were very different but bear enough resemblance to patterns in Mesoamerica to raise intriguing and still unanswerable questions. Did significant migrations northward from Mesoamerica ever take place? And if not, were there substantial trade links at times, allowing certain materials, techniques, ideas, and seeds to reach North American peoples? Or did the continent's distinctive societies, such as the Anasazi in the Southwest and the Cahokia mound builders on the Mississippi River, develop almost entirely independently?

Valleys of the Sun: The Mesoamerican Empires

Pre-Columbian Societies of the Americas

In Mesoamerica, the Maya and the Aztec established rich empires where worship of the sun was central to their religious beliefs. Mayan culture flourished between 300 and 900. The Maya controlled a domain stretching from the lowlands of the Yucatan peninsula to the highlands of what is now southern Mexico, Guatemala, Honduras, and El Salvador. They derived their elaborate calendar—a fifty-two-year cycle made up of twenty-day months—and many other aspects of their culture from the earlier Olmec, but they devised their own distinctive civilization. The Maya built huge stone temples and held ritual bloodletting ceremonies to appease their gods. Recently, researchers have deciphered the complex pictographs,

■ **MAP 1.1**
AMERICA BEFORE COLUMBUS   Distinctive cultures emerged in the Americas during the ten centuries
before 1500. But debate continues over the extent of trade and travel networks at any given time.

Indians of the Ancient Southwest
- Hohokam
- Anasazi
- Mogollon

Indians of Mesoamerica
- Maya   Toltec   Aztec

Indians of Eastern North America
- Hopewell
- Mississippian
- Northern Iroquoian

Indians of South America
- Moche
- Inca

or glyphs, that appear throughout Mayan art, yielding. New discoveries are pushing back
the earliest dates for Mayan culture.

The Maya declined rapidly after 750, and dominance in Mesoamerica moved farther west,
where great cities had arisen in central Mexico. The people who constructed the metropolis
of Teotihuacan in the Mexican highlands remain an enigma. They appear to have traded with
the Maya and perhaps with the Olmec before that. They laid out their immense city in a grid,
dominated by the 200-foot Pyramid of the Sun. By 500, the city held more than 100,000 inhabitants, making it one of the largest in the world. But Teotihuacan's society declined fast, for
unknown reasons, succeeded first by the Toltec and then by the Aztec.

The Aztec (or Mexica) had migrated to the central Valley of Mexico from the north in
the twelfth century. Looked down upon at first by the local people, they swiftly rose to power
through strategic alliances and military skill. According to legend, the Aztec's war god instructed
their priests to locate the place where a great eagle perched on a cactus. They found such a spot,

on a swampy island in Lake Texcoco. By the 1400s the Aztec had transformed the island into Tenochtitlán, an imposing urban center, located on the site of modern Mexico City.

The impressive city of Tenochtitlán, surrounded by Lake Texcoco and linked to shore by causeways, became the Aztec capital. Its architecture imitated the ruined temple city of Teotihuacan, which lay 35 miles to the north. The Aztec also adopted many other features of the cultures they had displaced. They used the cyclical fifty-two-year Mesoamerican calendar, and they worshipped the great god Quetzalcoatl, the plumed serpent associated with wind and revered by the Toltec, their predecessors in the Valley of Mexico.

> *Like the Inca of Peru, the Aztec imposed harsh treatment on the peoples they conquered, extracting heavy annual taxes.*

Eager to expand their empire, the Aztec launched fierce wars against neighboring lands. But their primary objective was not to kill enemies or gain more territory. Instead, Aztec warriors demanded tribute and took prisoners from the people they subdued. They then sacrificed numerous captives at pyramid temples to **placate** the gods. These deities, they believed, would in turn protect them as they conducted further wars of capture, leading to more tribute and sacrifices.

Like the Inca of Peru, the Aztec imposed harsh treatment on the peoples they conquered, extracting heavy annual taxes. This ruthless policy caused outlying provinces to resent Aztec authority and made the centralized empire vulnerable to external attack. When a foreign assault prompted the empire's downfall in the early sixteenth century, the challenge came from a direction Aztec priests and generals could not predict.

The Anasazi: Chaco Canyon and Mesa Verde

The great urban centers of Peru and Mesoamerica had no counterparts farther north. The peoples inhabiting North America in the millennium before Columbus never developed the levels of social stratification, urban dynamism, architectural grandeur, astronomical study, or intensive corn agriculture that characterized the Maya, Inca, or Aztec. Yet elements of all these traits appeared in North America, especially in the Southwest and the Mississippi Valley, with the emergence of increasingly settled societies and widening circles of exchange. Could north–south movements back and forth have occurred? Links of migration or trade would help to explain the dozens of ancient ball courts, similar to those in Mesoamerica, that archaeologists have excavated in Arizona. Recently, researchers have identified a north–south traffic in turquoise, highly prized in both Mexico and the Southwest.

Three identifiably different cultures were already well established in the North American Southwest by the year 500. The Mogollon occupied the dry, mountainous regions of eastern Arizona and southern New Mexico. Mogollon women were expert potters who crafted delicate bowls from the clay of the Mimbres River. Families lived in sunken pit houses that were cool in summer and warm in winter. The Hohokam, their neighbors to the west in south-central Arizona, constructed extensive canal and floodgate systems to irrigate their fields from the Gila and Salt rivers.

Farther north, where Utah and Colorado meet Arizona and New Mexico, lived the people remembered as the Anasazi, or "ancient ones." By 750 the Anasazi inhabited aboveground houses of masonry or adobe clustered around a circular ceremonial room dug into the earth. They entered this sunken religious chamber, known as a kiva, by descending a ladder through the roof. The climb back up symbolized the initial ascent of humans into the Upper World from below. European explorers later used the Spanish word for town, *pueblo*, to describe the Anasazis' multiroom and multistory dwellings.

Beginning in the 850s, Chaco Canyon in the San Juan River basin of northwest New Mexico emerged as the hub of the Anasazi world. Wide, straight roads radiating out from Chaco let builders haul hundreds of thousands of logs for use as roof beams in the nine great pueblos that still dot the canyon. The largest, Pueblo Bonito, rises five stories high in places and has 600 rooms arranged in a vast semicircle.

After 1130, a prolonged drought gripped the area, and the turquoise workshops of Chaco Canyon fell silent. Many of the inhabitants headed north, where dozens of Anasazi communities with access to better farming conditions dotted the landscape. Gradually—with populations growing, the climate worsening, and competition for resources stiffening—the Anasazi moved into sheltered cliff dwellings such as Cliff Palace at Mesa Verde in southwestern Colorado, with its 220 rooms and twenty-three kivas. Reached only by ladders and steep trails, these pueblos offered protection from enemies and shelter from the scorching summer sun. Still, another prolonged drought (1276–1299) forced the Anasazi to move once again by 1300. Survivors dispersed south into lands later occupied by the Hopi, Zuni, and Rio Grande peoples.

The Mississippians: Cahokia and Moundville

In the Mississippi Valley, the Hopewell people had prospered for half a millennium before A.D. 500 (during the era of Europe's Roman Empire). The Hopewell lived mainly in Ohio and Illinois. But their network of trade extended over much of the continent. Hopewell burial sites have yielded pipestone and flint from the Missouri River valley, copper and silver from Lake Superior, mica and quartz from Appalachia, seashells and shark teeth from Florida, and artwork made from Rocky Mountain obsidian and grizzly-bear teeth.

Hopewell trading laid the groundwork for larger mound-building societies, known as the Mississippian cultures, that emerged in the Mississippi Valley and the Southeast in roughly the same centuries as the great civilizations of Mesoamerica and the Anasazi in the Southwest. The Mississippian tradition developed gradually after 500. Then after 900, it flourished broadly for six centuries.

Shifts in technology and agriculture facilitated the rise of the Mississippians. Bows and arrows, long used in arctic regions of North America but little known elsewhere, began to see widespread use in the eastern woodlands around 700. At the same time, maize underwent a transformation from a marginal oddity to a central staple crop. Across the east, food supplies expanded as Native American communities planted corn in the rich bottomland soil along the region's many rivers. With greater productivity, commercial and religious elites took advantage of farmers and asserted stronger control over the community's increasing resources.

Separate Mississippian mound-building centers have been found as far apart as Spiro, in eastern Oklahoma, and Etowah, in northern Georgia. The largest complex was at Cahokia in the 25-mile floodplain below where the Illinois and Missouri rivers flow into the Mississippi. On Cahokia Creek, near East St. Louis, Illinois, dozens of rectangular, flat-topped temple mounds still remain after almost a thousand years. The largest mound—indeed, the largest ancient earthwork in North America—rises 100 feet in four separate levels, covering 16 acres and using nearly 22 million cubic feet of earth. Nearby, residents erected forty-eight posts in a huge circle, 410 feet in diameter. This creation, now called Woodhenge after England's Stonehenge, functioned as a calendar to mark the progression of the sun throughout each year.

IMAGE

Reconstructed View of Cahokia

Cahokia's mounds rose quickly in the decades after 1050, as the local population expanded beyond 10,000. A succession of powerful leaders reorganized the vicinity's small, isolated villages into a strong regional chiefdom that controlled towns on both sides of the Mississippi River. These towns provided the chiefdom's centralized elite with food, labor, and goods for trading. Around 1100, the population of Cahokia perhaps exceeded 15,000 people. It then waned steadily over the next two centuries as the unstable hierarchy lost its sway over nearby villages. As Cahokia declined, other regional chiefdoms rose along other rivers. The most notable appeared at Moundville in west-central Alabama, 15 miles south of modern Tuscaloosa. The site, with more than twenty flat-topped mounds, became a dominant ceremonial center in the thirteenth century. But by 1400, a century before the appearance of Europeans, Moundville's Mississippian elites had started to lose their power.

■ The most striking Mississippian earthwork to survive is the enigmatic Serpent Mound, built in the eleventh century by the Fort Ancient people in southern Ohio. The snake (holding an egg in its mouth) has links to astronomy because its curves are aligned toward key positions of the sun. The serpent may even represent Halley's Comet, which blazed in the heavens in A.D. 1066. Completely uncoiled, the earthwork would measure more than a quarter mile in length.

Linking the Continents

Estimates vary widely, but probably around one-sixth of the world's population—as many as 60 to 70 million people—resided in the Americas when Columbus arrived in 1492. Most of them lived in the tropical zone near the equator, but roughly one-tenth of the hemisphere's population (6 to 7 million) dwelt in North America, spread from coast to coast.

We cannot rule out the appearance in America of ancient ocean travelers on occasion. Around 400, Polynesian mariners sailed their double-hulled canoes from the Marquesas Islands in the South Pacific to the Hawaiian **archipelago**. Conceivably, in the millennium before 1500, one or two boats from Africa, Ireland, Polynesia, China, or Japan sailed—or were blown—to the American mainland. But any survivors of such a journey would have had little genetic or cultural impact, for no sustained back-and-forth contact between the societies occurred. Even the seafaring Norse from Scandinavia, known as Vikings, never established a lasting colony. Their brief settlement at L'Anse aux Meadows a thousand years ago is now well documented, but they remained only a few years at this coastal site in northern Newfoundland. Native American societies, therefore, knew nothing of the people, plants, animals, and microbes of the Eastern Hemisphere.

America's near isolation ended dramatically, beginning in the late fifteenth century, after innovations in deep-sea sailing opened the world's oceans as a new frontier for human exploration. Chinese sailors in the North Pacific or Portuguese mariners in the South Atlantic could well have been the first outsiders to establish ongoing contact with the peoples of the Western Hemisphere. Instead, it was Christopher Columbus, an Italian navigator in the service of Spain, who became the agent of this sweeping change. He encountered the Americas by accident and misinterpreted what he had found. But his chance encounter with a separate realm would spark new patterns of human migration, cultural transfer, and ecological exchange that would reshape the modern world.

Oceanic Travel: The Norse and the Chinese

Scandinavian settlers had colonized Ireland in the 830s and Iceland in the 870s. A century later, these seafarers—led by Erik the Red—reached Greenland in the 980s. When Erik's son Leif learned that Norse mariners blown off course had sighted land farther west, he sailed from Greenland to the North American coast. Here he explored a region near the Gulf of St. Lawrence that he named Vinland.

Around 1000, Leif Eriksson's relatives directed several return voyages to Vinland, where Norse Vikings built an outpost. The tiny colony of 160 people, including women and children, lived and grazed livestock in Vinland for several years until native peoples drove them away. The Greenlanders returned occasionally to cut timber, and they traded with inhabitants of northeastern Canada for generations. But by 1450 Norse settlements in Greenland had died out completely.

Whether sailors in Europe knew much about Norse exploits in the North Atlantic remains a mystery. What Europeans did know, vaguely, was the existence of the distant Chinese Empire. They called the realm Cathay, a term used by Italian merchant Marco Polo, who journeyed from Venice across Asia along the fabled Silk Road in the 1270s. Polo returned to Italy in 1292 to publish his *Travels*, an account of adventures in China during the reign of Kublai Khan.

Marco Polo told of many things unknown to Europeans, including rocks that burned like wood (coal) and spices that preserved meat. Asian spices such as nutmeg, cinnamon, pepper, ginger, and cloves, if they could be obtained, would offer new preservatives. When renewed Islamic power in the Middle East cut off the Silk Road to Cathay, Europeans searched for other ways to reach that far-off region.

The desire to obtain oriental spices at their source fueled European oceanic exploration, leading eventually to the transformation of the Americas. Yet it was China, not Europe, that first mastered ocean sailing on a large scale. Chinese strength in overseas exploration and trade reached its height in the early fifteenth century under Admiral Zheng He (pronounced "Jung Huh"). Between 1405 and 1433, this brilliant officer led seven large fleets to the Indian Ocean, sailing as far as east Africa. His immense treasure ships, 400 feet long and equipped with cannon, carried strange items—even giraffes—home to Asia.

Then, abruptly, China turned away from the sea, losing its opportunity to become the first global maritime power and to play a leading role in shaping oceanic trade and the destiny of North America. Within a century of Zheng He's accomplishments, the royal court grew dismissive of foreign trade and turned inward. Chinese officials destroyed the log books of earlier voyages and curtailed production of oceangoing vessels. Instead of powerful China on the Pacific, it was tiny Portugal, overlooking the Atlantic from the Iberian peninsula, that emerged as the leader in maritime innovation and exploration in the fifteenth century.

Portugal and the Beginnings of Globalization

Geography and religious zeal helped to spur Portugal's unlikely rise to world prominence. Its strategic location also exposed the tiny country to the ongoing conflict between Christianity and Islam. The religion founded by Muhammad (born at Mecca in 570) had spread rapidly across North Africa from Arabia. By the eighth century, followers of Islam (known as Muslims, Moslems, or Moors) had crossed the Straits of Gibraltar to establish a kingdom

Topkapi Serail Museum/AKG Photo

■ This Atlantic chart illustrates key aspects of Portuguese success in overseas exploration. Cape St. Vincent (A) where Prince Henry built his headquarters at Sagres, lies near the Strait of Gibraltar (B), the narrow entrance to the Mediterranean Sea. As Henry's mariners explored along the African coast for a sea passage to Asia, they also looked for possible allies such as Prester John, a mythical black king (C). They used the island groups of the eastern Atlantic to check their position: Azores (D), Madeiras (E), Canaries (F). Their small caravels (G) adopted the triangular lateen sail seen on traditional Arab boats in the Red Sea. Larger square-rigged ships that later sailed from Portugal to India (H) also incorporated lateen sails on a mast at the stern (I). A skilled Turkish navigator—who had never sailed on the Atlantic—made this unusual map in 1513. Piri Re'is used charts captured from a Christian ship in the Mediterranean; his inscriptions (J) are in Turkish.

in southern Spain. Centuries later, Spanish and Portuguese Christians rallied to force Islam out of the Iberian peninsula—a campaign that concluded in 1492—and to join other militant Europeans in fighting against Islamic power in the Middle East.

When Christian crusades to the holy land failed to defeat Islam and reopen overland trade routes to China, European strategists dreamed of skirting Africa by sea to reach Asia. The Portuguese were well positioned to lead this flanking movement around the areas under Muslim control. And if no such oceanic route to Asia existed, some speculated that Portuguese exploration south by sea still might provide links to a strong Christian ally. Fanciful rumors persisted regarding a wealthy black Christian ruler somewhere in Africa known as Prester John.

Intellectual and economic motives also existed for Portuguese ventures beyond the Sahara Desert, along the coast of sub-Saharan Africa. Such journeys, presenting new challenges in shipbuilding and navigation, could boost European knowledge of the unknown and open new markets. The first step involved an investment of leadership and resources, before early efforts could bear fruit and give the exploration process a momentum of it own.

Prince Henry of Portugal (1394–1460) provided these initial ingredients. In 1415 the young prince—later honored as "Henry the Navigator"—had crossed the Straits of Gibraltar to fight Muslims at Ceuta in North Africa. Committed to the campaign against Islam, Henry then waged a religiously inspired crusade-at-sea, building his headquarters at Sagres in southwest Portugal. From there, his sailors launched a far-reaching revolution in human communication and trade, perhaps the most momentous single step in a globalization process that continues to the present day.

Henry's innovative ships, known as caravels, pushed south along the African coast. Their narrow hulls were well suited for ocean sailing, and they used triangular lateen sails, an idea that Mediterranean sailors had borrowed from Arab boats on the Red Sea. The lateen sail let a vessel travel into the breeze, tacking back and forth on a zigzag course against a prevailing wind. (Vessels carryng only traditional square sails could not do this, making their voyages longer and more difficult.) Henry's experts at Sagres drew on the work of Jewish cartographers to develop state-of-the-art charts, astronomical tables, and navigational instruments. By the 1440s, his captains had mastered the winds and currents off western Africa. They began trading in gold and ivory, and, most ominously, they began buying African slaves and selling them in Europe. But when Henry died in 1460, his mariners had only sailed as far as what is now Sierra Leone.

Looking for the Indies: Da Gama and Columbus

During the 1480s, following a war with Spain, the Portuguese renewed their African designs. In 1482 they erected a trading fort called Elmina Castle on the Gold Coast (modern Ghana) to guard against Spanish competition and to support exploration toward the east. Finally, in 1487, Bartolomeu Dias rounded the southernmost tip of Africa, around the Cape of Good Hope, proving that a link existed between the Atlantic and Indian oceans. The Portuguese could now sail to India and tap into the rich spice trade. Success came a decade later with the voyage of Vasco da Gama (1497–1499). When his ship returned to Portugal from India laden with pepper and cinnamon, Europeans realized they had finally opened a southeastern sea route to the silk and spice markets of the East.

Meanwhile, the rulers of rival Spain, who were reconquering their realm from Muslim control at great expense, gambled on finding a profitable *westward* route to the Indies. In 1492, King Ferdinand and Queen Isabella finally succeeded in driving Islam from their realm by military means. The monarchs imposed Christian orthodoxy and forced Jews into exile. That same year, they agreed to sponsor an Atlantic voyage by an Italian-born navigator, Christopher Columbus. Leaving Spain with ninety men aboard three small vessels, Columbus headed for the Canary Islands and then sailed due west on September 6. After a voyage of three or four weeks, he expected to encounter the island of Cipangu (Japan), which Marco Polo had mentioned, or to reach the coast of Asia.

Why these huge misunderstandings? The mariner made several crucial mistakes. Like others, Columbus knew the world was round, not flat. He also accepted the idea of the ancient geographer Ptolemy that by using north–south lines, one could divide the globe into 360 degrees of longitude. But he questioned Ptolemy's estimate that each degree measures 50 nautical miles at the equator. (Each actually measures 60 miles.) Instead, Columbus accepted an alternative figure of 45 miles, making the circumference of his theoretical globe 25 percent smaller than the real distance around the earth. Besides *under*estimating the world's circumference, he compounded his error by *over*estimating two other crucial distances: the breadth of the Eurasian landmass and the extent of Japan's separation from China. The first distance is actually 130 degrees of longitude, and the second is 20. Columbus used authorities who suggested 225 and 30 degrees, respectively. His estimates placed Japan 105 degrees closer to Europe (at the longitude that runs through western Cuba) and well within reach.

Early on October 12, after weeks without sight of any land, the worried crew finally sighted a small island, naming it San Salvador after their Christian savior. The inhabitants proved welcoming, and Columbus recorded pleasure over the "gold which they wear hanging from their noses. But I wish to go and see if I can find the island of Cipangu." He did find a large and beautiful island (Cuba, not Cipangu), and he estimated that the Asian mainland of the Great Khan was only "a 10 days' journey" farther west. He claimed a nearby island as La Isla Española, the Spanish island, or Hispaniola (current-day Haiti and the Dominican Republic). He noted stories of hostile islanders farther south

Courtesy, Bancroft Library, University of California, Berkeley (SF309 G7 M25 1769 pl.20)

■ Horses, absent from the Americas for nearly 10,000 years, returned aboard Spanish ships. They awed Native Americans at first and played a crucial role in European conquests. "After God," the Spanish wrote, "we owe victory to the horses."

The largest Chinese vessels of Zheng He (400 ft.) were nearly five times longer than Columbus's flagship (85 ft.).

PACIFIC OCEAN

NORTH AMERICA

ATLANTIC OCEAN

Columbus (first voyage)

CUBA

Line created by Treaty of Tordesillas (1494)

Orinoco R.

SOUTH AMERICA

Magellan

Strait of Magellan

Major expeditions

- - - Marco Polo: from Venice (1271) to China along the Silk Road
——— Zheng He: from China to East Africa with a fleet of huge ships (1420s)
——— Prince Henry's ships: from Portugal as far as Sierra Leone (1420–1460)
——— Columbus: first voyage west from Spain via Canary Islands (1492–1493)
——— Da Gama: from Portugal to India via Cape of Good Hope (1497–1499)
——— Magellan's circumnavigation, completed by his crew (1519–1522)

■ **MAP 1.2**
OPENING NEW OCEAN PATHWAYS AROUND THE GLOBE, 1420–1520 In the 1420s, ships from Portugal and China explored opposite coasts of Africa. But China withdrew from oceanic trade, and European mariners competed to explore the world by sea. Within a century, Magellan's ship had circled the globe for Spain. The colonization in North America is a chapter in this larger saga of exploration.

called Caribs, or Caniba, who were said to devour their enemies. "I repeat," he asserted, "the Caniba are no other than the people of the Grand Khan." (Upon hearing of these fierce Caribs, Europeans soon fashioned the word *cannibal* and named the region the Caribbean.)

Bolstered by these encounters, the explorers returned hastily across the Atlantic on a more northerly route. They weathered a horrendous winter storm to reach Spain in March 1493. Columbus told the Spanish court that he had reached the Indies off the Asian coast, and he displayed several natives he called "Indians" to prove it. His three later voyages did not shake this belief, which he clung to until his death in 1506. Columbus had not reached the lands he sought, but his exploits would have immediate and extraordinary consequences.

DOCUMENT

From the Journal of Christopher Columbus

In the Wake of Columbus: Competition and Exchange

Within months of Columbus's return, the pope in Rome issued a papal bull, or decree. This pronouncement, titled *Inter Caetera*, viewed the whole world as the rightful inheritance of Christianity. It brashly divided the entire earth between two Christian powers, Spain and Portugal, by drawing a line down through the western Atlantic Ocean from the North

Pole to the South Pole. For 180 degrees west of the line, the Spanish alone could continue to seek access to Asia. East of the line, on the other half of the globe, Portugal would have a monopoly. The two Iberian powers affirmed this division of the earth in the Treaty of Torde-sillas (1494).

European navigators and cartographers quickly began to comprehend the geographic reality that Columbus had so thoroughly misunderstood. When Amerigo Vespucci, another Italian in the service of Spain, crossed the South Atlantic in 1499, he described what he saw not as part of Asia but as a *Mundus Novus*, or New World. European geographers wrote his name, *America*, across their maps. Meanwhile, a third Italian navigator—John Cabot (or Caboto)—obtained a license from the English king, Henry VII, to probe the North Atlantic for access to Cathay. In 1497 Cabot sailed west from Bristol across the Atlantic to Newfoundland and perhaps Nova Scotia. Clearly, the ventures of Columbus had sparked widespread excitement and curiosity in European ports, and increasing knowledge fueled greater transatlantic contact.

After thousands of years, the long separation of the hemispheres had been broken. The destinies of the world's most divergent continents swiftly became linked. Those links fostered human migrations of an unprecedented scale. With European ships came transfers of seeds and viruses, bugs and birds, plants and animals that forever reshaped the world. Scholars call this phenomenon the **Columbian Exchange**. The term also underscores the two-way nature of the flow. West across the Atlantic went horses, cows, sheep, pigs, chickens, and honeybees and important foods such as sugar cane, coffee, bananas, peaches, lemons, and oranges. But Europeans' westbound ships also carried devastating diseases unknown in the Americas, such as smallpox, measles, malaria, and whooping cough. East in the opposite direction traveled corn, potatoes, pumpkins, chili peppers, tobacco, cacao, pineapples, sunflowers, turkeys—and perhaps syphilis. The planet and all its inhabitants would never be the same again.

IMAGE

Early Botanical Illustrations— New World Plants

Spain Enters the Americas

Throughout the sixteenth century, European mariners, inspired by the feats of Columbus and da Gama, risked ocean voyaging in hopes of scoring similar successes. Those who survived brought back novelties for consumers, information for geographers, and profits for ship owners. New wealth prompted further investment in exploration, and expanding knowledge awakened cultural changes for both explorers and the people they met. The dynamic European era known as the Renaissance owed much to overseas exploration. Returning mariners brought reports of surprising places and people. Their experiences challenged the inherited wisdom of traditional authorities and put a new premium on rational thought, scientific calculation, and careful observation of the natural world.

In turn, Europe's Renaissance, or rebirth, stimulated ever wider exploration as breakthroughs in technology and navigation yielded practical results. Sailing south around Africa and then east, Portuguese caravels reached China by 1514 and Japan by 1543. Sailing west, Spanish vessels learned first that the Caribbean did not offer a passage to Asia and then in 1522—through Magellan's global voyage—that the ocean beyond America was enormous. In the West Indies, and then elsewhere in the Western Hemisphere, Native Americans began to pay dearly for the exchange that ships from Spain had initiated.

The Devastation of the Indies

Spanish arrival in the West Indies in 1492 triggered widespread ecological and human disaster within decades. Well-armed and eager for quick wealth, the early colonizers brought havoc to the Taino Indians and Caribs who inhabited the islands. The strange newcomers killed and enslaved native peoples and extracted tribute from the survivors in the form of gold panned from streams. Spanish livestock trampled or consumed native gardens, prompting severe food shortages. Worse, European diseases ravaged countless villages. The West Indian population plummeted as island societies totaling more than 1 million lost nineteen of every twenty people within a generation.

This near-extinction had three consequences. First, when Dominican friars reached Cuba in 1510, these devout missionaries denounced Spanish brutality as sinful. The Indians, they argued, possessed souls that only Christian baptism could save. A Spanish soldier named Bartholomé de Las Casas, who repented and joined the Dominican order, led the outcry for reform. In his scathing exposé titled *The Devastation of the Indies*, he opposed genocide and urged conversion.

Second, in response to the steep drop in population, Spanish colonizers began importing slaves from Africa to replace the decimated Indian workforce. The same Christians who bemoaned Native American enslavement (including Las Casas) justified this initiative and overlooked the contradictions. The first importation of Africans came in 1502, following the Portuguese **precedent** in the Azores.

Third, decimation in the islands prompted the Spanish to intensify their explorations. They sought new sources of Indian labor close at hand, fresh lands to exploit, and easy passageways to the Pacific. They pushed out from the Caribbean in several directions. In 1510, they established an outpost on the Atlantic coast of Panama. From there, Vasco Núñez de Balboa pressed across the **isthmus** to glimpse the Pacific in 1513. That same year, Juan Ponce de León sailed northwest from Puerto Rico, where he had amassed a fortune as governor. Despite later tales that he sought a fountain of youth, he actually hoped the nearby land, which he named Florida, would yield new gold and slaves. But the peninsula's Indians were already familiar with Spanish raiders; they turned Ponce de León away after he claimed the region for Spain.

The Spanish Conquest of the Aztec

By 1519, the Spanish had determined that the Gulf of Mexico offered no easy passage to Asia. They needed fresh alternatives. In Spain, crown officials sought someone to sail southwest, around the South American continent that Columbus and Vespucci had encountered. For this perilous task, they recruited a Portuguese navigator named Ferdinand Magellan, who had sailed in the Indian Ocean. On his epic voyage (1519–1522), Magellan located a difficult passage through the tip of South America—now called the Strait of Magellan—and revealed the vast width of the Pacific, which covers one-third of the earth's surface. Warring factions in the Philippines killed Magellan and twenty-seven of his men, but one of his ships made it back to Spain, becoming the first vessel to circumnavigate the globe.

As news of Magellan's voyage raced through Spain in 1522, word also arrived that a Spanish soldier, or *conquistador*, named Hernán Cortés had toppled the gold-rich empire of the Aztec in central Mexico. Like other ambitious conquistadores, Cortés had followed Columbus to the Caribbean. In 1519, hoping to march overland to the Pacific as Balboa had done, Cortés sailed along Mexico's east coast and established a base camp at Vera Cruz. He quickly realized he had reached the edge of a powerful empire.

As the Indian population of the Caribbean plummeted in the face of new diseases and exploitation, the Spanish began importing Africans to the New World as slaves. Many were put to work mining precious metals. Here men are forced to dig for gold nuggets beside a mountain stream, then wash them in a tub and dry them over a fire, before handing them to their Spanish master to weigh in his hand-held scale.

At Tenochtitlán the Aztec emperor, Moctezuma, reacted with uncertainty to news that bearded strangers aboard "floating islands" had appeared off his coast. If the newcomers' leader was the returning god Quetzalcoatl, the court had to welcome him with the utmost care. The emperor sent basketloads of precious objects encrusted with gold to Cortés's camp. But the elaborate gifts only alerted Cortés and his men to the Aztec's wealth.

Although the Spanish numbered scarcely 600, they had several key advantages over the Aztec. Their guns and horses, unknown in America, terrified the Indians. When Cortés found coastal peoples staggering under heavy Aztec taxes, he recruited them as willing allies. An Indian woman (christened Doña Marina, or La Malinche) acted as his translator and companion. In an aggressive show of force, Cortés marched directly to the capital and seized Moctezuma as his hostage.

The Spanish still faced daunting obstacles, but sickness worked decisively to their advantage. Smallpox was a disease the Aztec had never encountered before, so they lacked any immunity. The European illness reached the mainland with the invading army, and a crushing epidemic swept the Aztec capital in 1521. The disaster let Cortés conquer Tenochtitlán (which he renamed Mexico City) and claim the entire region as New Spain.

"These Gods That We Worship Give Us Everything We Need"

Three years after Cortés captured Tenochtitlán in central Mexico, 12 missionaries from the Franciscan Order arrived in the city to preach Christianity to the conquered Aztec. In several meetings with principal elders and priests, they explained their beliefs and laid out their plans through a translator. Similar talks would take place throughout America in later generations.

No transcript of the 1524 conversations exists, but another Franciscan, the famous preserver of Aztec culture Bernardino de Sahagún, gathered recollections of the encounter from both sides and reconstructed the dialogue. He published his version in 1564, creating parallel texts in Spanish and Nahuatl, the Aztec language. "Having understood the reasoning and speech of the twelve," Sahagún reports, the city leaders "became greatly agitated and fell into a great sadness and fear, offering no response." The next morning, they requested a complete repetition of the unsettling message. "Having heard this, one of the principal lords arose, asked the indulgence of the twelve,…and made the following long speech."

Our lords, leading personages of much esteem, you are very welcome to our lands and towns. . . . We have heard the words that you have brought us of the One who gives us life and being. And we have heard with admiration the words of the Lord of the World which he has sent here for love of us, and also you have brought us the book of celestial and divine words.

You have told us that we do not know the One who gives us life and being, who is Lord of the heavens and of the earth. You also say that those we worship are not gods. This way of speak-

Bibliothèque Nationale, Paris

ing is entirely new to us, and very scandalous. We are frightened by this way of speaking because our forebears who engendered and governed us never said anything like this.

On the contrary, they left us this our custom of worshiping our gods. . . . They taught us how to honor them. And they taught us all the ceremonies and sacrifices that we make. They told us that. . . we were beholden to them, to be theirs and to serve countless centuries before the sun began to shine and before there was daytime. They said that these gods that we worship give us everything we need for our physical existence: maize, beans, chia seeds, etc. We appeal to them for the rain to make the things of the earth grow.

These our gods are the source of great riches and delights, all of which belong to them. . . . They live in very delightful places where there are always flowers, vegetation, and great freshness, a place…where there is never hunger, poverty, or illness. . . . There has never been a time remembered when they were not worshiped, honored, and esteemed. . . . .

It would be a fickle, foolish thing for us to destroy the most ancient laws and customs left by the first inhabitants of this land. . . . We are accustomed to them and we have them impressed on our hearts. . . . How could you leave the poor elderly among us bereft of that in which they have been raised throughout their lives? Watch out that we do not

incur the wrath of our gods. Watch out that the common people do not rise up against us if we were to tell them that the gods they have always understood to be such are not gods at all.

It is best, our lords, to act on this matter very slowly, with great deliberation. We are not satisfied or convinced by what you have told us, nor do we understand or give credit to what has been said of our gods. . . . All of us together feel that it is enough to have lost, enough that the power and royal jurisdiction have been taken from us. As for our gods, we will die before giving up serving and worshiping them. This is our determination; do what you will.

Questions

1. Why would the Aztec priests fear an uprising of the common people under these circumstances? How would you respond to a similar situation?

2. As suggested near the end of this chapter, a similar religious confrontation was taking place in Europe in 1524, during the early years of the Protestant Reformation. Contrast and compare these two situations. ■

Source: Kenneth Mills and William B. Taylor, *Colonial Spanish America: A Documentary History* (Wilmington: Scholarly Resources, 1998), pp. 21–22.

Magellan and Cortés Prompt New Searches

Cortés's conquest of Mexico raised Spain's hopes of additional windfalls in the Americas. In 1531 Spanish raiders under Francisco Pizarro set sail from Panama for Peru, with plans to overthrow the Inca empire. Pizarro had limited resources (180 men and thirty-seven horses), but smallpox assisted him, as it had helped Cortés, and his invaders accomplished their mission. Marching overland to Cuzco in 1533, they killed the emperor, Atahualpa, and sacked the mountain capital for the gold it contained. The Spanish also pressed west across the Pacific from Mexico. One of three ships dispatched by Cortés for the Philippines actually reached its destination. Still, not until the 1560s did Spanish cargo ships, known as galleons, accomplish the arduous round trip from Acapulco to the Philippines and back across the Pacific.

In 1524, Italian navigator Giovanni da Verrazzano, sailing for the French, reached North America near modern Cape Fear, North Carolina, later cruising north to enter New York harbor and explore further along the coast. In 1526, Lucas Vásquez de Ayllón led 500 men and women from the Spanish Caribbean to the Santee River region (near present-day Georgetown, South Carolina) to settle and explore. But Ayllón fell sick and died, and the colony proved short-lived. Two years later, Pánfilo de Narváez directed an even greater disaster.

A rival of both Cortés and Ayllón, Narváez launched his expedition from Cuba in 1528. He landed near Florida's Tampa Bay, intending to bring wealth and glory to his 400 soldiers. But disease, hunger, and Indian hostilities plagued the party's journey along the Gulf Coast. Only four men—three Spanish and one North African black named Esteban—survived to make an extended trek on foot across the Southwest from Galveston Bay to Mexico City. Their leader, Álvar Núñez Cabeza de Vaca, wrote about the remarkable odyssey after he returned to Spain in 1537. Scholars now recognize Cabeza de Vaca's *Relation* (1542) as an early classic in North American literature.

Three New Views of North America

Even before Cabeza de Vaca published his narrative, Europeans initiated three more expeditions into North America. Each probed a separate region of the continent, hoping to gauge the land's dimensions, assess its peoples, and claim its resources. Together, the three enterprises made 1534 to 1543 the most extraordinary decade in the early European exploration of North America, for Native Americans and newcomers alike.

In the Northeast, Frenchman Jacques Cartier visited the Gulf of St. Lawrence in 1534 and bartered for furs with the Micmac Indians. He returned the next year and penetrated southwest up the St. Lawrence River into Canada. (The name comes from *kanata*, the Huron–Iroquois word for "village.") After a friendly reception at the large Indian town of Hochelaga near modern Montreal, the French returned downriver to camp at Stadacona, the future site of Quebec. Following a hard winter, in which he lost twenty-five men to scurvy, the explorer and his remaining crew sailed for France.

DOCUMENT

Jacques Cartier:
First Contact with
the Indians

Cartier came back to Quebec in 1541, seeking precious minerals and signs of a water passage farther west to the Pacific Ocean. He found neither, but a colonizing expedition followed in 1542, led by a nobleman named Roberval. It contained several hundred French settlers, including women for the first time. But again, scurvy and cold took a heavy toll at the Quebec campsite, and the weakened colony withdrew after a single winter. Despite a decade of effort, the French still had not established a beachhead in the New World. Nevertheless, they had demonstrated their resolve to challenge Spain's exclusive claim to American lands.

The Spanish, meanwhile, launched two intrusions of their own—one in the Southeast and one in the Southwest. News of Pizarro's 1533 triumph over the Incas in Peru helped renew the search for wealthy kingdoms to conquer. In 1537, Emperor Charles V of Spain granted one hardened veteran of the Peruvian campaign—Hernando de Soto—the right to explore in and beyond Florida, establishing a personal domain for himself. The conquistador spent

■ **Two decades after Verrazzano's explorations, this 1547 chart shows the early claims of France in North America. It depicts the men and women of Roberval's short-lived colonizing expedition as they disembarked in 1542, watched by Native Americans. Perhaps to feature the large St. Lawrence River, the European mapmaker put North at the bottom and South at the top. Hence, the Atlantic coast seems upside-down to our eyes, with Florida appearing in the upper–right-hand corner.**

most of his fortune assembling a force of more than 600 soldiers that reached Tampa Bay in 1539. The enterprise included several women and priests, along with scores of servants and African slaves, plus 200 horses. De Soto had also brought along a herd of 300 pigs that multiplied rapidly and provided food during the long march through the interior.

Over the next four years, de Soto's party traveled through parts of ten southern states. They hoped to find a city as wealthy as Cuzco in Peru or Tenochtitlán in Mexico. Instead, they encountered only scattered villages. Towns that refused to provide the intruders with porters or guides met with brutal reprisals that included the use of attack dogs. At Mabila near modern-day Selma, Alabama, de Soto's mounted army, brandishing swords and lances, killed several thousand Native Americans who had dared to attack them with bows and arrows. Still, Spanish frustrations grew due to difficult terrain, stiff Indian resistance, and failure to find riches. After exploring beyond the Mississippi River, de Soto died of a fever in 1542. His disheartened followers escaped downstream to the Gulf of Mexico the next year, leaving epidemic sickness in their wake.

At the same time, another encounter was unfolding in the Southwest. In Mexico, speculation about gold in the north had intensified after the appearance of Cabeza de Vaca. His

African companion, Esteban, guided a reconnaissance party north in 1539. Esteban was killed by the Zuni Indians, but exaggerated accounts of the region's pueblos prompted rumors about the seven golden cities known as Cibola. The next year, aspiring conquistador Francisco Vásquez de Coronado set out from northern Mexico to reach these wealthy towns before de Soto could. He left his post as a frontier governor and assembled a huge expedition with more than 300 Spanish adventurers and 1,000 Indian allies. However, his grandiose expectations were quickly dashed. The pueblos of the Zuni, he reported, "are very good houses, three and four and five stories high," but the fabled "Seven Cities are seven little villages."

The presence of Spanish forces soon imposed a heavy burden on the Pueblo Indians, as the newcomers demanded food and burned helpless towns. Desperate to get rid of Coronado, the Pueblo told him stories of a far-off, wealthy land called Quivira. They secretly recruited a Plains Indian to lead the Spaniards to some place where men and horses "would starve to death." In the spring of 1541, he guided Coronado's party northeast onto the Great Plains, with their endless herds of buffalo. But when Quivira proved to be a Wichita Indian village in what is now central Kansas, the Spanish strangled their deceitful guide and made their way back south to New Spain. At one point, as they crossed northern Texas, they even came within 300 miles of de Soto's ill-fated party in eastern Arkansas. But neither de Soto nor Coronado—nor Cartier in the north—ever discovered wealthy cities or a sea passage to the Far East.

> *Neither de Soto nor Coronado—nor Cartier in the north—ever discovered wealthy cities or a sea passage to the Far East.*

The Protestant Reformation Plays Out in America

In 1520, while Cortés vied with the Aztec for control in Mexico and Magellan maneuvered around South America, the pope excommunicated a German monk named Martin Luther. Three years earlier, Luther had mailed a list of ninety-five theses to the church door at Wittenberg, challenging papal authority. Luther's followers questioned lavish church spending and long-standing church practices such as the selling of religious pardons to raise money. They also rejected the church's elaborate hierarchy and criticized its refusal to translate the Latin Bible into modern languages. Luther's reform movement triggered the division of western Christianity into competing faiths. For their written protestations against the papacy, Luther and his fellow insurgents received the enduring name *Protestants*. Their movement became known broadly as the Reformation. Those who opposed it, siding with Rome, launched a Counter-Reformation to defend and revitalize the Roman Catholic Church.

For the first time in history, a controversy in Europe made waves that washed onto American shores. Throughout the remainder of the sixteenth century, European national and religious conflict played out in part overseas, a pattern that repeated itself in future centuries. France and Spain, competing in Europe, wrestled to claim control of Florida. England, an upstart Protestant monarchy with a rising population and an expanding navy, seized control of Ireland and launched its first attempt to plant a colony in North America.

Reformation and Counter-Reformation in Europe

Beginning in 1517, zeal for Luther's religious reforms spread across Europe, sparking armed conflict. In Switzerland, militant priests abolished the practice of confession, condemned the church calendar full of fasts and saints' days, and defied the tradition of a celibate clergy by marrying. The Swiss Reformation found its leader in a French Protestant named John Calvin who arrived in Geneva in 1541 and ruled the city as a church-centered state for more than two decades.

Calvin imposed his own strict interpretation on Lutheranism and drew dedicated followers to his church. Offended by expensive vestments and elaborate rituals, he donned a simple black "Geneva" robe. He argued that faith alone, not "good works," would lead Christians to be saved. Salvation, he preached, was determined by God, not bought by giving **tithes** to the church. Only a select few people, Calvin explained, were destined to be members of God's chosen elect. Moreover, only an informed clergy and the careful study of scripture could reveal signs of a person's status. Soon Calvinist doctrine helped shape Protestant communities across northern Europe: Huguenots in France, Puritans in England, Presbyterians in Scotland, and the Dutch Reformed Church in the Netherlands.

The Protestant Reformation that Luther had ignited coincided roughly with another important change in Europe, the emergence of the modern nation-state. Kings and queens gradually expanded court bureaucracies and asserted greater control over their subjects and economies. They strengthened their armies, gaining a near monopoly on the use of force, and they took full advantage of the new medium of printing. As religious ferment spread and local allegiances gave way to a broader sense of national identity, strong sovereigns moved to distance themselves from papal authority in Rome.

The emergence of England as a nation-state under the Tudor dynasty, founded by Henry VII in 1485, illustrates this shift in power away from Rome. In 1533, when the pope refused to grant England's next king an **annulment** of his first marriage, Henry VIII wrested control of the English church from papal hands and had Parliament approve his divorce and remarriage. The new Church of England, or Anglican Church, continued to follow much of the Catholic Church's doctrine. However, its "Protector and only Supreme Head" would now be the English monarch. During her long reign from 1558 to 1603, Henry VIII's daughter Queen Elizabeth I managed to steer the Church of England on a middle course between advocates of Catholicism and extreme Protestants.

Throughout Europe, as zealous believers on both sides of the debate staked out their positions, attempts to heal religious divisions gave way to confrontation. Challenges to the pope in Rome, whether from dissenting parishes or powerful monarchs, met with stiff resistance as Catholic leaders mobilized opposition. Their followers rallied to defend Roman Catholicism through efforts known collectively as the Counter-Reformation.

A militant new Catholic religious order called the Society of Jesus, or the Jesuits, represented one dimension of the Counter-Reformation. Led by a Spanish soldier named Ignatius Loyola and willing to give their lives for their beliefs, these dedicated missionaries and teachers helped to reenergize the Catholic faith and spread it to distant parts of the world. Another institution, the Inquisition, reflects a different side of the Counter-Reformation. In 1542, Catholic authorities established a new religious-judicial proceeding, known as the Inquisition, to help resist the spread of Protestantism. Heretics—persons accused of denying or defying church doctrine—were brought before the Inquisition's strict religious courts, and those who refused to renounce their beliefs suffered severe punishment. These heresy trials made clear to Inquisition leaders that the advent of printing was helping to spread the works of Luther and his Protestant allies. In 1557, therefore, the Vatican issued an "Index" of prohibited books.

In 1542, Catholic authorities established a new religious-judicial proceeding, known as the Inquisition, to help resist the spread of Protestantism.

In Spain, King Philip II, who ruled from 1556 to 1598, led an Inquisition to root out Protestant heresy. The Spanish monarch came close to overpowering Protestant England as well. In 1588 he sent a fleet of warships—the Spanish Armada—to England in hopes of reconquering it for the Catholic Church. A timely storm and hasty mobilization by the island nation foiled the Spanish king's invasion. But Philip II's confrontation with the navy of Elizabeth I epitomized the sharp new division between Catholic and Protestant power in Europe. This deepened antagonism—religious, ideological, and economic—shaped events overseas in the second half of the sixteenth century. The struggle became especially clear in Florida, the vague region claimed by Spain that encompassed Indian lands from Chesapeake Bay to the Gulf of Mexico.

Competing Powers Lay Claim to Florida

As Spain used force to obtain the dazzling wealth of New World societies, its European rivals looked on jealously. As early as 1523, French sea raiders had captured Spanish ships returning from Mexico with Cortés's Aztec bounty of gold, silver, and pearls. Ten years later, French pirates made a similar haul. To protect the flow of riches from America, the Spanish soon initiated a well-armed annual convoy to escort their wealth from Havana to Seville. Each year, Spain's huge West Indies treasure fleet made an enticing target as it followed the Gulf Stream along the Florida coast.

But France had its own designs on Florida, furthered by the special concerns of French Huguenots. Unsure of their future in a religiously divided country, these Protestants took a leading role in the colonization efforts of France. In 1562 French Huguenots established a settlement at Port Royal Sound (Parris Island, South Carolina), close to the route of Spain's annual treasure fleet. The effort lasted only two years and aroused Spanish suspicions of "Lutheran" intruders.

> *Each year, Spain's huge West Indies treasure fleet made an enticing target as it followed the Gulf Stream along the Florida coast.*

New York Public Library

■ In 1562, French Protestants established a short-lived colony at Port Royal Sound on the South Carolina coast. "The commander, on landing with some soldiers, found the country very beautiful, as it was well wooded with oak, cedar, and other trees. As they went through the woods, they saw Indian peacocks, or turkeys, flying past, and deer going by." Traveling upstream beyond Parris Island, they surprised an encampment of Indians, "who, on perceiving the boats, immediately took flight," leaving behind the meat "they were roasting."

■ MAP 1.3

THE EXTENT OF EUROPEAN EXPLORATION OF NORTH AMERICA BY 1592
By 1592, a century after Columbus's initial voyage, European explorers and colonists had touched the edges of North America, and a few had ventured far inland. But they had not found riches or a passageway to the Pacific, and only the Spanish had managed to establish a lasting foothold along the Florida coast.

North American exploration in the 16th century

- Ponce de León, 1513
- Verrazzano, 1524
- Ayllón, 1526
- Narváez, 1528
- Cabeza de Vaca and Esteban, 1528–1536
- Cartier, 1534/1535
- De Soto, 1539–1543
- Coronado, 1540–1542
- Pardo, 1566–1567
- Drake, 1577–1580

Undaunted, the French backed a larger colonizing effort to Florida in 1564. When French Protestants erected Fort Caroline on the St. John's River at present-day Jacksonville, the Spanish crown took swift action. In 1565 Philip II sent 300 soldiers and 700 colonists under Pedro Menéndez de Avilés to oust the French and secure Florida. Menéndez captured Fort Caroline and massacred hundreds of French Huguenots. The heretics, he feared, might attack the treasure fleet, forge alliances with Florida's Indians, or provoke revolt among slaves in the Spanish Caribbean. To prevent further French incursions on Florida's Atlantic coast, Menéndez established a new outpost at nearby St. Augustine. He also sent Juan Pardo far up the Savannah River to explore the interior.

With French threats defeated, the Spanish at St. Augustine attempted to plant strategic missions farther north to convert Native Americans to Christianity and secure Spain's land claims. In 1570, eight missionaries from Loyola's Society of Jesus sailed north from Florida to Chesapeake Bay. There, the Jesuits established a mission to convert local Indians and looked for "an entrance into the mountains and on to China." But the friars' rules and beliefs antagonized the Native Americans. By the time Menéndez visited the region in 1572, all the missionaries had been killed. Spain's failure to secure a foothold on Chesapeake Bay soon proved costly, as a new European rival appeared on the scene. Almost overnight, Protestant England emerged as a contending force in the Atlantic world. Now English adventurers began challenging Spanish dominance in the Caribbean and along North America's southeastern coast.

The Background of English Expansion

The voyages of John Cabot and the visits of Bristol fishing vessels to Newfoundland's Grand Banks had stimulated an early English interest in the Atlantic. But for several reasons this curiosity intensified after 1550. Henry VIII had used his power, plus the wealth he had seized from the Catholic Church, to build a sizable navy before he died in 1547. The merchant fleet grew as well, carrying English wool and cloth to Antwerp and other European ports. In addition, the English population, which had declined in the previous 150 years, grew steadily after 1500. Overall numbers more than doubled during the sixteenth century, creating pressure on limited resources, especially land. Adding to the squeeze, property owners, eager to enclose pastures for sheep grazing, pushed tenants off their land. This "enclosure movement" set even more people adrift to seek work in towns and cities. London's population soared from 50,000 in 1500 to 200,000 a century later. When Europe's saturated woolen textile market collapsed suddenly, English cloth exports fell 35 percent in 1551. Merchants searched hastily for new avenues of foreign commerce.

Starting in the 1550s, therefore, England's overseas exploration pushed in all directions. Investors in the new Muscovy Company sent ships north around Scandinavia through the Arctic Ocean, but they failed to find a northeastern route above the Asian landmass to China. Other English vessels sailed south to Morocco and the Gold Coast, challenging the Portuguese monopoly of the African trade. English mariner John Hawkins conducted three voyages to West Africa during the 1560s. Horning in on the growing transatlantic slave traffic, he purchased Africans and then sold them in Caribbean ports to Spanish buyers.

Philip II, having driven the French out of Florida, had had enough of Protestant interlopers. A Spanish fleet forced Hawkins and his young kinsman Francis Drake out of Mexican waters in 1568. But thereafter, English sea rovers, with quiet support from Queen Elizabeth I, stepped up their challenges to Spain on the high seas. Drake proved the most wide-ranging and successful. On a voyage to the Pacific (1577–1580) he plundered Spanish ports in Peru and landed near San Francisco Bay. He claimed California for England as New Albion and then sailed around the globe. In the 1580s, Drake continued, in his words, "to singe the Spaniard's beard." He sacked ports in the West Indies, encouraged slave uprisings against the Spanish, and attacked the settlement at St. Augustine. He also captured numerous treasure ships, sank two dozen enemy vessels in their home port at Cadiz, and helped to defeat Philip II's Spanish Armada in 1588.

England's anti-Catholic propagandists made Drake a national hero. Moreover, they painted Spanish cruelties toward Indians in the New World in the worst possible terms. To bolster their case, they translated the vivid writings of Las Casas into English. But the English were not blameless themselves. In the Elizabethan years, they established their own pattern of violence during their brutal conquest of Ireland. Many who played leading roles in this bloody takeover came to view a colony in America as the next logical step in England's aggressive overseas expansion.

Lost Colony: The Roanoke Experience

Sir Humphrey Gilbert, who had served in Ireland, was one Elizabethan with an eye on America. In 1576 Gilbert promoted the idea of a short northwestern passage to China, and Martin Frobisher, another veteran of the Irish campaign, undertook voyages to locate such a route. Writing an essay on "How Her Majesty May Annoy the King of Spain," Gilbert

© British Museum

■ John White took part in several voyages to Roanoke Island in the 1580s. A skilled artist, the Englishman made valuable firsthand drawings of Native Americans living in what is now coastal North Carolina, including the wife and daughter of a local leader. The woman kept her "haire trussed opp in a knott," had tattoos on her arms, wore "a chaine of great pearles," and often carried "a gourde full of some kinde of pleasant liquor." The girl holds an English doll, for Indian children "are greatly Delighted with puppetts . . . brought oute of England."

DOCUMENT

Charter to Sir
Walter Raleigh

proposed a colony in Newfoundland. The queen granted him a patent—a license giving him exclusive rights—for such a project. But shipwrecks and desertions doomed the venture to failure. When Gilbert died at sea on the homeward voyage, his half-brother, Walter Raleigh, obtained a similar patent to plant a colony in North America.

In 1584 Raleigh sent explorers to the Outer Banks, the string of coastal barrier islands below Chesapeake Bay that Verrazzano had glimpsed sixty years earlier. They brought back two Indian informants and positive reports about the land near Roanoke Island. The next month, Richard Hakluyt, England's foremost advocate and chronicler of overseas expansion, handed Elizabeth I an advisory paper entitled "Western Planting." The document called for the establishment of a strategic outpost on the North American coast, where the English could launch attacks against Spanish shipping, hunt for useful commodities, and convert Indians to Protestant Christianity.

Raleigh's three efforts to establish such an outpost failed in rapid succession. In 1585, he first sent Ralph Lane, a hardened veteran of the Irish campaigns, to build a fort at Roanoke Island. But storms at sea scattered his ships, and most of Lane's initial force never arrived. Those who did, including artist John White, fared badly because of scarce food, bad discipline, and hostile relations with the Indians. Francis Drake, arriving in 1586 after harassing the Spanish in the West Indies and Florida, expected to find a thriving enterprise. Instead, he carried the disheartened soldiers back to England. They had paid a price, Hakluyt commented, "for the cruelty and outrages committed by some of them against the native inhabitants of that country." A second expedition diverted to the Caribbean to prey on enemy shipping, after leaving a few men at Roanoke, who did not survive.

In May 1587 John White led a third English venture to America, with 110 people, including women and children. They planned to settle on Chesapeake Bay, but a contentious captain refused to carry them farther north after an initial stop at Roanoke Island. In August the settlers agreed to send White back to England for more supplies; they would leave a message for him if they moved. When he finally returned in 1590—delayed by England's clash with the Spanish Armada—he found the site deserted. The word *Croatoan* carved on a post suggested that survivors had joined the nearby Croatan Indians, but the Lost Colony's fate remains a source of endless speculation. The Spanish, worried by the English foray, drew up plans for a fortification at Chesapeake Bay, but warfare between Spain and England kept both countries preoccupied elsewhere until Philip II and Elizabeth I had died.

Conclusion

Over approximately 150 centuries, people of distant Asian ancestry had explored and settled the bountiful Western Hemisphere. In every region of North America, from the arctic North to the semitropical Florida Keys, they had adapted and prospered over countless generations. Then suddenly, in a single century, unprecedented intrusions by sea brought newcomers from foreign lands to the coasts of the Americas. Their numbers only increased with time. In the next century, the contest for European control of the Atlantic seaboard began in earnest.

Sites to Visit

Cahokia Mounds State Historic Site

Covering 2,200 acres just south of Highway 40 near Collinsville, in East St. Louis, Illinois, Mississippian earthworks dot this World Heritage Site. The Cahokia Mounds Museum Society conducts an archaeological field school each summer.

Chaco Culture National Historical Park

The most striking structure in this park is Pueblo Bonito, the largest building in North America until 1882. Lying in Chaco Canyon northwest of Albuquerque, New Mexico, these Anasazi ruins can be reached by driving south from Aztec (where there are several important museums) or north from Thoreau.

Makah Cultural and Research Center

This site, in Neah Bay, Washington, at the tip of Olympic Peninsula, houses thousands of artifacts from an ancestral Macah Indian village, at nearby Ozette, that was covered in a mudslide shortly before European contact and revealed by a 1970 winter storm.

Mesa Verde National Park

Located near Cortez, Colorado, this is the oldest archaeological national park in the United States. It covers 80 square miles in southwest Colorado, adjoining the Ute Mountain Indian Reservation. The park contains impressive Anasazi ruins, the most famous of which is Cliff Palace.

Moundville Archaeological Park

Located half a mile west of State Route 69, on the Black Warrior River outside Moundville, Alabama, just south of Tuscaloosa, this well-preserved Mississippian mound complex also contains an archaeological museum.

Poverty Point State Commemorative Area

A visitors' center is located near the center of the geometric earthworks from the late Archaic era on this 400-acre site on State Route 577 near Epps, Louisiana.

Pueblo Grande Museum

This downtown Phoenix, Arizona, museum, just off State Route 143, contains artifacts of the Hohokam culture. A large platform mound, a ball court, and ancient irrigation canals are preserved within the park.

Fort Raleigh National Historical Site

This site is on Route 64 at the north end of Roanoke Island, in eastern North Carolina. A reconstructed Elizabethan ship at nearby Manteo suggests the experience of England's sixteenth-century "lost colony." A drive or walk on the sandy Outer Banks (Route 12) recalls the coastline seen by Verrazzano in 1524.

Serpent Mound State Memorial

Four miles northwest of Locust Grove, Ohio, on State Route 73, this site includes a small museum and a viewing tower that allows visitors to look down on the winding effigy mound, now thought to be roughly 1,000 years old.

Digital Restorations of Ohio Valley Mounds
http://www.earthworks.uc.edu/

EarthWorks is an ongoing project at the University of Cincinnati's Center for the Electronic Reconstruction of Historical and Archaeological Sites (CERHAS). It is creating virtual reconstructions of pre-Columbian mounds and major earthen sites in the Ohio River valley, along with a CD-ROM and a videotape.

European Voyages of Exploration
www.acs.ucalgary.ca/applied_history/tutor/eurvoya/index.html

The University of Calgary has developed a course around this Web site titled "The European Voyages of Exploration: The Fifteenth and Sixteenth Centuries."

Cabeza de Vaca
www.pbs.org/weta/thewest/resources/archives/one/cabeza.htm

Read the narrative by Cabeza de Vaca of his journey across the Southwest in the 1530s.

Discoverers Web
www.win.tue.nl/cs/fm/engels/discovery/

See the "Discoverers Web" for numerous links concerning the era of European exploration.

For Further Reading

General

John Logan Allen, *North American Exploration, Vol. 1, A New World Disclosed* (1997).

Alfred W. Crosby, *Ecological Imperialism: The Biological Expansion of Europe, 900–1900* (1986; Canto edition, 1993).

Jared Diamond, *Guns, Germs, and Steel: The Fates of Human Societies* (1997).

Brian M. Fagan, *Ancient North America*, 3rd ed. (2000).

William H. Goetzmann and Glyndwr Williams, *The Atlas of North American Exploration: From the Norse Voyages to the Race to the Pole* (1992).

J. C. H. King, *First Peoples, First Contacts: Native Peoples of North America* (1999).

Charles C. Mann, *1491: New Revelations of the Americas Before Columbus* (2005).

Ancient America

Brian M. Fagan, *The Great Journey: The Peopling of Ancient America* (2004).

Francis Jennings, *The Founders of America* (1993).

Alice Beck Kehoe, *America Before the European Invasions* (2002).

Robert Silverberg, *Mound Builders of Ancient America: The Archaeology of a Myth* (1968).

A Thousand Years of Change: 500 to 1500

Sally A. Kitt Chappell, *Cahokia: Mirror of the Cosmos* (2002).

Alvin M. Josephy Jr., ed., *America in 1492: The World of the Indian Peoples Before the Arrival of Columbus* (1992).

Linda Schele and David Freidel, *A Forest of Kings: The Untold Story of the Ancient Maya* (1990).

David Hurst Thomas, *Exploring Native North America* (2000).

Linking the Continents

Alfred W. Crosby Jr., *The Columbian Exchange: Biological and Cultural Consequences of 1492* (1972).

William W. Fitzhugh and Elisabeth I. Ward, eds., *Vikings: The North Atlantic Saga* (2000).

Louise Levathes, *When China Ruled the Sea: The Treasure Fleet of the Dragon Throne* (1994).

Samuel Eliot Morison, *The European Discovery of America: The Northern Voyages, A.D. 500–1600* (1971).

J. H. Parry, *The Age of Reconnaissance: Discovery, Exploration, and Settlement, 1450–1650* (1963).

Spain Enters the Americas

Laurence Bergreen, *Over the Edge of the World: Magellan's Terrifying Circumnavigation of the Globe* (2003).

Cyclone Covey, trans. and ed., *Cabeza de Vaca's Adventures in the Unknown Interior of America* (1961).

W. J. Eccles, *France in America* (1972).

Charles Hudson, *Knights of Spain, Warriors of the Sun: Hernando de Soto and the South's Ancient Kingdoms* (1997).

Jerald T. Milanich, *Florida Indians and the Invasion from Europe* (1995).

Hugh Thomas, *Rivers of Gold: The Rise of the Spanish Empire, from Columbus to Magellan* (2003).

The Protestant Reformation Plays Out in America

Karen Ordahl Kupperman, *Roanoke: The Abandoned Colony* (1984).

Eugene Lyon, *The Enterprise of Florida: Pedro Menéndez de Avilés and the Spanish Conquest of 1565–1568* (1976).

Diarmaid MacCulloch, *The Reformation: A History* (2003).

John T. McGrath, *The French in Early Florida: In the Eye of the Hurricane* (2000).

David Beers Quinn, *England and the Discovery of America, 1481–1620* (1974).

Carl Ortwin Sauer, *Sixteenth Century America: The Land and the People as Seen by the Europeans* (1971).

For quizzes and other resources on these topics, go to www.longmanamericanhistory.com.

European Footholds in North America, 1600–1660

IN THE SUMMER OF 1621, AN ENGLISHMAN AND AN INDIAN LEFT PLYMOUTH VILLAGE ON FOOT TO visit a Native American leader named Massasoit and secure his support for the struggling English colony. During their 40-mile journey, Stephen Hopkins and Squanto saw numerous signs of a wave of disease that had swept the New England coast four years earlier, killing thousands of Indians. Unburied skulls and bones still lay aboveground in many places. The two men who encountered these grim scenes had come together from strikingly different backgrounds.

Back in 1609, Hopkins had left England in a fleet heading for Jamestown in Virginia. When a storm wrecked his ship on the uncharted island of Bermuda, he and others rebelled against their official leader. Accused of mutiny and sentenced to hang, Hopkins pleaded his case and narrowly escaped the noose. Hopkins made it back to England and started a family, but in 1620 he decided to return to America. At the English port of Plymouth, Hopkins, his pregnant wife Elizabeth, and several children and servants became paying passengers on a ship called the *Mayflower*. The vessel had been chartered to carry a group of English Protestants to America from their exile in Holland.

During the arduous passage, tensions mounted. Hopkins was among those who muttered "mutinous speeches" and argued that "when they came ashore, they should use their own libertie, for none had power to command them." But after Elizabeth gave birth, Hopkins joined the other forty men aboard in signing the Mayflower Compact. The agreement bound all the passengers together in a "Civil Body Politic" to be governed by laws "most meet and convenient for the general good." They reached New England in early winter, and Hopkins and others laid out the village of Plymouth in the snow. There, the newcomers met Squanto, a Native American with a command of English who helped them negotiate with local Indians.

Squanto had also endured Atlantic travel. He remembered the first French and English fishing vessels, which had appeared when he was a small boy. In 1614 Squanto was among twenty-seven

■ A *Mayflower* replica is now part of the restored Plymouth Colony site.

Indians taken hostage aboard an English ship. He spent time in Spain, England, and New-foundland before returning home in 1619, only to find his entire village swept away by disease.

The *Mayflower* pilgrims, arriving a year after Squanto's return, would also suffer heavy losses. Of the 102 settlers who had begun the voyage, half of them died in Plymouth Colony by the next spring. But in New England, as elsewhere in America, death seemed to play favorites in the following years. As colonization continued, recurrent epidemics took a particularly heavy toll on Native Americans, who lacked immunity when exposed to foreign diseases for the first time. In 1622 Squanto fell sick and died of a fever, leaving no relatives behind. In contrast, Stephen and Elizabeth Hopkins lived on to see numerous children and grandchildren thrive.

By the middle of the seventeenth century, English settlements had taken root in both the Chesapeake region and New England. The success of these colonies would exert a lasting influence on the future direction of American society. But their stories unfolded as part of a far wider North American drama that included a diversity of European groups and embraced both the Atlantic and the Pacific shores. Whether confronting newcomers from Spain, France, Holland, or England, scores of Native American communities faced new challenges that altered traditional Indian ways of living and sometimes threatened their very survival.

Spain's Ocean-Spanning Reach

In 1580 Spain's Philip II laid claim to the throne of Portugal. This consolidation (which endured until 1640) unified Europe's two richest seaborne empires but also created new problems. First, combining with Portugal put huge additional burdens on the overstretched Spanish bureaucracy. Second, the global success of the combined **Iberian** empires invited challenges from envious rivals in northern Europe. The new international competition came from the French, the Dutch, and the English, aspiring naval powers with imperial ambitions that touched the Pacific as well as the Atlantic.

By 1600, for example, a Dutch ship had entered the Pacific, defying Spanish claims for control of that ocean, and had reached Japan, where the new Tokugawa dynasty (1600–1868) was consolidating its control. The pilot, an Englishman named Will Adams, visited Edo—the rising military town that would grow into modern-day Tokyo. He even built a ship for the *shogun* (ruler). Adams's experience in Japan serves as a reminder that in the decades before the *Mayflower* sailed the Atlantic, the issue of who would dominate Pacific sea lanes to America was anything but clear.

Vizcaíno in California and Japan

In April 1607, a letter from the king of Spain reached Mexico City. The king commanded his viceroy in charge of affairs in Mexico (New Spain) to create an outpost on California's Monterey Bay. Spanish galleons returning from the Philippines through the North Pacific to the west coast of Mexico desperately needed a haven along the route, after crossing the immense ocean. Monterey Bay was well supplied with water, food, and timber. The sheltering harbor would provide a perfect way station, where ships could take on supplies and make repairs before heading south.

But the viceroy in Mexico City had other ideas. He diverted the necessary funds into a search for the fabled North Pacific isles of Rica de Oro ("Rich in Gold") and Rica de Plata ("Rich in Silver"). To search for the mysterious islands, in 1611 the viceroy dispatched Sebastián Vizcaíno, a seasoned Pacific navigator who had already explored the California coast. Vizcaíno found no isles of gold and silver, but he did visit Japan. When he finally returned across the

Pacific in 1613 aboard a vessel built in Japan, he brought 180 Japanese with him to Mexico. This unique delegation was bound for Spain and Italy to open doors between East and West. However, the Tokugawas soon began to persecute the European traders and Christian missionaries who had been allowed in the Japanese islands for a generation, so the frail link between Europe and Japan through Mexico never developed further.

Tokugawa officials, it seems, feared that tolerating foreigners in Japan's ports might foster the spread of Christianity and undermine their supremacy. Moreover, developing Japanese fleets might bring guns to warlords and disrupt hard-won peace. So Japan passed up an opportunity for naval expansion, just as Ming China had done two centuries earlier after the voyages of Zheng He. Instead, the new dynasty adopted a policy of commercial and cultural isolation that lasted for more than 200 years. Otherwise, the history of North America and the world would almost certainly have taken a very different path.

> *Spain wondered whether to maintain its existing North American colony in Florida and its newest frontier province: New Mexico.*

For the Spanish, Vizcaíno's Pacific adventure consumed crucial funds, and the possibility of a Spanish settlement at Monterey quickly disappeared. Concerned that their empire had already become overextended, Spanish officials postponed plans to colonize California's coast. In addition, Spain wondered whether to maintain its existing North American colony in Florida and its newest frontier province: New Mexico.

Oñate Creates a Spanish Foothold in the Southwest

In 1598 Juan de Oñate renewed the northern efforts of Coronado's expedition several generations earlier. Setting out from New Spain, he led 500 men, women, and children north into the upper Rio Grande valley to create the province of New Mexico. Aided by Franciscan friars (organized followers of St. Francis loyal to the pope), Oñate and his colonists expected to convert the Pueblo Indians to Christianity. Expanding outward from the compact apartment-like native towns, or pueblos, the intruders hoped to open a vast new colonial realm "greater than New Spain."

But Oñate drastically underestimated the difficulties. When embittered Indians at Acoma pueblo killed eleven of his soldiers in 1599, he retaliated by bombarding the mesa-top citadel, killing 800 inhabitants and enslaving nearly 600 others. Hearing of the brutal repression of the residents of Acoma, neighboring pueblos reluctantly submitted to Spanish demands for labor and food. Colonial reinforcements arriving in 1600 were dismayed by the harsh conditions; for the colony to prosper, Oñate needed new discoveries. In 1601 he launched an expedition east into the Great Plains, but the venture proved as futile as Coronado's earlier march had been.

To make matters worse, drought gripped the Rio Grande valley, and many of the recent settlers departed, complaining that the region lacked woods, pastures, water, and suitable land. When Oñate returned from the plains, he found that two-thirds of his tiny colony had given up and returned to Mexico. Foiled on the east and weakened along the Rio Grande, Oñate next pressed west to seek a link to the Pacific. When he reached the Gulf of California in 1605, he mistook it for the great ocean and envisioned a possible link to the Pacific trade.

In fact, however, Oñate's new "Mexico" remained isolated and impoverished. The desperate colonists, strapped for food and clothing, pressed hard on the native peoples. They demanded tribute in the form of cotton blankets, buffalo hides, and baskets of scarce maize. In winter, ill-equipped Spanish soldiers stripped warm robes off the backs of shivering women and children; in summer, they scoured each pueblo for corn, torturing residents to find out where food was hidden.

Meanwhile, a few hundred Pueblo Indians—intimidated by the Spanish, desperate for a share of the food they had grown, and fearful of attacks by neighboring Apache—began to accept Christian baptism and seek Spanish protection. By 1608, when the crown threatened to withdraw support from the struggling province, the colony's Franciscan missionaries

Spanish exploration by land and sea

■ Spanish territory, 1610
— Juan de Oñate, 1598–1601
— Juan de Oñate, 1604–1605
— Sebastián Vizcaíno, 1602–1603
— Sebastián Vizcaíno, 1611–1613
Present state boundaries provided for orientation

■ **MAP 2.1**
THE SPANISH SOUTHWEST IN THE EARLY SEVENTEENTH CENTURY

appealed that their converts had grown too numerous to resettle and too dependent to abandon. Their argument may have been exaggerated, but it caught the attention of authorities. Besides, England and France were launching new colonies in Virginia and Canada. Since mapmakers still could not accurately calculate longitude (to determine east–west distances on the globe), no one was sure whether these bases created by international rivals posed a threat that was dangerously close at hand. Worried Spanish officials finally agreed with the Franciscan friars that New Mexico must carry on. They replaced Oñate with a new governor and asserted royal control over the few dozen settlers who remained in the colony.

Kevin Fleming/CORBIS

■ Acoma, often called Sky City, sits atop a high sandstone mesa west of Albuquerque, New Mexico. The name means "place that always was," and the pueblo has been continuously inhabited for roughly 1,000 years. Acoma's Native American community survived a devastating attack by Spanish colonizers in 1599.

New Mexico Survives: New Flocks Among Old Pueblos

The Spanish decision to hold on in New Mexico reshaped life for everyone in the region. At least 60,000 Indians living in nearly sixty separate pueblos found their world transformed and their survival threatened over the next half-century. In 1610 the new governor, ruling over scarcely fifty colonists, created a capital at the village of Santa Fe. Within two decades, roughly 750 colonists inhabited the remote province, including Spanish, Mexican Indians, Africans, and mixed-race children.

The racial and ethnic diversity of New Mexico repeated the colonial pattern established in New Spain. Similarly, labor practices and religious changes also followed models established after the conquest of the Aztec in Mexico. As in New Spain, certain privileged people in the new colony received *encomiendas*; such grants entitled the holders (known as *encomenderos*) to the labor of a set number of Native American workers. With labor in short supply throughout the Spanish colonies, other settlers led occasional raids against nomadic Plains Indians, keeping some captives and shipping others south to toil as slaves in the Mexican silver mines.

Meanwhile, the number of Franciscan missionaries rose rapidly. They forbade traditional Pueblo celebrations, known as kachina dances, and destroyed sacred kachina masks. Their combination of intense zeal and harsh punishments prompted many Indians to learn Spanish and become obedient converts. However, it also drove the Indians' own religious practices

■ The Spanish made Santa Fe the capital of their New Mexico colony in 1610 and built the church of San Miguel there in 1626. Though destroyed in the Pueblo Revolt of 1680, it was rebuilt and has remained in use. "The floor is bare earth," wrote an eighteenth-century observer, "the usual floor throughout these regions."

underground—literally, into the hidden, circular kivas that had long been a focal point for Native American spiritual activities in the region. There, people kept their traditional faith alive in secret and passed sacred rituals along to the next generation.

The Spanish brought more than Christianity to New Mexico. The newcomers also transferred novel crops (wheat, onions, chilies, peas) and planted new fruits (peaches, plums, cherries). Settlers introduced metal hoes and axes to the area as well, along with donkeys, chickens, and other domesticated animals previously unknown to the native inhabitants. Horses and cattle, led north from New Spain, eventually revolutionized life across the North American West. But the most immediate impact came from Spanish sheep. Each friar soon possessed a flock of several thousand, and Pueblo artisans wove wool into cloth.

But the Pueblo world, like Squanto's world, was eroding under the onslaught of new European diseases. The large Pueblo population, cut in half in the sixty years after Coronado's appearance, still numbered more than 60,000 in 1600. Sickness, along with warfare and famine, cut this number in half again by 1650 and in half once more by 1680.

Conversion and Rebellion in Spanish Florida

By 1600 Spanish Florida also disappointed imperial officials. Dreams of gold-filled kingdoms and a strategic passage from the Southeast to the Orient had never materialized. The Spanish government regarded the outpost at St. Augustine as an undue burden and planned to disband the colony. But Franciscan missionaries won the day, as in New Mexico. They argued that scores of Indian towns appeared ready to receive Christianity. By 1608 the crown had decided to let the colony continue.

A handful of missionaries fanned out among the Indians of northern Florida, erecting small churches and mission schools. They recruited Indian students aggressively without regard to age or sex. In 1612 Francisco de Pareja published an illustrated, bilingual confessional in Castilian and Timucuan, the earliest text in any North American Indian language. The book enabled wary friars to ask villagers, "Have you said suggestive words?" and "Have you desired to do some lewd act with some man or woman or kin?"

Contact with Christian beliefs and books came at a steep price, for each inland village was expected to help feed the colonial garrison at St. Augustine. Local women neglected household crops to grow additional maize and grind it into meal. Annually, Spanish officials **requisitioned** Indian men from each village to transport the cornmeal overland to the Atlantic coast and return to the mission carrying supplies for the Franciscans. Imported candles, communion wine, and mission bells all had to be hauled inland.

Friars and Indian bearers traveling to the interior also carried sicknesses from St. Augustine. Epidemics of foreign diseases—

■ The Spanish found that glass beads, colorful and easy to transport, made fine gifts and trade items in their contacts with Florida Indians. Chiefs often received special quartz crystal beads and pendants to retain their loyalty.

measles, bubonic plague, malaria, typhus, smallpox, and influenza—took a devastating toll on the Native Americans. As whole villages disappeared, Spanish entrepreneurs began to expand cattle ranching across northern Florida. Faced with encroaching farms, crushing labor demands, and frightful mortality, local native leaders saw their power reduced and their communities depleted. These conditions sparked a short-lived revolt by Indians at Apalachee in 1647. Nine years later, when the governor at St. Augustine feared a possible attack by English ships, a wider Native American uprising shook Timucua in north-central Florida.

Native American Population Loss, 1500–1700

In the end, the English threat to Spanish Florida did not materialize in 1656, but the rumor underscored how much had changed in the preceding half-century. Two generations earlier, in 1600, no European power besides Spain had possessed a solid foothold in any portion of the Americas. But over the next six decades, France, Holland, and England all asserted claims on the American mainland.

France and Holland:
Overseas Competition for Spain

At the turn of the seventeenth century, interlopers from Holland had challenged Spanish colonizers in the Philippines and Portuguese traders in Japan. These Dutch efforts illustrated the growing competition between European powers for control of the world's oceans. In London, commercial leaders received a royal charter to create the English East India Company in 1600, and merchants in Amsterdam took a similar step. Hoping to capture Portugal's lucrative Asian trade, they established the Dutch East India Company in 1602. By 1652 their ships had invaded eastern oceans and had also founded a Dutch colony at Cape Town, on the southern tip of Africa.

The united powers of Spain and Portugal proved even more vulnerable in the Atlantic. To be sure, Spanish convoys continued to transport Mexican gold and silver to Europe annually, along with Asian silks and spices shipped to Mexico via the Pacific trade. Portuguese vessels carried Africans to the New World at a profit. But ships from rival European nations preyed on these seaborne cargoes with increasing success. Defiantly, they also laid claim to numerous islands in the Caribbean.

By 1660, the English had taken control of Barbados, Providence Island, Antigua, and Jamaica; the Dutch had acquired St. Maarten, St. Eustacius, Saba, and Curaçao; and the French had claimed Guadeloupe, Martinique, Grenada, and St. Lucia. For France, however, the most promising Atlantic prospects lay farther north in Canada. There, Spanish power was absent, hopes for a Northwest Passage persisted, and French imperial claims stretched back generations.

The Founding of New France

Since the time of Jacques Cartier, fishing boats from the coast of France had crisscrossed Newfoundland's Grand Banks. The trade increased after 1580 as crews built seasonal stations along the American coast for drying codfish. These stations prompted greater contact with Indians; soon Europeans were exchanging metal goods for furs on terms that pleased all. A Native American could trade a worn-out robe made from beaver skins for a highly valued iron kettle. A European artisan could fashion a beaver hat that proved fashionable and profitable.

As North Atlantic fishing and trading expanded, the domestic situation in France improved. In 1598 King Henry IV issued the Edict of Nantes, a decree granting political rights and limited toleration to French Protestants, or Huguenots. With religious wars curtailed, the king could contemplate new colonization initiatives in America. An experienced French soldier and sailor named Samuel de Champlain emerged as a key leader in this effort. From

1602 until his death in 1635, Champlain devoted himself to the St. Lawrence River region, where Acadia on the Atlantic coast and Canada along the extensive river valley made up the anticipated realm of New France.

In 1608 Champlain and several dozen other men established an outpost at Quebec, where Cartier and Roberval had wintered generations earlier. In June 1609 Champlain joined a band of Algonquin and Huron Indians in a raid on the Iroquois in modern New York. When they engaged their Iroquois enemies in battle, Champlain fired his gun—a novelty in the region—killing several war chiefs and sparking a rout. For the powerful **Iroquois League** south of the St. Lawrence (the Five Nation confederation composed of the Seneca, Cayuga, Onondaga, Oneida, and Mohawk Indians), the defeat spawned lasting bitterness. But for the French, their victory sealed good relations with the Algonquin and Huron, ensuring the survival of Quebec and spurring unprecedented commerce. Within fifteen years, Native Americans were trading 12,000 to 15,000 beaver pelts annually via the St. Lawrence River valley.

In 1627 the powerful first minister in France, Cardinal Richelieu, pressed for greater French settlement in Canada through a new private company. He banned Huguenots from participating and pushed to make sure that only Roman Catholics were allowed to migrate to Canada. But his expansive policies alarmed rival England, which captured Quebec briefly in 1629. When restored to French control several years later, the tiny outpost contained fewer than a 100 people. In an effort to expand the **meager** settlement and populate the fertile valley upriver from Quebec, French authorities began granting narrow strips of land with river frontage to any Catholic lord (seigneur) who would take up residence there and bring French tenants to his estate.

Competing for the Beaver Trade

Cardinal Richelieu's power in France epitomized the ongoing Counter-Reformation. This outpouring of Catholic zeal reached as far as North America. In 1635 Jesuits founded a college in Quebec, and in 1639 six nuns arrived to begin a school for Indian girls and a hospital. Other religious workers established a station farther west in 1641 in territory recently dominated by the Iroquois; the strategic outpost marked the beginnings of Montreal. From there, the French planned to control the beaver trade as it expanded west up the St. Lawrence. They also hoped to prevent the Iroquois League from diverting furs south to Holland's new colony on the Hudson River.

But the desperate Iroquois nations, facing collapse, took a stand. Increasing contact with Europeans and their contagious diseases had brought catastrophic epidemics to the Iroquois homelands below Lake Ontario. Beginning in 1633, sicknesses that were new to the region swept away some 10,000 people and cut the Five Nations' population in half within a decade, emptying the distinctive longhouses that made up Iroquois villages. According to Iroquois tradition, survivors must replace deceased individuals swiftly with captives to maintain the community's strength and continuity. Pressed by grieving families, Iroquois warriors initiated a generation of violent campaigns intended to capture and absorb neighboring groups. These so-called mourning wars are also remembered as the Beaver Wars because they included a clear economic as well as cultural motive. Besides captives, the Iroquois aggressors sought furs. If they could seize pelts before the valuable items reached the French, they could trade them to the Dutch for guns and powder. Well armed, they could then engage in further wars for captives and furs.

This spiral of aggression put the Iroquois on a collision course with the Huron and their allies, a small band of Jesuit missionaries willing to risk martyrdom in New France. Eager for Native American converts, the Jesuits focused their attention on the region east of Lake Huron, where 30,000 Huron Indians lived in large villages. The Jesuits erected chapels at four of these towns and constructed a central base at St. Marie near Georgian Bay. Having volunteered for hardship, they witnessed far more of it than they ever imagined.

■ **MAP 2.2**
EUROPEAN AND NATIVE AMERICAN CONTACT IN THE NORTHEAST, 1600–1660
French and English colonization efforts brought devastating diseases to the Five Nations of the Iroquois League. Eager to take captives and profit from the growing trade in furs, the Iroquois ranged north and west to make war on the French and their Huron Indian allies.

First came the same foreign epidemics that had wasted the Iroquois; smallpox cut down roughly two-thirds of the Huron population, or 20,000 people, between 1635 and 1640. Then came the Iroquois themselves, bent on capturing Huron women and children to revitalize their longhouses, swept by disease in the 1630s. Armed by Dutch traders eager for furs, 1,000 Iroquois warriors descended on the weakened Huron in March 1649. They burned villages, secured captives, tortured several priests to death, and seized large stocks of pelts. The Iroquois then launched raids on the St. Lawrence River valley, disrupting the fur trade and frightening the several thousand French inhabitants. By 1660 it seemed that New France—thinly settled, weakly defended, and poorly supplied—might face the same extinction that the much older and larger Huron community had suffered.

A Dutch Colony on the Hudson River

The Dutch traders who supplied firearms to the Iroquois in exchange for furs owed their start to English-born navigator Henry Hudson. In 1609, sailing for the Dutch East India Company, Hudson crossed the Atlantic in search of a western passage to the Orient. He visited Chesapeake Bay and Delaware Bay, then rediscovered modern-day New York harbor, the bay that Verrazzano had entered in 1524. Flying the Dutch flag above his vessel, the *Half Moon*, Hudson sailed north up the broad river that now bears his name. The Dutch moved quickly to gain a foothold in the region. Ships from Amsterdam appeared far up the Hudson, exchanging metal goods for beaver pelts. Soon the Dutch had established a year-round trading post at Fort Orange, near present-day Albany.

In 1621 responsibility for New Netherland—the region claimed between the Delaware and Connecticut rivers—fell to the newly chartered Dutch West India Company (DWIC). Modeled on the Dutch East India Company, the DWIC concentrated on piecing together an empire in the South Atlantic. Dutch ships seized part of sugar-rich Brazil (1632), the island of Curaçao near Venezuela (1634), and Portugal's African outpost at Elmina, on the coast of modern-day Ghana (1637). But the DWIC also laid plans for a North American colony.

To begin, the company transported a group of French-speaking Belgians to New Netherland in 1624. To secure the boundaries of the province, officials deposited farm families far up the Hudson at Fort Orange and along the Connecticut and Delaware rivers. However, Peter Minuit, the colony's director from 1626 to 1631, saw danger in this dispersal. To consolidate settlement, he purchased Manhattan Island at the mouth of the Hudson from the local Indians in 1626. By 1630 the village of New Amsterdam boasted 270 settlers at the southern tip of Manhattan.

When the company threw open the Indian trade to others besides its own agents, the careless and greedy actions of unregulated traders sparked a series of violent wars with coastal tribes. Also, the Dutch squabbled constantly with neighboring English settlers over fur-trading rights and other matters. The small colony of New Sweden, which materialized on the west side of the Delaware River in 1637, posed yet another problem. The settlers who built Fort Christina (now Wilmington, Delaware) were Swedes and Finns hoping to establish their own trade with the Indians. But in 1655, these several hundred Scandinavians were obliged to surrender to Dutch power.

"All Sorts of Nationalities": Diverse New Amsterdam

The symbol of Dutch power in the region, and the commander of the fleet that seized New Sweden, was Peter Stuyvesant. He ruled New Netherland aggressively for several decades before England seized the colony in 1664. Stuyvesant had served as governor of Dutch Curaçao, losing his right leg in a battle with the Spanish. When he arrived in New Netherland in 1647 as director general for the DWIC, he moved swiftly to assert control.

Stuyvesant limited beer and rum sales, fined settlers for promiscuity and knife fighting, and established a nine-member night watch. When a group of English Quakers, members of

■ **New Amsterdam Fort on Manhattan Island.**

the newly formed Society of Friends, arrived aboard a trading vessel in 1657, he attempted to expel the radical Protestants and fine any who gave them shelter. However, Dutch residents of Flushing, on Long Island, defied his ban and signed a public letter of objection stressing religious toleration.

To address the colony's chronic labor shortage, Stuyvesant endorsed trade in African slaves and used his Caribbean connections to expand this traffic. When the Portuguese forced Holland out of Brazil in 1654 and closed that sugar colony to Dutch slave vessels, some of the ships brought their cargoes to New Amsterdam instead. Like the Dutch-speaking blacks who already lived in the colony, most of these newcomers were enslaved for life. But the DWIC, the largest importer and owner of slaves in New Netherland, granted "half-freedom" to some whom it could not employ year-round. These people, in return for an annual fee, could travel and marry freely, acquire property, and hire out their labor. By 1664 black residents made up over 10 percent of New Netherland's population and 20 percent of New Amsterdam, the colony's capital.

New Amsterdam, home to fewer than 2,000 people, also had a small Jewish contingent, the first in mainland North America. In 1654, twenty-three Sephardic Jews reached Manhattan, forced out of Brazil by the Portuguese. Stuyvesant, strident in his anti-Semitism, claimed such "blasphemers of the name of Christ" would "infect and trouble this new colony." But the DWIC, which included Jewish stockholders and was eager for newcomers of all kinds, overruled the governor's request to expel the refugees. In the end, colony officials authorized a Jewish ghetto, or segregated neighborhood, where the newcomers could pray together freely in private. At first, however, they were not allowed to construct a synagogue for public worship.

In the early 1660s, the colony continued to grow, "slowly peopled by the scrapings of all sorts of nationalities," as Stuyvesant complained. Huguenots occupied New Paltz near the Hudson; farther north, other newcomers founded Schenectady in 1661. Swedes and Finns continued to prosper along the Delaware, and numerous English had settled on Long Island. Compared with New France, New Netherland seemed far more populous, prosperous, and ethnically diverse. But whereas the French colony to the north endured for another century, the Dutch enterprise soon was absorbed by England. For, despite a slow start, the English managed to outdistance all their European rivals and establish thriving North American colonies in the first half of the seventeenth century.

> *Compared with New France, New Netherland seemed far more populous, prosperous, and ethnically diverse.*

English Beginnings on the Atlantic Coast

When Queen Elizabeth I passed away in 1603, several important elements were already in place to help England compete for colonial outposts. Thousands of rural tenants had been pushed off farms; these landless people, who flocked to urban centers in search of work, formed a restless supply of potential colonists. Also, the country had an expanding fleet of English-built ships, sailed by experienced mariners. In addition, England had a group of seasoned and ambitious leaders. A generation of soldiers (many of them younger sons of the property-holding elite known as the gentry) had fought in Europe or participated in the brutal colonization of Ireland.

Because Elizabeth I died without heirs, the king of Scotland, James Stuart, succeeded her as ruler. During the reigns of James I (1603–1625) and his son Charles I (1625–1649), religious and economic forces in England prompted an increasing number of people to consider migrating overseas. With the expansion of the country's Protestant Reformation, religious strife escalated toward civil war, which erupted in 1642. During the tumultuous 1630s, English public officials were glad to transplant Puritans and Catholics alike to foreign shores. In turn, many **ardent** believers—weary of conflict or losing hope for their cause at home—welcomed the prospect of a safe haven abroad. Economically, the development of joint stock organizations enabled merchants to raise capital and spread the high risk of colonial ventures by selling numerous shares to small investors. At the same time, the fluctuating domestic economy prompted many people to consider seeking their fortunes elsewhere.

Nor had English geographers given up on finding a sea route somewhere in the Northern Hemisphere leading to the riches of Asia. Perhaps Virginia would prove no wider than the Isthmus of Panama, or a short passage to China would reveal itself farther north. With this latter prospect in mind, England pressed Henry Hudson into service in 1610, shortly after his voyage for the Dutch. The experienced explorer ventured far to the northwest, navigating the strait and bay in northern Canada that still bear his name. But Hudson's search for a Northwest Passage failed, and he was set adrift by his mutinous crew. English attention moved elsewhere.

The Virginia Company and Jamestown

For Richard Hakluyt, England's leading publicist for overseas expansion, the proper focus seemed clear: "There is under our noses," he wrote in 1599, "the great & ample countrey of Virginia." Great and ample, indeed, especially before the rival Dutch established New Netherland. On paper, the enormous zone that England claimed as Virginia stretched north to south from the top of modern-day Vermont to Cape Fear on Carolina's Outer Banks. From east to west, it spanned North America from the Atlantic to the Pacific, however narrow or wide the continent might prove to be.

In 1606 James I chartered the Virginia Company as a two-pronged operation to exploit the sweeping Virginia claim. Under the charter, a group of London-based merchants took responsibility for colonizing the Chesapeake Bay region. Meanwhile, merchants from the English seaports of Plymouth, Exeter, and Bristol took charge of developing the northern latitudes of the American coast. In 1607 two ships from Plymouth deposited roughly a hundred colonists at the Sagadahoc (Kennebec) River in Maine. The Sagadahoc settlers erected a fort and buildings, but frostbite, scurvy, and dwindling supplies prompted a retreat home in 1608.

Mural of Jamestown Settlement

A parallel effort by the Londoners proved more enduring—but just barely. In April 1607, three ships from the Thames sailed into Chesapeake Bay carrying 105 men. They disembarked on what appeared to be a secluded island near a broad river. Within months, these subjects of James I had named the waterway the James River and established a fortified village beside it called Jamestown. In June, hoping for quick rewards, they shipped to London various stones that they thought contained precious gems and gold ore.

When the rocks proved worthless, the colonists' dreams of easy wealth evaporated. So did their fantasies about pushing west to the Pacific. During the outpost's first winter, a fire destroyed the tiny settlement, and death from hunger, exposure, and sickness cut the garrison's population in half. The governor and council appointed by the Virginia Company bickered among themselves, providing poor leadership. Fully one-third of the early arrivals claimed to be gentlemen, from England's leisure class—a proportion six times higher than in England—and most proved unaccustomed to hard manual labor. Moreover, all the colonists were employees of the company, so any profits from their labor went to repay London investors.

Despite the unsuitable make-up of the garrison, conditions improved briefly with the emergence of John Smith as a vigorous leader. Captain Smith dealt brazenly with the local Powhatan Indian confederation, numbering more than 13,000 people. He reached a tenuous accommodation with the paramount chief, Powhatan, who had been steadily expanding his power across the Tidewater region. (Later, Smith claimed to have been assisted and protected by Powhatan's young daughter, Pocahontas.) Still, the Jamestown colony limped along with meager support, living in fear of Spanish attacks.

With hopes of a swift bonanza dashed, the London merchants decided to alter their strategy. They would salvage the venture by attracting fresh capital; then they would recoup their high initial costs by recruiting new settlers who could produce staple products suited for export—perhaps grapes, sugar, cotton, or tobacco. In 1609 the company began to sell seven-year joint stock options to the English public. Subscribers could invest money or they could sign on for service in Virginia. Company officials promised such adventurers at least a hundred acres of land when their investment matured in 1616. In June 1609, 500 men and 100 women departed for the Chesapeake aboard nine ships.

"Starving Time" and the Seeds of Representative Government

When the battered fleet arrived at Jamestown, the new arrivals found insufficient supplies. Moreover, the first settlers had failed to discover a profitable staple crop. The settlers, now numbering 500, depended heavily on the Native Americans for food, and Powhatan's Confederacy proved increasingly unwilling and unable to supply it. In a grim "starving time," the ill-equipped newcomers scavenged for berries and bark. Extreme hunger drove a few to cannibalize the dead before dying themselves. By the spring of 1610, seven of every eight people had died; scarcely sixty remained alive.

DOCUMENT

John Smith, "The Starving Time"

In June these survivors abandoned their ghost town altogether. But as they set sail for England, they encountered three long-overdue ships entering Chesapeake Bay with fresh supplies and 300 new settlers. Reluctantly, they agreed to try again. More years of harsh discipline, Indian warfare, and scarce resources followed. Another force—a severe dry spell—also conspired against the hapless newcomers. Indian and English crops alike shriveled from 1607 through 1612.

Relief came from an unexpected quarter: the "bewitching vegetable" known as Orinoco tobacco. The plant, grown in parts of the West Indies and South America, had captured English taste in the previous generation. Sales of this New World product in England sent profits to the Spanish crown and prompted James I to launch a vigorous antismoking campaign in 1604. But John Rolfe, reaching Jamestown in 1610, wondered whether the "noxious weed" might provide the colonists with a viable staple crop. Rolfe, a smoker himself, suspected that sweet-flavored Orinoco tobacco could prosper in Virginia soil. Within a year, Rolfe had somehow managed to obtain seeds, and by 1612 his patch of West Indian tobacco was flourishing. Desperate settlers and impatient London investors were delighted by Rolfe's successful experiment. Soon production of the leaf soared at Jamestown, to the neglect of all other pursuits.

National Geographic Society. © 1998. Photo by Steve Rawls

■ Inexperience prompted initial English difficulties at Roanoke and Jamestown, but so did poor weather. Scientists studying the region's bald cypress trees have recently shown (from certain narrow rings) that terrible droughts struck the coastal area in the late 1580s and again from 1606 through 1612. These two sequences of narrow annual rings are visible under the magnifying glass.

During Virginia's initial tobacco boom, recently starving settlers saw handsome profits within reach. Because land was plentiful, the only limitations to riches were the scarcity of workers and the related high cost of labor. Any farmer who could hire half a dozen field hands could increase his profits fivefold, quickly earning enough to obtain more land and import more servants. The company transported several shiploads of apprentices and servants to the labor-hungry colony. When a Dutch captain delivered twenty enslaved blacks in 1619, settlers eagerly purchased these first Africans to arrive in English Virginia. They also bid on the 100 women who disembarked the same year, shipped from England by the company to be sold as wives and workers. Still, men continued to outnumber women more than three to one for decades to come.

To encourage English migration further, the Virginia Company offered transportation and 50 acres to tenants, promising them ownership of the land after seven years of work. Men who paid their own way received 50 acres and an additional "**headright**" of 50 acres for each household member or laborer they transported. The Virginia Company went out of its way to assure its colonists access to such established English freedoms as the right to trial by jury and to a representative form of government. The company established civil courts controlled by English common law, and it instructed Virginia's governor to summon an annual assembly of elected **burgesses**—the earliest representative legislature in North America. First convened in 1619, the House of Burgesses wasted no time in affirming its commitment to fundamental English rights. The governor, the house said, could no longer impose taxes without the assembly's consent.

> *The Virginia Company went out of its way to assure its colonists access to established English freedoms.*

Launching the Plymouth Colony

To attract additional capital and people, the Virginia Company also began awarding patents (legal charters) to private groups of adventurers. The newcomers would live independently on a large tract, with only minimal control from the governor and his council. Two such small colonies originated among English Protestants living in exile in Holland because their separatist beliefs did not allow them to profess loyalty to the Church of England. The first group of 180, based in Amsterdam, departed for America late in 1618 on a crowded ship. Winter storms, sickness, and a shortage of fresh water destroyed the venture; scarcely fifty survivors straggled ashore in Virginia.

A second group of English Separatists, residing in the smaller Dutch city of Leiden, fared better. Most had migrated to Holland from northeast England in 1608. This group openly opposed the hierarchy, pomp, and inclusiveness of the Church of England. Instead, they wanted to return to early Christianity, where small groups of worthy (and often persecuted) believers formed their own communities of worship. After a decade in Holland, many of them had wearied of the foreign culture. Dismayed by the effect of worldly Leiden on their children, they also sensed, correctly, that warfare would soon break out in Europe. A few families pushed for a further removal to America, despite the obvious dangers of such a journey.

Possible destinations ranged from South America to Canada. But in the end, the Separatists decided to use a patent granted by the Virginia Company to a group of English capitalists. On the negative side, they had to work for these investors for seven years. They also had to take along paying passengers who did not share their beliefs. On the positive side, they received financial support from backers who paid to rent a ship. Moreover, instead of having their daily affairs controlled from London, they had the power to govern themselves.

DOCUMENT

Agreement Between the Settlers at New Plymouth (Mayflower Compact)

In September 1620, after costly delays, thirty-five members of the Leiden congregation and additional Separatists from England departed from Plymouth, along with other passengers. They were crowded aboard the *Mayflower*, a 160-ton vessel bound for Virginia. But a stormy two-month crossing brought them to Cape Cod, in modern-day Massachusetts, no longer considered part of the Virginia Company's jurisdiction. Sickly from their journey and with winter closing in, they decided to disembark at the spot they called Plymouth rather than push south to Chesapeake Bay. Earlier, they had signed a solemn compact aboard the *Mayflower* binding them together in a civil community.

William Bradford, the chronicler and longtime governor of Plymouth Colony, later recalled their plight: "They had now no friends to welcome them nor inns to entertain or refresh their weather-beaten bodies.... Besides, what could they see but a hideous and desolate wilderness." Bradford could scarcely exaggerate the challenge. His own wife drowned (an apparent suicide) shortly after the *Mayflower* dropped anchor. And by the time the ship departed in April, an illness had swept away half the colonists. When those remaining planted barley and peas, the English seeds failed to take hold.

Still, settlers had abundant fish and wildlife, along with ample Indian corn, and soon rein-forcements arrived from England bringing needed supplies. The newcomers also brought a legal patent for the land of Plymouth Plantation. With Squanto's aid, the settlers secured peaceful relations with Massasoit's villages. When survival for another winter seemed assured, they invited Massasoit and his Indian followers to join in a three-day celebration of thanksgiving so that, according to one account, all might "rejoice together after we had gathered the fruit of our labors."

AUDIO

"Plymouth Colony"

The Puritan Experiment

After more than a generation of costly colonization attempts, England still had little to show for its efforts when Charles I inherited the throne in 1625. Then two forces prompted rapid change: positive publicity about America and negative developments at home. John Smith, long a key promoter of overseas settlement, drew inspiration from the early efforts at Jamestown and Plymouth. In 1624 he published a best-seller predicting future success for these regions. Ironically, the book's popularity depended in large part on the grim religious, political, and economic conditions in England that suddenly gave such literature a broad appeal.

Formation of the Massachusetts Bay Company

European Christianity had taken a number of different forms since the religious upheaval sparked by Luther a century earlier. The first Protestants had demanded a reformation of the Roman Catholic Church and had questioned papal authority over Christians. Now many non-Catholic English worshippers doubted whether the Church of England (also known as the Anglican Church) had gone far enough toward rejecting the practices of Rome. They lamented what they saw as the church's bureaucratic hierarchy, ornate rituals, and failure to enforce strict observance of the Christian Sabbath each Sunday. They scoffed at the gaudy vestments of Anglican bishops, elaborate church music, and other trappings of worship unjustified by biblical scripture. Instead, they praised the stark simplicity that John Calvin had brought to his church in Geneva.

As English Calvinists grew in number, their objections to the Church of England increased. They protested that the Anglican Church, like the Catholic Church, remained inclusive in membership rather than selective. They argued for limiting participation only to the devout, and they protested that the Church of England should be independent and self-governing rather than tied to the monarchy. This keen desire for further cleansing and purity, so common to reformers, spurred the ongoing movement known as Puritanism.

VIDEO

"The Puritans"

Some of the most radical members of the broad Puritan coalition (including Bradford and the Plymouth pilgrims) became known as Separatists because they were committed to an extreme position: complete separation from what they saw as the corrupt Church of England. But many more Puritans (including most of the reformers who migrated to Massachusetts Bay) resisted separation. They hoped to stay technically within the Anglican fold while taking increased control of their own congregations—a practice known as congregationalism. Unwilling to conform to practices that offended them, these nonseparating Congregationalists remained determined to save the Anglican Church through righteous example, even if it meant migrating abroad for a time to escape persecution and demonstrate the proper ways of a purified Protestant church.

An emphasis on instructive preaching by informed leaders lay at the heart of the Puritan movement. Puritans believed that the sermon should form the center of the Christian worship service. Their churches resembled lecture halls, emphasizing the pulpit more than the altar. In

DOCUMENT

The Cambridge Agreement

preaching, Puritans stressed a "plain style" that all listeners could understand. Moreover, they urged listeners to play an active role in their faith—to master reading and engage in regular study and discussion of scripture. In response to mounting public interest in these practices, Puritan ministers intensified their preaching and published their sermons. In effect, they dared authorities to silence them.

Reprisals came swiftly, led by William Laud, bishop of London. Laud instructed all preachers to focus their remarks on biblical passages and avoid writing or speaking about controversial religious matters. As England's church grew more rigid and its monarchy more controlling, the nation's economy took a turn for the worse. Rents and food costs had risen more rapidly than wages, and workers paid dearly. Jobs became more scarce, and unemployed workers staged local revolts. In 1629 entrepreneurs who viewed New England as a potential opportunity teamed up with disaffected Puritans to obtain a charter for a new entity: the Massachusetts Bay Company. Through a generation of costly trial-and-error experiments, the English had amassed great expertise in colonization. And given the worsening conditions at home, especially among the Puritan faithful, proposals for overseas settlement attracted widespread attention.

"We Shall Be as a City upon a Hill"

During the next dozen years, more than 70,000 people left England for the New World. Two-thirds of them sailed to the West Indies. But a large contingent of Puritans embarked for the new Massachusetts Bay colony, adjacent to the Plymouth settlement. A loophole in the king's grant permitted them to take the actual charter with them and to hold their company meetings in America. This maneuver took them out from under the usual control of London investors and let them turn the familiar joint stock structure into the framework for a self-governing colony. By 1629 advance parties had established a post at Salem for people who "upon the account of religion would be willing to begin a foreign plantation."

In England, meanwhile, a Puritan squire named John Winthrop assumed leadership of the Massachusetts Bay Company. "God will bring some heavy Affliction upon this lande," he predicted to his wife, but the Lord "will provide a shelter & a hidinge place for us and others." In exchange, God would expect great things from these chosen people, as from the Old Testament Israelites. "We are entered into covenant with him for this work," Winthrop told his companions aboard the *Arbella* en route to America in 1630.

Winthrop laid out this higher Calvinist standard in a memorable shipboard sermon titled "A Model of Christian Charity." Far from hiding in obscurity, dedicated Puritans must set a visible example for the rest of the world, Winthrop declared. "We shall be as a city upon a hill."

The *Arbella* was one of seventeen ships that brought more than 1,000 people to New England in 1630. The English newcomers chose Winthrop as governor and established Boston as their port. By the time civil war erupted in England in 1642, nearly 20,000 people had made the journey, eager to escape the religious persecution and governmental tyranny of Charles I. Whole congregations migrated with their ministers; other people (more than 20 percent) crossed as servants. But most came as independent families, setting up stable households where

Worcester Art Museum, Worcester, MA. Gift of Mr. and Mrs. Albert W. Rice

■ Port records for 1635 show that groups leaving London varied markedly, depending on their colonial destination. Young children were common aboard ships heading for New England, as were women and girls. Among passengers for New England, eight of every twenty were female. In contrast, females made up only three in twenty of those going to Virginia and one in twenty among people heading for Barbados.

Anne Bradstreet: "The Tenth Muse, Lately Sprung Up in America"

The Puritans who migrated to America stressed literacy and education as part of their faith. They wrote down a great deal, and they left extensive records for posterity. But most of their sermons, diaries, and chronicles were drafted by men; few documents about the thoughts and experiences of New England's early migrants come from the pens of women. The poems and reflections of Anne Bradstreet provide a notable exception. "Here you may find," she reminded her children shortly before her death in 1672, "what was your living mother's mind."

The lifelong poet was born Anne Dudley in Lincolnshire, England, in 1612. She already "found much comfort in reading the Scriptures" by age seven. "But as I grew to be about 14 or 15," she recalled, "I found my heart more carnal, and . . . the follies of youth took hold of me. About 16, the Lord . . . smote me with the smallpox . . . and again restored me." That same year, she married Simon Bradstreet, the son of a minister. Two years later, despite a frail constitution, she sailed for Massachusetts Bay with her husband and her father (both future governors of the colony) aboard the Arbella.

Having left England at age eighteen, Anne Bradstreet was alert to all that seemed strange and different in America. When I "came into this country," she related, "I found a new world and new manners." The young couple set up housekeeping in the town of Cambridge, on the Charles River, but life was difficult at first. Anne suffered from "a lingering sickness like a consumption." Moreover, "It pleased God to keep me a long time without a child, which was a

Cambridge, on the Charles River near Boston, was a small village in the 1660s. The large building in the foreground is Harvard College, founded in 1636, and the smaller brick building beside it is the Indian College, built in 1655. The village was even smaller when Anne Bradstreet resided there briefly after her arrival in Massachusetts Bay.

COLLEGIUM CANTABRIGIAE A.D. CONDITUM — HARVARDIANUM IN NOVA ANGLIA MDCLXVIII A.D. MDCXXXVI

Courtesy of the Harvard University Archives

great grief to me and cost me many prayers and tears." Finally, she bore a son in 1633, and seven more children followed.

As the family grew and moved about, "Mistress Bradstreet" wrote poems and meditations, although detractors hinted that she should put down her quill pen and take up a sewing needle. "If what I do prove well, it won't advance," she lamented in rhyme; "They'l say it's stol'n, or else it was by chance." Nevertheless, a book of her poems was published in England in 1650, hailing her as "The Tenth Muse, Lately Sprung Up in America."

As a writer, Anne Bradstreet was more interested in spiritual improvement than literary grace. "Many speak well," she observed, "but few can do well." Throughout life, she followed a simple creed: "There is no object that we see; no action that we do; no good that we enjoy; no evil that we feel or fear, but we may make some spiritual advantage" of it.

Nothing epitomizes this belief more clearly than "some verses upon the burning of our house, July 10th, 1666." Bradstreet composed the lines on an unburned scrap of paper as she groped to make sense of the calamity. The poem helped her to mourn her loss, take stock of her blessings, and renew her faith. In part, it reads,

In silent night when rest I took,
For sorrow neer I did not look,
I waken'd was with thundring nois
And Piteous shreiks of dreadfull voice. . . .

I, starting up, the light did spye,
And to my God my heart did cry. . . .
Then coming out beheld a space
The flame consume my dwelling place.

And, when I could no longer look,
I blest his Name that gave and took,
That layd my goods now in the dust:
Yea so it was, and so 'twas just. . . .

When by the Ruines oft I past,
My sorrowing eyes aside did cast,
And here and there the places spye
Where oft I sate, and long did lye.

Here stood that Trunk, and there
  that chest;
There lay that store I counted best:
My pleasant things in ashes lye,
And them behold no more shall I. . . .

Then streight I gin my heart to chide,
And did thy wealth on earth abide?
Didst fix thy hope on mouldring dust,
The arm of flesh didst make thy trust? . . .

Thou hast a house on high erect
Fram'd by that mighty Architect. . . .
The world no longer let me Love,
My hope and Treasure lyes Above.

Questions

1. How might Anne Bradstreet's eventful life before age 20 have shaped her into a poet?

2. Imagine losing your home and belongings in a storm, flood, or fire. Would it deepen or weaken your religious beliefs? How about your need for material possessions? ■

Source: From "Verses upon the Burning of Our House," July 18th, 1666 by Anne Bradstreet.

women played important parts. They took an immediate role in crucial aspects of domestic manufacture and production, and their numerous children provided additional hands where labor was in short supply.

Initial settlers traded food, lodging, and building materials to later arrivals in exchange for textiles, tools, money, and labor. When new groups of church members wanted to establish a village, they applied for land to the General Court, a legislature made up of representatives elected from existing towns. By 1640 English settlements dotted the coast and had sprung up inland along the Connecticut River, where smallpox had decimated the Indians in 1633. There, English outposts rose at Hartford and Springfield, where English traders hoped to attract furs away from the French and Dutch.

Dissenters: Roger Williams and Anne Hutchinson

Like the biblical Hebrews before them, the Puritans—self-appointed saints—believed that God had chosen them for a special mission in the world. The Almighty, they believed, would watch carefully, punish harshly, and reward mightily. Inevitably, some devout people, raised to question authority in England, continued to dissent in New England. Not everyone accepted the idea that Puritans should dominate Indians or that women should defer to men. Roger Williams, a graduate of Cambridge University, and Anne Hutchinson, the talented daughter of an English minister, stand out as two of the earliest and most effective challengers to leadership in the Massachusetts Bay colony.

When Williams arrived in Boston, his Separatist leanings angered Bay Colony authorities, who still hoped to reform the Anglican Church rather than renounce it. Williams's other contentions proved equally distressing. The young minister argued that civil authorities, inevitably corrupt, had no right to judge religious matters. He even pushed for an unprecedented separation of church and state—to protect the church. He also contended that the colony's land patent from the king had no validity. The settlers, he said, had to purchase occupancy rights from the Native Americans. Unable to silence him, irate magistrates banished Williams from Massachusetts Bay in the winter of 1635. Moving south, he took up residence among the Narragansett Indians and built a refuge for other dissenters, which he named Providence. In 1643 he returned to London, where he persuaded leaders of England's rising Puritan revolution to grant a charter (1644) to his independent colony of Rhode Island.

A more explosive popular challenge centered on Anne Hutchinson, who had grown up in England with a strong will, a solid theological education, and a thirst for spiritual perfection. She married a Lincolnshire textile merchant and took an active part in religious discussions while also bearing fifteen children. When her Puritan minister, John Cotton, departed for New England, Hutchinson claimed that God, in a private revelation, had instructed her to follow. In 1634 the family migrated to Boston, where Hutchinson attended Cotton's church and hosted religious discussions in her home. The popularity of these weekly meetings troubled authorities, as did her argument that the "Holy Spirit illumines the heart of every true believer." Hutchinson downplayed outward conformity—modest dress or regular church attendance— as a route to salvation. Instead, she stressed direct communication with God's inner presence as the key to individual forgiveness.

Most Puritans sought a delicate balance in their lives between respected outer works and inner personal grace. Hutchinson tipped that balance dangerously toward the latter. To the colony's magistrates, especially Winthrop, such teaching pointed toward dangerous anarchy—more dangerous when it came from a woman. These officials labeled Hutchinson and her followers as Antinomians (from *anti*, "against," and *nomos*, "law"). But the vehement faction grew, attracting merchants who chafed under economic restrictions, women who questioned men's domination of the church, and young adults who resented the strict authority of their elders. By 1636 this religious and political coalition had gained enough supporters to turn Winthrop out as governor.

The Pull to Settle in America
1. Word-of-mouth information about America
2. Effective work and writing by recruiters
3. Appeal of land and economic opportunities
4. Desire to join earlier migrants to America
5. Safe pursuit of personal religious beliefs
6. Hope of educating and converting Indians

The Push to Leave Home in Europe
1. Escape from direct religious persecution
2. Fear regarding the religious future at home
3. Anxiety about political change in Europe
4. Dismay over economy; need for farmland
5. Relief from joblessness or personal adversity
6. Restlessness and desire for adventure

■ **FIGURE 2.1**
THE TOUGH CHOICE TO START OVER

Facing complete overthrow, members of the Puritan establishment fought back. They divided the opposition to win reelection for Winthrop, they established Harvard College to educate ministers who would not stray from the fold, they staged a flurry of trials for contempt and sedition (inciting resistance to lawful authority), and they made a special example of Hutchinson herself. After a two-day hearing in which she defended herself admirably, Winthrop sentenced his antagonist to banishment as "a woman not fit for our society." Forced into exile, Hutchinson moved first to Rhode Island and later to the vicinity of Dutch settlements near the Hudson. There she and most of her family were killed by Indians in 1643. A river and a parkway in Bronx, New York, still bear her name.

Expansion and Violence: The Pequot War

Immigration to New England slowed during the 1640s because of religious and political upheaval at home. In England, Puritans and supporters of Parliament formed an army and openly challenged royal authority during the English Civil War. After seizing power, these revolutionaries beheaded Charles I in 1649, abolished monarchy, and proclaimed England a republican Commonwealth. Settlers in Massachusetts Bay struggled to square such sweeping developments in England with Winthrop's earlier assurance that the eyes of God and humankind would be fixed on New England. Making matters worse, religious and economic controversies intensified as the next generation quickly came of age. Needing new farmland and intellectual breathing room, fresh congregations began to "hive off" from the original settlements like swarms of bees. By 1640 New Hampshire, Rhode Island, and Connecticut each had at least four new towns that would provide the beginnings for independent colonies.

But the northeastern forest was not an empty wilderness any more than the Chesapeake tidewater, the Florida interior, or the mesas of New Mexico had been. As the Hutchinsons discovered, newcomers who pushed inland were co-opting the land of longtime residents. Pressure on New England's Native Americans erupted in armed conflict in the Pequot War of 1637, at the height of the Antinomian Crisis. The neighboring Pequot Indians near the mouth of the Connecticut River had been English allies for several years, and a recent smallpox epidemic had weakened them dramatically. But Winthrop, whose son was leading a settlement effort in the area, fanned fears that the Pequot "would cause all the Indians in the country to join to root out all the English."

Recruiting Narragansett and Mohegan Indians to the English side, the colonists unleashed all-out war against the Pequot. The campaign culminated in a dawn raid on a stockaded Pequot town that sheltered noncombatants. The invaders torched the village (at Mystic, Connecticut) and shot or put to the sword almost all who tried to escape. Some 400 Indian men, women, and children died. The Puritans' Indian allies were shocked by the wholesale carnage. English warfare, they protested, "is too furious, and slaies too many men." Chastened by this intimidating display of terror and weakened by recurrent epidemics, the tribes of southern New England negotiated away much of their land over the next generation, trading furs to the expanding colonists and seeking to understand their perplexing ways.

Having gained the upper hand, the Bible-reading English made gestures to convert their Native American neighbors. The Massachusetts General Court encouraged missionary work, forbade the worship of Indian gods, and set aside land for "praying towns" to encourage "the Indians to live in an orderly way amongst us." In Roxbury, the Reverend John Eliot labored to create a 1,200-page Indian Bible. And in Cambridge, officials at Harvard, committed by their charter to the "education of the English and Indian youth of this Country," erected a well-publicized Indian College.

The Chesapeake Bay Colonies

On Chesapeake Bay, settlers' relations with the Indians remained strained at best during the first half of the seventeenth century. In 1608, in an effort to secure the support of Indian leadership, the English performed an elaborate ceremony granting a copper crown to Chief Powhatan and a scarlet cloak to replace his deerskin mantle. But two years later, suspicious that he was harboring runaway colonists, the English burned the nearest Indian villages and unthinkingly destroyed much-needed corn. One Indian woman leader, taken as a captive, watched English soldiers throwing her children in the river and shooting them in the head before she herself was stabbed to death.

For both sides, hopes of reconciliation rose briefly in 1614 with the match between Pocahontas, daughter of Powhatan, and John Rolfe, the prominent widower who had introduced tobacco. But the marriage proved brief; Pocahontas died in England three years later, after bearing one child. Leaders intended the wedding alliance as a diplomatic gesture toward peace. But it did little to curtail the settlers' bitterness over lingering dependence on Indian supplies, or Native Americans' resentment over English encroachment and arrogance.

The Demise of the Virginia Company

Powhatan's death in 1618 brought to power his more militant younger brother, Opechancanough, the leader of the Pamunkey tribe. His encounters with the English had been frequent and unfriendly. By 1618 the English tobacco crop was booming, and more newcomers were arriving annually. Over the next three years, forty-two ships brought 3,500 people to the Chesapeake colony. The influx disheartened the Indians, and Opechancanough and his followers in the Powhatan Confederacy sought ways to end the mounting intrusion. Briefly, disease seemed to work in the Indians' favor. Immigrants who made the long sea voyage with poor provisions often fell ill in the swampy and unhealthy environment of Jamestown. By 1622 the colony's inhabitants were dying almost as rapidly as newcomers arrived. Sickness had carried off 3,000 residents in the course of only three years.

Opechancanough sensed a chance to deliver the finishing blow. He planned a sudden and coordinated offensive along the lower James River. On March 22, 1622, his forces attacked the English, surprising the outlying settlements and sparing no one. Of the 1,240 colonists, nearly 350 lost their lives. Warned by an Indian, Jamestown survived the uprising, but hope for peaceful relations ended. The attack of 1622 fueled opposition to the Virginia Company among disgruntled English investors. In 1624 King James I annulled the company's charter, making Virginia a royal colony controlled by the crown. In the colony's first seventeen years, more than 8,500 people, almost all of them young, had embarked for the Chesapeake. Yet in 1624 scarcely 1,300 colonists (or three of every twenty arrivals) remained alive.

The colonists placed a bounty on Opechancanough's head, but attempts to ambush or poison him failed. The Indian leader lived on, nursing his distrust of the English. In 1644 he inaugurated a second uprising that killed some 500 colonists. But the English settlement had grown too large to eradicate. By this time old age forced the "Great General" to be carried on a litter. When the English finally captured him and brought him to Jamestown in 1646, Opechancanough was too old to walk unassisted. Still, he remained defiant until shot in the back by one of the Englishmen guarding him.

After two years of brutal warfare, the Pamunkey and their allies in the Powhatan Confederacy conceded defeat and submitted to English authority. From then on, they would pay a token annual tribute for the privilege to remain on lands that had once belonged to them. With the way cleared for expansion, land-hungry English settlers appeared in ever-increasing numbers near the shores of Chesapeake Bay. By 1660 roughly 25,000 colonists lived in Virginia and neighboring Maryland.

Maryland: The Catholic Refuge

Maryland, the smaller and the younger of the two English colonies on the Chesapeake, owed its beginnings to George Calvert. In a Protestant country, Calvert rose to become a respected Catholic member of England's government. He was named the first Baron of Baltimore, in Ireland, in 1625. Calvert, now Lord Baltimore, had a keen interest in colonization, and in 1632 he petitioned Charles I for land in the Chesapeake. The king granted him 10 million acres adjacent to Virginia, to be named Maryland in honor of the Catholic queen, Henrietta Maria. The Maryland charter gave the proprietor and his heirs unprecedented personal power, especially in the granting of lands to colonists without limitations based on religious belief.

DOCUMENT

The Charter of
Maryland (1632)

Because Calvert died before the royal charter took effect, his eldest son, the second Lord Baltimore, took charge of the settlement effort. In 1634 the *Ark* and the *Dove* carried more than 200 settlers—both Protestants and Catholics—to the new colony. There, they established a capital at St. Mary's, near the mouth of the Potomac River. With the execution of the king in 1649 and the creation of an anti-Catholic commonwealth in England, the Calvert family provided a haven in Maryland for their coreligionists. However, Catholics never became a majority in the Chesapeake colony.

In 1649 Maryland's assembly passed an Act Concerning Religion, guaranteeing toleration for all settlers who professed a belief in Jesus Christ. This assertion of religious toleration, though limited, proved too broad for many to stomach. In the 1650s, supporters of the English Puritan cause seized power in Maryland, repealed the act, and briefly ended the Calverts' proprietorship. But by 1660, with the restoration of the Stuart monarchy in England, proprietary rule returned to the prosperous farming colony.

The Chesapeake Region, 1600–1660

- ▨ Powhatan Confederacy in 1607
- ▨ English settlement by 1650
- ▨ New Sweden, 1637–1655
- ━━ Maryland boundary in 1632
- ━━ Current state boundaries

■ **MAP 2.3**
CULTURES MEET ON THE CHESAPEAKE
When the English founded Jamestown in 1607, the numerous tribes of the Powhatan Confederacy controlled a wide region south of the Potomac River. In 1632 King Charles I granted all of Virginia north of the Potomac River to Lord Baltimore for his Maryland colony. This domain, with its capital at St. Mary's, stretched from the headwaters of the Potomac to the Delaware River. It reached north to 40 degrees (above the current boundary of Maryland), and it included the settlement of New Sweden on the Delaware (1637–1655). By midcentury, European settlement remained confined along main waterways.

Tobacco Becomes a Way of Life

By 1660, Virginia and Maryland totaled roughly 35,000 settlers, scattered along the edges of the bay and its adjoining tidewater rivers. In contrast to New England, the Chesapeake still could not maintain its colonial population without steady infusions of newcomers. A sickly climate kept life expectancy low, and men continued to outnumber women by more than two to one. Early experiments with oranges, pineapples, and grapes led nowhere. Chesapeake lumber sold well at first, but it was John Rolfe's tobacco plant that emerged as the tidewater's unlikely crop of choice.

Virginia's annual tobacco exports rose from a total weight of 2,000 pounds in 1615 to 500,000 in 1626. By 1630, saturated markets and stiff taxes led to slumping tobacco prices, so Virginians diversified their efforts. The beginning of the Massachusetts Bay colony created a demand for food that Chesapeake farmers met with well-timed coastal shipments. In 1634 they reported selling to "their zealous neighbours of New England tenne thousand bushels of corne for their releefe, besides good quantities of beeves, goats and hoggs, whereof this country hath great plentie." Such diversification proved brief, however. By 1640, London was receiving almost 1.4 million pounds of tobacco annually.

Though tobacco prices remained low throughout much of the seventeenth century, newcomers to Virginia and Maryland still managed to eek out a profit. They could grow the plants amid stumps in partially cleared fields. They could learn the many necessary procedures—planting, weeding, worming, suckering, topping, cutting, stripping, and curing—as the crop progressed. In short, it took hard work, but little farming experience, to bring cured tobacco to waterfront docks. Since captains charged by volume rather than weight, planters reduced shipping costs by devising a uniform barrel size and developing ways to press more leaves into each cask.

Still, the problems were formidable. Tobacco depleted the soil rapidly, so crop yields dwindled after several years. Then farmers had to leave their plots fallow, allowing them to recover, while clearing new fields for planting. This time-consuming task forced them onto marginal land that was poorly drained and less fertile. It also moved them away from navigable rivers, raising transportation costs. Storms, droughts, and crop diseases posed constant threats, and dependence on a single product in a distant and uncertain overseas market created added dangers. By mid-century, Chesapeake planters worried about market saturation and overproduction. But by then, for better or worse, growing the noxious weed had become a way of life. Virginia and Maryland settlers found themselves enmeshed in the high-risk world of tobacco farming. Dependence on the troublesome crop would expand across the upper South for centuries to come.

Conclusion

During half a century, the French, Dutch, and English had all moved to challenge Spanish claims in North America. By 1660 all four of these maritime powers of western Europe had taken aggressive steps to establish permanent footholds on the fringes of the enormous continent. In each instance, the European colonizers benefited first from the presence of knowledgeable Native Americans and then from the sharp decline of those same people through warfare and the onslaught of new diseases.

Granted, warfare with foreign invaders and death from unknown diseases had become a part of Native American history in the preceding century. But the sixteenth century was an era of tentative European exploration. In contrast, the first half of the seventeenth century saw Europeans move beyond occasional forays to permanent colonization. Spain, France, Holland, and England each had formidable assets in Europe and on the high seas. By 1660 all had sponsored colonial settlements that had endured for several generations, and each had begun to taste the seductive fruits of empire in North America and elsewhere.

The English, slowest to become involved in overseas colonization, had caught up with their competitors by 1660. Among European countries, England had proven the most aggressive in forming expansive family-based colonies rather than military garrisons or trading outposts. By 1660 the population of England's fledgling North American colonies had already outstripped that of its rivals, and it was growing at an increasing rate. This emerging superiority in numbers was advantageous in the imperial clashes that lay ahead.

Sites to Visit

Acoma Pueblo

Located near Highway 40 west of Albuquerque, New Mexico, within the Acoma Indian Reservation, the Acoma Pueblo Visitors' Center offers guided tours of Sky City. On top of the 420-foot mesa, visitors can walk the streets of one of the oldest continuously inhabited sites in North America.

Mission San Luis Park

In northwest Tallahassee, archaeologists have excavated the Apalachee Indian town and Spanish mission that existed there in the seventeenth century. Mission San Luis Park, between Route 10 and

Route 90, contains an outdoor museum with reconstructed buildings, exhibits, and guided tours.

Mashantucket Pequot Museum and Research Center

This expansive modern museum at Mashantucket in southeast Connecticut contains impressive exhibits and features a dramatic film about the Pequot War. For information, call 1-800-411-6971.

New Netherland Museum and Half Moon Visitor Center

Located in Albany, New York, the museum maintains a full-scale replica of Henry Hudson's ship the *Half Moon*, which is usually docked at Albany and open for visitors. For information, contact the Main Office at 518-443-1609.

Plimoth Plantation
www.plimoth.org

This living history museum of seventeenth-century Plymouth is located off Route 3 south of Boston, Massachusetts. It recreates the pilgrim village as it appeared in 1627, with the *Mayflower II* and a Wampanoag Indian site nearby. Take a virtual tour at www.plimoth.org.

Historic Jamestown
www.history.org/nche/
www.ngdc.noaa.gov/paleo/drought/drght_james.html

At Historic Jamestown you can tour ruins, visit a glass-blowing exhibition, and see excavations of the original fort. Nearby, the Jamestown–Yorktown Foundation runs Jamestown Settlement, with reconstructed ships, fortifications, and Indian dwellings. These sites (busy during the 400th anniversary in 2007) are 7 miles from Williamsburg on Virginia's Colonial Parkway. They can be approached by ferry across the James River. The "Virtual Jamestown" Web site is a prize-winning educational resource on early Virginia. The severe seven-year Jamestown drought (1606–1612) is covered at the National Geographic Data Center site.

Wolstenholme Towne

This palisaded village, located near Jamestown, was destroyed in the 1622 Indian attack. The site is located at Carter's Grove Plantation, near Williamsburg. The Winthrop Rockefeller Archaeology Museum next door contains impressive exhibits on English settlement in Virginia.

Historic St. Mary's City

The site of Maryland's first capital lies off Route 5, near the mouth of the Potomac River, in southern Maryland, several hours' drive from Baltimore, Annapolis, and Washington, D.C. Since 1971 an annual summer archaeology field school has worked to excavate additional elements of the town.

For Further Reading

General

Bernard Bailyn, *The Peopling of British North America: An Introduction* (1985).
David Hackett Fischer, *Albion's Seed: Four British Folkways in America* (1989).
Henry Kamen, *Empire: How Spain Became a World Power* (2003).
Mary Beth Norton, *Founding Mothers and Fathers: Gendered Power and the Forming of American Society* (1996).
Alan Taylor, *American Colonies* (2001).

Spain's Ocean-Spanning Reach

Ramón A. Gutiérrez, *When Jesus Came, the Corn Mothers Went Away: Marriage, Sexuality, and Power in New Mexico, 1500–1846* (1991).
W. Michael Mathes, *Vizcaíno and Spanish Expansion in the Pacific Ocean* (1968).
Jerald T. Milanich, *Laboring in the Fields of the Lord: Spanish Missions and Southeastern Indians* (1999).
David J. Weber, *The Spanish Frontier in North America* (1992).

France and Holland: Overseas Competition for Spain

W. J. Eccles, *France in America* (1972).
Oliver A. Rink, *Holland on the Hudson: An Economic and Social History of Dutch New York* (1986).
Russell Shorto, *The Island at the Center of the World: The Epic Story of Dutch Manhattan and the Forgotten Colony That Shaped America* (2004).
Bruce G. Trigger, *Natives and Newcomers: Canada's "Heroic Age" Reconsidered* (1985).

English Beginnings on the Atlantic Coast

John Demos, *A Little Commonwealth: Family Life in Plymouth Colony* (1970).
Karen Ordahl Kupperman, *Indians and English: Facing Off in Early America* (2000).
Nathaniel Philbrick, *Mayflower—A Story of Courage, Community, and War* (2006).
Neal Salisbury, *Manitou and Providence: Indians, Europeans, and the Making of New England, 1500–1643* (1982).
Alden T. Vaughan, *American Genesis: Captain John Smith and the Founding of Virginia* (1975).

The Puritan Experiment

William Cronon, *Changes in the Land: Indians, Colonists, and the Ecology of New England* (1983).
Alison Games, *Migration and the Origins of the English Atlantic World* (1999).
Philip F. Gura, *A Glimpse of Sion's Glory: Puritan Radicalism in New England, 1620–1660* (1984).
Edmund S. Morgan, *The Puritan Dilemma: The Story of John Winthrop* (1958).

The Chesapeake Bay Colonies

Wesley Frank Craven, *The Southern Colonies in the Seventeenth Century, 1607–1689* (1949).
James Horn, *Adapting to a New World: English Society in the Seventeenth-Century Chesapeake* (1994).
Edmund S. Morgan, *American Slavery, American Freedom: The Ordeal of Colonial Virginia* (1975).
Helen C. Rountree, *The Powhatan Indians of Virginia* (1989).

For quizzes and other resources on these topics, go to www.longmanamericanhistory.com.

Controlling the Edges of the Continent, 1660–1715

CHAPTER

3

O N THE MONTREAL WATERFRONT IN APRIL 1704, MARGUERITE MESSIER LOADED A LARGE canoe, with help from her five children. She worked with her brother and a guide to prepare for an expedition to meet her husband at a new French outpost on the Gulf of Mexico. At twenty-eight, Messier had already been married half her life, having wed explorer-trader Pierre-Charles Le Sueur in 1690 when he was thirty-four and she was only fourteen.

Messier was deeply involved, through family ties, in the dramatic changes taking place throughout the vast North American hinterland claimed by France. Her cousin, an adventurous Canadian named Pierre Le Moyne d'Iberville, had established the French colony of Louisiana near the mouth of the Mississippi River in 1699, and three years later Iberville and his younger brother Bienville had started the village of Mobile (near present-day Mobile, Alabama) to serve as the first capital. In 1702 Messier's husband, long active in Canada's far-flung western trade, had paddled down the Mississippi, taking furs to the new outpost at Mobile. There he constructed a house for his family; then he accompanied Iberville back to France.

In 1704, confident about the future success of the Louisiana venture, Le Sueur sent word to his wife in Montreal to attempt the inland journey of nearly 2,000 miles to Mobile. He himself departed from France aboard the *Pelican* for the same destination, hoping to reunite with his family. Messier and her party set out from Montreal on April 30, 1704, making their way up the St. Lawrence and passing through Lake Ontario and Lake Erie. After more than a year, they reached Kaskaskia in southern Illinois and began to descend the Mississippi River. Messier's brother and a daughter died before the travelers finally reached their destination. When the survivors arrived at Mobile in August 1705, more bad news awaited them: the voyage of the *Pelican* had met with disaster.

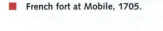
■ French fort at Mobile, 1705.

Messier's husband had boarded the ship in France, joining missionaries, soldiers, and potential brides recruited to go to Mobile. But at a stopover in Cuba, he had caught yellow fever and died, along with many others, before the immigrants reached Mobile. The town—home to just 160 men and a dozen women—hardly had enough food and shelter for the sickly newcomers, and yellow fever spread quickly. The epidemic swept away forty residents in two months and decimated nearby Indian villages.

Still, life at the outpost persisted. Townsmen welcomed the *Pelican*'s eligible young women, ages fourteen to eighteen, and priests celebrated thirteen marriages within the first three weeks. By 1705, when Marguerite Messier arrived from Montreal, new children were being born. Moving into the house her late husband had built, Messier determined to stay on and make a fresh start in the Louisiana colony.

Many of the changes that took place in North America during Marguerite Messier's lifetime occurred within a broad international context. During the second half of the seventeenth century, European maritime powers were caught up in a global race to expand and protect their overseas empires, and the chessboard was constantly changing. By the 1670s, Dutch authorities had been forced to withdraw entirely from North America, for example. As the Dutch departed, the Spanish, French, and English intensified their competition, starting towns wherever possible in order to stake out their claims.

In the East, England expanded the number and size of its coastal colonies, and English ports multiplied along the Atlantic seaboard. English newcomers also pressed inland along numerous rivers to found towns. Many of these towns (such as William Byrd's trading post that became Richmond, Virginia) appeared at the "fall line," the point where waterfalls blocked passage upstream and provided water power to run grist mills. Pushing up from the South, meanwhile, Spain struggled to retain its foothold in Florida and New Mexico and to lay claim to parts of Arizona and Texas as well. New Spanish towns appeared at Albuquerque, El Paso, and Pensacola. Of the three competing powers only France, pressing in from the St. Lawrence Valley, managed to penetrate the interior of the continent extensively. Its government created a string of forts from the Great Lakes to the Gulf of Mexico: Detroit, Peoria, and Mobile all came into being under the French flag.

One fundamental question recurred in numerous places during the decades after 1660: Who has the right to govern? Often, boundaries were vague and structures of control were tenuous; religious dissenters and political rebels who felt excluded or exploited could openly question the legitimacy of those in charge. In congregations, towns, and whole colonies, challenges to authority arose repeatedly. Disruptions and violence became familiar experiences for thousands of people inhabiting North America.

France and the American Interior

The potential wealth of the North American interior had long intrigued government ministers in France. If Canadian fur traders (known as *voyageurs*) could explore this vast domain and befriend its Indian inhabitants, France might control some of the continent's most fertile farmland and keep its extensive natural assets out of the hands of European rivals. If the French could recruit enough Native Americans as loyal allies, they might even threaten the rich mines of the Spanish empire in Mexico and challenge the growing English colonies lying to the east of the Appalachian Mountains. But for France to realize such wide ambitions, the French king, Louis XIV, would need to make North American colonization a national priority, and the extent of his commitment remained uncertain.

The Rise of the Sun King

King Louis XIV stood at the center of France's expanding imperial sphere. Indeed, so much seemed to revolve around him that he became known as the "Sun King." In 1661, at age twenty-two, he assumed personal control of a realm of 20 million people. During most of his long rule—until his death in 1715 at age seventy-seven—Louis dominated European affairs. Always a builder of monuments, he expanded the Louvre in Paris and then dazzled the French nobility and clergy with his opulent new palace at Versailles.

In religion, the Sun King challenged the Catholic pope on one hand and suppressed French Protestants (Huguenots) on the other. In politics, he centralized the monarchy's power as never before. His administration consolidated the laws of France, strengthened the armed forces, built roads, and expanded commerce. His government ministries foreshadowed modern nation-states by regulating industry and imposing tariffs and taxes.

Throughout Louis XIV's reign, his officials followed a set of policies known as **mercantilism**, a system in which a government stressed economic self-sufficiency and a favorable balance of trade. By avoiding foreign debts and drawing in valuable resources from its competitors and its own colonies, a state could pay for wars abroad and costly projects at home. The French mercantilist strategy was to exploit labor efficiently and import raw materials cheaply, while exporting expensive manufactured products, such as glassware, wine, silk, and tapestries, in exchange for gold and silver. France's colonists, like those of Spain and England, were expected to generate much-needed natural resources and to serve as eager consumers for the mother country's manufactured goods.

■ Portrait of Louis XIV, the Sun King.

In Paris, finance minister Jean-Baptiste Colbert emerged as the chief architect of this strategy of aggressive mercantilism. At home he taxed foreign imports, removed domestic trade barriers, and improved internal transportation. Moreover, he reduced worker holidays and outlawed strikes. Colbert improved France's ports and created a code to regulate maritime shipping. He expanded the naval fleet and pressed French sailors into its service. Pushing still harder, he organized overseas trading companies and provided insurance for their expensive ventures. In addition, he sanctioned France's involvement in the African slave trade. Colbert yearned to acquire new territory to increase the empire's self-sufficiency and keep overseas resources out of enemy hands. To that end, he and his successors encouraged French exploration of North America on an unprecedented scale.

The government of Louis XIV assumed direct control over New France from a private company in 1663. Colbert hoped to diversify production away from the fur trade, so he shipped artisans to the colony, along with livestock and tools. To promote domestic life and population growth, the government also transported young single women and announced cash incentives for early marriages and large families. Many of the soldiers sent to protect New France from Iroquois and English threats stayed on to establish farms.

On balance, however, Colbert's plans for a prosperous, well-populated colony failed. The small population of New France—10,000 by 1680—never grew as rapidly as French imperial strategists desired. The harsh winters and short growing seasons hindered the expansion of agriculture. Also, Louis XIV imposed restrictions to make sure that any colonist sent overseas was a pious and loyal Catholic. In 1685, when he revoked the Edict of Nantes (which had granted French Protestants their legal rights), thousands of frightened Huguenots prepared to leave the country. But the king forbade the dissenters from traveling to France's colonies. In contrast to the English, the French did not use their overseas colonies as havens for outcasts, troublemakers, and religious dissidents.

Exploring the Mississippi Valley

Encouraged by the government of Louis XIV, French Canadian explorers had probed steadily across the Great Lakes, reaching the western shores of Lake Michigan in 1634. There, Winnebego Indians (today's Ho-Chunk Nation) told of a river called the "Messisipi," and rumors of this river circulated among the French for a generation. Finally, in 1673, trader Louis Jolliet,

Montréal
Lachine

Lake Superior

Sault-Ste-Marie
Ft. Michilimackinac

Ft. Frontenac

Minnesota R.

Mississippi R.

Wisconsin R.

Fox R.

Lake Michigan

Lake Huron

Ft. Conti

L. Ontario

Detroit

Lake Erie

Missouri R.

Peoria
(Ft. St.Louis)

Ft. St.Joseph

Illinois R.

Ft. Crèvecoeur

Wabash R.

Ohio R.

Kansas R.

Cahokia

Ft. de Chartres

Kaskaskia

Arkansas R.

Arkansas Post

Mississippi R.

Ft. Toulouse

Brazos R.

Colorado R.

Red R.

Natchez
(Ft. Rosalie)

Neches R.

Trinity R.

Natchitoches

Mobile
(Ft. St. Louis)

Biloxi
(Ft. Maurepas)

Pensacola
(1698)

San Antonio
(1718)

La Salle
killed

New Orleans
(1718)

San Juan Bautista
(1700)

English
Turn

Ft. St.Louis

Gulf of
Mexico

Rio Grande

Matagorda
Bay

Routes of important French explorations

La Salle, 1670	La Salle's party, 1687
Joliet and Marquette, 1673	Iberville, 1699
La Salle, 1679–1682	St. Denis, 1714
La Salle and colonists from France, 1685	La Harpe, 1719
French Fort	
Spanish Missions 1716–1717	Spanish settlements

Present state boundaries provided for orientation

■ **M A P   3 . 1**
FRANCE IN THE AMERICAN INTERIOR, 1670–1720

joined by a Jesuit priest named Jacques Marquette, entered the upper Mississippi and descended the great stream to the mouth of the Arkansas River. If the Mississippi waterway flowed south into the Gulf of Mexico, instead of west to the Pacific as some explorers hoped, perhaps the river could give France a path to the wealth of New Spain and provide French settlers with access to a warm-water port.

Officials in Quebec moved to exploit these western prospects, making effective use of an experienced young adventurer: René-Robert Cavelier, Sieur de La Salle. In 1679, inspired by word of Jolliet's exploits, La Salle and his men pushed west through the Great Lakes to erect forts on the Illinois River, a tributary of the Mississippi. These outposts strengthened French trading ties with local Indians and provided a launching point for more exploration. In 1682 La Salle led a contingent of French and Indians south from the Illinois to explore the lower Mississippi. He returned to confirm that the great river indeed emptied into the Gulf of Mexico. He claimed the rich land drained by all its tributaries for Louis XIV, naming the entire river basin "Louisiana" after his king.

But La Salle, hindered by poor maps and crude navigational instruments, had mislocated the mouth of the Mississippi. Therefore, when he tried to return by sea, sailing from France with four ships and several hundred colonists, he mistakenly disembarked on the Texas coast early in 1685. Slowly, the entire colonization plan unraveled. When one ship sank near shore, the hapless settlers lost valuable supplies and any hope of relocating. Jealous lieutenants eventually killed La Salle before he could find the Mississippi River. Most of the colonists he had brought from France perished in the Texas wilderness.

King William's War in the Northeast

The French colonizers had overreached themselves. They had failed to challenge Spanish power in the Gulf of Mexico or to establish a southern port. Spread thin by the widening fur trade, French Canadians were in a weak position to repel renewed Iroquois attacks along the St. Lawrence River in the 1680s. Moreover, a strengthened Protestant regime emerged in London with the ascent of William III to the English throne in 1689. This transition started more than 100 years of conflict between Protestant England and Catholic France, an ideological and military struggle that often included North America.

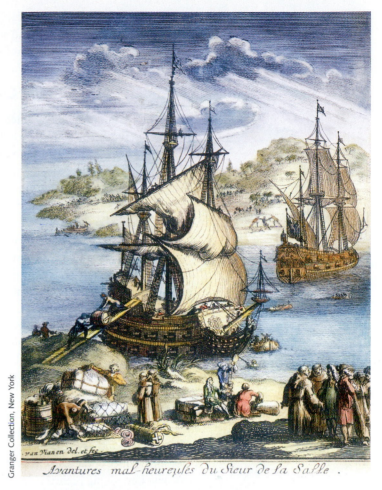

Avantures mal-heureuses du Sieur de la Salle.

■ When La Salle's colonizing expedition landed on the Texas coast in 1685, one supply ship, the *Belle*, sank in Matagorda Bay during the unloading process. Lost and discouraged, the French colony faded away within two years. In 1995 archaeologists found the *Belle* in shallow water and salvaged its remains.

The American conflict began in the Northeast with the outbreak of King William's War in 1689, when the Iroquois, well supplied with English arms, launched raids near Montreal. The French struck back, sending parties south to terrorize the English frontier, setting fire to outposts in New York and New England. At Fort Loyal (modern Portland, Maine) raiders butchered 100 English men, women, and children who had surrendered, and they took others captive. Leaving their dead unburied, the survivors fled south toward Salem and Boston in Massachusetts. Many who experienced the attack viewed it as part of a wider design to undo the Reformation and expand the authority of the Catholic Church.

After eight years of bloodshed, King William's War ended in a stalemate in 1697. Hurt by the hostilities, the Iroquois soon promised to remain neutral during any future colonial wars between France and England, a pledge they generally honored for more than half a century. The French, having strengthened their position in Canada, revived the "southern strategy" of colonization that had so obsessed Colbert and La Salle.

A turn in European events opened the door for renewed French efforts in the American heartland. King Carlos II of Spain fell ill without an immediate heir, and the royal courts of Europe competed to determine his successor. Louis XIV, eager to acquire Spain's European realm and American dominions for France, proposed that his grandson, Philip of Anjou, receive the Spanish crown. But England supported an opposing candidate, so the War of Spanish Succession (1701–1714) broke out soon after Carlos died.

Founding the Louisiana Colony

Even before new hostilities erupted in Europe in 1701, Louis XIV and his ministers took steps to secure French claims in the Gulf of Mexico, despite Spain's naval dominance in the area. By renewing La Salle's plan for a Louisiana colony, France could strengthen its hand in the impending war over succession to the Spanish throne. A colony on the Gulf of Mexico would provide a southern outlet for the French fur trade and a strategic outpost to counter Spain's new fort at Pensacola in western Florida.

England also saw advantages to establishing a base on the lower Mississippi. Such a post could challenge Spanish and French claims to the gulf region and increase English trade with the Chickasaw and other southern Indians. In 1698 a London promoter quietly made plans to transport a group of Huguenot refugees to the mouth of the Mississippi. Catching wind of this scheme, the French organized their own secret expedition to the Gulf of Mexico under an aspiring Canadian officer, Pierre Le Moyne d'Iberville.

Coming from a large and well-connected Montreal family, the Le Moynes, Iberville quickly drew several siblings into the gulf colonization plan, including his teenage brother, Bienville. Iberville and his party sailed for the Gulf of Mexico from the French port of Brest in 1699. Their ship entered the mouth of the Mississippi in time to repel the English expedition at a site on the river still known as English Turn. They also managed to build a fort at nearby Biloxi Bay before returning to France.

The two brothers were now well on their way to creating the Gulf Coast colony that La Salle and his followers had failed to establish. A second voyage let Iberville conduct further reconnaissance of the lower Mississippi. On a third trip, in 1702, he established Fort Louis, near Mobile Bay, giving French traders access to the Choctaw Indians. Young Bienville, placed in charge of Fort Louis, labored to sustain the tiny outpost at Mobile. Iberville himself left to pursue other schemes and died an early death in 1706.

Enmeshed in the War of Spanish Succession, France ignored its new Gulf colony. Epidemics took a heavy toll on Louisiana's newcomers and a far heavier toll on Indian neighbors. Settlers drawn from Canada, with prior wilderness experience, maintained close ties with local Native Americans and resented the incompetence and haughtiness of colonists sent from France. The latter complained about the poor living conditions and looked down on the uneducated Canadians. However, despite social friction and a chronic lack of supplies from France, the small community at Mobile survived, including the widow Marguerite Messier and her children.

Far to the north, additional posts reinforced French territorial claims, fostered the fur trade, and protected neighboring Indians against Iroquois raids. The village of Peoria sprang up on the Illinois River in 1691. Catholic missions appeared nearby at Cahokia (1697) and Kaskaskia (1703). Later, Fort de Chartres arose in southern Illinois in 1719. Further north, the French established two other strategic posts. In 1689 they laid out a garrison where Lake Huron joins Lake Michigan. In 1701 they created a lasting town on the strait (*le détroit* in French) connecting Lake Erie to Lake Huron. This outpost—called Detroit—was founded by a Monsieur Cadillac, who foresaw a prosperous future for the village. The Iroquois had pledged their neutrality, so the new trading post, Cadillac wrote, lay open "to the most distant tribes which surround these vast sweet water seas."

In 1712 the French crown, its resources depleted by a decade of warfare in Europe, granted control over Louisiana to a powerful Paris merchant, Antoine Crozat. Drawing Cadillac from Detroit to serve as Louisiana's governor general, Crozat hoped to develop connections

"Marry or do not marry"

Father Jacques Gravier (1651–1708) visited French posts from Mackinac to Mobile. The Jesuit spent most of his time at Fort St. Louis (modern Peoria) among several thousand Illinois Indians, compiling a dictionary of their language and seeking to win converts. In 1691, he built a chapel outside the fort and erected a 35-foot cross. He concentrated on teaching young people, offering prizes—colored beads, needles, rosaries, small knives— to those who learned the catechism. The daughter of powerful Chief Rouensa (a girl named Aramepinchone, whom Gravier called Marie) proved especially interested. But French traders and Indian leaders remained wary of his message.

I was surprised by the indifference to instruction,…notwithstanding the politeness with which the old men received me. One of them told me in confidence that his tribesmen had resolved to prevent the people from coming to the chapel to listen to me, because I spoke against their customs. Many children and young people were sick, and I had not as free access to all of them as I would have wished. . . . They cry out against me as if I were the cause of the disease. . . . I was looked upon in most of the cabins as the bird of death; and people sought to hold me responsible for the disease and the mortality.

[In 1694 Marie's] father and mother…brought her to me in company with the Frenchman whom they wished to have for a son-in-law. [Michel Accault was a wealthy and experienced trader whom La Salle had sent to explore the Upper Mississippi in 1680. But Marie indicated] that she did not wish to marry;

Chief of an Illinois Tribe, Charles Becard de Granville, about 1700. New York Public Library; Astor, Lenox, and Tilden Foundations.

An Illinois chief, holding a calumet (c. 1700). "They are tattooed behind from the shoulders to the heels, and as soon as they have reached the age of twenty-five, on the front of the stomach, the sides, and the upper arms."

that she had already given her heart to God, and did not wish to share it. . . . I told [Accault and the parents] that God did not command her not to marry, but also that she could not be forced to do so. . . . The father…told me that inasmuch as I was preventing his daughter from obeying him, he would also prevent her from going to the chapel. That very night her father gathered the chiefs of the four villages, and told them that, since I prevented the French from forming alliances with them…he earnestly begged them to stop the women and children from coming to the chapel.

I thought I should not remain silent after so great an insult had been offered to God. I went to the commandant of the fort,…who answered in an insulting manner that I had drawn all this upon myself, through my stubbornness in not

allowing the girl to marry the Frenchman, who was then with him. [The Jesuit demanded that the commandant support him against the chiefs. The French leader] replied coldly that he would speak to the chiefs; but, instead of assembling them at once, he waited until the afternoon of the following day, and even then I had to return to him from the purpose. [Then Gravier advised Marie:] My daughter, God does not forbid you to marry; neither do I say to you: 'Marry or do not marry.' If you consent solely through love for God, and if you believe that by marrying you will win your family to God, the thought is a good one.

Marie, age 16, married Accault and bore two sons before he died. By 1704 she had married another French trader, Michel Philippe, and moved to the new town of Kaskaskia. There Philippe turned to farming and amassed a sizable estate, including an Indian servant and five black slaves. Marie raised six more children before her death in 1725. Her will, dictated in French and then translated into the Illinois language, withheld property from one son who continued to live as an Indian. Her priest, Father Gravier, had been shot in the arm by an Indian in 1705. The arrowhead could not be removed, and he died three years later.

Questions

1. *Regarding the Rouensa-Accault marriage, explore the differing motives of Marie, her parents, Michel Accault, and Father Gravier.*
2. *Can you recreate an argument in 1720 at Kaskaskia between Catholic Marie and the son remaining loyal to the ways of Chief Rouensa?* ■

---

to mineral-rich Mexico and to discover precious metals in the Mississippi watershed. But probes on the upper Mississippi, the Missouri, and the Red rivers yielded no easy bonanza. Instead, explorers established three new trading posts: Natchitoches on the Red River, Fort Rosalie (at Natchez), and Fort Toulouse (near modern Montgomery, Alabama).

When Louis XIV died in 1715, the colonial population of Lower Louisiana stood at scarcely 300 people. But over two generations, the French had established a solid claim on

French America 1608–1763

Over two generations, the French had established a solid claim on the American interior.

the American interior. Their position was an ongoing challenge to English and Spanish competitors. The crescent of wilderness outposts arcing north and then east from the Gulf Coast offered a useful network for additional exploration, Indian trade, and military conquest. French control of the Mississippi Valley remained a real possibility until the era of Thomas Jefferson and Napoleon Bonaparte nearly a century later.

The Spanish Empire on the Defensive

Whereas France's power expanded during Louis XIV's reign, Spain's overextended empire continued to weaken. This decline opened the door for Louis to maneuver his own grandson onto the Spanish throne in 1700 as Philip V. Meanwhile, Spanish colonizers struggled to defend vast territorial claims in North America that spread—on paper—from the Gulf of California to the Florida peninsula.

In Spain's remote colonies of New Mexico and Florida, local administration often proved corrupt, and links to imperial officials at home remained waek and cumbersome. For several generations, the Indian majority had resented the harsh treatment and strange diseases that came with colonial contact. Now, cultural disruptions and pressures from hostile Indian neighbors fanned the flames of discontent. In the late seventeenth century, a wave of Native American rebellions swept the northern frontier of New Spain.

The Pueblo Revolt in New Mexico

DOCUMENT

Pedro Hidalgo, Legal Statement (1680)

The largest and most successful revolt took place along the upper Rio Grande. There, Pueblo Indians from dozens of separate communities (or pueblos) united in a major upheaval in August 1680. They murdered twenty-one of the forty friars serving in New Mexico, ransacked their churches, and killed more than 350 settlers. After laying siege to Santa Fe, the rebels drove the remaining Spanish colonists and their Christian Indian allies south out of the province and kept them away for more than a decade. Several thousand stunned survivors took refuge at what is now El Paso and soon began questioning Indian informants to find an explanation for the fearsome uprising.

Diverse pressures had combined to ignite the Pueblo Revolt of 1680. First, a five-year drought beginning in 1666 had inflicted a famine with long-lasting effects on the peoples of New Mexico. Second, around the same time, neighboring Apache and Navajo stepped up their hostilities against the small colonial population and the numerous Pueblo Indians who had been linked with the Spanish over several generations. The attackers were embittered by the continuing Spanish slave raids that took Indian captives to work in the Mexican silver mines. In retaliation these raiding parties, riding stolen Spanish horses, killed livestock and seized scarce food. When Spanish soldiers proved unable to fend off the hit-and-run attacks, their credibility among local Pueblo Indians weakened.

Third, a smoldering controversy over religion flared during the 1670s. When an epidemic struck in 1671, Spanish missionaries could not stem the sickness with Christian prayers. In response, traditionalist Indian priests revived age-old Pueblo religious customs. Horrified, the Spanish friars and government officials punished what they saw as backsliding within a Pueblo population that seemed to have accepted key elements of the Catholic faith. At Santa Fe in 1675, they hanged three Indian leaders for idolatry and whipped and imprisoned forty-three others—including a militant leader from San Juan pueblo named Popé. Before the captives could be sold into slavery, armed Indians successfully demanded the release of Popé and the other prisoners.

Popé withdrew to Taos, the northernmost pueblo in New Mexico. From there, he negotiated secretly with like-minded factions in other pueblos, unifying resistance to Spanish dom-

Southwest in the era of the Pueblo Revolt

- Spanish colonization up to 1680
- Pueblo Revolt, 1680
- Navajo settlements, 1600
- Navajo settlements, 1800
- Navajo Reservation boundaries, 2000
- Fr. Kino's missionary travels, 1681–1711
- Indian pueblos
- Spanish towns
- Mission at San Xavier del Bac

Present state names and boundaries are provided for orientation, and Navajo Indian relocation is shown over 400 years

■ MAP 3.2

CHANGES IN THE SOUTHWEST The 1680 Pueblo Revolt (green) overwhelmed Spain's small New Mexico colony. In the next three decades, Father Kino and other Jesuits moved the mission frontier north into what is now Arizona. Over time, the Navajo relocated their homelands; they remain an important presence in the region.

ination and forging an underground movement. In part, he built support around widespread resentment of the Spanish **encomienda** system (requiring Indian communities to supply labor or pay tribute) and the Catholic Church (which forbade traditional Indian religious ceremonies). Indian women whom Spanish priests or soldiers had abused took Popé's side in this cultural clash. The movement also received covert support from numerous **mestizos** and **mulattos**, mixed-race people whose lack of "pure" Spanish blood cost them any chance for advancement. Popé sent runners to each conspiring pueblo, fixing the date for the rebellion. When the time came, his Pueblo warriors swiftly routed their adversaries. Unified in triumph,

Harald Sund/Getty Images

■ Horses and sheep arrived in the Southwest with the Spanish, and both became central to the Navajo (or Diné) culture in northern Arizona and New Mexico. Navajo women continue to herd sheep and weave their wool into rugs and blankets, as they have done for more than three centuries.

the zealous victors smeared excrement on Christian altars and bathed themselves to remove the stigma of baptism.

But initial cohesion gave way to friction. The successful rebels soon quarreled over who should hold power and how best to return to ancient ways. Kivas would replace churches, and the cross would give way to the **kachina**. But what other parts of the imported culture should the Indians abandon after eight decades of intermingling with the newcomers? Various Pueblo groups could not agree on which Spanish words, tools, and customs to discard or which foreign crops and animals to retain.

In 1681 the Pueblo fended off a Spanish attempt at reconquest. But they remained divided among themselves and more vulnerable than ever to Apache raids. Within a decade, rival factions had deposed Popé, and another Spanish army, under Governor Diego de Vargas, had entered New Mexico. It took the new governor several years to subdue the province, and the Pueblo managed another full-scale rebellion in 1696. But Vargas anticipated the revolt and crushed the opposition, just as Oñate had done a century earlier. In 1706 several families established the town of Albuquerque on its present site. Learning from prior mistakes, Spanish officials did not reimpose the hated encomienda system. A new generation of Franciscan missionaries tolerated indigenous Pueblo traditions as long as the Indians also attended Catholic mass.

Navajo and Spanish on the Southwestern Frontier

The repercussions of rebellion and reconquest along the upper Rio Grande echoed through the Southwest. To the north, Pueblo refugees joined the Navajo and brought valuable experience as corn farmers. Corn, already known to the Navajo, now became an increasingly important food and sacred symbol for them. Moreover, the new arrivals had learned from the Spanish how to plant peach orchards and raise sheep. Navajo women—the weavers in their society—soon owned large flocks and created wool blankets on their traditional portable looms. The Pueblo also brought more Spanish horses, a key asset that let the Navajo spread their domain west into fine grazing country in what is now northeast Arizona. Farther north, the Ute and Comanche also acquired horses after the Pueblo Revolt. Eventually, the Comanche pressed southeast onto the Texas plains.

In Mexico City, despite limited resources, authorities sent missionaries north to spread Christianity to hostile Indians near the Gulf of California. Year by year, these friar-explorers edged toward what is now southern Arizona until they reached the cactus-studded landscape of the Sonoran Desert in the 1690s. Eusebio Kino, a tireless Jesuit missionary born in Italy and educated in Germany, spearheaded the early exploration. In 1701 this padre on horseback established a mission at San Xavier del Bac, below modern Tucson, Arizona. But Father Kino's missions languished after his death in 1711. Twenty-five years later, a silver strike at "Arizonac," near present-day Nogales on the U.S.-Mexican border, provided a new name for the region, which would eventually become the state called Arizona.

Borderland Conflict in Texas and Florida

The encounters on Spain's other North American frontiers took different forms, in part because European rivals appeared on the scene. Conflict with the French led the Spanish to found missions in Texas, a land they named after the local Tejas Indians. At first, responding to news about La Salle's ill-fated French colony, the Spanish made a brief attempt to establish a Texas mission in 1690, departing again in 1693. They renewed their effort two decades later, after Louisiana's Governor Cadillac (the founder of Detroit) sent explorers from Louisiana across eastern Texas to forge ties with Spanish communities south of the Rio Grande. Eager to open trade with the Spanish, the French visitors reached San Juan Bautista, below the modern U.S.-Mexican border, in 1714.

Spanish authorities, taken by surprise, dusted off plans for colonizing Texas. By 1717 they had established half a dozen small missions near the Sabine River, the boundary between modern Texas and Louisiana. The next year, to expand their missionary activities and secure the supply route from San Juan Bautista to these distant outposts in east Texas, the Spanish built a cluster of settlements beside the San Antonio River, at a midpoint in the trail. Within two decades, a string of missions stretched along the river. Indian converts tended herds of cattle and sheep and constructed aqueducts to irrigate new fields of wheat and corn. The earliest mission, San Antonio de Valero (1718), provided a nucleus for the town of San Antonio. Later known as the Alamo, the mission also strengthened Spanish claims to Texas against threats of French intrusion.

During the second half of the seventeenth century, the Indians of Florida, like the Pueblo in New Mexico, debated whether to reject generations of Spanish rule. The Columbian Exchange had altered their lives in dramatic ways. They ate new foods such as figs, oranges, peas, and cabbages. They used Spanish words—*azucár* (sugar), *botija* (jar), *caballo* (horse)— and metal hoes from Europe allowed them to produce more corn. But expanding contact with missionaries created major problems as well. By 1660 devastating epidemics had whittled away at Florida's Native American towns. The Indians still outnumbered the newcomers more than ten to one, but they had to expend enormous energy raising, processing, and hauling food for the Spanish. When colonists grew fearful of French and English attacks after 1670, they forced hundreds of Indians to perform even more grueling labor: constructing the stone fortress of San Marcos at St. Augustine.

Nothing proved more troubling to Florida's Indians than the spread of livestock farming. St. Augustine's elite had established profitable cattle ranches on the depopulated savannas of Timucua, near present-day Gainesville in north-central Florida. These entrepreneurs ignored requirements to keep cows away from unfenced Indian gardens, and they enforced harsh laws to protect their stock. Any Florida Indian who killed cattle faced four months of servitude; people caught raiding Spanish herds had their ears cut off.

> *During the second half of the seventeenth century, the Indians of Florida, like the Pueblo in New Mexico, debated whether to reject generations of Spanish rule.*

Resentment grew in Florida's scattered mission villages. Restless Indian converts wondered whether the English, who had founded their Carolina colony in 1670, might make viable allies. The English seemed eager to trade for deerskins, and they offered the Native Americans a steadier supply of desirable goods than the Spanish could provide. Several Indian communities moved closer to Carolina to test this new alternative for trade. But when France and Spain joined forces against the English after 1700, Florida's Indians found themselves caught up in a struggle far larger than they had bargained for.

Ever since the days of Francis Drake, the English had schemed to oust the Spanish from St. Augustine. In 1702 English raiders from Carolina, under Governor James Moore, rampaged through the town. Yet the new stone fortress of San Marcos held firm, protecting the inhabitants. Two years later, Moore invaded Apalachee (near modern Tallahassee). His troops crushed the mission towns, killing hundreds and carrying away more than 4,000 Indian captives. Most of them were women and children, whom the English sold as slaves. By 1706 the mission villages in Apalachee and Timucua lay in ruins. "In all these extensive dominions," wrote a troubled Spanish official from St. Augustine, "the law of God and the preaching of the Holy Gospel have now ceased."

England's American Empire Takes Shape

In 1660, as Louis XIV began his long reign in France and Spanish missionaries labored in obscurity in New Mexico and Florida, England experienced a counterrevolutionary upheaval that influenced American colonial affairs dramatically. In the 1640s, amid violent civil war, rebels supporting Puritans and the Parliament had overthrown the ruling Stuart family, beheaded Charles I, and abolished hereditary monarchy altogether.

For a brief period, England became a republican commonwealth without a king. But Oliver Cromwell, the movement's dictatorial leader and self-styled Lord Protector, died in 1658. Pressures quickly mounted to undo the radical Puritan Revolution and return to monarchical government. In May 1660, a strong coalition of conservative interests welcomed the late king's son back from exile and "restored" him to the throne as King Charles II, an act known as the **Restoration**. For this reason, the last three decades of the Stuart dynasty (1660–1688) are remembered in English politics and culture as the **Restoration Era**.

The shift in London's political winds could hardly have been more sudden, and Charles II moved quickly in 1660 to underscore the end of England's Puritan experiment. He ordered the execution of those who had beheaded his father in 1649. Many who had fought to end the monarchy and strengthen Parliament sought refuge in the American colonies when their religious and political beliefs abruptly fell out of favor at home. But other elements of colonial demographics—early marriage, high birth rates, and a low level of mortality in most places—did even more to prompt expansion up and down the Atlantic coast.

Monarchy Restored and Navigation Controlled

Because most English colonists still lived within 50 miles of the Atlantic, an increase in people steadily broadened the opportunities for seaborne trade. Growing ship traffic, in turn, sparked government desires to regulate colonial navigation to bring mercantilist advantages to the restored monarchy. In 1660 Parliament passed a major new law designed to promote British shipping and trade.

Tabacum latifolium.

The Navigation Act of 1660 laid out important conditions that shaped England's colonial commerce for generations. First, merchants could not conduct trade to or from the English colonies in foreign-owned ships. Second, key non-English products imported from foreign lands—salt, wine, oil, and naval stores (the tar, pitch, masts, and other materials used to build boats)—had to be carried in English ships or in ships with mostly English crews. Third, the law contained a list of "enumerated articles" produced overseas. The items listed—tobacco, cotton, sugar, ginger, indigo, and dyewoods—could no longer be sent directly from a colony to a foreign European port. Instead, merchants had to ship them to England first and then reexport them, a step that directly boosted England's domestic economy. Another Navigation Act, in 1663, required that goods moving from the European continent to England's overseas colonies also needed to pass through the island. Moreover, they had to arrive and depart on English ships.

Ten years later, yet another measure—the Plantation Duty Act of 1673—tried to close loopholes regarding enumerated articles. The new act required captains to pay a "plantation duty" before they sailed between colonial ports with enumerated goods. Otherwise, colonial vessels carrying such goods had to post bond before leaving harbor to ensure that they would sail directly to England. To enforce these rules, the government sent customs officers to the colonies for the first time. Backed by the Navigation Acts, England's fleets grew, and colonial trade became a major sector in England's economy.

Even the Great Plague, which swept England in 1665, could not blunt this mercantile growth. And when a catastrophic fire destroyed most of London the next year, planners redesigned the city with the broad streets and impressive buildings that suited the prosperous hub of an expanding empire. The fashionable coffee shops that sprang up as a novelty in late-seventeenth-century London became common meeting places for exchanging news and views about England's increasingly profitable activities overseas.

Dutch New Netherland Becomes New York

At the beginning of his reign, Charles II knew he had to build loyalty and strengthen an economy weakened by civil war. The king, with expensive tastes and a depleted treasury, found that he could reward loyal family members and supporters, at no cost to the crown, by granting them control over pieces of England's North American domain. With this prospect in hand, he and his ministers sought to bolster foreign trade, strengthen the royal navy, and outstrip England's commercial rivals, focusing first on the Dutch.

As London stepped up its search for new profits, English officials moved to strengthen control over existing colonies and establish (or seize) new ones wherever possible. The Navigation Acts cut sharply into the Dutch carrying trade and spurred a decade of renewed warfare between England and Holland. For the most part, these intermittent Anglo-Dutch Wars ended in stalemate. But at the final Peace of Westminster in 1674, the English emerged with several important gains in Africa and America.

In West Africa, the English captured and held several key coastal outposts: an island at the mouth of the river Gambia (renamed James Fort for the Duke of York) and Cape Coast Castle on the Gold Coast (near Elmina, the African headquarters of the Dutch West India Company). This encroachment challenged Dutch dominance of commerce with Africa for gold and ivory. It also gave England the footholds it needed to force its way into the Atlantic slave trade. Charles II had already moved to take advantage of the situation. He granted a monopoly to the Royal Adventurers into Africa (1663) and then the Royal African Company (1672) to exploit the grim but highly profitable slave traffic. Within several generations, this ruthless initiative reshaped England's American colonies at enormous human cost.

Across the Atlantic, the English had seized the Dutch colony of New Netherland and its poorly defended port of New Amsterdam. Charles II claimed that the land had belonged to

Pepys Library, Magdalene College, Cambridge[

■ **Images of the Great Plague in London (1665).**

DOCUMENT
Navigation Acts

England from the time his grandfather endorsed the Virginia Company in 1606. In 1664 the king used his royal prerogative to regain control of this domain. He issued a charter putting the entire region between the Delaware and Connecticut rivers under the personal control of his brother James, Duke of York. That same year, James sent a fleet to claim his prize. When Governor Peter Stuyvesant surrendered the Dutch colony without a fight, both the province and its capital on Manhattan Island each received the name New York. Fort Orange on the Hudson became Albany because England's traditional name was *Albion*.

James now controlled an enormous domain (including the Dutch and English settlements on Long Island), and he wielded nearly absolute power over his new dukedom. He never visited New York, but as proprietor, he chose the colony's governor. That official ruled with an appointed council and enforced "the Duke's Laws" without constraint by any assembly. English newcomers to the colony resented the absence of an elected legislature, and the governor finally authorized an elected body in 1683. But when the new assemblymen approved a Charter of Liberties endorsing government by consent of the governed, the Duke of York disallowed the legislature.

Married women living in the New York colony lost ground in the transition to English rule. Dutch law codes had ensured their full legal status, whereas English common law assigned wives to an inferior status (known as **coverture** or *feme covert*). They could not own property or keep control over money they earned, and they lacked any independent standing before the law.

As the English asserted political control over New York, the Dutch presence remained evident everywhere. Many English married into Dutch families and worshipped in the Dutch Reformed Church. English-speaking New Yorkers borrowed such Dutch words as *waffle*, *cookie*, *coleslaw*, and *baas* (boss). Anyone who was bilingual, such as Albany merchant Robert Livingston, had a special advantage. Livingston, an immigrant from Scotland, had learned to speak Dutch in Holland in his youth. His marriage linked him to powerful Dutch families in the Hudson Valley, and much of his early wealth came from his ability to translate commercial documents between English and Dutch.

DOCUMENT

Church Record of
a Marriage
Conflict, Brooklyn
(1663)

New Restoration Colonies: New Jersey, Pennsylvania, and Carolina

Charles II had spurred England's seizure of New Netherland by issuing a charter for control of the contested region to his brother, the Duke of York. To reward supporters, the king continued issuing royal charters for American land, hoping to expand colonization at no cost to the crown. In 1670, for example, he granted a charter to the Hudson's Bay Company. The deal gave the company's proprietors a monopoly on trade, minerals, and land across northern Canada. Farther south, Charles used charters to redistribute control along major portions of the Atlantic coast. His actions prompted an unprecedented scramble for colonial property and profits. Within decades, the English launched important settlement clusters along the Delaware River valley and the Carolina coast. Each depended upon lucrative charters for a small network of friends.

> *Charles II had spurred England's seizure of New Netherland by issuing a charter for control of the contested region to his brother, the Duke of York.*

Most of these well-placed people belonged to the Councils for Trade and Plantations in London. Created in 1660, these advisory groups linked England's powerful merchants with crown officials. When Charles II issued a charter for Carolina in 1663, five of its eight initial proprietors served on those councils. In 1665 two of these same eight men became the proprietors of New Jersey. In addition, three of the eight played an active role in the Royal African Company, four became founders of the Hudson's Bay Company, and five became initial proprietors of the Bahamas. But Charles reached beyond this small group as well. In 1679 he made New Hampshire a proprietorship (an ill-fated experiment that lasted to 1708). In 1681 he paid off a debt to Quaker aristocrat William Penn by granting him a charter for Pennsylvania. (The generous arrangement included the "Lower Counties" that became Delaware in 1704.)

Penn's "holy experiment" to create a Quaker refuge benefited from earlier colonization south of New York. Dutch and Swedish settlers had inhabited the lower Delaware River valley for more than a generation. In 1665 the Duke of York carved off a portion of his vast proprietorship, granting the area between the Delaware and the Hudson to two friends: Lord John Berkeley and Sir George Carteret. They named the area New Jersey because Carteret had been born on the Isle of Jersey in the English Channel and had harbored Charles II when he took refuge there in 1649. Berkeley and Carteret promptly announced liberal "Concessions"—a representative assembly and freedom of worship—to attract rent-paying newcomers from England and the existing colonies. But their plans for profit made little headway.

In 1674 the proprietors divided these fertile lands into two separate provinces. East Jersey—where Newark was established in 1666—attracted Puritan families from New England, Dutch farmers from New York, and failed planters from Barbados. West Jersey was sold to members of the Society of Friends (including William Penn) who inaugurated a Quaker experiment along the Delaware River. Filled with egalitarian beliefs, the Quakers created a unicameral (single body) legislature, used secret ballots, and gave more power to juries than to judges. Their idealistic effort foundered within decades, and by 1702 all New Jersey came under crown control as a royal colony.

But by then, the Quakers had established a foothold in the neighboring colony of Pennsylvania. Its capital, the market town of Philadelphia, laid out by proprietor William Penn in 1682, already had more than 2,000 inhabitants. An earnest Quaker, Penn professed pacifism. He made it a point to deal fairly with the Lenni-Lenape (Delaware) Indians. After purchasing their land, he resold it on generous terms to English, Dutch, and Welsh Quakers who agreed to pay him an annual premium, called a **quitrent**. He also emphasized religious toleration. A growing stream of German Protestants and others facing persecution in Europe began to flow into Pennsylvania after 1700.

DOCUMENT

Penn, Description of Pennsylvania (1681)

Penn drew inspiration from James Harrington, the English political philosopher. Harrington's book *Oceana* (1656) argued that the best way to create an enduring republic was for one person to draft and implement its constitution. After endless tinkering, Penn devised a progressive "Frame of Government" that allowed for trial by jury, limited terms of office, and no use of capital punishment except in cases of treason and murder. But he remained ambivalent about legislative democracy. Settlers resented his scheme for a lower house that could approve acts drafted by the governor but could not initiate laws. In a new Charter of Privileges in 1701, Penn agreed to the creation of a **unicameral legislature** with full lawmaking powers. Penn's expansive proprietorship belonged to his descendants until colonial rule ended in 1776.

Anthony Ashley-Cooper, leader of the Carolina proprietors, also drew inspiration from Harrington, but for a very different undertaking. *Oceana* had stressed that distribution of land determined the nature of any commonwealth, and Ashley-Cooper (later the first earl of Shaftesbury) was eager to establish a stable aristocratic system. With his young secretary, John Locke (later an influential political philosopher), he drew up a set of "Fundamental Constitutions" in 1669. They proposed a stratified society in which hereditary nobles controlled much of the land and wealthy manor lords employed a lowly servant class of "leetmen." Their unrealistic document tried to revive the elaborate feudal hierarchy of medieval times.

The new government framework also endorsed racial slavery, declaring that "Every Freeman of Carolina shall have absolute Power and Authority over his Negro Slaves." This endorsement was not surprising, given the proprietors' involvement with England's new slave-trading monopoly in Africa and their initial recruitment of settlers in 1670 from the sugar island of Barbados. When Carolina colonists founded Charlestown (later Charleston) between the

Ashley and Cooper rivers in 1680, the proprietors had already modified aspects of their complicated scheme, setting aside feudalism to encourage greater immigration. Nevertheless, their endorsement of slavery shaped the region's society for hundreds of years.

Bloodshed in the English Colonies: 1670–1690

The appearance of English settlements along the Atlantic coast did little, in most places, to alter the traditional rhythms of life. Year after year, the daily challenges of subsistence dominated American life for Indians and colonists alike. The demanding seasonal tasks of clearing fields, planting seeds, and harvesting crops remained interwoven with the incessant chores of providing clothing, securing shelter, and sustaining community.

Over time, however, changing circumstances in America and Europe introduced new pressures up and down the Atlantic seaboard. On occasion after 1670, familiar routines gave way to episodes of bloodshed that threatened to tear whole colonies apart. Elsewhere in North America, Pueblo rebels were resisting the Spanish in New Mexico, and Iroquois warriors were challenging the French in Illinois country. The English, with their larger numbers, posed an even greater cultural and economic problem for Native American inhabitants.

In 1675 embittered Indians rose up across southern New England in Metacom's War (or King Philip's War). The next year, frontier tensions in Virginia sparked the upheaval known as Bacon's Rebellion. A decade later, events in England prompted further tremors. In London, mounting opposition forced the unpopular James II to surrender the English throne to William of Orange, and Parliament emerged from this "Glorious Revolution" with enhanced powers. In America, the end of rule by the Stuart dynasty was punctuated by controversy and violence in one colony after another.

> *On occasion after 1670, familiar routines gave way to episodes of bloodshed that threatened to tear whole colonies apart.*

Metacom's War in New England

By 1675 the Indians of southern New England, like the Pueblo in New Mexico, had endured several generations of colonization. Yet they disagreed over how much English culture they should adopt. Many used English words for trading, English pots for cooking, and English weapons for hunting. Some had converted to Christianity, living in protected "praying towns." Several young men had enrolled in Harvard's Indian College, where they learned to write English and Latin with an eye toward entering the ministry.

Massasoit, the Wampanoag **sachem** (leader) who had assisted the Pilgrims at Plymouth, made sure that his sons, Wamsutta and Metacom, learned English ways. The two men raised pigs and fired guns, and the colonists called them Alexander and Philip, after the kings of ancient Macedon. But when Wamsutta died in the 1660s, shortly after succeeding his father, Metacom (now called King Philip) suspected foul play by the English. And Metacom had other grievances. Colonial traders made the Indians drunk and then cheated them. English livestock trampled Wampanoag corn, and if Indians shot the cattle, colonial courts imposed punishments. Worst of all, colonists now outnumbered the remaining 20,000 Indians in southern New England by more than two to one.

When a white man shot and wounded a Native American in 1675, it triggered a long-expected conflict. Metacom's warriors ravaged towns along the Connecticut River valley and closer to the coast, using the victories to recruit additional Indian allies. The colonists, unprepared after forty years of peace and unchallenged dominance, were caught off guard. Distrusting even the Christian Indians, Massachusetts officials relocated whole praying towns of Indian converts to barren windswept islands in Boston Harbor.

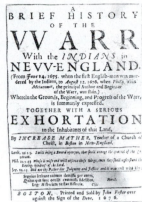

By December, the Connecticut and Rhode Island colonies, terrified of being wiped out, united with Plymouth and Massachusetts Bay to create a force of more than 1,000 men. An Indian captive led them to a stronghold of the still-neutral Narragansett in a swamp a dozen miles west of Newport, Rhode Island. The colonists surprised and overwhelmed the fortified village, setting it ablaze during the fierce fighting. Indian survivors fled, leaving behind more than 600 dead. Many of the men, women, and children were "terribly Barbikew'd," minister Cotton Mather later recorded.

This "Great Swamp Fight," reminiscent of an earlier battle in the Pequot War, infuriated the Narragansett survivors, who joined Metacom's much-feared confederacy. But as spring arrived in 1676, the coalition weakened and the tide turned. Sickness broke out among the fighters, who lacked food and gunpowder. The powerful Mohawk of the Iroquois Confederacy opposed Metacom from the west. Numerous Christian Indians joined the colonial forces, despite their painful internment at Boston's Deer Island.

With Metacom facing defeat, defections increased. In August, a former ally betrayed the resistance leader, shot him, and delivered his head to the English. As the struggle ground to a close, the colonists captured Metacom's wife and child, selling them into slavery in the West Indies along with hundreds of other prisoners of war. New England's remaining Indians became second-class inhabitants, confined to enclaves in the areas they had once dominated, while the colonists soon rebuilt and extended their domain.

Bacon's Rebellion in Virginia

While smoke still billowed over New England, new flames broke out in Virginia. Social unrest had been growing under the stern governorship of Sir William Berkeley. England's wars with the Dutch cut into the tobacco trade, and unfree tobacco workers—more than 6,000 indentured Europeans and nearly 2,000 enslaved Africans—chafed against their harsh treatment. On the frontier, colonists resented the dependent Indians (Occaneechi, Pamunkey, and others) who traded furs in exchange for protection from enemy tribes. Settlers also feared the well-armed Susquehannock living near the Potomac River. "Consider us," Berkeley wrote to the king in 1667, "as a people press'd at our backes with Indians, in our Bowills with our Servants . . . and invaded from without by the Dutch."

By 1676 tensions in Virginia reached the breaking point. Officials had increased taxes to pay for fortifications, servant plots and mutinies abounded, and corruption ran rampant among Berkeley's close associates. The aging governor ruled from Green Spring, his huge estate near the capital, Jamestown. Fearing the hostile views of free men who did not own property, Berkeley had revoked their right to vote. He had not dared to call an election in fourteen years. He also dreaded outspoken preachers, free schools, and printing presses. "How miserable that man is," he wrote, "that Governes a People where six parts of seaven at least are Poore Endebted Discontented and Armed."

Even wealthy newcomers such as Nathaniel Bacon had trouble gaining access to Berkeley's inner circle. When Bacon arrived from England in 1674 at age twenty-seven, he received a council seat because of his connections. But rivals denied the ambitious gentleman a license to engage in the fur trade. Impatient, Bacon condemned Berkeley's ruling Green Spring faction as sponges who "have sukt up the Publique Treasure." When frontier tensions erupted into racial violence, Bacon threw himself into the conflict, challenging Berkeley's leadership and launching aggressive campaigns. His frontier followers, eager for Indian land, killed friendly Occaneechi as well as hostile Susquehannock.

Benjamin Henry Latrobe, *View of Greenspring House*, 1796. Maryland Historical Society, Baltimore, MD (II-33)

■ Green Spring, the largest mansion in Virginia at the time of Bacon's Rebellion, symbolized the autocratic rule of Governor William Berkeley and his "Green Spring Faction." The estate was seized by Bacon's forces in 1676 and later restored by Berkeley's widow.

DOCUMENT

Bacon's
Declaration
(1676)

VIDEO

Bacon's Rebellion

Bacon's army continued to grow as backcountry leaders joined landless poor and runaway workers—both black and white—to support his anti-Indian cause. When the desperate governor called for a rare election to assert his strength, Bacon's supporters dominated the new House of Burgesses. Berkeley retreated to Virginia's eastern shore.

Throughout the summer of 1676, rumors swirled that Bacon might join malcontents in Maryland and in the Albemarle region of northeastern North Carolina to carve out an independent enclave and seek aid from the Dutch or the French. The new assembly quickly restored the vote to propertyless men and forbade excessive fees. It limited sheriffs to one year in office and passed other measures to halt corruption and expand participation in government. As an incentive for enlistment in the frontier war, the assembly granted Bacon's recruits the right to sell into slavery any Indians they captured.

For their part, slaves and indentured servants took advantage of the breakdown in public controls to leave their masters and join Bacon. Networks of "news wives" (women who used facts and rumors to fan worker discontent) spread stories of oppressive conditions. In June rebel soldiers talked openly of sharing estates among themselves, and in August they took over Green Spring Plantation, where Berkeley kept sixty horses and 400 head of cattle. A month later, Bacon's army burned Jamestown to the ground. But by October Bacon was dead, struck down by dysentery, and reinforcements for Berkeley were on the way from England. With armed vessels patrolling the rivers, Berkeley worked up enough nerve to return from the eastern shore. Soon propertied men who had joined with Bacon were changing sides again and receiving amnesty from the governor.

The revolt had been crushed, but the impact of the tumult proved huge. On the frontier, Bacon's violent campaign against the Indians had killed or enslaved hundreds and fostered bitter hatreds. In the Tidewater, the uprising had raised a frightening prospect for wealthy tobacco planters: a unified and defiant underclass of white and black workers. From then on, Virginia's gentry applied themselves to dividing the races and creating a labor force made up of African slaves. In London, the recently formed Royal African Company stood ready to further such a design.

The "Glorious Revolution" in England

No sooner had peace returned to New England and Virginia than Stuart policies brought a new round of turmoil on both sides of the Atlantic. In England, debate revived over who would succeed Charles II on the throne. The irreligious Charles, an Anglican in name only, had no legitimate children. Therefore, his brother James, a convert to Catholicism, was first in line to inherit the crown.

In 1678 rumors spread regarding a "Popish Plot" by Catholics to kill the king so that James could take power. The House of Commons, fearful of rule by a Catholic king, urged that James be excluded from the line of succession. Instead of James, House members argued, why not consider James's Protestant daughters by his first marriage: either Mary (recently wedded to her Dutch cousin, William of Orange) or Anne? Angered by such interference, Charles II dissolved Parliament in 1681 and ruled on his own for the last four years of his life.

When Charles II died in 1685, the traditional rule of succession prevailed: James II took over the English throne. In France that same year, Louis XIV revoked the Edict of Nantes, which had protected French Protestants. Fear spread among England's Protestant majority that their country's new Catholic ruler, James II, might also sanction persecution of non-Catholics. These concerns mounted when James disbanded Parliament, raised a standing army, and placed a Catholic in command of the navy. Then in 1688, James's queen gave birth to a male heir. Protestant anxieties about a pending Catholic dynasty erupted into open resistance.

United by their fear of Catholicism, rival factions among England's political elite (known for the first time as "Whigs" and "Tories") papered over their differences temporarily. They invited the Protestant William of Orange, James's Dutch son-in-law, to lead an army from Holland and take the English crown. In November 1688, he crossed the English Channel with 15,000 men, prompting James to **abdicate** the throne and escape into exile. William and Mary were proclaimed joint sovereigns in 1689, accepting a Bill of Rights that limited royal power.

Its position now enhanced, Parliament moved to grant toleration to Protestant dissenters, establish limited freedom of the press, and ensure regular parliamentary sessions. It also imposed limits on any permanent, paid military forces, known as standing armies, because they could accrue their own power and jeopardize civil authority. The English had thus preserved Protestantism and curtailed royal absolutism, all without bloodshed. Parliament hailed King William III as "our great Deliverer from Popery and Slavery." The propertied classes, who benefited most from the peaceful transition, hailed it as the "Glorious Revolution."

The "Glorious Revolution" in America

The succession of James II in 1685 did not bode well for England's American colonies. The new king not only professed

Jan Wyck, *William III Landing at Torbay*, 1688. National Maritime Museum Picture Library

■ Protestants in England and America opposed to King James II welcomed news that William of Orange (above) had arrived from Holland with his army in 1688 to take over the English throne.

the Catholic faith but also cherished absolute monarchy and distrusted elected assemblies. In colonial affairs, James favored revenue-generating reforms and direct obedience to the crown. He detested the powerful leaders in Massachusetts since, as Congregationalists, they believed in a decentralized Protestant church. James also resented the fact that they disobeyed the Navigation Acts and asserted their right to self-rule, even after the crown revoked their charter in 1684. Moreover, he rejected the notion that colonists possessed the precious right claimed by the English at home: not to be taxed without giving their consent. The king envisioned an extensive reorganization of the American colonies.

When James assumed the throne, his own colony of New York automatically became a royal province. Convinced of his divine right to set policy, the king nullified the charters of certain colonies in order to bring them under his control. As the cornerstone of his reorganization plan, James linked the New England colonies (plus New York and New Jersey in 1688) into one huge *Dominion of New England*. This consolidation, under an appointed governor general, would make it easier for England to suppress dissent, enforce shipping regulations, and defend the Dominion's frontiers—at least in theory.

In practice, the effort to forge a Dominion of New England proved a disaster. The move met such stiff resistance in America that a similar design for England's southern colonies never materialized. Control of the Dominion went to a military officer, Sir Edmund Andros. The heavy-handed Andros attempted to rule from Boston through a council he appointed, made up of loyal associates, without aid or interference from any elected legislature. He asserted the crown's right to question existing land patents, and he requisitioned a Congregational church for Anglican services. Worse, he offended local leaders by strictly enforcing the Navigation Acts to collect revenue. When participants in democratic town meetings raised objections, he jailed the leaders.

> *Colonists seethed with resentment toward this revival of Stuart absolutism, which claimed total obedience to the king and his officers as a divine right for the Stuart monarchy.*

Colonists seethed with resentment toward this revival of Stuart absolutism, which claimed total obedience to the king and his officers as a divine right for the Stuart monarchy. Rumors of French invasions and Catholic plots swirled among staunch Protestants. In April 1689, welcome news that the Protestant William of Orange had invaded England inspired a revolt in Boston. Mobs showed public support for overthrowing the Stuart regime, and local leaders locked Governor Andros in jail.

The success of William and the demise of the Dominion of New England did not end royal efforts to tighten imperial control over New England. The new Massachusetts charter of 1691 consolidated neighboring Plymouth and Maine into the Massachusetts Bay colony. Moreover, it proclaimed that future governors would be appointed by the monarchy, as in other colonies. The men of Massachusetts, who had elected their own governor since the days of John Winthrop, would no longer have that right.

Emboldened by Boston's actions in 1689, New Yorkers ousted their own Dominion officials and set up a temporary government headed by Jacob Leisler. This German-born militia captain was a staunch Calvinist and hostile to the town's growing English elite. In Leisler's Rebellion, long-standing ethnic and religious rivalries merged with lower-class hostilities: Leisler's supporters resented their treatment at the hands of the rich. They freed imprisoned debtors and attacked the houses of leading merchants. After a new governor arrived to take charge in 1691, the elite fought back. They lowered artisan wages and executed Leisler as a rebel, although they could find no carpenter willing to provide a ladder for the gallows.

Similar tremors shook the Chesapeake region. In Maryland, where the Catholic proprietor ruled over a large and restive Protestant population, the governing Calvert family waited too long to proclaim its loyalty to King William. Fearing a "Popish" plot, assemblyman John Coode and a force of 250 armed Protestants marched on St. Mary's City and seized the government by force. The "happy Change in England" had replaced divine right rule with a more balanced constitutional monarchy, and Maryland settlers were determined to show their support.

Consequences of War and Growth: 1690–1715

The success of the Glorious Revolution hardly brought peace to England or its empire. On the contrary, warfare marked the reign of William and Mary and also that of Mary's sister, Queen Anne, who ruled from 1702 until her death in 1714. William immediately became involved in bloody campaigns to subdue highland clans in Scotland and overpower Catholic forces in Ireland. Moreover, English involvement against France in two protracted wars on the European continent had implications for colonists and Indians living in eastern North America. The War of the League of Augsburg in Europe became known to English colonists in America as King William's War (1689–1697), and the protracted War of Spanish Succession was experienced in America as Queen Anne's War (1702–1713).

Nowhere was the impact of these imperial wars more evident than in the rapidly growing colonies of the Northeast. Indeed, the earlier bloodshed of Metacom's (King Philip's) War, starting in 1675, had already aroused consternation and soul-searching in Bible-reading New England, and the violent decades that followed were viewed by many as a harsh test or a deserved punishment from the Almighty. They believed that the initial Puritan errand into the wilderness had been closely watched by God. Could it be, ministers now asked from the pulpit, that the Lord had some special controversy with the current generation? As communities grew more prosperous and became caught up in the pursuit of worldly success, were church members forgetting their religious roots and leading less pious lives? Invoking the Old Testament prophet Jeremiah, clerics interpreted personal and collective troubles as God's punishment for the region's spiritual decline.

But such a sweeping explanation of misfortune only raised deeper questions. New Englanders could see clearly that the consequences of rapid change were not spread equally among all towns, congregations, and families. As in most war eras, some people and localities suffered more than others. Certain individuals and groups seemed to benefit economically while others fell behind. Some anxious believers saw the hand of Satan in the day-to-day struggles of village life. Others argued that the worldly success and wartime profits of an expanding elite had undermined the community ideals of earlier generations. While flames engulfed isolated Massachusetts communities such as Deerfield and portions of the Maine frontier, fiery passions were also being aroused in older settlements, such as Salem and Boston.

DOCUMENT

Benjamin Wadsworth, from *A Well-Ordered Family* (1712)

Salem's Wartime Witch Hunt

One of the most memorable disruptions, the Salem witch hunt, occurred in Essex County, Massachusetts, a two-day ride on horseback from the embattled Maine frontier. In 1692 an outburst of witchcraft accusations engulfed the farm community of Salem Village. The strange episode remains one of the most troubling in American history.

Among European Christians, a belief in witches with a supernatural power to inflict harm stretched back for centuries. In the 1600s, witchcraft trials abounded in Europe, and in New England zealous believers had executed several dozen supposed witches in isolated cases. Three-fourths of those accused (and even more of those executed) were women. Most were beyond childbearing age, often poor or widowed, with limited power to protect themselves in the community. But the hysteria in Salem went far beyond other colonial incidents, with more than 200 people accused and twenty put to death.

Early in 1692, more than half a dozen young women in Salem Village, ranging in age from nine to twenty, began to suffer violent convulsive fits. With reduced appetites and temporary loss of hearing, sight, and memory, they also experienced choking sensations that curtailed their speech. Vivid hallucinations followed. By April the girls had accused ten people of being witches. Then some of the ten named others in their elaborate confessions, and the hysteria snowballed.

In a world where people considered satanic influence very real, frightened authorities seriously weighed the girls' stories of people appearing to them as devilish specters and apparitions. Overriding tradition, jurists allowed such "spectral evidence" in court, and convictions mounted. The court ordered public hangings on Gallows Hill that continued through September. Only when accusations reached too high in the social hierarchy and when several accusers recanted their stories did the new governor finally intervene. He emptied the jails, forbade further imprisonments, and pardoned the surviving accused until the tremor could subside.

Why this terrible outburst? Some writers wonder whether the girls' symptoms suggest food poisoning (perhaps from a fungus on rye used in baking bread) or an epidemic of mosquito-borne encephalitis (an inflammation of the brain). Others note political factions within the village. Strained relations between farm families and more prosperous urban residents nearby may have influenced the craze. Still others emphasize the zeal and gullibility of those first assigned to investigate. Some speculate that the absence of central authority, until Governor Phips arrived in the colony, allowed a troubled situation to spin out of control. Finally, commentators stress a perverse psychological dynamic that arises in any witch hunt, ancient or modern. In such cases, accused suspects often can save their own lives by supplying damaging and vivid confessions implicating others rather than by offering heartfelt denials of guilt. One or more of these factors surely came into play.

DOCUMENT

Ann Putnam, Deposition (1692)

DOCUMENT

Ann Putnam, Confession (1706)

Yet devastation on the Maine frontier also contributed to what happened in Salem Village. The little Massachusetts town had numerous links to the war zone. A recent minister, George Burroughs, much disliked in the village, had come from Maine and had returned there when the contentious parish refused to pay him. Traumatized survivors from King William's War—the current conflict against the Abenaki and French—had trickled into the community. Significantly, more than half the young women who had accused others of witchcraft had lost one or both parents in the brutal frontier wars. On February 5, just weeks before the first accusations, attackers had burned the Maine village of York 80 miles north of Salem, killing forty-eight people, and taking seventy-three captives. Word of the raid no doubt triggered shocking memories among Salem's war refugees, especially the orphans who worked as servants in local households.

Fears deepened in April when one of the accused testified that the Devil had tempted her while she had been living in Maine. Then it was reported that the specter of Reverend Burroughs "appeared" to an accuser. Charged with promoting witchcraft and encouraging the hostile Indians (whom the colonists saw as Satan's helpers), Burroughs was arrested in Maine and hanged on Gallows Hill. A servant named Mercy Short, who had been captured and orphaned by Indians, recalled disturbing dreams of the Devil. She told minister Cotton Mather that in her dreams Satan and his minions (who had "an Indian colour") had made "hideous assaults" upon her. Much of what Mather and others recorded as the work of Satan may actually have been posttraumatic stress in a frayed community during wartime.

The Uneven Costs of War

Throughout the 1690s and beyond, King William's War and then Queen Anne's War made conflict a constant element of colonial life, but the burdens fell unevenly. For many colonial families, incessant warfare brought only death and dislocation. But for others, it offered new opportunities as the colonial economies expanded. Farmers with access to port towns shifted away from subsistence agriculture and grew crops for commercial sale. In doing so, they exposed themselves to greater financial risks, given transportation costs and market fluctuations. But they hoped to reap large profits. Overseas trade and wartime smuggling offered investors even higher gains and larger risks. The crews of **privateers** (boats licensed to harass enemy shipping in wartime) made money if they captured a foreign vessel as a prize. Profits

New York Public Library

■ For protection, the pirate Blackbeard often brought his ship into the shallow waters behind the barrier islands that form North Carolina's Atlantic coast. There, his crew bartered stolen goods at Ocracoke Island and reveled on the beach with local inhabitants.

for outright pirates were greater still. Therefore, some colonial mariners chose to become buccaneers who operated for their own gain while avoiding the arm of the law. Englishman Edward Teach, known as Blackbeard, won notoriety as a privateer-turned-pirate, haunting the Carolina coast until his death in 1718.

Everywhere, poorer families were most likely to sink under the burdens of war. **Regressive taxes**, requiring the same amount from a poor carpenter as from a rich merchant, obviously hurt impoverished people the most. So did high wartime prices for food and other basic necessities. Furthermore, many of the poor men recruited by the military became casualties of combat or disease, increasing the number of widows living in poverty. As towns expanded, the growing distance between rich and poor struck local residents. The moral ties and community obligations—known as the social covenant—that Puritan elders had emphasized two generations earlier were loosening. In their place emerged a focus on secular priorities and a new, individualistic spirit.

In Boston, troubled ministers decried the hunger and poverty that they saw deepening in their parishes alongside unprecedented displays of wealth. Between 1685 and 1715, the share of all personal wealth in the town controlled by the richest 5 percent climbed from 26 percent to 40 percent. Angry writers published irate pamphlets encouraging working people to take political action. They charged once-respected elites with studying "how to oppress, cheat, and overreach their neighbours." Predictably, when an English fleet of sixty warships carrying 5,000 men docked at Boston in 1711, powerful merchants who controlled the flow of provisions reaped huge rewards from this windfall.

Storm Clouds in the South

Peace returned to New England's frontier villages and port towns in 1711, as negotiations began for ending Queen Anne's War in America and the related War of Spanish Succession in Europe. British diplomats gained favorable terms from France and Spain when they signed a treaty at

Utrecht two years later. (The formal union of England and Scotland in 1707 under the name *Great Britain* had transformed the *English* empire into the *British* empire.) But London officials could not prevent fresh violence in North America, given the expansion of their British colonies. The Wampanoag, Narragansett, and Abenaki Indians had attempted to roll back the advancement of northeastern settlers into Connecticut, Massachusetts, and Maine. Now Native Americans in the Southeast sought to counter the encroachments of newcomers along the Carolina coast.

By the 1660s, settlers drifted into what would become the North Carolina colony. Some were English radicals fleeing the Restoration. Others, such as John Culpeper, had moved north from the Carolina settlement on the Ashley River, where they disapproved of the hierarchical plans drawn up by Shaftesbury and Locke giving Carolina proprietors firm control over the new colony. Still others were runaway servants from Virginia and refugees escaping the aftermath of Bacon's uprising. In 1677 these newcomers, led by Culpeper, seized control in the Albemarle region. The proprietors suppressed "Culpeper's Rebellion," but in 1689 they agreed to name a separate governor for the portion of Carolina "That Lies north and east of Cape Feare." Another disturbance, "Cary's Rebellion" in 1710, led to official recognition of "North Carolina, independent of Carolina," the next year. (Surveyors marked off the dividing line with Virginia in 1728.)

Native American Population Loss, 1500–1700

In 1680 Native Americans still outnumbered newcomers in eastern North Carolina by two to one, but within thirty years that ratio had been reversed. The Naval Stores Act of 1705, passed by Parliament to promote colonial production of tar and pitch for shipbuilding, drew a stream of settlers to the pine forests of eastern North Carolina. By 1710 English communities existed on Albemarle Sound, at what is now Edenton, and on Pamlico Sound, at Bath (where Blackbeard and other pirates were frequent visitors). Farther south, Protestant immigrants from Bern, Switzerland, had staked out the town of New Bern on the site of a Native American village. John Lawson, who had explored the Carolinas before helping to lay out Bath and New Bern, conceded that the Indians had been "better to us than we are to them."

Eventually, the Tuscarora Indians struck back. Frustrated by corrupt traders and land encroachment, they killed Lawson and launched a war in 1711 to drive out the intruders. But they had waited too long. Within two years, the settlers—aided by a South Carolina force of several dozen whites and nearly 500 Yamasee Indians—had crushed Tuscarora resistance. Most of the Tuscarora survivors migrated north, where they became the sixth nation within the powerful Iroquois Confederacy.

Yamasee warriors from the Savannah River region helped British colonists quell the Tuscarora uprising. But in 1715 they led their own rebellion against advancing settlers and corrupt traders linked to Charleston. They received support from Creek Indians, Spanish settlers in Florida, and French traders at the new Alabama outpost of Fort Toulouse. The still-powerful Cherokee in Appalachia opted not to join in the Yamasee War. Otherwise, the Indians might have overwhelmed the South Carolina colony.

Conclusion

European Claims in America, c. 1750

Inspired by the exploits of LaSalle and a generation of voyageurs and missionaries, the French had made inroads into the heart of the continent, glimpsing the huge Mississippi Valley. But most European intrusions remained confined to the fringes of the vast continent. The French established themselves in Louisiana, and small numbers of Spanish held onto footholds in New Mexico and Florida, while venturing into parts of Arizona and Texas.

The English newcomers, far more numerous, remained clustered along the Atlantic seaboard. When their rising numbers prompted expansion up local river valleys away from the coast, warfare with traditional inhabitants ensued. Along the length of eastern North America, from the Kennebec River to the Savannah, hundreds of settlers and Indians died violently

■ MAP 3.3
VIRGINIA AND THE CAROLINAS, c. 1710   After John Lawson made a 1,000-mile journey through the Carolina interior (1700–1701), he became an advocate for colonial growth. The expanding settlements of North Carolina and South Carolina pressed the Tuscarora and Yamasee Indians, who staged wars of resistance after 1710.

during the half-century before 1715. Often the frontier struggles became entwined with wider conflicts between the rival European empires. These wilderness skirmishes seem minute compared with the battles raging in Europe at the same time. Despite the small scale of the conflicts in North America, however, Europe's imperial wars had started to influence developments in the English colonies.

Another element of Europe's expansion overseas—the transatlantic slave trade—had also begun to alter the shape of England's North American colonies. What had seemed only a small cloud on the horizon in the early seventeenth century had grown into an ominous force, with a momentum of its own, by the early eighteenth century. The storm hit hardest along the Southeast coast, where the arrival of thousands of Africans soon shaped a distinctive and depressing world of enslavement and exploitation that endured for generations. No sooner had the English gained control along the Atlantic edge of North America than they orchestrated a "terrible transformation" that placed thousands in bondage and altered the shape of American history.

Sites to Visit

Mission San Xavier del Bac

Lying 7 miles south of Tucson, Arizona, off Interstate 19 is the mission Father Eusebio Kino founded in 1700. The current church was created in 1783. A short drive south on Highway 19, the Tumacacori National Historical Park preserves ruins of three early Spanish missions.

Jesuit Missionary Records

puffin.creighton.edu/jesuit/relations/

In the late nineteenth century, Reuben Gold Thwaites compiled and edited more than seventy volumes titled *The Jesuit Relations and Allied Documents*. Creighton University has made almost the entire English translation of these valuable documents available on this Web site. The documents are also available on CD-ROM from Quintin Publications.

Fort Toulouse

In 1717 the French built Fort Toulouse where the Coosa and Talapoosa rivers converge, just north of Montgomery, Alabama. On the third weekend each month between April and November, volunteers conduct a French Colonial Living History program in and around the reconstructed French fort, with displays of blacksmithing and musket firing.

Straits of Mackinac

The Straits of Mackinac joining lakes Huron and Michigan was once a strategic spot. Here, Interstate 75 now links Upper and Lower Michigan. North of the Mackinac Bridge, a memorial at St. Ignace honors Father Marquette. At the south end, Colonial Michilimackinac is a reconstructed village reflecting French and English frontier life.

Castillo de San Marcos

www.nps.gov/casa/home/home.htm

This stone fort guarding St. Augustine, Florida, was built in 1672–1695. The National Park Service maintains this fortress as a national monument and also provides a virtual tour online.

Old Deerfield National Historic Landmark

This site lies just east of Interstate 91 and surrounds a beautiful village in the hills of northwestern Massachusetts. Historic Deerfield, incorporated in 1952, maintains fourteen restored houses, open for a self-guided walking tour, and the Flynt Center of Early New England Life displays New England life from 1650 to 1850.

Salem Village Witchcraft

www.nhc.rtp.nc.us:8080/tserve/eighteen/ekeyinfo/salemwc.htm

A good Web introduction to "Witchcraft in Salem Village" appears as part of a project on "Religion and the National Culture" at this Web site of the National Humanities Center. Salem Village (Danvers, Massachusetts) has a memorial to victims of the 1692 witchcraft persecutions.

Eastern North Carolina

www.ah.dcr.state.nc.us/sections/hs/bath/bath.htm

North Carolina's earliest colonial ports at Edenton, Bath, and New Bern (ranging from north to south) still contain rich evidence of eighteenth-century life. This Web site for Historic Bath has links on explorer-naturalist John Lawson, Blackbeard the Pirate, and the Tuscarora War.

For Further Reading

General

Elaine G. Breslaw, *Witches of the Atlantic World: A Historical Reader and Primary Source Book* (2000).

Wesley Frank Craven, *The Colonies in Transition, 1660–1713* (1968).

Elizabeth A. H. John, *Storms Brewed in Other Men's Worlds: The Confrontation of Indians, Spanish, and French in the Southwest, 1540–1795* (1975).

Alvin M. Josephy Jr., *The Patriot Chiefs: A Chronicle of American Indian Resistance* (1969).

France and the American Interior

Marcel Giraud, *A History of French Louisiana, Vol. One: The Reign of Louis XIV, 1698–1715* (1974).

Eric Hinderaker, *Elusive Empires: Constructing Colonialism in the Ohio Valley, 1673–1800* (1997).

Robert S. Weddle, *The Wreck of the* Belle, *the Ruin of La Salle* (2001).

Richard White, *The Middle Ground: Indians, Empires, and Republics in the Great Lakes Region, 1650–1815* (1991).

The Spanish Empire on the Defensive

Ramón A. Gutiérrez, *When Jesus Came, the Corn Mothers Went Away: Marriage, Sexuality, and Power in New Mexico, 1500–1846* (1991).

Andrew L. Knaut, *The Pueblo Revolt of 1680: Conquest and Resistance in Seventeenth-Century New Mexico* (1995).

Jerald T. Milanich, *Florida Indians and the Invasion from Europe* (1995).

David J. Weber, ed., *What Caused the Pueblo Revolt?* (1999).

England's American Empire Takes Shape

Alan Gallay, *The Indian Slave Trade: The Rise of the English Empire in the American South, 1670–1717* (2002).

Joyce D. Goodfriend, *Before the Melting Pot: Society and Culture in Colonial New York City, 1664–1730* (1992).

Brendan McConville, *These Daring Disturbers of the Public Peace: The Struggle for Property and Power in Early New Jersey* (1999).

Gary B. Nash, *Quakers and Politics: Pennsylvania, 1681–1726* (1968).

Robert M. Weir, *Colonial South Carolina: A History* (1983).

Bloodshed in the English Colonies: 1670–1690

John Demos, *The Unredeemed Captive: A Family Story from Early America* (1994).

Jill Lepore, *The Name of War: King Philip's War and the Origins of American Identity* (1998).

David S. Lovejoy, *The Glorious Revolution in America* (1972).

Stephen S. Webb, *1676: The End of American Independence* (1984).

Consequences of War and Growth: 1690–1715

Verner W. Crane, *The Southern Frontier, 1670–1732* (1928).

Evan Haefeli and Kevin Sweeney, *Captors and Captives: The 1704 French and Indian Raid on Deerfield* (2003).

James H. Merrell, *The Indians' New World: Catawbas and Their Neighbors from European Contact Through the Era of Removal* (1989).

Gary B. Nash, *The Urban Crucible: The Northern Seaports and the Origins of the American Revolution* (1986, abridged edition).

Mary Beth Norton, *In the Devil's Snare: The Salem Witchcraft Crisis of 1692* (2002).

Marcus Rediker, *Villains of All Nations: Atlantic Pirates in the Golden Age* (2004).

For quizzes and other resources on these topics, go to www.longmanamericanhistory.com.

PART TWO

A Century of Colonial Expansion to 1775

O N APRIL 19, 1775, NEW ENGLAND FARMERS BATTLED BRITISH soldiers at Concord Bridge. The confrontation marked the start of the American Revolution. (Each spring in Massachusetts, the date is still set aside as Patriots' Day and celebrated with the running of the Boston Marathon.) But how did colonies that were weak outposts before 1700 become strong enough to challenge the power of the British Empire in the second half of the eighteenth century? The answer is not a simple one. Life changed in dramatic ways during the century before 1775, not only in New England but throughout much of North America.

The rapid spread of Spanish horses across the West allowed Native Americans, such as the Comanche and Sioux, to become mounted buffalo hunters on the Great Plains. The arrival of Russian fur traders disrupted traditional cultures on the Aleutian Islands and the coast of Alaska. At the same time, the gradual success of the new Louisiana colony gave France access to much of the Mississippi River valley. But the potential for a dominant French-speaking empire in America evaporated with the stunning defeat of French forces by the British in the Seven Years' War. As that global conflict ended in 1763, the Spanish also lost ground in North America. After claiming Florida for 200 years, they finally ceded the peninsula to the British, even as they began to extend Spanish missions up the coast of California.

Other changes were even more dramatic. In the eighteenth century, race slavery became an established aspect of colonial society in North America. Hints of coming change appeared even in the generation before 1660. During the next half century, race slavery rapidly took hold as a dominant institution in the coastal Southeast. The English had come late to the transatlantic slave trade, but they became aggressive participants in the lucrative traffic in human beings. English colonizers fashioned harsh slave-based societies in the Caribbean, then in the Chesapeake colonies of Virginia and Maryland, next in North and South Carolina, and finally, after 1750, in the recently established colony of Georgia.

Race slavery transformed the mainland colonies in terrible ways and had far-reaching results. Thousands of Africans arrived in North American ports in the eighteenth century. Strikingly, they were only a small fraction of the much greater transport of Africans to the Caribbean and Central and South America. Nevertheless, by 1750 there were nearly 250,000 African Americans living in North America. Most lived in the South, and most were enslaved, including several hundred in Spanish East Florida and several thousand in French Louisiana. By 1775 the number exceeded half a million. By then, blacks made up more than 20 percent of the population of the British colonies, and the legal and social constraints that shackled their world remained tighter than ever.

Newcomers from Europe, as well as from Africa, altered the make-up of Atlantic colonies that had once been almost entirely English. Many of these newly arrived Europeans, unable to afford the cost of passage, had to pledge their labor for a period of years. But in contrast to the Africans, most European migrants came to America voluntarily and were free from obligations within a few years. The Atlantic crossing could be harrowing, of course, but for thousands the long-term advantages outweighed the short-term drawbacks. Artisans of all kinds were in high demand, and land was cheap. Colonial governments ruled with a light hand in comparison to the monarchies of Europe, and they competed with one another to attract newcomers. This competition for new arrivals bred relative religious and ethnic tolerance.

Pushed by events in Europe and drawn by opportunities in America, non-English families flocked to Britain's North American colonies. This new flow from Europe and the British Isles, combined with the African slave trade, quickly generated a far more diverse colonial society on the foundations laid by earlier English immigrants. Prior generations of colonists had laid out towns, formed governments, and founded the rudimentary institutions of colonial social life. They had established an ambiguous pattern of interaction with Native Americans that involved warfare and displacement as well as trade and intermarriage. Also, they had located harbors, carved out roads, and started to build an economic infrastructure.

As numbers rose and diversity increased, a series of regional economies emerged along the eastern seaboard. Each sustained the local inhabitants while also serving the wider needs of the British Empire. For much of the eighteenth century, the British crown promoted economic growth in the colonies through a workable combination of protectionist controls and benign neglect.

But the British victory over the French brought drastic new problems to eastern North America after 1763. Native Americans lost a valued trading partner and military ally when the French withdrew. Britain faced an enormous war debt and looked to its burgeoning colonies as a source of much-needed revenue. Within little more than a decade, Britain's North American colonists went from resentment and resistance to overt rebellion and an anticolonial war of independence.

1759	Quebec falls to the British
1760	George III becomes king of England French surrender Montreal to British
1763	Treaty of Paris ends the French and Indian War Proclamation Line limits expansion of British colonies Pontiac's Rebellion
1764	Sugar Act; Currency Act
1765	Quartering Act; Stamp Act Virginia Resolves; Stamp Act demonstrations Tenant riots in Hudson Valley
1766	Stamp Act repealed Declaratory Act Bougainville explores the South Pacific
1767	Townshend Acts
1768	James Cook makes first of three voyages to explore the Pacific Massachusetts Circular Letter
1770	Boston Massacre
1771	Battle of Alamance ends the Regulator Movement in North Carolina
1772	Burning of the *Gaspée*
1773	Boston Tea Party
1774	Intolerable Acts First Continental Congress meets The Suffolk Resolves
1775	Battles of Lexington and Concord Spanish enter San Francisco Bay

African Enslavement: The Terrible Transformation

O N A WINTERY DAY IN JANUARY 1656, A MULATTO SERVANT NAMED ELIZABETH KEY WENT BEFORE the local court in Northumberland County, Virginia. She was twenty-five years old. The late Colonel John Mottrom, a justice of the peace, had held Elizabeth as a slave, kept in perpetual bondage. She objected strongly, and she wanted to sue the executors of Mottrom's estate for her freedom and back pay. Bess, as she was known, presented a threefold argument. First, as the daughter of a free man, she should inherit her father's legal status according to English law. Second, as a baptized Christian, she should not be enslaved. And third, she could produce a document showing that as a small child she had been "put out" to work until she was fourteen, following local custom. Such contracts for apprenticing a child for a fixed number of years were common in America, where labor was in short supply. But her term of work had expired long ago.

Key was accompanied in court by her white attorney and lover, William Greensted. They had had two children together and would marry six months later, when they finally won a favorable verdict. The young couple produced witnesses who testified that Bess was the daughter of Thomas Key, a white man serving in the Virginia General Assembly, and his "Negro woman." One witness told the jury that Bess's mother had lived openly with Mr. Key and had said that the girl was Key's daughter. Further testimony established that in 1636, not long before he died, Key had bound little Bess to Humphrey Higginson, a member of the Council of State. Higginson "promised to use her as well as if shee were his own Child"; that is, "more Respectfully than a Comon servant or slave." He even stood as her godfather when Bess was christened.

To be raised in a Christian church was no small matter at a time when Europeans viewed non-Christians captured in wars to be uniquely vulnerable to legal enslavement. For Bess, this circumstance helped her cause greatly, for she proved

■ Africans arriving in America often had ornamental scarification (known as "country marks") on their bodies, as well as brands inflicted by slave traders and physical scars from the middle passage.

"able to give a very good account of her fayth." Furthermore, she produced clear evidence that her father had sold her to Higginson for nine years. Mr. Key had demanded that Higginson not dispose of her to any other person, such as to Colonel Mottrom. Rather, he was to give her the usual "freedom portion" of corn and clothes "and lett her shift for her selfe," either in England or Virginia, when her term expired.

The local jury accepted Elizabeth Key's three-part argument and pronounced her free. But the General Court overturned the verdict on appeal, only to be overruled in turn by a committee of the General Assembly. In the end, the committee determined that "Elizabeth ought to bee free." The assemblymen also argued that her last master owed her a "freedom portion," plus back pay "for the time shee hath served longer than Shee ought to have done." Still, the matter generated debate among settlers. Several decades later, Elizabeth's case would have been decided differently. Moreover, the courts of Virginia might well have enslaved her children for life. And their offspring would have inherited slavery status as well.

A terrible transformation was under way in English colonial culture that would warp American society for centuries to come. It spread gradually, like a cancer, revealing a different pace and pattern in each mainland colony. During the 1620s and 1630s, a few black servants were working alongside white servants. But well before the end of the century, a fateful transition had occurred, and the grandchildren of those workers had been separated into two distinct categories based upon skin color and physical appearance, or race. Free blacks persisted in the English colonies, but in most communities they became anomalies, for the tide was flowing against them. From now on, people of African ancestry were to be legally enslaved for life. Elizabeth Key and her children and grandchildren experienced the painful transition firsthand.

The Descent into Race Slavery

Some major transitions in human affairs evolve gradually. This was the case for the descent of North American society into sanctioned race slavery. Nothing shaped colonial cultures more forcefully than the European colonists' commitment to the legal enslavement of hundreds of thousands of people and their descendants. It is important to examine the slippery slope that led to perpetual servitude based on race.

The Caribbean Precedent

The roots of race slavery in the Americas extend back to the era of Columbus, when warfare, sickness, and exploitation quickly decimated the native populations of the Caribbean after 1492. Hungry for human labor, the Spanish intruders began to import people from Africa to grow crops and dig for gold in the Caribbean islands. As the native population declined sharply through epidemics, the traffic in black newcomers expanded.

Spanish pressure for labor in the New World intensified further with the discovery of additional mines for precious metals in Mexico and Peru. To meet the growing demand, Spain's king even issued a contract (called the *asiento*) that allowed other European powers—such as Portugal, France, or the Netherlands—to import African slaves to the Spanish colonies. High profits drew eager participation. In the half-century between 1590 and 1640, more than 220,000 people arrived in chains from Africa at the Spanish empire's ports in Central and South America.

Meanwhile, the Portuguese purchased enslaved Africans to work their own expanding sugar plantations. They imported more than 75,000 slaves, mostly from the Congo River region of West Central Africa, to the Atlantic island of São Tomé in the sixteenth century. When

Portuguese sugar production spread to coastal Brazil, so did the exploitation of African labor. By 1625 Brazil imported the majority of slaves crossing the Atlantic each year and exported most of the sugar consumed in Europe.

Long before the 1660s, therefore, Europeans had set a precedent for exploiting African workers in New World colonies. Religious and secular authorities frowned on actively enslaving people, especially if they were fellow Christians. But they tolerated buying so-called infidels (those who followed other religions), particularly if slavery had already been imposed on them elsewhere. West African victims were non-Christians, and most had already been enslaved by others, captured by fellow Africans in war.

Confident in this rationale, the Spanish and Portuguese adapted their laws to accept the enslavement of Africans. Moreover, the condition would be passed on, with children inheriting at birth their mother's legal status. The Catholic Church backed the new labor system, though priests occasionally worked to alleviate suffering among Africans in the Americas. The pope did nothing to condemn the growing traffic, nor did the Protestant Reformation have a dampening effect. On the contrary, the rising Protestant sea powers of northern Europe proved willing to assist in the slave trade and take part in the dramatic "sugar revolution," growing sugar on a massive scale for expanding Atlantic markets.

The Dutch, for example, ruled Brazil for a generation in the first half of the seventeenth century, importing slaves to South America and exporting sugar. When the Portuguese regained control of Brazil at midcentury, they pushed out Dutch settlers. These outcasts took their knowledge about managing sugar plantations to the islands of the Caribbean. Some appeared in the new English possessions of Barbados and Jamaica, and soon they were directing African slaves in cutting, pressing, and boiling sugar cane to make molasses. The thick molasses could then be processed further to make rum and refined sugar for export. By the 1650s slavery and sugar production were engulfing England's West Indian possessions, just as these twin features had already become central to the New World colonies controlled by Spain and Portugal. A looming precedent had been set. But as late as 1660, it was not at all clear that African slavery would gain a prominent place, or even a lasting foothold, in any North American colonies.

> *As late as 1660, it was not at all clear that African slavery would gain a prominent place, or even a lasting foothold, in any North American colonies.*

Ominous Beginnings

As far back as the sixteenth century, African men had participated in Spanish explorers' forays into the Southeast, and some had remained, fathering children with Indian women. African slaves had helped to establish the small Spanish outpost at St. Augustine in 1565, but a century later no additional coastal colonies had yet appeared on the mainland anywhere south of Chesapeake Bay.

Granted, Africans were present farther north in the fledgling settlements of the French, Dutch, and English. But their numbers remained small—several thousand at most—and few of these newcomers had come directly from Africa. Most had lived for years in the Caribbean or on the mainland, absorbing colonial languages and beliefs. So they and their children, like Bess Key, were not viewed as complete outsiders by the Europeans. The legal and social standing of these early African Americans remained vague before the 1660s. Everywhere, workers were in demand, and most black newcomers found themselves laboring alongside unfree European servants, each person bound by an "**indenture**" for a period of years.

In the Massachusetts Bay colony early Puritan settlers, casting about for sources of labor and for markets, exchanged goods for slaves in the Caribbean. In 1644 seafaring New Englanders even attempted direct trade with Africa. But the following year, Massachusetts authorities ordered a New Hampshire resident to surrender a black worker he had purchased in Boston. They argued that the man had been stolen from Africa, not captured in war, and should be returned to his home. In 1652 Rhode Island passed a law limiting all involuntary service—for Europeans or Africans—to no more than ten years.

Along the Hudson River, the Dutch colonists had close ties with the sugar islands of the West Indies where race slavery was already an accepted system. In New Netherland, therefore, the laws discriminated against black workers and limited their rights. But the statutes also provided loopholes that permitted social and economic advancement to the community's Africans, most of whom spoke Dutch.

Chesapeake Bay lay even closer to the main routes of the Atlantic slave traffic. In 1619 a Dutch warship brought to Virginia more than twenty African men and women acquired as slaves in the Caribbean. Like people deported from England to the Chesapeake, they were sold as servants. Terms of service varied, and some black newcomers earned their freedom quickly and kept it. But others saw their terms extended arbitrarily. In 1640 Virginia's General Court considered punishment for "a negro named John Punch" and two other servants who had escaped to Maryland. When apprehended, the Dutchman and the Scotsman each received four additional years of service, but the African was sentenced to unending servitude "for the time of his natural life." That same year, Virginia passed a law that prevented blacks from bearing arms. A 1643 law taxing productive field hands included African American women but not white women.

These early efforts to separate Africans from Europeans by law set an ominous precedent in the use of skin color as a distinguishing marker. Still, rules governing the lives of people of color and their offspring remained ambiguous for several decades, and (as the case of Bess Key makes clear) efforts at exploitation could often be undone in court. But new forces would come into play in the mainland American colonies after 1660, consolidating the transition to hereditary African slavery.

Anonymous, Vue du Cap Francais et Du nvr La Marie Seraphique de Nantes, 1772–1773. Le jour de l'Ouverture de sa Vente, Troisieme Voyage d'Angole. Musée du Château des Ducs de Bretagne (950.4.3)

■ **This summary of an African slave-trading voyage shows wealthy planters boarding a French ship upon its arrival in the West Indies in order to buy slaves newly arrived from Angola. The crew has used an iron fence dividing the deck to protect against revolt during the voyage. The captain conducts business under an awning in the stern.**

Alternative Sources of Labor

For African newcomers to English North America, their legal status became distinctly clearer and less hopeful in the decades after 1660. The transatlantic slave trade, already more than a century old, provided certain English colonies with a ready source of African workers at a time when more obvious streams of inexpensive labor—captured Native Americans and impoverished Europeans—were dwindling.

For labor-hungry colonists, Native Americans were close at hand and knew the country well. They took captives when fighting one another, so colonists could buy Indian prisoners or seize them in frontier warfare. Europeans felt they could enslave such people in good conscience, since they were non-Christians who had been taken captive in war. But Native American numbers were declining steadily, owing to epidemics. And those who did become enslaved knew the countryside well enough to escape. Besides, traffic in Indian slaves disrupted the profitable deerskin trade, undermined wilderness diplomacy, and sparked conflict on the frontier.

Efforts to maintain a steady flow of cheap labor from Europe ran into different problems. The Great Plague of 1665 devastated the English population, and the London Fire the following year created a new need for workers of all kinds to rebuild the capital. England's labor surplus, which had been a boon to the initial colonies half a century earlier, rapidly disappeared. The use of indentures persisted, whereby the poor could buy their passage by agreeing to sell their labor for a fixed term. But when these workers reached America, they served for only a few years and then had to be replaced.

Equally important, when indentured servants were mistreated, they had little difficulty in relaying their complaints home to other potential workers. The flow of ships back and forth between Europe and North America grew steadily in the century after 1660, so word of places where indentured servants were regularly abused or swindled quickly reached the other side of the Atlantic. In contrast, the African slave trade lacked any similar "feedback loop." As a result, the brutal treatment of black workers never had a chance, through accurate feedback across the Atlantic, to influence the future flow of deportations from Africa.

The Fateful Transition

In general, powerful Chesapeake tobacco planters were encouraged in 1660 by news of the Restoration of Charles II, since England's new king was likely to support their interests and reward their loyalty. These men had noticed the rising profits that sugar growers were making by using slaves in the Caribbean. In Virginia and Maryland, therefore, planters passed a series of laws that sharpened distinctions between servants working for a fixed period and slaves consigned to labor for life.

In shaping new legislation, local leaders even challenged long-standing English legal traditions, such as the right of children to inherit their father's status. In 1662 Virginia's General Assembly considered whether any child fathered "by an Englishman upon a negro woman should be slave or Free." In a crucial reversal of precedent, the legislature said that in such cases children shall be "bond or free *only according to the condition of the mother.*" From now on, the infant of any female slave would be enslaved from birth. Slavery was becoming a hereditary condition.

Could enslaved persons receive their freedom if they accepted Christianity, as sometimes happened in Spanish colonies? A 1664 Maryland law closed off that prospect.

The act made clear that the legal status of non-Christian slaves did not change if they experienced religious conversion. Three years later, Virginia's government agreed that "the conferring of baptisme doth not alter the condition of the person as to his bondage." By taking religion out of the question, legislators shifted the definition of who could be enslaved from someone who was not Christian to someone who did not look European.

> *In scarcely a generation, black bondage had become a hereditary institution, and the conditions of life had grown markedly worse for African Americans.*

In scarcely a generation, black bondage had become a hereditary institution, and the conditions of life had grown markedly worse for African Americans. Increasingly, they faced corporal punishments: whippings and mutilation. Black slaves—and often free blacks—lost their right to accuse, or even testify against, a white person in court. "And further," stated Virginia's formative slave law of 1680, "if any Negro" raises a hand, even in self-defense, "against any Christian, he shall receive thirty lashes, and if he absent himself . . . from his master's service and resist lawful apprehension, he may be killed."

The Growth of Slave Labor Camps

Over two generations, beginning in the late seventeenth century, tobacco growers in the Chesapeake and rice producers in the new colony of South Carolina embraced the system of hereditary race slavery that had developed in the Caribbean. For those forced to cut the trees, drain the swamps, and harvest the crops, the shift in production strategy represented—in modern terminology—the emergence of slave labor camps. After all, these

Alice Ravenel Huger Smith, *The Threshing Floor with a Winnowing-House (The Carolina Rice Plantation Series).* Gibbes Museum of Art/CAA, 37.09.22

■ Rice plantations that emerged in coastal South Carolina around 1700 became labor camps where enslaved blacks were confined for generations, without wages or legal rights. In the 1850s, distant descendants of the region's first African workers were still being forced to plant, harvest, and process the huge rice crops that made their masters rich.

people received no wages for their labor, had no legal rights, and could be deported to some other location at any time. This deterioration in conditions occurred first, and most dramatically, in Virginia, where several thousand African Americans lived and labored by the 1670s.

Black Involvement in Bacon's Rebellion

Nothing did more to consolidate Virginia's slide toward race slavery than Bacon's Rebellion, the major uprising that shook the Chesapeake region in 1676 (see Chapter 3). The episode pitted aspiring gentry, led by Nathaniel Bacon, against beleaguered Indian groups on the frontier and an entrenched elite in Jamestown.

Free men, would-be farmers in search of land, made up part of Bacon's following, but diverse unfree workers also proved eager recruits. Such ill-treated people remained legally bound to large landholders for varying terms, and many of the Africans were undoubtedly bound for life. Together, they raised the colony's annual tobacco crop, and the backbreaking labor prompted frequent unrest. These ragged workers, however long their term of service might be, had the most to gain and the least to lose from Bacon's revolt. According to the Virginia Assembly, "many evil disposed servants . . . taking advantage of the loosenes of the tymes . . . followed the rebells in rebellion." When Bacon died in October 1676, many of his wealthier supporters reasserted their loyalty to the colonial government. But bound workers who had escaped from their masters continued the fight.

A letter reaching London that fall suggested that at the height of the rebellion Bacon had "proclam'd liberty to all Servants and Negro's." Clearly, the widespread unrest had given hope to downtrodden tobacco pickers, about a quarter of whom were black. When military reinforcements arrived in Chesapeake Bay from England in November, the commander, Captain Thomas Grantham, found hundreds of laborers still in active revolt.

Impressed by their strength, Grantham chose to use deceit when he met with 800 heavily armed rebels, both white and black, at their headquarters near the York River. Making vague promises regarding pardons and freedom, he persuaded most of the white men to surrender and return home. Only about "Eighty Negroes and Twenty English" demanded "their hoped for liberty and would not quietly laye downe their armes." But when these last holdouts boarded a sloop, Grantham disarmed the rebels and chained them below decks for return to their masters.

The Rise of a Slaveholding Tidewater Elite

With Bacon's death and the arrival of British ships, propertied Virginians had narrowly averted a successful multiracial revolution, fueled from below by workers who resented their distressed condition. But clearly some future revolt might succeed, and so the great planters of the Chesapeake region moved to tighten their hold on political and economic power. After Bacon's Rebellion, a strategy of divide and conquer seemed in order. They moved to improve conditions for poor whites in ways that would ensure deference and racial solidarity among Europeans. At the same time, they further reduced the legal status of blacks and solidified their enslavement for life.

For precedent, the aspiring planters had the model provided by slavery-based colonial societies in the West Indies, including the English sugar island of Barbados. Their uneasiness continued over importing non-Christian strangers who spoke little, if any, English. But such doubts were more than offset by the prospect of laying claim to the children of slaves and to the lives and labor of all generations to come.

Increasing life expectancy in the Chesapeake region, resulting from sturdier dwellings and more stable living conditions, meant that Africans enslaved for life would yield profitable service for an increasingly long time. And they would be more likely than ever to produce healthy offspring. Boys and girls who survived childhood could then be forced to clear more land to grow additional crops.

Among a circle of wealthy investors, the enticement of such an economic bonanza overcame any cultural anxieties or religious scruples. Seizing the moment, these aggressive entrepreneurs established themselves as the leading families of Virginia. These ambitious merchant-planters expected that the English-speaking Africans already present could assist in teaching newcomers to receive orders. They also assumed that slave laborers from diverse African societies could not communicate well enough with one another to cause dangerous disturbances. And of course, having now made skin color a determining feature of social order, they knew that black runaways could be spotted and apprehended readily in the free white community.

Closing the Vicious Circle in the Chesapeake

As the profitability of the slavery option increased, so did its appeal. By 1700 some 4,500 people were enslaved in Maryland in a total population of 35,000. And the colony's assembly was actively encouraging the importation of slaves. Growing demand meant that merchants and sea captains who had only dabbled in the transportation of slaves now devoted more time and larger ships to the enterprise. Expansion of the slave-trading infrastructure made African workers readily available and affordable.

As the supply of enslaved black newcomers grew larger, planters eager to strengthen their position manipulated the established headright system. Traditionally, under this system, the colonial government granted to any arriving head of household 50 acres for every family member or hired hand he brought into the colony. The incentive was intended to spur migration from Europe, expand the free population, and develop the land through the establishment of family farms. But the wealthy planters who saw African slavery as a profitable labor source also controlled Virginia's legal system. For their own benefit, therefore, they extended the headright system so that a land bonus also went to anyone who purchased an African arrival as a lifelong slave. Thus, before the seventeenth century closed, a Virginia investor buying twenty slaves could also lay claim to headrights worth 1,000 acres of land.

To consolidate their new regime, planters worked through the church and the legislature to separate whites from blacks socially and legally. They undermined the position of free blacks and stigmatized interracial ties. A 1691 Virginia statute decried the "abominable mixture and spurious issue" that resulted from "Negroes, mulattoes and Indians intermarrying" with English or other white people. All such couples were "banished from this dominion forever." It also prohibited masters from freeing any black or mulatto unless they paid to transport that person out of the colony within six months.

> *To consolidate their new regime, planters worked through the church and the legislature to separate whites from blacks socially and legally.*

Virginia's Negro Act of 1705 further underscored the stark new boundaries. It mandated that white servants who were mistreated had the right to sue their masters in county court. Slaves, in contrast, had no such right. Any enslaved person who tried to escape could be tortured and even dismembered in hopes of "terrifying others" from seeking freedom. When masters or overseers killed a slave while inflicting punishment, they were automatically free of any felony charge. If slaves were killed or put to death by law, the owners would be paid public funds for the loss of their "property." In scarcely forty years, a dire and long-lasting revolution had transformed the labor system of the Chesapeake with the full backing of the law.

DOCUMENT

Of the Servants and Slaves in Virginia (1705)

England Enters the Atlantic Slave Trade

The Atlantic slave trade remains the largest and longest-lasting deportation in human history. In nearly four centuries, more than 10 million people were torn from their homelands against their will and transported to the Caribbean and to Central, South, and North America. Several million more perished in transit. By 1700, more Africans than Europeans had already crossed the Atlantic to the Western Hemisphere. Their numbers grew over the following century as the traffic reached its height. The importation of Africans to North America expanded after 1700, but it remained a small proportion of the overall Atlantic slave trade.

England took little part in the trade at first. However, the development of Barbados as a lucrative sugar colony and the expansion of English overseas ambitions changed matters quickly after 1640. With the restoration of the English monarchy in 1660, Charles II immediately granted a monopoly on African trade to a small group of adventurers, and in 1672 he chartered the powerful new Royal African Company (RAC).

The RAC dispatched a steady flow of merchant ships along a **triangular trade** route. The first leg took captains to English outposts along the coast of West Africa, where they exchanged textiles, guns, and iron bars for gold, ivory, and enslaved Africans. After a transatlantic **middle passage** of one to three months, the captains sold slaves and took on sugar in the West Indies before returning to England on the final leg of the triangle. When the company's monopoly ended officially in 1698, English slave trading ballooned. By the 1730s, British ships controlled the largest share of the Atlantic slave trade. They continued to dominate the traffic for the next seventy years.

The Slave Trade on the African Coast

By the 1680s, it had been two centuries since Portuguese sailors had visited Africa's western shores and established a post at Elmina, in modern-day Ghana. Dozens of these depots, controlled by

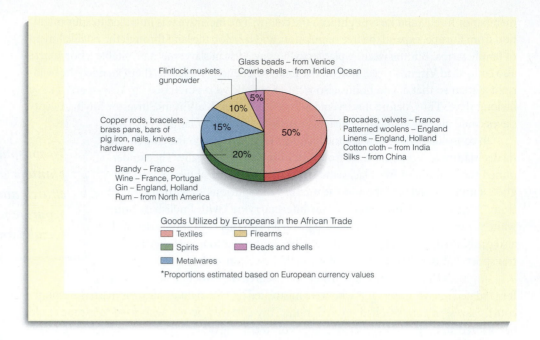

Glass beads – from Venice
Cowrie shells – from Indian Ocean

**Flintlock muskets,
gunpowder**

**Copper rods, bracelets,
brass pans, bars of
pig iron, nails, knives,
hardware**

5%

10%

15%

50%

20%

**Brocades, velvets – France
Patterned woolens – England
Linens – England, Holland
Cotton cloth – from India
Silks – from China**

**Brandy – France
Wine – France, Portugal
Gin – England, Holland
Rum – from North America**

Goods Utilized by Europeans in the African Trade

Textiles   Firearms
Spirits   Beads and shells
Metalwares

*Proportions estimated based on European currency values

■ **FIGURE 4.1**
GOODS TRADED IN AFRICA As European ship captains expanded trade along the African coast, they tailored their cargoes to suit the demands of local markets.

rival European powers and their local allies, dotted the sub-Saharan coastline. (They became known as *factories*—an early use of the word—since a *factor*, or manager, ran each imperial trading post.) This string of European outposts began at the mouth of the Senegal River, just above Cape Verde, the continent's westernmost point; it ended below the mouth of the Congo River, in present-day Angola. In between, the coastline curved some 5,000 miles. It embraced diverse geographic environments—from open savannas to thick forests—and scores of distinctive cultures. All along this coastline, villagers caught fish and gathered salt for trade with herders and farmers living farther inland.

Generations of contact with oceangoing ships brought new pressures and opportunities to African coastal communities. Local merchants, who traded gold and ivory to sea captains for imported textiles and alcohol, formed alliances with European trading partners in response to the growing demand for human labor. They consolidated their positions near suitable harbors and navigable rivers. From there, they bartered local servants and war captives to white agents (factors). In return, they obtained linen, beads, metalwares, and muskets, items that enhanced their prestige and let them extend their inland trading networks.

Inland traders, alert to the rising demand for slaves in the port towns, annually brought thousands of captives from the backcountry to the coast. The traders traveled by land and water, binding their prisoners together in small groups to form a **coffle** (from the Arabic word for "caravan"). The overseas goods they received as payment included firearms, gunpowder, and knives, which they used to prosecute additional wars and raids to secure more captives.

By the 1660s and 1670s, the pace of deportation across the Atlantic had reached an average rate of nearly 15,000 people each year. It rose steadily to a high of more than 65,000 people per year a century later. As the traffic grew, it became increasingly organized, competitive, and routine. Shrewd African traders played one European vessel against another for the best deals. When they saw that a ship was eager to depart, they increased their prices. Hardened European agents stockpiled the wares that African traders most wanted. They also learned to curry favor with local officials and to quell unrest among captives, confined in the holding pens known as **barracoons**. Experienced captains timed their ventures to avoid the months when sickness was most rampant in the tropics. Through repeated voyages,

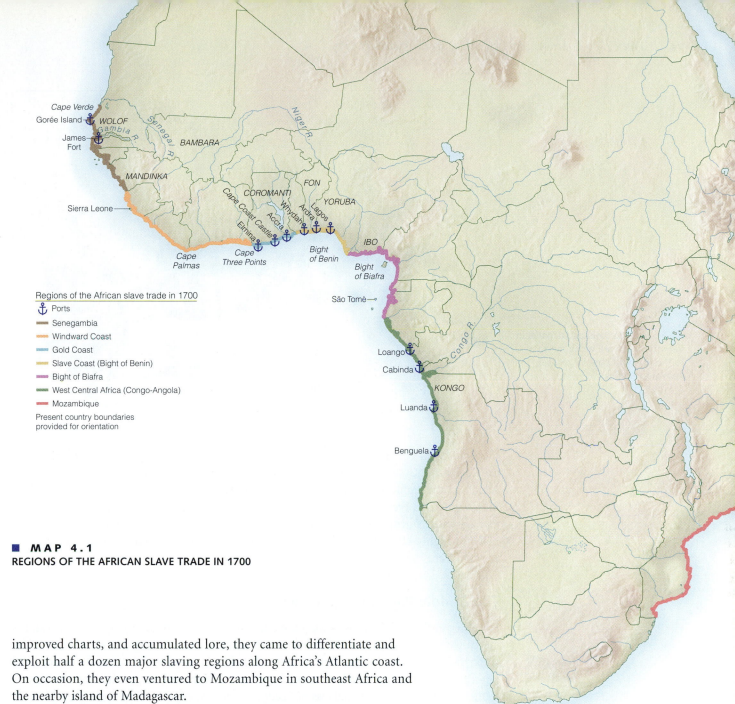

MAP 4.1
REGIONS OF THE AFRICAN SLAVE TRADE IN 1700

Regions of the African slave trade in 1700
- Ports
- Senegambia
- Windward Coast
- Gold Coast
- Slave Coast (Bight of Benin)
- Bight of Biafra
- West Central Africa (Congo-Angola)
- Mozambique

Present country boundaries provided for orientation

improved charts, and accumulated lore, they came to differentiate and exploit half a dozen major slaving regions along Africa's Atlantic coast. On occasion, they even ventured to Mozambique in southeast Africa and the nearby island of Madagascar.

The closest market where Europeans bargained for goods and slaves was Senegambia, or the northern parts of Guinea, between the Senegal River and the Gambia River. Gorée Island, off the coast of Senegal, and James Fort, located in the mouth of the Gambia, served as slave-trading centers. The long Windward Coast extending to the southeast beyond Sierra Leone became known for its pepper, grain, and ivory. Further east, from the area of Cape Three Points and Elmina to the factory at Accra, stretched the Gold Coast. There, the Portuguese had established Elmina to draw trade from the Asante gold fields in the interior. Farther east, the Slave Coast reached along the Bight of Benin to the huge delta of the Niger River. Trading depots at Whydah, Ardra, and Lagos drew captives from secondary ports in between. Beyond the Niger, where the African coast again turns south near Cameroon, lay the Bight of Biafra. English captains quickly learned the preferences for trade goods in each district, carrying textiles to the Gold Coast and metals to the Bight of Biafra.

The largest and most southerly region, known as Congo-Angola or West Central Africa, was the only one below the equator. Here, Catholic missionaries established

■ Slaves were held as prisoners in the interior before being marched to the African Coast in groups known as coffles.

footholds, and Portuguese traders exported slave labor for sugar production in Brazil and the Caribbean. Before 1700 more than half of all Atlantic slaves departed from West Central Africa. In the eighteenth century the proportion remained over one-third. Later, north of the Congo River, French and English interests came to dominate the slave traffic out of Loango and Cabinda. During the entire span of the slave trade, the Congo-Angola hinterland furnished roughly 40 percent of all Atlantic deportees: more than 4.5 million men, women, and children.

The Middle Passage Experience

DOCUMENT

Equiano, the Middle Passage (1788)

For every individual the exodus was different, a harrowing personal story. Nevertheless, the long nightmare of deportation contained similar elements for all who fell victim to the transatlantic trade. The entire journey, from normal village life to enslavement beyond the ocean, could last a year or two. It unfolded in at least five stages, beginning with capture and deportation to the African coast. The initial loss of freedom—the first experience of bound hands, harsh treatment, and forced marches—was made worse by the encounters with strange landscapes and unfamiliar languages. Hunger, fatigue, and anxiety took a steady toll as coffles of young and old were conveyed slowly toward the coast through a network of traders.

The next phase, sale and imprisonment, began when a contingent reached the sea. During this stage, which could last several months, African traders transferred "ownership" of the captives to Europeans. Many buyers subjected their new property to demeaning inspections and burned brands into their skin. Then they were put in irons alongside hundreds of other captives and guarded in a secure spot to prevent escape. From there, canoes transported the captives through the surf to a waiting vessel. (Their hands were bound, so if a canoe capsized, it meant certain drowning.) Once aboard, they might languish in the sweltering hold for weeks while the captain cruised the coast in search of additional human cargo. Crew members sometimes raised nets surrounding the deck to prevent attempts at escape or suicide.

IMAGE

Diagram of a Slave Ship

The ship's captain decided when to begin crossing the Atlantic, the harrowing third phase that constituted the middle passage. The Africans aboard each ship now faced an utterly alien plight, trapped in a strange wooden hull. When the crew finally raised anchor and unfurled the vessel's huge sails, the captives could only anticipate the worst. Already the crowded hold had become foul, and the large wooden buckets used as latrines had taken on a loathsome smell. The rolling of the ship on ocean swells brought seasickness and painful chafing from lying on the bare planks. Alexander Falconbridge, who sailed as a surgeon on several slave ships, recorded that "those who are emaciated frequently have their skin and even their flesh entirely rubbed off, by the motion of the ship, from the . . . shoulders, elbows and hips so as to render the bones quite bare."

Historians have documented more than 27,000 slave voyages from Africa to the Americas, and in each one an array of variables came into play to shape the Atlantic crossing. These included the exact point of departure, the planned destination, the season of the year, the length of the journey, the supplies of food and fresh water, the navigational skills of the captain and crew, the condition of the vessel, the health and resolve of the prisoners, the vagaries of piracy and ocean warfare, and the ravages of disease. A change in weather conditions or in the captain's mood could mean the difference between life and death.

While the grim details varied, the overall pattern remained the same. The constant rolling of the vessel; the sharp changes in temperature; the crowded, dark, and filthy conditions; and the relentless physical pain and mental anguish took a heavy toll. Pregnant mothers gave birth or miscarried; women were subjected to abuse and rape by the crew. Crews threw the bodies of those who died to the sharks and even used corpses as bait to catch sharks, which they fed to the remaining captives.

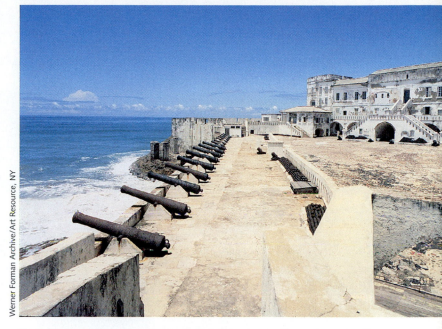

Werner Forman Archive/Art Resource, NY

■ England's Royal African Company maintained more than a dozen small posts along the Gold Coast. Each outpost funneled slaves to this strong seventy-four-gun fortress known as Cape Coast Castle. Cut into rock beneath the parade ground, the vaulted dungeon inside could "conveniently contain a thousand Blacks . . . against any insurrection."

DOCUMENT

Falconbridge, the African Slave Trade (1788)

Saltwater Slaves Arrive in America

For the emaciated survivors of the Atlantic ordeal, two further stages remained in their descent into slavery: the selling process and the time called "seasoning." The selling process on American soil could drag on for weeks or months after the ship dropped anchor. Prospective owners examined and prodded the newcomers in dockside holding pens. Those purchased were wrenched away from their shipmates with whom they had formed strong links during their miseries at sea. Slaves often were auctioned in groups, or parcels, to ensure sale of the weak along with the strong. Then another journey brought them to the particular plantation where they were fated to work and probably to die.

Most newcomers did not begin their forced labor immediately. Instead, they entered a final stage, known as seasoning, which lasted several months or longer. The arrivals were distinguished as "saltwater slaves"—in contrast to "country-born slaves" who had grown up in America from birth—and seasoning gave them time to mend physically, regain their strength, and begin absorbing the rudiments of a new language. Inevitably, many suffered from what we would now describe as posttraumatic stress syndrome.

As adults and children recovered from the trauma of the middle passage, they faced a series of additional shocks. They confronted strange foods, unfamiliar tasks, and even new names. Worst of all, they encountered a master or his overseer who made every effort to break the wills of these fresh arrivals and to turn them into compliant bondservants. Repeatedly, the powerful stranger used arbitrary force to demand the slaves' obedience, destroy their hope, and crush any thoughts of resistance.

IMAGE

Slave Dealers

TO BE SOLD on board the Ship *Bance-Island*, on tuesday the 6th of *May* next, at *Ashley-Ferry*; a choice cargo of about 250 fine healthy **NEGROES**, just arrived from the Windward & Rice Coast.
—The utmost care has already been taken, and shall be continued, to keep them free from the least danger of being infected with the SMALL-POX, no boat having been on board, and all other communication with people from *Charles-Town* prevented. .

Austin, Laurens, & Appleby.

N. B. Full one Half of the above Negroes have had the SMALL-POX in their own Country.

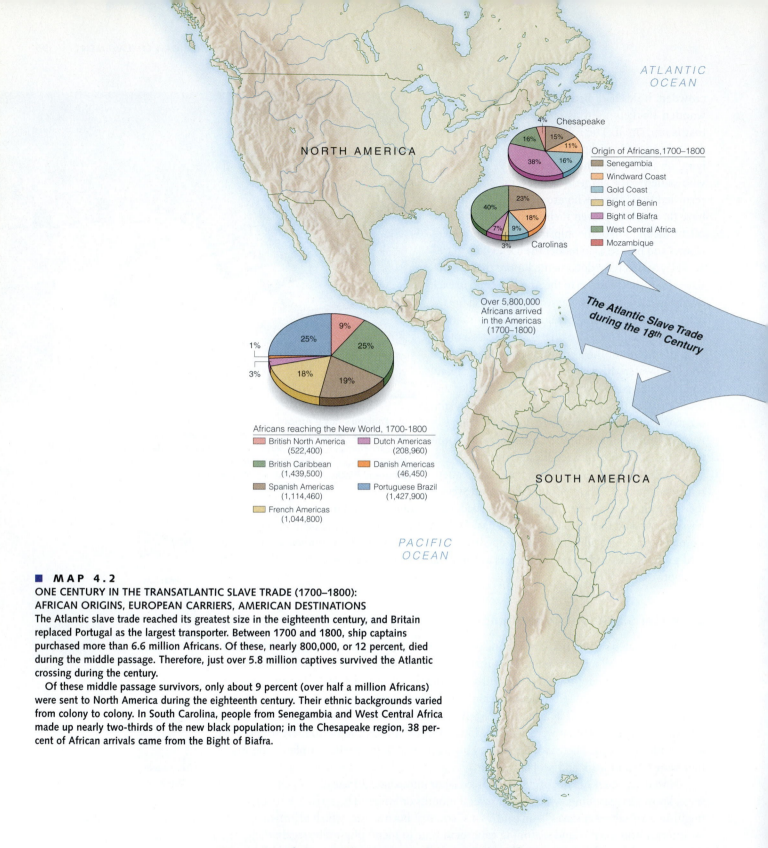

ATLANTIC OCEAN

NORTH AMERICA

4% Chesapeake

Origin of Africans, 1700–1800
- Senegambia
- Windward Coast
- Gold Coast
- Bight of Benin
- Bight of Biafra
- West Central Africa
- Mozambique

Carolinas

Over 5,800,000 Africans arrived in the Americas (1700–1800)

The Atlantic Slave Trade during the 18th Century

SOUTH AMERICA

Africans reaching the New World, 1700-1800

- British North America (522,400)
- British Caribbean (1,439,500)
- Spanish Americas (1,114,460)
- French Americas (1,044,800)
- Dutch Americas (208,960)
- Danish Americas (46,450)
- Portuguese Brazil (1,427,900)

PACIFIC OCEAN

■ MAP 4.2

ONE CENTURY IN THE TRANSATLANTIC SLAVE TRADE (1700–1800): AFRICAN ORIGINS, EUROPEAN CARRIERS, AMERICAN DESTINATIONS
The Atlantic slave trade reached its greatest size in the eighteenth century, and Britain replaced Portugal as the largest transporter. Between 1700 and 1800, ship captains purchased more than 6.6 million Africans. Of these, nearly 800,000, or 12 percent, died during the middle passage. Therefore, just over 5.8 million captives survived the Atlantic crossing during the century.

Of these middle passage survivors, only about 9 percent (over half a million Africans) were sent to North America during the eighteenth century. Their ethnic backgrounds varied from colony to colony. In South Carolina, people from Senegambia and West Central Africa made up nearly two-thirds of the new black population; in the Chesapeake region, 38 percent of African arrivals came from the Bight of Biafra.

Survival in a Strange New Land

By 1700 race slavery was accepted throughout the mainland colonies, so Africans found themselves scattered from New England to Louisiana. But their distribution was far from even. Among roughly 247,000 slaves in the North American colonies in 1750, only 30,000 (or 12 percent) resided in the North, where they made up just 5 percent of the overall population from Pennsylvania to New Hampshire. More than one-third of these northerners (11,000) lived in the colony of New York, where they constituted 14 percent of the colonial inhabitants. All

African Slave Trade

ATLANTIC OCEAN

EUROPE

AFRICA

INDIAN OCEAN

1%
5%
3%
16%
47%
28%

Nations participating and their share
in the slave traffic, 1700-1800

- Britain (3,100,100)
- The Netherlands (349,600)
- Portugal (1,846,900)
- Denmark (52,770)
- France (1,028,950)
- British Colonies/U.S.A. (211,100)

SENEGAMBIA

Roughly 800,000 Africans perished at sea

Approximately 6,600,000 departed from Africa (1700–1800)

WINDWARD COAST

GOLD COAST

BIGHT OF BENIN

BIGHT OF BIAFRA

WEST CENTRAL AFRICA

MOZAMBIQUE

2%
6%
8%
11%
37%
18%
18%

Africans taken to the Americas, 1700-1800

- Senegambia (389,150)
- Bight of Biafra (1,174,050)
- Windward Coast (521,100)
- West Central Africa (2,440,000)
- Gold Coast (758,550)
- Mozambique (131,000)
- Bight of Benin (1,187,300)

the rest of the people of African descent in North America—some 217,000 men, women, and children by the mid-eighteenth century—lived and worked in the Chesapeake region and the lower South. Fewer than 5,000 of these black southerners resided in French Louisiana.

African Rice Growers in South Carolina

Throughout the eighteenth century, by far the most North American slaves lived in Virginia or Maryland: 150,000 African Americans by 1750. But the highest *proportion* of enslaved workers lived in South Carolina, where Africans began outnumbering Europeans as early as 1708. By 1750 this black majority (40,000 people) constituted more than 60 percent of the colony's population. Almost all had arrived through the deepwater port of Charleston. Sullivan's Island, near the entrance to the harbor, with its so-called **pest house** to quarantine incoming slaves and reduce the spread of shipborne disease, has been called the Ellis Island of black America.

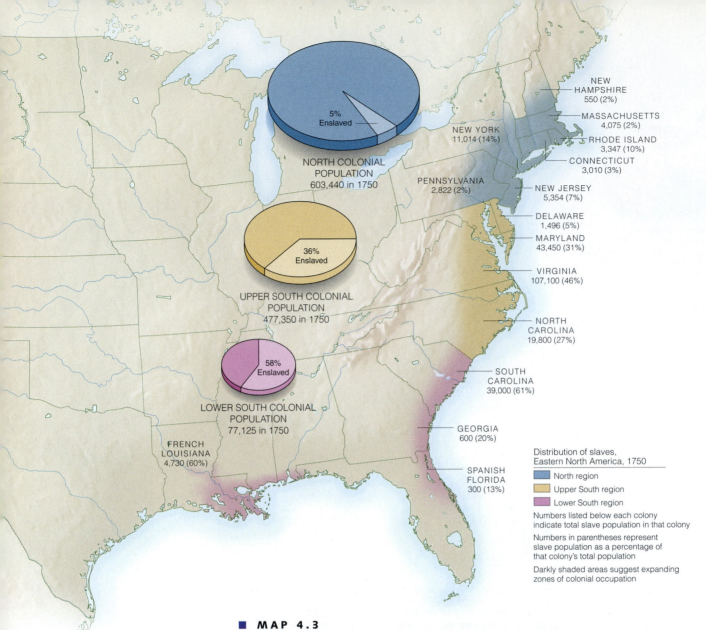

NEW
HAMPSHIRE
550 (2%)

MASSACHUSETTS
4,075 (2%)

NEW YORK
11,014 (14%)

RHODE ISLAND
3,347 (10%)

CONNECTICUT
3,010 (3%)

5%
Enslaved

NORTH COLONIAL
POPULATION
603,440 in 1750

PENNSYLVANIA
2,822 (2%)

NEW JERSEY
5,354 (7%)

DELAWARE
1,496 (5%)

MARYLAND
43,450 (31%)

36%
Enslaved

VIRGINIA
107,100 (46%)

UPPER SOUTH COLONIAL
POPULATION
477,350 in 1750

NORTH
CAROLINA
19,800 (27%)

58%
Enslaved

SOUTH
CAROLINA
39,000 (61%)

LOWER SOUTH COLONIAL
POPULATION
77,125 in 1750

GEORGIA
600 (20%)

FRENCH
LOUISIANA
4,730 (60%)

SPANISH
FLORIDA
300 (13%)

Distribution of slaves,
Eastern North America, 1750

■ North region
■ Upper South region
■ Lower South region

Numbers listed below each colony
indicate total slave population in that colony

Numbers in parentheses represent
slave population as a percentage of
that colony's total population

Darkly shaded areas suggest expanding
zones of colonial occupation

■ MAP 4.3

ENSLAVED PEOPLE LIVING IN NORTH AMERICA IN 1750: DISTRIBUTION BY COLONY, PERCENTAGE OF TOTAL POPULATION By 1750 nearly a quarter of a million people lived as slaves in eastern North America—more than 21 percent of the colonial population. Almost all were Africans or the descendants of Africans, along with a few thousand Native American and mixed-race slaves. In the North, slaves made up a small fraction of a large population. By far the greatest number of slaves lived in the Chesapeake area, where they made up more than a third of the total population. Enslaved people were less numerous but much more concentrated in the lower South, making up a clear majority of the overall inhabitants. White settlers had already smuggled several hundred slaves into the fledgling colony of Georgia, even though the exploitation of slave labor did not become legal there until 1751.

What explains the emergence of South Carolina's slave concentration? For one thing, the colony was closer than Virginia to Africa and to the Caribbean. Moreover, it had been founded in 1670, just as the English were embracing plantation slavery and the African trade. Indeed, some of the colony's original proprietors owned stakes in the Royal African Company. Also, some of Carolina's influential early settlers came directly from Barbados, bringing enslaved Africans and planter ambitions with them.

In the earliest days of colonization in South Carolina, newcomers lacked sufficient labor to clear coastal forests and plant crops. Instead, they let their cattle and pigs run wild. With easy foraging and warm winters, the animals reproduced rapidly. The settlers slaughtered them and shipped their meat to the Caribbean, along with firewood for boiling sugar cane and wooden barrels for transporting sugar. Ship captains also carried enslaved Native Americans to the West Indies and brought back African slaves.

The arriving Africans understood South Carolina's subtropical climate, with its alligators and palmetto trees, better than their European owners did. Many of these enslaved newcomers were already familiar with keeping cattle. Others, obliged to feed themselves, began growing rice in the fertile swamplands just as they had in West Africa. Slave owners quickly realized that this plant, unfamiliar to much of northern Europe, held the answer to their search for a profitable staple crop. Soon, people who had tended their own irrigated rice crops near the Gambia River were obliged to clear cypress swamps along the Ashley and Cooper rivers to grow rice for someone else.

Before long, merchants were shipping tons of Carolina rice to Europe, where it proved a cheap grain for feeding soldiers, orphans, and peasants. By the middle of the eighteenth century, their fortunes improved even more when indigo, another African crop, joined rice as a profitable export commodity. Outnumbered by their enslaved workers, South Carolina's landowners passed strict Negro Acts patterned on those of the Caribbean. Legislation prohibited slaves from carrying guns, meeting in groups, raising livestock, or traveling without a pass. Everywhere, mounted patrols enforced the regulations with brutal severity.

Patterns of Resistance

In South Carolina and elsewhere, enslaved African Americans pushed against the narrow boundaries of their lives. Like any other imprisoned population, they used every possible means to negotiate slivers of freedom, including spreading rumors, refusing to work, breaking tools, feigning illness, and threatening violence. In response, their owners tried to divide them in order to control them. Masters rewarded workers who were obedient and diligent or who informed on fellow slaves. They imposed harsh punishments—whipping, mutilation, sale, or death—on those suspected of taking food, sowing dissent, or plotting revolt. And they encouraged the formation of black families, not only to gain another generation of laborers at no cost but also to create the emotional ties that they knew would hold individuals in check for fear of reprisals against loved ones.

Owners confined residents in the slave labor camps with curfews and pass systems and kept them from learning to read and from communicating freely with neighbors and relatives. They also refused to allow any impartial system for expressing grievances or appealing arbitrary punishments. Faced with such steep odds, many slaves submitted to the deadening routine of the prison camp to survive. But others resorted to diverse strategies to improve their situation or undermine their masters' dominance. Running away, even for a brief period, provided relief from forced work and deprived owners of the labor they depended on. Because arson created serious damage and was difficult to detect, some slaves burned down barns at harvest time. Others succeeded in killing their masters or overseers. Such acts of pent-up rage usually proved suicidal, but they also confirmed slave owners' worst fears.

Above all, the prospect of open rebellion burned in the minds of prisoners and jailers alike. Often, therefore, it is hard to untangle episodes of white paranoia from incidents of actual revolt. Many innocent slaves were falsely accused. But countless others did discuss plans for resistance, and a few freedom fighters avoided detection or betrayal long enough to launch serious uprisings. Word of one upheaval, real or imagined, could spark others.

An early wave of slave unrest erupted in the dozen years after 1710, highlighted by violence in New York City in the spring of 1712. The leaders of the conspiracy were "Coromantee," or Akan people from Africa's Gold Coast region. Several dozen enslaved Africans and Indians, determined to obtain their freedom and kill all the whites in the town, set fire to a building. As citizens rushed to put out the blaze, the rebels attacked them with guns, clubs, pistols, staves, and axes, killing eight and wounding more. When the militia captured the insurgents, six of them committed suicide. Authorities executed eighteen, burning some at the stake, hanging others and leaving their bodies on display.

A Wave of Rebellion

A second wave of black resistance swept the mainland colonies after 1730, fueled by the largest influx of Africans to date. In Louisiana, the French had moved their capital to the new town of New Orleans on the Mississippi River (1722) and had joined their Choctaw allies in a devastating war to crush the Natchez Indians and seize their lands (1729–1731). As French landowners staked out riverfront plantations, they also imported African slaves. The several thousand black workers soon outnumbered European settlers.

Fearful of attack, Louisiana's whites broke up two presumed slave plots in 1731. One involved a scheme to rebel while Catholic colonists attended a midnight mass on Christmas. Another apparent plot was revealed by the careless boast of a black servant woman in New Orleans. It included several hundred Bambara newcomers from Senegal who aspired to massacre whites, enslave other Africans, and take control of the region. The leader was a man known as Samba Bambara, a former interpreter at Galam on the Senegal River. Bambara had lost that post and been deported to Louisiana, where he became a trusted slave, supervising workers owned by the French Company of the Indies. When torture by fire failed to force confessions from the key suspects, officials hanged the servant woman. Then Bambara and half a dozen other men were "broken on the wheel" (put to death slowly by being tied to wagon wheels and having their bones broken).

The largest slave uprising in colonial North America broke out in 1739 near the Stono River, 20 miles southwest of Charleston. Several factors fueled the Stono Rebellion. By 1739 blacks exceeded whites nearly two to one among South Carolina's 56,000 people. The proportion of recently imported slaves had reached an all-time high. In addition, working conditions had worsened steadily as rice production expanded. Moreover, for several decades the Spanish in Florida had been luring slaves from South Carolina, knowing that the promise of freedom might destabilize Carolina's profitable slave regime. More than a hundred fugitives had escaped to Florida by 1738, when Florida's governor formed them into a free black militia company at St. Augustine. Hoping to win more defections, he allowed thirty-eight African American households to settle north of the town and build a small fortress—Fort Mose.

Meanwhile, the wider commercial rivalries of the British and Spanish continued elsewhere, leading to open warfare between the two Atlantic empires in 1739. The slave uprising at Stono erupted just after word reached Charleston that war had broken out between Spain and Britain. Other factors may also have influenced the rebels' timing. An epidemic in Charleston had disrupted public activities, and a new Security Act requiring all white men to carry arms to church was to take effect before the end of September.

Early on Sunday, September 9, 1739, twenty slaves from a work crew near the Stono River broke into a local store. There they seized weapons and exe-

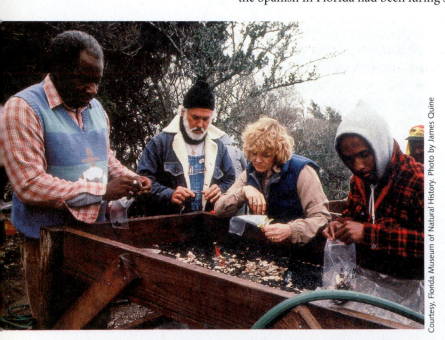

Courtesy, Florida Museum of Natural History. Photo by James Quine

■ Archaeologists have recently excavated the site of Fort Mose, near St. Augustine, Florida. Dozens of slaves who escaped from South Carolina received their freedom from the Spanish and established an outpost there in the 1730s.

cuted the owners, then raised a banner and marched south, beating drums and shouting "Liberty!" The insurgents burned selected plantations, killed a score of whites, and gathered more than fifty new recruits. But armed colonists overtook them and blocked their escape to St. Augustine. Dozens of rebels died in the ensuing battle. In the next two days, militia and hired Indians killed twenty more and captured an additional forty people, whom they immediately shot or hanged.

DOCUMENT

Oglethorpe, Stono Rebellion (1739)

Yet even these reprisals could not quell black hopes. In June 1740 several hundred slaves plotted to storm Charleston and take arms from a warehouse. However, a comrade revealed the plan. According to a report, "The next day fifty of them were seized, and these were hanged, ten a day, to intimidate the other negroes." In November, a great fire of suspicious origin consumed much of Charleston.

Fire also played a role in hysteria that broke out in New York City in 1741. In March, a blaze consumed the residence of New York's governor and a local fort. Other fires soon focused suspicions on a white couple, John and Sarah Hughson, who had often entertained blacks at their alehouse. The Hughsons—thought to fence stolen goods for a black crime ring—were accused of inciting working-class unrest. In exchange for her freedom, a sixteen-year-old Irish indentured servant at the Hughsons' tavern testified that she had overheard the planning of an elaborate plot.

In a gruesome spiral of arrests and executions, New York authorities put to death thirty-four people, including four whites, and banished seventy-two blacks. On one hand, the debacle recalled the Salem witch trials, as a fearful community engaged in judicial proceedings and killings on the basis of rumors and accusations. On the other hand, the New York Slave Plot recalled Bacon's Rebellion, for evidence emerged of cooperation between impoverished blacks and whites eager to see a redistribution of property. According to his accusers, a slave named Cuffee had often observed that "a great many people had too much, and others too little." He predicted that soon his master "should have less, and that he (Cuffee) should have more." Instead, he was burned at the stake.

The Transformation Completed

The mechanisms for extorting labor from tens of thousands of people were firmly in place. But to maintain the slave labor system, local governments had to be vigilant and repressive, prompting debates within the white population. Some colonists saw slavery as too morally degrading and physically dangerous to maintain. Powerful supporters of the institution, however, found it too rewarding to give up and suggested modifications instead. Following the Stono uprising in South Carolina, for example, leaders imposed a heavy import duty on new African arrivals for several years, hoping to increase the ratio of whites to enslaved blacks in the lowcountry. At a time of growing humanitarian concerns in Enlightenment Europe, it took great effort to maintain the rationale for enslavement in America. But free people who questioned the institution met stiff resistance from those with vested interests, as the experience of the new colony of Georgia demonstrates.

Voices of Dissent

As race-based slavery expanded, white colonists treated the continuing presence of free blacks as a contradiction and a threat. As early as 1691, the Virginia assembly passed an act restricting **manumissions** (grants of individual freedom by masters) because "great inconvenience may happen to this country by setting of negroes and mulattoes free." According to the act, such people fanned hopes of freedom among enslaved blacks. Besides, when they grew old and infirm, their care at public expense could constitute "a charge upon the country." By 1723 additional Virginia statutes prevented free people of color from voting, taxed them unfairly, and prevented them from owning or carrying firearms. Lawmakers went on to prohibit all manumissions, except when the governor rewarded "meritorious service," such as informing against other enslaved workers.

While the southern slave colonies labored to intimidate, divide, and reduce their free black communities, free blacks in the North faced growing discrimination in their efforts to hold jobs, buy land, obtain credit, move freely, and take part in civic life. Northern slave populations, though small in comparison to those in the South, were growing steadily. As the North's involvement in the Atlantic slave trade expanded, its economic and legal commitment to race slavery increased. Rhode Island's slave ranks jumped from 500 in 1720 to more than 3,000 in 1750. Everywhere, new laws made manumission more difficult and African American survival more precarious. Only in the century after 1760 did northern free black communities gain the numerical and social strength to offer effective opposition to enslavement.

The Colonies to 1740

Whereas free blacks lacked the means to oppose slavery, prominent white Christians lacked the will. Even in Massachusetts, where religion remained a dominant force at the turn of the century and the number of slaves had scarcely reached 1,000 people, many leaders already owned black servants, and most ministers defended the practice. The protests that did appear were ambivalent at best. In 1700 Judge Samuel Sewell questioned African enslavement in a tract titled *The Selling of Joseph.* But he also revealed his sense of superiority and his skepticism that blacks could play a part in "the Peopling of the Land." African Americans, Sewell commented, "can seldom use their freedom well; yet their continual aspiring after their forbidden Liberty, renders them unwilling servants." Reverend Cotton Mather, a slave owner who once berated Sewell as one who "pleaded much for Negroes," was even more ambivalent. In *The Negro Christianized* (1706), the influential Puritan stressed that conversion and Christian instruction, far from earning African slaves their freedom, would make them into "better servants."

The conversion and instruction of slaves, rather than the abolition of slavery, also became a mission for pious English philanthropist Thomas Bray, a well-to-do Anglican committed to spreading the Anglican faith in America among Europeans, Indians, and Africans. In 1701 Bray established the Society for the Propagation of the Gospel in Foreign Parts (SPG). The SPG strengthened the Church of England abroad in the eighteenth century by providing dozens of ministers to serve in the colonies.

But this Anglican foothold came at a steep price. Southern planters made SPG ministers agree that any hopes they offered to slaves regarding heavenly salvation would not include hints of earthly freedom. With few exceptions, the Anglican clergy gave in, strengthening religious support of race slavery. In 1723 a heartfelt petition from a mulatto slave to the Bishop of London, in which the author protested "Cruell Bondegg" in Virginia, went unanswered. That same year, Bray set up a trust of "Associates" to carry on his work. With limited success, they focused on converting blacks in the British plantation colonies.

By the 1730s, only a few whites in Europe or America dared to press publicly for an end to slavery. Christian Priber, who arrived in the South in 1735, was one such activist. The idealistic German hoped to start a utopian community in southern Appalachia. But his radical proposal for a multiracial "Paradise" uniting Indians, Africans, and Europeans posed a huge threat to South Carolina authorities. Priber's brief career as a social agitator challenging the status quo ended in 1743, when he was arrested and brought to jail in Charleston. He died—or was killed—before his case could be heard in court.

At the same time, a New Jersey tailor and bookkeeper named John Woolman posed a less defiant but more enduring threat to race slavery. In 1743, at age twenty-three, this shy Quaker began to question his role in writing out bills of sale when his fellow Quakers purchased slaves. It struck him forcefully that "to live in ease and plenty by the toil of those whom violence and cruelty have put in our power" was clearly not "consistent with Christianity or common justice." Woolman traveled widely to Quaker meetings, north and south, pressing an issue

"Releese Us Out of This Cruell Bondegg"

As researchers pay increasing attention to African bondage in the colonial era, new pieces of evidence continue to appear. This appeal, written in Virginia in 1723 by a mulatto Christian slave, was rediscovered in a London archive in the 1990s and transcribed by historian Thomas Ingersoll. It is addressed to Edward Gibson, the newly appointed Bishop of London, whose position gave him religious oversight over all the Anglican parishes in England's American colonies, including Virginia. Gibson, through his pamphlets, had shown an interest in the Christianization of enslaved Africans, but like many contemporary church leaders, he had less interest in the liberation of slaves. This heartfelt document, prepared with great labor and at enormous risk, was simply filed away with the bishop's vast correspondence. It never received a response or prompted any further inquiry into conditions in Virginia.

When abolition of the slave trade finally became a public issue in England in the 1780s, British artists painted scenes criticizing the traffic. But two generations earlier, pleas from New World slaves aroused no response, even from the Bishop of London, who supervised the Church of England in the American colonies.

George Morland, Traite Des Negres, 1790–91. Colonial Williamsburg Foundation

August the forth 1723

to the Right Raverrand father in god my Lord arch Bishop of Lonnd. . . .

this coms to sattesfie your honour that there is in this Land of verJennia a Sort of people that is Calld molatters which are Baptised and brouaht up in the way of the Christian faith and followes the ways and Rulles of the Chrch of England and sum of them has white fathars and sum white mothers and there is in this Land a Law or act which keeps and makes them and there seed Slaves forever. . . .

wee your humbell and poore partishinners doo begg Sir your aid and assisttancce in this one thing . . . which is that your honour will by the help of our Sufvering [i.e., sovereign] Lord King George and the Rest of the Rullers will Releese us out of this Cruell Bondegg. . . .

/and here it is to bee notd that one brother is a Slave to another and one Sister to an othe which is quite out of the way and as for mee my selfe I am my brothers Slave but my name is Secrett/

wee are commandded to keep holey the Sabbath day and wee doo hardly know when it comes for our task mastrs are has hard with us as the Egypttions was with the Chilldann of Issarall. . . . wee are kept out of the Church and matrimony is deenied us and to be plain they doo Look no more upon us then if wee ware dogs which I hope when these Strange lines comes to your Lord Ships hands will be Looket in to. . . .

And Sir wee your humble perticners do humblly beg . . . that our childarn may be broatt up in the way of the Christtian faith and our desire is that they may be Larnd the Lords prayer the creed and the ten commandments and that they may appear Every Lord's day att Church before the Curatt to bee Exammond for our desire is that godllines Shoulld abbound amongs us and wee desire that our Childarn be putt to Scool and Larnd to Reed through the Bybell

My Riting is vary bad. . . . I am but a poore Slave that writt itt and has no other time butt Sunday and hardly that att Sumtimes. . . . wee dare nott Subscribe any mans name to this for feare of our masters for if they knew that wee have Sent home to your honour wee Should goo neare to Swing upon the gallass tree.

Questions

1. In 1723, do these mulatto petitioners identify more closely with their African and non-Christian relatives who are enslaved or with their European and Anglican relations who are free? Explain.

2. Using the same kind of poor spelling and good logic, draft a paragraph or two that might further strengthen this petition and prevent the bishop of London from setting it aside. ■

Source: Thomas N. Ingersoll, "'Releese Us out of This Cruell Bondegg': An Appeal from Virginia in 1723," *William and Mary Quarterly*, Third Series, 51 (October 1994): 776–782.

that most Quakers preferred to ignore. When he drafted *Some Considerations on the Keeping of Negroes* (1754), members of the Quaker Yearly Meeting in Philadelphia published his booklet and circulated it widely. Four years later, led by Anthony Benezet, this group outlawed slaveholding among its local members. They set a precedent that many Quakers followed in the next generation, and they challenged other denominations to do the same.

Oglethorpe's Antislavery Experiment

Oglethorpe, "Establishing Georgia" (1733)

The most sustained early challenge to the slavery system in the American South came in the Georgia colony. In 1732 a group of well-connected London proprietors (known as trustees) obtained a twenty-year charter for the region between English South Carolina and Spanish Florida. Ten of the twenty-one initial trustees were members of Parliament. They included James Oglethorpe, who had recently organized and chaired a "committee on jails" to investigate the condition of debtors in English prisons. The trustees foresaw three related purposes—charitable, commercial, and military—for their experimental colony, which they named after King George II. Georgia would provide a haven for England's worthy poor, selected members of the neediest classes who could be transported across the Atlantic and settled on small farms. These grateful newcomers would then produce warm-weather commodities—olives, grapes, silk—to support the empire. Their prosperity would create a growing market for English goods. Finally, their presence would provide a military buffer to protect South Carolina from further warfare with the Yamasee and Creek Indians and from possible invasion by the Spanish in St. Augustine.

With Oglethorpe as their governor, an initial boatload of 114 settlers arrived in 1733 and began building a capital at Savannah. By 1741 the town, located on a bluff 15 miles up the Savannah River, boasted more than 140 houses. By then, more than a thousand needy English, plus 800 German, Swiss, and Austrian Protestants, had journeyed to Georgia at the trustees' expense. Another thousand immigrants had paid their own way. Like earlier colonizers, Georgia's first arrivals had trouble adjusting to a strange environment. Alligators, rattlesnakes, and hurricanes tested their resolve. Tension over governance only deepened their discouragement.

The idealistic trustees in London declined to accumulate property and profits for themselves in the colony, but they felt justified in controlling every aspect of Georgia's development. For example, they knew that gin was becoming a source of debt and disruption in Europe and that rum and brandy sold by traders was poisoning colonial relations with southeastern Indians. So in 1735 they outlawed the use of every "kind of Spirits" while still allowing consumption of wine and beer. Georgia's early experiment with prohibition of hard liquor proved difficult to implement, and officials quietly stopped enforcing the law in 1742.

Other efforts at control from above went further. The trustees refused to set up a legislature or to let settlers buy and sell land. Instead, they gave 50 acres of farm land to each family they sent over, plus a house lot in a local village, so all new towns could be well defended. But they parceled out land with little regard for variations in soil fertility. They also stipulated that owners could pass land on to sons only. To prevent the concentrations of wealth that they saw developing in other colonies, the trustees said that no one could own more than 500 acres. Prohibiting massive estates would allow for thicker settlement and therefore greater manpower to defend the colony militarily.

But the most important prohibition, by far, involved slavery. Oglethorpe began his career as a deputy governor of the Royal African Company, but he died in 1785 opposing the slave trade. His sojourn in Georgia turned him against slavery. In neighboring South Carolina, he saw firsthand how the practice degraded African lives, undermined the morals of Europeans, and laid that colony open to threats of revolt and invasion. So Oglethorpe persuaded the trustees to create a free white colony, convincing them to enact a law in 1735 that prohibited slavery and also excluded free blacks. He believed that this mandate would protect Georgia from the cor-

William Hogarth, To Inquire Into the State of the Gaols of This Kingdom. National Portrait Gallery, London

■ In 1729 James Oglethorpe (seated, right front) chaired a parliamentary committee exposing the harsh conditions in English jails. When William Hogarth portrayed the committee's visit to Fleet Street Prison, the artist showed Oglethorpe's concern for a dark-skinned prisoner, a hint of the philanthropist's future opposition to slavery in Georgia.

ruptions of enslavement while also making it easier to apprehend black runaways heading to Florida from South Carolina.

In 1739, the Stono Rebellion and the outbreak of war between England and Spain strengthened Oglethorpe's belief that slavery undermined the security of the English colonies by creating internal enemies who would support any foreign attackers. He saw further evidence in 1740, when he failed in a wartime attempt to capture St. Augustine from Spain. Unable to take the Florida stronghold, the governor managed to seize neighboring Fort Mose, which had been erected by anti-English slaves who had escaped from Carolina. When a Spanish force retook Fort Mose, relying heavily on Indian and African American fighters, Oglethorpe saw the intensity with which ex-slaves would fight the English, their former masters.

The next year, fearing a counterattack, Oglethorpe issued a warning to imperial officials. He predicted that if Spanish soldiers captured Georgia, a colony inhabited by "white Protestants and no Negroes," they would then send agents to infiltrate the vulnerable colonies farther north and stir black rebellion.

The End of Equality in Georgia

As Britain's war with Spain continued, few whites could deny the Georgia governor's assertion that slavery elsewhere in British America was a source of internal weakness and strategic danger. In 1742, as the governor had predicted, Spain pushed from Florida into Georgia with an eye toward destabilizing the colonies farther north. Oglethorpe's troops repulsed the invading Spanish force in the crucial Battle at Bloody Marsh on St. Simon's Island. The victory reduced the immediate threat to Britain's North American colonies, especially neighboring

■ Savannah, the capital of Oglethorpe's Georgia, was one year old when this view was sketched in 1734. The following year, Georgia's trustees officially outlawed slavery, creating a sharp contrast with the other British colonies in North America, especially neighboring South Carolina on the opposite bank of the Savannah River.

South Carolina, where Oglethorpe and his idealistic policies had numerous powerful opponents. These opponents now joined a group of so-called Malcontents in Savannah to question Georgia's continued prohibition against slavery. When this coalition challenged the trustees' antislavery stance, it prompted the first protracted North American debate about enslavement.

In the face of numerous ills—including a sickly climate, poor soil, restrictive land policies, and lack of representative government—a well-organized Georgia faction argued that slavery was the one thing needed for the colony to prosper, since it would provide profits to slave owners regardless of Georgia's many drawbacks. Not everyone agreed. In 1739 Scottish Highlanders living at Darien on the Altamaha River had contacted Oglethorpe to lay out their practical arguments against importing Africans. Their petition expressed shock "that any Race of Mankind, and their Posterity, Should be sentenced to perpetual slavery." Immigrants from Salzburg, Germany, residing at Ebenezer on the Savannah River drafted a similar statement. But Georgia's Malcontents pushed back, demanding the right to import slaves. They drew encouragement and support from powerful merchant-planters in South Carolina, eager to expand their trade in slaves from Africa and to extend their successful rice operations into coastal Georgia.

Oglethorpe warned that the proslavery lobby, hungry to create large estates, seemed bent on "destroying the Agrarian Equality" envisioned in Georgia's initial plan. But the colony's trustees in London grew less unified, committed, and informed over time. Eventually, the persistent efforts of the proslavery pamphleteers bore fruit. In 1750 the trustees gave in on the matter of land titles. They allowed acreage to be bought and sold freely in any amount, which opened the door for the creation of large plantations. From there, it was just one more step to allowing slavery. The trustees finally gave in on the question of bondage, letting Georgians exploit slaves after January 1, 1751. The 1750 law permitting slavery made futile gestures to ensure kind treatment and Christian education for slaves, but the dam had bro-

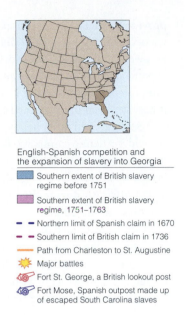

■ MAP 4.4

ENGLISH-SPANISH COMPETITION AND THE EXPANSION OF SLAVERY INTO GEORGIA   The Spanish and the British had competing land claims along the southeast coast after 1670. Creation of the Georgia colony in 1732 intensified the rivalry. The Spanish in Florida offered freedom to any slaves who escaped from South Carolina to St. Augustine, sparking the Stono Revolt in 1739. During the war between Britain and Spain (1739–1743), Georgians defeated the Spanish at Bloody Marsh and secured the disputed "Sea Island" region for the British. Within a decade, slavery became legal in Georgia, and scores of new labor camps appeared between the Savannah and the St. Mary's River, producing rice for export.

ken. Hundreds of slave-owning South Carolinians streamed across the Savannah River to invest in land. In 1752 the trustees disbanded, their patent expiring, their vision undone. By 1754 Georgia had become a royal colony.

Slave labor camps producing rice and indigo for export soon dotted the lowcountry on both sides of the Savannah River. Georgia's assembly passed a harsh slave code in 1755, based on South Carolina's. Two years later, it legislated a system of patrols to keep the brutal new regime in place. Georgia's effort to counter race slavery in North America had failed, a case of too little too late. After holding out for nearly two decades, the colony fell victim to the same divisive institution that had already taken root elsewhere.

Slave Quarter, Hermitage Plantation, Savannah, Georgia

Conclusion

Bit by bit, the slavery system gained a firm foothold in North America during the century after 1660. In southern colonies the system shaped the entire economy and social structure, creating a society based on race slavery. Farther north, where the institution never dominated, it still persisted as a disturbing element of colonial life. Two final observations provide a wider Atlantic context. First, the influx of African slaves into English North America occurred long after the **diaspora**, or dispersion, to Mexico, Brazil, and the Caribbean was well established. The North American portion of the gigantic African traffic did not expand steadily until after the 1670s. A century later, on the eve of the American Revolution, the proportion of blacks in the colonial population (over 20 percent) was higher than it has ever been in the United States since then.

Second, even at its height, the North American trade remained marginal in relation to the wider Atlantic commerce in African labor. For example, whereas roughly 50,000 enslaved men and women reached all the docks of North America between 1721 and 1740, the small West Indian islands of English Barbados and French Guadeloupe *each* received more than 53,000 Africans during the same period. In the next two decades, while Britain's mainland colonies purchased just over 100,000 Africans, Caribbean Islands such as English Jamaica (120,000) and French Saint Domingue (159,000) absorbed many more slaves.

During this single forty-year span (1721–1760), Brazil bought 667,000 African workers—more than would reach North America during the entire slave trade. All told, scholars currently estimate that some 650,000 Africans were brought to North America over several centuries. They represented roughly 6 percent of the total Atlantic commerce in enslaved people. Still, the number of mainland slaves expanded from scarcely 7,000 in 1680 to nearly 29,000 in 1700 and to more than 70,000 in 1720. Half a century later in 1770, because of importation and natural increase, 470,000 individuals were confined to enslavement from New Hampshire to Louisiana.

A century had passed since Elizabeth Key's generation saw the terrible transformation begin. Relative openness had given way to systematic oppression, and slavery's corrosive effects were felt at every level of society. An English visitor to the South in 1759 found provincial planters "vain and imperious," subject "to many errors and prejudices, especially in regard to Indians and Negroes, whom they scarcely consider as of the human species." It took another century before pressures developed that could unseat race slavery, sanctioned by law, as a dominant institution in the land.

Sites to Visit

The Slave Trade in Global Memory
http://digital.nypl.org/lwf/flash.html

The United Nations proclaimed 2004 as the International Year to Commemorate the Struggle Against Slavery and Its Abolition. The UNESCO Slave Route Project and New York's Schomberg Center for Research in Black Culture created an exhibit and Web site entitled "Lest We Forget: The Triumph Over Slavery."

Fort Mose
http://www.oldcity.com/sites/mose/

The site of Fort Mose sits on the eastern edge of a marsh, 2 miles north of St. Augustine, Florida. Under Spanish protection, people who had escaped from slavery in South Carolina built this fortified free black community in the 1730s. Archaeologists rediscovered the site, and it is being made into an exhibition area.

Africans in America
www.pbs.org/wgbh/aia/home.html

This four-part television series prepared for PBS provides an overview of slavery from its beginnings to the end of the Civil War. Part One deals with "The Terrible Transformation," offering resources and insights on the era from 1450 to 1750.

New Hampshire's Early Black History
www.SeacoastNH.com

Billed as "the biggest website for America's smallest seacoast," this site contains an excellent section on New Hampshire's black history, which stretches back more than 350 years. Links connect to the Portsmouth Black Heritage Trail, which leads to two dozen sites in Portsmouth, describing where early black residents lived and worked.

Drayton Hall

This National Trust historic site on the Ashley River outside Charleston, South Carolina, features the oldest plantation house in America open to the public, built by Europeans and African Americans at the time of the 1739 Stono Rebellion. The staff has developed a "Gullah Connection" to explore black culture with local schools.

Cultural Landscape of the Plantation
www.gwu.edu/~folklife/bighouse/intro.html

American studies professor John Michael Vlach has created this online exhibition using images of plantation buildings from the Library of Congress and linking them with the testimonies of former slaves recorded during the 1930s.

Somerset Place

This is just one of many historic plantations across the South steadily improving the ways in which they present the slave experience. Somerset Place is a huge estate created after the American Revolution beside Lake Phelps, in Creswell, North Carolina. The site has reconstructed slave buildings, and it hosts a biannual black homecoming.

Sunken Slave Ship *Henrietta Marie*

http://melfisher.org/henriettamarie/overview.htm

The Mel Fisher Maritime Museum in Key West, Florida, explains how underwater archaeologists have recovered artifacts relating to the slave ship *Henrietta Marie,* which sank near Key West in 1700.

Images of the Atlantic Slave Trade and Slave Life

http://hitchcock.itc.virginia.edu/Slavery/

This database contains 1,000 images, arranged in 18 categories, relating to the transatlantic slave trade and slave life in the Americas.

For Further Reading

General

Ira Berlin, *Many Thousands Gone: The First Two Centuries of Slavery in North America* (1998).

——, *Generations of Captivity: A History of African-American Slaves* (2003).

David Eltis, *The Rise of African Slavery in the Americas* (2000).

Michael A. Gomez, *Reversing Sail: A History of the African Diaspora* (2005).

John Thornton, *Africa and Africans in the Making of the Atlantic World, 1400–1800* (1992).

Peter H. Wood, *Strange New Land: Africans in Colonial America* (2003).

The Descent into Race Slavery

T. H. Breen and Stephen Innes, *"Myne Owne Ground": Race and Freedom on Virginia's Eastern Shore, 1640–1676* (1980).

Kathleen M. Brown, *Good Wives, Nasty Wenches, and Anxious Patriarchs: Gender, Race, and Power in Colonial Virginia* (1996).

Winthrop D. Jordan, *White over Black: American Attitudes Toward the Negro, 1550–1812* (1968).

Edmund S. Morgan, *American Slavery, American Freedom: The Ordeal of Colonial Virginia* (1975).

Anthony S. Parent, *Foul Means: The Formation of a Slave Society in Virginia, 1660–1740* (2003).

The Growth of Slave Labor Camps

Judith A. Carney, *Black Rice: The African Origins of Rice Cultivation in the Americas* (2001).

Jay Coughtry, *The Notorious Triangle: Rhode Island and the American Slave Trade, 1700–1807* (1981).

Sylvia R. Frey and Betty Wood, *Come Shouting to Zion: African American Protestantism in the American South and British Caribbean to 1830* (1998).

Allan Kulikoff, *Tobacco and Slaves: The Development of Southern Cultures in the Chesapeake, 1680–1800* (1986).

England Enters the Atlantic Slave Trade

Madeleine Burnside, *Spirits of the Passage: The Transatlantic Slave Trade in the Seventeenth Century* (1997).

Robert Harms, *The Diligent: A Voyage Through the Worlds of the Slave Trade* (2002).

Herbert S. Klein, *The Atlantic Slave Trade (New Approaches to the Americas)* (1999).

Randy J. Sparks, *The Two Princes of Calabar: An Eighteenth-Century Atlantic Odyssey* (2004).

James Walvin, *Black Ivory: A History of British Slavery* (1994).

Survival in a Strange New Land

Michael A. Gomez, *Exchanging Our Country Marks: The Transformation of African Identities in the Colonial and Antebellum South* (1998).

Jane Landers, *Black Society in Spanish Florida* (1999).

Jill Lepore, *New York "Burning": Liberty, Slavery, and Conspiracy in Eighteenth-Century Manhattan* (2005).

Peter H. Wood, *Black Majority: Negroes in Colonial South Carolina from 1670 Through the Stono Rebellion* (1974).

The Transformation Completed

Harold E. Davis, *The Fledgling Province: Social and Cultural Life in Colonial Georgia, 1733–1776* (1976).

Gwendolyn Midlo Hall, *Africans in Colonial Louisiana: The Development of Afro-Creole Culture in the Eighteenth Century* (1992).

A. Leon Higginbotham Jr., *In the Matter of Color: Race and the American Legal Process, the Colonial Period* (1978).

Phillips P. Moulton, ed., *The Journal and Major Essays of John Woolman* (1997).

Betty Wood, *Slavery in Colonial Georgia, 1730–1775* (1984).

For quizzes and other resources on these topics, go to www.longmanamericanhistory.com.

CHAPTER 5

An American Babel, 1713–1763

I N 1749 PEACE SEEMED A WELCOME PROSPECT IN THE SPANISH SETTLEMENT OF SAN ANTONIO IN south-central Texas. On an August morning, hundreds of people gathered in the town plaza. Captain Turibio de Urrutia, the local military commander, was there along with Father Santa Ana, who presided over the local missions.
Across from them stood four Apache chiefs with many of their people. In the center of the plaza, Spanish and Indian workers began to dig a deep pit with steep sides. Those attending were about to witness one of the most important events in the town's brief history.

Three decades earlier, in the spring of 1718, a small Spanish expedition had established the town next to the San Antonio River. The newcomers built houses and excavated irrigation ditches to divert river water onto their fields. But they had occupied contested ground. In 1720 Apache bands, moving south under pressure from the Comanche, attacked several settlers. The Spanish responded with their own raids, capturing Apache women and children and selling them into Mexico as slaves.

Father Santa Ana protested such harsh tactics. The cleric hoped to make peace with the Apache and draw them into the expanding mission system, where they would learn Spanish and accept Christianity. At Santa Ana's urging, Captain Urrutia modified his approach in 1749. After the spring raids, he ordered humane treatment for the 175 prisoners brought back to San Antonio. Rather than sell them as slaves, he merely detained them and sent several captives back to Apache country with a proposal for peace.

■ Mission San Francisco de la Espada, at San Antonio, had 1,100 cattle, 80 horses, and 16 pairs of oxen when this chapel was being constructed in the 1740s. By the time the United States annexed Texas a century later (1845), the church had fallen into disrepair.

When these messengers (two women and a man) returned with word that important Apache chiefs were prepared to negotiate, the townsfolk welcomed the Apache delegation. There was feasting, important for such occasions, and the four chiefs attended a mass conducted by Father Santa Ana. After two days of discussion through translators, the Spanish released some Apache prisoners as a goodwill gesture, and both sides agreed to hold a formal peace ceremony in the plaza.

The next day all gathered to watch the workers digging the deep pit. Then the longtime adversaries buried their differences in an elaborate symbolic ritual. They lowered a live horse into the hole, along with other emblems of warfare: a lance, a hatchet, and a bundle of arrows. Next, the four chiefs linked hands and walked solemnly around the pit, accompanied by the Spanish leaders. At a signal, all the onlookers suddenly grabbed up loose earth and tossed it into the hole. The horse was completely buried—a sacrifice for peace—and the ceremony broke up with shouts and celebration.

Though striking, the encounter between the Spanish and Apache at San Antonio was not unique. During the same era, Europeans and Native Americans met to parley and trade in Detroit, Albany, Philadelphia, Charleston, St. Augustine, Mobile, New Orleans, and other colonial towns. Such formal occasions highlight a wider process of contact and interaction throughout the North American colonies in the half-century between 1713 and 1763. Everywhere, colonial expansion brought together Europeans, Africans, and Native Americans in surprising new contacts. Equally important, it forced different peoples *within* each of these three categories, despite contrasting backgrounds, to rub shoulders with one another in unfamiliar ways.

These encounters had all been set in motion by the colonization process. Spanish missionaries lived among Tejas Indians in eastern Texas; French explorers dominated, and then lost, the Mississippi Valley; escaped African slaves fought militiamen from Georgia on the outskirts of St. Augustine. Everywhere, motives differed, accents jarred, and cultures clashed. In Philadelphia, Benjamin Franklin, a newcomer from Boston, protested the way in which Germans "swarm into our settlements, and by herding together establish their language and manner to the exclusion of ours."

For many Christians, the new confusions recalled the story of Babel. The people in that biblical city, despite their high ambitions, could not undestand one another well enough to work together. Eventually, they scattered abroad across the face of the earth. Bible-reading Americans no doubt recalled that tale, especially during the great religious awakening that shook the English colonies in the 1740s, when the prospect of building something new and transcendent seemed close at hand. The German-born utopian Christian Priber even attempted to establish an egalitarian realm in Appalachia where Europeans, Africans, and Native Americans could live peaceably together. Such dreams were not to be, however. Instead, the existing colonies continued to build up regional economies of their own, under British protection, and elements of a dominant Anglo-American culture began to emerge amid the Atlantic Babel's many voices.

New Cultures on the Western Plains

It makes sense that the Apache chose to bury a horse during their elaborate ceremony at the Spanish **presidio** in 1749. By this time the horse, recently introduced to the Indians, was transforming life on the Great Plains. It also makes sense that they buried arrows and hatchets rather than guns. Traditionally, the Spanish aspired to make the Indians into loyal subjects and Christian converts. From the time of Spain's arrival in the New World, therefore, official Spanish policy had forbidden the sale of firearms to Native Americans.

In contrast, the French, Dutch, and English desired trade at almost any cost. They showed less hesitation about supplying Indians with guns in return for furs, so firearms had become familiar to many eastern Indians in the seventeenth century. In the eighteenth century, guns began to spread across the Mississippi River as well. Combined with the movement of horses from the south, this development had enormous consequences. New patterns of warfare altered Indian cultures, and more powerful hunting techniques affected the regional economies and ecologies of the Native American West.

The Spread of the Horse

Although small horses once roamed the ancient West, they migrated into Asia thousands of years ago and became extinct in America. They returned with the early Spanish explorers. Around 1600, when New Mexico's early colonists brought mares north for breeding, horse herds developed in the Rio Grande valley. After the Pueblo Revolt in 1680, horses taken from the Spanish entered Indian trading networks and rapidly moved north from one culture to another.

By 1690 the Ute had obtained horses and traded them to the Shoshone. Before the mid-eighteenth century, horses had moved west of the Rocky Mountains to the Nez Perce and north to the Blackfoot. The Apache brought horses east to the Caddoan cultures near the Red River and then north to the Pawnee, Arikara, and Hidatsa. Even tribes in the Southeast acquired Spanish horses from the West before they obtained English horses from the Atlantic coast. When a Chickasaw leader drew a regional map on deerskin in 1723, he showed a Native American leading a horse east of the Mississippi River.

For all Indians, the first horses seemed utterly strange. One elder recalled that "the people did not know what they fed on. They would offer the animals pieces of dried meat." "He put us on mind of a Stag that had lost his horns," another remembered, "and we did not know what name to give him. But as he was a slave to Man, like the dog, which carried our things, he was named the Big Dog." For generations, Native Americans had used

■ The horse offered new mobility for hunting, as in this modern painting of Navajo riders. Tribes that had once tracked buffalo on foot at the edge of the Great Plains could now pursue herds across miles of open grassland. This was true for the Cheyenne, who were living in fixed villages in what is now South Dakota in the early eighteenth century. "After they got the first horses," recalled John Stands-in-Timber, "they learned there were more of them in the South and they went there after them." Cheyenne life would never be the same again.

Harrison Begay, *Night Chant Ceremonial Hunt*, 1947. Museum purchase, The Philbrook Museum of Art, Tulsa Oklahoma (1947.40)

dogs to pull provisions and bedding on a **travois**, an A-frame device made with tent poles. A larger animal could haul bigger loads, including longer tent poles that allowed for more spacious tipis.

Whether or not a tribe used tipis as dwellings, it could readily use the horse as a new source of food and as an aid in hunting. As herds expanded and horsemanship improved, warriors rode into battle. On horses, they could conduct lightning raids over long distances. Soon, raising, trading, and stealing horses became important activities, and a family's wealth and status depended partly on the number of horses at its command.

The Rise of the Comanche

By the 1770s, mounted Comanche warriors commanded respect and fear across a vast domain. Their territory stretched south nearly 600 miles from western Kansas to central Texas, and it spanned 400 miles from eastern New Mexico to what is now eastern Oklahoma. This area, known as the Comanchería, roughly equaled all the English settlements on the Atlantic coast in size, but its origins were recent and humble. The Comanche's Shoshone-speaking ancestors had been hunter-gatherers on the high plains of Wyoming, living on small game, roots, and berries. The arrival of the horse around 1690 changed everything, allowing family bands to migrate southeast from the Rockies to hunt the buffalo herds that grazed along the western edges of the Great Plains. From there, they could trade buffalo hides for additional horses at Taos and Santa Fe.

The Comanche were not the first to make their homes in what is now eastern Colorado. For generations, groups of Apache had settled in the region near the upper reaches of the Platte and Arkansas rivers. The Apache settlements—with their irrigated gardens and herds of horses—provided easy targets for Comanche newcomers. Within two decades, the Comanche had hammered their enemies south through one river valley after another. Apache bands soon reached San Antonio, where they stole livestock from the new Spanish settlement to survive. Threatened by the Comanche moving into central Texas, the hard-pressed Apache chose to seal a pact with the Spanish at San Antonio in 1749.

Not long after they buried the horse in the plaza, the Spanish began plans for a mission and **presidio** (military post) among their Apache allies. The outpost would lie 150 miles northwest of San Antonio on the San Saba River, near present-day Menard, Texas. But the post had been established for less than a year when the Comanche attacked it in 1758. They returned the next year, capturing 700 horses. "The heathen of the north are innumerable and rich," exclaimed a Spanish officer at San Saba. "They dress well, breed horses, [and] handle firearms with the greatest skill." The Comanche onslaught continued, and the attacks finally forced the Spanish to withdraw from San Saba in 1767.

In less than two decades, the Comanche had overrun most of Texas. They continued to absorb smaller Native American groups and swell in numbers. By 1780 they had grown into a proud Indian nation of more than 20,000 people. Their domain, the Comanchería, remained a powerful entity in the Southwest for decades.

The Expansion of the Sioux

Comanche strength depended not only on mounted warfare but also on using the horse as a trade commodity to obtain guns. Because Spanish policy prohibited the sale of firearms to Native Americans, the Comanche looked east for weapons. They discovered that by selling horses to their eastern allies, such as the Wichita Indians, they could receive French muskets from Louisiana in return. But the Comanche were not alone; the Sioux also took advantage of the gun frontier as it inched steadily west.

By 1720 the French had established settlements at Peoria, Cahokia, and Kaskaskia in Illinois and at New Orleans, Natchez, and Natchitoches in Louisiana. French traders at these

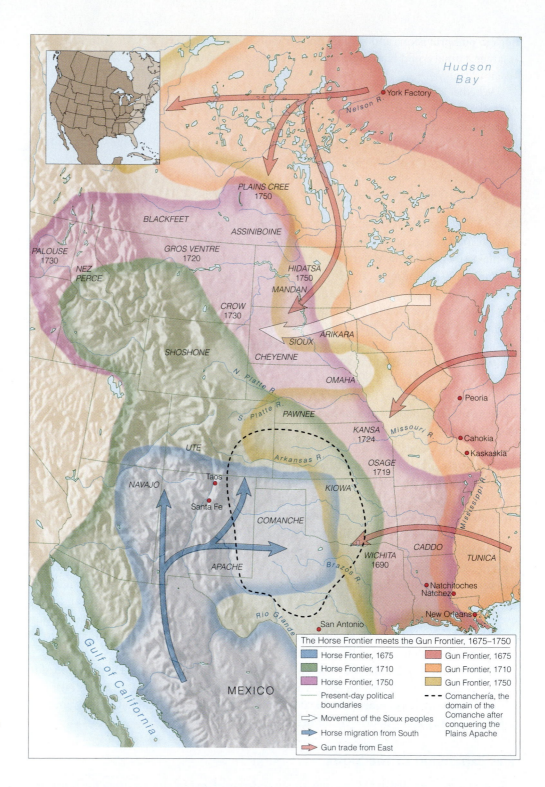

■ **MAP 5.1**
**THE HORSE FRONTIER MEETS
THE GUN FRONTIER, 1675–1750**

sites provided guns and other metal goods to Indians in exchange for salt, deerskins, beaver pelts, horses, or war captives. Native American groups that took advantage of this trade included the Tunica beside the Mississippi, the Caddo and Wichita along the Red and Arkansas rivers, and the Osage, Pawnee, and Omaha tribes near the Missouri.

Farther north, muskets carried west from French posts on the Great Lakes and south from English bases in subarctic Canada proved especially important among the Sioux peoples, who trapped game and gathered wild rice by the lakes of their northern Minnesota homeland. The

Comanche had mastered horses and then acquired guns; the Sioux, given their different location, first absorbed firearms and then adopted the horse. But the results proved equally dramatic.

When the Sioux first encountered a gun from French voyageurs in the mid-seventeenth century, they called it *mazawakan*, meaning "mysterious or sacred iron." Initially, they used the few muskets they could obtain to fight their less well-armed Indian neighbors. By 1700 French traders, moving from the east, had established direct trade with the Sioux, offering a steady supply of guns and powder in exchange for furs.

For a generation, several Sioux bands (the Teton and Yanktonai) walked between two worlds. In the summers, they followed the buffalo onto the prairies, with dogs pulling travois and women carrying heavy burdens. As cold weather approached, they retreated to the edge of the woodlands to gather firewood and seek beaver. In the spring, after trading meat and pelts to the French for guns and ammunition, they returned to the edge of the plains. They glimpsed their first horses not long after 1700. But it was several generations before the western Sioux had acquired enough mounts and developed sufficient confidence to drop their old customs and adopt a horse-centered way of life.

By midcentury, the horse frontier on the northern Great Plains had met the gun frontier. Saukamappee, a Cree Indian living with the Blackfoot, remembered vividly the surprise of the initial encounter. When he was a young man, his war party—well-armed and on foot—had gone into battle against the Shoshone. "We had more guns and iron headed arrows than [ever] before," he recalled years later. "But our enemies . . . had Misstutim [Big Dogs, that is, Horses] on which they rode, swift as the Deer."

Indian women remembered the arrival of the horse and the gun with ambivalence. These new assets improved food supplies and made travel less burdensome, but the transition brought disadvantages as well. Violent raids became more common, and young men who fought as warriors gained status in the community compared to older men and women. Also, the hard task of processing slain buffalo increased, creating new work for women even as it provided fresh resources for the whole community.

As the overlap of horse and gun proceeded after 1750, Sioux men bearing muskets continued to acquire mounts and fight for control of the buffalo grounds. Their competitors, all of whom had recently acquired horses, now had guns as well. But within several decades, the Sioux had pushed their domain west to the Missouri River. Like the Comanche farther south, they had emerged as a dominant power on the Great Plains.

Britain's Mainland Colonies: A New Abundance of People

West of the Mississippi, horses and guns brought dramatic shifts as the eighteenth century progressed. But east of the Appalachian Mountains, a different force prompted striking change: population growth. Several factors came together to push the demographic curve upward at an unprecedented rate after 1700. From our vantage point in the twenty-first century, the colonial seaports and villages appear tiny, and rural settlement seems sparse. But by the mid-eighteenth century, the coastal colonies represented the largest concentration of people that had ever occupied any portion of the continent.

On both sides of the North Atlantic, population growth characterized eighteenth-century life. But in Europe numbers rose at a gradual pace, while the population along the eastern seaboard of North America surged at an astounding rate. England in 1700 had 5.1 million people, and that figure increased a mere 14 percent to 5.8 million by 1750. In contrast, during the same half-century, the colonial population in British North America more than quadrupled, from 260,000 to nearly 1.2 million.

During these same decades, the Atlantic seaboard colonies also made a permanent and dramatic shift away from a population that was almost entirely of English origin. Never before had North America seen such extensive ethnic and racial diversity. As the numerous cultures and languages indigenous to western Europe, western Africa, and eastern North America mixed and mingled, they gave rise to an American Babel.

Population Growth on the Home Front

Natural increase—more births than deaths each year—played an important role in colonial population growth. Marriages occurred early, and the need for labor created an incentive for couples to have large families. Benjamin Franklin, who rose to become the best-known colonist of his generation, was born in Boston in 1706. He grew up in a household of seventeen children. Large families had long been commonplace, to compensate for frequent deaths among children. What made the Franklin family unusual was that all the children survived childhood and started families of their own.

Although a high birth rate typified most preindustrial cultures, it was the low death rate and long average life span that pushed up American population numbers. With no huge urban centers, colonial epidemics proved less devastating than in Europe. Food was plentiful, and housing improved steadily. Newborns who survived infancy could live a long life. (Franklin himself lived eighty-four years.) Moreover, the 1720s and 1730s proved peaceful compared to earlier decades, so soldiering did not endanger lives among men of military age. For women, death related to pregnancy and childbirth still loomed as a constant threat. (Franklin's own mother was his father's second wife; the first wife died after bearing seven children.) Yet women still outnumbered men among people living into their seventies and eighties.

Although grandparents often endured far into old age, the average age for the total population stayed remarkably young. (See Figure 5.1.) The reasons seem clear. The ratio between men and women was becoming more even over time, the marriage rates for women remained extremely high, and there was no effective means of contraception. Women could resort to sexual abstinence to avoid pregnancy, and mothers could extend the time between births by nursing their infants for a long period (since lactation reduces the chances of conception). Not surprisingly, children abounded.

"Packed Like Herrings": Arrivals from Abroad

Frequent births and improving survival rates were only part of the population story. Immigration—both forced and free—also contributed mightily to the colonies' growth. The unfree arrivals came in two different streams from two separate continents and faced very different prospects. The largest flow of unfree arrivals came from Africa, and these forced migrants faced a bleak new life with few options for improvement. By the 1730s, the expanding transatlantic slave trade brought at least 4,000 Africans to the colonies every year, and the rate increased steadily.

A separate stream of unfree laborers came to the colonies from Europe. It included prisoners forced from crowded jails and also indentured servants unable to pay their own way to America. By comparison to enslaved Africans, the long-term prospects of these European migrants were far more promising. Every year, hundreds of detainees in British jails were offered transportation to the colonies and a term of service laboring in America as an alternative to prison time or execution.

Deported felons joined the larger flow of unfree migrants from Europe: poor people, unable to pay for their own passage, who accepted transportation to America as indentured servants. All were sold to employers to serve as workers, with scant legal rights, until their indenture expired, usually after three to six years. In the 1720s, Philadelphia shippers

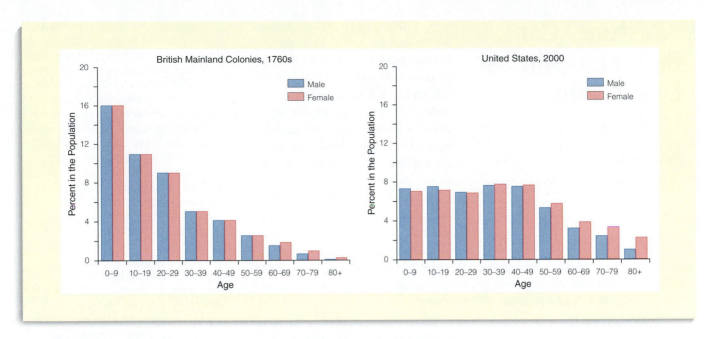

■ **FIGURE 5.1**

COMPARISON OF OVERALL POPULATION STRUCTURE BY AGE COHORT AND SEX: BRITISH MAINLAND COLONIES, 1760S, AND UNITED STATES, 2000   In the mid-eighteenth century, more than half of all people in the British mainland were under age twenty and fewer than two in ten were forty or older. In contrast, among all the living Americans at the start of the twenty-first century (281.4 million people), fewer than three in ten are under twenty, and more than four in ten are age forty or older.

devised a variation on indentures known as the redemption contract. Under this **redemption system**, agents in Europe recruited migrants by contracting to loan them money for passage and provisions. On arrival in America, the recruits could then sign a pact with an employer of their own choosing. That person agreed to pay back the shipper, "redeeming" the original loan that had been made to the immigrant. In exchange, the newcomer (called a redemptioner) promised to work for the employer for several years, receiving no more than room and board. After that, the redemptioners were on their own, and their prospects usually improved.

Besides Africans who remained unfree for life and Europeans who gained freedom after a period of service, a smaller stream of newcomers involved free families arriving from Europe who could pay their own way. Poor conditions at home pushed these risk-takers to try their luck in the New World, and glowing descriptions of abundant land at bargain rates caught their attention. American land speculators hoped to rent forest tracts to immigrant farmers who would improve the value of the land by clearing trees and building homes. Britain's imperial administrators also sought to recruit European immigrants to the American colonies. Their frontier settlements could bolster colonial defenses against foreign rivals and provide a buffer to ward off Indian attacks.

Even for those newcomers who could pay their own way, the Atlantic passage was a life-threatening ordeal. "The people are packed densely, like herrings," Lutheran minister Gottlieb Mittelberger recorded after a voyage to Pennsylvania. "During the journey the ship is full of pitiful signs of distress—smells, fumes, horrors, vomiting, various kinds of sea sickness, fever, dysentery, headaches, heat, constipation, boils, scurvy, cancer, mouth-rot, and similar afflictions." Despite such hardships, newcomers found economic opportunities awaiting them in America. They often wrote home glowing accounts of colonial life, and their letters helped boost the rising population further.

DOCUMENT

"The Passage of Indentured Servants" (1750)

"Pastures Can Be Found Almost Everywhere": Joshua von Kocherthal Recruits Germans to Carolina

Joshua von Kocherthal grew up in southern Germany and trained to be a Lutheran minister. On a visit to London at the start of the eighteenth century, he learned of England's desire to recruit settlers to its American colonies. Because fellow Germans faced hard times at home, he led several groups to New York, where they established Neuberg (Newburgh) on the Hudson River. In 1706 Kocherthal published a German-language tract promoting migration to South Carolina. The popular booklet went through several editions in his homeland.

The winter of 1708–1709 was especially harsh east of the Rhine River. In the spring of 1709, a stream of German refugee families migrated north along the Rhine and then west to England. From there, they hoped to obtain passage across the Atlantic to South Carolina. Many carried Kocherthal's simple pamphlet, and they focused on the numerous advantages outlined in his brochure, especially the abundance of land. According to Kocherthal, the colonial government registered all land grants "to prevent errors or future arguments," and it exempted newcomers from taxes for several years. Best of all, food was plentiful, no feudal obligations or serfdom existed, and members of Protestant denominations had "freedom of religion and conscience."

South Carolina is one of the most fertile landscapes to be found…preferable in many respects to the terrain in Germany, as well as in England. . . . Game, fish, and birds, as well as waterfowl such as swans, geese, and ducks, occur there in such plentiful numbers that…newcomers can sustain themselves if necessary…until they have cleared a piece of land, sown seeds, and gathered in a harvest. . . . Among other things, there can be found in the wild so-called "Indian chickens" [turkeys], some of which weigh about 40 pounds or even more. These exist in incredible numbers. . . .

Hunting game, fishing, and bird-catching are free to anyone, but one shouldn't cross the borders of neighbors or of the Indians [who] live in complete peace and friendship with our families. In addition, their number decreases while the number of our people (namely the Europeans) increases. . . . Lumber can be found there in abundance, especially the most beautiful oaks, but also many of the nicest chestnuts and nut trees which are used by many for building and are considered better than oaks. One can also find beeches, spruces, cypresses, cedars, laurels, myrtle, and many other varieties.

Hogs can be raised very easily in great numbers at little cost, because there are huge forests everywhere and the ground is covered with acorns. . . . Above all, the breeding of horses, cows, sheep, hogs and many other kinds of domestic livestock proceeds excellently, because pastures can be found almost everywhere, and the livestock can remain in the fields the whole year, as it gets no colder in Carolina in the middle of winter than it does in Germany in April or October. . . . Because of the multiplication of livestock, almost no household in Carolina (after residing there a few years) can justifiably be called poor.

Non-English Newcomers in the British Colonies

DOCUMENT

Elizabeth Sprigs, Letter to Her Father (1756)

Colonies that were thoroughly English at their origin became decidedly more varied after 1700. By far the largest change came from North America's increasing involvement in the Atlantic slave trade. By 1750, 240,000 African Americans made up nearly 20 percent of the population of the British colonies. Native Americans had been drawn into the mix in small numbers as slaves, servants, spouses, and Christian converts. But four out of five colonists were of European descent. Among them, as among the Africans and Indians, many spoke English with a different accent, or as a second language, or not at all.

The New England colonies remained the most homogenous, but even there, 30 percent of the residents had non-English roots by 1760. The new diversity was most visible in New York because of the colony's non-English origins. A 1703 census of New York City shows that the town remained 42 percent Dutch, with English (30 percent) and Africans (18 percent) making up nearly half the population. The remainder included a Jewish community (1 percent) and a growing number of French Protestants (9 percent).

The French New Yorkers had fled to America after Louis XIV ended protection for the Protestant minority of France. When the king revoked the long-standing Edict of Nantes in

Courtesy, Dartmouth University Library

LONDON: Printed for J. Baker, at the Black-Boy in Pater-Noster-Row. 1710.

In 1709, roughly 13,000 German immigrants seeking passage to America encamped for months at Blackheath, near London. The British government supplied them with tents, blankets, bread, and cheese, and churchgoers prayed for their welfare. But other Britons protested that the German strangers took "bread out of the mouths of our native handicraft men and laboring people, and increase the number of our poor which are too many and too great a burden to our nation already." Most of the refugees reached North America, serving as the vanguard for later German migration.

As far as vegetables and fruits are concerned, Indian corn predominates, thriving in such a way that one can harvest it twice a year and grow it wherever one wants to. Our local cereals such as wheat, rye, barley, and oats do well, but above all, rice thrives there as excellently as in any other part of the world, and it grows in such amounts that it can be loaded on ships and transported to other places. And as the inhabitants use rice so much and make much more profit from it than any other cereal, they are most keen on growing rice and there has been very little cultivation of other cereals.

All kinds of our fruits can be planted there, but...future arrivals would do well to bring along seedlings of any kind, or at least the seeds. . . . There can already be found different kinds of our local apples. . . . As far as cabbage, beets, beans, peas, and other garden plants are concerned, not only do our local plants grow very well, but there are also many other varieties with excellent taste that are completely unknown to us. . . . Newcomers will do well to acquire all sorts of iron tools and bring these along. . . . If someone has lived in Carolina for a time and he wants to go to another country, he may do so freely at any time.

Questions

1. Study the picture and caption regarding German refugees near London. Is that situation similar to, or different from, conditions in a modern refugee camp that you have read about or seen in the news? Be specific.

2. Do any of Kocherthal's observations about the natural world relate to the ongoing Columbian Exchange described in Chapter 1? ■

Source: Translations by Dorothee Lehlbach from Joshua von Kocherthal, *Ausfeuhrlicher und umstaendlicher Bericht von der beruehmten Landschaft Carolina, in dem engellaendischen American gelegen* (Frankfurt: Georg Heinrich Oehrling, 2nd ed., 1709), in the Special Collections Library of Duke University.

1685, he also prohibited Huguenot emigration, but several thousand French Protestants escaped illegally and sought refuge in America. They established small communities such as New Rochelle in New York. Everywhere, they intermarried with the English and prospered in commerce. By the 1760s, several families with humble Huguenot origins, such as the Laurenses in Charleston, had amassed enormous fortunes.

At a time when France and Great Britain were at war, another infusion of French-speaking refugees, the Acadians, fared less well. In 1755 authorities evicted French Catholics from Acadia in British Nova Scotia, fearing they might take up arms for France. Officials burned their homes and deported 6,000 of them to the various coastal colonies farther south. Mistreated for their Catholicism and feared as enemies during wartime, the Acadians struggled to get by. Resented in their new homes, many moved on to French Louisiana, where the Acadians, or Cajuns, became a lasting cultural force.

Scotland provided a much larger flow of migrants than France, stemming from two different sources. A growing stream of families, at least 30,000 people by 1770, came from Scotland itself. They were pushed by poverty, land scarcity, famines, and a failed political rebellion in 1745. In addition, a larger group known as the Scots-Irish came from Ulster

John Wollaston, *Mary Spratt Provoost Alexander*, undated. Museum of the City of New York, Gift of William Hamilton Russell (50.215.4)

■ Like many New Yorkers of her generation, shopkeeper Mary Spratt Provoost Alexander (1693–1760) spoke both Dutch and English. Her Dutch mother had married a Scottish immigrant, and Mary was the wife of a local attorney who also came from Scotland.

in Northern Ireland. The British had encouraged these Scottish Presbyterians to settle in Ireland in the seventeenth century, displacing rebellious Irish Catholics. But the Scottish newcomers in Ulster soon faced restrictions from Parliament and the Anglican Church. By 1770 nearly 60,000 Scots-Irish had opted to leave Ireland for America.

Another stream, German-speaking immigrants, nearly equaled the combined flow of Scots and Scots-Irish settlers. They began to arrive shortly after 1700, as religious persecution, chronic land shortages, and generations of warfare pushed whole communities out of southern Germany and neighboring Switzerland. By 1770 the total had reached 85,000. These refugees generally came as whole families, and they usually took up farmland on the fringes of the colonies. Germans occupied New York's Mohawk Valley and Virginia's Shenandoah Valley, and they fanned out from Germantown across the rich farmland of Pennsylvania. Swiss founded New Bern, North Carolina, in 1710.

Almost all of the white, non-English newcomers were Protestant Christians. Many clung to their language and traditions. But most arrivals learned English, and their children intermarried with English settlers. A French visitor described a typical American "whose grandfather was an Englishman, whose wife is Dutch, whose son married a French woman, and whose present four sons have now four wives of different nations."

The Varied Economic Landscape

Population growth had consequences, and the changes began at the water's edge. Ships carrying newcomers docked most often at Boston, New York, Philadelphia, or Charleston. Each of these ports grew from a village to a commercial hub, absorbing manufactured goods from Britain and shipping colonial produce abroad. All four towns developed an active coastal trade with secondary ports located on nearby rivers. In contrast, Chesapeake Bay had no single dominant port. There, Baltimore, Annapolis, Alexandria, Norfolk, and Newport News all expanded. But given the bay's many rivers, Atlantic ships often visited separate riverside plantations and villages to do business.

Colonial Products

In Chesapeake Bay and elsewhere, inland commerce was conducted by boat wherever possible. Hartford on the Connecticut River, Albany on the Hudson, Trenton on the Delaware, and Augusta on the Savannah all become riverside trading centers. Trails and former Indian paths connected these river-based communities, easing the way for travelers in the hinterland. By the 1740s, a pathway known as the Great Wagon Road headed southwest from Philadelphia to Winchester in Virginia's Shenandoah Valley and then south through gaps in the Blue Ridge Mountains to the Piedmont region of Carolina.

Widening networks of contact, using boats and wagons, extended inland from the primary ports. And expanding fleets of ships tied each major hub to distant Atlantic ports. As a result, farmsteads and villages that had been largely self-sufficient before 1710 gradually became linked to wider markets. Local production still met most needs. But increasingly, the opportunity existed to obtain a new tool, a piece of cloth, or a printed almanac from far away. The new possibility of obtaining such goods lured farmers to grow crops for market rather than plant only for home consumption.

As local commercial systems gained coherence and strength, a string of regional economies developed along the Atlantic seaboard. Coastal vessels and a few muddy roads linked them ten-

John Moale, engraving, 1752. I. N. Phelps Stokes Collection, New York Public Library

BALTIMORE IN 1752,

■ In 1729 Maryland planters founded Baltimore to provide a port on Chesapeake Bay for shipping tobacco. The community had only 50 homes and 200 inhabitants when this early sketch was made in 1752, but the town grew rapidly after that.

uously to one another. But geographical and human differences caused each to take on a character of its own. Migration patterns reinforced this diversity, since arrivals from Europe often sought out areas where others already spoke their language or shared their form of worship. The influx of German farmers through Philadelphia, for example, gave unique traits to Pennsylvania. (Because the newcomers spoke German, or *Deutsch*, they became known as Pennsylvania Dutch.) Likewise, the rising importation of Africans helped shape the economy and culture of Chesapeake Bay, and the same held true for coastal South Carolina. Besides the diversity among arriving peoples, American ecological differences played a role as well. Variations in land and climate contributed to the emergence of five distinctive economic regions along the Atlantic coast: Georgia and South Carolina; North Carolina; the Chesapeake; New England; and the so-called middle colonies of New York, New Jersey, and Pennsylvannia.

Sources of Gain in the Carolinas and Georgia

Two related but distinctive regions took shape along the southeastern coast, linked respectively to the two Carolina colonies. The larger one centered on the lowcountry of coastal South Carolina. There, the warm Gulf Stream current provided a long growing season; it also assured mild winters, meaning that cattle and hogs could forage unattended for most of the year. As livestock multiplied, settlers sold meat, barrel staves, and firewood to the sugar islands of the West Indies, purchasing African slave labor in return.

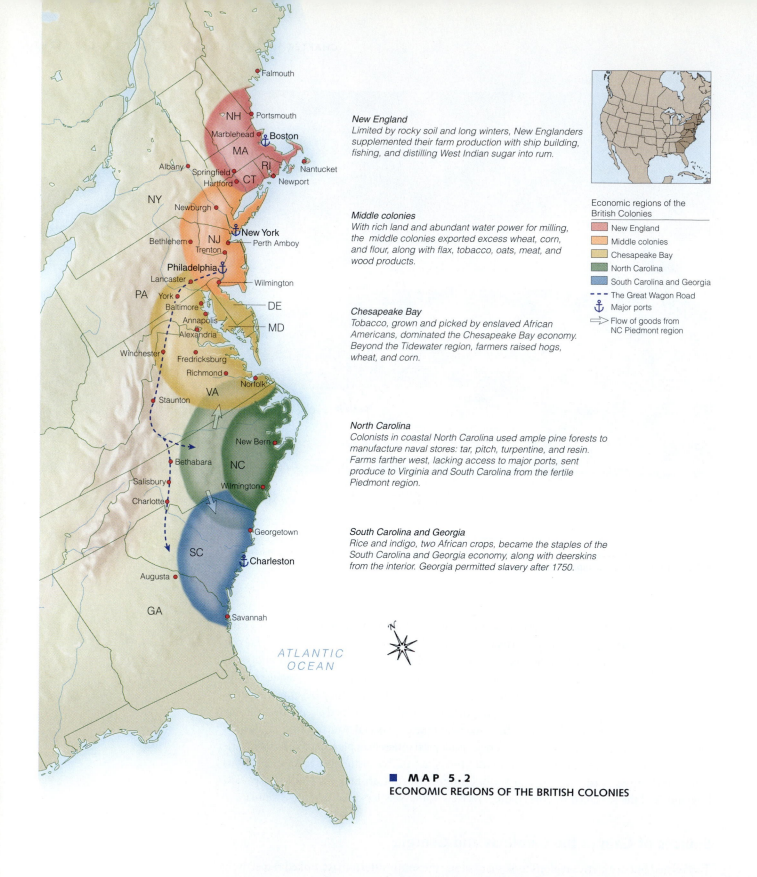

New England
Limited by rocky soil and long winters, New Englanders supplemented their farm production with ship building, fishing, and distilling West Indian sugar into rum.

Middle colonies
With rich land and abundant water power for milling, the middle colonies exported excess wheat, corn, and flour, along with flax, tobacco, oats, meat, and wood products.

Chesapeake Bay
Tobacco, grown and picked by enslaved African Americans, dominated the Chesapeake Bay economy. Beyond the Tidewater region, farmers raised hogs, wheat, and corn.

North Carolina
Colonists in coastal North Carolina used ample pine forests to manufacture naval stores: tar, pitch, turpentine, and resin. Farms farther west, lacking access to major ports, sent produce to Virginia and South Carolina from the fertile Piedmont region.

South Carolina and Georgia
Rice and indigo, two African crops, became the staples of the South Carolina and Georgia economy, along with deerskins from the interior. Georgia permitted slavery after 1750.

Economic regions of the British Colonies

- New England
- Middle colonies
- Chesapeake Bay
- North Carolina
- South Carolina and Georgia
- - - The Great Wagon Road
- Major ports
- Flow of goods from NC Piedmont region

■ **MAP 5.2**
ECONOMIC REGIONS OF THE BRITISH COLONIES

Some of the newcomers had grown rice in Africa before their enslavement. In planting rice for their own use, they soon showed that the crop could thrive in Carolina. Once African know-how made clear the potential for rice cultivation, a system of plantation agriculture, imported from Barbados, took hold quickly after 1700. Rice production spread to Georgia after that colony legalized slavery in 1751. Another African plant, indigo, also took root as a money-making staple crop. For several generations after 1740, indigo from South Carolina provided the blue dye for England's textile industry.

On Charleston's docks, casks of deerskins piled up beside barrels of rice and indigo. The deerskin trade in South Carolina and Georgia depended on the Creek and Cherokee men who hunted the animals and the Indian women who processed hides. At the trade's height in the 1730s, Indian and white hunters killed more than a million deer per year.

In North Carolina, a second regional economy evolved. North of Cape Fear, the sandy barrier islands known as the Outer Banks prevented easy access for oceangoing vessels and hindered efforts to promote staple crop agriculture. So colonists turned to the pine forest to make a living. An extensive band of longleaf pine stretched inland for a hundred miles. With labor, this pine forest yielded naval stores: the tar and pitch used by sailors to protect their ships and rigging. Workers hauled the finished products to Wilmington on the Cape Fear River, the colony's best outlet to the sea. By the 1770s, the port was well known for exporting naval stores, and a dozen sawmills dotted the river.

Farther inland, Scots-Irish and German families moved down the Great Wagon Road after 1740 to carve out farms across the Carolina Piedmont on lands controlled largely by several absentee owners in Britain. By 1763 Ben Franklin estimated that Pennsylvania had lost 10,000 families to North Carolina. Typical of this migration were the Moravians, who established towns at Nazareth and Bethlehem, Pennsylvania, in the 1740s. In 1753 members of this German-speaking religious group bought a tract near modern-day Winston-Salem, North Carolina. They named it Wachovia, meaning "Peaceful Valley," and they quickly developed prosperous farms, a pottery shop, and a tannery around their initial settlement, called Bethabara. The newcomers bartered seeds and tools with one another and shipped extra produce overland, traveling northeast to South Carolina or northeast to coastal Virginia.

Chesapeake Bay's Tobacco Economy

North of the Carolinas, farmers in the colonies bordering Chesapeake Bay committed to tobacco production in the seventeenth century and clung to that staple crop during a long decline in its market price. After 1710, demand for tobacco revived, in part because snuff (pulverized tobacco inhaled through the nostrils) became popular among Europeans. Tobacco continued to dominate the Chesapeake economy, but local conditions in parts of Virginia and Maryland prompted crop diversification as the century progressed.

For one thing, constant tobacco planting depleted the soil. For another, most farms lay far from any navigable river, and rolling huge casks of tobacco many miles to market proved expensive. Wheat and corn thus emerged as important secondary **staples**, along with flax, hemp, and apples for making cider. The new crops provided a buffer against poor tobacco harvests and spurred related activities such as building wagons, making barrels, and constructing mills. These trades, in turn, produced widening networks of local exchange and prosperity for white **yeoman** families, with or without slaves.

Before 1700, all the mainland colonies could be described as *societies with slaves*. After that, the northern colonies continued to allow enslavement, but they never relied on it. In contrast, the southern colonies, except for certain inland farmlands settled from the north, shifted early in the eighteenth century to become something different: full-fledged *slave societies*, tied economically and culturally to slavery. By midcentury, plantation owners remained less wealthy than their counterparts in the West Indies who lived off the profits of slave-grown sugar. But on average, members of the southern elite controlled far more wealth than their counterparts in the North. The profits of the plantation system spread widely through the rest of the European American community. By the 1770s, whites in the South averaged more than twice as much wealth per person as whites in the North. An estimate for 1774 puts the average net worth among white southerners at £93, a sharp contrast to their counterparts in the middle colonies (£46) and New England (£38).

New England Takes to the Sea

North of Chesapeake Bay, two overlapping economic regions emerged: the long-established New England colonies and the somewhat newer and more prosperous middle colonies. New England faced peculiar disadvantages, beginning with the rocky soil. As imports from London increased, New Englanders found no staple crop that could be sold back directly to Britain to create a balance of trade. All the beaver had been hunted, and much of the best land had been occupied. The region's farm families had adapted well to the challenging environment and short growing seasons. Both men and women worked on handicrafts during the long, hard winters, and networks of community exchange yielded commercial prosperity in many towns. But with a rapidly growing population, successive generations had less land to divide among their children.

By 1770 three out of every four ships sailing from New England to a British port were owned by colonial residents.

Increasingly, young men with little prospect of inheriting prime farmland turned to the sea for a living. In timber-rich New England, shipbuilding prospered. Colonists established shipyards at the mouth of nearly every river, drawing skilled carpenters and willing deckhands to the coast. By 1770 three out of every four ships sailing from New England to a British port were owned by colonial residents. In contrast, in the southern colonies from Maryland to Georgia, the proportion was only one in eight.

On Nantucket Island off Cape Cod, whaling became a new source of income. For generations, the islanders had cooked the blubber of beached whales to extract oil for lamps. In 1715 they outfitted several vessels to harpoon sperm whales at sea and then return with the whale blubber in casks to be rendered into oil. In the 1750s, they installed brick ovens on deck and began cooking the smelly blubber at sea in huge iron vats. This change turned the whaling vessel into a floating factory, and it allowed longer voyages in larger ships. By the 1760s, Nantucket whalers were cruising the Atlantic for four or five months at a time and returning loaded with barrels of oil.

The fishing industry prospered as well. All along the coast, villagers dispatched boats to the Grand Banks, the fishing grounds off Newfoundland. When the vessels returned, townspeople graded, dried, and salted the catch. The colonists sent the best cod fish to Europe in exchange for wine and dry goods. Yankee captains carried the lowest grade to the Caribbean sugar islands, where planters bought "refuse fish" as food for their slaves. In return, skippers brought back kegs of molasses to be distilled into rum. By 1770, 140 American distilleries, most of them in New England, produced 5 million gallons of rum annually. Much of it went to colonial taverns and Indian trading posts. But some also went to Africa, aboard ships from Britain and New England. American rum, along with various wines and spirits from Europe, made up one-fifth of the total value of goods utilized to purchase African slaves.

As the New England economy stabilized, it became a mixed blessing for women. On the farm, their domestic labors aided the household economy and helped to offset bad harvests. Mothers taught their daughters to spin yarn, weave cloth, sew clothes, plant gardens, raise chickens, tend livestock, and churn butter. The products from these chores could be used at home or sold in a nearby village to buy consumer goods. While the husband held legal authority over the home, a good wife served as a "deputy husband," managing numerous household affairs, or perhaps earning money as a midwife to help make ends meet. She took charge entirely if her husband passed away or went to sea.

But for all their labors, women seemed to lose economic and legal standing to men as New England towns became larger and more orderly. Networks of local officials, consisting entirely of men, drafted statutes and legal codes that reinforced male privileges. Women found it difficult to obtain credit or receive a business license, and the law barred married women from making contracts, limiting their chance for activities outside the home. Gradually, male apothecaries and physicians with a smattering of formal training shouldered traditional midwives away from the bedside. Overseers of the poor had the power to remove children from a widowed mother and place them in the **almshouse**, a home for persons in need of charity.

Economic Expansion in the Middle Colonies

The fifth regional economy, the one that flourished in the middle colonies between New England and Chesapeake Bay, improved upon these two neighboring worlds. The Europeans who resettled Indian lands in Delaware, Pennsylvania, New Jersey, and New York found a favorable climate, rich soil, and numerous millstreams. Unlike New Englanders, they developed a reliable staple by growing an abundance of grain. They exported excess wheat, flour, and bread as effectively as southerners shipped tobacco and rice. But unlike the planters in Virginia and Maryland, middle-colony farmers did not become locked in the vicious cycle of making large investments in enslaved workers and exporting a single agricultural staple. Instead, they developed a more balanced economy, using mostly free labor. Besides grain products, they also exported quantities of flaxseed, barrel staves, livestock, and pig iron. Large infusions of money from Britain, sent to support the war effort in America during the long conflict against France in the 1750s, gave a further lift to this prosperous economy.

Whereas the Chesapeake had no dominant seaport, the middle colonies boasted two major ports of entry. European craftsmen, unwilling to compete with unpaid slave artisans in the South, flocked to the middle-colony seaports instead. Both Philadelphia and New York grew faster than rival ports in the mid-eighteenth century, passing Boston in size in the 1750s. By 1763 Philadelphia had more than 20,000 people, New York had nearly as many, and both cities faced a set of urban problems that had already hit Boston.

As the port towns grew, so did economic and social distance between rich and poor. Large homes and expensive imports characterized life among the urban elite. In contrast, the poorest city dwellers lacked property and the means to subsist. By the 1760s, Philadelphia's almshouse and the new Pennsylvania Hospital for the Sick Poor were overflowing. In response, Philadelphia's Quaker leaders established a voluntary Committee to Alleviate the Miseries of the Poor, handing out firewood and blankets to the needy. They also built a "Bettering House," patterned on Boston's workhouse, that provided poor Philadelphians with food and shelter in exchange for work. To limit urban poverty, New York and Philadelphia authorities moved newcomers to the countryside, where Dutch and German settlers had already established an efficient farming tradition. As immigration rose, the region slowly expanded its economy far up the Hudson Valley, east into Connecticut and Long Island, and south toward Maryland.

AUDIO

"The Connecticut Peddler"

The farm frontier pushed west as well. The acquisitive Thomas Penn had inherited control of Pennsylvania from his more idealistic father, founder William Penn. In 1737 the young proprietor defrauded the Delaware Indians out of 1,200 square miles of potential farmland west of the Delaware River. In the infamous Walking Purchase, Penn claimed a boundary that could be walked in a day and half. Then Penn hired runners who covered more than 55 miles in 36 hours, giving him title to a huge tract. Land-hungry settlers pressed the reluctant Delaware west toward the Allegheny Mountains and occupied the rich river valleys of eastern Pennsylvania. Land agents and immigrant farmers called the fertile region "the best poor man's country."

Matters of Faith: The Great Awakening

Philadelphia epitomized the commercial dynamism of the eighteenth-century British colonies. The city was a hub in the fastest-growing economic region on the Atlantic seaboard. Ben Franklin, arriving there in 1723 at age seventeen, achieved particular success. Within seven years he owned a printing business. Within twenty-five years he was wealthy enough to retire, devoting himself to science, politics, and social improvement. He created a lending library, developed an efficient stove, promoted schools and hospitals, supported scientific and philosophical organizations, and won fame experimenting with electricity.

The outburst of scientific inquiry and religious skepticism spreading through the Atlantic world at the time became known as the Enlightenment, and its spirit of rational questioning and reason was greatly aided by the printing press. In America, Franklin and his fellow printers personified the new Age of Enlightenment. By 1760 the British mainland colonies had twenty-nine printing establishments, more presses per capita than in any country in Europe. These presses squeezed out eighteen weekly newspapers and countless public notices, fostering political and business communication throughout the colonies. But American printers also published an array of religious material, for the colonial spirit of worldly enterprise existed uneasily beside a longing for spiritual community and social perfection.

VIDEO

The Great Awakening

In the first half of the eighteenth century, colonists witnessed breakthroughs in religious toleration and controversies within the ministry. They also experienced a revivalist outpouring with roots in Europe and America, later known as the **Great Awakening**. This stirring began in the 1730s, and it gained momentum through the visits from England of a charismatic preacher named George Whitefield (pronounced Whitfield). The aftershocks of the Great Awakening persisted for a full generation.

Seeds of Religious Toleration

The same population shifts that made Britain's mainland colonies more diverse in the eighteenth century also created a new Babel of religious voices that included many non-Christians. Africans, the largest of all the new contingents, brought their own varied beliefs across the Atlantic. Some slaves from Portuguese Angola had had exposure to Catholicism in their homeland. But most Africans retained much of their traditional cultures and showed skepticism toward Christianity. Efforts to convert Native Americans also had mixed results. A minister living near the Iroquois reported that Indians would beat a drum to disrupt his services and then "go away Laughing."

Another non-Christian contingent, Jewish immigrants, remained few in number, with only several hundred families by 1770. Merchants rather than farmers, they established communities in several Atlantic ports, beginning in Dutch New Amsterdam (1654) and Newport (1658). Most were Sephardic Jews; that is, their ancestral roots were in Spain and Portugal. They came by way of the Caribbean, reaching Charleston in 1697, Philadelphia after 1706, and Savannah in 1733. A few of their children married into the Protestant culture, but more than 80 percent of Jewish young people found partners within their own small communities.

The majority of eighteenth-century newcomers to the British colonies were Christians. A few, such as the Acadians, were Catholics, but the rest had some Protestant affiliation. In the two centuries since the Reformation, numerous competing Protestant denominations had sprung up across Europe. Now this wide array made itself felt in America, as Presbyterians, Quakers, Lutherans, Baptists, Methodists, and smaller sects all increased in numbers. To attract immigrant families, most colonies did away with laws that favored a single established church. Nevertheless, New England remained firmly Congregational, and the southern gentry (plus merchant elite everywhere) concentrated within the Anglican Church.

Paul Rocheleau Photography

▲ Members of the Jewish community in Newport started Touro Synagogue in 1759, a century after the arrival of their first ancestors in the Rhode Island seaport. Completed in 1763, this gem of colonial architecture is the oldest existing synagogue in the United States.

Rhode Island had emphasized the separation of church and state from the start, and Pennsylvania had likewise favored toleration, both as a matter of principle and as a practical recruitment device to attract new settlers. Since migration from Europe was a demanding ordeal, those who took the risk were often people with strong religious convictions. Such newcomers looked for assurances that they could practice their religion freely, and colonies competed to accommodate them. In many places, religious tests still limited who could hold public office, but tolerance for competing beliefs was expanding.

Many felt that if any institution threatened the growing religious toleration in the colonies, it was, ironically, the British king's own denomination. The monarch headed the Anglican Church, and it had influential American members, including almost every colonial governor. Therefore, repeated talk by the Church of England about installing a resident bishop in America aroused suspicions among colonists who worshipped in other denominations. This was especially true in New England, where Congregationalists had long opposed ideas of religious hierarchy. Boston, which had eighteen churches, rose up against a plan for an Anglican bishop in 1750. In a passionate sermon, Reverend Jonathan Mayhew preached that the town must keep "all imperious bishops, and other clergymen who love to lord it over God's heritage, from getting their feet into the stirrup."

The Onset of the Great Awakening: Pietism and George Whitefield

As relative toleration became a hallmark of the British colonies, no one benefited more than German-speaking Protestant groups. Numerous religious sects, such as the Moravians, Mennonites, Schwenkfelders, and Dunkers, were escaping from persecution as well as poverty at home. Their numbers multiplied after 1730, and hymns in German became a common sound on Sabbath day. In 1743, before any American printer produced an English-language Bible, a press in Pennsylvania put out a complete German edition of Luther's Bible, using type brought from Frankfurt.

Collectively, these newcomers were part of a European reform movement to renew piety and spiritual vitality among Protestant churchgoers in an age of increasing rationalism and worldliness. Pietism, as this "Second Reformation" was called, had roots in eastern Germany and stressed the need to restore emotion and intensity to worship that had become too rational and detached. The German pietists reached out after 1700 to inspire Huguenots in France and Presbyterians in Scotland. They influenced reformers in the Church of England such as John Wesley, the founder of Methodism and a teacher at Oxford University. Through Wesley, pietist ideas touched George Whitefield, a preaching prodigy in Oxford's class of 1736. Over the next decade, "the boy parson" sparked a widespread religious awakening in the American colonies.

Whitefield's mentor, Wesley, had preached briefly in Georgia. So in 1738, at age twenty-three, Whitefield spent several months in the new colony, where he laid plans for an orphanage near Savannah. Arriving back in England, Whitefield quickly achieved celebrity status, drawing large crowds with fiery sermons that criticized the Anglican Church. His popularity preceded him in 1739 when he returned to America for an extended tour, the second of seven transatlantic journeys during his career. Building upon religious stirrings already present in the colonies, Whitefield preached to huge and emotional crowds nearly 350 times in fifteen months. He made appearances from Savannah to Boston, something no public figure had ever done. "God shews me," he wrote in his journal, "that America must be my place for action."

The timing was perfect. Whitefield's brother was a wine merchant who understood the expanding networks of communication and consumption in the British Atlantic world. So Whitefield realized that in America, as newspapers multiplied and roads improved, he could advertise widely and travel extensively. He had little taste for Protestant debates over church organization and sectarian differences. Instead, he believed that an evangelical min-

When George Whitefield visited America in 1739, his preaching spurred the Great Awakening.

DOCUMENT

Edwards, "Sinners in the Hands of an Angry God"

IMAGE

Jonathan Edwards

ister should simply preach the Bible fervently to a wide array of avid listeners. Everywhere he went, Whitefield served as a catalyst for religious activity.

"The Danger of an Unconverted Ministry"

The heightened commotion in American churches had local origins as well. The same tension felt in European parishes—between worldly, rational pursuits and an emotional quest for grace and salvation—also troubled colonial congregations. Occasional local revivals had taken place in America for decades. The most dramatic one occurred in Northampton, Massachusetts, in 1734–1735, spurred by a talented minister named Jonathan Edwards. As the colonies' most gifted theologian, Edwards anticipated Whitefield's argument that dry, rote "head-knowledge" made a poor substitute for "a true living faith in Jesus Christ." "Our people do not so much need to have their heads stored," Edwards observed, "as to have their hearts touched."

In a fast-growing society, who would prepare suitable church leaders for the next generation? Candidates for the ministry could train at Harvard College (founded 1636), William and Mary (1693), Yale (1707), or one of several small academies. But these institutions could not instruct sufficient numbers. The shortage of educated ministers, combined with geographic expansion, meant that one preacher might oversee several parishes. Even if he tended only a single parish, the great distances separating parishioners made it hard for any pastor to travel widely enough to address their needs.

Problems in the pulpit went beyond quantity to include issues of quality as well. Many college graduates had too much "head-knowledge." Their fluency in Latin and Greek often earned them more disdain than respect from down-to-earth congregations. Most foreign-born ministers, such as Anglicans sent from England and Presbyterians from Scotland, had failed to land good positions at home. Too often, they showed limited appreciation for the local church members who paid their salaries, and they resented those who criticized their ministries. One such critic was William Tennent, a Scots-Irish immigrant who arrived in Pennsylvania with his family in 1716. Dismayed by the cold, unemotional outlook of Presbyterian ministers, Tennent opened a one-room academy in a log house to train his four sons and other young men for the ministry. But local Presbyterian authorities challenged his credentials and disparaged the teachings of his "Log College." Eventually, the school moved and grew, becoming linked to the new College of New Jersey in 1746, which later evolved into Princeton University. But before this happened, Tennent's preacher sons allied themselves with Whitefield and managed to shake the colonial religious establishment to its roots.

One of Tennent's sons, Gilbert, eventually led a Presbyterian church in Philadelphia created by Whitefield's supporters. In 1740, at the time of Whitefield's triumphal tour, young Gilbert Tennent delivered a blistering sermon entitled "The Danger of an Unconverted Ministry" that became a manifesto for the revival. Cutting to the heart of the matter, he condemned the "sad security" offered by incompetent, uncaring, and greedy ministers. "They are as blind as Moles, and as dead as Stones," he charged, "without any spiritual Taste and Relish." He argued that congregations should turn away from these "Letter-learned . . . Old Pharisee-Teachers" and listen to traveling preachers instead.

The Consequences of the Great Awakening

Whitefield hailed Gilbert Tennant and his brothers as "burning and shining lights" of a new kind. All the ministers and worshipers who joined in the movement began to call themselves "New Lights." Opponents, whom they dismissed as "Old Lights," continued to defend a learned clergy, emphasized head-knowledge on the difficult road to salvation, and opposed the disruptions caused by **itinerant ministers** who moved freely from parish to parish without invitation. The New Lights, in contrast, appealed to people's emotions and stressed the prospect of a more democratic salvation open to all. They defended their itinerant wanderings, which made them more accessible to a broader public and less likely to become set in their ways. "Our Blessed Saviour was an Itinerant Preacher," they reminded their critics; "he Preach'd in no other Way."

Just as New Light preachers moved readily across traditional parish boundaries, they also transcended the lines between different Protestant sects. Their simple evangelical message reached across a wide social spectrum to diverse audiences of every denomination. Moreover, their stress on communal singing, expressive emotion, and the prospects for personal salvation drew special attention from those on the fringes of the culture, such as young people, women, and the poor. Not surprisingly, New Light ministers also made headway in spreading Christianity within various African American and Native American communities.

Members of the religious establishment, once secure as unchallenged leaders in their communities, now confronted a stark choice. Some powerful churchmen acknowledged their New Light critics and reluctantly welcomed the popular renegades into the local pulpits. Such a strategy might blunt the thrust of the revival, and it would surely raise church attendance. Other Old Lights, however, took the opposite approach; they clung to tradition and stability, challenging their new rivals openly. They condemned itinerancy and disputed the interlopers' right to preach. They mocked the faddish popularity of these overemotional zealots and even banned the New Light itinerants from local districts for the good of the parishioners.

In the end, neither tactic stemmed the upheaval, which peaked in the North in the 1740s and in the South during the 1750s and 1760s. But the long-term consequences of the Great Awakening were mixed. Zealous New Light men and women tried to transcend the competing denominations and create a broad community of Protestant believers. But the reformers could never create such unity, and they left behind no new set of doctrines or institutional structures. Nevertheless, they created an important legacy. First, they infused a new spirit of piety and optimism into American Christianity that countered older and darker Calvinist traditions. Second, they established a manner of fiery evangelical preaching that found a permanent place in American life. Finally, and most importantly, they underscored democratic tendencies in the New Testament gospels that many invoked in later years when faced with other apparent infringements of their liberties.

> *Zealous New Light men and women tried to transcend the competing denominations and create a broad community of Protestant believers.*

The French Lose a North American Empire

In 1739, while George Whitefield launched his tour of the English colonies and the Stono slave rebellion erupted in South Carolina, the French dreamed of expanding their American empire. When Pierre and Paul Mallet set out up the Mississippi River from New Orleans that year, the two French Canadians suspected that the Missouri River, the Mississippi's mightiest tributary, stretched to New Mexico. If so, they hoped to claim a new trading route for France. Pausing in Illinois to gather seven French Canadian recruits, the Mallet brothers pushed up the Missouri, hoping it flowed from the southwest.

Jean-Pierre Lassus, *Vue et Perspective de la Nouvelle-Orleans,* 1726. C.A.O.M. Aix-en-Provence (France) DFC Louisiane 71 (pf6B)

But the river flowed from the northwest instead. Disappointed, the party left the river in Nebraska, purchased horses at an Omaha Indian village, and set off across the plains, reaching Santa Fe in July. After a nine-month stay, most of them returned east across the southern plains the next year. When the Mallets completed their enormous circuit and returned to New Orleans, they brought word from the West of Indian and Spanish eagerness to engage in greater trade. From their perspective, the future of France in America looked bright indeed. But the promise disappeared entirely within their lifetimes.

Prospects and Problems Facing French Colonists

In 1740 French colonists had grounds for cautious optimism. France already claimed a huge expanse of North America, and its wilderness empire ran strategically through the center of the continent. The potential for mineral resources and rich farmland seemed boundless. Moreover, no Europeans had shown greater skill in forging stable and respectful relations with Native Americans. French forts stretched up the Mississippi River and then east to the lower Great Lakes and the St. Lawrence Valley. These posts facilitated trade with Native Americans and secured ties between Canada and Louisiana. With Indian support, more outposts could be built farther east near the Appalachian Mountains to contain the English settlers and perhaps one day to conquer them.

At least three problems marred this scenario. First, the French population in America paled in comparison to the large number of English settlers. Canada still had fewer than 50,000 colonial inhabitants in 1740, whereas Britain's mainland colonies were rapidly approaching a million. Louisiana contained only 3,000 French people, living among nearly 4,000 enslaved Africans and 6,000 Native Americans. Second, French colonists lacked sufficient support from Paris to develop thriving communities and expand their Indian trade. The importation of goods from France was still meager and unpredictable. Finally, an ominous trickle of British hunters and settlers was beginning to cross the Appalachian chain. Carolina traders already had strong ties with the Chickasaw Indians living near the Mississippi River, and Virginia land speculators were eyeing lands in the Ohio Valley.

What seemed a promising situation for the French in 1740 was soon put to the test. Britain and France had long been on a collision course in North America. Colonial subjects of the

■ By 1726 New Orleans, with 100 cabins and nearly 1,000 inhabitants, was receiving shipments of trade goods from France and distributing them up the Mississippi River and its tributaries. Following a Louisiana hurricane in 1722, the levies along the waterfront were expanded, but flooding remains a threat to the low-lying city even today, as the devastation of Hurrican Katrina in 2005 made clear.

two European superpowers had already clashed in a series of wars. After several decades of peace, warfare was about to resume. King George's War (1744–1748) and the French and Indian War (1754–1763) preoccupied colonists and Native Americans alike over the next two decades. In 1763 the Treaty of Paris ended the French and Indian War, part of a far broader conflict known in Europe as the Seven Years' War. At that point, less than a quarter century after the Mallet brothers' optimistic journey through the heartlands, the British gained the upper hand. The expansive French empire in North America suddenly vanished.

British Settlers Confront the Threat from France

These colonial conflicts of the mid-eighteenth century, generally linked to wider warfare in Europe, had a significant impact on everyone living in the British mainland colonies. A few people took advantage of the disturbances to become rich. They provisioned troops, sold scarce wartime goods, sponsored profitable privateering ventures, or conducted forbidden trade with the enemy in the Caribbean. But many more people paid a heavy price because of war: a farm burned, a job lost, a limb amputated, a husband or father shot in battle or cut down by disease. From London's perspective, the Americans made ill-disciplined and reluctant soldiers. But from the colonists' viewpoint, they received too little respect and inadequate assistance from Britain.

Adding insult to injury, a hard-won victory in North America could be canceled out at the peace table in Europe. In 1745, during King George's War, Massachusetts called for an attack on Louisburg, the recently completed French fortress on Cape Breton Island that controlled access to the St. Lawrence River and nearby fishing grounds. After a long siege, New England's forces prevailed. But British diplomats rescinded the colonial victory, handing Louisburg back to France in 1748 in exchange for Madras in India.

Whatever their differences, the American colonists and the British government saw potential in the land west of the Appalachian Mountains, and both were eager to challenge French claims there. In 1747 colonial speculators formed the Ohio Company of Virginia to develop western lands. Two years later the crown granted them 200,000 acres south of the Ohio River, if they would construct a fort in the area. Moving west and north, the Virginians hoped to occupy a valuable spot (modern-day Pittsburgh, Pennsylvania) where the Monongahela and Allegheny rivers come together to form the Ohio River. But the French had designs on the same strategic location.

131

In 1753 the Virginia governor sent an untested young major in the colonial militia named George Washington—at age twenty-one already regarded as a promising officer—to warn the French to leave the area. The next spring Virginia workers began erecting a fort at the Fork of the Ohio, but a larger French force drove them off and constructed Fort Duquesne on the coveted site. When Major Washington returned to the area with troops, he probed for enemy forces. In a skirmish on May 28, 1754, near modern Uniontown, Pennsylvania, his men killed ten French soldiers, the first casualties in what eventually became history's first truly global war. With 450 men and meager supplies, Washington fortified his camp, calling it Fort Necessity, and dug in to prepare for a counterattack.

Throughout the British colonies in the early summer of 1754, fears spread about the dangers of the French offensive and the loyalties of Native American allies. Officials in London requested that all the colonies involved in relations with the Iroquois send delegates to a special congress in Albany, New York, to improve that Indian alliance. Seven colonies sent twenty-three representatives, who hoped to strengthen friendship with the Iroquois nations and also discuss a design for a union of the colonies. The delegates to the Albany Congress adopted a proposal by Benjamin Franklin for a colonial confederation. The colonies would be unified by an elected Grand Council and a president general appointed by the crown. But no colonial legislature ever ratified Franklin's far-sighted Albany Plan. "Everyone cries, a union is necessary," Franklin wrote, "but when they come to the manner and form of the union, their weak noodles are perfectly distracted."

> *"Everyone cries, a union is necessary, but when they come to the manner and form of the union, their weak noodles are perfectly distracted."*

DOCUMENT

Albany Plan
of Union

The main distraction came from Pennsylvania, with word that on July 3 the French had defeated Washington's small force at Fort Necessity. But the British were not willing to give up their claims to the Ohio Valley without a fight. The crown responded by dispatching General Edward Braddock and two regiments of Irish troops to America. Early in 1755, his force arrived in Virginia, where preparations were already under way for a campaign to conquer Fort Duquesne. In June Braddock's combined British and colonial army of 2,500 began a laborious march west to face the French.

An American Fight Becomes a Global Conflict

IMAGE

The Seven
Years' War

The early stages of the war in America could hardly have been more disastrous for Britain or more encouraging for France. A French and Indian force ambushed Braddock's column in the forest near Fort Duquesne, cutting it to pieces in the most thorough defeat of the century for a British army unit. Elsewhere, Indian raids battered the frontiers, spreading panic in the northern colonies. With the local militia away at war, fears of possible slave uprisings swept through the South. The French commander, the Marquis de Montcalm, struck into New York's Mohawk Valley from Lake Ontario in 1756, then pushed south down Lake Champlain and Lake George in 1757. After a seven-day siege, he took 2,000 prisoners at Fort William Henry. In an episode made famous in *The Last of the Mohicans*, France's Huron Indian allies killed more than 150 men and women after their release from the fort.

The change in British fortunes came with the new ministry of William Pitt, a vain but talented member of the House of Commons. Pitt was an expansionist committed to the growth of the British Empire at the expense of France. He brought a daring new strategy to the war effort, and he had the determination and bureaucratic skill to carry it out. Stymied in Europe by the military might of the French army, the British would now concentrate their forces instead on France's vulnerable and sparsely populated overseas colonies. Under Pitt, the British broadened the war into a global conflict, taking advantage of their superior naval power to fight on the coasts of Asia and Africa and in North America as well. By 1758 Britain had undertaken a costly military buildup in America, with nearly 50,000 troops.

To win colonial support for his plan, Pitt promised to reimburse the colonies generously for their expenses. In the South, guns, ammunition, and trade goods flowed freely to Britain's

British conquest of New France

- 🟦 French settlements
- 🟥 British settlements
- 🟨 Iroquois settlements
- --- Land claimed by the Ohio Company of Virginia
- ✶ French victories
- ✶ British victories
- 🔫 French forts
- 🔫 British forts

1 Washington gives up Ft. Necessity to French, July 3–4, 1754

2 Braddock's army destroyed near Ft. Duquesne, July 9, 1755

3 British yield Ft. William Henry to Montcalm, Aug. 9, 1757

4 British capture French fort at Louisburg, July 26, 1758

5 British take Ft. Frontenac from the French, Aug. 27, 1758

6 Johnson captures Ft. Niagara from the French, July 25, 1759

7 Wolfe defeats Montcalm, Plains of Abraham, Sept. 13, 1759

8 Amherst accepts French surrender of Montreal, Sept. 8, 1760

■ **MAP 5.3**
THE BRITISH CONQUEST OF NEW FRANCE, 1754–1760

Native American allies. In the North, France lost Louisburg again in July 1758. Fort Frontenac on Lake Ontario fell in August. In November, the French destroyed and abandoned Fort Duquesne. The British seized the strategic site at the Fork of the Ohio, erecting a new post (Fort Pitt), and laying out the village of Pittsburgh beside it.

In Canada, autumn brought a poor harvest, followed by the worst winter in memory. Ice in the St. Lawrence, plus a British naval blockade, cut off overseas support from France. The Marquis de Montcalm huddled in Quebec with his ill-equipped army.

In the spring of 1759, the British pressed their advantage, moving against Canada from the west and the south. Britain's superintendent of Indian affairs in the region, Sir William Johnson, sensed that many Native Americans were eager to support the winning side. Johnson successfully recruited 1,000 formerly neutral Iroquois to join 2,000 British regulars on the shores of Lake Ontario to lay siege to Fort Niagara. The fort fell in July, a British victory that effectively isolated enemy posts farther west and obliged the French to abandon them. In August, a British force under Jeffery Amherst captured Ticonderoga and Crown Point on Lake Champlain. The stage was set for an assault on Quebec.

Thomas Johnson, engraving, 1759. I. N. Phelps Stokes Collection of American Historical Prints, Prints Division, New York Public Library

■ *Quebec, the Capital of New France,* by Thomas Johnson. A Boston printer, eager to celebrate the fall of Quebec, took an old image of the city from a French map. It shows the Catholic churches and seminaries that Louis XIV had promoted in the previous century. But in 1759 much of the town had been devastated by British cannon fire.

Quebec Taken and North America Refashioned

In London, William Pitt knew that capturing Quebec would conquer Canada. Months earlier, he had ordered James Wolfe "to make an attack upon Quebeck, by the River St. Lawrence." Wolfe's **flotilla**, with 8,500 troops, anchored near the walled city in late June. But the French held their citadel despite weeks of heavy shelling. Desperate and sick, Wolfe resorted to a ruthless campaign against the countryside that left 1,400 farms in ruins. Even this strategy failed to draw Montcalm's forces out to fight.

As a last resort, Wolfe adopted a risky plan to climb a steep bluff and attack the vulnerable west side of the city. On the night of September 12, 1759, he dispatched troops to float quietly past French sentries and scale the formidable cliffs. At daybreak, twelve British battalions emerged on a level expanse known as the Plains of Abraham. The future of the continent and its inhabitants hinged on a pitched battle between opposing European armies. Montcalm and Wolfe staked everything in the clash, and both lost their lives in the encounter. By nightfall, the British had won a decisive victory, and four days later the surviving French garrison surrendered the city of Quebec.

Montreal fell to Britain the following year, and fighting subsided in America. But Pitt continued to pour public money into the global war, and one military triumph followed another. The British conquered French posts in India, took French Senegal on the West African coast, and seized the valuable sugar islands of Martinique and Guadeloupe in the French West Indies. When Spain came to France's aid in 1762, British forces captured the Philippines and the Cuban city of Havana. But British taxpayers resented the huge costs of the war, and they worried that the effort to humiliate France and Spain could spark retaliation. Rising criticism pushed Pitt from office, and peace negotiations began.

In a matter of months, the European powers redrew the imperial map of North America. Their complex swaps constituted the largest single rearrangement of real estate in the history of the continent. First, France ceded to Spain the port of New Orleans and all of the Louisiana territory west of the Mississippi River. Then, in the 1763 Treaty of Paris, Spain turned over East Florida to Britain, receiving back Havana and the Philippines in return. France gave Britain its holdings between the Appalachians and the Mississippi River as well as the parts of Canada not already claimed by the Hudson's Bay Company. For this vast acquisition, the British returned the sugar islands of Martinique and Guadeloupe, and they allowed France to retain fishing rights off Newfoundland.

Those negotiating the peace agreed that French Canadians could choose between leaving Canada or becoming British subjects. But the Paris treaty made no mention of the thousands of Native Americans whose homelands were being reassigned. The final results were striking. Britain emerged as the world's leading colonial power, and, after two centuries, the empire of France in North America abruptly disappeared.

Conclusion

For half a century, the complex currents of colonial life had recalled the ancient tale of Babel, as told in the Book of Genesis in the Bible. A confusion of voices, interests, and cultures competed and interacted over a wide expanse in North America. In the process, a string of related economic regions emerged along the eastern seaboard. The British colonies that composed these regions varied in ethnic make-up, but they were all expanding rapidly in population. In 1763, Britain's mainland colonies contained more than 1.6 million people. The figure had quickly come to dwarf all the other population totals on the continent. Amazingly, in the thirteen years between 1750 and 1763, the British mainland colonies added more than 400,000 people. This number of new inhabitants—reflecting natural increase, European immigration, and the slave trade combined—exceeded the entire population that had been living in those same British colonies five decades earlier, in 1713.

The growth in numbers during the decades to come would be equally rapid, and the changes for the continent proved even more dramatic and long lasting. In the dozen years after 1763, the same colonies that had failed to embrace Franklin's Albany Plan of 1754 proved increasingly willing to cooperate in their opposition to new and troubling British policies. As their shared identity grew in these years leading up to the outbreak of the War of Independence in 1775, the colonists, for the first time, frequently referred to themselves—rather than to the Indians—as *Americans*.

Sites to Visit

San Saba Mission

The ruins of the mission, abandoned by the Spanish after Comanche attacks in the 1750s, lie 2 miles east of Menard, Texas, off US 190, near the San Saba River. Two miles west of Menard, on Highway 29, the fully restored San Saba Presidio contains a small museum in the rebuilt chapel. Menard is 150 miles northwest of San Antonio.

Winchester, Virginia

Founded in 1744 as a stop on the Great Wagon Road, Winchester is located 70 miles west of Washington, D.C., at Interstate 81, "where the Shenandoah Valley begins and history never ends." Young George Washington worked as a land surveyor in this frontier town, and his office is now a museum.

Old Salem

www.oldsalem.org

This reconstruction of a village founded in 1766 is in Winston-Salem, North Carolina. The site includes the Winkler Bakery, a cemetery, and the Museum of Early Southern Decorative Arts (MESDA). Take a virtual tour of the site at www.oldsalem.org. Nearby is Bethabara, a Moravian community founded in 1753, also open to the public.

George Whitefield

www.crta.org/documents/Whitefield.html

The texts of 59 sermons of the Reverend George Whitefield are available online at this Web site. The Bethesda Orphanage, founded by Whitefield in 1740, is located on 650 acres beside the Moon River outside Savannah, Georgia. It is now the Bethesda Home for Boys, America's oldest existing children's home.

Rice Museum

Located in the Old Market Building in Georgetown, South Carolina, the museum contains dioramas and exhibits describing rice cultivation. The Caw Caw Interpretive Center, west of Charleston on the Savannah Highway (Route 17S) in Ravenel, South Carolina, provides a fascinating view of eighteenth-century rice fields.

French and Indian War
www.frenchandindianwar250.org/default.aspx

This Web site offers an introduction to the 250th anniversary of the French and Indian War. PBS has made a four-hour TV program on "The War That Made America," narrated by actor Graham Greene, an Oneida Indian whose ancestors fought in the war.

Fort William Henry and Fort Ticonderoga
www.fort-ticonderoga.org/

Fort William Henry, at the south end of Lake George, was the location for events in 1757 depicted in the novel and film *The Last of*

the Mohicans. Guided tours relating to the British–French struggle are available there and at larger Fort Ticonderoga, on Lake Champlain. Both sites are east of Interstate 87, north of Albany, New York.

Old Fort Western
www.oldfortwestern.org/

Old Fort Western is located at 16 Cony Street on the east bank of the Kennebec River in Augusta, Maine. The fort, built in the opening year of the French and Indian War, celebrated its 250th anniversary in 2004. It is the oldest surviving wooden fort in the country and is open daily during the summer.

For Further Reading

General

John J. McCusker and Russell R. Menard, *The Economy of British America, 1607–1789* (1991).

Gary B. Nash, *The Urban Crucible: The Northern Seaports and the Origins of the American Revolution* (abridged edition, 1986).

Carla Gardina Pestana, *Liberty of Conscience and the Growth of Religious Diversity in Early America, 1636–1786* (1987).

Marcus Rediker, *Between the Devil and the Deep Blue Sea: Merchant Seamen, Pirates, and the Anglo-American Maritime World, 1700–1750* (1987).

Daniel Richter, *Facing East from Indian Country: A Native History of Early America* (2001).

New Cultures on the Western Plains

Gary Clayton Anderson, *Kinsmen of Another Kind: Dakota–White Relations in the Upper Mississippi Valley, 1650–1862* (1984).

James F. Brooks, *Captives and Cousins: Slavery, Kinship, and Community in the Southeast Borderlands* (2002).

Elizabeth A. H. John, *Storms Brewed in Other Men's Worlds: The Confrontation of Indians, Spanish, and French in the Southwest, 1540–1795* (1975).

Britain's Mainland Colonies: A New Abundance of People

Kirsten Fischer, *Suspect Relations: Sex, Race, and Resistance in Colonial North Carolina* (2002).

A. G. Roeber, *Palatines, Liberty, and Property: German Lutherans in Colonial British America* (1993).

Laurel Thatcher Ulrich, *Good Wives: Image and Reality in the Lives of Women in Northern New England, 1650–1750* (1982).

Marianne S. Wokeck, *Trade in Strangers: The Beginnings of Mass Migration to North America* (1999).

The Varied Economic Landscape

Kathryn E. Holland Braund, *Deerskins and Duffels: Creek Indian Trade with Anglo-America, 1685–1815* (1993).

Elaine Forman Crane, *Ebb Tide in New England: Women, Seaports, and Social Change, 1630–1800* (1998).

Margaret Ellen Newell, *From Dependency to Independence: Economic Revolution in Colonial New England* (1998).

Daniel Vickers, *Farmers and Fishermen: Two Centuries of Work in Essex County, Massachusetts, 1630–1850* (1994).

Michael Zuckerman, *Peaceable Kingdoms: New England Towns in the Eighteenth Century* (1970).

Matters of Faith: The Great Awakening

Patricia U. Bonomi, *Under the Cope of Heaven: Religion, Society, and Politics in Colonial America* (1986).

Philip Greven, *The Protestant Temperament: Patterns of Child-Rearing, Religious Experience, and the Self in Early America* (1977).

Timothy D. Hall, *Contested Boundaries: Itinerancy and the Reshaping of the Colonial American Religious World* (1994).

Jacob R. Marcus, *The Colonial American Jew* (1970).

The French Lose a North American Empire

Fred Anderson, *The War that Made America: A Short History of the French and Indian War,* (2005).

Fred Anderson, *A People's Army: Massachusetts Soldiers and Society in the Seven Years' War* (1984).

Colin G. Calloway, *The Scratch of a Pen: 1763 and the Transformation of North America* (2006).

John Mack Faragher, *A Great and Noble Scheme: The Tragic Story of the Expulsion of the French Acadians from Their American Homeland* (1998).

Ian K. Steele, *Betrayals: Fort William Henry and the "Massacre"* (1990).

Daniel H. Usner Jr., *Indians, Settlers, and Slaves in a Frontier Exchange Economy: The Lower Mississippi Valley Before 1783* (1992).

For quizzes and other resources on these topics, go to www.longmanamericanhistory.com.

The Limits of Imperial Control, 1763–1775

B
Y THE 1760S, BOSTON HAD GROWN INTO A BUSY SEAPORT OF 16,000 PEOPLE. WITH THIS expansion, the gap between rich and poor had widened steadily, and the Seven Years' War (the French and Indian War) had only worsened the growing inequality. During the war, wealthy Boston families such as the Hancocks multiplied their fortunes, building stately homes and importing elegant fashions. In 1764 young John Hancock, heir to his uncle's vast shipping business, inherited an immense fortune of £80,000.

■ Some wealthy colonists, like the Hancocks of Boston, joined the Patriot opposition during the 1760s and 1770s. Gradually, out of necessity, these merchants and planters forged a loose and convenient alliance with colonial artisans and workers who came from a very different world.

However, most Bostonians lived in a very different world. Half the townspeople had property and savings worth less than £40, and half of those possessed £20 or less. George Hewes, five years younger than Hancock, was born into this other Boston in 1742. At age seven, Hewes lost his father, a butcher who also sold soap and candles. But unlike Hancock, George had no rich uncle; he became an apprentice shoemaker at age fourteen.

Despite the town's growth, rich and poor still encountered one another on occasion. If anything, those contacts increased during the tumultuous decade that gave rise to the American Revolution. Politics—both imperial and local—heated up in the 1760s, opening rifts in the ruling elite. Throughout the colonies, British officials and other people who supported the crown's policies became known as Loyalists, or Tories. The wealthy among them saw social and economic dominance as their birthright and scorned their rivals for courting favor with the poor. In contrast, leaders of the emerging opposition (known as Whigs or Patriots) consisted of less conservative—often young and ambitious—members of the educated and professional classes. These people downplayed their rank and privilege to win popular support from those beneath them on the social scale.

In Boston, John Hancock was one such person. In 1763, after Hewes repaired an expensive shoe for Hancock, the merchant invited the young cobbler to a New Year's open house at his impressive mansion. In his old age, Hewes still recalled the occasion vividly. Intimidated by the wealth around him, he remembered being scared "almost to death" when the magnate toasted him and gave him a silver coin.

The two men met again on very different terms after a decade had passed. In December 1773 the shoemaker joined other activists, disguised as Indians, to empty chests of British tea into Boston Harbor. Recalling that night as an old man, Hewes was one of the first to refer to the event as a "tea party." And he swore that in the darkness he had rubbed elbows with Hancock himself and had joined him in smashing a crate of tea. Symbolically, the two men were now working shoulder to shoulder. They came together across class lines in a coalition that would soon challenge Europe's strongest empire, Britain, and spark the Atlantic world's first successful anticolonial revolution.

America's implausible alliance between a portion of the colonial elite and a wide spectrum of working people developed gradually and imperfectly. During the decade before 1776, class and regional interests still divided British colonists on many occasions. Urban artisans, rural farmers, enslaved African Americans, and numerous wives and widows, for example, did not necessarily share common views and concerns. Indeed, they were frequently at odds. Nevertheless, within half a generation enough of these diverse people—many as distant from one another socially as Hancock and Hewes—came together to wage a successful struggle for political independence.

What shared experiences and beliefs caused this unlikely and unstable partnership to emerge? What events shaped it and prompted it to gather momentum by July 1776, when John Hancock, as president of the Second Continental Congress, applied the first and largest signature to the American colonies' Declaration of Independence? In retrospect, we know that between 1763 and 1775, for the first time, colonists from separate regions and backgrounds began to speak of themselves as Americans—a term that had previously applied only to Indians. At times, of course, this self-conscious new identification with North America went too far, as in the creation of a *Continental* Congress; it was not, of course, a body of the entire North American continent at all.

In fact, in the Midwest in 1763, thousands of Native Americans under the leadership of Pontiac were fighting to assert their own independence from European encroachment. On the Great Plains, the Comanche and Sioux contended for new territories. Still farther west, other peoples experienced the initial shocks of colonial contact. Suddenly, inhabitants of the Hawaiian Islands and the Alaskan coast were encountering European intruders for the first time. For rival European empires, competing globally for mastery in the Atlantic, Pacific, and Indian Oceans, North America remained only one prize in a wider imperial contest.

Following the departure of the French, the push of rival powers to establish permanent control over the North American continent continued. But geographic ignorance, limited resources, weak bureaucracies, huge distances, strong-willed colonists, and resilient native inhabitants all posed limits for maintaining and expanding far-flung empires. Russia's foothold in Alaska and Spain's presence in California were new and tenuous at best. Spanish dominance at older outposts in Arizona, New Mexico, and Texas remained partial, and Spain's grip on its newly acquired Louisiana territory was even more nominal. East of the Mississippi River, long-term British control finally seemed to be assured. But even Britain, secure after its victory over France, would soon be fighting a losing battle to retain much of North America that it confidently claimed to control.

New Challenges to Spain's Expanded Empire

With Spain's acquisition of Louisiana from France in 1763, the Spanish held nominal title to the entire West, from the Mississippi to the Pacific, populated by more than one million Native Americans. But whether Spain could explore and defend this vast domain, stretching north toward Alaska, remained an open question. After all, envious rivals were already probing North America's Pacific coast. French and British exploration voyages challenged Spain's dominance in the Pacific, and Russian colonization in Alaska spurred the Spanish to establish posts along the coast of California. These rivalries, in turn, brought new pressures to bear on the West's diverse Indian peoples, even before the United States emerged as a separate entity with expansionist ambitions of its own.

Pacific Exploration, Hawaiian Contact

Defeat in the Seven Years' War removed the French from North America in 1763. Burdened with heavy war debts, France sought fresh prospects in the unexplored South Pacific. Not to be outdone, British captains pressed their own Pacific explorations. The most skilled and successful was James Cook, who ranged from the Arctic Circle to Antarctica during three momentous voyages beginning in 1768. In January 1778, during Cook's final voyage, his two vessels happened upon the Hawaiian Islands, eight major volcanic islands, plus 114 minor isles, stretching over 300 miles. More than thirteen centuries earlier (A.D. 300–500), seafaring Polynesians had migrated here in ocean-sailing canoes. They had arrived from the Marquesas Islands far to the south, and their descendants, perhaps as many as 300,000 people, lived in agricultural and fishing communities dominated by powerful chiefs.

The Hawaiians treated Cook with hospitality and respect. "No people could trade with more honisty," the captain observed. During the next twelve months, Cook cruised up the west

John Webber, *A View of Kealakekua Bay,* c. 1781–1783. Dixson Library, State Library of New South Wales, Sydney

■ When Captain Cook anchored at Hawaii's Kealakekua Bay in 1779, he wrote in his journal that the islanders crowded aboard his two vessels and paddled around them in "a multitude of Canoes." Hundreds of others swam around the ships, along with "a number of men upon pieces of Plank." One such surfboarder is visible in the foreground.

coast of North America, two centuries after Francis Drake's visit. English mariners still hoped to find a sea passage through North America to shorten voyages from the Atlantic to Asia, but Cook encountered a solid coastline stretching all the way to Alaska. Along the way, he traded with Northwest Coast Indians for sea otter pelts.

Cook's vessels returned south in 1779, and they were again greeted with fanfare on the big island of Hawaii. But admiration turned to resentment as the English outstayed their welcome, and an angry crowd of Hawaiians killed Cook and four of his mariners. After the captain's death, his two sloops stopped at Macao in China, where the crew sold their furs at a huge profit. They then sailed back to England in 1780 with word of money to be made selling North American sea otter pelts in China. The voyagers also confirmed a disturbing rumor: Russia already had a foothold in this lucrative Pacific traffic.

The Russians Lay Claim to Alaska

In 1728 Vitus Bering, a Danish captain in the Russian naval service, completed a three-year trek across Siberia. Reaching the Kamchatka peninsula on the Pacific Ocean, he built a boat and sailed north between Asia and America through the strait that bears his name. The journey ended European speculation that Asia was linked to North America. On a second expedition in 1741, Bering visited the Alaskan mainland and claimed it for Russia. He lost his life on the return voyage after a winter shipwreck on a frozen island.

Bering's crew finally returned to Kamchatka with valuable pelts. Over the next generation, Russian merchants sent several expeditions to Alaska each year, bringing back furs that they traded with the powerful Chinese Empire. In Alaskan waters, the Russian trappers lacked the numbers and the skill to collect furs on their own. So they captured native women and children as hostages, then ransomed them back to their men in exchange for a fixed number of furs. Native Alaskans resisted these rough intruders where possible, but many eventually submitted in a desperate effort to survive.

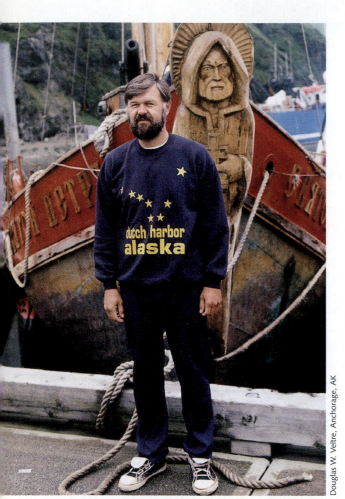

■ In 1991, 250 years after Vitus Bering's voyage to Alaska, Russians from Kamchatka sailed replicas of Bering's three small vessels across the North Pacific to Alaska. Aleksandr Maslov-Bering, a descendant of the explorer, poses beside the carved bow of one boat.

Douglas W. Veltre, Anchorage, AK

In the quarter-century before 1780, thirty different companies sponsored expeditions to Alaskan waters. Harsh conditions and stiff competition between ships made the traffic risky for the Russians and far worse for the Aleutian Islanders. The newcomers, bringing diseases, firearms, and their brutal hostage-taking system, reduced the population of the islands. As the number of humans and animals on the Aleutian Islands declined, the Russians pushed farther east in search of new hunters and hunting grounds.

The voyages from Kamchatka were growing longer and more expensive, so a Russian organizer, Grigorii Shelikov, planned an Alaskan base to facilitate operations. Shelikov and a partner formed a new company in 1781 and founded a permanent colonial settlement on Kodiak Island east of the Aleutians in 1784, despite fierce opposition from the island's native residents. By 1799 the firm had absorbed smaller competitors to become the Russian-American Company, with a monopoly from the **czar**.

In 1790, with the Kodiak base secure, Russians forced more than 7,000 island inhabitants to embark on vast fur hunts in their versatile two-seat **kayaks**. That same year, Shelikov hired Alexander Baranov to oversee the Kodiak post and expand operations down the Alaskan coast. In 1799 Baranov established an additional outpost at Sitka in southeast Alaska. Called

New Archangel at the time, the post became the capital of Russian America in 1808. From here, Baranov eventually extended the company's reach south toward California, seeking new hunting grounds and a longer growing season.

Spain Colonizes the California Coast

The Seven Years' War had left Spain's king, Carlos III, with vast new land claims in western North America. With only limited resources, the bureaucrats administering Spanish America struggled to control the huge domain. Many of the Native Americans across the Southwest resisted several decades of military suppression and slave raids. In addition, clerics offered their own resistance to government designs. The powerful Jesuits opposed administrative reform in the colonies, and in 1767 Carlos III expelled them from the Spanish realm. Unruly colonists posed a threat of their own. French inhabitants of New Orleans led a brief rebellion against Spanish rule in 1768. Finally, officials feared challenges in the Pacific from the British and the Russians. As early as 1759, a Spanish Franciscan had published *Muscovites in California*, warning of Russian settlements.

With the threat of Russians in mind, Spanish leaders in Mexico City concentrated on establishing a token presence along the Pacific coast. In 1769 they sent a small vanguard north from lower (Baja) California, led by Gaspar de Portolá and Franciscan friar Junípero Serra, to establish an initial outpost at San Diego Bay. Portolá then pressed farther up the coast, building a presidio (or military garrison) at Monterey in 1770 to "defend us from attacks by the Russians, who," he believed, "were about to invade us."

After the removal of all Jesuits from Spanish America in 1767, numerous Franciscan missionaries, members of a competing Catholic order, expanded their work and took on new responsibilities. Following the lead of Father Serra, other Franciscans soon planted several missions between San Diego and Monterey. These included the San Gabriel mission in 1771, where colonists established the town of Los Angeles ten years later. In 1775 a Spanish captain sailed into San Francisco Bay, and the next year a land expedition laid out the presidio and mission of San Francisco. A town sprang up at nearby San José the following year. As Franciscan fathers labored to convert the coast's diverse Indians, Spanish vessels pushed far up the Pacific shoreline. Captain Ignacio de Arteaga reached the Gulf of Alaska in 1779, fourteen months after Captain Cook had been there.

Since Spanish ships had difficulty supplying the few dozen settlers in California, authorities looked for an overland supply route. In 1774 Juan Bautista de Anza set out in search of a land route to California from the presidio he commanded at Tubac, south of Tucson. Accompanied by a Franciscan named Father Garcés, he forded the Colorado River and then crossed desert and mountains to reach the coast at San Gabriel. The next year, Anza led 240 reinforcements—mostly Spanish women and children—along a similar route, pausing at San Gabriel and heading north to San Francisco Bay.

Further explorations in 1776 proved less successful. Trying to find a usable route between California and New Mexico, Father Garcés meandered through the southwestern deserts without success. Two other Franciscans, Fathers Domínguez and Escalante, left Santa Fe on horseback in July 1776. They headed northwest across Colorado and Utah in search of a more northern route to Monterey on the Pacific coast. But no such trail existed. Instead, their 1,800-mile trek revealed the huge expanse of the Great Basin.

Moreover, the path to California that Anza had established proved short-lived. The Yuma Indians, who had helped his party cross the Colorado River in 1774, soon grew to resent Spanish trespassers, and they rebelled in the summer of 1781. Father Garcés and more than 100 Spanish men, women, and children died in the bloody Yuma Revolt, and hopes for a rapid expansion of the Spanish colony in California died with them.

■ MAP 6.1

SPANISH EXPLORATION AFTER 1760 AND THE START OF THE CALIFORNIA MISSIONS

Map legend: The Spanish entry into Alta (upper) California
- Fort
- † Mission
- ▪ Presidio
- ● Town
- Mission and Presidio
- Town and Presidio
- —— Portolá, 1769
- —— Anza and Garcés, 1774
- —— Anza, 1775–1776
- —— Garcés, 1776
- —— Domínguez and Escalante, 1776
- —— Modern state boundaries shown for orientation
- (1769) Years indicate the date of founding

Despite these problems, Spain managed to retain control over its recently expanded North American empire. The same could not be said for the British in their own newly enlarged empire farther east. They had taken French Canada, and their military might dominated the Atlantic world. But their fortunes in North America were about to change.

New Challenges to Britain's Expanded Empire

VIDEO

The Struggle for Dominance

In September 1760, French forces at Montreal submitted to British commander Jeffery Amherst. For Native Americans living east of the Mississippi, the French defeat in Canada had an immediate impact. General Amherst, who despised Indians as "contemptible," intended to alter Native American relations in the interior to reflect the new balance of power. He promptly sent James Grant to South Carolina with instructions "to chastise the Cherokees," who had taken up arms against the growing number of English traders and settlers in western Carolina. With 2,800 soldiers, Grant invaded Cherokee country in 1761. His men burned fifteen villages, without sparing women or children, and destroyed 1,500 acres of beans and corn.

With the Cherokee chastened in the South, Amherst turned his attention to the Indians north of the Ohio River. Here his harsh policies brought a sudden retaliation from the Native Americans that took many lives and cost Amherst his command. And if Indians in the Midwest posed fresh challenges to Britain, so did the colonists themselves.

Midwestern Lands and Pontiac's War for Indian Independence

As soon as the British unseated their French competitors in the Ohio River valley, they prohibited traffic with Indians in such goods as knives, tomahawks, muskets, powder, and lead. As French traders withdrew, the British took over their strategic posts at Detroit and at Michilimackinac. English settlers built new forts in the Ohio Valley and erected Fort Pitt over the ruins of Fort Duquesne. Indians at Niagara Falls commented in dismay at "so many Men and so much artillery passing by." Then, early in 1763, word spread among Indians that France would cede Louisiana to Spain and give up Canada and the entire Midwest to Great Britain. For Native Americans, this shocking news undercut moderate leaders willing to accommodate the English, and it strengthened the hand of pro-war factions.

Word that a treaty in far-off Paris might disrupt the entire region drew attention to Neolin, a Delaware Indian prophet urging a return to ancient ways and a sharp separation from the corrupting Europeans. Neolin's vision of renewing independence by driving out the British appealed to many Native Americans in the Midwest including Pontiac, a militant Ottawa warrior. In April, Pontiac addressed a secret council of more than 400 Ottawa, Potawatomie, and Huron, meeting within 10 miles of Fort Detroit. Invoking the Delaware Prophet's vision, he announced that the Master of Life resented the British and wanted them removed: "Send them back to the lands which I have created for them and let them stay there." By May, Pontiac had mobilized a coalition and laid siege to Detroit.

Soon Indians from eighteen nations had joined in Pontiac's widespread uprising. By mid-June 1763, both Detroit and Fort Pitt were under siege, and the British had lost every other Ohio Valley and Great Lakes outpost. As Indian raiding parties ravaged white communities in western Virginia and Pennsylvania, embittered settlers responded with racial killing. In December, white men from Paxton Creek descended on Christian families of Conestoga Indians near Lancaster, Pennsylvania, executing more than thirty peaceful converts. When easterners protested this outrage, the "Paxton Boys" marched on Philadelphia to demand increased protection on the frontier. General Amherst ordered his officers to spread smallpox if possible, and to take no prisoners. The Indians deserved extermination, he ranted, "for the good of mankind."

The violence ended in a stalemate. Without French support, Native American munitions ran short, and Detroit and Fort Pitt endured. Indian militancy waned, and Pontiac was killed by a Peoria Indian in 1765. Still, the uprising proved costly for the British and prompted a shift in policy. To avoid further expensive warfare, officials moved to restore the Indian trade, keep squatters and debt evaders out of Indian country, and prevent colonial speculation in western lands. In October 1763, Major General Thomas Gage replaced Amherst in command of British forces.

In England, the crown went further. Late in 1763, it issued a proclamation forbidding colonial settlers from moving west across the Appalachian summit. Beyond that dividing line, all the land east of the Mississippi River valley would be reserved for Indians and a few authorized British soldiers and traders. While the Proclamation Line of 1763, drawn along the crest of the Appalachians, had only limited success, it frustrated Virginia's gentry. Such prominent men as George Washington and Thomas Jefferson were investors in land companies that speculated in large western tracts, hoping to obtain property cheaply from Native Americans and sell small parcels to eager settlers at a steady profit. But the British government, fearful of sparking unified Indian opposition and additional warfare, denied the Virginians' wishes and aroused their resentment.

Grenville's Effort at Reform

In 1763 King George III appointed Robert Grenville to head a new government in London. Grenville's ministry immediately faced a series of intertwined problems. Britain's victory over the French in the Seven Years' War had proved costly, nearly doubling the national debt to a staggering £146 million. As England's postwar depression deepened, returning soldiers swelled the ranks of the unemployed. In addition, rural mobs protested a new tax on domestic cider, imposed to help whittle away at the war debt.

No one promoted opposition to the government more than John Wilkes, a flamboyant member of Parliament (MP) who published the *North Briton*, an outspoken periodical which attacked the king's peace settlement with France and the king himself. Grenville reacted by arresting the publisher, despite his status as an MP. Angered by government suppression of dissent, protesters made "Wilkes and Liberty!" a popular rallying cry.

Pressured at home, Grenville set out to impose order on Britain's growing American colonies through a series of reforms. The first step was to maintain a considerable military presence of nearly 7,000 troops in North America. The move would protect newly acquired territories while keeping young British men employed overseas rather than jobless at home. Strapped for funds, Grenville hoped to pay for the transatlantic forces with money drawn from the very colonies the troops were defending.

Raising money in this way would remind the British colonies of their subordination to the sovereign power of Parliament. Colonists had grown wealthy by sidestepping the elaborate Navigation Acts and trading illegally with foreign powers, even during wartime. Sympathetic colonial juries had looked the other way. Worse, American legislatures had used their power of the purse to withhold money from any British governor who did not favor local interests. Finally, lax customs officers assigned to colonial ports often collected their salaries while remaining in England, without even occupying their posts.

As a preliminary step, Grenville ordered absentee customs officials to their colonial stations and dispatched forty-four navy ships to assist them. Next, he moved his first reform through Parliament: the American Duties Act of 1764, also known as the Sugar Act. The new revenue law increased the duty on sugar and various other products entering the empire from non-British ports, and it cut in half the import duty of sixpence per gallon on foreign molasses. Officials hoped that New England rum distillers, who had been secretly importing cheap molasses from the French West Indies without paying customs, would be willing to pay threepence per gallon. If enforced, the act would reduce smuggling and boost revenues while saving merchants from the heavy costs of bribing port officials.

To ensure compliance, the Sugar Act strengthened the customs officers' authority to seize goods off arriving ships, and it established the first of several vice-admiralty courts. The court sat at Halifax, Nova Scotia, so defendants had large travel expenses, and they faced a single appointed judge instead of a favorable local jury. "What has America done," protested critics, "to be stripped of so invaluable a privilege as the trial by jury?"

> *"What has America done," protested critics, "to be stripped of so invaluable a privilege as the trial by jury?"*

Additional statutes followed quickly. The Currency Act of 1764 prohibited colonial assemblies from issuing paper money or bills of credit to be used as legal tender to pay off debts. The move only worsened the money shortage in British America, where a lopsided trade balance was already draining gold and silver from the colonies to England. Colonial merchants had to pay Grenville's new duties using scarce hard money.

The next year Parliament passed a Quartering Act that obliged colonists to assist the army by allowing soldiers to use vacant barns and other buildings as temporary quarters. The local governor was to supply the soldiers, at colonial expense, with certain basic necessities they would expect at any inn: firewood, candles, bedding, salt, vinegar, utensils, and rations of beer and cider. Colonial assemblies had willingly voted such support during colonial wars. However, these peacetime requisitions, ordered by a distant Parliament, seemed to challenge their authority and smacked of indirect taxation.

DOCUMENT

Otis, "The Rights of the British Colonies Asserted and Proved"

The Stamp Act Imposed

There was nothing indirect about Grenville's most important reform: the Stamp Act. Early in 1765, Parliament approved the new statute "for raising a further revenue" to pay for "defending, protecting, and securing" the British colonies in America. The new act was patterned on a similar law in England, and it required stamps (like those on modern packs of cigarettes) to appear on a variety of articles in America after November 1, 1765. The list included legal contracts, land deeds, liquor licenses, indentures, newspapers, almanacs, and playing cards. Colonial lawyers and printers were to purchase these stamps from designated agents; the official stamp distributor in each colony would receive a handsome fee from all stamp sales. The British treasury anticipated taking in £100,000 per year, to be spent only for government operations in America.

Stamp Act
Stamps

Grenville's stamp bill generated little debate in England. Granted, colonists had no actual representation in the Parliament, but neither did the majority of subjects in England. Most of them did not have the right to vote, yet all were said to be "virtually" represented by MPs, who supposedly had the interests of the entire country at heart. If members of Parliament looked out for nonvoting subjects at home, surely they could provide the same sort of "virtual representation" for British subjects throughout the realm.

Whether or not they spoke for colonists in America, most MPs viewed Grenville's stamp measure as appropriate and well conceived. They saw no legal distinction between external duties used to regulate trade and internal taxes imposed by Parliament within the colonies themselves to raise revenue. Because the stamp tax applied to daily articles used throughout the colonies, it would be widely and evenly distributed. Even better, revenues would grow steadily and automatically as colonial economic activity continued to expand.

So as not to cause alarm in the colonies, Parliament set initial stamp prices in America lower than those charged in England, although it could always raise the rates as colonists grew accustomed to the tax. Moreover, the tax was to be gathered quietly by Americans themselves in the course of doing business rather than extracted from citizens by tax collectors. Prominent colonists were eager to accept the lucrative stamp distributorships, and no one predicted an upheaval. But the Stamp Act soon unleashed a storm of organized resistance in ports where the stamps were to be sold.

The Stamp Act Resisted

At first, colonial assemblies had mixed responses to the burdensome new tax. But in late May, the youngest member of the Virginia House of Burgesses—a rising country attorney named Patrick Henry—galvanized American resistance to the Stamp Act. As the House session was winding down, Henry introduced a series of fiery resolves challenging Parliament's right to impose taxes. The twenty-eight-year-old orator managed to gain narrow passage of five separate resolutions.

Henry's fifth and most provocative resolve asserted that Virginia's assembly had the "sole exclusive right and power to lay taxes" on the colony's inhabitants. The resolution passed by just one vote. In fact, opponents reintroduced it the next day, after Henry left town, and voted it down. But the spark had been struck. Distant newspapers were soon reprinting Henry's "Virginia Resolves," including the resolution that had been voted down plus two that had been drawn up but never introduced for a vote. These provocative draft resolutions said that Virginians were "not bound to yield obedience" to such a tax, and anyone arguing otherwise must "be deemed an enemy" to the colony.

In Massachusetts, the assembly took a different approach. It issued a call for each colony to send delegates to a Stamp Act Congress in New York in October 1765 to "implore relief" from Parliament. Local citizens, inflamed by Virginia's resolutions and squeezed by an economic depression, prepared to take more direct action. In Boston, a small group of artisans and merchants known as the Loyal Nine mobilized to force the designated stamp distributor,

1765 Stamp Act
Protest

Library of Congress

■ Lawyers and artisans in the Sons of Liberty encouraged demonstrations against the Stamp Act. But they ran the risk, suggested here, that poor workers, black slaves, and women in the crowds might give their own meanings to the shouts of "Liberty!"

DOCUMENT

Franklin, Testimony Against the Stamp Act

Andrew Oliver, to resign before the stamps arrived from England. On August 16, a crowd of several thousand hanged an effigy of Oliver and tore down his Stamp Office. The protesters ransacked Oliver's elegant house, drinking his wine and smashing his furniture. The next day, Oliver resigned his appointment.

As word of the protest spread, crowds took to the streets in scores of towns. Often the mobs were encouraged by local leaders who opposed the Stamp Act. These prominent citizens had started to organize themselves in secret groups, which they called the Sons of Liberty. The crowds forced the resignation of potential stamp distributors in ports from New Hampshire to the Carolinas. When a shipment of stamps finally arrived in New York City, nearly 5,000 people risked open warfare to confiscate the hated cargo.

Throughout the second half of 1765, the Sons of Liberty promoted street violence against specific targets. But they could not always control the demonstrations, since the debtors, sailors, blacks, and women drawn to such crowds all had separate grievances of their own. For example, on August 26 in Boston, just ten days after the raid on Oliver's house, a second mob launched a broader assault. Without sanction from the Loyal Nine or the Sons of Liberty, the crowd went after the homes of several wealthy office holders, including the house of Lieutenant Governor Thomas Hutchinson. Because he also served as chief justice of the Superior Court, Hutchinson had offended townspeople by issuing numerous warrants for debtors and collecting large fees for administering bankruptcies. Hutchinson recounted how he fled when "the hellish crew fell upon my house with the Rage of devils and . . . with axes split down the doors," pillaging his entire estate.

In South Carolina several months later, the spirit of insurrection also went well beyond the careful boundaries intended by the Sons of Liberty. They were pleased when Charleston artisans hanged a stamp distributor in effigy, with a sign reading, "Liberty and no Stamp Act." And they gave tacit approval when white workers harassed the wealthy slave trader and potential stamp distributor Henry Laurens with chants of "Liberty, Liberty!" Soon, however, enslaved African Americans also took to the streets, raising their own defiant cry of "Liberty, Liberty!" Fearing an insurrection by South Carolina's black majority, the same people who had sanctioned earlier street demonstrations quickly shifted their focus, believing that ideas of freedom had spread too far. The colonial assembly temporarily banned further importation of Africans. Local leaders expanded slave patrols and placed Charleston briefly under martial law.

Elsewhere, too, the colonial elites took steps to contain the turbulence. Many moved—often reluctantly—toward more radical positions, joining the Sons of Liberty and ridiculing the British concept of virtual representation. Colonial assemblies condemned Grenville's intrusive reforms. The Stamp Act Congress passed resolutions vehemently protesting both the Sugar and Stamp acts. But even as they challenged Parliament, these same local leaders stressed their loyalty to the crown and moved to control the violence, some of which was directed at them. Such moderation appealed to cautious merchants in Atlantic seaports, who reluctantly agreed to stop ordering Britain goods. They hoped that exporters in Britain, feeling the economic pinch of a colonial boycott, might use their political strength to force a repeal of the Stamp Act and defuse the tense situation.

Hudson Bay
Company

Quebec

Three Rivers

Lake
Nipissing

Montreal

St. Lawrence R.

Nova Scotia

Halifax

ME
(part of Mass.)

Annapolis
Royal

Ft. Edward Augustus,
abandoned June 15, 1763

Ft. Michilimackinac,
June 2, 1763

Ft. Niagara

NH

Portsmouth
Windham   Salem
                       Marblehead
Albany   Lebanon   Boston
           Hartford   MA Pomfret
NY   Wethersfield   Plymouth
           Wallingford   RI
           New Haven CT Newport
Ft. Presque Isle,   West Haven   Norwich
June 14–17, 1763   Milford Lyme New London
                                         Stratford
Ft. Detroit   PA   Woodbridge Fairfield
                              Paxton Piscataway New York
Ft. Venango,   Amwell Twp. Elizabeth Town
June 13, 1763   Perth Amboy
Ft. St. Joseph,   Ft. Le Boeuf,   Brunswick
May 25, 1763   June 18, 1763 Lancaster NJ Philadelphia
        Ft. Sandusky, Ft. Pitt Conestoga Salem
        May 16, 1763
                            Baltimore
Ft. Miami,   Frederick Town Elk Ridge Landing
May 27, 1763   Annapolis Talbot DE
                              Dumfries Lewes
Ft. Ouiatenon,   MD
May 31, 1763
                              Leeds
                              Tappahannock
                       VA
Ft. Chartres   Williamsburg
                              Norfolk

Indian
reserve
(by proclamation 1763)

Spanish
Louisiana

Mississippi R.

NC

Cross Creek   New Bern
        Duplin

ATLANTIC
OCEAN

Wilmington
Brunswick
        Fort Johnson

SC

Proclamation Line 1763

GA   Charleston

Savannah

Boundary after 1764

West Florida

Boundary in 1763

Mobile
New Orleans
        Pensacola

Ft. Apalachee

St. Mary's R.

St. Augustine

East
Florida

Gulf of
Mexico

British dominance in eastern North America

- Acquired by Britain from France
- Acquired by Britain from Spain
- Prior British colonies, as of 1763
- Reserved to Indians under British rule
- Spanish Louisiana

Points of violence, 1763–1766

- British forts seized during Pontiac's Rebellion in 1763
- Towns demonstrating against the Stamp Act in 1765

Distribution of British troops

- British posts 100–250 soldiers
- British posts 250–600 soldiers
- British posts over 600 soldiers

■ MAP 6.2
BRITISH NORTH AMERICA, 1763–1766   In 1763 the British
worked to govern their new provinces in Canada and Florida while
suppressing an Indian uprising in the Midwest. With widely
dispersed troops, they also tried to keep colonists out of the
Mississippi Valley and halt opposition to the 1765 Stamp Act.

When politics in London prompted Grenville's sudden removal from office, hopes rose in America for a possible compromise resolving the Stamp Act crisis. In March 1766, these hopes were nearly fulfilled. The new ministry of Lord Rockingham, responding to merchant pressure as predicted, and also to the compelling rhetoric of William Pitt, persuaded Parliament to repeal the Stamp Act. But colonial victory had a hollow ring to it, for the repeal bill was accompanied by a blunt Declaratory Act. In it, the members of Parliament declared clearly that they reaffirmed their power "to make Laws . . . to bind the Colonists and People of America . . . in all Cases whatsoever."

"The Unconquerable Rage of the People"

As news of the Stamp Act repeal spread, the Sons of Liberty organized elaborate celebrations in British America. But word of the Declaratory Act had a sobering effect. Clearly, the problems surrounding colonial taxation and representation remained unresolved. The atmosphere of mutual suspicion and righteous indignation that had erupted during the Stamp Act crisis divided colonists further in the years ahead.

A flurry of pamphlets from colonial presses broadened awareness of the issues, sharpened arguments, and inspired new coalitions. As colonial leaders collaborated, they discovered a shared viewpoint that gave added meaning and importance to each new event. This emerging ideology had deep roots stretching back into English history.

Power Corrupts: An English Framework for Revolution

The radical ideas that had appeared during England's Civil War in the 1640s, when English subjects briefly overthrew their monarchy and proclaimed a Puritan Commonwealth, lived on long after the Restoration in 1660. English Whigs who led the Glorious Revolution in 1688 invoked some of these principles when they limited the monarchy's power and strengthened Parliament's authority. Succeeding generations hailed the rights of English subjects and congratulated themselves that Great Britain (as England and Scotland became known in 1707) had achieved a truly balanced government. They drew on the ancient Greek philosopher Aristotle to explain their accomplishment.

DOCUMENT

Magna Carta

Aristotle, his modern readers noted, had observed a cycle in politics. He believed that too much power vested in a king could eventually corrupt the monarchical form of government. Unbounded royal power led to a tyranny, misrule by a despot wielding absolute control. When nobles then asserted themselves against the tyrant (as English barons had done when they forced King John to sign the Magna Carta in 1215), the resulting aristocracy could easily turn corrupt. Abuse of power by such an oligarchy of self-serving nobles could then prompt the common people, known as the commons, to rise up. If the commons gained sway, they might build a democracy, but it too could degenerate, leaving only anarchy. Such a "mobocracy" paved the way for an opportunistic leader to once more seize the scepter of royal power and start the cycle over again.

Confident Whigs claimed that England had halted this vicious cycle by balancing the power of the nation's three estates: the king epitomized the legitimate interests of monarchy, the House of Lords represented the aristocracy, and the House of Commons represented the rest of the population. However, a few of the more radical Whig theorists continued to oppose this consensus view long after 1700. Calling themselves the Real Whigs, these skeptics charged that the existing mixed government—which claimed an ideal and lasting balance between monarchy, aristocracy, and commons—was actually less perfect and more vulnerable than most people suspected.

A truly balanced government, they argued, is hard to achieve and difficult to maintain, for power inevitably corrupts. Schemers who obtain public office can readily disrupt such a fragile system, so its protection, these critics stressed, demanded constant vigilance. They urged citizens to watch for the two surest signs of decay: the concentration of wealth in a few hands and the political and social corruption that inevitably follows. Where others saw stability in England's exuberant growth, these Real Whigs perceived sure signs of danger in the powerful new Bank of England, the expanding stock market, and the rise in public debt.

No Real Whigs proved more vigilant than John Trenchard and Thomas Gordon. The two men sensed around them the same luxury and greed that had undermined the Roman Republic. They pored over the works of ancient writers such as the Roman statesman Cato, who described and challenged corrupt behavior. In 1721 they published their own *Cato's Letters: Essays on Liberty*, cautioning against "the Natural Encroachments of Power" and warning that "public corruptions and abuses have grown upon us."

Trenchard and Gordon took special offense at Britain's corrupt patronage system. Public positions seemed designed to reward loyal support, and too many people appeared to gain a post (often in the colonies) through political ties rather than through skill or training. The authors of *Cato's Letters* saw each individual act of corruption as representing a dangerous precedent, if unopposed. They reminded their readers that tyranny is usually imposed through small, subtle steps, for "if it is suffered once, it is apt to be repeated often; a few repetitions create a habit." Before citizens realize that they are losing their liberties, the permanent "Yoke of Servitude" is in place, supported by military force. All hope of successful protest has disappeared. The encroachment of power over liberty, Trenchard and Gordon concluded, is "much easier to prevent than to cure."

Americans Practice Vigilance and Restraint

Though these writers attracted only limited attention in England, they earned a wide American following. The popularity of *Cato's Letters* and related tracts continued to spread in the colonies during the 1760s, for colonists saw disturbing parallels between the warnings of Real Whig authors and current events in America. Now, as throughout history, a government tainted by corruption might deny adequate representation, initiate unjust taxes, or replace jury trials with arbitrary courts. Officials might curtail freedoms of press or religion to consolidate their power. Moreover, weak ministers might advise the king poorly or keep citizens' pleas from reaching his ears. If the populace relaxed its guard, these ministers might even sanction a standing army in peacetime to impose arbitrary rule over their own population.

> *During the 1760s, colonists saw disturbing parallels between the warnings of Real Whig authors and current events in America.*

According to Real Whig doctrine, ordinary people must be alert but circumspect; a measured response to threats was all-important. One stubborn or mistaken act by officials did not prove a pattern of conspiracy, and it could be counterproductive to raise alarms too often. So prudent citizens should turn first to legal methods of **redress**. If the system was functioning properly, claims of real abuses would bring forth proper corrections. Even if forced to take to the streets as a last resort, crowds should be organized and purposeful, not uncontrolled. They should threaten property before people and hang effigies, not actual office holders.

For the most part, the Stamp Act demonstrations had followed this logic of restraint and had gained the desired effect. "In every Colony," wrote John Adams, "the Stamp Distributors and Inspectors have been compelled, by the unconquerable Rage of the People, to renounce their offices." But did individual demands for liberty have limits? Could slaves seek liberty from their masters? What about wives from husbands? Could tenants press for redress from rich landlords, or debtors from powerful creditors? Such questions generated widespread, heated debate in the turbulent quarter-century ahead.

Rural Unrest: Tenant Farmers and Regulators

For colonists, certain events in Europe after 1765 seemed to confirm the views that the Real Whigs had passed down. When John Wilkes was repeatedly elected to Parliament but expelled from the Commons for his radical views, his American supporters rallied on his behalf. Similarly, British colonists embraced the short-lived cause of Pasquale Paoli, who fought to free the Mediterranean island of Corsica from domination by Genoa. Many colonists christened their sons after Wilkes or Paoli, and Pennsylvanians named new towns after these overseas heroes. The two men seemed to embody the universal struggle of liberty against tyranny—a contest that often flared up closer to home as well.

In local controversies, both large and small, the "Rage of the People" frequently boiled up from below. "The People, even to the lowest Ranks, have become more attentive to their Liberties," John Adams observed, "and more determined to defend them." While stamp protesters demonstrated in New York City, aggrieved tenant farmers staged a violent revolt against powerful landholders in the Hudson River valley. They chose an Irish immigrant as their leader, established a council, organized militia companies with elected captains, and broke open jails to free debtors. They even set up their own peoaple's courts to try captured Hudson Valley gentry, before British troops finally suppressed the revolt.

Unrest also shook the Carolinas in the interior region known to colonists as the backcountry, or the Piedmont. In South Carolina, the absence of civil government beyond the coastal parishes fostered lawlessness among white settlers until the governor extended circuit courts into the interior in 1769. In North Carolina, migrants seeking fertile land moved south from Virginia and Pennsylvania in a steady stream. When they arrived in the Piedmont, they found a local elite already appointed to county posts by the governor. The newcomers disliked these grasping office holders who possessed strong family and financial ties to powerful planters and merchants farther east. They seemed to epitomize, at the local level, the sorts of corruption that had long troubled Real Whig pamphleteers.

As backcountry settlers grew in numbers, they protested against their inadequate representation in the colonial assembly. They began organizing into local groups to better "regulate" their own affairs, and they soon became known as Regulators. These small farmers, many in debt, protested loudly against regressive taxes that imposed the same burden on all colonists, regardless of their wealth. The Regulators' discontent turned into outrage when coastal planters who dominated the assembly voted public funds to build a stately mansion in New Bern for William Tryon, the colonial governor. By this act, the eastern slaveholding elite hoped to establish North Carolina's permanent capitol building on the coast, and yet Piedmont farmers would bear most of the cost of constructing the mansion.

The decision to erect "Tryon's Palace" at public expense confirmed backcountry suspicions that the governor and his associates were looking out for their own interests at the expense of the public. Both sides dug in their heels. In 1771 Governor Tryon finally called out the militia and marched into the Piedmont. After defeating several thousand angry farmers at the battle of Alamance in May 1771, Tryon hanged six Regulator leaders in Hillsborough and forced backcountry residents to swear an oath of loyalty. Many refused, migrating farther south to Georgia or west to the Appalachian Mountains. Their leader, a Quaker named Herman Husband, barely escaped with his life. In North Carolina, just as in the Hudson Valley, well-to-do members of the Sons of Liberty dismissed the organized and militant farmers as misguided rabble.

"Squez'd and Oppressed": A 1768 Petition by 30 Regulators

Photo courtesy of Tryon Palace Historic Sites & Gardens

In 1768 the creation of Tryon's Palace, a mansion for the North Carolina governor at New Bern, prompted backcountry protests. Irate farm families, feeling heavily taxed and poorly represented, joined the Regulator Movement. They filed petitions, withheld taxes, closed courts, and harassed corrupt officials, protesting the "unequal chances the poor and weak have in contentions with the rich and powerful."

In the 1760s, corruption prevailed among appointed officials in central North Carolina. Often holding numerous offices at once, these men managed elections, controlled courts, and gathered taxes. Apparently not all the tax money they collected made it to the public treasury. Nevertheless, any farmer who resisted paying might lose the plow horse or the milk cow that sustained the family. It could be "seized and sold" to cover a small tax payment or minor debt, with "no Part being ever Return'd" from the proceeds.

Banding together to better regulate their own affairs, these farmers sought relief through every possible legal means. By 1768 these organized Regulators had exhausted most avenues of peaceful protest. The western counties where they resided were badly underrepresented in the colonial assembly. As a new session prepared to convene, they fired off a final round of petitions, assuring legislators that they were law-abiding citizens willing to pay their legal share of taxes. In this message of October 4, 1768, thirty Regulators begged for the appointment of honest public officials.

To the Worshipful House of Representatives of North Carolina

Your Poor Petitioners [have] been Continually Squez'd and oppressed by our Publick Officers both with Regard to their fees as also in the Laying on of Taxes as well as in Collecting. . . . Being Grieved thus to have our substance torn from us [by]…such Illegal practices, we applied to our public officers to give us some satisfaction…which they Repeatedly denied us.

With Regard to the Taxes,…we labour under Extreem hardships. . . . Money is very scarce…& we exceeding Poor & lie at a great distance from Trade which renders it almost Impossible to gain sustenance by our utmost Endeavours….

To Gentlemen Rowling in affluence, a few shillings per man may seem trifling. Yet to Poor People who must have their Bed and Bedclothes, yea their Wives Petticoats, taken and sold to Defray, how Tremenious [tremendous]…must be the Consequences….Therefore, dear Gentlemen, to your selves, to your Country, and in Pity to your Poor Petitioners, do not let it stand any longer to Drink up the Blood and vitals of the Poor Distressed.

After seeking relief from existing taxes, the petitioners went on to question new burdens, such as the law imposing an additional tax "to Erect a Publick Edifice" for Governor Tryon in New Bern.

Good God, Gentlemen, what will become of us when these Demands come against us? Paper Money we have none & gold or silver we can Purchase none of. The Contingencies of Government Must be Paid, and…we are Willing to Pay, [even] if we [must] sell our Beds from under us. And [yet] in this Time of Distress, it is as much as we can support….If, therefore, the Law for that Purpose can be happily Repealed,…May the God of Heaven Inspire you with sentiments to that Purpose.

We humble Begg you would…Use your Influence with our Worthy, Virtuous Governor to discontinue…such Officers as would be found to be ye Bane of Society, and [instead to] Put in the Common Wealth [officials willing] to Encourage the Poor and…to stand [up] for them. This would Cause Joy and Gladness to Spring from every Heart. This would cause Labour and Industry to prevail over Murmuring Discontent. This would Raise your poor Petitioners…to a flourishing Opulent and Hoping People. Otherwise…disatisfaction and Melancholy must Prevail over such as Remain, and Numbers must Defect the Province and seek elsewhere an Asylum from Tyranny and Oppression….

We leave it to you…in your great Wisdom…to pass such Act or Acts, as shall be Conducive to the welbeing of a whole People over Whose welfare ye are plac'd as Guardians. . . . For the Lords Sake, Gentlemen, Exert your selves this once in our favour.

Questions

1. *How, specifically, do the tone and content of this petition reflect the widespread political outlook, combining vigilance and restraint, described in Cato's Letters?*

2. *Pick some current issue that concerns you deeply and draft a brief, impassioned petition to your legislators. In compelling language, lay out your best arguments for action. Then see if 30 people will sign your petition.* ■

Source: William S. Powell, James K. Huhta, and Thomas J. Farnham, eds., *The Regulators of North Carolina: A Documentary History, 1759–1776* (Raleigh: State Department of Archives and History, 1971), pp. 187–189. Some corrections have been made for readability.

A Conspiracy of Corrupt Ministers?

Numerous sharp divisions—some leading to armed conflict—continued to separate colonists of different classes and regions. But ill-timed steps by successive administrations in London attracted widening attention throughout British America, prompting uneasy new alliances. Colonists familiar with the dire warnings of Real Whig pamphleteers asked themselves a question: in the weak and short-lived ministries that succeeded Grenville's, were the leaders simply ill-informed, or were they actively corrupt? Colonists wondered whether some official conspiracy existed to chip away at American liberties. Even loyal defenders of the crown expressed frustration with new policies that appeared too harsh to calm irate colonists, yet too weak to force them into line.

Parliament's first new imposition after repeal of the Stamp Act was the Revenue Act of 1766. The act offered an additional reduction in the molasses duty, from threepence per gallon to a single penny, to further discourage smuggling and raise revenue. Colonial merchants accepted this measure as an external tax designed to regulate imperial trade. They paid the new duty, and customs revenues rose. But Real Whigs reminded them that compliance with even the most innocuous measure could set a dangerous precedent.

The skeptics had a point, for Parliament soon imposed new hard-line measures. Before his sudden death in 1767, Charles Townshend, the Chancellor of the Exchequer (or chief finance minister) put these distasteful statutes in motion. Townshend's new duties sparked angry responses from colonists. The most telling came from John Dickinson, a moderate Philadelphia lawyer. He drafted a series of widely circulated "Letters from a Farmer in Pennsylvania," urging colonists to respond "peaceably—prudently—firmly—jointly." He dismissed any distinction between external and internal taxation, and he also rejected the idea that Americans had virtual representation in Parliament. "We are taxed without our own consent," Dickinson proclaimed to his readers. "We are therefore—SLAVES."

DOCUMENT

John Dickinson, "Letters…"

The Townshend Duties

In search of funds, Parliament passed the Townshend Revenue Act of 1767, which created new duties on colonial imports of glass, paint, lead, paper, and tea. Proceeds were to be spent in the colonies for "the administration of justice, and the support of civil government," a seemingly benevolent gesture. But Dickinson and other colonists pointed out what these two phrases actually meant. "The administration of justice" cloaked expanded searches of American homes and shops in which customs officers used hated "writs of assistance" to ferret out smuggled goods. "The support of civil government" ensured that governors and appointed office holders could draw their pay directly from the new duties instead of depending on an annual salary grant from the local assembly. In short, the new act removed from colonial legislatures one of their strongest bargaining tools in dealing with the crown: the power to pay or withhold yearly salaries for key officials sent from Britain.

Similar acts and instructions followed. Asserting its sovereignty, Parliament disciplined the New York Assembly for defying the Quartering Act of 1765. The crown instructed governors in America, now less dependent for their salaries on colonial lower houses, to disapprove any measures from legislatures asserting their traditional control over how members were chosen, what their numbers should be, and when they would meet. Equally galling, the Customs Act of 1767 established a separate Board of Customs for British North America. Ominously, the commissioners would live in Boston rather than London. To strengthen the board's hand, in 1768 Britain expanded the number of vice-admiralty courts in North America from one to four, adding new courts in Boston, Philadelphia, and Charleston. Furthermore, to look after its troublesome mainland colonies, the British government created a new American Department, overseen by Lord Hillsborough. It also began to move British troops in America from remote frontier outposts to major Atlantic ports, both as a cost-cutting measure and as a show of force.

Americans found these measures threatening, especially when considered as a whole. In February 1768, the Massachusetts legislature, led by forty-six-year-old Samuel Adams, petitioned the king for redress. The legislators circulated a call to other colonial assemblies for similar protests. Condemning the Townshend Revenue Act as unconstitutional, they argued that it imposed taxation without representation. By removing control of the governors' salaries from colonial legislatures, they said, Parliament set the dangerous precedent of making royal officials "independent of the people." Lord Hillsborough demanded an immediate retraction of this provocative "Circular Letter" and ordered the dissolution of any assembly that took up the matter.

In June, events in Boston took a more radical turn. Defying Hillsborough, the Massachusetts assembly voted against rescinding its circular letter. On June 5, a dockside crowd faced down a "press-gang" from a British warship and protected local sailors from being forced (or "pressed") into naval service. Five days later, customs officials seized John Hancock's sloop, *Liberty*, and demanded that he pay import duties for a cargo of Madeira wine. This move sparked a huge demonstration as citizens dragged a small customs boat through the streets and then burned it on Boston Common. Impatient Sam Adams was heard to say, "Let us take up arms immediately and be free."

AUDIO

"The Liberty Song"

Emotions ran high. But most leaders sensed that any escalation of the violence would be premature and perhaps suicidal. They reined in demonstrations and instead initiated a boycott of British goods. Nonimportation plans called upon colonists to refrain from imported luxuries and opt instead for virtuous self-sufficiency. The prospect of nonviolent resistance held broad appeal. As the nonimportation movement expanded, women of all ranks, self-proclaimed Daughters of Liberty, turned to making and selling homespun garments. Local associations sprang up, pledging to forgo imported tea and London fashions. A dozen colonial assemblies voted to halt importation of selected goods. In New York, the value of imports from Britain shrank from £491,000 to just £76,000 in a single year.

> *Impatient Sam Adams was heard to say, "Let us take up arms immediately and be free."*

IMAGE

Signing an Anti-Tea Agreement

The damage to English shipping proved substantial. Britain was losing far more revenue in colonial trade than it was gaining through the expanded customs duties. Soon influential British exporters were pressing their government for relief. When Baron Frederick North, who succeeded Townshend, established a new ministry in January 1770, he received the king's consent to work toward a better arrangement with the colonies. On March 5, 1770, Lord North persuaded Parliament to repeal all the Townshend Duties except the one on tea. The move defused the colonial boycott, but it offered too little too late. Like the earlier Declaratory Act, this measure reaffirmed Parliament's disputed right to tax the colonists at will. Moreover, it came on the exact day that violence and bloodshed were escalating in Boston.

The Boston Massacre

After the *Liberty* riot in June 1768, tensions had mounted in Boston, especially with the arrival in October of two regiments of British soldiers, well armed and dressed in their traditional red coats. According to Real Whig beliefs, any appearance by a standing army in peacetime constituted danger. Artisans in a sluggish economy welcomed the increased business that the men in uniform generated, but numerous unemployed workers resented the soldiers' "moonlighting," trying to earn extra pay by applying for local jobs. With 4,000 armed men encamped in a seaport of scarcely 16,000, confrontation seemed inevitable. Affairs "cannot long remain in the state they are now in," wrote one observer late in 1769; "they are hastening to a crisis. What will be the event, God knows."

DOCUMENT

Boston Gazette, Description of the Boston Massacre

In March 1770, protesters took to the streets after a run-in between local workers and job-seeking soldiers. Rumors spread about a larger confrontation, and on March 5, around 9 p.m.,

Library of Congress

■ In Paul Revere's image of the 1770 Boston Massacre, a moon lights up the night scene. British soldiers defend the hated customs house, which Revere labels clearly as "Butcher's Hall." The partisan engraving spread an anti-British view of the bloody event.

a crowd gathered outside the customs house. When a harassed sentry struck a boy with his rifle butt, angry witnesses pelted the guard with snowballs. As fellow soldiers pushed through the mob to assist him, firebells summoned more townspeople to the scene. The British loaded their rifles and aimed at the crowd, their bayonets fixed.

Into this tense standoff marched several dozen sailors, waving banners and brandishing clubs. Their leader was Crispus Attucks, an imposing ex-slave who stood 6 feet 2 inches. The son of a black man and an Indian woman, he had run away from his master and then taken up a life at sea. Damning the soldiers and daring them to fire, Attucks pressed his band of colonial sailors to the front, waving a long stick in the moonlight. In the mayhem, a British gun went off, prompting a volley of fire from the other soldiers. The crowd recoiled in disbelief at the sight of dead and wounded Americans lying in the street. According to a printed report, Attucks and four others had been "killed on the Spot." The anti-British cause had its first martyrs.

By grim coincidence, the bloody episode in New England occurred only hours after Lord North addressed the House of Commons to urge removal of most Townshend Duties. His effort at reconciliation immediately became lost in a wave of hostile publicity. Paul Revere, a Boston silversmith, captured the incident in an inflammatory engraving. The Sons of Liberty quickly named the event of March 5 the Boston Massacre. "On that night," John Adams remarked, "the foundation of American independence was laid."

The *Gaspee* Affair

The overzealous conduct of customs officers gave colonists further cause for distrust. In 1769, after crown agents confiscated John Hancock's vessel, the *Liberty*, and converted it into a customs vessel, citizens in Newport, Rhode Island, destroyed the sloop. In the Delaware River region, residents jailed a customs collector in 1770, and the next year local protesters stormed a customs schooner and beat up the crew. In June 1772, the *Gaspee*, another customs boat said to harass local shipping, ran aground near Pawtuxet, Rhode Island. In a midnight attack, more than a hundred raiders descended on the stranded schooner and set fire to the vessel.

The destruction of the *Gaspee* renewed sharp antagonisms. The irate Earl of Hillsborough, secretary of state for the American colonies, sent a royal commission from London to investigate and to transport suspects to England for trial. But many of the attackers, such as John Brown of Providence, came from important Rhode Island families. Even a £500 reward could not induce local inhabitants to name participants. Besides, many viewed the order to deport accused citizens to England as a denial of their fundamental right to trial by a jury of their peers.

When the colonists took action, Virginia's House of Burgesses again led the way, as it had in the Stamp Act crisis. In March 1773, Patrick Henry, Thomas Jefferson, and Richard Henry Lee pushed through a resolution establishing a standing committee to look into the *Gaspee* affair and to keep up "Correspondence and Communication with our sister colonies" regarding the protection of rights. Following Virginia's example, ten other colonial legislatures promptly established their own Committees of Correspondence. In Massachusetts, similar committees sprang up linking individual towns. Within months a new act of Parliament, designed to rescue the powerful East India Company from bankruptcy, gave these emerging communication networks their first test.

Launching a Revolution

In 1767, before Parliament imposed the Townshend Duties, Americans annually imported nearly 870,000 pounds of tea from England. But the boycott movement cut that amount to less than 110,000 pounds by 1770; colonists turned to smuggling Dutch blends and brewing homemade root teas. When nonimportation schemes lapsed in the early 1770s, purchase of English tea resumed, though a duty remained in effect. Encouraged by this apparent acceptance of parliamentary taxation, Lord North addressed the problem facing the East India Company, which owed a huge debt to the Bank of England and had 18 million pounds of unsold tea rotting in London warehouses. Many MPs held stock in the East India Company, so Parliament passed a law to assist the ailing establishment.

The Tempest over Tea

The Tea Act of 1773 let the struggling East India Company bypass the expensive requirement that merchants ship Asian tea through England on its way to colonial ports. Now they could send the product directly to the colonies or to foreign ports, without paying to unload, store, auction, and reload the heavy chests. Any warehouse tea destined for the colonies would have its English duty refunded. These steps would reduce retail prices and expand the tea market. They would also quietly confirm the right of Parliament to collect a tea tax of threepence per pound.

The company promptly chose prominent colonial merchants to receive and distribute more than 600,000 pounds of tea. These consignees would earn a hefty 6 percent commission. But wary colonists in port towns, sensing a repetition of 1765, renewed the tactics that had succeeded against the Stamp Act. Sons of Liberty vowed to prevent tea-laden ships from docking, and crowds pressured local distributors to renounce participation in the scheme. "If they succeed in the sale of that tea," proclaimed New York's Sons of Liberty, "then we may bid adieu to American liberty."

In Boston, where tea worth nearly £10,000 arrived aboard three ships in November, tension ran especially high. The credibility of Governor Thomas Hutchinson, who had taken a hard line toward imperial dissent, had suffered in June when Benjamin Franklin published private correspondence suggesting the governor's willingness to trim colonial rights. When Hutchinson's sons were named tea consignees, the appointments reinforced townspeople's suspicions. The governor could have signed papers letting the three vessels depart. But instead he decided to unload and distribute the tea, by force if necessary.

On December 16, the largest mass meeting of the decade took place at Boston's Old South Church. A crowd of 5,000, including many from other towns, waited in a cold rain to hear whether Hutchinson would relent. When word came that the governor had refused, the cry went up, "Boston Harbor a teapot tonight!" A band of 150 men, disguised as Mohawk Indians and carrying hatchets, marched to the docks and boarded the ships.

The Bostonians Paying the Excise-Man, or Tarring and Feathering (1774). Library of Congress

■ A 1774 London cartoon expressed anger that Boston's Sons of Liberty, defying British authority, could overturn the Stamp Act, tar and feather revenue agents, dump East India Company tea, and use their "Liberty Tree" to hang officials in effigy.

As several thousand supporters looked on, this disciplined crew spent three hours methodically breaking open chests of tea and dumping the contents overboard. The well-organized operation united participants representing all levels of society—from merchants such as John Hancock to artisans such as George Hewes—and news of the event spurred similar acts of defiance in other ports. Sixty years later, as one of the oldest veterans of the Revolution, Hewes still recalled with special pride his role in "the destruction of the tea."

The Intolerable Acts

"The crisis is come," wrote General Thomas Gage, commander of British forces in America, responding to the costly Tea Party in Boston Harbor; "the provinces must be either British colonies, or independent and separate states." Underestimating the strength of American resolve, Parliament agreed with King George III that only stern measures would reestablish "the obedience which a colony owes to its mother country." Between March and June 1774, it passed four so-called Coercive Acts to isolate and punish Massachusetts.

The first of the Coercive Acts, the Boston Port Act, used British naval strength to cut off the offending town's sea commerce—except for shipments of food and firewood—until the colonists paid for the ruined tea. By the Administration of Justice Act, revenue officials or soldiers charged with murder in Massachusetts (as in the Boston Massacre) could have their trials moved to another colony or to Great Britain. The Quartering Act gave officers more power to requisition living quarters and supplies for their troops throughout the colonies. Most important, the Massachusetts Government Act removed democratic elements from the long-standing Massachusetts Charter of 1691. From now on, the assembly could no longer elect the colony's Upper House, or Council. Instead, the governor would appoint council members, and he would even forbid town meetings unless he gave written permission.

Lord North's government went even further. It replaced Hutchinson with Gage, installing the general as the governor of Massachusetts and granting him special powers and three additional regiments. It also secured passage of the Quebec Act, new legislation to address nagging problems of governance in Canada after a decade of English rule. The act accommodated the Catholic faith and French legal traditions of Quebec's inhabitants. Moreover, it greatly expanded the size of the colony to draw scattered French settlers and traders under colonial government. Suddenly, Quebec took in the entire Great Lakes region and all the lands north of the Ohio River and east of the upper Mississippi River.

Expanding the province of Quebec to the Ohio River might extend British government to French wilderness outposts and help to regulate the Indian trade. But the move also challenged the western land claims of other American colonies. The Quebec Act appeared to favor French Catholics and Ohio Valley Indians—both recent enemies of the crown—over loyal English colonists. Resentment ran especially high in New England, where Protestants had long associated Catholicism with despotism. The Quebec Act, which denied the former French province a representative assembly and jury trials in civil cases, set an ominous precedent for neighboring colonies.

The Coercive Acts and the Quebec Act—lumped together by colonial propagandists as the Intolerable Acts—brought on open rebellion against crown rule. Competing pamphlets debated the proper limits of dissent. In *A Summary View of the Rights of British America*, Thomas Jefferson went beyond criticisms of Parliament to question the king's right to dispense land, control trade, and impose troops in America. Within months, Massachusetts called for a congress of all the colonies and established its own Provincial Congress at Concord, a village 17 miles west of Boston. Out of reach of British naval power, this **de facto** Massachusetts government reorganized the militia into units loyal to its own Committee of Public Safety. These farmer-soldiers became known as Minutemen for their quick response to Gage's repeated efforts to capture patriot gunpowder supplies.

Hudson Bay Company

Lake Nipissing

Quebec

Ft. Michilimackinac

Ft. Niagara

Ft. Detroit

Three Rivers

Quebec

Montreal

St. Lawrence R.

NH

Concord · Lexington
Woodstock · MA · Marshfield
New Haven · CT · RI
Fairfield
New York

NY

ME
(part of Mass.)

PA

NJ

MD

DE

Baltimore
Alexandria
Fredericksburg
King William
Williamsburg
Chowan
Edenton

VA

Alamance · Hillsborough
New Bern
Onslow

NC

Wilmington

SC

GA

Kaskaskia

Indian Reserve

Spanish Louisiana

Mississippi R.

West Florida

Mobile
Pensacola

St. Mary's R.

East Florida

St. Augustine

Gulf of Mexico

ATLANTIC OCEAN

Boundary by Carleton's commission 1774

Boundary of Quebec Act 1774

Nova Scotia

44°30′
43°15′
41°
40°30′
36°15′

HALIFAX, Regional Vice-Admiralty Court for everything above 43 degrees, 15 minutes

BOSTON, Regional Vice-Admiralty Court for everything between 44 degrees, and 40 degrees 30 minutes

PHILADELPHIA, Regional Vice-Admiralty Court for everything between 41 degrees, and 36 degrees 15 minutes

CHARLESTON, Regional Vice-Admiralty Court for everything below 36 degrees, 15 minutes

N

British dominance in eastern North America

- British-ruled providence of Quebec, 1774
- Boundary set by Quebec Act of 1774
- British-ruled providence of East Florida
- British-ruled providence of West Florida
- Reserved to Indians under British Rule
- Spanish Louisiana
- Major battles

Distribution of British troops

- British posts 100–300 soldiers
- British posts 300–500 soldiers
- British post 4,800 soldiers

The spread of news concerning the battles of Lexington and Concord, April 19, 1775

- Within 1–7 days
- Within 8–14 days
- More than 14 days

■ **MAP 6.3**
BRITISH NORTH AMERICA, APRIL 1775   Rising colonial unrest brought strong countermeasures. The British government organized regional vice-admiralty courts to punish smugglers; it greatly expanded Quebec in 1774; and it reallocated troops to the Boston area. When warfare erupted there in April 1775, the news spread throughout the colonies within weeks.

From Words to Action

While Massachusetts chafed under new restrictions, shifting coalitions in each colony, ranging from conservative to radical, vied for local political control. Extralegal committees, existing outside the authorized structure of colonial government, took power in hundreds of hamlets. In Edenton, North Carolina, fifty-one women signed a pact to abstain from using imported products for the "publick good." London cartoonists mocked the action as the "Edenton Ladies' Tea Party," but women in other colonies made similar agreements to boycott British tea and textiles. During the summer, all colonies except Georgia selected representatives to the First Continental Congress.

In September 1774, fifty-six delegates convened at Carpenters Hall in Philadelphia. Most had never met before, and they disagreed sharply over how to respond to the Intolerable Acts. Joseph Galloway, a wealthy lawyer and land speculator from Pennsylvania, urged a compromise with Britain modeled on the Albany Congress of 1754. His plan called for the creation of a separate American parliament, a grand council with delegates elected by the colonial legislatures. The less conservative delegates opposed this idea for a colonial federation, under a president-general appointed by the king. Led by Patrick Henry of Virginia, they managed to table the Galloway Plan by a narrow vote.

When Paul Revere arrived from Boston on October 6, bearing a set of militant resolves passed in his own Suffolk County, further rifts appeared. Moderates from the South expressed sympathy for Massachusetts but still resisted calls for a nonexportation scheme that would withhold southern tobacco, rice, and indigo from Great Britain. By the time the Congress adjourned in late October, it had issued a Declaration of Rights and passed a range of measures that seemed to balance competing views. On one hand, the Congress endorsed the fiery Suffolk Resolves, which condemned Parliament's Coercive Acts as unconstitutional and spoke of preparation for war. On the other, it humbly petitioned the king for relief from the crisis and professed continued loyalty. But in practical terms, Galloway and the more conservative members had suffered defeat. Most importantly, the delegates signed an agreement to prohibit British imports and halt all exports to Britain except rice. They called for local committees to enforce this so-called Association, and they set a date—May 10, 1775—for a Second Congress.

Before delegates could meet again in Philadelphia, the controversy that had smoldered for more than a decade on both sides of the Atlantic erupted into open combat. Predictably, the explosion took place in Massachusetts, where General Gage had received secret orders to arrest the leaders of the Massachusetts Provincial Congress and regain the upper hand before the strained situation grew worse. He was to use force, even if it meant the outbreak of warfare.

DOCUMENT

"Give Me Liberty or Give Me Death"

■ The shots fired at dawn by British troops, dispersing local militia from Lexington's town green, were the opening volley of the American Revolution. Amos Doolittle, a Connecticut soldier who responded to the alarm, later depicted the events of April 19, 1775. The date is still honored in New England as Patriots' Day.

On April 18, Gage ordered 700 elite troops from Boston to row across the Charles River at night, march 10 miles to Lexington, and seize John Hancock and Sam Adams. Next, the soldiers were to proceed 7 miles to Concord to capture a stockpile of military supplies. Alerted by signal lanterns, express riders Paul Revere and William Dawes eluded British patrols and spurred their horses toward Lexington along separate routes to warn Hancock and Adams. Bells and alarm guns spread the word that the British were coming. By the time the British soldiers reached Lexington, shortly before sunrise, some seventy militiamen had assembled on the town green. When the villagers refused to lay down their arms, the redcoats dispersed them in a brief skirmish that left eight militiamen dead.

DOCUMENT

Warren, "Account of the Battle of Lexington"

The British column trudged west to Concord and searched the town for munitions. Four hundred Minutemen who had streamed in from neighboring communities advanced on the town in double file, with orders not to shoot unless the British fired first. At the small bridge over the Concord River, British regulars opened fire. "The shot heard 'round the world" killed two men. The Americans loosed a volley in return, killing three. By noon, exhausted British forces were retreating toward Boston in disarray. The redcoats made easy targets for the more than 1,000 Americans who shot at them from behind stone walls. A relief party prevented annihilation, but the British suffered severe losses: seventy-three killed and 200 wounded or missing. The Americans, with only forty-nine dead, had turned the tables on General Gage, transforming an aggressive raid into a punishing defeat.

Conclusion

For Britain, festering administrative problems in America had suddenly become a military emergency. A decade of assertive but inconsistent British policies had transformed the colonists' sense of good will toward London into angry feelings of persecution and betrayal. The years of incessant argument and misunderstanding reminded many, on both sides of the Atlantic, of watching a stable, prosperous household unravel into mutual recrimination. A once-healthy family was becoming increasingly dysfunctional and troubled. The assertive children grew steadily in strength; the aging parents chafed at their diminished respect. Predictably, authorities in London found the once-dependent colonists to be ungrateful, intemperate, and occasionally paranoid. With equal assurance, the American subjects saw Parliament, government ministers, and eventually the king himself as uninformed, selfish, and even deceitful.

Britain's overseas empire, which had expanded steadily for two centuries, now seemed on the verge of splitting apart. As the limits of imperial control in North America became more evident, colonists worked to overcome the regional and ethnic differences that had long been a fact of eighteenth-century life. Political independence no longer seemed implausible. With effort, class hostilities and urban-rural divisions could also be overcome. Redirecting old local resentments toward the British crown could increase a sense of unity among people with different personal backgrounds and resources.

Nor would British colonists be alone if they mounted a rebellion. On one hand, they could make the unlikely choice of liberating half a million slaves, empowering colonial women, and embracing the anti-British cause of Pontiac and numerous Native Americans. Such revolutionary moves would increase their strength dramatically in one direction. On the other hand, they could also take a more cautious and less democratic route. If men of substance could gain control of the forces that were being unleashed, they might curb potential idealism among slaves, women, tenant farmers, and the urban poor, giving precedence instead to policies that would win vital support from the continent of Europe in an American fight for independence. France, recently evicted from North America, and Spain, anxious about British designs in the Pacific, might both be willing allies, despite their commitment to monarchy. Such an alliance, if it ever came about, could push the limits of British imperial control to the breaking point.

Sites to Visit

Anza-Borrego Desert State Park
http://anza.uoregon.edu

This isolated and beautiful state park covers 600,000 acres 80 miles east of San Diego, California. The Web site, which focuses on the exploration of Alta, California, 1774–1776, contains maps, resources, and documents in both English and Spanish concerning Juan Bautista de Anza's two overland expeditions.

Museums in Alaska

Located near the ferry landing in Kodiak, Alaska, the Baranov Museum is housed in one of the few remaining structures from the Russian colonial era. In Fairbanks, the University of Alaska's impressive Museum of the North has added a new wing. The Anchorage Museum of History and Art contains an Alaska Gallery.

Fort Ross State Historic Park

This reconstruction of the outpost built by the Russians on the northern California coast in the early nineteenth century is located on a scenic bluff 11 miles northwest of the town of Jenner on Highway 1, about a two-hour drive from San Francisco.

Pontiac Marker

In 1977 Michigan placed a marker concerning Pontiac on a building at 3321 East Jefferson Avenue, near the Renaissance Center in downtown Detroit. It commemorates the Battle of Bloody Run, in July 1763, which marked the height of Pontiac's siege of Detroit. The city of Pontiac, named for the Ottawa leader, lies 25 miles northwest.

Boston's Freedom Trail
http://www.nps.gov/bost/freedom_trail.htm

This 2.5-mile self-guided walking tour begins at Boston Common. Stops include the Boston Massacre site, the Old South Meeting House where the Boston Tea Party began, Paul Revere's house, and the Granary Burial Ground, where Revere, John Hancock, Samuel Adams, and Crispus Attucks are all buried.

Colonial Williamsburg
http://www.history.org

This tourist site in Virginia, suitable for all ages, features shops, homes, and public buildings as they existed in the 1770s. In the Capitol Building on Duke of Gloucester Street, Patrick Henry stirred the House of Burgesses to oppose the Stamp Act in 1765. Costumed guides offer interpretations and candlelight tours.

Tryon's Palace

Governor William Tryon erected this building in New Bern, North Carolina, in 1768 over the protests of Regulators. The Georgian mansion, with a handsome garden overlooking the Trent River, served as the colony's first capitol. Now restored, Tryon Palace Historic Sites and Gardens is 112 miles east of Raleigh, the current capital.

Alamance Battleground

At this site, located on Route 62 near Burlington, North Carolina, Governor Tryon's forces defeated the Regulators in 1771. In historic Hillsborough, 30 miles east, a plaque on a hillside at the end of King Street on the east side of the town marks the site where Regulator leaders were hanged.

For Further Reading

General

Jack P. Greene, ed., *Colonies to Nation: A Documentary History of the American Revolution* (1975).
Merrill Jensen, *The Founding of a Nation: A History of the American Revolution, 1763–1776* (1968).
Pauline Maier, *From Resistance to Revolution: Colonial Radicals and the Development of American Opposition to Britain, 1765–1776* (1972).
Robert Middlekauff, *The Glorious Cause: The American Revolution, 1763–1789* (1982).
Alfred F. Young, ed., *The American Revolution: Explorations in the History of American Radicalism* (1976).

New Challenges to Spain's Expanded Empire

John Francis Bannon, *The Spanish Borderlands Frontier, 1513–1821* (1970).
Lydia T. Black, *Russians in Alaska, 1732–1867* (2004).
Richard Hough, *Captain James Cook* (1994).
John L. Kessell, *Spain in the Southwest: A Narrative History of Colonial New Mexico, Arizona, Texas, and California* (2002).
Mark Santiago, *Massacre at the Yuma Crossing: Spanish Relations with the Quechans, 1779–1782* (1998).
Barbara Sweetland Smith and Redmond J. Barnett, eds., *Russian America: The Forgotten Frontier* (1990).

New Challenges to Britain's Expanded Empire

John K. Alexander, *Samuel Adams: America's Revolutionary Politician* (2002).
John L. Bullion, *A Great and Necessary Measure: George Grenville and the Genesis of the Stamp Act, 1763–1765* (1982).
Colin G. Calloway, *The Scratch of a Pen: 1763 and the Transformation of North America* (2006).
Arthur H. Cash, *John Wilkes: The Scandalous Father of Civil Liberty* (2006).
Gregory E. Dowd, *A Spirited Resistance: The North American Indian Struggle for Unity, 1745–1815* (1992).
Edmund S. Morgan and Helen M. Morgan, *The Stamp Act Crisis: Prologue to Revolution*, 3rd ed. (1995).

"The Unconquerable Rage of the People"

Bernard Bailyn, *The Ideological Origins of the American Revolution* (1967).
Edward Countryman, *A People in Revolution: The American Revolution and Political Society in New York, 1760–1790* (1981).
Ronald Hoffman, *A Spirit of Dissention: Economics, Politics, and the Revolution in Maryland* (1973).
Marjoleine Kars, *Breaking Loose Together: The Regulator Rebellion in Pre-Revolutionary North Carolina* (2002).

A Conspiracy of Corrupt Ministers?

Bernard Bailyn, *The Ordeal of Thomas Hutchinson* (1974).

Woody Holton, *Forced Founders: Indians, Debtors, Slaves, and the Making of the American Revolution in Virginia* (1999).

Peter D. G. Thomas, *The Townshend Duties Crisis: The Second Phase of the American Revolution, 1767–1773* (1987).

John W. Tyler, *Smugglers and Patriots: Boston Merchants and the Advent of the American Revolution* (1986).

Launching a Revolution

David Hackett Fischer, *Paul Revere's Ride* (1994).

Benjamin Woods Labaree, *The Boston Tea Party* (1964).

Peter D. G. Thomas, *Tea Party to Independence: The Third Phase of the American Revolution, 1773–1776* (1991).

Alfred F. Young, *The Shoemaker and the Tea Party: Memory and the American Revolution* (1999).

For quizzes and other resources on these topics, go to www.longmanamericanhistory.com.

PART THREE

The Unfinished Revolution, 1775–1803

I N 1775 GREAT BRITAIN STILL POSSESSED ALL OF NORTH AMERICA EAST of the Mississippi River, from Hudson Bay to the Gulf of Mexico. If the British could suppress the troublesome rebellion along the Atlantic seaboard, their prospects for expansion in America looked promising. Farther west, Spain had recently acquired the vast Louisiana Territory from France. The Spanish retained their dominance in the Southwest, and they were finally beginning to expand their claim to California by building a series of new missions and presidios.

By 1803, however, the broad picture had changed markedly. In the Pacific Ocean, Europeans had encountered the Hawaiian Islands for the first time, Russian fur traders had consolidated their hold in Alaska, and Spanish vessels along the Pacific coast faced increasing competition from the ships of rival nations. The British still held Canada and Florida, but the thirteen rebellious colonies had become an independent republic and had started to acquire new territories. The most spectacular acquisition was the Louisiana Territory, which the United States purchased in 1803, after Spain returned the region to the control of France.

Few could have foreseen such an unlikely series of events in such a brief span of time. Thomas Jefferson drafted the Declaration of Independence in 1776 at age thirty-three. His generation had reluctantly become the effective leaders of a revolutionary movement by the mid-1770s. They contended ably with those who pushed for greater democratization, those who desired the stability of military rule, and even those who longed for the protection of the British monarchy.

These unlikely revolutionary leaders were by no means united in all their views and actions. They argued fervently over constitutional issues, domestic policies, and foreign alignments. Most managed to reap personal rewards from the new society's collective success. And they saw to it that these rewards reached far beyond their own households. Urban artisans, frontier farmers, and immigrant newcomers benefited from the removal of monarchy.

Such positive developments inspired optimism for many, both at home and abroad. Yet although the revolutionary era fulfilled the expectations of numerous citizens, it failed to meet the hopes and aspirations of other

Americans. Many American merchants and planters, indebted to British interests before 1776, gained by the separation from Great Britain as creditors and investors in the new society. Many frontier farmers and army veterans, on the other hand, faced burdensome debts after the Revolutionary War.

Women worried that the numerous written constitutions of the period were unresponsive to their interests. In 1776 New Jersey gave the vote to "all free inhabitants" who were also property holders. This included some single women, and in 1790 the state's election law referred specifically to "he or she" among voters. But this novel provision was undone a generation later, in 1807, when New Jersey men objected to the idea of any women having the right to vote. From New Hampshire to Georgia, committed "Daughters of Liberty" had made possible colonial boycotts through their industry and had managed families, farms, and businesses during the dislocations of war. Female access to education and the courts improved somewhat in the last quarter of the eighteenth century, but for most American women the advances were more symbolic than real.

For African Americans the disappointments were greater still. British offers of freedom prompted thousands of southern slaves to take up the Loyalist cause at great personal risk. Other free blacks and slaves, primarily in the North, shouldered arms for the Patriots, drawn by the rhetoric of liberty and the prospect of advancement. Even though they had chosen the winning side, they reaped few benefits. Although the number of free blacks expanded after the Revolutionary War, the African slave trade to the United States resumed and gained official protection. Slavery itself gained renewed significance with the transition to cotton production in the South and a federal constitution that sanctioned the power of slaveholders. Even in the North, where gradual emancipation became the norm by the end of the century, free blacks found their welcome into white churches and schools to be so half-hearted that many began organizing their own separate institutions.

Eastern Indians, like African Americans, had good reason to distrust the Revolution and its leaders. The majority, including most Iroquois and Cherokee warriors, sided with the British and paid a steep price in defeat. Throughout the Mississippi Valley, Native Americans who still remembered the benefits of French trade and British military support faced relentless pressure as American speculators, soldiers, and settlers dissected their homelands. After 1803, government officials promised that the newly acquired lands beyond the Mississippi would become an Indian Territory, providing a refuge for displaced eastern tribes. If so, what was to become of the Native American nations that already inhabited the western plains?

Like most political upheavals, the American Revolution left many questions unanswered and much business unfinished. Even the new federal government itself, in operation for little more than a decade by 1803, remained a work in progress. The specific roles and relative power of the government's three separate branches spurred endless debate, as did the proper place of the military and the most suitable direction for foreign policy. The Constitution ratified in 1789 seemed promising, but it remained an uncertain and largely untested framework.

1791 Bill of Rights is ratified
Saint Domingue slave revolt
Alexander Hamilton, "Report on the Subject of Manufactures"
Samuel Slater constructs first spinning machine on U.S. soil
Bank of the United States is chartered

1792 Washington is reelected president
Mary Wollstonecraft, *Vindication of the Rights of Woman*

1793 Washington issues Neutrality Proclamation
Eli Whitney invents the cotton gin

1794 U.S. troops defeat forces of Ohio Confederacy
Whiskey Rebellion

1795 Jay's Treaty
Treaty of San Lorenzo

1796 Washington's farewell address
John Adams is elected president

1797 XYZ Affair

1798 Quasi War with France (to 1800)
Alien and Sedition Acts
Kentucky and Virginia Resolutions (1798–1799)

1799 Seneca Leader Handsome Lake proclaims *gai'wiio*, or "Good Message"

1800 Thomas Jefferson is elected president
Gabriel plot is exposed in Richmond, Virginia

1801 Judiciary Act of 1801
War against Barbary pirates
Spain secretly cedes Louisiana Territory to France

1803 Louisiana Purchase
Marbury v. Madison

CHAPTER 7

Revolutionaries at War, 1775–1783

I N 1775 AFRICAN-BORN THOMAS PETERS WAS A THIRTY-SEVEN-YEAR-OLD SLAVE IN WILMING- ton, North Carolina. As a young man, he had been taken from what is now Nigeria and shipped to Louisiana aboard a French slave ship. Forced to cut sugar cane, Peters rebelled so often that his owner sold him to a merchant on North Carolina's Cape Fear River. There he received his English name, operated a grist mill, and started a family. Still enslaved, Peters was working as a millwright and living with his wife, Sally, age twenty-two, and their four-year-old daughter, Clairy, by the eve of the Revolutionary War.

During the fifteen years between Peters's abduction from Africa in 1760 and the outbreak of hostilities between America and Britain in 1775, nearly 225,000 people had streamed into the British mainland colonies. More than half came from the British Isles (125,000), and another 15,000 arrived from elsewhere in Europe. But the remaining 85,000 newcomers—or four in every ten— had all been purchased in Africa and enslaved in the coastal South. Thomas Peters, entering from Louisiana, was among the recent arrivals in British America.

In the summer of 1775, Peters must have heard talk about possible slave revolts in Virginia and the Car- olinas. Before the end of the year, he certainly knew that Virginia's gover- nor, Lord Dunmore, had offered free- dom to slaves who would take up arms for the British. The following March, ships of the Royal Navy arrived at Cape Fear River. The fleet offered to provide safe haven for any slaves escaping from Patriot masters. Joining other black

■ Escaped slave Thomas Peters took part in the British fleet's unsuccessful attempt to seize control of Charleston Harbor in June 1776. A South Carolina soldier painted this view of British ships afire the morning after the attack.

families, Tom and Sally Peters risked arrest to gain their personal liberty by bolting to the British vessels.

Peters was with the British fleet when General Henry Clinton's forces tried to take Charleston, South Carolina, in June 1776. Throughout the war, Peters served in a unit called the Black Pioneers. Wounded twice, he rose to the rank of sergeant and earned the promise of a farm in British Canada. In 1783, as defeated Loyalists left New York City at the end of the war, he joined other Black Pioneers aboard the *Joseph James*, bound for Nova Scotia. With him were Sally, Clairy, and eighteen-month-old John. Departing in November, the ship was blown off course by foul weather. The ex-slaves spent the winter at Bermuda before finally joining 3,500 other black Loyalists in Nova Scotia in May 1784.

After he and others had been stripped of promised farmland in Nova Scotia, Peters ventured to London in 1790 to protest their treatment. In England, he met with British abolitionists who were planning a colony of former slaves in West Africa. Returning to Canada with this news, he led 1,200 African Americans to Sierra Leone, where he died at Freetown in 1792. In thirty-two years, Peters had seen New Orleans, Wilmington, Charleston, Philadelphia, New York, Bermuda, Halifax, and London. (See Map 7.1.) He had escaped after sixteen years of enslavement and gone to war, fighting for his freedom and for the safety of family and friends.

Though Thomas Peters's saga is unusual, it helps to illustrate that the War of American Independence was not a two-sided struggle, with English colonists unified to oppose the English monarchy. Instead, like most revolutions, it was a conflict fought by shifting coalitions. In a time of strife, there were countless possibilities for forging political "marriages of convenience" between different regions, groups, and interests.

Within each small community, and within the Atlantic theater as a whole, alliances often proved the old adage that "My enemy's enemy is my friend." Thomas Peters escaped servitude to join the British in part because the man holding him in slavery was a leading member of the local Sons of Liberty. Likewise, powerful merchants like John Hancock and Henry Laurens threw in their lot with the people because they had grown disillusioned with Parliament's political and commercial controls. On the international scale, the monarchies of France and Spain swallowed their dislike for American rhetoric to join in a war that allowed them an opportunity to attack their long-standing rival, Britain. On the other hand, many Cherokee and Iroquois Indians, disillusioned by contact with land-hungry settlers, cast their lot with the British forces from overseas.

These numerous alliances remained problematic and incomplete. Not all Iroquois warriors or African slaves sided with the British, and by no means all New England merchants or Virginia planters embraced the Patriot cause. In a landscape marked by uncertainty, large numbers of people at all levels of society opted for cautious neutrality as long as they could, while others shifted their allegiance as the winds changed. The final outcome of the conflict, therefore, remained a source of doubt. Looking back, Americans often view the results of the Revolutionary War as inevitable, perhaps even foreordained. In fact, the end result—and thus independence itself—hung in the balance for years.

IMAGE

Patriots and Slaves Toppling Statue of George III

■ **MAP 7.1**

BRITAIN AT WAR: THE GLOBAL CONTEXT, 1778–1783   For Britain, the war that began in 1775 expanded into a worldwide conflict against rival European powers within three years. By 1783 the British lost American colonies while expanding their hold in India. The lifetime journey of African-born Thomas Peters, shown here, is clearly exceptional, but extensive movements figured in many lives during these years of warfare. General Cornwallis, for example, went on to serve the British in India after his defeat at Yorktown in 1781.

"Things Are Now Come to That Crisis"

VIDEO

The American Revolution

New England's Minutemen had rallied swiftly at Lexington. In the ensuing months, Congress took the initial steps to form a Continental Army. It also launched efforts to force the British out of Boston and to pull Canada into the rebellion. If these predominantly Protestant rebels hoped to draw the French Catholics of Quebec into their revolt, would free whites also be eager to include the blacks of Boston, Williamsburg, and Charleston in the struggle for liberty? Or would it be the British who recruited more African Americans such as Thomas Peters and furnished them with arms? The answers to such questions became clear in the fifteen months between the skirmish at Lexington and the decision of Congress to declare political independence from Britain in July 1776.

The Second Continental Congress Takes Control

DOCUMENT

Royal Proclamation of Rebellion

Enthusiasm ran high in Philadelphia in May 1775 as the Second Continental Congress assembled, and the delegates moved quickly to put the colonies on a wartime footing. They instructed New York to build fortifications, and they paid for a dozen companies of riflemen to be sent north to aid the Minutemen surrounding Boston. They created an Army Department under the command of a New York aristocrat, General Philip Schuyler, and approved an issue of $2 million in currency to fund the military buildup.

In late May, word arrived from Lake Champlain in New York of a victory for soldiers under Benedict Arnold of Connecticut and for the Green Mountain Boys, Vermont-area farmers led by Ethan Allen. They had captured Fort Ticonderoga, along with its cannons, and the new Army Department badly needed all such heavy arms. This initiative not only secured the Hudson Valley against a British attack from the north; it also allowed Schuyler to propose a strike against Montreal and Quebec via Lake Champlain. Congress approved the assault, to be led by General Richard Montgomery. It also approved a daring scheme submitted by Arnold. He planned to lead separate forces up the Kennebec River. They would assist Montgomery in seizing Quebec and winning Canada before the region could become a staging ground for British armies.

But no single action by Congress had greater implications than the one taken on June 15, 1775. That day, members voted unanimously to appoint George Washington, a forty-three-year-old delegate from Virginia, "to command all the continental forces." Colonel Washington already headed a committee drawing up regulations to run the new army, and he had notable military experience. But his strongest asset may have been his southern roots. Northern delegates sensed the need to foster colonial unity by placing a non–New Englander in charge of the army outside Boston. In military and political terms, the selection of Washington proved auspicious. The tall, imposing planter from Mount Vernon emerged as a durable and respected leader in both war and peace. But putting a slaveholder in command also closed certain radical options. It signaled the beginning of an important alliance between the well-to-do regional leaders of the North and South, contributing to the particular shape of the Federal Constitution a dozen years later.

Charles Willson Peale, *George Washington in the Uniform of a British Colonial Colonel*, c. 1772. Washington-Custis-Lee Collection, Washington and Lee University, Lexington, VA

■ In June 1775, Congress selected a wealthy Virginia planter to command its army. The choice of George Washington reassured southern slave owners and disappointed blacks and whites in the North who saw slavery as a contradiction in the struggle for freedom.

"Liberty to Slaves"

The selection of Washington sent a strong message to half a million African Americans, spurring many of them to risk siding with the British. For their part, the British sensed an opportunity to undermine rebellious planters. In June 1775, the British commander in America, Thomas Gage, wrote to London: "Things are now come to that crisis, that we must avail ourselves of every resource, even to raise the Negros, in our cause."

In the South, rumors of liberation swept through the large African American community during 1775. Slaveholding rebel authorities countered with harsh measures to quell black unrest. In South Carolina that spring, attention focused on a prominent free black man named Thomas Jeremiah, a skilled pilot in the busy port of Charleston. In April, Jeremiah supposedly told an enslaved dockworker of a great war coming and urged slaves to seize the opportunity. Weeks later, nervous Patriot planters made the well-known free black into a scapegoat, accusing him of involvement in a plot to smuggle guns ashore from British ships to support a slave uprising. In August 1775, despite a lack of hard evidence against him, Jeremiah was publicly hanged and then burned.

That September, a Georgia delegate to Congress made a startling comment. If British troops were to land on the southern coast with a supply of food and guns, he said, and offer freedom to slaves who would join them, 20,000 blacks from Georgia and South Carolina would materialize in no time. In November, the beleaguered royal governor of Virginia, Lord Dunmore, attempted just such a scheme. Dunmore issued a proclamation granting freedom to the slaves of rebel masters who agreed to take up arms on behalf of the king. Hundreds responded to Dunmore's proclamation. They formed the Ethiopian Regiment and wore sashes proclaiming "Liberty to Slaves."

The Siege of Boston

In the North, British forces had been confined in Boston ever since the Battle of Lexington. They would remain isolated on the town's main peninsula for nearly a year, supported by the Royal Navy. In early July 1775, Washington arrived at nearby Cambridge to take up his command and oversee the siege of Boston. He quickly set out to improve order among his men, tightening discipline, calming regional jealousies, and removing incompetent officers. In addition, he wrote scores of letters to civilian political leaders and the president of Congress to muster support for his feeble army.

Washington made clear that nearly everything was in short supply, from tents and uniforms to muskets and cannons. He dispatched twenty-five-year-old Henry Knox, a former bookseller and future general, to retrieve the cannons captured at Ticonderoga. The Patriots' siege could not succeed without heavy fieldpieces to bombard the city from the heights at Dorchester and Charlestown that lay across the water from Boston.

Even before Washington's arrival, the British and the Americans had vied for control of these strategic heights. Indeed, General Gage drew up plans to secure Charlestown peninsula by seizing its highest point, Bunker Hill. But the Patriots learned of the scheme. On the night of June 16, 1775, they moved to fortify the area. The next afternoon, 1,500 Patriots confronted the full force of the British army in the Battle of Bunker Hill.

Gage might easily have sealed off Charlestown peninsula with his naval power. Instead, he used 2,500 British infantry to launch three frontal attacks from the shoreline. The first two uphill charges fell back, but a third assault finally dislodged the Americans. Although the battle of Bunker Hill was technically a British victory, success came at a terrible price. The encounter left forty-two percent of British troops (1,054 men) wounded or dead—the worst casualty figures of the war. Gage lost his command, replaced by General William Howe, and the Royal Army no longer appeared invincibile.

With Washington and his army encamped outside Boston, Henry Knox worked to retrieve the British **ordnance** captured at Ticonderoga. Using oxen, sledges, and local volunteers, he hauled forty-three heavy cannons east, across trails covered with snow and ice, from the Hudson Valley to the coast. His men delivered the guns in late winter, and in March 1776 the Americans, in a surprise move, placed them on Dorchester Heights, where they could bombard the enemy huddled in Boston. Threatened, and unable to counterattack, Britain's General Howe evacuated his army, retreating by ship to Halifax, Nova Scotia. There, he made plans to attack the rebels again at New York, where Loyalist support was stronger.

Declaring Independence

As Washington laid siege to Boston, other Americans converged on British forces in Canada. General Montgomery's troops seized Montreal in November 1775. They then descended the St. Lawrence River to join Benedict Arnold's men, who had struggled north toward Quebec under brutal winter conditions. Their combined force attacked the walled city during a fierce snowstorm on the night of December 30. But their assault failed, and Montgomery perished in the fighting. When British reinforcements reached Quebec in May, the Americans retreated toward Lake Champlain. They left behind most of their baggage and hundreds of sick companions, dying from smallpox. Hundreds more died during the withdrawal or spread the deadly pox as they returned to New England towns. Everywhere, strained loyalty to the British was turning to explosive anger.

DOCUMENT

"Common Sense"
by Thomas Paine

"Time to Part"

In January 1776, a brilliant pamphlet, *Common Sense*, captured the shifting mood and helped propel Americans toward independence. The author, a former corsetmaker named Thomas

Paine, had endured personal and economic failures in England before sailing to Philadelphia in 1774 at age thirty-seven. To this passionate man, with his gift for powerful prose, America represented a fresh start, and Paine poured his energy into bold newspaper essays.

Common Sense sold an amazing 120,000 copies in three months. Paine promised to lay out "simple facts, plain arguments, and common sense" on the precarious American situation. He lambasted "the so much boasted constitution of England," attacking hereditary monarchy and the divine right of kings. "One honest man," Paine proclaimed, is worth more "than all the crowned ruffians that ever lived." He urged the creation of an independent constitutional republic that could become "an asylum for all mankind." "Reconciliation is now a fallacious dream," he argued: "'TIS TIME TO PART."

Paine's **avid** readers agreed. In the spring of 1776, one colony after another instructed its representatives to the Second Continental Congress to vote for independence. But many among the well-to-do held strong social and economic ties to London. They feared the loss of British imperial protection and the startling upsurge of democratic political activity among the lower orders. At first, Congress vacillated. Finally, with no sign of accommodation from England, most members agreed with Robert Livingston of New York that "they should yield to the torrent if they hoped to direct its course." In early June, young Livingston, age thirty, joined the committee assigned to prepare a formal statement declaring independence from Great Britain. The Committee of Five also included Benjamin Franklin, John Adams, Roger Sherman, and the second youngest member of the Continental Congress, Thomas Jefferson.

The thirty-three-year-old Jefferson willingly took responsibility for crafting the document. He framed a stirring preamble, drawing on British philosopher John Locke's contract theory of government. Locke (1632–1702) believed that the sovereign power ultimately resided not in government but in the people themselves, who chose to submit voluntarily to civil law to protect property and preserve basic rights.

According to Locke, rulers possessed conditional, not absolute, authority over the people. Citizens therefore held the right to end their support and overthrow any government that did not fulfill its side of the contract. For any people facing "a long train of abuses," Jefferson wrote, "it is their right, it is their duty, to throw off such government and to provide new guards for their future security." He went on to catalogue the "repeated injuries and usurpations" committed by King George III. On July 2, when Congress voted on a statement affirming that "these United Colonies are, and of right, ought to be, Free and Independent States," twelve colonies approved, with the New York delegation abstaining. Having made the fundamental decision, the delegates then considered how to "declare the causes" behind their momentous choice to separate from Great Britain.

Over the next two days, Congress members edited the draft declaration submitted by the Committee of Five. They kept Jefferson's idealistic assertion that "all men are created equal." But they removed any reference to slavery, except for the charge that the king had "excited domestic insurrections amongst us," a veiled reference to the Thomas Jeremiah debacle in Charleston and to Lord Dunmore's proclamation. With other changes in place, they finally voted to approve the revised Declaration of Independence on July 4, 1776.

John Hancock, the president of the Congress, signed the document with a flourish, and printers hastily turned it into a published broadside. The other signatures (contrary to folklore) came two weeks later, after New York had finally offered its approval. Then fifty-six delegates gathered to sign their names to "The unanimous declaration of the thirteen United States of America." They did so at great risk, for signing the document exposed them to charges of treason, punishable by death.

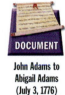

DOCUMENT

John Adams to Abigail Adams (July 3, 1776)

VIDEO

Declaration of Independence

IMAGE

Signing of the Declaration of Independence

The British Attack New York

While the Second Continental Congress debated independence, the British maneuvered to suppress the rebellion. Strangling the revolt with a naval blockade appeared impossible, given

"Revoking Those Sacred Trusts Which Are Violated": One of Many Proclamations of Independence (South Carolina, May 1776)

Young Martha Ryan used her cipher-book to do more than practice writing. She also drew American ships and flags and embellished the popular rallying cry, "Liberty or Death."

Throughout the late spring of 1776, provincial assemblies, town meetings, and grand juries in the thirteen colonies began issuing their own pronouncements regarding a break with Great Britain. The authors drew on historical precedent, legal tradition, and emotional sentiment. They mixed lofty theory and Real Whig ideology with local concerns. They also incorporated rhetoric and ideas from current pamphlets, speeches, and newspaper essays.

At least ninety of these proclamations survive. Most are more impressive for their strong feelings than for their literary merit. *But taken together, they suggest the sentiments, arguments, and words that were in the air when Jefferson drafted the Declaration of Independence. This document was drawn up and signed by fifteen members of the Cheraw District grand jury who came together for their regular court session in* Long Bluff, South Carolina, on Monday, May 20, 1776.

The Presentments of the Grand Jury of and for the Said District

I. When a people, born and bred in a land of freedom and virtue…are convinced of the wicked schemes of

the length of the American coastline. But two other strategies emerged—one southern and one northern—that shaped British planning throughout the conflict.

The southern design rested on the assumption that loyalty to the crown remained strongest in the South. If the British could land forces below Chesapeake Bay, support from white loyalists and enslaved blacks might enable them to gain the upper hand and push north to reimpose colonial rule elsewhere. In June 1776, troops under General Henry Clinton arrived off the South Carolina coast with such a mission in mind. On June 28, British ships bombarded Sullivan's Island, at the mouth of Charleston harbor. But the Americans' log fortress withstood the cannon fire, and the attackers withdrew. The British did not renew their southern design for several years, concentrating instead on a separate northern strategy.

According to Britain's northern plan, troops would divide the rebellious colonies in two at the Hudson River valley, seizing New York City and advancing upriver while other forces pushed south from Canada. Then, having sealed off New England, they could finally crush the radicals in Massachusetts who had spearheaded the revolt while restoring the loyalties of inhabitants farther south. Lord George Germain, the aggressive new British cabinet min-their treacherous rulers to fetter them with the chains of servitude, and rob them of every noble and desirable privilege which distinguishes them as freemen,—justice, humanity, and the immutable laws of *God,* justify and support them in revoking those sacred trusts which are so impiously violated, and placing them in such hands as are most likely to execute them in the manner and for the important ends for which they were first given.

II. The good people of this Colony, with the rest of her sister Colonies, confiding in the justice and merited protection of the King and Parliament of *Great Britain,* ever…esteemed such a bond of union and harmony as the greatest happiness. But when that protection was wantonly withdrawn, and every mark of cruelty and oppression substituted;…self-preservation, and a regard to our own welfare and security, became a consideration both important and necessary. The Parliament and Ministry of *Great Britain,* by their wanton and undeserved persecutions, have reduced this Colony to a state of separation from her…as the only lasting means of future happiness and safety…. Cast off, persecuted, defamed, given up as a prey to every violence and injury, a righteous and much injured people have at length appealed to *God!* and, trusting to his divine justice and their own virtuous perseverance, taken the

only and last means of securing their own honour, safety, and happiness.

III. We now feel every joyful and comfortable hope that a people could desire in the present Constitution and form of Government established in this Colony; a Constitution founded on the strictest principles of justice and humanity, where the rights and happiness of the whole, the poor and the rich, are equally secured; and to secure and defend which, it is the particular interest of every individual who regards his own safety and advantage.

IV. When we consider the publick officers of our present form of Government now appointed, as well as the method and duration of their appointment, we cannot but declare our entire satisfaction and comfort; as well in the characters of such men, who are justly esteemed for every virtue, as their well-known abilities to execute the important trusts which they now hold.

V. Under these convictions,… we…recommend it to every man…to secure and defend with his life and fortune a form of Government so just, so equitable, and promising;…that the latest posterity may enjoy the virtuous fruits of that work, which the integrity and fortitude of the present age had, at the expense of their blood and treasure, at length happily effected.

VI. We cannot but declare how great the pleasure, the harmony, and

political union which now exists in this District affords; and having no grievances to complain of, only beg leave to recommend that a new Jury list be made for this District, the present being insufficient.

And lastly, we beg leave…that these our presentments be printed in the publick papers.—PHILIP PLEDGER, Foreman [and 14 other signatures]

Questions

1. *While Thomas Jefferson was preparing the Declaration of Independence (see the text of the document in the Appendix, pp. A-3–A-4), many local presentments were in circulation. How does the South Carolina example compare in form, content, emotion, and clarity to Jefferson's document?*

2. *If many ideas and arguments present in the Declaration of Independence were indeed commonplace in the colonies early in 1776, how does this information enhance or alter your understanding of Thomas Jefferson's accomplishment?* ■

Source: Pauline Maier, *American Scripture: Making the Declaration of Independence* (New York: Knopf, 1997), pp. 229–231.

ister in charge of American affairs, favored this plan. An overwhelming strike, he asserted, could "finish the rebellion in one campaign."

Early in 1776, Germain set out to generate a land and sea offensive of unprecedented scale. He prodded the sluggish admiralty for ships, and he rented troops from abroad. Russia declined a request for 20,000 soldiers, but the German states produced 18,000 mercenaries. Eventually, 30,000 German troops traveled to America, so many of them from the state of Hesse-Cassel that onlookers called all of them Hessians. Canada, having already repulsed an American invasion, could provide a loyal staging ground in the north. "I have always thought Hudson's River the most proper part of the whole continent for opening vigorous operations," observed "Gentleman Johnny" Burgoyne, the dapper and worldly British general who arrived at Quebec with reinforcements in May 1776.

But plans for a strike south from Canada had to wait. Britain made its first thrust toward the mouth of the Hudson River by sea. In June, a convoy under General William Howe sailed from Halifax to Staten Island, New York, with 9,000 soldiers. By August, the general had received 20,000 reinforcements from across the Atlantic. His brother, Admiral Richard Howe, hovered nearby with 13,000 sailors aboard seventy naval vessels. On

■ John Trumbull spent years gathering portraits for his famous painting *The Declaration of Independence*. This engraving identifies individuals in the painting with their signatures. The artist placed the Drafting Committee in the center (31–35). He omitted signers for whom he had no likeness, and he included several nonsigners, such as John Dickinson.

orders from Congress, General Washington moved south to defend New York City, a difficult task made harder by ardent Loyalist sentiment. Short on men and equipment, the general weakened his position further by dividing his troops between Manhattan and Brooklyn Heights on nearby Long Island.

A month after Congress members signed the Declaration of Independence, Washington nearly lost his entire force—and the cause itself. General Howe moved his troops by water from Staten Island to the Brooklyn area and then outflanked and scattered the poorly trained Americans in the Battle of Long Island on August 27. Remarkably, the British leader called off a direct attack that almost certainly would have overrun the American batteries on Brooklyn Heights. When his equally cautious brother failed to seal off the East River with ships, rebel troops escaped disaster by slipping back to New York City in small boats under cover of night and fog.

"Victory or Death": A Desperate Gamble Pays Off

New York Burning (1776)

Washington's narrow escape from Long Island in August 1776 was the first of numerous retreats. His army left New York City on September 15. The rebels withdrew from upper Manhattan and Westchester in October and from Fort Washington and Fort Lee on the Hudson—with heavy losses—in November. The Americans "fled like scared rabbits," one Englishman wrote. With winter at hand, the Continental forces retreated southwest toward Philadelphia.

As the ragged American army withdrew from New York late in 1776, General William Howe repeatedly failed to press his advantage. The British commander and his brother had received a commission from Lord North, who headed the government in London, permit-

William Mercer, *Battle of Princeton*, date unknown. Courtesy of the Historical Society of Pennsylvania Collection, Atwater Kent Museum of Philadelphia

■ This picture showing the noise and movement of the American victory at the Battle of Princeton was created by deaf painter William Mercer, whose father, Brigadier General Hugh Mercer, died in the battle.

ting them to negotiate a peace settlement with the Americans whenever possible. They hoped that a strong show of force, without a vicious offensive that might alienate civilians, could bring the enemy to terms. Howe's troops offered pardons to rebels and encouraged desertions from Washington's army. In early December, the dwindling American force hurried through Princeton and slipped across the Delaware River into Pennsylvania. Confident of victory, the British failed to pursue them, instead making camp at Trenton. Washington realized that unless circumstances changed quickly, "the game will be pretty well up."

Distressed by civilian talk of surrender, Tom Paine again took up his pen. In the *Pennsylvania Journal* for December 19, he launched a new series of essays ("The American Crisis") that began with the ringing words "These are the times that try men's souls." Paine mocked "the summer soldier and the sunshine patriot" who shrank from extreme trials. "Let it be told to the future world, that in the depth of winter, when nothing but hope and virtue could survive," vigilant citizens, "alarmed at one common danger, came forth to meet and to repulse it."

Action soon followed words. On Christmas Day 1776, Washington issued a new code phrase for sentinels: "Victory or Death." He ordered Paine's words read aloud to the troops. Then, after dark, his men recrossed the windswept Delaware River in a driving snowstorm and advanced on Trenton. Holiday festivities and foul weather had left the enemy unprepared, and intelligence of the impending attack seems to have been ignored. The Americans inflicted a startling defeat, killing several dozen and capturing more than 900 Hessian soldiers. As Washington advanced again on December 30, Howe sent fresh troops forward under Charles Cornwallis to confront the rebels, pinning them down near Trenton. But when the British paused before attacking, the Americans left their campfires burning and slipped out of reach. They then circled behind Cornwallis to defeat his reinforcements at Princeton on January 3. It was not the last time that Washington bested Cornwallis.

The Struggle to Win French Support

Revolutionary War: Northern Theater, 1775–1780

The success at Trenton and Princeton restored a glimmer of hope for the tattered Continental Army and its supporters. As American forces took up winter quarters at Morristown, Howe withdrew his army from much of New Jersey to await the spring campaigns. As a result, anxious civilians in the region who had sworn their loyalty to the crown felt deserted. Public sentiment again swung toward the rebels.

More importantly, news of the victories spurred support overseas for the American cause. French officials, eager to see their European rival bogged down in a colonial war, dispatched secret shipments of munitions to aid the revolutionaries.

One young aristocrat, the idealistic Marquis de Lafayette, was already on his way from France to volunteer his services to General Washington. But drawing forth an official French commitment to the American cause would take a larger show of success. That triumph finally came at the end of the next campaign season, with the Americans' stunning victory at Saratoga, deep in the Hudson Valley, 185 miles above New York City.

Breakdown in British Planning

Among the Americans, two years of grim conflict had dampened the initial zeal that had prompted citizens to enlist. Washington believed that the armed resistance could scarcely continue unless many more men made longer commitments to fight. He also insisted that his soldiers needed tighter discipline and better pay. In response, Congress expanded his disciplinary powers and offered a bonus to those who enlisted for a three-year term.

In a slumping economy, numerous recruits answered the call, including immigrants and unemployed artisans. All lacked training, supplies, and experience. Many rural recruits also lacked immunity to smallpox, since they had never been exposed to the disease. When smallpox broke out among the soldiers at Morristown, Washington ordered a mass inoculation. Because the process brings on a mild case of the disease, he anxiously counted the days until his rebuilding army could be ready to fight. "If Howe does not take advantage of our week state" Washington Commented on April 1777, "he is very unfit for his trust."

By seeking a decisive blow and a negotiated settlement in 1776, the British had achieved neither objective.

Despite American vulnerability, the British were slow to move. Lord North's ministry had fallen victim to its own contradictions. By seeking a decisive blow *and* a negotiated settlement in 1776, the British had achieved neither objective. They had also underestimated the persistence of Washington's army. During the 1777 campaigns, they learned further lessons about the difficulty of their task and the need for coordinated plans.

General Burgoyne, returning to London for the winter, won government support for a major new offensive. He planned to lead a large force south from Canada, using the Hudson Valley to drive a wedge through the rebellious colonies. In support, a combined British and Indian force would strike east from Lake Ontario, capturing Fort Stanwix and descending eastward among the Mohawk River to meet Burgoyne at Albany. William Howe would push north from New York City to complete the design.

But General Howe had formed a different plan. Assuming Burgoyne would not need his help in the Hudson Valley, he intended to move south against Philadelphia. The two generals

The Revolutionary War in the North

— British
— Patriots
✸ British victories
✸ Patriot victories

1 Arnold leads winter journey to Quebec, 1775
2 Montgomery fails to conquer Canada, 1775–1776
3 Knox hauls cannon from Ft. Ticonderoga, 1776
4 William Howe withdraws from Boston to Halifax, 1776
5 Howe brothers capture New York with huge force, 1776
6 Washington retreats, then re-crosses the Delaware, 1776–1777
7 William Howe sails from New York, moves on Philadelphia, 1777
8 Washington meets Howe at Brandywine and Germantown, 1777
9 Burgoyne tries to seize Hudson Valley from Canada , 1777
10 Arnold defeats British near Ft. Stanwix, 1777
11 Gates forces Burgoyne's surrender at Saratoga, 1777
12 Clinton retreats from Philadelphia to New York, 1778
13 Marching from Valley Forge, Washington wins at Monmouth, 1778
14 Brant/Butler attack Wyoming Valley, 1778; Cherry Valley, 1779
15 Sullivan attacks Iroquois villages, 1779

■ **M A P 7 . 2**
THE REVOLUTIONARY WAR IN THE NORTH

never integrated their separate operations, and the results were disastrous. In one six-month span, the British bungled their best chance for victory and handed their enemies an opening that permanently shifted the course of the war.

Saratoga Tips the Balance

The isolated operations of Burgoyne and Howe got off to slow starts in late June 1777. Howe took two months to move his troops by sea from New York harbor to the headwaters of Chesapeake Bay. This delay gave the Americans time to march south, but an engagement at Brandywine Creek on September 11, 1777, failed to check the British advance on Philadelphia. The British finally entered the city in late September only to find that the rebel Congress had retreated to York, Pennsylvania.

At Germantown, just north of Philadelphia, Washington launched a surprise attack against the large Hessian garrison on October 4, but morning fog created so much confusion that the inexperienced Patriot troops allowed victory to slip away. Yet as the battered army took up winter quarters at nearby Valley Forge, the defeats at Brandywine and Germantown seemed worth the price. The Americans had gained combat experience and had made Howe pay heavily for his hollow capture of Philadelphia. "Now," Washington wrote, "let all New England turn out and crush Burgoyne."

Moving south from Canada in late June, "Gentleman Johnny" saw little likelihood of being crushed. The British officers believed their huge army to be invincible. The worried Americans fell back from Crown Point and Ticonderoga on Lake Champlain. But as British supply lines lengthened, the crown's army grew less certain of victory. Burgoyne's soldiers expended valuable time cutting a roadway through the wilderness. Also, the reinforcements anticipated from the West had been turned back by Benedict Arnold's men at Fort Stanwix. Even worse, American militia near Bennington badly mauled a British unit of 600 sent to forage for corn and cattle. With cold weather approaching and supplies dwindling, Burgoyne pushed toward Albany, unaware that Howe would not be sending help up the Hudson to meet him.

As Burgoyne's situation worsened, the American position improved. An arrogant British proclamation demanding submission from local residents only stiffened their resolve and drew out more rebel recruits. While Burgoyne's army crossed to the Hudson River's west bank at Saratoga, General Horatio Gates's American forces dug in on Bemis Heights, 10 miles downstream.

On September 19, 1777, Patriot units under two aggressive officers, Benedict Arnold and Daniel Morgan, confronted the enemy at Freeman's Farm, not far from Saratoga. In the grueling battle, British forces suffered 556 dead or wounded, nearly twice the American losses. Gates's refusal to commit reinforcements prevented the Patriots from achieving total victory. Nevertheless, the American ranks swelled with new recruits who sensed a chance to inflict losses on Burgoyne's forces. On October 7, the beleaguered British tried once more to smash southward, only to suffer defeat in a second battle at Freeman's Farm. Morgan and Arnold once again played key roles, though Arnold suffered a crippling leg wound. When Burgoyne's entire army of 5,800 surrendered at nearby Saratoga ten days later, Gates took full credit for the stunning triumph.

Forging an Alliance with France

Ever since declaring independence, Congress had maneuvered to win international recognition and aid for the new nation. It sent Benjamin Franklin to Paris as part of a commission seeking European support. Uncertain about the rebellion's chances for success, especially after the fall of Philadelphia, the French government moved cautiously, confining itself to covert assistance in money and arms.

Word of the American victory at Saratoga suddenly gave Franklin greater leverage. When he hinted to the French that he might bargain directly with London for peace, France's foreign minister, Comte de Vergennes, moved immediately to recognize American independence. France agreed to renounce forever any claim to English land in North America, and Franklin promised that the Americans would help defend French holdings in the Caribbean. Both parties pledged to defend the liberty of the new republic, and each agreed not to conclude a separate peace with Great Britain or to cease fighting until U.S. independence had been ensured by formal treaty. In May 1778 the Continental Congress approved this alliance. The next month, France entered the war, adding its enormous wealth and power to the American cause. A year later, Spain—unwilling to ally itself directly with the upstart republic but eager to protect its vast American assets from Great Britain—entered the war on the side of France.

For the British, what had been a colonial brushfire swiftly flared into a global conflict reminiscent of the Seven Years' War. These new hostilities with France meant possible invasions at home and inevitable attacks on outposts of Britain's empire. French ships seized Senegal in West Africa, took Grenada in the West Indies, and burned trading posts on Hudson Bay in Canada. London's annual war expenditures climbed from £4 million in 1775 to £20 million in 1782.

As war costs mounted in Britain, domestic opposition to the conflict in America intensified. Some members of Parliament pushed for a swift settlement. In 1778 a peace commission led by Lord Carlisle offered concessions to the Continental Congress, hoping to tear the French alliance apart. But the Carlisle Commission failed to win a reconciliation. Other Britons went further in opposing the war. Their diverse reasons included fear of French power, desire for American trade, disgust over war profiteering, ties to friends in America, and idealistic belief in the revolution's principles. Many drank toasts to General Washington and openly supported the American cause.

Faced with growing economic and political pressure, the king and his ministers briefly considered withdrawing all troops from the rebellious colonies and focusing on the French threat. But instead, when General Howe resigned as commander in chief in America, they instructed his successor, Sir Henry Clinton, to retreat from Philadelphia to New York and devote his main resources to attacking the French in the Caribbean. Over the next four years, discontent within Britain continued to escalate, and no strategy proved sufficient to pacify the Americans or to crush their rebellion.

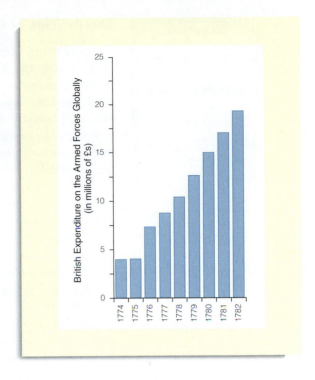

■ **FIGURE 7.1**
BRITISH GOVERNMENT EXPENSES ON ARMED FORCES THROUGHOUT THE WORLD (IN MILLIONS OF POUNDS), 1774–1782   Britain's war budget soared after France entered the conflict in 1778, but major resources flowed toward India and the Caribbean, limiting the share available for North America.

Legitimate States, a Respectable Military

Even with the new French alliance, the rebellious American states faced serious challenges on both the civilian and military fronts. They had thrown out their colonial governors and embarked on a dangerous war, but two fundamental questions still confronted them: How would the once-dependent colonies govern themselves? And how could they shape a military force with enough unity and resources to offer protection but not so powerful and unchecked as to seize control from their new civil governments?

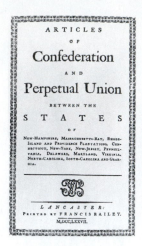

The Articles of Confederation

The Continental Congress that the rebelling states created had taken prompt initiative. Without clear authority, it had declared independence, raised an army, issued currency, borrowed money from abroad, and negotiated an alliance with France. Then it moved to bring greater stability and legitimacy to its work. In 1777, one month after the victory at Saratoga, it approved Articles of Confederation and presented this formal plan for a lasting and unifying government to the states for ratification. In every region, citizens were already debating how much authority each new state government would have in relation to the larger federation. Who would have the power to levy taxes, for example, and who would control the distribution of land?

The Articles declared "The United States of America" to be a "firm league of friendship" between the thirteen former colonies. The final document proposed a weaker confederation than the one outlined in an earlier draft by John Dickinson. In the finished charter, each state would retain all independent rights and powers not "expressly delegated" to the Confederation Congress. Indeed, ties between the sovereign states seemed so loose that France considered sending thirteen separate ambassadors to America.

VIDEO

Articles of Confederation

According to the Articles, Congress could not collect taxes or regulate trade; it could only requisition funds from the states. Proportions would vary depending on each state's free population. Moreover, the Confederation had no separate executive branch; executive functions fell to various committees of the Confederation Congress. In addition, to the dismay of land speculators, the Congress would not control the western domains that several large states had claimed. Maryland, a small state without western claims, protested this arrangement and refused to ratify. To win the required approval from all thirteen states, drafters changed the plan and granted the Confederation control of western lands. After four years, the Articles finally won ratification in 1781.

Given the importance of the states, the task of designing new state governments seemed a higher priority to many than inventing a confederation structure. Some leaders in the Continental Congress returned home to help implement this state-level process. In May 1776, for example, two of Jefferson's friends in the Virginia delegation in Philadelphia departed for Williamsburg. They left their younger colleague behind, but they carried his written draft for a possible state constitution. Those already at work in Virginia accepted Jefferson's proposed preamble, and on June 29, 1776, Virginia led the way, adopting the first republican state constitution.

Virginia had already pioneered in another respect. Two weeks earlier, Virginia representatives approved a Declaration of Rights drawn up by George Mason. He affirmed the revolutionary concepts that all power derives from the people and that magistrates are their servants. He went on to endorse trial by jury, praise religious freedom, and condemn hereditary privilege. Over the next eight years, many states adopted a similar bill of rights to enumerate the fundamental limits of government power.

Creating State Constitutions

Though diverse, the thirteen states shared practical needs. Each had removed a functioning colonial government and needed to reestablish the rule of law under a new system. Britain possessed no written constitution, but the colonists had been ruled under published charters, and they believed in the value of such clear and open arrangements. Thus they readily envisioned an explicit controlling document, or constitution, for each new state. Besides, the novel idea that government flowed from the people—as an agreement based on the consent of the governed—called for some all-encompassing, written legal contract.

A new written constitution, whether for a state or a union of states, represented something more fundamental and enduring than a regular law. It needed to be above day-to-day legal statutes and political whims. Somehow, the people, through chosen representatives, had to prepare a special document that citizens would affirm, or ratify, only one time. After the new government structure was in place, the constitution itself would be difficult, though not impossible, to change.

In 1779 Massachusetts legislators, under pressure from the public, fixed upon a method for providing the elevated status and popular endorsement for such a new document. Local voters in town meetings chose representatives for a specific constitution-drafting convention. These delegates, building on a model suggested by John Adams, crafted a suitable document, and their proposed constitution was then submitted to all the state's free men (regardless of race or property) for ratification. This widened constituency was intended to give special weight to the endorsement process.

DOCUMENT

John Adams,
Thoughts on
Government

Approval of the Massachusetts document was hotly debated. Many objected to the limits on popular power that were part of Adams's novel design. A reluctant revolutionary, Adams had composed a tract titled *Thoughts on Government* to counter the democratic enthusiasm of Tom Paine's *Common Sense*. Adams argued that "interests" (like-minded groups), rather than people, should receive equal representation. In addition, he proposed sharing legislative responsibilities between a house, a senate, and a chief executive. Property requirements for these offices were steep, so wealthy interests would have power far beyond their numbers. The Massachusetts state constitution, ratified by a narrow margin, implemented these ideas. They signaled a turn away from the strongest popular radicalism of 1776 and foreshadowed the more conservative balance of interests that James Madison championed in the federal Constitution drafted in 1787.

This extended experiment in constitution writing was unprecedented. Never before in history, John Adams observed, had several million people had numerous opportunities "to form and establish the wisest and happiest government that human wisdom could contrive." Initial state efforts yielded varied results as citizens debated novel approaches to self-government. By 1780 the desire of prominent and well-established elites to rein in democratic power was evident. Yet in comparison to the overseas monarchy they had rejected, even the most conservative new state constitutions seemed risky and bold.

At least three common threads ran through all the documents. First, fearing executive might, drafters curtailed the power of state governors to dismiss assemblies, raise armies, declare war, fill offices, or grant privileges. Colonial governors had been appointed from above, by proprietors or the crown, and they could serve terms of any length. In contrast, state governors would now be elected annually, usually by the assembly. Moreover, their service was subject to impeachment and controlled by term limits. In Pennsylvania, the most radical of the new constitutions did away with a single governor altogether, placing executive power in the hands of a twelve-member council elected by the people.

Second, drafters expanded the strength of legislatures and increased their responsiveness to the popular will. They made elections more frequent, and they enlarged the size of assemblies to allow greater local involvement. They also reduced property requirements for holding office and changed limits on the right to vote to allow wider participation.

Third, the constitution-makers feared the possible corruptions that came when people held more than one office at the same time. Having experienced these glaring conflicts of interest firsthand, they stressed the separation of executive, legislative, and judicial posts. Preventing members of the executive branch from also holding a legislative seat removed any prospect for a cabinet-style government along the lines of the British model.

Tensions in the Military Ranks

A new republican order, whatever its nature, could not defend itself without a suitable fighting force. Just as defunct colonial administrations gave way to new state governments after much debate, colonial militia companies transformed into state militia amid serious arguments. In the state militias and in Washington's national army, which was controlled and paid by the Continental Congress, tensions emerged from the start. Animated discussions erupted as to what

IMAGE

George Washington at Valley Forge

constituted equitable pay, appropriate discipline, suitable tactics, and a proper distribution of limited supplies. Others argued over whether wealth, popularity, vision, military experience, political savvy, European training, or influential ties should play a role in determining who received, or retained, the cherished right to command.

One heated topic involved the election of officers. Wealthy gentry assumed that they would command the state militias, while citizen soldiers demanded the right to choose their own leaders. Another source of tension concerned the right of a prosperous individual to buy exemption from military service or to send a paid substitute. In 1776, as Washington's army had retreated into Pennsylvania, militia in Philadelphia had chastised "Gentlemen who formerly Paraded in our Company and now in the time of greatest danger have turn'd their backs." They asked whether state authorities meant "to force the poorer kind into the field and suffer the Rich & the Great to remain at home?"

Three years later, some of these same Philadelphia militia, bitter that the burdens of the war always fell disproportionately on the poor, took part in what became known as the Fort Wilson Riot. Staging a demonstration in October 1779 spurred by soaring food prices, they intentionally marched past the stately home of James Wilson, where wealthy Patriots had gathered. "The time is now arrived," the demonstrators' handbill proclaimed, "to prove whether the suffering friends of this country, are to be enslaved, ruined and starved, by a few overbearing Merchants, . . . Monopolizers and Speculators." Shots were exchanged, and six died in the melee at "Fort Wilson." (Wilson himself went on to become a leader of the 1787 Constitutional Convention.)

Subtle class divisions also beset the Continental Army, where jealousies over rank plagued the status-conscious officer corps. Congressional power to grant military commissions, often on regional and political grounds, only intensified disputes. Also, Americans representing Congress abroad were empowered to promise high military posts to attract European officers. Some of these recruits served the American cause well, such as Johann de Kalb and Friedrich von Steuben (both born in Germany) and Thaddeus Kosciusko and Casimir Pulaski from Poland. In France, at age nineteen, the Marquis de Lafayette secured a commission to be a major general in America, and he assisted Washington impressively throughout the war.

In contrast, other foreign officers displayed arrogance and spread dissension. Irish-born Thomas Conway, for example, courted congressional opponents of Washington and encouraged the desires of General Horatio Gates to assume top command. Whether or not a concerted "Conway Cabal" ever existed, Washington managed to defuse tensions from Valley Forge during the hard winter of 1777–1778. His numerous letters helped to consolidate his position with Congress and to patch frayed relations with Gates.

Another rival for command of the army, English-born Charles Lee, met disfavor several months later, when Washington ordered him to attack the rear guard of Clinton's army as it withdrew from Philadelphia to New York. Lee mismanaged the encounter at Monmouth, New Jersey, on June 28, 1778, and only Washington's swift action stopped a premature retreat. The Battle of Monmouth ended in a draw, but American troops claimed victory and took pride in their swift recovery and hard fighting.

Shaping a Diverse Army

George Washington at Valley Forge

The army's improved effectiveness came in large part from the efforts of Friedrich von Steuben, a European officer recruited by Benjamin Franklin after charges of homosexuality disrupted his German military career. He had arrived at Valley Forge in February 1778, offering to serve without pay. There he found soldiers with poor food, scant clothing, and limited training. Many Americans still wanted to see a more democratic citizen army, with elected officers and limited hierarchy. But Washington hoped to mold long-term soldiers into a more "Europeanized" force, and Steuben suited his needs. The German worked energetically to drill soldiers who, in turn, trained others.

Pennsylvania Capitol Preservation Committee

■ More than a century after the grim winter at Valley Forge, artist Edwin Abbey composed this mural of Steuben drilling Washington's soldiers in February 1778.

DOCUMENT

Letter from a
Revolutionary War
Soldier

New discipline helped boost morale. Still, terms of service and wage levels remained sources of contention. So did the disparities in treatment and pay between officers and enlisted men. There were other grievances: inept congressional committees overseeing the war effort, incompetent officers filling political appointments, and a frustrating shortage of new recruits. Arguments also persisted over whether women or African Americans could serve in the army.

Women organized in diverse ways to assist the war effort, making uniforms and running farms and businesses for absent husbands. A few American women, such as Deborah Sampson of Massachusetts, disguised themselves as men and fought. Far more accompanied the troops to cook and wash in the camps. Earning scant pay, they carried water to the weary and wounded on the battlefield. Serving in these capacities, they formed a presence in both armies. As many as 20,000 women may have accompanied the American army during the war. Mary Hays, wife of a Pennsylvania soldier, endured the winter at Valley Forge and later hauled pitchers of water on the battlefield at Monmouth. When her husband was wounded, she is said to have set down her jug and joined his gun crew, earning folk legend status as the cannon-firing "Molly Pitcher."

After petitioning to fight, free blacks were allowed to join the revolutionary army. Rhode Island even formed an African American regiment. But repeated proposals to arm southern slaves met with defeat. South Carolina and Virginia went so far as to move in the opposite direction, offering to give away slaves captured from Loyalist planters as a bonus to white recruits. Thus it is no surprise that thousands of enslaved people, especially in the South, risked their lives to escape to British lines.

The War at Sea

Even as the Americans' army grew into a respectable force, their lack of naval strength proved a constant disadvantage. As early as October 13, 1775, the Continental Congress had agreed to arm two vessels to prey on British supply ships. The vote marked the birth of the American navy. Despite objections, Congress promptly appointed a committee to acquire sailing craft, and most of the thirteen states built up their own small navies, adding to the confusion. The lack of central coordination proved deadly. When Massachusetts sent its ships along the Maine coast to challenge a Loyalist buildup at Castine in 1779, British vessels cornered the fleet at Penobscot Bay and crushed the enterprise.

Despite its strength, the British navy faced increasing challenges as more European powers joined the fray: France in 1778, Spain in 1779, and Holland in 1780. The English feared possible invasion, and French corsairs harassed Britain's coastline, joined by American captains. One such captain, a Scottish immigrant named John Paul Jones, arrived in European waters from America in early 1778. In April, Jones raided the port of Whitehaven in his native Scotland, and the propaganda triumph of an American success in British waters proved huge. The brazen young captain won an even greater victory the next year when his crew managed to board Britain's sleek new H.M.S. *Serapis* and capture the frigate before their own vessel sank.

In all, the Continental Navy equipped more than fifty vessels and captured nearly 200 British craft as prizes. But these numbers pale in comparison to the activities of American privateers. More than a thousand private shipowners obtained licenses from Congress to seize enemy ships and divide the proceeds among themselves and their crew. With international commerce curtailed, shipowners and sailors were eager to try their luck. Their small, quick boats swarmed the Atlantic like troublesome gnats, frustrating England's mighty navy. By war's end the British had surrendered 2,000 ships, 12,000 men, and goods valued at £18 million. And privateering drew merchant investors into the Patriot war effort, helping to bind the coastal elite more firmly to the American cause.

The Long Road to Yorktown

By July 1778, Clinton's British forces had returned to New York City, and their situation had not improved. Frustrated in New England and the middle tier of states, Clinton revived the southern strategy discussed at the beginning of the war. Less thickly settled than the North, the South appeared more vulnerable. It supposedly contained a wide array of Loyalists who would offer support. Also, the South's lengthy growing season meant more fodder for wagon horses and cavalry mounts. The long southern coastline had little protection, and Washington's distant army would have trouble defending the region. Moreover, nearly 500,000 slaves posed a threat to Patriot planters and represented potential support for British invaders. Finally, the same whites who dreaded slave rebellion also feared war with Native Americans, so the possible use of Indian allies also entered Britain's strategic calculation.

Indian Warfare and Frontier Outposts

Most Native Americans in eastern North America remained loyal to the British. Exceptions existed, such as the Oneida, Tuscarora, and Catawba, but many Indians had long-standing grievances about white encroachments. In Appalachia, colonial land investors and colonists had defied the king's Proclamation Line for more than a decade. When dissident Cherokee, led by a young war chief named Dragging Canoe, attacked intruders on the Watauga River in July 1776, whites struck back. In all, 6,000 troops from four southern states pushed into the mountains, laying waste to Cherokee villages.

Daniel Boone had already led migrants through Cumberland Gap in western Virginia to establish a fort on the Kentucky River at Boonesborough in 1775. By 1777 these pioneer families faced Indian adversaries who were fighting for their homelands. The Native Americans were also being urged on by Henry Hamilton, the British commandant at far-off Detroit. In one six-month span, Hamilton, who became known as the Hair Buyer, received seventy-seven prisoners and 129 scalps from this frontier warfare. Along the upper Ohio, violence escalated in 1777, when Americans killed Shawnee leader Cornstalk and his son during a truce. The next

The Revolutionary War in the West

━━━ British and their Indian allies

━━━ Patriots and their Spanish allies

✴ British victories

✴ Patriot victories

⬛ Spanish Louisiana

⬛ British West Florida

🔫 Fort

─── Several present state lines included for orientation

① Daniel Boone moves through Cumberland Gap to establish Boonesborough, 1775

② Shawnee Indians cross the Ohio River to attack Boonesborough, 1778

③ Patriot raiders from Ft. Pitt descend the Mississippi River to capture Natchez, 1778

④ George Rogers Clark secures Kaskaskia and Cahokia, 1778

⑤ Henry Hamilton moves from Ft. Detroit to Vincennes, 1778

⑥ Clark takes Vincennes from the British and captures Hamilton, 1779

⑦ Sioux, Chippewa, Sauk attack Spanish St. Louis, 1780

⑧ Bernardo de Gálvez seizes Mobile, 1780; Pensacola, 1781

⬛ **MAP 7.3**
THE REVOLUTIONARY WAR IN THE WEST

year, they murdered the neutral Delaware leader, White Eyes. Four years later, at the village of Gnadenhutten (south of modern-day Canton, Ohio), militia from Pennsylvania massacred 100 peaceful Delaware men, women, and children who had been converted to Christianity by missionaries of the Moravian Church.

By then, conflict involving Native Americans had also flared farther north. Joseph Brant, a mixed-race Mohawk leader educated in New England and loyal to the British, pushed south from Fort Niagara on Lake Ontario, attacking poorly guarded frontier settlements. First in the Wyoming Valley of northeastern Pennsylvania and later in New York's Cherry Valley, the raiders killed hundreds of non-Indian settlers. In the summer of 1779, American General John Sullivan led a campaign to annihilate Indian towns in reprisal.

■ The British used Fort Niagara (on the southwest edge of Lake Ontario, at the mouth of the Niagara River) to launch attacks on American settlements and to shelter Indian allies. During the harsh winter of 1779–1780, 5,000 Iroquois refugees, made homeless by the scorched-earth campaign of General John Sullivan, camped near the fort in 5 feet of snow.

Sullivan's revenge-minded troops, numbering more than 4,000, destroyed forty villages of the four tribes in the Iroquois Confederacy most linked to the British cause: the Mohawk, Onondaga, Cayuga, and Seneca. They avoided towns of the two Iroquois groups sympathetic to the Americans—the Oneida and Tuscarora—but elsewhere they chopped down orchards, torched crops, and sent Indian refugees streaming to Fort Niagara. Hunger and retaliatory raids haunted the region until the end of the war.

While the British were passing arms and supplies to the divided Iroquois Confederacy through Fort Niagara, they were also using several western posts to arm other Indian allies and seek an advantage in the interior. Soldiers at Fort Michilimackinac recruited Sioux, Chippewa, and Sauk warriors for an unsuccessful attack on Spanish-held St. Louis in 1780. At Fort Detroit, Hamilton continued to equip war parties of Ottawa, Fox, and Miami Indians to attack American newcomers migrating into the Ohio Valley.

In 1778, with support from his home state of Virginia, a young Patriot surveyor named George Rogers Clark organized a foray west to counter these raids and lend support to Spanish and French allies in the upper Mississippi Valley. He secured settlements on the Mississippi River, and in February 1779 he led a grueling winter march to the fort at Vincennes in southern Indiana. In surprising that outpost on the Wabash River, the Americans managed to capture Henry Hamilton, but they failed to seize Detroit.

The Unpredictable War in the South

The rebel war effort beyond the Appalachian Mountains expanded south in 1778, when Patriot raiders captured Natchez on the lower Mississippi and seized property in British West Florida. But it was the energetic governor of Spanish Louisiana, Bernardo de Gálvez, whose actions proved decisive. Living in New Orleans, Gálvez maintained a careful neutrality between the Americans and their British rivals through 1778. But when Spain allied with France and declared war on Britain the next year, the governor acted quickly to keep the British from gaining ground on the Gulf Coast.

Moving from west to east, Governor Gálvez drove the British from the Mississippi River in 1779, seized their fort at Mobile in 1780, and conquered Pensacola, the capital of British West Florida, in 1781. The fall of Mobile and Pensacola cut British supply lines to the southeast-

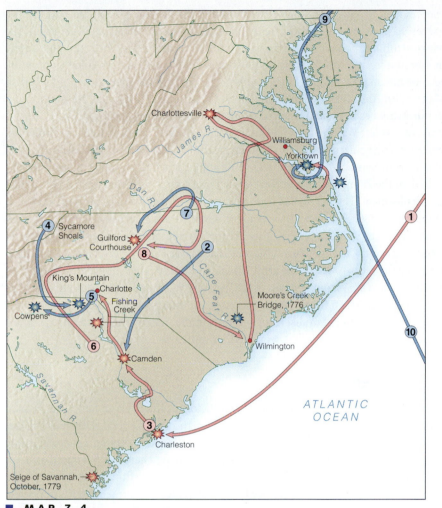

The Revolutionary War in the South
— British and their Loyalist allies
— Patriots and their French allies
✸ British victories
✸ Patriot victories

1 Clinton and Cornwallis force surrender of Charleston, May 1780
2 Gates moves the American army to Camden, August 1780
3 Cornwallis bests Gates at Camden and moves North, August 1780
4 Americans defeat Ferguson at Kings Mountain, October 1780
5 Morgan meets British at Cowpens, defeats Tarleton, January 1781
6 Cornwallis pursues Greene's army across the Dan River, February 1781
7 Greene confronts Cornwallis at Guilford Courthouse, March 1781
8 After a retreat to Wilmington, Cornwallis moves to Virginia, April 1781
9 Washington moves south, pins Cornwallis at Yorktown, August 1781
10 De Grasse from West Indies, defeats the British fleet, September 1781

■ **MAP 7.4**
THE REVOLUTIONARY WAR IN THE SOUTH

ern interior, hurting Creek and Cherokee warriors. Without additional guns, knives, and powder, the Indians could offer little assistance in Britain's ambitious plan to win back the South. It was support the British could ill afford to lose.

Still, the crown's forces regained control of most of Georgia from the rebels in 1778. The next year, they blocked American and French efforts to retake Savannah. Early in 1780, British generals Clinton and Cornwallis ferried troops by sea from New York to South Carolina, and by May they had isolated Charleston and forced the surrender of 5,500 American troops—the largest loss of American men and weapons during the entire war. A confident Clinton returned to New York, leaving Cornwallis in command in South Carolina as fierce fighting erupted across the state. Banastre Tarleton's British cavalry, along with Loyalist supporters, went head to head against the guerrilla bands led by Thomas Sumter, Andrew Pickens, and Francis Marion.

In June 1780, Congress appointed Horatio Gates to take command of southern operations, and he hurried to the Carolinas with fresh troops. On August 16, Gates's army confronted Cornwallis at Camden, South Carolina, 120 miles north of Charleston. The Americans, short on rest, food, and leadership, suffered another huge defeat. Two days after the Camden disaster, as Gates fled north, Tarleton's cavalry landed another blow. They surprised Sumter's band of 800 partisans at Fishing Creek near the Catawba River and took 300 prisoners. Suffering almost no losses themselves, the cavalry inflicted 150 casualties and freed several hundred Loyalists and British regulars.

That September, as Washington absorbed word of the defeats at Camden and Fishing Creek, he received another rude shock. Benedict Arnold—in command of West Point, the key outpost controlling the Hudson River—had plotted to defect and yield the post to the British. An admired leader, Arnold was also self-centered. When Congress failed to promote him, he became alienated from the Patriot cause. The capture of General Arnold's British contact, Major John André, alerted Washington to the scheme. He hanged the major as an enemy spy, but Arnold escaped and received command of British troops.

Five years of war left Washington and Congress facing severe problems: soaring inflation, scarce resources, sinking citizen morale, and mounting disobedience among enlisted men. Early in 1780, soldiers from Massachusetts, New York, and Connecticut had mutinied in separate incidents. Members of the Pennsylvania and New Jersey Lines soon staged similar strikes over disputed terms of enlistment. The British had reason for optimism as Cornwallis pressed into North Carolina in the fall of 1780. But the next twelve months saw a dramatic reversal in their fortunes.

That reversal began in October with a surprising Patriot victory at King's Mountain in the southern backcountry, where Cornwallis had sent Major Patrick Ferguson with a troop of South Carolina Loyalists to guard the army's flank and **harry** rebel supporters. More than 800 frontiersmen rallied at Sycamore Shoals in the Watauga Valley and raced south to challenge the British. On October 6, just below North Carolina's southern border, these sharpshooters surrounded and decimated the Loyalist troops. Ferguson died in the one-sided affair, and his force lost more than 1,000 men—killed, wounded, or captured.

The Final Campaign

A shrewd change in American leadership followed the victory at King's Mountain. Congress, on Washington's advice, replaced Gates in the southern command with General Nathanael Greene, an experienced Rhode Islander who had served as the army's quartermaster general. Greene arrived in Charlotte, North Carolina, in December 1780, taking charge of a tattered army of 1,600. Shocked by the violence of partisan warfare and conscious of the need to win public support, he urged restraint on such experienced guerrilla fighters as Sumter and Marion while weaving them into his overall plans to conduct an elusive "fugitive war." Greene decided to divide his small army and send half his men into South Carolina under the seasoned Daniel Morgan to harass the British flank. "It makes the most of my inferior force," he explained, "for it compels my adversary to divide his, and holds him in doubt as to his own line of conduct."

Cornwallis took the bait and dispatched Tarleton, who caught up with Morgan at Hannah's Cowpens, west of King's Mountain, on January 17, 1781. The outnumbered rebel militia lacked experience and discipline, but Morgan turned this weakness to an advantage at the Battle of Cowpens. He stationed the militia units in front of his Continental forces with orders to fire two rounds and fall back. Sensing an enemy retreat, the British force of 1,100 advanced too far too fast. Morgan's men promptly overwhelmed them. Tarleton managed to escape, but he left behind 100 dead, 800 prisoners, and most of his horses and ammunition. Morgan's victorious Patriot force suffered only 148 casualties. He rightly called the Battle of Cowpens "a devil of a whipping."

Though frustrated, Cornwallis clung to the belief that "a successful battle may give us America." He discarded all excess baggage and pursued the rebel army 200 miles across North Carolina. Greene, continuing his elusive "fugitive war," directed a speedy retreat over swollen rivers to the Virginia border. Then he doubled back to confront the weary British in the Battle of Guilford Courthouse on March 15. Although the American forces eventually withdrew from the field, Cornwallis sustained such heavy losses that he was forced to alter his plans.

The British retreated to the coast at Wilmington, North Carolina, and then marched north in early summer 1781 to Yorktown, Virginia. There, Cornwallis hoped to obtain reinforcements by sea, rally Loyalists in the Chesapeake region, and divide the rebelling colonies. The design's success hinged on naval superiority and timely support from General Clinton in New York. But Cornwallis could be assured of neither.

■ The joint American-French victory at the siege of Yorktown, Virginia, in October 1781 ended British hopes for preventing American independence. As Cornwallis's troops marched out to lay down their arms, a band played "The World Turned Upside Down." "Finally," Lafayette wrote proudly, "everything came together at once, and we had a sensational turn of events. . . . The play is over."

In August the French fleet in the Caribbean set out for Chesapeake Bay. Admiral François De Grasse planned to spend eight weeks in North American waters. The move gave Washington (still in the north) brief access to impressive naval power, and he seized his chance. He sent word south to Lafayette in Virginia to keep Cornwallis contained at Yorktown. Then, to hold Clinton's forces in New York, he ordered his men to make a show as if preparing for a lengthy siege. But instead of besieging New York City, American soldiers and their French allies slipped away, secretly marching south to lay a trap for the British army.

Admiral De Grasse reached Chesapeake Bay with two dozen ships at the end of August. On September 5, he repulsed a British fleet off the mouth of the bay, dashing Cornwallis's hopes for relief by sea and allowing Washington to tighten the noose. When 9,000 Americans and 7,800 French converged on Yorktown in late September, they outnumbered their 8,000 opponents by more than two to one, and the siege proved brief. Plagued by sickness and shortages of food and munitions, the British surrendered on October 19, 1781. For Washington and his army, Yorktown was a stunning victory. Intermittent warfare continued for another year. But the Americans finally had powerful leverage to bargain for peace and force Britain to recognize their independence.

Winning the Peace

After Yorktown, the final phase of the war played out in European courts. There, the diplomatic maneuvering proved complicated and risky, with Benjamin Franklin, John Adams, and John Jay as the key American players. Often at odds, the three men nevertheless managed to achieve a final triumph that proved as unlikely and momentous as Washington's victory in Virginia. They did it, wrote the immodest Adams, "in spite of the malice of enemies, the finesse of Allies, and the mistakes of Congress."

For the British, the road to the peace table had been long and unpleasant. Early feelers about a negotiated settlement—from the Howes in 1776 and the Carlisle Commission in 1778—had not mentioned independence. But conditions changed drastically after Yorktown. Domestic unrest in Britain had already boiled into riots, and the expanded war was going poorly in India and the West Indies. "O God, it is all over!" Lord North muttered when he received the news of Cornwallis's defeat in Virginia.

MAP

The American Revolution

Benjamin West, *Signing of the Peace Treaty.* Courtesy, Winterthur Museum

■ The final American victory in the War of Independence came at the peace table, when negotiators John Jay, John Adams, and Benjamin Franklin won favorable terms in the 1783 Treaty of Paris. Benjamin West's unfinished painting also includes the absent Henry Laurens (rear) and Franklin's grandson (right), the delegation's secretary.

Within months, Sir Guy Carleton replaced Clinton in command of the remaining British forces in America, the hawkish Lord Germain stepped down from the Cabinet, and North resigned after twelve years as prime minister. Even the king spoke of abdicating. But instead, he approved a new ministry more suited to the rising antiwar sentiment in Parliament. The Earl of Shelburne became prime minister in July 1782. Even before he assumed office, he had authorized peace discussions with his old acquaintance, Benjamin Franklin.

Franklin was in a difficult position. The crucial alliance he had negotiated with France stated that the Americans would not sign a separate peace with Britain. Moreover, Congress, grateful for vital French military and financial support, had instructed the American negotiators to defer to the wishes of Vergennes. The Americans did not realize that the French foreign minister had already entertained thoughts of a truce that would leave London in control of all the territory it currently held in America, including New York City and parts of the lower South. Vergennes opposed the Americans' republican principles, and he refused to treat the American diplomats as equal partners.

Still, the American peace commissioners fared surprisingly well in the treacherous waters of European diplomacy, starting with Franklin's first informal talks with the British. He laid out four "necessary" points, leading with the recognition of American independence. To this he added the removal of British troops, the right to fish in Newfoundland waters, and the revision of the Canadian border, which the Quebec Act of 1774 had pushed south to the Ohio River. Franklin then noted some "desirable" items for later bargaining. The British, he suggested, should consider paying an indemnity for war damages, an act that would officially acknowledge their own blame for the war. Perhaps they should cede Canada to the United States as well.

For its part, Britain sought compensation for roughly 70,000 American Loyalists who had been driven from their homes, plus the right to collect old debts that colonists had owed to British merchants before 1776. Hoping to disrupt the American-French alliance and to reestablish trade with their former colonies, the British negotiated preliminary peace terms with the Americans in November 1782. In return for independence, troop withdrawal, and fishing rights, the Americans agreed vaguely that their Congress would "recommend" that individual states approve compensation for confiscated Loyalist property.

On the Canadian boundary question, the Americans scored another success, but one that came at the expense of Indian nations. By giving up their bid for all of Canada, the negotiators persuaded Britain to relinquish the Ohio Valley and accept a northern boundary for the United States defined by the Great Lakes and the St. Lawrence River. In the west, the United States would reach to the Mississippi River, and Americans would gain free navigation on that waterway, despite Spanish opposition. In the South, the thirty-first parallel, above East and West Florida, would provide the American boundary.

The diplomats endorsed the final peace terms at Versailles, France, in September 1783. Amid all the other treaty terms, the British yielded East and West Florida to Spain. In the process, however, they made no mention of the Indians who had served as allies in the American conflict. Abandoned, the Native Americans had to confront their new situation alone. To end up "betrayed to our Enemies & divided between the Spaniards and the Amer-

MAP

Territorial Campaigns in Eastern America after Treaty of Paris icans is Cruel & Ungenerous," protested the Creek leader, Alexander McGillivray. His people had been "most Shamefully deserted."

Conclusion

The War for Independence that began at Lexington had lasted eight years. Like any lengthy armed struggle, it took a heavy toll on combatants and noncombatants alike. Personal survival was far from certain, as encounters with sickness and the enemy carried off enlisted men. American forces lost an estimated 25,000 soldiers, a huge number in proportion to the small overall population.

For those who avoided death, lesser dangers abounded. Uprooting from home became commonplace, losses of property were extensive, and indebtedness proved widespread. Despite constant uncertainties at the individual level, a makeshift revolutionary army, learning as it marched, had forced the British to concede American independence.

As in all wars, some of the most decisive action occurred far from the battlefield. In London, weakness in the chain of command, a lumbering bureaucracy, and divided public sentiment undermined the British war effort. Elsewhere in Europe, skillful American diplomats built the international alliances needed to secure victory and won peace terms that promised survival to the new confederation of states. A flurry of constitution writing unprecedented in history had launched more than a dozen newly independent states, and the Articles of Confederation, approved after long delay, had knit them together into a formal league with a common Congress. The new and difficult art of republican self-government remained a work in progress, with some of the most difficult and contentious choices still to come. The fragile unity built on fighting a common enemy would be strained to the limit as new debates erupted over the meaning and direction of the unfinished revolution.

Sites to Visit

Saratoga National Historical Park

The National Park Service maintains a visitor center and has arranged a self-guided battlefield tour that includes the locations for the British and American camps during the crucial engagement of October 1777 at this park, which is located 10 miles south of Saratoga Springs, New York, on Route 50.

Brandywine Battlefield State Park

This park is located on Highway 202 west of Philadelphia, Pennsylvania, not far from the borders of Delaware and Maryland. (At nearby Chadds Ford, the Wyeth Museum celebrates one of America's great artistic families.)

The Continental Congress
http://lcweb2.loc.gov/ammem/amlaw/lawhome.html

This Web site in the American Memory series of the Library of Congress contains materials, starting from 1774, that concern the First and Second Continental Congress.

Virginia Runaways Project
http://people.uvawise.edu/history/runaways/

This digital database of runaway slave and servant advertisements contains transcripts and images of all runaway ads placed in Virginia newspapers from 1736 to 1777. It contains a new search interface and updated support material.

Cowpens National Battlefield
http://www.nps.gov/cowp/index.htm

The actual site of the battle where Daniel Morgan's troops defeated Banastre Tarleton's British forces (January 17, 1781) is located 10 miles west of Gafney, South Carolina, off Highway I-85. The battle was dramatized in Hollywood's film *The Patriot* (2000).

Spy Letters of the American Revolution
http://www.si.umich.edu/spies/index-timeline.html

This Web site, maintained by the Clements Library at the University of Michigan, contains facsimiles and transcriptions of diverse spy letters contained in the Sir Henry Clinton collection and provides some context for each letter.

Old Fort Niagara
http://www.oldfortniagara.org/

This New York State Historic Site overlooks Lake Ontario at the mouth of the Niagara River. Built by the French in 1727, the fort is located just off the Robert Moses Parkway, not far from Niagara Falls, at Youngstown, New York.

Birth of the Navy of the United States
http://www.history.navy.mil/

Visit the Naval Historical Center Web site (Early History Branch) to learn about the history of the U.S. Navy in the Revolutionary era.

For Further Reading

General

Colin G. Calloway, *The American Revolution in Indian Country: Crisis and Diversity in Native American Communities* (1995).

Gregory Fremont-Barnes and Richard Alan Ryerson, *The Encyclopedia of the American Revolutionary War: A Political, Social, and Military History,* 5 vols. (2006).

Don Higginbotham, *The War of American Independence* (1971).

Piers Mackesy, *The War for America, 1775–1783* (1965).

Robert Middlekauff, *The Glorious Cause* (1982).

Gordon S. Wood, *The Creation of the American Republic, 1776–1787* (1969).

Alfred F. Young, ed., *Beyond the American Revolution: Explorations in the History of American Radicalism* (1993).

"Things Are Now Come to That Crisis"

Ira D. Gruber, *The Howe Brothers and the American Revolution* (1972).

Mary Beth Norton, *Liberty's Daughters: The Revolutionary Experience of American Women, 1750–1800* (1980).

Ray Raphael, *A People's History of the American Revolution: How Common People Shaped the Fight for Independence* (2001).

Richard A. Ryerson, *The Revolution Is Now Begun: The Radical Committees of Philadelphia, 1765–1776* (1978).

Simon Schama, *Rough Crossings: Britain, the Slaves, and the American Revolution* (2006).

Declaring Independence

David Hackett Fischer, *Washington's Crossing* (2004).

Eric Foner, *Tom Paine and Revolutionary America* (1976).

Pauline Maier, *American Scripture: Making the Declaration of Independence* (1997).

Barnet Schecter, *The Battle for New York: The City at the Heart of the American Revolution* (2002).

Gordon S. Wood, *The Americanization of Benjamin Franklin* (2004).

The Struggle to Win French Support

Wayne Bodle, *The Valley Forge Winter: Civilians and Soldiers at War* (2002).

Stephen Conway, *The British Isles and the War of American Independence* (2000).

Jonathan R. Dull, *A Diplomatic History of the American Revolution* (1985).

Sylvia R. Frey, *The British Soldier in America: A Social History of Military Life in the Revolutionary Period* (1981).

Max M. Mintz, *The Generals of Saratoga: John Burgoyne and Horatio Gates* (1990).

Legitimate States, a Respectable Military

Willi Paul Adams, *The First American Constitutions: Republican Ideology and the Making of the State Constitutions in the Revolutionary Era* (1980).

Jeff Broadwater, *George Mason: Forgotten Founder* (2006).

Elisha P. Douglass, *Rebels and Democrats: The Struggle for Equal Political Rights and Majority Rule During the American Revolution* (1955).

Charles Patrick Neimeyer, *America Goes to War: A Social History of the Continental Army* (1996).

Evan Thomas, *John Paul Jones: Sailor, Hero, Father of the American Navy* (2003).

Alfred F. Young, *Masquerade: The Life and Times of Deborah Sampson, Continental Soldier* (2004)

The Long Road to Yorktown

Robert M. Calhoon, *The Loyalists in Revolutionary America, 1760–1781* (1973).

Max M. Mintz, *Seeds of Empire: The American Revolutionary Conquest of the Iroquois* (1999).

Richard B. Morris, *The Peacemakers: The Great Powers and American Independence* (1965).

Steven Rosswurm, *Arms, Country, and Class: The Philadelphia Militia and the Lower Sort During the American Revolution* (1987).

J. Barton Starr, *Tories, Dons, and Rebels: The American Revolution in British West Florida* (1976).

Carl Van Doren, *Mutiny in January: The Story of a Crisis in the Continental Army* (1943).

For quizzes and other resources on these topics, go to www.longmanamericanhistory.com.

New Beginnings: The 1780s

During the Revolutionary War years, between 1775 and 1782, a huge smallpox epidemic ricocheted relentlessly across broad sections of North America. At times the epidemic entwined itself with the war, traveling on supply ships and moving with marching troops. In the Northeast, it struck during the siege of Boston and the attack on Quebec. In the South, it cut down hundreds of Virginia slaves who had escaped at the start of the war to join Governor Dunmore's "Ethiopian Regiment." The disease found additional victims during the British siege of Charleston in 1780.

Like the war itself, smallpox erupted first in Massachusetts. But the devastating contagion spread far more widely than the military destruction, proving truly continental in scope. It gained a foothold in New Orleans, Mexico City, and the trading posts that dotted the Canadian interior. In 1781 the disease ravaged Indian villages on the Northwest Coast, devastated missions on the Baja Peninsula, and erupted at California's San Gabriel Mission, where Spanish-speaking newcomers were building a village named Our Lady of the Angels (the start of modern-day Los Angeles). On the Atlantic coast, smallpox menaced Virginia as French and American troops surrounded the British at Yorktown. As the War of Independence ended, the transcontinental epidemic also drew to a close.

The contagion left a patchwork of destruction from the Atlantic to the Pacific. Smallpox losses were greatest among Native Americans, and few groups or regions remained untouched. British sea captain George Vancouver, probing Puget Sound in 1792, observed numerous skulls, ribs, and other human remains "scattered about the beach."

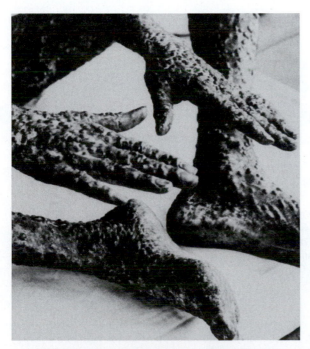

■ Smallpox "spread like lightning through all the missions," causing "havoc which only those who have seen it can believe. The towns and missions were . . . deserted, and bodies were seen in the road." Time and again, "the poor little children, abandoned beside the dead, died without help" (Father Luis Sales, Baja California, 1781). This modern photo shows that smallpox persisted until its global eradication in the 1970s.

■ **MAP 8.1**

THE SPREAD OF SMALLPOX ACROSS NORTH AMERICA, 1775–1782   A great smallpox epidemic swept North America during the Revolutionary era. In 1781 it moved up the Baja Peninsula with settlers heading for San Gabriel, the Spanish mission that became Los Angeles, California.

The spread of smallpox, 1775–1782
— Known transmission route
— Probable transmission route
Modern state and provincial boundaries are provided for reference

When Vancouver's pilot, Peter Puget, pressed farther into the sound that is named for him, he found deserted villages that only a dozen years earlier had bustled with people. In its eight-year course, the fearsome virus took more than 130,000 North American lives, many times the total of 25,000 Americans lost in service during the Revolution.

As the dual scourges of epidemic and war subsided, fresh problems confronted North America's inhabitants. Great Britain's mainland colonies had won their independence, but questions remained as to which European powers would exert the most influence on the huge continent. British power ruled Canada; Spanish authority claimed much of the West; and French officials still dreamed of regaining control over the Mississippi Valley. In the North Pacific, Russians intruded on the Alaskan coast, and soon the prospect of trade with China lured sea captains from the United States to seek furs along the Northwest Coast.

In the woodlands between the Appalachian Mountains and the Mississippi River, Indians whom Pontiac had sought to unify once again endured sudden transfers of their ancestral land between distant powers. But now the rapid incursion of American settlers added new urgency to their situation. Farther east, inhabitants of the Atlantic seaboard faced an array of thorny problems after warfare and smallpox loosened their grip. Half a million people remained legally enslaved, and they were potential allies for any European power seeking to disrupt the fragile new **federation**.

In addition, members of the Confederation's Continental Congress in Philadelphia had a restless army to pay, a weak government to reform, and enormous war debts to confront. Acceptance of the Articles of Confederation in 1781 had not come easily, and all assumed that the basic structure of governance would demand further revision and adjustment. However, few could foresee that within eight years it would be set aside for a more centralized federal design.

Beating Swords into Plowshares

At first, in the wake of military victory over Britain, the short-term survival of the new United States of America seemed assured, thanks to years of intense fighting and skillful diplomacy. The former colonies had banded together under the Articles of Confederation, finally ratified in 1781, which placed specific governmental powers in the hands of an elected national legislature, or Continental Congress. But deeper questions persisted regarding the new republican experiment. With peace at hand, how would citizens transform their "swords into plowshares," as urged by the Biblical prophet, Isaiah? Should power rest primarily with the victorious army, the wealthy merchants, or the artisans and farmers central to the revolutionary movement? Should authority be consolidated in the hands of a well-educated, new national elite, or should it be widely dispersed, with local communities and states empowered to manage their own affairs? Equally important, what cultural patterns would take hold within the fledgling society in these postwar years?

Women Petition for War Compensation

Will the Army Seize Control?

After their triumph at Yorktown, Washington's men had moved north to press British forces to evacuate New York City. More than 10,000 American troops and 500 officers encamped at Newburgh, on the Hudson River. Exhausted soldiers were eager to receive long-overdue pay and return home. Clearly, they could negotiate best for promised wages while they were still together and armed. Officers were especially reluctant to disband without certain assurances of money. In 1780 they had extracted from the Congress a promise of half pay for life. In December 1782, with no sign of compensation in sight, disgruntled officers sent a delegation to Philadelphia to press their claims.

Within Congress, the men around financier Robert Morris, including James Wilson and Alexander Hamilton, wanted to bolster and centralize the Confederation's finances. To that end, they sought a new duty of 5 percent on imported goods to raise money from the states. Revenue from this "continental impost" could make the Confederation solvent and allow it to

Demobilization: "Turned Adrift Like Old Worn-Out Horses"

*Joseph Plumb Martin was born in western Massachusetts in 1760. He enlisted in the Continental Army before his sixteenth birthday and was encamped at West Point, New York, when peace finally arrived. Later, in a compelling narrative of his wartime experiences, he recalled the **demobilization** process from the perspective of a common soldier.*

[On April 19, 1783,] we had general orders read which satisfied the most skeptical, that the war was over and the prize won [after] eight tedious years. But the soldiers said but little about it; their chief thoughts were closely fixed upon their situation. . . . Starved, ragged and meager, not a cent to help themselves with, and no means or method in view to remedy or alleviate their condition. This was appalling in the extreme. . . .

At length, the eleventh day of June 1783, arrived. "The old man," our captain, came into the room, with his hands full of papers. . . . He then handed us our discharges, or rather furloughs,. . . permission to return home, but to return to the army again if required. This was policy in government; to discharge us absolutely in our present pitiful, forlorn condition, it was feared, might cause some difficulties. . . .

Some of the soldiers went off for home the same day that their fetters were knocked off; others stayed and got their final settlement certificates, which they sold to procure decent clothing and money. . . . I was among those. . . . I now bid a final farewell to the service. I had obtained my settlement certificates and sold some of them and purchased some decent clothing, and then set off from West Point. . . .

When those who engaged to serve during the war enlisted, they were promised a hundred acres of land, each. . . . When the country had drained the last

drop of service it could screw out of the poor soldiers, they were turned adrift like old worn-out horses, and nothing said about land to pasture them upon. . . . Congress did, indeed, appropriate lands, . . . but no care was taken that the soldiers should get them. [Instead,] a pack of speculators. . .were driving about the country like so many evil spirits, endeavoring to pluck the last feather from the soldiers. The soldiers were ignorant of the ways and means to obtain their bounty lands. . . . It was, soldiers, look to yourselves; we want no more of you.

We were, also, promised six dollars and two thirds a month. . . . And what was six dollars and sixty-seven cents of this "Continental currency," as it was called, worth? It was scarcely enough to procure a man a dinner. . . . I received one month's pay in specie while on the march to Virginia, in the year 1781, and except that, I never received any pay worth the name while I belonged to the army. . . . It is provoking to think of it. The country was rigorous in exacting my compliance to *my* engagements. . .but equally careless in performing her contracts with me, and why so? One reason was

that she had all the power in her own hands and I had none. Such things ought not to be.

After the war, Martin settled on the Maine frontier, and a speculator bought his right to 100 acres of bounty land in Ohio. In 1818, as a disabled laborer with a large family, he successfully petitioned Congress for a small pension to support the household. He died poor in 1850.

Questions

1. *Why did the government worry about discharging soldiers such as Martin in 1783, and why did many of them sell their final settlement certificates?*

2. *Do elements in Martin's complaints relate to the situation of modern American combat veterans?* ■

Source: James Kirby Martin, ed., *Ordinary Courage: The Revolutionary War Adventures of Joseph Plumb Martin,* 2nd ed. (New York: Brandywine Press, 1999), pp. 159–164.

William Ranney painted *Revolutionary War Veterans Returning Home* in 1848, when the United States was at war with Mexico. The image offered a positive reminder of earlier American military success. But some soldiers leaving the Continental Army in 1783 had clearly fared better than others.

William Ranney, *Veterans of 1776 Returning from the War*, c. 1848. Dallas Museum of Art, Museum League Fund, Special Contributors and General Acquisitions Fund assume responsibility for paying off war debts. In turn, this commitment would tie the interests of wealthy citizens to the Confederation government's success. Morris even threatened to resign his post if the "nationalists" did not get their way. Rumblings from the officer corps would help these politicians push through the impost measure, crucial to their long-term goals. So they quietly encouraged the military dissidents in Newburgh.

In March 1783, anonymous petitions circulated among officers encamped at Newburgh. These inflammatory "addresses" contained a veiled threat of military takeover in order to impose stability after a turbulent revolution. They suggested that officers should sit tight, neither fighting nor laying down their arms, until Congress guaranteed their payment. Without Washington's approval, the officers at Newburgh arranged a meeting to discuss their plight.

If the plotters hoped to draw Washington into the scheme, they were sorely disappointed. He did attend the officers' meeting on March 15, but he used his commanding presence to discredit the ill-advised plan. His eyes weakened by endless wartime correspondence, he drew a pair of spectacles from his pocket, a surprising gesture that underscored his years of dedication and sacrifice. He then read a letter from Congress containing assurances of support, and he urged his officers not to take any actions that would undermine the honor they had earned. Within Congress, the frightening prospect of a coup dissolved resistance to certain demands from the officers. Chastised by Washington, the officers disavowed the "infamous propositions" and accepted a congressional offer of full pay for the next five years. In April 1783, word spread that preliminary articles of peace had been signed in Paris. By June most soldiers were headed home.

DOCUMENT

George Washington, The Newburgh Address

The Society of the Cincinnati

Washington's strong stance against the suspected Newburgh conspiracy reminded his admirers of the familiar story of Cincinnatus, a general in Rome's early Republic. The Roman Senate called Cincinnatus from his farm to command an army against invaders. After defeating the enemy, he put down his sword and took up his plow again rather than seize power as a military ruler. His selfless act earned Cincinnatus the lasting respect of the Roman people. Similarly, at a crucial moment for the American republic, Washington urged fellow officers to respect the fragile principle of civilian control over the military. Your action, Thomas Jefferson told Washington, "has probably prevented this revolution from being closed as most others have been by a subversion of that liberty it was intended to establish."

Still, Jefferson and others had grounds to fear that some military officers might meddle in politics while hiding behind the noble name of Cincinnatus. In May 1783, General Henry Knox announced formation of the Society of the Cincinnati. The new organization invoked the name of the famous Roman, in a plural form, to put its members in the best light. But it was open only to officers in the Continental Army, their descendents, and invited honorary members, so some onlookers sensed that the "Cincinnati Club" had a sinister purpose. After all, members contributed to a charitable fund that resembled a political **war chest**, and they maintained contact with each other through newsletters concerning "the general union of the states." Critics feared a separate, self-perpetuating aristocracy of the very kind Americans had fought to erase.

Washington was automatically a member of the society, but Jefferson and other friends urged the general not to accept a leadership position. Struck by this "formidable" opposition, Washington suggested changes in the society, including doing away with the hereditary and honorary memberships. However, he never played a central role in the organization, and Washington's well-publicized alterations were never implemented. The Cincinnati exerted influence as a pressure group before receding from politics in future generations.

Renaming the Landscape

The controversy over the Society of the Cincinnati represented part of a larger debate about the direction of postwar life. Many Americans—despite continuing disagreements—set out to build a national culture and a shared identity. Like the Puritans before them, they aspired to provide new models for the Atlantic world.

They began with names. Everywhere, people christened new towns, counties, streets, and schools and renamed old ones. They replaced numerous British names, such as those of hated prewar governors, so Virginia's Dunmore County received the Indian name *Shanando* (later spelled *Shenandoah*). Because most people found references to royalty distasteful, King Street in Boston quickly became State Street. Still, royal figures who had aided the revolution received their due. Newcomers on the Ohio River named their town Louisville, honoring America's wartime alliance with King Louis XVI of France.

Political leaders popularized Christopher Columbus as well. For generations, the English had downplayed the explorer's importance as they contested Spanish claims in the Western Hemisphere. Now, American writers coined the ringing term *Columbia* for their land to stress its separation from Britain. In South Carolina, citizens named their new capital Columbia in 1786. Five years later, the proposed national capital was christened the District of Columbia. In New York City, when King's College reopened in 1784 under local governance, it was called Columbia College (later Columbia University).

Of all the new names, those honoring individual war heroes became the most popular. Citizens hailed foreign supporters of the revolution—such as Lafayette, Pulaski, and Steuben—by using their names on streets and towns. They saluted American officers the same way. Washington's name was used most often, but those of Montgomery, Wayne, Greene, Lincoln, Mercer, Marion, and others popped up as well. North Carolina named one of its trans-Appalachian forts on the Cumberland River Nashborough, after General Francis Nash, who had died at the battle of Germantown. Citizens changed the fort's name to Nashville in 1784. Two years later, inhabitants of a site on the Tennessee River named their new town Knoxville in honor of General Knox, who had become the Confederation's secretary of war the previous year.

An Independent Culture

New names were just part of the story. Many felt that the American language needed to be made more independent and accessible. Noah Webster, a schoolteacher who had fought against Burgoyne, believed that "as an independent nation, our honor requires us to have a system of our own, in language as well as government." In his *American Spelling Book* (1783), Webster championed a simple, uniform written language that rejected English conventions. Words such as *colour* and *labour* lost their silent *u*, *theatre* became *theater*, and *plough* was shortened to *plow*. The New Englander followed this success with an influential grammar book and a popular reader. Webster went on to produce *An American Dictionary of the English Language* (1828) that incorporated 5,000 new words, many of them reflecting Indian origins (*tomahawk*) and American nature (*rattlesnake*).

> *Noah Webster believed that "as an independent nation, our honor requires us to have a system of our own, in language as well as government."*

Webster also joined other reformers in lobbying state legislatures for copyright laws to protect the literary works that poured from the pens of ambitious writers. Philip Freneau, a classmate of James Madison at Princeton, drafted a poem titled "The British Prison Ship" (1781), about his war experiences. Authors living near Hartford, known as the Connecticut Wits, wrote similarly nationalistic poetry. Timothy Dwight, future president of Yale College, created "The Conquest of Canaan" (1785), and Joel Barlow composed an epic titled "The Vision of Columbus" (1787), heralding a bright future.

Increasingly, the land itself captured the imagination of Americans. In 1784 a Connecticut silversmith engraved the first map of the new United States, and a recent Yale graduate, Jedidiah Morse, published *Geography Made Easy*, which went through twenty-five editions. (Five years later, Morse created *The American Geography* and earned his reputation as the "Father of American Geography.") In Philadelphia, Quaker naturalist William Bartram drafted a pioneering nature book about his travels throughout the Southeast, and the versatile painter and patriot Charles Willson Peale launched a museum to promote interest in art and the natural world. At Monticello, Thomas Jefferson corresponded with Peale and pursued his own fascination with the American landscape. He promoted exploration, tested new crops, and excavated ancient Indian mounds. In *Notes on the State of Virginia* (1785), Jefferson detailed his region's geography, society, and natural history.

In 1782 Hector St. John de Crèvecoeur, a Frenchman who made his home in America, published *Letters from an American Farmer*, posing the question "What is an American?" According to Crèvecoeur, free people flourished in America because of "a new mode of living, a new social system" that nurtured community growth. Societies for bettering jails, assisting debtors, and building libraries had existed before independence, but after the war Crèvecoeur watched a new generation creating voluntary associations at an unprecedented rate. Reformers launched more than thirty new benevolent organizations between 1783 and 1789, offering aid to the poor, the sick, and the disabled.

In 1785 prominent New Yorkers John Jay and Alexander Hamilton joined like-minded citizens to form a Society for the Promotion of the Manumission of Slaves. In Connecticut, citizens banded together in an early temperance organization to stop the abuse of liquor. Similar efforts to reform and improve the new nation sprang up everywhere. Amid such optimism, no sooner had the former British colonists disentangled themselves from the British Empire than they began to speak of shaping an expansive empire of their own.

Natural History Museum, London

■ Exploring near the Altamaha River in Georgia, John Bartram and his botanist son William found "several curious shrubs, one bearing beautiful good fruit." They named it the Franklin tree after their scientist friend in Philadelphia, Benjamin Franklin. William drew a watercolor of the rare plant and saved seeds to protect the species.

Competing for Control of the Mississippi Valley

"It has ever been my hobby-horse," John Adams wrote in 1786, "to see rising in America an empire of liberty, and a prospect of two or three hundred millions of freemen, without one noble or one king among them. You say it is impossible. . . . I would still say, let us try the experiment." Westward expansion became a persistent American theme. But during the postwar decade, interest and activity centered mostly on the land just beyond the Appalachian Mountains, territory reserved for Indians by the British until Britain ceded the lands to the United States at the end of the Revolution.

In the South in the 1780s, pioneer families searching for land pushed west through Cumberland Gap and spread out across parts of the lower Mississippi River valley, a region that eventually became known as the Old Southwest. These homesteaders promptly faced resistance from Native American inhabitants and their Spanish supporters. At the same time, north of the Ohio River, other American migrants were flocking to newly claimed woodlands later remembered as the Old Northwest. They, too, met stiff opposition from Native Americans and their British allies in neighboring Canada. By the time the Constitutional Convention met in Philadelphia in the summer of 1787, the Continental Congress of the existing Confederation government was busy revising an elaborate plan to draw this territory into the Union.

Map legend:

- Major Southeastern Indian groups
- Attempted state of Franklin
- Spanish boundary claim
- U.S. boundary set in 1783 treaty with England
- Spanish Louisiana, eastern boundary
- Spanish East Florida, northern boundary
- Spanish West Florida
- Natchez Trace

■ MAP 8.2

SOUTHERN LAND DEBATES AFTER 1783   Following the Revolution, competing forces collided in the trans-Appalachian South. The United States claimed land reaching the Mississippi River down to 31 degrees latitude, and the Spanish claimed territory north to the Tennessee River. Although major Indian tribes continued to possess much of the region, coastal states also claimed sweeping jurisdiction. In Georgia, for instance, settlement remained confined near the Savannah River, but the state sold speculators large tracts as far west as the Yazoo River.

Disputed Territory: The Old Southwest

For a generation, Spain had been rebuilding its position north of the Gulf of Mexico and east of Texas in the Old Southwest. The Spanish had acquired Louisiana from France in 1763 and had conquered West Florida. In a 1783 treaty, Britain gave back East Florida to the Spanish and agreed that Spain would retain West Florida as well. The Spanish occupied St. Augustine, Pensacola, New Orleans, and Natchez, as well as St. Louis farther north.

Because Spain controlled both banks of the lower Mississippi, the Spanish determined who could use the huge river for trade. Since 1763 they had let British subjects navigate freely on the Mississippi, so trans-Appalachian fur traders had become accustomed to using this thoroughfare. Louisiana merchants paid for goods in Spanish silver, and settlers upriver needed the hard currency. During the Revolutionary War, Americans had retained access to the river, and the Spanish in New Orleans depended on produce from the north. Still, Spanish authorities feared American expansion into the Mississippi Valley. They debated whether to resist migrants pushing from the east, or to co-opt newcomers and profit from their trade.

In 1783 Spain was shocked when Britain, through its separate treaty with the United States, granted the Americans a generous southern boundary: the thirty-first parallel. The treaty terms also included the right of Americans to navigate the Mississippi. The Spanish believed that they should be the only ones to decide whose boats had access to the Mississippi. Moreover, Spain had good reason to claim that its West Florida province stretched north *above* 31 degrees at least to the mouth of the Yazoo River and perhaps as far as the Tennessee River.

For its part, the new Confederation had the force of numbers working to its advantage. The threat of Indian attacks had dammed up westward expansion since 1775. After the war, Americans migrated by the thousands to three existing centers of Anglo settlement in the Old Southwest. By 1785, 10,000 recent migrants clustered along several rivers above Knoxville. Nearly three times that many newcomers had already staked claims to the rich land between Lexington and Louisville. In addition, another 4,000 were clearing farms along the Cumberland River around Nashville, and aggressive Americans talked about pushing even farther. They imagined establishing a foothold on the Mississippi at Chickasaw Bluffs (modern Memphis) or perhaps seizing Natchez or New Orleans.

American Claims and Indian Resistance

Powerful land speculators pressed southern legislatures to support expansion. Georgia, unlike many other states, had not relinquished its western lands to the Confederation. The state's 35-million-acre Yazoo claim stretched west from the Chattahoochee River (Georgia's present boundary with Alabama) to the Mississippi River and from the lower border of modern-day Tennessee to the thirty-first parallel. "I look forward to a time, not very far distant," wrote Judge George Walton, when Georgia "will be settled and connected . . . from the shores of the Atlantic to the banks of the Mississippi." By 1789 Walton had been elected governor of the state, and the land business boomed. During his tenure, Walton signed warrants for huge tracts up to 50,000 acres, sometimes selling unusable or even nonexistent acreage.

Unlike Georgians, pioneers from Virginia and the Carolinas faced a rugged mountain barrier. But they still trekked west through Cumberland Gap. In the decade after the war, backwoodsman Daniel Boone worked as a surveyor for these migrants in the trans-Appalachian region of Virginia that became Kentucky in 1792. During that same decade, North Carolina issued more land patents than it had created during the entire colonial era, most of them deeds for homesteads west of the mountains. Some of North Carolina's western landholders tried to create their own separate jurisdiction: the mountain state of Franklin. Without recognition from the Confederation government, their venture soon failed. Instead, all of North Carolina's western territory—from the Appalachians to the Mississippi— became the state of Tennessee in 1796.

Native American southerners, living in all these lands, suddenly found themselves caught between the competing claims of Spain and the United States.

Native American southerners, living in all these lands, suddenly found themselves caught between the competing claims of Spain and the United States. The Cherokee, Creek, Choctaw, and Chickasaw—numbering roughly 40,000 people—all debated over which leaders and strategies to follow. Some responded to their new situation by selecting leaders with European-American ties. Among the Creek, for example, Alexander McGillivray rose to prominence. The son of a wealthy Scottish trader and a Creek woman, he had been raised on his father's Georgia plantation before becoming the Creek leader in 1782. He was well equipped to bargain with Spanish and American officials.

The renegade Cherokee warrior Dragging Canoe, who had split with tribal elders before the Revolution broke out, offered a different approach. Hundreds of militant Indians, discouraged by the compromises of their leaders, had joined his band of guerrilla fighters known as the Chicamauga living along the Tennessee River. From this well-protected location—near where Alabama, Georgia, and Tennessee now meet—the Chicamauga recruited allies and led forays to stop American encroachment. But Dragging Canoe died in 1792 before he could build a strong alliance with Indians north of the Ohio River.

"We Are Now Masters": The Old Northwest

Native Americans in the North also struggled to maintain their way of life and resist the new-comers. But white Americans lost no time in claiming Indian domains ceded by Britain in the 1783 Treaty of Paris. "We are now Masters of this Island," General Philip Schuyler boasted to the Iroquois, "and can dispose of the Lands as we think proper." Britain refused to vacate western forts on the pretext that Americans still owed prewar debts to London merchants. Even so, the British could provide little material support to the region's Indians.

American delegations moved quickly to draft treaties with the Iroquois and the Ohio Valley tribes. Delegates bluntly asserted the right of the new United States government to Indian lands, treating the Native Americans as dependents rather than equals. The negotiators even took hostages to force the Indians to accept their terms. Ordinary Americans sealed these claims with a surge of migration into western Pennsylvania and beyond. "The Americans . . . put us out of our lands," Indian leaders complained to the Spanish in 1784, "extending themselves like a plague of locusts in the territories of the Ohio River which we inhabit."

Americans initially remained divided among themselves over who would control the region. Connecticut retained a "western reserve" of 4 million acres south of Lake Erie that it used to satisfy claims from the state's war veterans. Similarly, Virginia held onto land rights for an even larger "military district" to repay soldiers and war victims. But one by one, the states of Massachusetts, New York, Connecticut, and Virginia ceded large territorial claims to the Confederation government.

These western acquisitions transformed the Confederation into something more than a league of states. With lands of its own to organize, the Confederation government took on attributes of a sovereign ruling body. As the number of cessions increased, Congress put Thomas Jefferson in charge of a committee to draft "a plan for the temporary Government of the Western territory." Before he departed for Europe to replace Benjamin Franklin as the American minister to France, Jefferson drew up a design for western land distribution.

Western Land Claims Ceded by the States

■ A sketch by Congressman Thomas Jefferson shows his proposal to divide the new interior territories into fourteen states (with Number 7 to be named Saratoga after the crucial Revolutionary War victory). By suggesting numerous compact states, Jefferson hoped to maximize the congressional voting power of western farmers. Others, eager to limit western power in Congress, pushed successfully for fewer, larger states.

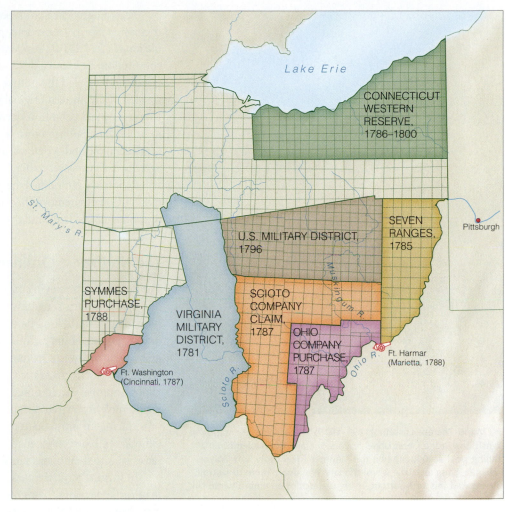

■ **MAP 8.3**

SETTLERS' OHIO, AFTER 1785   In 1785 the American government began to impose a novel grid system on the territory northwest of the Ohio River. Later, surveyors laid our similar straight geometric boundaries for states and counties accross the natural landscape of the American West.

After Jefferson sailed for France, his report became the basis for the Land Ordinance of 1785. Jefferson knew that in the South, where surveyors often staked out piecemeal claims on a first-come, first-served basis, the best property had gone to wealthy investors. Moreover, boundary **litigation** over odd-shaped lots had proved endless. To avoid these complications, the 1785 ordinance called for surveyors to lay out a grid of adjoining townships, beginning at the point where the Ohio River flowed out of Pennsylvania. A township would contain thirty-six numbered sections, each 1 mile square (640 acres). The ordinance reserved the income from one valuable section near the heart of every township to support public education.

But orderly surveying and public education were just parts of Jefferson's plan. Hoping to populate the region with self-sufficient yeomen farmers, he proposed that the government give away land in small parcels. He envisioned self-government for these new inhabitants, not colonial status. For Jefferson, the more weight these independent farmers obtained in the American government the better, so he urged the rapid entry of numerous new territories into the Union on an equal footing with the thirteen original states. He suggested creating up to fourteen small, rectangular districts in the west. At least nine would be north of the Ohio River, and each could become a separate state with voting rights in Congress.

Courtesy, Monroe County Historical Commission, Monroe, MI

■ Marie-Thérèse Lasselle (1735–1819) witnessed a generation of transitions in the Great Lakes region. She and her husband ran a trading post at Kekionga on the Maumee River (now Fort Wayne, Indiana). Long after the Revolutionary War drove them to Detroit, she created this self-portrait, using watercolor on embroidered silk.

DOCUMENT

Northwest
Ordinance (1787)

According to Jefferson's report, the first settlers arriving in a district were to form a temporary government. When the local population reached 20,000, residents could call a convention, frame a constitution, and send a delegate to Congress. When the district's population equaled the number of free inhabitants living in the smallest of the thirteen original states, that district could enter the Union if certain conditions were met. Each new state must agree to support a republican form of government, remain part of the Confederation, and accept a share of the federal debt. It must also agree to exclude slavery after 1800. Congress accepted Jefferson's report, but then it modified the plan greatly. In its Land Ordinance of 1785, Congress removed his call for numerous districts, dismissed the notion of free land, and dropped the idea of ending slavery.

The Northwest Ordinance of 1787

The huge task of surveying the wilderness north of the Ohio River into neat geometric squares would take years to complete. Almost immediately—and long before the initial ordinance could take hold—political shifts produced an entirely new law from Congress: the Northwest Ordinance of 1787. This law determining how territories north of the Ohio River would be governed contained a number of additional changes to Jefferson's original plan. For example, it reversed direction on the slave question once again, introducing an immediate prohibition of slavery north of the Ohio River. However, it made arrangements to deport fugitive slaves back to their owners in slaveholding states.

In various ways, the new ordinance proved less democratic than earlier versions. Congress cut the possible number of new states from the Old Northwest, specifying there could be only three to five new states. This move limited the potential political weight of the vast territory. In addition, the ordinance increased property requirements for citizens who wanted to vote or hold office. It also slowed the process by which new states could gain admission to the Union. Eventually, Congress granted statehood to five new entities, but the process took more than half a century.

Most members of Congress feared democratic governance in the Old Northwest and the prospect of giving a strong voice to people with different regional interests. To retain control over the domain, they provided for the appointment of territorial officials—a governor, a secretary, and three judges—instead of allowing elected governments. Even when territorial legislatures formed, the governor would have veto power over their actions. James Monroe, head of the committee that moved the bill through Congress, wrote candidly to Jefferson, "It is in effect to be a colonial gover[nme]nt similar to wh[at] prevailed in these States previous to the revolution."

These changes benefited eastern speculators—some of whom were members of Congress—who hoped to control these lands for profit. In 1786 former army officers in New England, joined by five surveyors, organized the Ohio Company to buy up western land. They dispatched Massachusetts minister Manasseh Cutler to lobby Congress to sell a huge tract at bargain rates. Cutler joined forces with congressional insiders associated with another venture, the Scioto Company. Together, they engineered a deal providing 1.5 million acres to the Ohio Company and another 5 million acres for Scioto investors.

Whatever suspicious bargains surrounded congressional passage of the Northwest Ordinance of 1787, the new law still granted basic rights to western residents. These guarantees—following state bills of rights—included religious freedom, trial by jury, and access to common-law judicial proceedings. Most important, the western territories were assured of full entry into the Union as equal states rather than receiving dependent status as permanent colonies. This system established an orderly method for bringing new regions into the Union, starting when Vermont became the fourteenth state in 1791.

Debtor and Creditor, Taxpayer and Bondholder

T he end of the Revolutionary War brought widespread economic depression. The money spent by foreign armies for goods and services dried up, and the split with Britain disrupted established patterns of commerce. When peace returned, merchants and artisans scrambled to find new markets and to locate new routes of profitable trade. At the same time, those who had preserved their holdings or made money during the war paid to buy goods from abroad that had been scarce during the fighting. These foreign purchases drained hard currency away from the states and increased the Confederation's debt.

Citizens everywhere felt the **brunt** of the postwar slump as prices dropped and the money supply shrank. As credit tightened, merchants called in their loans and unpaid bills. Families in debt, especially poor artisans and subsistence farmers, suddenly faced the threat of **foreclosure** and loss of their property. They fought back in local elections, in state legislatures, and even in the streets. Violence broke out in state after state, from New Hampshire to Georgia, as hard-pressed people, many of them veterans, decried fiscal policies that favored wealthy bondholders. Onerous taxes were being used to pay annual interest on bonds held by members of the moneyed classes. When armed conflict erupted in Massachusetts, the rebellion helped prompt a drastic effort to restructure and strengthen the national government through a special, closed-door convention in Philadelphia.

New Sources of Wealth

In 1783, the British government managed to fire one parting shot at the former colonies. To nurture Britain's maritime trade and punish New England shippers, it restricted Americans from trading with the British West Indies. The move barred American ships from a key portion of Britain's imperial commerce, forcing merchants to seek out new avenues of trade. In 1784 an American vessel entered the Baltic Sea and established trade relations with Russia. Meanwhile, the seaports of Nantucket and New Bedford stepped up their search for whales to provide oil for American lamps. Captains had no trouble finding sailors in need of work, and ships sailed wherever they sensed possible profits.

Early in 1783, a Savannah merchant named Joseph Clay commented that a "vast number" of slaves had fled the South in wartime. As rice plantations renewed production, African workers were "exceeding scarce and in demand." Sensing a profit, foreign slave traders shipped 15,000 Africans to Georgia and South Carolina by 1785. New England captains soon joined in, sailing ships to Africa in hopes of renewing a trade that had been interrupted during the war. Antislavery sentiment had increased with the idealism of the Revolution, and several states, including Virginia, had outlawed slave imports. Still, American ships transported Africans to the Spanish West Indies, South Carolina, and Georgia. "The Negro business is a great object with us," Clay reported in 1784. "It is to the Trade of this Country, as the Soul to the body."

Financier Robert Morris took a global perspective, realizing that profits could be made by opening new trade routes to the Orient. The project would take an enormous investment— ten times the amount needed to send a ship to Europe—but the potential rewards were irresistible. Morris's first vessel, the *Empress of China*, left New York harbor for Canton by way of the Indian Ocean early in 1784. It carried almost 30 tons of ginseng root—procured from western Virginia—highly prized by the Chinese. The ship also carried 2,600 furs, and $20,000 in hard currency, a huge drain on New York's economy.

This painting on glass shows Northwest Coast Indians menacing the American ship *Columbia* from their large war canoes. Captain Robert Gray was conducting trade for sea otter pelts to transport across the Pacific Ocean to China, where the soft fur was highly valued.

ATACKTED at JUAN. DE. FUCA. STRAIT'S.

George Davidson, *Attacked at Juan de Fuca Straits,* c. 1792. Oregon Historical Society, OrHi 85076

In six months, the American ship reached Canton, China's outlet for foreign commerce. "The Chinese had never heard of us," one sailor noted, "but we introduced ourselves as a new Nation" and gave them "a description of our Country." Chinese merchants welcomed trade with "the new people" and called their strange country "the flowery flag kingdom" because the stars on the American flag resembled blossoms. In May 1785 the *Empress of China* returned to New York loaded with tea, chinaware, and silk. Morris and his partners raked in a hefty 20 percent return on their investment.

Other traders took notice. In 1787 the Browns, wealthy merchants in Providence, diverted a slave ship from the African trade to the China tea trade. That same year, six Boston investors sent several vessels around Cape Horn to trade for furs on the American Northwest Coast, pioneering new Pacific routes for American ships. Among the Nootka Indians, Captain Robert Gray exchanged cloth and iron goods for sea otter pelts. Then he sailed the *Columbia* across the Pacific, pausing at Hawaii for supplies. Reaching Canton in 1789, Gray traded profitably and proceeded home through the Indian Ocean, making the *Columbia* the first American ship to circumnavigate the globe.

Because Gray's voyage affirmed the rewards of trade along the Northwest Coast, a diplomatic controversy flared the following year at Nootka Sound, on the west side of Vancouver Island. Although Spain protested British and American trading activities in the area, Gray was back on the Northwest Coast by 1792. He entered a powerful stream—where Washington and Oregon now meet—and named it the Columbia River, after his ship. When he planted the American flag at the mouth of this major waterway, his action foreshadowed later territorial claims by the United States in the Oregon region.

While American merchants probed for new markets abroad, they also moved to strengthen their economic and political position at home. Some wealthy investors bought up a variety of loan certificates, paper notes, and wartime securities issued by state governments and the Continental Congress, paying only a small fraction of the original value. Certificates issued to soldiers at the end of the war became part of this speculative market when the original recipients sold their notes to prosperous speculators for needed cash. In Maryland, for example, the claims on $900,000 owed by the state became concentrated in the hands of only 318 people by 1790. Moreover, sixteen of these people controlled more than half of the total value, and these wealthy investors took an increasing interest in political events. They realized that whoever controlled the reins of power at the state and national levels would determine how the various notes of credit might be redeemed. Speculators who had purchased large quantities of these notes for a fraction of their face worth stood to reap enormous profits from any government that would pay interest on, and then buy back, all these paper arrangements at their original high value.

"Tumults in New England"

The few people who had acquired most of the paper securities wanted their holdings redeemed for hard money. But the majority of citizens, faced with rising debts amid an economic downturn, resented the heavy taxes needed to pay interest on the debt to these wealthy speculators. Favoring much easier credit, they urged their states to issue new paper money. But local elites wanted to limit paper money in ways that favored their new position as powerful creditors and holders of wartime certificates. Their opponents argued that issuing paper money could take the pressure off cash-strapped farmers and help retire enormous war debts. In seven states, these advocates of economic relief carried the day. State government presses put additional notes in circulation.

Local battles over debt, credit, and currency issues hit hardest in the Northeast. In Massachusetts, a legislature sympathetic to creditors consolidated the state's huge war debts in a way that placed extreme tax burdens on ordinary citizens. Also, Britain's move to ban American ships from the British West Indies cut off the lucrative trade that New Englanders had created. For generations, these American captains had sold fish, grain, and lumber to the islands in exchange for hard currency. Sudden exclusion from Britain's Caribbean colonies dried up the flow of much-needed cash into New England and undermined that region's economy.

Sudden exclusion from Britain's Caribbean colonies dried up the flow of much-needed cash into New England and undermined that region's economy.

These changes had an immediate impact. In New Hampshire courts, debt cases rose sixfold from 1782 to 1785. Even if the debts themselves were not large, the heavy costs of traveling to court and paying high legal fees pushed thousands of rural families into bankruptcy. Judges routinely ordered the seizure and sale of property. Embittered farmers watched as their horses, cows, wagons, and household goods disappeared in auction at low prices. Hard times often spark drastic responses, and New England's pot soon boiled over. Early in 1787, Washington's secretary in Virginia noted that the "tumults, insurrections, and *Rebellion* in New England have of late much engrossed the minds of the people here."

Newspaper accounts told of disturbing events in Rhode Island. There, rural politicians seeking relief for indebted farmers swept into power during the elections of April 1786. Their triumph freed the assembly from its longtime domination by rich Providence merchants. The newcomers, elected on their paper-money platform, wasted no time in implementing their ballot-box revolution. The Rhode Island region had a withered economy, and the state government carried a burdensome war debt. To address these matters, assemblymen approved a huge outlay of paper money: £100,000. The assembly planned to distribute the new money among the towns and lend it to citizens on equitable terms. The revenue received back in taxes as the economy rebounded would then be used to pay off the state's debts and retire the paper currency. To ensure the plan's success, legislators declared the money as legal tender that all creditors had to accept as payment.

Not surprisingly, creditors and speculators resented Rhode Island's currency law. Moreover, they fumed at the new legislature's unwillingness to assume a share of the national debt and pay interest to wealthy bondholders, as other states had done. Without control over the legislature, these speculators feared they would be left holding all the continental securities they had acquired. They took swift action. Though heavily outnumbered, members of the moneyed class in Providence used their economic strength to fight back. Many merchants closed their stores rather than accept payments in the new medium of exchange. Some even left the state to avoid being forced to accept debt payments in paper money. When the controversial new statute expired, creditors everywhere sighed with relief. Their elite newspapers condemned the "Rogues' Island" currency law as a dire example of the dangers of democracy.

The Massachusetts Regulation

In Massachusetts and New Hampshire, unlike Rhode Island, powerful merchants retained control over the state assemblies, and they resisted public pressure to generate more paper money. Instead, these creditors pushed to enforce debt collection by the courts. As in other states, wealthy speculators had bought up, at bargain rates, most of the public securities and certificates issued during the war. They anticipated huge profits if a government they controlled could redeem these notes, in gold and silver, at their full face value.

In New Hampshire, by 1785, securities valued at nearly £100,000 belonged to just 4.5 percent of the state's adult male population: 1,120 men among approximately 25,000. A mere 3 percent of this group—thirty-four men—controlled more than a third of this vast speculative investment. Most of these men had close ties to the prevailing government, situated in Exeter, near the coast. When farmers organized conventions to voice their economic grievances, merchants infiltrated and disrupted their meetings. In September 1786, 200 citizens, many of them armed war veterans, marched on Exeter to demand money reforms before conditions "drive us to a state of desperation." Officials organized cavalry units to confront the furious citizens, arresting their leaders from the crowd "as a butcher would seize sheep in a flock." As soon as the state's president, General John Sullivan, had suppressed the dissenters, he issued a proclamation forbidding further conventions. He then wrote to Massachusetts governor James Bowdoin, offering to help crush similar unrest in the neighboring state.

DOCUMENT

Military Reports on Shays' Rebellion

Early in 1786, the Commonwealth of Massachusetts had imposed a heavy direct tax on its citizenry. Western farmers lacked sufficient cash and already faced a wave of foreclosures for debt. They protested the tax law at town meetings and county conventions. When their complaints fell on deaf ears, they took action, "regulating" events as the North Carolina Regulators had done two decades earlier. The Massachusetts Regulation became known as Shays's Rebellion when a former army officer named Daniel Shays emerged as one of its popular leaders. At first, these New England Regulators focused on closing the courts. In August 1786, 1,500 farmers marched against the Court of Common Pleas in Hampshire County and shut it down. The next month, another band closed the court in Worcester.

■ **FIGURE 8.1**
CONCENTRATION OF SECURITY NOTES IN THE HANDS OF A FEW: THE EXAMPLE OF NEW HAMPSHIRE IN 1785

The confrontation escalated as winter set in. By January more than 1,000 Shaysites, knowing that their allies in New Hampshire had been defeated, moved to seize the federal arsenal in Springfield. But Governor Bowdoin had mobilized an army, financed largely by wealthy merchants in Boston. This private militia overpowered the westerners and forced all who did not flee to sign an oath of allegiance. Disarmed but not silenced, the dissidents succeeded in extracting some relief from the legislature. They also managed to defeat Bowdoin in the next election and replace him with a more popular governor, John Hancock.

> *The unrest in New England played into the hands of those advocating a stronger national government. (Rumors even circulated that nationalists had provoked the violence to rally support for their cause.)*

The unrest in New England played into the hands of those advocating a stronger national government. (Rumors even circulated that nationalists had provoked the violence to rally support for their cause.) In May 1787, Henry Knox expressed fear to General John Sullivan that "we are verging fast to anarchy." He urged Sullivan to send delegates from New Hampshire to a crucial meeting that was about to begin in Philadelphia.

Drafting a New Constitution

Even before Yorktown, Alexander Hamilton, Washington's youthful Caribbean-born aide-de-camp, had proposed a convention to restructure the national government. Now he worked with another young nationalist, James Madison, and their energetic supporters to bring it about. Congress had made earnest efforts toward reform, but any changes to the Confederation's governing articles required approval from all thirteen states. Thus, vital amendments—which would let Congress regulate commerce, raise revenue, and establish a judiciary, for example—proved nearly impossible. For some powerful leaders, especially merchants and creditors, a major political revision seemed in order.

Alexander Hamilton – Portrait

"Many Gentlemen both within & without Congress," wrote Madison, desire a "Convention for amending the Confederation." Still, it would take impressive leadership—Madison provided much of it—to seize the initiative and then generate enough momentum to change the rules of national government. Extensive compromise, both between elite factions and toward resistant popular forces, would be necessary at every stage. After all, it would take an enormous push to engineer such a convention, to guide it to restructure the government along nationalist lines, and finally to persuade voting Americans to ratify the proposed changes and accept their legitimacy. To begin such a task, would-be reformers needed to convince the Confederation Congress to allow their revision plans to move forward. For that, they needed to recruit the enormous prestige of George Washington.

Statue of George Washington

Philadelphia: A Gathering of Like-Minded Men

The path began at Mount Vernon in 1785 when Washington hosted commissioners appointed by Maryland and Virginia to resolve state boundary disputes regarding the Potomac River. During the gathering, these men (including James Madison) scheduled a broader meeting on Chesapeake trade for the next year at Annapolis, Maryland. They invited all the states to send representatives. Only twelve delegates from five states showed up at Annapolis in September 1786, but news of the unrest in New England prompted talk of a more extended meeting.

Mount Vernon

Alexander Hamilton, as a representative from New York, persuaded the other delegates to call for a convention in Philadelphia the following May to discuss commerce and other matters. Madison won endorsement for the proposal from the Virginia legislature and then from Congress. Reform-minded congressmen, such as James Monroe, saw an opportunity to amend and improve the existing Confederation structure. But when the states sent delegates to Philadelphia the following spring, many of the appointees thought that amendments might not go far enough. They were open to the more sweeping changes that Madison and other nationalists had in mind. So the gathering called to consider commercial matters and propose improvements to the Articles of Confederation soon became a private meeting to design and propose an entirely new structure for governing the United States.

Madison reached Philadelphia in early May 1787. He immediately began drafting plans for drastic change and lobbying delegates, some of whom came early to attend a secret gathering of the Society of the Cincinnati. On May 25, when representatives from seven states had arrived, they launched the convention and unanimously chose Washington as the presiding officer. Participants agreed that they would operate behind closed doors and each state delegation would have one vote. There would be no public discussion or official record of their proceedings. Soon, delegates from twelve states had joined the gathering. Only Rhode Island opted not to send representatives.

The fifty-five delegates had much in common. All were white, male, and well educated, and many already knew one another. These members of the national elite included thirty-four lawyers, thirty public creditors, and twenty-seven members of the Society of the Cincinnati. More than a quarter of the participants owned slaves, and nearly a dozen had done personal business with financier Robert Morris of the Pennsylvania delegation. Not surprisingly, all seemed to agree that the contagion of liberty had spread too far. Indeed, Elbridge Gerry of Massachusetts called the current situation "an excess of democracy."

Specifically, these men feared recent legislation that state assemblies had adopted to assist hard-pressed citizens: laws that delayed tax collection, postponed debt payments, and issued paper money. Most delegates hoped to replace the existing Confederation structure with a national government capable of controlling finances and creating creditor-friendly fiscal policy. To be effective, they believed, a strengthened central government must have greater control over the states. Only Robert Yates and John Lansing of New York and Luther Martin of Maryland staunchly resisted expanding central power.

Many delegates, especially those from heavily populated states, thought the national legislature should be based on proportional representation according to population rather than each state receiving equal weight regardless of its numbers. Also, most wanted to see the single-house (unicameral) Congress of the Confederation replaced by an upper and lower house that would reflect the views and values of different social classes. John Adams had helped create such a two-house (bicameral) system in the Massachusetts constitution, thereby limiting pure democracy and giving more political power to propertied interests.

Besides calling for checks within the legislative branch itself, Adams had also laid out strong arguments for separating, and checking, the powers of each competing branch of government. For a sound and lasting government, Adams had argued, there should be **separation of powers**; the legislative branch should be balanced by separate executive and judicial branches that are equally independent. Most delegates agreed with this novel system of **checks and balances**, intended to add stability and remove corruption.

Compromise and Consensus

DOCUMENT

The Debates in the Federal Convention of 1787 reported by James Madison

The Philadelphia gathering, which lasted through the entire summer, would later be known as the Constitutional Convention of 1787. Even as a consensus emerged within the small meeting, countless personal, practical, and philosophical differences persisted. Hamilton delivered a six-hour speech in which he staked out an extremely conservative position. He underscored "the imprudence of democracy" and stressed a natural separation between "the few and the many"—the "wealthy well born" and the "turbulent and changing" people. Hamilton's conservative oration called for the chief executive and the senators to be chosen indirectly, by elected representatives rather than by the people themselves, and he recommended that these high officials should serve for life. Such ideas undoubtedly appealed to many of his listeners, but all of the delegates knew that a majority of citizens would never accept such proposals. Pierce Butler of South Carolina invoked Solon in ancient Greece, "who gave the Athenians not the best government he could devise but the best they would receive."

This attentiveness of convention members to what the public would accept is illustrated by their approach to voting rights. Property ownership was no longer a universal voting requirement, and state constitutions varied on whether religion, race, or gender could determine eligibility. James Wilson of Pennsylvania, second only to Madison in working to build a practical nationalist majority in the convention, pointed out that "it would be very hard and disagreeable" for any person, once franchised, to give up the right to vote. Accordingly, the delegates proposed that in each state all those allowed to vote for the "most numerous branch of the state legislature" would also be permitted to cast ballots for members of the House of Representatives. But they shied away from accepting direct election for the Senate or the president, and they deferred suffrage matters to the states.

Time and again during the sixteen-week convention, these like-minded men showed their willingness to bargain and compromise. Lofty principles and rigid schemes often gave way to balancing and improvisation. The unlikely creation of the electoral college for selecting a president is one example. Delegates who differed over the length for the chief executive's term of office and right to run for reelection also disagreed on the best method of presidential selection. Some of them suggested that ordinary voters should elect the president; others proposed that the state governors, or the national legislature, or even electors chosen by the lower house should choose the chief executive.

Finally, the aptly named Committee on Postponed Matters cobbled together an acceptable system: a gathering (or "college") of chosen electors from each state would cast votes for the presidency. This **electoral college** plan had little precedent, but it managed to balance competing interests. Under the scheme, state legislatures would set the manner for selecting electors. The least populous states would get a minimum of three electoral votes, and states with more people would choose more electors in proportion to their numbers, giving them added weight in the decision. The people could also participate in the voting process, though only if their state legislatures called for it. If no candidate won a majority in the electoral college, the House of Representatives had the right to determine the president, with each state having one vote. The system was far from elegant or democratic, but it placated varied interests, and it won prompt approval.

Questions of Representation

As deliberations stretched across the long, hot summer of 1787, two central issues threatened to unravel the convention: political representation and slavery. Questions of representation pervaded almost every discussion, pitting the states with the largest populations, such as Virginia, Pennsylvania, and Massachusetts, against the less populated states. Madison's well-organized Virginians offered a comprehensive blueprint outlining a new national government that would have three separate branches. This design, called the "Virginia Plan," recommended a bicameral national legislature with proportional representation in each body. The House of Representatives would be chosen by popular election, the Senate by the lower house.

Madison's system clearly favored populous states. Not surprisingly, a coalition of small-state delegates led by William Paterson of New Jersey submitted an alternative "New Jersey Plan." This less sweeping revision built on the current Articles of Confederation. It called for a continuation of the existing unicameral legislature, in which each state received an equal vote. A committee chaired by Benjamin Franklin managed to break the impasse. The idea of an upper house, or Senate, would be retained, and each state, whatever its size, would hold two senate seats. Seats in the House of Representatives would be determined proportionally, according to the relative population of each state. Moreover, this lower house would have the power to initiate all bills dealing with finance and money matters.

To implement proportional representation in a fast-growing society, the delegates devised a radical innovation: a national census every ten years. This regular headcount in turn raised a thorny

> *As deliberations stretched across the long, hot summer of 1787, two central issues threatened to unravel the convention: political representation and slavery.*

question. Should slaves—people enumerated in the census yet denied the rights of citizens—be counted in determining a state's proportional representation in the national government? Slave-holding states wanted their human property to count because that would give those states more representation. The convention resolved this dilemma in mid-July with a "three-fifths" formula that made every five enslaved people equivalent to three free people in apportionment matters.

In an ironic twist, the same week the Constitutional Convention delegates approved the notorious three-fifths clause, the existing government of the United States leaned in the opposite direction. Meeting in New York, members of the Confederation's Congress passed the Northwest Ordinance, which outlawed slavery in the new territory above the Ohio River. Because there was much contact between the two meetings, some scholars speculate that powerful Southerners agreed to give away the prospect of slavery north of the Ohio River in exchange for more support of slavery within the new plan taking shape in Philadelphia.

Slavery: The Deepest Dilemma

During the debate over the three-fifths clause, Madison commented that the greatest division in the United States "did not lie between the large & small States: it lay between the Northern & Southern," owing to "the effects of their having or not having slaves." This highly charged issue continued to simmer beneath the surface for most of the summer.

In late August, with most other matters resolved, delegates could no longer postpone questions surrounding slavery. Yet again, a committee deliberated, and a bargain was struck. But this time, hundreds of thousands of human lives were at stake. Planter delegates from Georgia and South Carolina refused to support any document that regulated the slave trade or curtailed slavery itself. They asserted that such a charter could never win acceptance at home.

In part they were bluffing. Constraints against slavery had wide popular appeal in the expanding backcountry of the Deep South, where independent farmers outnumbered planters, ministers questioned slavery, and pioneers wanted national support in confronting powerful Indians.

Yet few delegates challenged the proslavery posture, possibly because strong antislavery opinions could have prolonged or even deadlocked the convention. Weary participants were eager to complete their work and fearful of unraveling their hard-won consensus. Rather than force the matter, even those who disapproved of slavery rushed to compromise, heaping a huge burden on future generations. Southern delegates dropped their protests against giving Congress the power to regulate international shipping. In exchange, the framers approved a clause protecting the importation of slaves for at least twenty years. They also added a provision governing fugitive slaves that required the return of "any person held to service or labor." Through a calculated bargain, delegates had endorsed slavery and drawn the South into the Union on terms that suited that region's leaders. The word *slave* never appeared in the finished document.

In early September, the convention members put the finishing touches on their proposal and wondered whether Americans would accept it. Winning state-by-state approval would involve an uphill battle, especially given the absence of a bill of rights. George Mason, who had drawn up Virginia's Declaration of Rights eleven years earlier, reminded members that such a set of guarantees "would give great quiet to the people." But in the convention's closing days, many delegates resisted the notion, and all were eager to adjourn. They overwhelmingly voted down Mason's suggestion.

Without a bill of rights, Mason and Gerry refused to endorse the final document, along with Edmund Randolph of Virginia. Other delegates who dis-

■ In a crucial decision, members of the Constitutional Convention chose to protect the slave trade and preserve slavery. One African American who had already taken matters in her own hands was Mumbet, a slave in Massachusetts and widow of a Revolutionary War soldier. In 1781 she sued for her freedom on the grounds that "all were born free and equal." Her court victory proved a landmark in New England. Proudly, she took the name Elizabeth Freeman.

sented had already departed. Of the seventy-four delegates chosen at the convention's outset, fifty-five actually attended the proceedings, and only thirty-nine agreed to sign the finished plan. It was approved "by the unanimous consent of the States present" on September 17, 1787.

Ratification and the Bill of Rights

Committed nationalists now faced their most difficult task: winning public acceptance for an alternative structure that defied existing law. After all, the proposed constitution ignored the fact that the Articles of Confederation—the document governing the United States at the time—could be amended only with the approval of all thirteen states. Instead, the text drafted in Philadelphia stated that ratification (acceptance through voting) by conventions in any nine states would make the new document take effect in those places. Moreover, the proposed ratification process left no room for partial approval or suggested revisions. Each state, if it wanted to enter the debate at all, had to accept or reject the proposed frame of government as offered.

The Campaign for Ratification

The Confederation Congress had acquiesced in allowing the 1787 convention to occur in the first place. Most congressional representatives had expected the meeting to produce proposals for amending the current government, not discarding it. But now that the Philadelphia **conclave** had ended, the Congress sitting in New York City balked at endorsing the revolutionary document. To avoid a lengthy and troublesome debate, proponents of the new constitution urged Congress simply to receive the frame of government as a possible proposal and then transmit it to the states without an endorsement. Congress did so on September 28, 1787, and the document's advocates portrayed the unanimous vote as an expression of approval.

Supporters had no time to lose because Pennsylvania's assembly was set to adjourn on the next day. An early victory in that large and central state would be crucial in building momentum, so they rushed the congressional letter of transmittal from New York to Philadelphia. There, the assembly faction dominated by Robert Morris won a hasty vote to schedule a state ratifying convention. Over the next three months, towns and counties elected delegates, a convention met, and Pennsylvania voted to approve the new plan. Delaware had approved it unanimously on December 7, and New Jersey and Georgia followed suit. By the end of January, Connecticut had also ratified. Other states had called elections and scheduled conventions. Only Rhode Island, which had not sent delegates to the drafting convention, refused to convene a meeting to debate ratification.

By seizing the initiative early, the proponents of the new framework shaped the terms of debate. The drafters, anything but a cross-section of society, worked to portray themselves as such. They noted that their document began with the ringing phrase "We the people of the United States," a last-minute addition by Gouverneur Morris of New York. And Madison told the public that the text sprang from "*your* convention."

Most important, in a reversal of logic and contemporary usage, the nationalists who supported the new constitution took for themselves the respected name of **Federalists**. They gave their opponents the negative-sounding term **Anti-Federalists**. The Federalists then used their ties to influential leaders to wage a media war for public support. They dashed off letters and published essays praising the proposed constitution.

The strongest advocacy came from Alexander Hamilton and James Madison. The two men composed eighty essays for the New York press under the pen name *Publius*. John Jay added five more, and in the spring of 1788 the collection appeared as a book titled *The Federalist*.

DOCUMENT

Madison Defends
the Constitution

In 1788 newspapers tracked ratification of the new "federal superstructure" state by state. Massachusetts ratified the proposed U.S. Constitution in March—apparently aided by the Hand of God! New Hampshire provided the "ninth and sufficient pillar" in June, followed by Virginia four days later.

In the most famous piece, "Number 10," Madison challenged the widely accepted idea that a republic must be small and compact to survive. Turning the proposition around, he argued that minority opinions would fare better in a large nation, where diverse competing interests would prevent a unified majority from exerting control.

Dividing and Conquering the Anti-Federalists

Opponents of the new plan found themselves on the defensive from the start. Many of them had supported some government change, and most conceded the presence of economic difficulties. But Federalist predictions of impending chaos seemed exaggerated. "I deny that we are in immediate danger of anarchy," one Anti-Federalist writer protested.

DOCUMENT

Henry, Against the Ratification of the Constitution

Richard Henry Lee, president of the Confederation Congress, condemned the Federalists as a noisy "coalition of monarchy men, military men, aristocrats and drones." Other prominent figures joined him in opposition: George Clinton in New York; Luther Martin in Maryland; and Patrick Henry, George Mason, and Benjamin Harrison in Virginia. Such notables became the spokespeople for a far wider array of skeptics.

Many opponents of the proposed constitution protested the plan's perceived threat to local political power. Despite Madison's reassurances in *Federalist* Number 10, they believed that local and state governments represented voters more fairly and responded to their needs more quickly than a distant national authority could. For some critics this belief expressed a radical democratic principle; for others it represented their provincial bias. In short, Anti-Federalists were too diverse to speak with a single voice. Their ranks included subsistence farmers living far from urban markets and war veterans who saw their influence in republican government diminished by the proposed system. Many indebted people also opposed ratification, fearing that a strong national government would favor the interests of bondholders and foreign creditors ahead of the economic well-being of ordinary citizens.

If Anti-Federalists were numerous in the remote countryside, Federalists predominated in coastal commercial centers. Using a variety of tactics, they pressed their advantages in the fight to control state ratifying conventions. They lured prominent Anti-Federalist delegates with hints of high office, and they ridiculed vocal opponents as Shaysite extremists. In state after state, they forged coalitions linking commercial farmers living near towns and rivers with aspiring artisans and city-based entrepreneurs. Through intensive politicking, they garnered approval in Massachusetts in February 1788, but only by a thin margin (187 votes to 168 in the ratifying convention). This commitment

Collection of the New-York Historical Society, (#1176)

■ Celebrations in July 1788 hailed the new Constitution of the United States. "Columbus" on horseback led New York City's parade, followed by artisan groups. The silk banner of the pewterers proclaimed that under the Federal Plan, "All Arts Shall Flourish in Columbia's Land, And All Her Sons Join as One Social Band."

from "the Bay State" helped to sway Maryland in April, South Carolina in May, and New Hampshire in June. The Federalists could now claim the nine states needed to implement their plan, and in July they staged parades to hail the new Constitution of the United States.

The approved Constitution promptly became the law of the land. But in Massachusetts, the Federalists had triumphed only by promising to add an explicit bill of rights that gave written protection for valued civil liberties. They had to make similar assurances to secure slim majorities in Virginia (89 to 79) and New York (30 to 27). North Carolinians had voted down the proposed frame of government at their first ratifying convention because it lacked a bill of rights. A second North Carolina convention, called in 1789, withheld approval until a bill of rights had actually been introduced into the first Federal Congress as proposed amendments to the Constitution. In 1790, Rhode Island narrowly voted approval for the new framework (34 to 32) rather than risk being left in economic and political isolation.

Adding a Bill of Rights

In a society consisting of almost 3 million people, the franchise remained a limited privilege, open primarily to white men with property. All told, only about 160,000 voters throughout the country took part in choosing representatives to the state ratifying conventions. And only about 100,000 of these people—less than 7 percent of the entire adult population—cast votes for delegates who supported the Constitution. Federalists knew, therefore, that they would have to fulfill their pledge to incorporate a bill of rights. Madison, goaded by Jefferson, promised Virginians that he would push for the inclusion of specific rights as amendments to the Constitution. He had several motives. First, he hoped to ensure his own election to the nation's new House of Representatives. Second, he wanted to head off talk of another convention "for a reconsideration of the whole structure of government."

In compiling a list of protections, or bill of rights, Madison drew from scores of proposals for explicit amendments put forward by the state ratifying conventions. He selected those, mostly dealing with individual rights, that could pass a Federalist-dominated Congress and would not dilute any of the proposed new government's powers. He set aside suggestions for limiting the government's right to impose taxes, raise a standing army, or control the time and place of elections. True to his word, he pushed twelve less controversial statements through the Congress as constitutional amendments, despite congressional apathy and opposition. Within two years, three-fourths of the states ratified ten of these short but weighty pronouncements. Hence, the first ten amendments—the Bill of Rights—quickly became a permanent part of the U.S. Constitution.

Many of the protections provided by the **Bill of Rights** harked back to lessons learned in earlier struggles with Parliament. The ten amendments guarded the right of the people to bear arms, limited government power to quarter troops in homes, and banned unreasonable searches or seizures. They also ensured the right to trial by jury, outlawed excessive bail and fines, and prohibited "cruel and unusual punishments." The First Amendment secured freedom of speech and of the press, protected people's right to assemble and petition, and prohibited Congress from meddling in the exercise of religion. By securing these freedoms, Madison engineered a final set of compromises that ensured the acceptance and **longevity** of the Constitution he had done so much to frame.

Conclusion

The War for Independence exhausted the new nation. Managing the difficult task of demobilization and reconstruction consumed American energy and resources in the 1780s. So did the new western domain, where Americans had to balance prospects for national expansion against the military threats posed by European empires and Native American groups that claimed the region. Also, economic differences set aside during the war quickly reemerged; questions of wealth and property loomed large.

Therefore, when confederation leaders imposed unprecedented taxes to pay off the war bonds gathered up by wealthy speculators, irate farmers and veterans protested that Congress was gouging "the Many" to enrich "the Few." These numerous dissenters pressured state governments to provide debt relief and issue paper money. But wealthy creditors reacted forcefully: these like-minded men maneuvered to create a new and stronger central government that could support their interests and override state-level economic measures favoring the common people. Sidestepping the existing government, they drafted a new constitution at a closed convention in Philadelphia in 1787, and they campaigned successfully for its ratification by 1789.

The reins of power, which nearly slipped from the hands of established American leaders during the tumultuous 1770s, had been securely restored by the end of the 1780s, in the face of bitter and varied opposition. But the fierce debate over ratification of the constitution raised fresh uncertainties about the long-term survival of the union. Much hinged on selection of the first president. Inevitably, George Washington emerged as the overwhelming favorite to become the first chief executive of the new republic.

Sites to Visit

Washington's Newburgh Headquarters

For sixteen months in 1782–1783, the farmhouse of Jonathan Hasbrouck served as Washington's headquarters in Newburgh, New York, 12 miles north of West Point. The state of New York purchased the stone building on Lafayette Street in 1850 and opened it as the first publicly operated historic site in the United States.

Fraunces Tavern

http://www.francestavernmuseum.org/index.html

Here, at 54 Pearl Street near the tip of Manhattan, Washington bid farewell to his officers in 1783. From 1785 to 1787, while New York served as the capital city, the building held the departments of foreign affairs, the treasury, and war. Now it houses a museum with exhibits relating to the eighteenth century.

Mount Vernon
www.mountvernon.org/

During the nineteenth century, concerned women rallied to preserve Mount Vernon, George Washington's estate on the Potomac River. It is still maintained by the Mount Vernon Ladies' Association. If you cannot visit the plantation itself, 8 miles south of Alexandria, Virginia, you can visit the Web site.

Independence National Historical Park in Philadelphia
http://www.nps.gov/inde/

Covering 45 acres and containing twenty buildings, this site includes Independence Hall, where the Constitutional Convention met in the summer of 1787. The Visitor Center is at Third and Walnut Streets. On the Market-Frankfurt Subway, use the 5th Street and Market station.

Natchez Trace Parkway
http://www.nps.gov/natr/

Running 444 miles from Natchez, Mississippi, to the outskirts of Nashville, Tennessee, this one-time Chickasaw Indian trail became a pathway for boatmen returning north after floating their goods down the Mississippi. It is now a scenic road maintained by the National Park Service.

Congress and the Constitution
http://lcweb2.loc.gov/ammem/amlaw/lawhome.html

This Library of Congress Web site has the complete text of Max Farrand's *Records of the Federal Convention*, published in 1911, plus Paul H. Smith's *Letters of Delegates to Congress*, and many excellent post-1789 documents.

James Madison: His Legacy
http://www.jmu.edu/madison/madison.htm

The James Madison Center at James Madison University in Virginia maintains this Web site, which provides ready access to materials on Madison's life and interests, along with links to numerous documents and Web sites.

Historic Bartram's Garden
http://www.ushistory.org/tour/index.html

This Web site is part of LibertyNet's Virtual Tour of Historic Philadelphia. The garden itself, located at 54th Street and Lindbergh Boulevard, is run by the John Bartram Association, named for William Bartram's botanist father. Visit www.bartramtrail.org/ to learn more about backpacking Bartram's Trail through the South.

For Further Reading

General

Merrill Jensen, *The New Nation: A History of the United States During the Confederation, 1781–1789* (1948).

Richard B. Morris, *The Forging of the Union, 1781–1789* (1987).

Kenneth Silverman, *A Cultural History of the American Revolution* (1976).

Larry E. Tise, *The American Counterrevolution: A Retreat from Liberty, 1783–1800* (1998).

Gordon S. Wood, *The Creation of the American Republic, 1776–1787* (1969).

Beating Swords into Plowshares

Elizabeth A. Fenn, *Pox Americana: The Great Smallpox Epidemic of 1775–82* (2001).

Richard H. Kohn, *Eagle and Sword: The Federalists and the Creation of the Military Establishment in America, 1783–1802* (1975).

Henry F. May, *The Enlightenment in America* (1976).

Competing for Control of the Mississippi Valley

Gregory Evans Dowd, *A Spirited Resistance: The North American Indian Struggle for Unity, 1745–1815* (1992).

R. Douglas Hurt, *The Ohio Frontier: Crucible of the Old Northwest, 1720–1830* (1996).

Peter S. Onuf, *Statehood and Union: A History of the Northwest Ordinance* (1987).

Arthur Preston Whitaker, *The Spanish American Frontier, 1783–1795* (1927, reprinted 1969).

Debtor and Creditor, Taxpayer and Bondholder

E. James Ferguson, *The Power of the Purse: A History of American Public Finance, 1776–1790* (1961).

Jackson Turner Main, *The Anti-Federalists: Critics of the Constitution, 1781–1788* (1961).

Edmund S. Morgan, *Inventing the People: The Rise of Popular Sovereignty in England and America* (1988).

Leonard L. Richards, *Shays' Rebellion: The American Revolution's Final Battle* (2002).

Drafting a New Constitution

Charles A. Beard, *An Economic Interpretation of the Constitution of the United States* (1913).

Carol Berkin, *A Brilliant Solution: Inventing the American Constitution* (2002).

Christopher Collier and James Lincoln Collier, *Decision in Philadelphia: The Constitutional Convention of 1787* (1986).

Leonard W. Levy and Dennis J. Mahoney, eds., *The Framing and Ratification of the Constitution* (1987).

John P. Kaminski, ed., *A Necessary Evil? Slavery and the Debate over the Constitution* (1995).

Jack N. Rakove, *Original Meanings: Politics and Ideas in the Making of the Constitution* (1996).

Ratification and the Bill of Rights

Akhil Reed Amar, *The Bill of Rights: Creation and Reconstruction* (1998).

Saul Cornell, *The Other Founders: Anti-Federalism and the Dissenting Tradition in America, 1788–1828* (1999).

Michael Kammen, *A Machine That Would Go by Itself: The Constitution in American Culture* (1986).

Richard E. Labunski, *James Madison and the Struggle for the Bill of Rights* (2006).

Garry Wills, *Explaining America: The Federalist* (1981).

David Siemers, *The Antifederalists: Men of Great Faith and Tolerance* (2003).

For quizzes and other resources on these topics, go to www.longmanamericanhistory.com.

Revolutionary Legacies, 1789–1803

AMERICA'S REVOLUTIONARY WAR WAS OVER, BUT COMPETING IDEAS OF LIBERTY AND EQUALITY swirled throughout the Atlantic world, reinforced by the rhetoric of the French Revolution of 1789. In August 1800, Gabriel Prosser, an enslaved blacksmith in Richmond, Virginia, plotted to seize the state capitol and overthrow the slave regime. His plan gave voice to the egalitarian principles articulated in Philadelphia in 1776 and then in the Caribbean island of Saint-Domingue in 1791, when slaves had staged a bloody revolution against their French masters. (In 1804 they renamed the country Haiti.) Gabriel's rebels used the words of the nation's founders to justify their actions, rallying around the cry "Death or Liberty." One even compared himself to George Washington in his struggle to "obtain the liberty of [his] countrymen." Gabriel's plans failed when informants betrayed him and a hurricane-force storm washed out any hope for the uprising's success. Yet Gabriel's rebellion, even though foiled, is indicative of the ongoing struggles among almost all Americans regarding the legacy of the Revolution.

Among Native Americans, the American Revolution destroyed one Indian confederation and led to the creation of another. The Iroquois Confederacy in present-day New York State had suffered greatly during the war. Then, in the late 1780s, some survivors migrated westward, away from their ruined fields and still smoldering villages. Regrouping in Detroit, they forged a new political alliance, this time with other Indians living along the Ohio River and in the Great Lakes region. Mohawk leader Joseph Brant urged the Algonquin, Shawnee, Delaware, and others to join in common purpose to resist U.S. territorial aggression. Members of the Ohio Confederacy, he claimed, should "eat

■ Artist Gilbert Stuart painted this portrait in 1786 of Mohawk leader Joseph Bryant (born Thayendanegea).

out of one bowl with one spoon." Gaining military strength from political unity (just as the American colonists had done), they could now resist the tide of newcomers sweeping into the trans-Appalachian West—the area that is today Kentucky, Ohio, Indiana, and Michigan. Their resistance proved effective, drawing the army of the infant nation into an expensive and bloody war.

Slaves and Native Americans were not the only ones wrestling with the unfinished revolution. As the century ended, a number of groups challenged dominant notions about race, gender, wealth, and standing in the community. In New England and the Upper South, a rapidly growing class—free people of color—struggled to assert their rights. Throughout the new states, some women maintained a high degree of political engagement; New Jersey even granted well-to-do women the right to vote, if only for a brief period. Artisans also sought to wield new political clout, taking part in the new and surprising formation of national parties. Free blacks, women voters, and artisan-politicians all revealed the social tensions mounting in the new republic as well as the promise it offered to these same groups.

The first census of the United States, conducted in 1790, tallied 4 million people. Of this number, 750,000 (more than 18 percent) were black. People of various ethnicities clustered together in pockets throughout the states. German-born people accounted for one-third of all Pennsylvanians, and almost one-fifth of New York residents were Dutch. Numbers of Northerners and Southerners were about equal. However, ethnic and regional differences proved less significant in shaping the emerging two-party system than the persistent split between urban-based merchants and rural interests such as southern planters. The Revolution also unleashed enormous creative energy, as some people, unfettered by restrictions imposed by the crown, pursued new economic opportunities. In contrast, many artisans and small farmers continued to stagger under a burden of debt and new federal taxes. For them, the Revolution was a betrayal of their vision for America.

Competing Political Visions in the New Nation

In the first two decades of the new nation, domestic politics remained entwined in relations with the great European powers. For all their bold talk of freedom and liberty, the heirs of the Revolution continued to formulate public policies based upon the models offered by Great Britain and France. Specifically, some Americans found much to admire in British traditions of social order and stability, traditions shaped by a strong central authority in the form of a monarchy. Other Americans derived inspiration from the French Revolution, which began in 1789. They believed that, for all its bloody excesses, the revolution represented an ideal of true democracy, an ideal at odds with entrenched privilege in the form of monarchies and aristocracies. The British model appealed to Federalists, supporters of a strong central government. In contrast, the French model appealed to Anti-Federalists, soon to be called Democratic-Republicans, supporters of the rights of the states and of the active participation of ordinary citizens in politics. These divergent views shaped both foreign and domestic policy in the 1790s.

Within this contentious atmosphere, George Washington assumed the presidency in 1789, backed by the unanimous endorsement of the electoral college. Neither the ratification of the Constitution nor Washington's election silenced the continuing debate over civil liberties and the nature of the national government. Responding to the concerns of the Anti-Federalists, Congress quickly passed ten amendments to the Constitution, collectively called the Bill of Rights. Ratified by the necessary number of states in 1791, the amendments were intended to protect white men from the power of government, whether local, state, or national. The Judiciary Act of 1789 established a national, federal court system that included a five-member Supreme Court and the office of attorney general, charged with enforcing the nation's laws.

Like other public figures of the time, Washington believed that ideological differences between political leaders should never become institutionalized in the form of separate parties. These leaders believed politicians should debate issues freely among themselves, without being

VIDEO

The Hamiltonian
System

bound by partisan loyalty to one view or political candidate over another. However, by the late 1790s, the intense rivalry between Alexander Hamilton, Washington's secretary of the treasury, and Thomas Jefferson, his secretary of state, had produced a **two-party system** that proved remarkably durable. Representing two competing political visions, Hamilton and his supporters (known as Federalists) and Jefferson and his supporters (called Democratic-Republicans) disagreed on foreign diplomacy and domestic economic policies. Hamilton advocated a strong central government that would promote commerce and manufacturing. In contrast, Jefferson favored states' rights bolstered by small, independent farmers who would serve as the nation's moral and political center.

In 1792 Washington ran for and won a second term. Four years later, Washington declined to run for a third term. His successor was his vice president, John Adams, an unabashed Federalist who rankled Jefferson and other more egalitarian-minded citizens. Between 1789 and 1800, the clash between the Federalists and the Democratic-Republicans reverberated on the high seas, in Indian country, and in the halls of Congress.

Federalism and Democratic-Republicanism in Action

An outspoken Federalist, Hamilton took bold steps to advance the commercial interests of the new nation. In 1789, as Washington's secretary of the treasury, he persuaded Congress to enact the first U.S. **tariff** on imported goods. He argued this move would encourage home manufactures and raise money for the treasury.

DOCUMENT

Alexander
Hamilton, "Bank"

Hamilton also sought to strengthen the federal government through **monetary policy**. At his prodding, in 1790 Congress agreed to fund the national debt—that is, to assume responsibility for repaying the government's creditors including paying interest on the debt (a total of $54 million). Congress also assumed responsibility for debts that the individual states had incurred during the Revolution. To pay for all this, federal officials stepped up debt collection and imposed new taxes on individuals. In 1791 Congress also issued a twenty-year charter to the first Bank of the United States. Hamilton believed this institution, modeled after the Bank of England, would help stimulate the economy by circulating surplus funds held by the government.

An advocate of agricultural interests and the power of individual states, Jefferson disagreed with Hamilton on all these issues. Jefferson bitterly opposed the Bank of the United States, arguing that only the states could issue charters for financial institutions. He favored a lower tariff, urging that high-priced imports hurt farmers and other small consumers. The leader of the Democratic-Republicans believed that the government should not interfere in the lives of its citizens by imposing new taxes on individual households or on imported goods. According to Jefferson, governments, like individuals, should exercise restraint in their spending and should avoid accumulating debt. Hamilton and Jefferson's opposing views of government shaped the American political party system for generations to come.

The different views epitomized by Hamilton and Jefferson found expression in American reactions to Europe's political turmoil surrounding the French Revolution. Since France had recently been a crucial wartime ally, most Americans at first supported the dramatic events unfolding there in 1789. By imposing constitutional constraints on their king, Louis XVI, the French seemed engaged in a heroic struggle much like that of the Patriots of 1776, who had challenged the enormous power of the British monarch. But when French radicals launched what became known as the Reign of Terror, American public opinion grew more critical.

In January 1793, leaders in Paris beheaded the French king and went on to execute aristocrats and presumed opponents of the revolution. In response, Federalist politicians argued that the bloody excesses in France should push American citizens toward a moderate and stable central government for the United States, more like that of Great Britain. Months later, when

France and England went to war over territorial claims in Europe and the West Indies, American public opinion was divided. Fearing dangerous entanglements, President Washington issued a Proclamation of Neutrality at the outbreak of the war, but few Americans could resist taking sides.

Tensions between France and the United States took a turn for the worse when France's first envoy to the United States, Citizen Edmund Genêt, ignored the Neutrality Proclamation and tried to enlist American support for French designs on Spanish Florida and British Canada. Nor did Britain endear itself to its former American subjects during these years. Pursuing French military forces in 1793, the British navy seized 300 American merchant ships plying the West Indian seas, forcing American sailors into service. In a practice known as **impressment**, British sea captains boarded American ships and captured sailors at gunpoint. Meanwhile, along the United States' northwest border, British officials were supplying the Indians of the Ohio Confederacy with guns, alcohol, and encouragement in their fight against the Americans. Feeling squeezed by foreign powers in such ways, many Americans hoped that economic growth could assist the fledgling United States in resisting pressures from European rivals.

Planting the Seeds of Industry

During the late eighteenth century, most manufacturing still took place in individual households. Master artisans employed journeymen (skilled workers) and apprentices as well as their own wives and children. Throughout New England and the Mid-Atlantic, family businesses made everything from soap and candles to cloth and shoes.

In the 1790s, however, signs of a novel manufacturing economy emerged, especially in the region stretching from New England to New York, New Jersey, and Pennsylvania. This area had all the ingredients for an American Industrial Revolution: water power from rushing rivers, a faltering agricultural economy that western producers would soon eclipse, capital from successful merchants, and a dense population offering both workers and consumers.

Key individuals helped spark the early changes, including Samuel Slater, a twenty-one-year-old English inventor who arrived in the United States in 1791. With financial support from Moses Brown, a wealthy merchant of Providence, Rhode Island, Slater constructed the first American machine for spinning cotton thread and launched his Steam Cotton Manufacturing Company in nearby Pawtucket. The nine boys and girls (ages seven to twelve) hired by Slater to operate the machinery were among America's first factory workers.

In 1793 another innovator, Massachusetts-born Eli Whitney, invented the cotton gin. This machine gave a tremendous boost to both the southern plantation economy and the fledgling northern industrial system. By quickly removing the seeds and other impurities from raw cotton, Whitney's cotton gin fostered the emergence of a new cotton economy. Southern planters expanded their holdings in land and slaves, rushing to meet the rising demand for cotton from mill owners in both England and New England.

By the mid-1790s, Hamilton and his supporters were praising the nation's economic growth and regional specialization. Traditional

Ralph Earl, *Elijah Boardman*. Metropolitan Museum of Art. Bequest of Susan W. Tyler, 1979. (1979.395)

■ **Elijah Boardman of New Milford, Connecticut, poses at his desk in 1789. The portrait highlights Boardman's success as a merchant. His business prospered because wealthy Americans wanted to dress fashionably, as he did, with his ruffled sleeves, silk stockings, and fancy shoe buckles. By the late eighteenth century, New England merchants were at the center of a thriving worldwide exchange of goods between Europe, the United States, and China. Their profits helped to finance the country's industrial revolution.**

■ This logo advertises the Hampshire machine. A precursor of the canal lock, the machine consisted of a pulley that carried a canal barge in a cart up an inclined plane. Invented in 1795, it was used on the Connecticut River in western Massachusetts. However, it proved too cumbersome in the long run. Most canals used locks, sections closed off with gates so that the water level could be raised or lowered.

products of the Atlantic seaboard—tar and turpentine in North Carolina, tobacco in the Chesapeake region, wheat in the Mid-Atlantic states—flourished once again, as early canal and turnpike construction encouraged new markets. In New England, shipbuilding prospered, free from earlier British restrictions, and the fishing and whaling fleets expanded. The forests of Maine and New Hampshire produced wood for hulls, masts, planks, and barrels. In the Deep South, enslaved workers raised cotton, first in South Carolina and Georgia, later in the fertile lands of Alabama and Mississippi. Between 1792 and 1800, annual cotton production jumped from 3 million to 35 million pounds. The figure would soar to 93 million pounds by 1815.

The Whiskey Rebellion: A Tax Revolt in the Countryside

Despite Hamilton's optimism about the economy, Washington's administration faced violent resistance on occasion, particularly with regard to Hamilton's "hard money" policy. By favoring **hard currency** (coinage) and limiting paper money, the government constricted financial credit. With less money to lend, creditors charged high interest rates for loans. Courts forced debtors such as small farmers to repay loans, even when money was extremely scarce. Those who could not pay their taxes or repay their loans faced foreclosure on their property.

Eager to strengthen the federal government and reduce the national debt, Hamilton devised a federal excise tax on whiskey. The plan was aimed at distillers rather than consumers, and it imposed a higher rate on small producers. Therefore, the tax fell especially hard on backcountry farmers, who distilled their bulky grain harvest into whiskey for efficient shipment to eastern markets. In 1794, opposition boiled over into a defiant "Whiskey Rebellion" in Pennsylvania, where cash-strapped farm families felt they were being saddled with an unfair burden.

These farmers, using the tactics of the Stamp Tax rioters a generation earlier, attacked officials and tarred and feathered a man charged with collecting the whiskey tax. They closed courts, blocked roads, and organized mass protests.

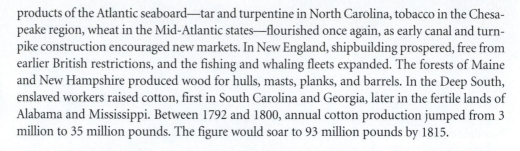

DOCUMENT

Washington
Whiskey Rebellion
Address

Hamilton, believing that a show of force would strengthen the federal government, urged the president to make western Pennsylvania a test case for enforcing the tax. In September, the government federalized 13,000 men from state militias to subdue the rebellion. To underscore the supremacy of the national government over the states, Washington personally led the troops into western Pennsylvania. However, when the soldiers arrived, they found that organized resistance had collapsed.

Washington claimed that the Whiskey Rebellion had been incited by ignorant men who perverted the facts with their "suspicions, jealousies, and accusations of the whole government." Yet he failed to gauge the extent of country dwellers' economic distress. By defying federal authority so openly, the farmers expressed the general grievances of westerners who felt underrepresented in state legislatures and the halls of Congress. They also revealed the deep current of resentment against Federalist policies that was running through rural America.

Securing Peace Abroad, Suppressing Dissent at Home

DOCUMENT

The Jay
Treaty (1794)

In 1795 the president sent Chief Justice John Jay to England to negotiate a key treaty. The negotiations were intended to address four problems: British forts in the Northwest Territory, American debts owed to British creditors, British seizure of American ships and sailors in the West Indies, and the right of individual Americans to trade freely with European belligerents in wartime. Jay obtained a treaty but failed to extract meaningful compromises from England.

England grudgingly agreed to evacuate its northern forts and to stop seizing American ships. Jay, however, acquiesced to English demands that individual Americans pay the debts they had owed to English creditors since before the Revolution. The Americans believed that

Frederick Kemmelmeyer, General George Washington Reviewing the Western Army at Fort Cumberland the 18th of October, c. 1794. Winterthur Museum (58.2780).

■ This 1794 painting seemingly evokes the American Revolution, when General Washington reviewed American troops. However, in this scene, President Washington is surveying some of the 13,000 state militiamen he commanded in an effort to suppress the Whiskey Rebellion in western Pennsylvania. Farmers objected to the new government tax on whiskey. With cries of "Liberty and No Excise," the protesters harassed federal tax collectors, reminiscent of anti–Stamp Act demonstrations three decades before. The Whiskey Rebellion melted away quickly. Critics objected to Washington's willingness to use such a huge force against the protesters.

their victory in the war exempted them from long-standing financial obligations to their English creditors. The Democratic-Republicans took alarm at Jay's concessions. In their view, the new agreement humiliated all Americans and threatened southern planters in particular.

Western agricultural interests did better with the Pinckney Treaty of 1795 (the Treaty of San Lorenzo). Under this agreement, Spain allowed the United States to navigate the Mississippi River freely and to land goods at New Orleans free of taxes for three years.

With their eye on the next presidential election, the Democratic-Republicans began a vigorous campaign in favor of their own candidate, Virginia's Thomas Jefferson. They contrasted Jefferson, the friend of the small farmer, with the Federalists' choice, Vice President John Adams of Massachusetts, an advocate of strong central government run by the educated and wellborn. Jefferson's party expressed particular dismay over Washington's haste to crush the rebellious Pennsylvania farmers in 1794 and over Jay's Treaty. Backed by the New England states, Adams won the election, though narrowly. Because Jefferson received the second largest number of electoral votes—68 to Adams's 71—the Virginian became the new vice president according to the terms of the Constitution then in effect (Article II, section I).

DOCUMENT

The Treaty of San Lorenzo

In his farewell address, printed in newspapers but not delivered in person, Washington warned against the "insidious wiles of foreign influence" and against entangling alliances with foreign powers that could compromise America's independence and economic well-being. Nevertheless, upon assuming the presidency in 1797, Adams found that European powers still had a hold on American domestic and foreign relations. France began to seize American merchant vessels (300 of them by mid-1797) in retaliation for what it saw as favoritism toward England in Jay's Treaty. In October of that year, President Adams sent John Marshall and Elbridge Gerry to join the U.S. ambassador to France, Charles Pinckney, to negotiate a new treaty with France. However, French intermediaries (referred to only as X, Y, and Z in the Americans' dispatches) demanded that the three U.S. commissioners arrange for a loan of $12 million to France and pay a $250,000 bribe. Only then would the envoys be allowed to speak to the foreign minister, Charles Talleyrand. The sentiments of the American public, outraged at the idea of paying a bribe and willing to defend their new nation against all aggressors, were captured in the cry "Millions for defense, but not one cent for tribute." Adams called the commissioners home, ending the "XYZ Affair."

Federalists throughout the country called for war against France, and the Adams administration sought to shore up the country's military forces by creating the Navy Department and the Marine Corps. Hoping to rid U.S. coastal waters of French ships that were preying on American vessels, in May 1798 Congress authorized American captains to seize such armed "pirates" sent from the Republic of France. Over the next two years, the undeclared so-called Quasi War pitted the American navy against its French counterpart until the two nations signed a treaty, called the Convention of 1800, in Paris.

Conflicts also continued to simmer on the domestic front. The Federalist-dominated Congress passed the Alien and Sedition Acts in 1798 to suppress the rising chorus of criticism from rural people, Democratic-Republican leaders, and newspaper editors. Such dissent, they charged, amounted to **sedition**—an act of insurrection against the government. These new laws made it more difficult for immigrants to become resident aliens, gave the president the power to deport or imprison aliens, and branded as traitors any people (U.S. citizens included) who "unlawfully combine or conspire together, with intent to oppose any measure or measures of the government of the United States."

Even though the Alien and Sedition Acts were unconstitutional—they violated the First Amendment's guarantee of freedom of speech—the Federalist-dominated Supreme Court upheld them. Consequently, Democratic-Republicans were by definition guilty of treason, for they advocated policies and supported candidates opposed by the Federalists, the party in power.

Ten newspaper editors were convicted, and many others charged and jailed, under the Sedition Act. Some Democratic-Republican lawmakers also spent time in jail because their speech offended their partisan rivals. Congressman Matthew Lyon of Vermont (founder of a newspaper called Scourge of Aristocracy) went to prison for suggesting that President Adams showed "unbounded thirst for ridiculous pomp, foolish adulation, and selfish avarice."

In 1798 and 1799, the state legislatures of Kentucky and Virginia issued a series of resolutions condemning the Alien and Sedition Acts. Outraged at what they saw as the Federalists' blatant power grab, the two legislatures proposed that individual states had the right to

TABLE 9-1

The Election of 1796

Candidate	Political Party	Electoral Vote
John Adams	Federalist	71
Thomas Jefferson	Democratic-Republican	68
Thomas Pinckney	Federalist	59
Aaron Burr	Democratic-Republican	30

DOCUMENT

The Alien and
Sedition Acts

declare such measures "void and of no force." Thomas Jefferson (for Kentucky) and James Madison (for Virginia) wrote the actual resolutions. In declaring that states could essentially ignore congressional authority, the two Founding Fathers unwittingly laid the theoretical framework for Southerners to attempt to nullify federal laws in the future.

DOCUMENT
The Virginia and Kentucky Resolutions

People of Color: New Freedoms, New Struggles

In the late eighteenth century, despite the rhetoric of equality, North American elites demonstrated a preoccupation with race as a means of categorizing people. Spanish officials in colonial New Mexico conducted a 1790 census that divided the population into groups based on ethnicity, with specific terms to designate varieties of mixed-race parentage. In the United States, a 1790 Naturalization law limited naturalized U.S. citizenship to "free white persons," mocking the oft-heard claim that all people were equal under the law.

The crosscurrents of the revolutionary legacy showed themselves most obviously in the status of African Americans. Most remained enslaved, and their numbers were increasing

New Bedford Whaling Museum (#803)

■ After the Revolution and well into the early nineteenth century, African Americans, both enslaved and free, served as sailors in disproportionate numbers. This picture suggests the dangers faced by all men who labored on whaling ships. By the 1790s, American whalers were searching for sperm whales as far away as the South Pacific. These whales were the source of several prized substances, including sperm oil (a fuel), spermaceti (used to make candles), and ambergris (an ingredient in expensive perfumes). During the heyday of the sperm whale industry, American fleets were killing 10,000 whales annually.

annually, due to the continuation of the Atlantic slave trade. But even free African Americans faced an uphill struggle in their efforts to achieve political rights and economic well-being. Free people of color created educational and religious institutions that affirmed their sense of community and shared heritage. But persistent white prejudice, sanctioned by law, limited their employment options and condemned many to poverty. For them, the Revolution remained an unfulfilled promise, not to be forgotten. According to Jeremiah Asher, an African American born in New Jersey in 1785, "my first ideas of the right of the colored man to life, liberty, and the pursuit of happiness" came from "the lessons taught me by the old black soldiers of the Revolution."

Blacks in the North

Between 1790 and 1804, all the northern states abolished slavery. Some, such as New York and New Jersey, did so gradually, stipulating that the children of slaves must serve a period of time (as long as twenty-eight years in certain states) before they could gain their freedom. In 1800 over 36,500 blacks in the North were still enslaved, and some 47,000 were free. Pennsylvania did not liberate its last slave until 1847. Yet throughout the North, blacks—whether enslaved or free—were only a small percentage of the total population, ranging from less than 1 percent in Vermont to almost 8 percent in New Jersey. Most black men worked as farm hands or manual laborers, most black women as domestic servants or laundresses. Nevertheless, some whites saw black men as rivals for their jobs and as a threat to the well-being of the white population.

At both the state and national levels, most free blacks lacked basic citizenship rights. In 1792, two years after Congress limited naturalized U.S. citizenship to "free white persons," it restricted the militia to white men. State legislatures in New England and the Mid-Atlantic region imposed various other restrictions on free people of color. These measures limited blacks' right to vote, serve on juries, and move from place to place. Rectifying an "oversight" in their state constitutions, New Jersey and Connecticut later took special pains to disfranchise African American men. Massachusetts offered free blacks the most rights, including the right to vote (for men) and the right of blacks and whites to intermarry.

As slaves, African Americans had served in a variety of skilled capacities in the North. Yet as free people, they faced mounting pressures in trying to live independently. Certain jobs, such as those with the federal postal service, remained closed to them by law. And municipal authorities refused to grant them licenses to ply their trades, such as wagon driving. Lacking the means to buy tools and equipment and the ability to attract white customers, many black artisans had to take menial jobs. Increasingly, free black men worked as laborers, sailors, and domestic servants, and black women worked mostly as domestic servants and laundresses.

Still, free blacks in the North set about creating their own households and institutions. They moved out of the garrets and back rooms in houses owned by whites and set up housekeeping on their own. In Boston in 1790, one in three African Americans lived outside white households; thirty years later, eight in ten did so. In response to efforts of white Methodists to segregate church seating, Philadelphia black leaders formed the Free African Society in 1787. The first independent black church in the North, St. Thomas Protestant Episcopal Church, was founded in Philadelphia in the early 1790s. Black people also continued to celebrate their own festivals, typically featuring parades in which black people came together to strut their finery, play drums and other African musical instruments, and proclaim their identity as a free people. The festivals gave men and women alike an opportunity to escape the confines of the workplace, even if only for a short time, and eat, drink, and dance with other people of color.

The Old Plantation, c. 1790–1800. Abby Aldrich Rockefeller Folk Art Museum. Colonial Williamsburg Foundation, Williamsburg, VA

■ An anonymous artist captured this scene, probably in the slave quarters of a South Carolina plantation, in 1800. It is unknown what kind of entertainment or celebration the musicians and dancers are engaged in. The two men on the right are playing musical **instruments** of west African origin: a banjo and a *quaqua*, or skin-covered gourd used as a drum. On large lowcountry plantations especially, Africans and their descendants preserved traditional musical forms and social rituals.

Manumissions in the South

In 1782 the Virginia state legislature lifted a fifty-nine-year-old ban on manumission, a process by which owners released selected people from bondage. Over the next ten years, approximately 10,000 Virginia slaves gained their freedom through manumission. Some planters believed that the Revolution was the will of God, and they came to believe that slavery violated their religious principles. Some, taking to heart the rhetoric of the Revolution, objected to the glaring contradiction between the ideal of liberty and the reality of bondage. In 1802 a Maryland woman freed her slaves because, she said, the institution went against "the inalienable Rights of Mankind."

In the Upper South, especially, private manumissions dramatically increased the free black population. There, the emergence of a more diversified economy, including craft shops and grist mills, had lowered slave prices and encouraged abolitionist sentiment among some lawmakers, clergy, and slave owners.

Virginia planters George Washington and Robert Carter were unusual in terms of the numbers of slaves they manumitted (several hundred) and their efforts to ease the transition to freedom for people who possessed neither land nor financial resources. Providing for manumission in his will, Washington arranged apprenticeships for younger freed blacks and pensions for aged ones. In 1792 Carter granted his older slaves small plots of land. In general, however, newly emancipated men and women had difficulty finding employment as free workers. Nor was their freedom guaranteed: the 1782 Virginia manumission law provided that black debtors could be returned to slavery.

Some slaves, inspired by the growing community of free people of color in their midst and by the example of the black revolutionaries in Saint-Domingue in 1791, freed themselves. They ran away, heading for the anonymity of a nearby town or a haven such as Philadelphia or New York. Despite the growth in the free black population, the number of slaves actually increased in the Upper South, from over 520,000 in 1790 to almost 650,000 in 1810. In the South, slavery proved to be an extraordinarily durable institution.

■ MAP 9.1

THE NORTHWEST TERRITORY   After the Revolution, the Northwest Territory became a battleground. Indians—both long-term residents and newcomers—as well as European American squatters and speculators vied for control of the land. The Northwest Ordinance of 1787 provided for territorial governments before an area could apply for statehood. The present-day states of Ohio, Indiana, Michigan, Illinois, and Wisconsin were carved out of the Northwest Territory. All had gained statehood by 1848, but only after almost sixty years of bloodshed between Indians and U.S. troops in the region.

Continuity and Change in the West

Western communities tended to duplicate their eastern counterparts. The opening of federal lands proved a boon for speculators, who extended credit to homesteaders and profited from the sale of small land parcels. Charged high prices for their purchases and forced to buy expensive supplies transported across the Appalachians, some newcomers rapidly sank into debt. Nor did black Americans fare well, whether slave or free. Before 1800, many white families seeking a fresh start in the trans-Appalachian South took slaves with them into the new states of Kentucky and Tennessee. Even in the Northwest Territory (above the Ohio River), where slavery was prohibited by law, African American arrivals faced the same prejudices that shaped social relations in the East. Rather than extend the bounds of liberty, western settlement solidified ideas about white supremacy.

From the Canadian border to Georgia, the trans-Appalachian West had become a cultural battlefield. European Americans warred against Indians, but Indian leaders also disagreed bitterly with one another about how to respond. Should they defend their hunting grounds to the death or seek refuge elsewhere? For most, the answer was neither total resistance nor complete **capitulation** to an alien culture. Yet one generalization holds true for all inhabitants: the abundance of land and natural resources, combined with the clash of cultures and the prevalence of armed men of different backgrounds, made life particularly dangerous in the borderlands.

Indian Wars in the Great Lakes Region

Native Americans residing in the Northwest Territory in the 1790s included peoples who had long occupied the Great Lakes region and the Upper Midwest, such as the Miami, Potawatomi, Menominee, Kickapoo, Illinois, Fox, Winnebago, Sauk, and Shawnee. Also present were refugees from the East: Ottawa, Ojibway, Wyandot, Algonquin, Delaware, and Iroquois displaced by the Revolutionary War. As they resettled in villages, they managed to retain some elements of their cultural identity, but in the seven years immediately after the Revolution, thousands died in Indian-white clashes in the region.

What caused this violence? By encouraging European Americans to stake their claim to the area, the Northwest Ordinance inflamed passions on both sides: whites' determination to occupy and own the land and Indians' equal determination to resist this incursion. In 1790, under orders from President Washington, Brigadier General Josiah Harmar led a force of about 1,500 men into the Maumee River Valley in the northwest corner of modern-day Ohio. Orchestrating two ambushes in September, Miami chief Little Turtle and his men killed 183 of Harmar's troops, driving the general back in disgrace. The next year, Washington chose another officer, General Arthur St. Clair, to resume the fight. But when St. Clair's men met Little Turtle's warriors in November 1791 near the upper Wabash River, the Americans suffered an even greater defeat, losing over 600 men.

Washington tried once more to find a commander equal to Little Turtle. This time he chose General Anthony Wayne, a Revolutionary War hero dubbed "Mad Anthony" for his bold recklessness. Wayne mobilized a force of 3,000 men and constructed a string of new forts as well. At the battle of Fallen Timbers in August 1794, near present-day Toledo, hundreds of Indians perished before Wayne's forces. The withdrawal of British support helped to doom the Ohio Confederacy. On August 3, 1795, 1,100 Indian leaders met at Fort Greenville (in western Ohio) and ceded to the United States a vast tract of Indian land: all of present-day Ohio and most of Indiana. Little Turtle helped negotiate the agreement.

Indian Acculturation in the West

White newcomers swiftly made clear their belief that men should farm and herd sheep and cattle, while women should milk cows, raise chickens, tend the garden, spin thread, and weave cloth. However, Indian groups differed in their responses to the various attempts to persuade—or force—them to "acculturate" by adopting novel customs. At first, all learned from each other, as newly arrived settlers and indigenous peoples traded foodways, folk remedies, and styles of dress, adopting foreign habits while still retaining some old ways. Little Turtle himself chose among European American cultural traits; he drank tea and coffee, kept cows, and shunned leather breeches in favor of white men's clothing. The fact that his wife made butter suggested that she was skilled in the ways of European American homemakers.

Adopting some habits of European Americans—for example, liquor consumption—amounted to self-destruction. Alcohol was a prized trade item. Moreover, European Americans and Indians often used it to lubricate political negotiations and cultural rituals. Yet conflicts over liquor, and tensions vented under the influence of liquor, became increasingly common—and deadly. Some Indian leaders, such as Joseph Brant and Little Turtle, came to view the drinking of alcohol as a full-blown crisis among their people. Both believed that Indians must reject the white man's bottle if they were to survive.

But liquor was only one piece of a larger cultural puzzle, as the experience of the Cherokee, Chickasaw, Choctaw, Creek, and Seminole Indians in the southeastern United States revealed. The migration of whites into their hunting grounds rapidly depleted their game supply and devastated their crop fields. Unable to hunt efficiently for food, many in these groups took up new forms of agriculture after the Revolution, and they became known to whites as

Courtesy, Museo de America, Madrid. Photo by Iris Engstrand

■ In 1791, an artist made this sketch of the wife of a Spanish soldier stationed at the presidio, or military garrison, in Monterey, California. Many elite Spaniards in the Americas went to great lengths to dress like their European counterparts. This woman is wearing the elegant dress, elaborate jewelry, and dainty shoes that befit her status. One eighteenth-century resident of New Mexico wrote that, despite the hot climate, European Americans "will go up to their ears in debt simply to satisfy their pride in putting on a grand appearance." However, most *nuevomexicanos* adopted some elements of Indian-style clothing, such as practical leather moccasins and garments made of buckskin and coarse woolens.

the Five Civilized Tribes. Women, who had traditionally tended crops using hoes, gave way in the fields to men, often using plows provided by the federal government. Protestant missionaries encouraged Indian women to learn to spin thread and weave cloth. For more than a generation, the willingness of these southern tribes to accommodate themselves to European American law and divisions of labor allowed them to stay in their homeland and retain key elements of their cultural identity.

In southwest and far west borderland areas, Spanish officials met with mixed success in their attempts to convert Indians to Christianity and encourage them to engage in **sedentary farming**. For example, between 1772 and 1804, Spanish priests established five missions among the Chumash, hunter-gatherers living in permanent villages along the California coast. When large numbers of the Indians moved to these settlements, they forfeited their traditional kin and trade networks, and their distinctive culture began to fade. Birth rates plummeted due to disruptions in family life (more women than men lived in the missions), and mortality rates increased dramatically as contact with the Spanish introduced new diseases.

In contrast, along the Texas Gulf Coast, the Spanish made little headway in their efforts to bring the Karankawa Indians into the missions. Members of this nomadic tribe arrived at the mission gates only when their own food reserves were low; in essence, the Karankawa simply included the missions in their seasonal migrations between the Gulf Coast and the coastal prairie.

Land Speculation and Slavery

The West was not necessarily a place of boundless economic opportunity for all people who settled there. Eager investors and creditors thwarted many homesteaders' quest for cheap land. Schemes such as the Ohio Company of Associates foreshadowed the significance of **land speculation** in shaping patterns of settlement and property ownership further west in later generations. With backing from wealthy investors, the Ohio Company quickly bought up tracts of land and then sold parcels to family farmers at inflated rates. A similar venture was initiated in Georgia in 1795, when speculators bribed state legislators for the right to resell huge tracts to the west of the state, land that the state did not even own. The state legislature passed the so-called Yazoo Act (named for a Georgia river) because of these bribes. The act resulted in the defrauding of thousands of buyers, whose land titles were worthless.

By protecting slavery and opening new territory to European American settlement, the new nation condemned southern blacks to a kind of legal bondage that stood in stark contrast to revolutionary principles. Many settlers relied on slave labor. By the late eighteenth century, Kentucky slaves numbered 40,000—more than 18 percent of the state's total population. On wilderness homesteads, where farmers owned just one or two slaves, African Americans faced a kind of isolation unknown on large plantations in the East.

Patterns of land use directly affected the spread of slavery into the West. Despite eastern planters' use of European soil conservation techniques (crop rotation, use of manure as fertilizer), many of them had to contend with depleted soil in the Upper South. Generations of tobacco growers had worn out the land, depriving it of nutrients. As a result, many growers were forced to abandon tobacco. Some of them moved west into Indian lands in the Mississippi Territory to cultivate cotton. The scarcity of labor motivated slave owners to push work-

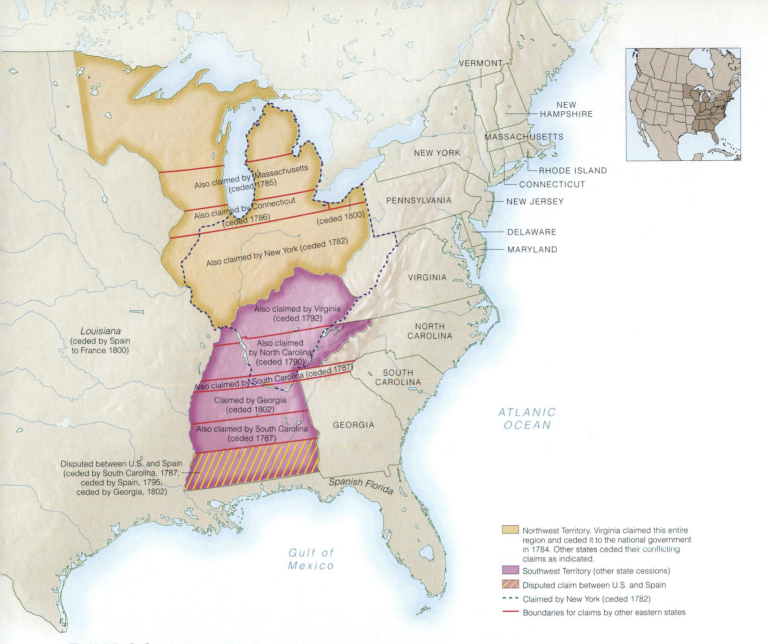

MAP 9.2

WESTERN LAND CLAIMS OF THE STATES   Several of the original thirteen colonies, including Massachusetts, Connecticut, New York, Virginia, South Carolina, North Carolina, and Georgia, claimed land west of the Appalachian mountains. By 1802 these states had ceded their western lands to the federal government. The Land Ordinance of 1785 provided that this expanse be auctioned off in parcels no less than 640 acres each, with a minimum price of one dollar per acre—too expensive for many family homesteaders, thus opening the way for investors to purchase and profit. Hoping to raise money through land sales, the federal government did not object to speculation.

ers to the limits of their endurance. Slaves cleared potential farmland, rooted out tree stumps, and prepared the ground for cultivation. Once cotton could be planted, these same slaves worked in gangs under the sharp eye of a white overseer or black driver. Men, women, and children labored as human machines, planting, hoeing, and harvesting as much cotton as quickly as possible.

Many free people of color also found a less than hospitable welcome in the West. In 1802 delegates to the first Ohio territorial convention moved to restrict blacks' economic and political opportunities, even though fewer than 400 were living in Ohio at the time. Although slavery was outlawed in Ohio and other territories, blacks still lacked the right to vote. Soon after Ohio became a state in 1803, the legislature took steps to prevent the in-migration of free blacks altogether. In 1803 the territorial legislature of Indiana passed a "black law" prohibiting blacks or Indians from testifying in court against white people. Black families in the Northwest Territory were also vulnerable to kidnapping: some white men seized free blacks and sold them as slaves to plantation owners in the South.

Shifting Social Identities in the Post-Revolutionary Era

The nation's founders had argued for an egalitarian society, one in which people prospered according to their talents and ambition. Of course, their definition of egalitarianism encompassed only white men. Still, it was a revolutionary idea and led to challenges of social hierarchies after the Revolution. These hierarchies included the patriarchal (male-headed) family, established Protestant denominations, power systems based on social standing, and ideas about race and gender. Ordinary men and women penned letters to local newspapers, glorifying common laborers and questioning the claim to power of elite citizens.

In the early nineteenth century, voluntary reform organizations multiplied across the nation. As their numbers proliferated, both the possibilities and limitations of reform became clear. Some groups—for example, white working men—sought to advance their own self-interest without showing much concern for the plight of African American laborers. In other cases, peo-

Shaker Village of Pleasant Hill, Harrodsburg, KY

■ Men and women participate in a Shaker worship service in New Lebanon, New York. The formal name of the church was the United Society of Believers in Christ's Second Appearance. The group's more familiar name derived from their peculiar worship style, which involved trembling and shaking. Members of the group reconfigured traditional family relations. They forbade marriage and sexual intercourse, depending on new converts to expand their ranks. Like several other Protestant denominations, encouraged congregants to call each other brothers and sisters.

ple banded together to target the behavior of a specific group: drunkards, slave owners, the irreligious, or prostitutes. These moral reform groups welcomed diversity among members, as long as new converts supported the cause.

Artisan-Politicians and the Plight of Post-Revolutionary Workers

In the decades after the Revolution, residents of port cities along the eastern seaboard grew accustomed to public parades marking special occasions: a visit from George Washington, the ratification of the Constitution, the Fourth of July. Most of these parades consisted of groups of artisans marching together, carrying the banners of their respective occupations. As one example, the bricklayers' flag declared, "Both Buildings and Rulers Are the Works of Our Hands."

Proud of their role in the Sons of Liberty and other revolutionary organizations, bricklayers—along with tanners, carpenters, glassblowers, weavers, and other groups of artisans—proclaimed themselves the proud citizens of the new nation. American worker organizations built on a distinct revolutionary heritage that stressed the equality of all (white) freeborn men. Master artisans in several cities—including Boston, Albany, Providence, Portsmouth, Charleston, Savannah, and New York—created organizations called the General Society of Mechanics and Tradesmen that brought together skilled workers from a variety of fields. The proliferation of newspapers let these artisans participate in a new, more open public forum. Such participation in turn helped them to gain greater influence within local politics. In some towns, as many as 85 percent of adult men owned property of some kind and thus were eligible to vote. Indeed, artisans' organizations soon became quasi-political groups, extending their reach in ways that pre-Revolutionary trades-based associations had not.

But not all workers were so secure. The diggers who constructed the early canals of the 1790s included men from all walks of life: part-time farmers, indentured servants, slaves, and white transients. Moving around in search of work, they led an unsettled existence that contrasted greatly with the more predictable life of urban artisans. Canal diggers represented a transition workforce of sorts, bridging the worlds of traditional, outdoor work with the more disciplined, regimented pace of the factory.

The plight of menial laborers (in the countryside and the cities) suggests the ironies that accompanied the decline of indentured servitude and the rise of the "free laborer." To be sure, master artisans attained a degree of economic independence. But for men and women who lacked skills, money, and wealthy patrons, freedom often meant financial insecurity and, in some cases, reliance on public or private charity. Those who did find work usually had the kinds of jobs that came with the booming economy of the late eighteenth century: moving goods from one place to another, building new structures, and providing personal services for the merchants who profited from all this commercial activity.

"Republican Mothers" and Other Well-Off Women

Some well-educated women in the United States read English writer Mary Wollstonecraft's *Vindication of the Rights of Woman* published in England and America in 1792. In that manifesto, Wollstonecraft argued that young men and women should receive the same kind of education. She objected to a special female curriculum that exclusively emphasized skills such as needlepoint and musical accomplishments; this "false system of education," she charged, left women "in a state of perpetual childhood."

In 1801 an anonymous "American Lady" published an essay titled "A Second Vindication of the Rights of Woman." In it, she claimed that "a good kitchen woman [that is, a household drudge], very seldom makes a desirable wife, to a man of any refinement." The anonymous "American Lady" and others who shared her opinion celebrated a new kind of woman—the

A Sailmaker Discusses "Means for the Preservation of Public Liberty" on the Fourth of July, 1797

Urban skilled artisans (also called mechanics) played a significant role in the American fight for independence. In the years after the conflict, many artisans remained active in politics. They believed that the success of the new nation depended on the ability of its citizens to remain informed about and engaged in the political process.

In a speech delivered on July 4, 1797, a New York sailmaker, George James Warner, warned that citizens must strive to preserve the hard-won gains of the Revolution.

We must guard as a most valuable privilege, the freedom and rights of election. WHEREVER the wealthy by the influence of riches, are enabled to direct the choice of public officers, *there* the downfall of liberty cannot be very remote. It is our own fault if an influence so dangerous, has become in any measure prevalent among us. It would not be the case if the people did not consent to become the dupes of design. It is because tradesmen, mechanics, and the industrious classes of society consider themselves of TOO LITTLE CONSEQUENCE to the body politic that *any thing* belonging to the system of oppression at all obtains. We ought to spurn from us with disdain, the individual who would not solicit our vote, from motives of personal consideration. He ought not to be listened to, who would *demand* it as the price of friendship, or who would *expect* it from regard to his superior riches. It too often happens that men only capable of attracting public notice by an ostentatious display of their wealth, are deemed best qualified to protect the rights of the people, and consequently receive their suffrages; while our choice ought only to be directed to men of TALENTS and VIRTUE whatever their situation in life might be. The *possession* of riches is not necessarily accompanied by superior understanding or goodness of heart. On the contrary, the experience of ages confirms this opinion, that a state of mediocrity is more favorable to them both.

If, instead of improving on it original plan, our government, at any future period, should be irresistibly impelled in an unalterable course toward despotism, the dividing line between the *rich* and the *poor* will be distinctly marked, and the *latter* will be found in a state of vassallage [slavery] and dependence on the former.

Be it your care then, my fellow-citizens, to guard with unceasing vigilance against the growth of this evil; assume the native dignity of your character and maintain with a modest but determined spirit, the liberty of opinion. Suffer no one to DICTATE imperiously what line of conduct you are to pursue; but at the same time let no one be sacrificed at the alter of public vengeance, for a candid and liberal expression of his sentiments....

We must endeavor to acquaint ourselves with the political situation and relative interests of our country. Without this information, we shall either be unable to form an accurate opinion on our own, or often become the dupes of the designing. The PUBLIC PRINTS naturally present themselves as the vehicles of this necessary knowledge. Those conducted in a spirit of liberality, yet altogether consonant to the principles on which our revolution was achieved, should employ the public attention and meet its decided support. It will be found, that a JUST and EQUAL GOVERNMENT will ever derive additional stability, as the PEOPLE obtain a more general knowledge of its principles and operations. The result is, that every sincere friend to our NATIONAL CONSTITUTION ought sedulously to promote the dissemination of this knowledge, as a barrier to

---

"**Republican mother**"—who provided cultured companionship for her husband and reared her children to be virtuous, responsible members of society. This image of womanhood led to a new notion: that well-off women should dedicate themselves to tending the home fires rather than aspiring to a more public role in business or politics.

Prior to the Revolution, women tended to bear many children, since additional hands were needed to labor in the fields. But as the sons of farmers became store managers and bookkeepers, they had less need for the unpaid labor of their own children. The decline in white women's fertility rates after the Revolution suggests that the economy had shifted. And some women could now buy products their grandmothers had made at home. In particular, a small but influential group of well-to-do women in the cities were shedding their roles as producers of candles, soap, and textiles. Instead, they became consumers of these staples and of luxury goods, and they managed household servants. As "Republican mothers," these women participated in the public life of the new nation as the guardians of the home and the socializers of children.

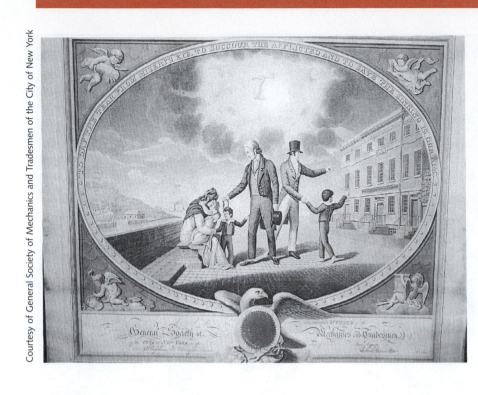

The New York City Mechanics' Society was founded in 1785 and incorporated in 1792. The society included many different kinds of artisans. In addition to representing the interests of skilled artisans, it served as a mutual aid association, lending money to members and distributing charity to the poor. This certificate of membership combines the traditional symbol of arts and crafts, the arm and hammer, with images of American patriotism (the eagle in the center foreground) and prosperity (waterways and fields on the left, urban townhouses on the left). Children are prominently featured here. In 1820 the General Society opened a school for the children of its members, and began offering classes to women in 1821.

the risings of sedition, as well as to the encroachments of arbitrary power.

In his speech, Warner also called for "the practice of all the moral virtues" and the education of children "as to the RIGHTS which they possess, and the DUTIES which they owe society." Warner himself became active in New York's Democratic-Republican party.

Questions

1. According to Warner, in what ways do wealthy politicians threaten to undermine a robust form of democracy?

2. How are the principles of an educated citizenry and a free press related to the preservation of American liberty?

3. How would an African American sailor react to Warner's speech? How would a New York woman employed as a domestic servant react to Warner's speech? ■

Source: George James Warner, Means for the Preservation of Public Liberty (New York, 1797); reprinted in Howard B. Rock, The New York City Artisan, 1789–1825 (Albany: State University of New York Press, 1989), pp. 6–11.

But the idea of the "Republican mother" also suggested a more radical notion. If such a woman wanted to earn the respect accorded all intelligent human beings, she must strive for an education equal to that of men. In the 1790s, a number of academies for "young ladies" opened in New England. These schools offered courses in such "womanly pursuits" as needlework, etiquette, and music. But many also offered a classical curriculum consisting of mathematics, foreign languages, and geography. This system of study encouraged young women to think for themselves. In this respect, female academies challenged the view that women were intellectually inferior to and necessarily dependent on men.

A Loss of Political Influence: The Fate of Nonelite Women

Many Native American women, feeling the pressure of non-Indian cultures, found their traditional roles had been weakened by the end of the eighteenth century. For example, among

James Peale, *The Artist and His Family*, 1795. Pennsylvania Academy of the Fine Arts, Philadelphia (1922.1.1). Gift of John Frederick Lewis

■ James Peale completed this painting of his family in 1795. Peale came from a distinguished family of artists. The picture represents the ideal of post-Revolutionary citizenship and family life. Husband and wife are both featured prominently, although their roles differ. The husband represents the household in the public, political sphere. The wife, a devoted mother, is responsible for preparing the children to be virtuous citizens of the new republic. Growing up in a well-to-do home, these playful children are exempt from the hard labor associated with childhood in the colonial period and, in the 1790s, still characteristic of childhood among enslaved, rural, and poor families.

the Cherokee, the introduction of a European American division of labor lessened women's customary political influence as leaders and diplomats. Most European Americans believed that only men should serve in positions of authority, and so Cherokee women felt pressed to refrain from taking part in political negotiations and to subordinate themselves to men.

In the West, Indian women registered the brunt of ongoing conflicts between their own people and European American settlers. In New Mexico, female Indian captives from Plains tribes (such as the Apache, Comanche, and Kiowa) became *indios servientes* in Hispanic households. In the East, Native American women dispossessed of their land pieced together a meager existence. For example, in Natick, Massachusetts, women turned to weaving and peddling baskets and brooms while their men scrounged for wage labor.

For some Americans, the postwar years brought unprecedented opportunities to buy, sell, and trade. However, commercial development, combined with race and gender discrimination, offered only modest possibilities for many impoverished women and women of color. Like other free blacks, Chloe Spear of Boston "worked early and late" at a number of jobs, such as laundering and ironing clothes. Eventually, she managed to purchase her own home. In Rhode Island, Elleanor Eldrige started her work career at age ten in 1795. Thereafter, she worked as a domestic servant, spinner, weaver, dairymaid, and nurse. She finally went into business, first as a soapboiler and then as a wallpaperer and house painter. However, like many free blacks, Eldrige remained vulnerable to the machinations of white men who tried to defraud her of her hard-won earnings.

Commercial development, combined with race and gender discrimination, offered only modest possibilities for many impoverished women and women of color.

Some white women also felt the effects of fluctuations in the market economy. In Philadelphia in the mid-1790s, two former servants—Polly Nugent (married to a blacksmith who had just lost his job) and Grace Biddle (newly widowed)—had to plead for assistance from their former mistress, Elizabeth Drinker. The city's "Bettering House" for indigent people housed men and women, blacks and whites. Many women had neither the resources nor the opportunities to improve their lot after the Revolution.

The Election of 1800: Revolution or Reversal?

The campaign of 1800 pitted Thomas Jefferson and his vice-presidential running mate, Aaron Burr, against the incumbent, John Adams, and his vice-presidential nominee, Charles Pinckney. Certain elements of the campaign were predictable. The Democratic-Republicans blasted Alexander Hamilton's economic policies and the Adams administration's military buildup. Jefferson's party also condemned the Alien and Sedition Acts, used to silence Adams's political opponents. For their part, the Federalists portrayed Jefferson as a godless supporter of the French Revolution. They also charged that he had fathered children by one of his slaves, Sally Hemings. (Two centuries later, DNA evidence suggested that this assertion might be true.)

TABLE 9-2		
The Election of 1800		
Candidate	**Political Party**	**Electoral Vote**
Thomas Jefferson	Democratic-Republican	73
Aaron Burr	Democratic-Republican	73
John Adams	Federalist	65
Charles C. Pinckney	Federalist	64

Jefferson prevailed in the 1800 election, but his victory did not come easily. The electoral college allowed delegates to vote separately for president and vice president, and as a result Jefferson tied with Burr. Each man received 73 votes. Then the decision went to the House of Representatives, which was dominated by Federalists. After a series of tied votes, Jefferson finally gained a majority. His selection in February 1801 marked the orderly transfer of power from the Federalists to the Democratic-Republicans, a peaceful revolution in American politics.

As chief executive, Jefferson did little to change the direction of the country. Aware of his razor-thin victory, he retained many Federalist appointees. And his eagerness to expand the boundaries of the United States—which culminated in the Louisiana Purchase of 1803—solidified the Hamiltonian principles that favored commerce and trade over agrarian values.

The Enigmatic Thomas Jefferson

Who was Thomas Jefferson? In 1800 Jefferson, the presidential candidate, wrote, "I have sworn upon the altar of God eternal hostility against every form of tyranny over the mind of man." Yet Jefferson's own views on ordinary people were less heroic. Specifically, his deep skepticism about African American equality and the viability of Indian cultures helped to justify violent assaults on both groups in the early nineteenth century.

Many Americans know Jefferson as the author of the Declaration of Independence. But he also sought to justify slavery as a central institution in the new republic, and he regarded blacks as lacking in imagination and intelligence. Jefferson wrote much about the noble calling of the yeoman farmer. Yet he assigned the task of tilling the soil on his own estate (Monticello, near Charlottesville, Virginia) to his enslaved workers.

The president's views on Indians also did nothing to reverse the course of aggression in the West. He believed that land ownership created the stable institutions necessary for civilized behavior. Yet the system of private property, and the violent methods that whites used to enforce it, spelled the destruction of traditional Indian ways of life.

"Jefferson and Liberty"

It is tempting to excuse Jefferson's racist beliefs by saying he merely reflected his time. But in fact, a significant number of Jefferson's contemporaries were voicing their misgivings about slavery. While Jefferson acknowledged their arguments, he did not share their beliefs. A citizen of a trans-Atlantic "republic of ideas," he corresponded with political thinkers—from John Adams to the Marquis de Lafayette—who understood the inherent tension between freedom for whites and slavery for blacks. Obviously, Jefferson knew that some of the northern states had written constitutions that incorporated the sentiments of the Declaration of Independence in ways that justified the abolition of slavery. Moreover, a notable number of Jefferson's wealthy Virginia compatriots (including George Washington) had chosen to free their slaves, either by their own hand or through provisions of their wills, to practice in their own households what they preached to British tyrants.

> *The United States provided the political theory and rhetoric to inspire abolitionists around the globe, but within the new nation, the debate over the institution of slavery continued to rage.*

Jefferson lived in an age when revolutionary enthusiasm was sweeping the western world. Challenges to slavery had rocked Europe; France outlawed the practice in 1794, although Napoleon later reinstated it. Abolition had also transformed the Western Hemisphere with the successful rebellion of the Saint-Domingue slaves in 1791. The United States provided the political theory and rhetoric to inspire abolitionists around the globe, but within the new nation, the debate over the institution of slavery continued to rage. The southern states, in particular, took decisive steps to solidify the institution within their own boundaries.

Protecting and Expanding the National Interest: Jefferson's Administration to 1803

As president, Jefferson reconsidered his original vision of the United States: a compact country in which citizens freely pursued modest agrarian interests without interference from the national government or distractions from overseas conflicts. Indeed, during his years in office, the federal government moved toward increasing its power.

Just before Jefferson assumed the presidency, the Federalist-dominated Congress had strengthened the national court system by passing the Judiciary Act of 1801. The act created sixteen circuit (regional) courts, with a judge for each, and bolstered support staff for the judicial branch in general. President Adams appointed these judges (so-called midnight judges because they were appointed right before Jefferson took office). Before stepping down, Adams had also appointed Secretary of State John Marshall as chief justice of the Supreme Court.

Adams's last-minute acts had long-term consequences. Marshall remained on the bench for thirty-four years. He presided over the court when it rendered its landmark *Marbury v. Madison* decision in 1803, which established the judiciary's right to declare acts of both the executive and legislative branches unconstitutional. Chief Justice Marshall wrote: "It is emphatically the province and duty of the judicial department to say what the law is."

In the realm of international affairs, Jefferson asserted his own authority. Challenges from foreign powers prompted the Democratic-Republican president to take bold steps to protect U.S. economic and political interests abroad and along the country's borders. In 1801 Jefferson's administration launched a war against Barbary pirates in North Africa when Tripoli (modern-day Libya) demanded ransom money for kidnapped American sailors. (Together, the North African kingdoms of Tunis, Tripoli, Algeria, and Morocco were known as the Barbary States.) The war against Tripoli, which spanned four years, revealed the extent of U.S. trade interests even at this early point in the nation's history. The United States signed a peace treaty with Tripoli in 1805 and paid $60,000 for the release of the American captives.

VIDEO
Louisiana
Purchase

At the beginning of the nineteenth century, the European powers continued their operations in the territory west of the United States. In 1801 Napoleon persuaded the King of Spain to secretly cede the trans-Mississippi region called Louisiana to France. Retaining control of New Orleans, Spain denied Americans the right to use that city as a depository for goods awaiting shipment. In 1803 Jefferson sent his fellow Virginian, and prominent Anti-Federalist, James Monroe to Paris. Together with American ambassador Robert Livingston, Monroe set out to secure American trading rights to New Orleans. To the Americans' surprise, Napoleon agreed to sell the whole area to the United States. At the time, Louisiana included most of the territory between the Mississippi River and the Rocky Mountains—a total of 828,000 square miles. The United States agreed to pay $15 million for the Louisiana Purchase.

The Louisiana Purchase reversed the roles of Jefferson and his Federalist rivals. The president advocated territorial expansion, but his opponents remained suspicious of the move. Devoted to a strict interpretation of the Constitution, Jefferson traditionally favored limiting federal authority. Yet he sought to justify the purchase by pointing out that it would finally rid the area of European influence. He proposed shifting Indians from the Mississippi Territory (part of present-day Alabama and Mississippi) to the West so that American newcomers could have the eastern part of the country to themselves. For their part, the Federalists feared that Louisiana would benefit mainly agrarian interests and eventually dilute New England's long-standing political influence and power. They suspected Jefferson of attempting to expand the influence of his own political party.

Conclusion

In his first inaugural address, Jefferson suggested that both parties, despite their differences, shared similar views about the role of government and the importance of economic opportunity for ordinary people. Seeking unity after a partisan campaign, he reminded political leaders, "We are all Republicans, we are all Federalists." Indeed, most public officials at the time held a common suspicion of groups that professed religious beliefs that lay outside the mainstream of Protestantism or liberal Deism (a general belief in God without ties to a particular religious denomination). Most considered slavery less a moral issue than a political matter that individual states must address. And most agreed that women, as well as black and Indian men, should have no formal voice in governing the nation.

Despite such widely shared assumptions, officeholders often defined political interests in "either-or" terms: either the French system of political equality or the British monarchy; either the individual states or the federal government; either the farm or the factory. Such thinking suited the emerging two-party system, and was reinforced by that system's growth. But it also promoted narrow views regarding the promise of the United States, already a society of great economic and ethnic diversity. After all, a candidate's political victory depended on his winning more votes than his opponent, and the electoral system provided no avenues for different groups to share power. This system made it extremely difficult for people who had no place in it to find their own political voice and claim the Revolutionary legacy as their own.

At the same time, the new nation gave white men opportunities practically unknown in the rest of the world. Regardless of their background, many white men could aspire to own property, to enjoy impressive legal rights, and to participate in the political process. The federal government supported economic growth by facilitating territorial expansion, technological innovation, and the protection of private property. As much for the prosperity it promoted as for the noble ideas it nourished, the Revolution continued to inspire liberation movements within the United States and throughout the world.

Sites to Visit

Thomas Jefferson
www.pbs.org/jefferson/
This site is the companion to the Public Broadcasting System series on Jefferson. The site includes material on how people understand Jefferson today.

Archiving Early America
earlyamerica.com
Old newspapers provide a window into the issues of the past. This site includes the Keigwin and Matthews collection of early newspapers.

Alexander Hamilton
http://www.alexanderhamiltonexhibition.org
This site, developed by the New York Historical Society, provides an introduction to Hamilton's life and influence in the United States.

XYZ Affair
gi.grolier.com/presidents/aae/side/xyzaffr.html
This site examines the XYZ affair.

Whiskey Rebellion
www.whiskeyrebellion.org
This site devoted to the 1794 Whiskey Rebellion includes a narrative of events and a timeline.

Native Languages of the Americas
www.geocities.com/bigorrin/miam.htm
This site provides information on the language of the Miami and Illinois Indians, a dialect of the same Algonquin language spoken in Indiana and later in Oklahoma.

The Quasi War, 1798–1800
www.yale.edu/lawweb/avalon/quasi.htm
This site for the Avalon Project at the Yale Law School explores the Quasi War between the United States and France.

Marshall Cases
odur.let.rug.nl~usa/D/1801-1825/marshallcases/marxx.htm
John Marshall, and the cases he heard, shaped the form and function of the judicial system in the United States.

National Museum of the American Indian
www.si.edu/nmai
The Smithsonian Institution maintains this site, which provides information about the new museum in Washington D.C., that is dedicated to the history and culture of Native Americans.

For Further Reading

General Works

Joyce Appleby, *Inheriting the Revolution: The First Generation of Americans* (2000).

Joseph J. Ellis, *Founding Brothers: The Revolutionary Generation* (2000).

Richard H. Kohn, *Eagle and Sword: The Beginnings of the Military Establishment in America* (1975).

Richard White, *The Middle Ground: Indians, Empires, and Republics in the Great Lakes Region, 1650–1815* (1991).

Bernard A. Weisberger, *America Afire: Jefferson, Adams, and the Revolutionary Election of 1800* (2000).

Competing Political Visions in the New Nation

Joyce Appleby, *Capitalism and the New Social Order: The Republican Vision of the 1790s* (1984).

Albert Bowman, *The Struggle for Neutrality: Franco-American Diplomacy During the Federalist Era* (1974).

William Hogeland, *The Whiskey Rebellion* (2006).

James Roger Sharp, *American Politics in the Early Republic: The New Nation in Crisis* (1995).

People of Color: New Freedoms, New Struggles

Ira Berlin, *Slaves Without Masters: The Free Negro in the Antebellum South* (1981).

Douglas R. Egerton, *Gabriel's Rebellion: The Virginia Slave Conspiracies of 1800 and 1802* (1993).

James O. Horton and Lois Horton, *In Hope of Liberty: Culture, Community, and Protest Among Northern Free Blacks, 1700–1860* (1997).

Leon Litwack, *North of Slavery: The Negro in the Free States, 1790–1860* (1961).

Matthew Mason, *Slavery and Politics in the Early Republic* (2006).

Continuity and Change in the West

Henry W. Bowden, *American Indians and Christian Missions: Studies in Cultural Change* (1981).

Gregory Evans Dowd, *A Spirited Resistance: The North American Indian Struggle for Unity, 1745–1815* (1992).

Robert V. Hine and John Mack Faragher, *The American West: A New Interpretive History* (2000).

Reginald Horsman, *Expansion and American Indian Policy, 1783–1812* (1967).

Shifting Social Identities in the Post-Revolutionary Era

Paul Gilje, *Liberty on the Waterfront: American Maritime Culture in the Age of Revolution* (2003).

Nathan O. Hatch, *The Democratization of American Christianity* (1989).

Linda Kerber, *Women of the Republic: Intellect and Ideology in Revolutionary America* (1980).

William G. McLaughlin, *Cherokee Renascence in the New Republic* (1986).

Billy G. Smith, *The "Lower Sort": Philadelphia's Laboring People, 1750–1800* (1990).

The Election of 1800: Revolution or Reversal?

Doron Ben-Atar and Barbara B. Oberg, eds., *Federalists Reconsidered* (1998).

Gordon S. Brown, *Toussaint's Clause: The Founding Fathers and the Haitian Revolution* (2005).

Joseph J. Ellis, *American Sphinx: The Character of Thomas Jefferson* (1996).

John Ferling, *Adams vs. Jefferson: The Tumultuous Election of 1800* (2004).

Peter S. Onuf, *Jefferson's Empire: The Language of American Nationhood* (2000).

Garry Wills, *"Negro President": Jefferson and the Slave Power* (2003).

For quizzes and other resources on these topics, go to www.longmanamericanhistory.com.

P A R T   F O U R

Expanding the Boundaries of Freedom and Slavery, 1803–1848

I N THE FIRST HALF OF THE NINETEENTH CENTURY, FEW IF ANY NATIONS
could rival the United States' remarkable record of growth. At its
founding, the country consisted of 4 million people living in thirteen
states that hugged the eastern seaboard of North America. By the mid-
nineteenth century, the nation's population had grown to 22.5 million
people as a result of reproduction, foreign immigration, and the conquest
of indigenous and Spanish-speaking peoples. Because of a mix of diplomatic pressure and military aggression, dramatic geographic expansion
accompanied the burgeoning population growth. By 1850 the country
sprawled the breadth of the continent to the Pacific Ocean.

Territorial expansion, economic growth, and increasing ethnic diversity profoundly shaped American politics in the first half of the nineteenth century. Innovations in transportation (the steamboat),
communication (the telegraph), and the production of crops and textiles
(reapers and mechanical looms) allowed Americans to move materials,
people, and information more quickly and to produce food and goods
more efficiently. Meanwhile, the immigration of large numbers of western
Europeans, the rapid expansion of the free black population, and the conquest of Spanish-speaking peoples in the Southwest in 1848 challenged
the United States' view of itself as an exclusively Anglo-Protestant nation.

Some citizens declared that the United States had a God-given duty
and God-given right to expand its borders in opposition to the British
and Russians in the Northwest and in opposition to Spain and later
Mexico in the South and Southwest. Thus, territorial expansion brought
the United States into conflict with other countries and groups that
claimed the land. America's victory in the War of 1812 secured the
nation's Great Lakes border and at the same time proved that American
soldiers and sailors were the equal of England's seasoned fighting forces.

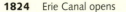

In 1823, fearful that European powers would take advantage of independence movements in Latin America, the United States issued the Monroe Doctrine, stating that the era of colonization of the Americas was over.

Nevertheless, Indian tribes continued to resist the incursion of European Americans who believed that land was a commodity to be wrested from native peoples and then bought and sold. In the southern part of the country, the Five Civilized Tribes and other Native American groups occupied territory coveted by both gold seekers and cotton growers. Many American voters demanded that their political leaders work to expand the nation's boundaries through a variety of means: treaty, negotiation, or military force.

Andrew Jackson, who assumed the presidency in 1828, seemed a fitting symbol and a representative politician of the age. Determined to expand the power of the executive branch of government, Jackson claimed to represent the interests of ordinary people in his political battles against the Second Bank of the United States and the Supreme Court and in his forceful removal of Indian tribes from the Southeast to Indian Territory (present-day Oklahoma). Like other politicians of the time, Jackson conceived of citizenship as a system of rights and privileges for white men only.

Still, European Americans trumpeted the arrival of a new era of egalitarianism. Western settlers laid claim to political power, and suffrage restrictions based on property ownership crumbled in the wake of egalitarian legislation and rhetoric. Americans were restless, moving out west and back east again, around the countryside, and in and out of cities. Believing that people could and should work together to reform society, many created reform associations, embraced new religious beliefs, and joined political parties. New forms of association yielded new kinds of communities in an era characterized by great geographic mobility.

At the same time, two distinct power systems coalesced to ensure that certain groups would monopolize the political and economic life of the country. In the South, cotton planters launched an aggressive defense of the institution of slavery. In the North, an emerging class system extended the differences between the political influence and material well-being of factory owners and machine operatives.

For the country, therefore, growth brought great promise and great peril. Abolitionists, associations of working people, nativists (people hostile to immigrants), women's rights advocates, and a variety of other groups proclaimed their agendas for social change. Most significantly, by 1848 it was becoming more difficult for national legislators to resolve the question of whether to allow slavery in the territories. As passions rose, few could imagine a political compromise that would satisfy abolitionists and proslavery advocates alike. As midcentury approached, more and more Americans seemed prepared to express their convictions—or their prejudices and resentment—through violent means.

1826	American Society for the Promotion of Temperance founded
1827	Workingmen's Party founded in Philadelphia
1828	*Cherokee Phoenix* begins publication
1829	Gold discovered on Cherokee lands in Georgia
1831	Nat Turner leads slave rebellion in Virginia William Lloyd Garrison publishes *The Liberator*
1832	Nullification crisis *Worcester v. Georgia* Jackson vetoes Second Bank of the United States Black Hawk War
1833	Great Britain abolishes slavery National Road completed
1834	Cyrus McCormick patents reaper First strike at Lowell mills Whig Party organized
1835	Alexis de Tocqueville, *Democracy in America* Texas revolts against Mexico
1836	Congress passes gag rule on antislavery petitions Republic of Texas founded
1837	Panic of 1837 John Deere invents steel plow
1838	Pennsylvania revokes black male suffrage Cherokee removal begins; Trail of Tears
1840	Liberty Party founded
1841	John Tyler assumes presidency after death of William Henry Harrison Supreme Court rules in favor of *Amistad* Africans
1844	Mormon leader Joseph Smith killed by mob in Nauvoo, Illinois
1845	Irish potato famine Frederick Douglass, *Narrative of the Life of Frederick Douglass* Texas becomes twenty-eighth state
1846	Great Britain cedes southern part of Oregon Country to United States Mexican-American War begins
1847	United States wins battles of Buena Vista, Vera Cruz, Mexico City Capture of San Patricio soldiers, Battle of Churubusco
1848	Treaty of Guadalupe Hidalgo ends Mexican-American War Women's Rights convention in Seneca Falls, New York Popular revolutions sweep Europe

CHAPTER 10

Defending and Expanding the New Nation, 1803–1818

I
N EARLY NOVEMBER 1804, A GROUP OF SOLDIERS WORKED FEVERISHLY TO CONSTRUCT A ROUGH military garrison on the north bank of the Missouri River, near several Mandan Indian villages just west of modern Washburn, North Dakota. The soldiers knew they had to work quickly. Within a month, winter would descend on the northern Great Plains, and the temperature would plummet. In fact, not long after Fort Mandan was completed, the temperature registered at 45 degrees Fahrenheit below zero.

Louisiana Purchase and Exploration of the Trans-Mississippi West

The garrison provided shelter for an expedition party led by Meriwether Lewis and William Clark. Both captains in the U.S. Army, Lewis and Clark had been commissioned by President Thomas Jefferson to explore the upper reaches of the newly acquired Louisiana Territory, which had doubled the size of the country. With the ultimate goal of reaching the Pacific Coast in what today is Oregon, their party spent the winter at Fort Mandan and joined the buffalo hunts and nightly dances sponsored by their hosts, the Mandan Indians. Between November 1804 and March 1805, Lewis and Clark also found time to record their observations on all manner of things natural and cultural. In their journals and their letters to President Jefferson, they described the language of the Hidatsa Indians and the beadwork of the Arikara, the medicinal properties of native plants, and the contours of the Missouri River. In a shipment prepared for the president, they included deer horns, pumice stones, and the pelt of a white weasel. Among an assortment of live animals, only a magpie and a prairie dog survived the journey to Washington, D.C.

Lewis and Clark's trek took twenty-eight months to complete and covered 8,000 miles. Their expedition's purpose was partly scientific, but Jefferson had also commissioned them to chart a northwestern waterway

CHAPTER OUTLINE

The British Menace

The War of 1812

The "Era of Good Feelings"?

The Rise of the Cotton Plantation Economy

Conclusion

Sites to Visit

For Further Reading

■ Captain Meriwether Lewis posed in Indian dress for this watercolor completed in 1807 by French artist C. B. J. Févret de Saint-Mémin.

242

The Lewis and Clark expedition to the Pacific

—— Pittsburgh to Camp Wood, 1803
—— Camp Wood to Pacific and return, 1804–1805
- - - Continental Divide
⚔ Fort   ⛺ Camp

Lewis and Clark returned east from the Pacific to St. Louis by slightly different routes in 1806

Present state names and boundaries provided for orientation

■ **MAP 10.1**

LEWIS AND CLARK This map, showing the route of the Lewis and Clark expedition, suggests the importance of interior waterways in facilitating travel and exploration in the West. Spain feared, rightly, that the Americans would use western rivers to establish trade links with the Indians and thereby challenge Spain's northern border with the United States.

passage to the Pacific coast. The president hoped to divert the profitable fur trade of the far Northwest away from British Canada and into the hands of Americans by locating a river connecting this larger Northwest directly to eastern U.S. markets. Jefferson also instructed Lewis and Clark to initiate negotiations with various Indian groups, to pave the way for miners and ranchers to move into the area.

Lewis and Clark's party consisted of a diverse group of people, including British and Irish enlisted men, and Lewis's African American slave, York. At Fort Mandan, the group picked up Toussaint Charbonneau, a French Canadian, and his fifteen-year-old wife, Sacajawea, a Shoshone Indian. The explorers came to rely on Sacajawea's skills as an interpreter. And because women never traveled with Indian war parties, Sacajawea's presence reassured suspicious Native Americans that the goal of the expedition was peaceful.

During the first two decades of the nineteenth century, the United States faced a number of challenges from within and outside its borders, challenges that had long-lasting political and economic effects. Indians in general were a persistent threat to the new nation. Indeed, in the Great Lakes region, various tribes maintained political

The Louisiana Purchase

William Clark, *Eulachon (T. Pacificus)*, 1806, Voorhis Journal #2. William Clark Papers, Missouri Historical Society Archives

■ Lewis and Clark were not only explorers; they were also pioneering naturalists committed to gathering, recording, and studying plants and animal life in the West. William Clark drew this sketch of a eulachon, also called a candlefish, as part of his journal entry for February 25, 1806. Pacific Indians dried the oily fish and used it as a torch.

and military alliances with the British in Canada. Nevertheless, in this period the United States successfully met its most severe test to date: a war with Great Britain that raged from 1812 to 1815. The effects of this so-called Second American Revolution were far-reaching. The conflict eliminated the British from the Old Northwest once and for all. The war also spurred industrialization and stimulated commerce. In the South, the cotton plantation system began to shape the political and economic life of the entire region, in the process stimulating the expansion of human bondage.

The British Menace

In the election of 1804, Democratic-Republican Thomas Jefferson and his vice-presidential running mate, George Clinton, easily defeated their Federalist opponents, Charles C. Pinckney and Rufus King. Developments overseas preoccupied Jefferson during his second term in office. England and France continued to challenge each other as the reigning powers of Europe. In 1805 the British navy, under the command of Lord Nelson, defeated the French and Spanish fleets in the Battle of Trafalgar off the coast of Spain. That same year, France reveled in its own triumph on land when Napoleon conquered the Austrian and Russian armies at the Battle of Austerlitz. Supreme on the seas, England in 1806 passed the Orders in Council, which specified that any country that wanted to ship goods to France must first send them to a British port and pay taxes on them. Many Americans believed that England's policies amounted to acts of military and economic aggression against the United States.

The Embargo of 1807

Not content to control trade across the Atlantic as decreed by the 1806 Orders in Council, the British also seized sailors from American ships, claiming that these men were British seamen who had been lured away from their own vessels by American captains promising them higher wages. In some cases these claims were probably true. However, U.S. political leaders charged that an estimated 6,000 U.S. citizens had been seized by the British navy between 1808 and 1811, including an unknown number of African Americans, many of whom were working as mariners. With limited economic opportunities on shore, black sailors accepted the danger and long absences from home. However, neither black nor white sailors had bargained for enforced service in His Majesty's Royal Navy. Seizure, or impressment, reminded Americans of their pre–Revolutionary War days, when British "press gangs" prowled the docks of American port cities and seized colonial merchant sailors. In 1807 the tensions over impressment erupted into violence. Just 10 miles off the shore of Virginia, the American ship *Chesapeake* came under attack from a British vessel. British naval officers claimed that the Americans were harboring four British deserters. In the ensuing exchange of cannon fire, three Americans were killed and eighteen wounded. Jefferson demanded that England leave American sailors and ships alone, but he was rebuffed.

TABLE 10-1		
The Election of 1804		
Candidate	Political Party	Electoral Vote
Thomas Jefferson	Democratic-Republican	162
Charles C. Pinckney	Federalist	14

In 1807 President Jefferson decided to place an **embargo** on all exports to the European powers in an effort to force those nations to respect the rights of Americans on the high seas. The Embargo Act passed by Congress halted the shipment of goods from the United States to Europe. Because Europe—including England—relied heavily on American grain and timber, Jefferson hoped that the move would force England to respect American independence. The president saw this measure as preferable to either war or capitulation to England. But the move aroused intense opposition in Federalist-dominated New England, where the regional economy depended heavily on foreign trade. As the effects of the embargo took hold, the New England grain growers saw the markets for their products dry up, and the timber industry suffered when local shipbuilding ground to a standstill. Southern tobacco and cotton planters faced similar hardship because of the embargo. By 1808 some of them had joined with Northerners to circumvent the embargo by moving their goods through Canada and then to Europe.

Yet Jefferson held his course, prodding Congress to enforce the unpopular act. His efforts provoked a backlash as New England politicians threatened to take their states out of the union. Despite all the uproar, the embargo did benefit Americans by promoting industrialization at home. At the same time, the embargo seemed only to intensify, not lessen, tensions between England and the United States.

On the Brink of War

Both the Federalists and the Democratic-Republicans suffered a blow to their leadership in 1804. That year, the Federalist party lost one of its original leaders with the death of Alexander Hamilton at the hand of his rival, Aaron Burr. Both successful New York attorneys, the two men had risen together through the political ranks in the 1780s and 1790s. Burr served as Jefferson's running mate in the election of 1800; four years later he ran for governor of New York. Incensed by a report that Hamilton had claimed he was "a dangerous man, and one who ought not to be trusted with the reins of government," as well as "still more despicable rumors," Burr challenged his antagonist to a pistol duel at Weehawken, New Jersey, in July 1804. Hamilton, mortally wounded in the affair, died the next day, and Burr's political career fell into ruin.

Jefferson, declining to run for a third presidential term in 1808, left the stage as well. Soon after the inauguration of the new president, James Madison, Congress repealed Jefferson's embargo and replaced it with the Non-Intercourse Act, which eased the complete ban on exports to Europe. This measure permitted American exporters to ship their goods to all European countries except for France and England, still at war with one another. New Englanders opposed even this limited embargo.

The original partisan division within Congress—the Federalists, with their emphasis on a strong national government, against the localist Democratic-Republicans—gradually eased. By 1810 a different split had emerged—between young, hotheaded representatives from the West and their more conservative seniors from the eastern seaboard. The western group, or "**war hawks**," called on the nation to revive its former glory. Americans must uphold U.S. honor, they declared, by opposing European, especially British, claims to military dominance. The war hawks also yearned to vanquish the Indians who impeded settlement of the area west of the Mississippi.

TABLE 10-2		
The Election of 1808		
Candidate	Political Party	Electoral Vote
James Madison	Democratic-Republican	122
Charles C. Pinckney	Federalist	47
George Clinton	Democratic-Republican	6

Library of Congress

■ This lithograph of the Prophet (Tenskwatawa) was based on an 1824 painting of the Shawnee mystic and holy man. Early in life, he suffered an accident with bows and arrows, losing his right eye. He and his older brother Tecumseh called on all Indians to resist the encroachment of their lands by whites and to renounce the way of life followed by whites, including the use of liquor. After the Indians' defeat at the Battle of Tippecanoe in 1811, the Prophet retreated to Canada. He returned to the United States in 1826. By that time he no longer wielded influence as a leader of the Shawnee.

Looking eastward, the war hawks saw an England determined to defile the honor of their young nation. Looking westward, these same men saw an equally threatening menace: the rise of an ominous Indian resistance movement that blended military strength with native spirituality. The movement was led by Shawnee brothers Tecumseh and Tenskwatawa (also known as the Prophet), who founded Prophet's Town in Indiana in 1808. They envisioned a sovereign Indian state and the preservation of Native American culture. Tenskwatawa spoke of a time and place where Indians would reject alcohol and scorn "the food of whites" as well as the "wealth and ornaments" of commercial trade. Tecumseh set out to deliver the message to as many Indian groups as possible, traveling the broad swath of territory from Florida to Canada.

In 1809, the territorial governor of Indiana, William Henry Harrison, plied a group of Indian leaders with liquor, then got them to agree to sell 3 million acres to the U.S. government for just $7,600. Upon hearing of the deal, Tecumseh decried a new form of American aggression: "treaties" between U.S. officials and Indians who lacked the authority to sell their people's homeland. "All red men," Tecumseh proclaimed, must "unite in claiming a common and equal right in the land, as it was at first, and should be yet; for it never was divided, but belongs to all, for the use of each."

In November 1811, Harrison led 1,000 U.S. soldiers in an advance on Prophet's Town. But before they could reach the settlement, several hundred Shawnees under the command of Tenskwatawa attacked their camp on the Tippecanoe River. The Indians suffered a sound defeat before the superior U.S. weapons, and Harrison burned Prophet's Town to the ground.

■ MAP 10.2

THE PUBLIC DOMAIN IN 1810
This map indicates the expanse of western lands owned by the U.S. government in 1810, after the Louisiana Purchase. American war veterans received land warrants in return for military service in the Revolutionary War and the War of 1812. A warrant entitled the bearer to settle a specific number of acres of unoccupied lands. Warrants could be transferred, sold, and traded like stocks and bonds. After the War of 1812, the government issued 29,186 land warrants for a total of 4.8 million acres.

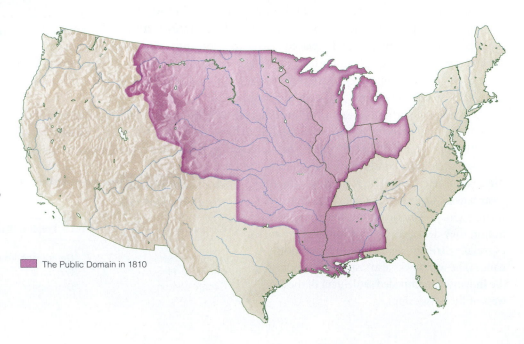

The Public Domain in 1810

The War of 1812

The defeat of the Shawnees at Tippecanoe encouraged western war hawks' resolve to break the back of Indian resistance altogether. But to achieve this goal, the United States would have to invade Canada and eliminate the British arms suppliers who had been trading with the Indians. Claiming the mantle of patriotism, western and southern members of the House of Representatives agitated for a war that would eliminate both the British threat on the high seas and the Canada-based Indian-British alliance. These Americans wanted a war that would win for them a true independence once and for all. "On to Canada! On to Canada!" became the rallying cry of the war hawks.

TABLE 10-3		
The Election of 1812		
Candidate	**Political Party**	**Electoral Vote**
James Madison	Democratic-Republican	128
De Witt Clinton	Federalist	89

The War of 1812

In a secret message sent to Congress on June 1, 1812, President Madison listed Americans' many grievances against England: the British navy's seizure of American citizens, the blockades of American goods, and continued conflict "on one of our extensive frontiers," the result of "savages" who had the backing of British traders and military officials. Madison left it up to Congress whether Americans would continue to endure these indignities or would act "in defense of their natural rights." Seventeen days later, the House voted 79 to 49 and the Senate voted 19 to 13 to declare war on England and, by extension, the western Indians.

While uniting Americans behind a banner of national expansion, the War of 1812 also exposed dangerous divisions between regions of the country and between political viewpoints. Many New Englanders saw the conflict as a plot by Virginia Democratic-Republicans primarily to aid France in opposition to England and to add agrarian (that is, slave) states to the Union. In an ironic twist, the New England Federalists—usually staunch defenders of the national government—argued that states should control their own commerce and militias.

Pushing North

Although the Americans were better armed and organized than the western Indians, they were at a disadvantage when they took on the soldiers and sailors of the British Empire. The United States had not invested in the military and thus was ill-prepared for all-out war. The American navy consisted merely of a fleet of tiny gunboats constructed during the cost-conscious Jefferson administration. The charter for the Bank of the United States had expired in 1811, depriving the country of a vital source of financial credit. Suffering from a drop in tax revenues as a result of the embargo on foreign trade, the nation lacked the funds to train and equip the regular army and the state militias. Nevertheless, in the fall of 1812, the Americans launched an ambitious three-pronged attack against Canada, striking from Niagara, Detroit, and Lake Champlain. All three attempts failed miserably.

In the West in late 1812, Tecumseh (who had accepted a commission as a brigadier general in the British army) and British General Isaac Brock captured Detroit. Yet the Americans scored some notable successes in 1813. That September, Commodore Oliver

Courtesy, Dartmouth College Library

BIG DICK AT THE 'MERMAID'S RETREAT.' SEE CHAPTER II.

■ In 1815 approximately 6,000 American prisoners of war were confined to Britain's dank Dartmoor Prison in Devonshire, England. Many of them were African Americans, who represented one-fifth of all sailors who fought in the war. Among that group was Richard Crafus. An imposing man, Crafus earned the title "King Dick" by serving as the leader of the central barracks at Dartmoor, where blacks were held. He strolled through the cell block, carrying a large club and settling disputes between the prisoners.

MAP 10.3

THE NORTHERN FRONT, WAR OF 1812   Much of the fighting of the War of 1812 centered in the Great Lakes region. It was there, the war hawks charged, that the British were inciting Indians to attack American settlements. Conducted in 1812 and 1813, the campaign against Canada was supposed to eliminate the British threat and, some Americans hoped, win Canadian territory for the United States.

H. Perry defeated a British fleet at Put-in-Bay on Lake Erie. Exhilarated, he declared, "We have met the enemy and they are ours." Perry's hard-won victory forced the British back into Canada, over Tecumseh's objections. General William Henry Harrison followed in hot pursuit. British Colonel Henry Proctor marched his troops to eastern Ontario, leaving Tecumseh to try holding the Americans at bay. At the Battle of the Thames that October, Harrison defeated the Indians. Many perished, Tecumseh among them.

Later that autumn, an American campaign against Montreal failed. The Americans trudged back into New York state, the British close behind them. Flush with their victory in Montreal, the British captured Fort Niagara and set Buffalo and other nearby towns aflame.

By mid-1814, the English and their allies had also crushed Napoleon in Europe. This success freed up 15,000 British troops, who promptly sailed for North America. Still, in July 1814 the Americans, under the leadership of Major General Jacob Brown and Brigadier General Winfield Scott, managed to defeat the British at the Battle of Chippewa, across the Niagara River from Buffalo. But by the end of that year, the Americans had withdrawn to their own territory and relinquished their goal of invading and conquering Canada. The arrival of fresh British troops forced the Americans to defend their own soil.

Fighting on Many Fronts

For the Americans, the most humiliating episode of the war came with the British attack on the nation's capital. On August 24, 1814, the British army, backed by the Royal Navy, sailed into Chesapeake Bay. At the Battle of Bladensburg, Maryland, they scattered the American troops they encountered. The Redcoats then advanced to Washington, where they torched the Capitol building and the White House, causing extensive damage to both structures.

Residents of the capital city had received word that the British were advancing. On Sunday, August 21, public officials frantically packed up their books and papers. Private citizens gathered up their furniture and other belongings and left town. By Tuesday, the city stood nearly empty. As a ragtag American force succumbed to the British, a Baltimore newspaper reported, President Madison "retired from the mortifying scene, and left the city on horseback."

Yet the Americans rallied, pursued the British, and bested them in the Battle of Baltimore. This victory inspired an observer, Francis Scott Key, to write "The Star Spangled Banner" as he watched "the bombs bursting in air" over Baltimore's Fort McHenry. The Americans scored another crucial victory in September, when U.S. naval commander Thomas McDonough crushed the British fleet on Lake Champlain near Plattsburgh, New York.

In the Southeast, Tecumseh's message of Indian unity had resonated with particular force among Native Americans once the war broke out. Some Cherokee and Choctaw cast their lot with the United States. However, a minority of Creek were emboldened by Tenskwatawa's call to war against the whites. By 1813 a group of warriors called Red Sticks (for their scarlet-painted weapons) stood ready to do battle with U.S. forces. Yet they faced opposition from some of their own people, the White Sticks, who counseled peace. The Red Sticks finally decided to attack Fort Mims, north of Mobile.

In response, Andrew Jackson, leader of the Tennessee militia, received a commission as major general. His mission was to retaliate against the Indians. Jackson had speculated in Indian lands in Mississippi Territory, and he called Native Americans "blood thirsty barbarians." Even in a country where anti-Indian sentiment ran high, his views were extreme. He often boasted about collecting the scalps of all his Indian victims, and he relished his new assignment.

DOCUMENT

Dolley Madison to Her Sister as the British Approach (1814)

Library of Congress

■ This engraving, published in 1814, depicts the bombardment of Fort McHenry by British warships in September of that year. When he witnessed the battle, Francis Scott Key, a Washington lawyer, was aboard a prisoner exchange boat in Baltimore Harbor. He was seeking release of a friend captured by the British. After penning the poem "The Star Spangled Banner," Key set the words to music, using the tune of a popular English drinking song. Congress declared the song the national anthem in 1931.

Jackson's 3,500 troops laid waste to Creek territory. Regiments of Cherokee, Choctaw, and Chickasaw Indians, as well as White Sticks, helped them. During a monumental battle in March 1814, more than three-quarters of the 1,000 defending Red Sticks and a number of Indian women and children died at Horseshoe Bend (in modern-day Alabama). In the Treaty of Horseshoe Bend that followed, the Americans forced the Creek Nation to give up 23 million acres. The remnants of the Red Sticks fled to the swamps of Florida, where they joined additional Creeks, other Florida Indians, and numerous fugitive slaves in an emerging group known as the Seminoles.

Jackson next marched to New Orleans to confront the British. Knowing he would be facing some of Europe's finest soldiers, he assembled 7,000 men, U.S. soldiers and militiamen from the states of Louisiana, Kentucky, and Tennessee. Two Kentucky regiments consisted of free Negro volunteers, about 400 men in total. The Battle of New Orleans, fought on January 8, 1815, began with a ferocious assault by British soldiers. But within just half an hour, 2,000 of them lay dead or wounded. The Americans lost only seventy. Jackson's back country sharpshooters had vanquished the army of Europe's greatest military power.

Later, many Americans associated Andrew Jackson with the war's decisive battle and most glorious victory. But in fact, American and British negotiators had actually signed a peace agreement ending the war two weeks before the British defeat in New Orleans. The Battle of New Orleans might have been a glorious victory for the Americans, but it was hardly the decisive battle of the war.

An Uncertain Victory

In the fall of 1814, Madison had decided to end the war. He dispatched John Quincy Adams, son of former president John Adams, to the Belgian city of Ghent to start negotiations. Representative Henry Clay and three other American envoys accompanied Adams. At first, English representatives at the meeting made two demands. The Americans, they said, must agree to the creation of an Indian territory in the upper Great Lakes region. They must also cede much of the state of Maine to England. The Americans refused, and the negotiations dragged on.

In the meantime, the New England states had grown increasingly impatient with what they called "Mr. Madison's war." As with the embargo, they saw the effort as a mistake and a threat to their regional commercial interests. In December 1814, Massachusetts, Connecticut, Rhode Island, New Hampshire, and Vermont sent delegates to a gathering in Hartford, Connecticut, to consider a course of action. The delegates demanded that the federal government give their states financial aid to compensate for the revenue they had lost as a result of disrupted trade. Some delegates even hinted that their states wanted to secede from the union. Although most delegates shied away from immediate action, the majority of them apparently wanted to leave open the possibility of actual **secession**.

After Congress ratified the Treaty of Ghent in February 1815, the Americans and the British never again met each other across a battlefield as enemies.

Back in Ghent, the British had reversed their initial position by late December. They had lost recent battles in upper New York and in Baltimore and, as always, were still worried about new threats from France. They dropped their demands for territory and for an Indian buffer state in the upper Midwest. They also agreed to an armistice that, in essence, represented a draw: both combatants would retain the same territory they had possessed when the war began. The British made no concessions to the Americans' demands that they stop impressing American sailors and supplying the western Indians with arms or that they revoke the Orders in Council. Still, most U.S. citizens considered the war a great victory for the United States. After Congress ratified the Treaty of Ghent in February 1815, the Americans and the British never again met each other across a battlefield as enemies.

DOCUMENT

The Treaty of Ghent (1814)

The "Era of Good Feelings"?

In the 1816 presidential election, Democratic-Republican candidate James Monroe benefited from several developments that had mortally wounded the Federalist party: the War of 1812 victory, presided over by a Democratic-Republican chief executive; the New England Federalists' flirtation with secession (and treason) during the war years; and the strong nationalist tendencies of both the Jefferson and Madison administrations, which had stolen the Federalists' thunder.

Addressing Congress in December 1817, President Monroe expressed optimism about the state of the nation. The country's boundaries were secure, and the Indians had little choice but to retreat farther and farther west. The president predicted that, shortly, "Indian hostilities, if they do not altogether cease, will henceforth lose their terror." Equally inspiring, the Americans had once again defied the British Empire and won. Two treaties with Britain—the Rush-Bagot of 1817 and the pending Convention of 1818—set the U.S.-Canadian border at the forty-ninth parallel and provided that the two countries would jointly occupy Oregon Territory for ten years.

Monroe called on Congress to acknowledge "the vast extent of territory within the United States [and] the great amount and value of its productions" and to facilitate the construction of roads and canals. It was this "happy situation of the United States," in Monroe's words, that ushered in what some historians called "The Era of Good Feelings." Although voters continued to disagree over some issues of the day—such as the national bank, sectionalism, and **internal improvements**—they did not necessarily express those disagreements in the form of bitter partisan wrangling. Still, the term "good feelings" may fully apply only to a narrow group of **enfranchised citizens**, men who shared common beliefs about territorial expansion and economic development.

TABLE 10-4		
The Election of 1816		
Candidate	Political Party	Electoral Vote
James Monroe	Democratic-Republican	183
Rufus King	Federalist	34

DOCUMENT

Western Country Ohio (1816)

Praise and Respect for Veterans After the War

American veterans of the War of 1812 won the praise of a grateful nation. Even the British expressed a grudging respect for Americans' fighting abilities. One British naval officer admitted, "I don't like Americans; I never did, and never shall." He had "no wish to eat with them, drink with them, or consort with them in any way." But, he added, he would rather not fight with "an enemy so brave, determined, and alert, as they have always proved." To reward veterans for their service, Congress offered them 160-acre plots of land in the territory between the Illinois and Mississippi rivers. These grants did much to encourage families to emigrate west and establish homesteads.

Some military heroes of the war parlayed their success into impressive political careers. Andrew Jackson won election to the presidency in 1828 and 1832, as did William Henry Harrison in 1840. Countless others earned recognition within their own community, and European American veterans were not the only ones to gain status and influence as a result of the conflict. For example, a Cherokee leader named the Ridge earned the gratitude of American officials for his contributions to the war effort. He had accepted the government's attempts to press the Cherokee to adopt European American ways, settling in a log cabin rather than in a traditional Cherokee dwelling when he married a Cherokee woman named Susanna Wickett in the early 1790s. During the war against the Red Sticks, the Ridge served under Andrew Jackson and earned the title of major. For the rest of his life, the Cherokee leader was known as Major Ridge. His wife devoted herself to tending an orchard, keeping a garden, and sewing clothes,

Cherokee Women Petition Against Further Land Sales to Whites in 1817

In traditional Cherokee society, men took responsibility for foreign affairs while women focused on domestic matters, leading to a roughly equal division of labor. However, European American diplomats, military officials, and traders dealt primarily with Indian men. As a result, beginning in the eighteenth century, Cherokee women's traditional influence was eroding within their own communities. In this new world, Indian warriors wielded significant power.

Nevertheless, Cherokee women insisted on presenting their views during the crisis of 1817–1819, when men of the group were deciding whether to cede land to U.S. authorities and move west. The following petition was supported by Nancy Ward, a Cherokee War Woman. This honorific title was bestowed on women who accompanied and attended to the needs of war parties. Ward had supported the colonists' cause during the American Revolution.

Amovey [Tennessee] in Council 2nd May 1817

The Cherokee Ladys now being present at the meeting of the Chiefs and warriors in council have thought it their duties as mothers to address their beloved Chiefs and warriors now assembled.

Our beloved children and head men of the Cherokee nation we address you warriors in council we have raised all of you on the land which we now have,

In 1987, Wilma Mankiller became the first woman to be elected Principal Chief of the Cherokee Nation of Oklahoma.

which God gave to us to inhabit and raise provisions we know that our country has once been extensive but by repeated sales has become circumscribed to a small tract, and [we] never have thought it our duty to interfere in the disposition of it till now, if a father or mother was to sell all their lands which they had to depend on which their children had to raise their living on which would indeed be bad and to be removed to another country we do not wish to go to an unknown country [to] which we have understood some of our children wish to go over the Mississippi but this act of our children would be like destroying your mothers. Your mothers your sisters ask and beg of you not to part with any more of our lands, we say ours. [Y]ou are our descendants and take pity on our request, but keep it for our growing children for it was the good will of our creator to place us here and you know our father the great president [James Monroe], will not allow his white children to take our country away for if it was not they would not ask you to put your hands to paper for it would be impossible to remove us all for as soon as one child is raised, we have others in our arms for such is our situation and will consider our circumstance.

Therefore children don't part with any more of our lands but continue on it and

enlarge your farms and cultivate and raise corn and cotton and we your mothers and sisters will make clothing for you which our father the president has recommended to us all we don't charge anybody for selling any lands, but we have heard such intentions of our children but your talks become true at last and it was our desire to forewarn you all not to part with our lands.

Nancy Ward to her children[:] warriors to take pity and listen to the talks of your sisters, although I am very old yet cannot but pity the situation in which you will hear of their minds. I have great many grand children which I wish they do well on our land.

In addition to Nancy Ward, 12 Cherokee women signed the petition. Their names suggest the varying degrees of assimilation to white ways on the part of Cherokees in general. Petitioners included Cun, o, ah and Widow Woman Holder, as well as Jenny McIntosh and Mrs. Nancy Fields.

It is unclear what effect, if any, this petition had on Cherokee male leaders. The Cherokee nation did halt land cessions to whites between 1819 and 1835.

Questions

1. How and why did motherhood confer authority on Cherokee women?
2. What is the significance and meaning of the land in Cherokee culture?
3. Does this petition provide evidence for the view that early nineteenth-century Cherokee men and women were adopting elements of European American culture? If so, what elements, and in what ways? ■

Source: Cherokee Women to Cherokee Council, May 2, 1817, series 1, Andrew Jackson Presidential Papers, Library of Congress Manuscripts Division, Washington, D.C. Reprinted in Nancy F. Cott, Jeanne Boydston, Ann Braude, Lori Ginzberg, and Molly Ladd-Taylor, eds., *Root of Bitterness: Documents of the Social History of American Women* (Boston: Northeastern University Press, 1996), pp. 177–178.

tasks traditionally performed by European American but not Native American women. Eventually, the family prospered, bought African American slaves, and became Christians as well.

The Ridge's battlefield experiences earned him the respect of other Cherokee who embraced the "civilization" program that missionaries and government officials promoted. At the same time, the Ridge vehemently resisted U.S. officials' attempts to persuade the Chero-

Unidentified Artist, *Benjamin Hawkins and the Creek Indians*, c. 1805. Greenville County Museum of Art, Greenville, SC. Gift of The Museum Association, Inc., with funds donated by Corporate Partners: Ernst and Young; Fluor Daniel; Director's Circle Members: Mr. and Mrs. Alester G. Furman III; Mr. and Mrs. M. Dexter Hagy; Thomas P. Hartness; Mr. and Mrs. E. Erwin Maddrey II; Mary M. Pearce; Mr. and Mrs. John Pellett, Jr.; Mr. W. Thomas Smith; Mr. and Mrs. Edward H. Stall; Eleanor and Irvine Welling; Museum Antiques Show, 1989, 1990, 1991, Elliott, Davis and Company, CPAs, sponsor; Collector's Group 1990, 1991

■ **Southeastern** Indians varied widely in their willingness to adopt European American ways. Some argued that the best way to preserve their community and remain on the land of their forebears was to accommodate themselves to white practices of trade, textile production, and farming. This 1805 painting shows Benjamin Hawkins, a government Indian agent, at a Creek settlement near Macon, Georgia. Hawkins expresses evident satisfaction with the Indians' neat cabins, well-tended fields, flocks of sheep, and bountiful harvest of vegetables.

kee to give up their lands to whites and move west. He believed that his people should adopt some elements of white culture but should also hold fast to their native lands in opposition to white settlers and politicians.

A Thriving Economy

The end of the War of 1812 saw an upsurge in internal migration. New Englanders, especially, pushed west in search of new opportunities. Between 1800 and 1820, the population of Ohio grew from 45,000 to 581,000. New means of transportation—and new means to fund them—facilitated the movement of goods and people. In 1807 an entrepreneur named Robert Fulton piloted the *Clermont*, his new kind of boat powered by steam, up the Hudson River from New York City. Steamboats traveled upriver, against the current, ten times faster than keelboats, which had to be pushed, pulled, or hauled by men or mules. Within a few years, therefore, such vessels were plying the Mississippi River and its major tributaries.

Improvements in land transportation stimulated economic growth. The profits that the Philadelphia and Lancaster Turnpike raked in by charging travelers tolls inspired other local private corporations to invest in roads. By 1810 several thousand such corporations were building roads up and down the East Coast. Funding came from a variety of sources, both public and private. Philadelphia textile mill owners financed transportation links with the city's **hinterland** (rural areas to the west) to carry their goods to the largest number of customers. Individual cities also invested in routes westward. The state of Virginia authorized a board of public works to expend funds for roads and other internal improvements. Western politi-

> *Improvements in land transportation stimulated economic growth.*

cians flexed their political muscle in 1806 by securing congressional authorization for the building of the Cumberland (later National) Road, which snaked through the Allegheny Mountains and ended at the Ohio River.

The acceleration of commerce in the West, combined with the disruption in trade from Europe that had come with the Embargo of 1807 and the War of 1812, stimulated manufacturing throughout the United States. Philadelphia's growth proved particularly dazzling. During the war, the city's craft producers did not have to worry about foreign competition. Local merchant-financiers, who otherwise might have been pouring their money into trade ventures, began to invest in manufacturing. As early as 1808, the city's new factories had compensated for the glass, chemicals, shot, soap, lead, and earthenware that no longer flooded in from England. Philadelphia soon took the lead in production of all kinds, whether carried out in factories, artisans' shops, or private homes. Metalworking, ale brewing, and leather production counted among the array of thriving industries that made Philadelphia the nation's top industrial city in 1815. Still, in 1820 about two-thirds of all Philadelphia workers labored in small shopd employing fewer than six people.

Transformations in the Workplace

Even the earliest stages of the Industrial Revolution transformed the way people lived and worked. Some crafts—for example, the production of leather, barrels, soap, candles, and newspapers—expanded from small shops with skilled artisans into larger establishments with unskilled wage earners. In these cases, production was reorganized; now wage earners under the supervision of a boss replaced apprentices and journeymen who had formerly worked alongside a master artisan. These workers performed a single task many times a day instead of using their specialized skills to see a production process through to completion.

New England rapidly became the center of mechanized textile production in the United States. By the late eighteenth century, Boston shippers were making handsome profits by supplying Alta California (the area north of San Diego, encompassing present-day California, Nevada, and parts of Arizona and Utah) with cloth, shoes, and tools, selling western otter pelts in China, and returning home laden with Chinese porcelains and silks. These profits helped to finance New England's mechanized textile industry. By 1813 seventy-six cotton mills housing over 51,000 spindles were operating within the vicinity of Providence, Rhode Island.

Faced with a shortage of adult men (many were moving west), New England mill owners sought other local sources of labor. The Rhode Island system of production had relied on child spinners working in small mills. This system gave way to the Lowell model, based in Waltham and Lowell, Massachusetts, which brought young women from the surrounding countryside to work in gigantic mills. Many of the women were eager to earn cash wages and to escape the routine of farm life. Still, New England mill owners realized that they had to reassure Yankee parents that their daughters would find the factories safe, attractive places to work. Mill owners offered the young women housing in dormitory-like boardinghouses staffed by older women, called matrons, who looked after them.

The Market Revolution

In the North, wage earning gradually replaced family labor and indentured servitude as the dominant labor system. Factory workers quickly and efficiently proccessed raw materials—leather into shoes, cotton into clothing. With the advent of steamboats and toll roads, traditional barriers separating farms from towns and the West from the East began to crumble. Together, all of these rapid economic transformations in the early nineteenth century fueled what some scholars have called the **Market Revolution**. Driven by improvements in transportation, increasing commercialization, and the rise of factories, powerful economic changes affected ordinary Americans and their everyday routines at home and on the job.

The gradual changes of the Market Revolution were driven by investment. Wealthy New England merchants led the way, but a wide variety of private individuals and public institutions proved willing to invest their money and energy in new economic opportunities. Profits from foreign trade helped to build the textile factories that dotted the northeastern landscape. States and even towns used the money of taxpayers and private investors to build turnpikes and later to finance canals and railroads. **Entrepreneurs** pioneered the **putting out** system, a form of production (of hats and other forms of clothing, for example) that enlisted the efforts of single women in the cities, as well as farm families during the winter season. These workers received raw materials from a **merchant-capitalist** and engaged in piecework in return for wages. Combined public-private investment in new forms of business organization and technology spurred American economic growth.

These changes spilled over into American social and religious life, encouraging some people to adopt an optimistic worldview about the possibilities inherent in American life—possibilities that included moving from one place to another, making money by selling new products, altering the natural landscape to make way for canals or factories, and aspiring to buy goods rather than produce goods at home. Foreign visitors often commented on the "restlessness" of Americans, their "acquisitiveness," and their impatience with tradition.

Not all Americans adopted this new way of looking at the world, but almost all groups felt its effects. Slave owners pushed black men, women, and children to work even harder in the fields of the South so that more cotton and rice could be exported to northern and European markets. Western Indians suffered the effects of European American conquest, as whites chopped down forests and cleared the land for farms, violently displacing native populations in the process. In New England textile mills, women and children operated the machines that produced cloth. These operatives served as the vanguard of the Industrial Revolution in America.

By the second decade of the nineteenth century, America had clearly defined itself as a nation that embraced many different kinds of change in transportation and technology. Yet traditional forms of inequality and hierarchy endured, serving as distinguishing features of the Market Revolution.

The Rise of the Cotton Plantation Economy

The growth and spread of the cotton economy redefined the institution of slavery, the southern political system, and, ultimately, all of American history. With the invention of the cotton gin and the acquisition of the Louisiana Territory, cotton production boomed, and the enslaved population expanded. About 700,000 slaves resided in the United States in 1790; just two decades later, that figure had jumped to 1.1 million. Beginning in 1808, the United States outlawed the importation of new slaves. However, the astounding profitability of cotton heightened the demand for labor. Planters began to rely on the domestic slave trade—the forced migration of slaves from the upper South to the lower South.

The institution of slavery was marked by increasingly sharp regional variations, reflecting the impact of cotton cultivation on local economies. At the same time, the contours of an African American culture emerged. This culture had certain characteristics regardless of place, such as strong ties that bound nuclear and extended family members, rich oral and musical traditions heavily influenced by West African customs, and individual and collective resistance to slavery. White people as a group understood little of this culture; they viewed black people primarily as workers who would never become citizens. As U.S. military strength and nationalistic pride grew, southern planters imposed a harsher, more regimented system of slavery on the black population. The tension between the rhetoric of freedom and equality and the reality of slavery continued to shape southern—and American—life for the next four decades.

Regional Economies of the South

Throughout the South, shifts in production methods transformed the demographic and economic make-up of specific regions. For example, by the early nineteenth century, the Chesapeake tobacco economy had declined as a result of worn-out lands and falling prices. In its place arose a more diversified economy based on crafts, the cultivation of corn and wheat, and the milling of flour. Owners put enslaved men to work making barrels and horseshoes while forcing their wives, sisters, and daughters to labor as spinners, weavers, dairymaids, personal servants, and livestock tenders.

Plantation and Southern Commerce

The lower South states of Georgia and South Carolina also saw their economies change during this period. The indigo export business never recovered from the Revolution, since colonial cultivators of the plant had relied heavily on British **subsidies** to shore up their profits. European customers now had to turn to Louisiana and Central America for indigo. In contrast, the lowcountry (coastal) South Carolina rice economy recovered and flourished after the war. In a particularly rich rice district, All Saints Parish, one out of two slaves lived on a plantation with more than a hundred slaves in 1790; thirty years later, four out of five lived on such large establishments. In these areas, the plantation owners themselves often lived elsewhere, and black people constituted almost the entire population.

Adding to the wealth of South Carolina and Georgia was the rapid development of cotton cultivation, especially in the interior, away from the coast. There, prosperous cotton planters began to rival their lowcountry rice-growing counterparts in social status and political influence, and these slaveholders pushed steadily for further western expansion. Cotton planters rushed into the newly-purchased Louisiana Territory after 1803. They accelerated an economic process that had begun in the late eighteenth century: the replacement of a frontier exchange economy with plantation agriculture. (Sugar dominated the New Orleans region; cotton, the rest of the lower Mississippi Valley.) By 1800 slaves in lower Louisiana were producing 4.5 million pounds of sugar annually and more than 18,000 bales of cotton.

The reaches of the lower Mississippi took on an increasingly multicultural flavor. A strong Spanish influence persisted as a vestige of colonial days. French-speaking planter-refugees and their slaves from revolutionary Saint-Domingue came to New Orleans while the city was still in French hands (1800 to 1803). Between 1787 and 1803, nearly 3,000 slaves arrived from Africa, Spanish West Florida, and the Chesapeake to be sold in New Orleans, followed by even larger numbers of slaves from the North after 1803. Slave owners who settled in Natchez, on the banks of the Mississippi River, grew cotton—and grew rich.

Black Family Life and Labor

The number of enslaved persons in the United States grew from 700,000 in 1790 to more than 1.5 million in 1820 and continued to increase rapidly over the next four decades. Since importation of Africans ended officially in 1808, these numbers suggest a tremendous rate of natural increase. Some planters continued to buy slaves brought into the country illegally after 1808. But most of the increase stemmed from births. The preferences of both slave owners and slaves account for this development. Southern planters encouraged black women to bear many children. At the same time, enslaved African Americans valued the family as a social unit; family ties provided support and solace for a people deprived of fundamental human rights. Even under harsh conditions, black people fell in love, married (albeit informally, without the sanction of law), had children, and reared families. Despite the lack of protection from local, state, and national authorities, the slave family proved a remarkably resilient institution.

Enslaved African Americans valued the family as a social unit; family ties provided support and solace for a people deprived of fundamental human rights.

The stability of individual slave families depended on several factors, including the size and age of the plantation and the fortunes and life cycle of the slave owner's family. Very large

John Antrobus, *Plantation Burial*, c. 1860. Historic New Orleans Collection, accession no. 1960.46

■ British artist John Antrobus titled his 1860 painting *Plantation Burial*. Held at night, after the workday, slave funerals provided an opportunity for the community—including slaves from nearby plantations—to come together in mourning. Planters remained suspicious of such gatherings, which were marked by African musical forms and religious rituals. Whites feared that slaves would conspire under the cover of darkness.

or long-established plantations had more two-parent slave families than did the small or newer holdings, which tended to have more unrelated people. Slave families were broken up when whites died and their "property" was bequeathed to heirs. Slaves might also be sold or presented to other family members as gifts. Many slave families suffered disruption in response to the growing demand for slaves in the fresh cotton lands of Alabama and Mississippi. The forced migration from upper South to lower South necessarily severed kin ties, but slaves often reconstituted those ties in the form of symbolic kin relationships. Families adopted new, single members of the slave community, and the children called these newcomers "Aunt" or "Uncle."

Since plantations functioned as slave labor camps, owners generally showed little or no inclination to take family relationships into account when they parceled out work assignments to men, women, and children. Rather, those assignments, and the conditions under which slaves performed them, reflected the size and crops of a particular plantation. An estimated 75 percent of (prewar) **antebellum** slaves worked primarily as field hands. On large plantations the division of labor could be quite specialized. Men served as skilled carpenters, blacksmiths, and barrelmakers, and women worked as cooks, laundresses, nursemaids, and personal maids.

Rice slaves continued to work under the task system. Each day, after they completed a specific assigned task, they spent their time as they chose, within limits. Even in the cotton-growing regions, where blacks labored under the regimented gang system, slaves tried to work for themselves in the little free time they had on Saturday afternoons and Sunday. In Louisiana, one white observer noted that the slave man returning to his living quarters after a long, hot day in the fields "does not lose his time. He goes to work at a bit of the land which he has planted with provisions for his own use, while his companion, if he has one, busies herself in preparing some for him, herself, and their children." Family members who grew or accumulated a modest surplus—of corn, eggs, vegetables—in some cases could sell their wares in a nearby market or to slaves on another plantation.

Some slaves appropriated goods from their master's storeroom and barn and sold or traded them to other slaves or to poor whites. These transactions often took place under the cover of darkness. Planters complained of slaves who stole their cattle, hogs, chickens, sacks full of cotton, farm equipment, and stores of ham and flour. Thus slaves' various forms of labor fell into at least three categories: work performed at the behest of and directly under the supervision of whites, labor performed by and for family members within the slaves' living quarters, and the sale (or sometimes clandestine exchange) of goods with masters, other slaves, and poor whites.

Resistance to Slavery

In 1817 the New Orleans City Council decreed that slaves could sing and dance at a stipulated place—Congo Square—every Sunday afternoon. Thereafter, a variety of groups came together to make music. These groups included recent émigrés from Saint-Domingue and slaves newly imported from Africa; slaves from neighboring plantations, in town for the day; and free people of color (**Creoles**), who often blended Spanish and French classical music traditions. In towns and on plantations throughout the South, black people drew from West African musical styles, using drums as well as banjolike instruments, gourd rattles, and mandolins. Over the generations several uniquely American musical styles flowed from Congo Square and other southern gathering places: the blues, gospel, ragtime, jazz, swing, and rock 'n' roll.

In their artistic expression, dress, hairstyles, and language, slaves sought to preserve their cultural uniqueness and create an existence that slaveholders could not touch. In the South Carolina lowcountry, slaves spoke Gullah. Originally a pidgin—a blend of words and grammatical structures from West African languages and English—Gullah later developed into a more formal Creole language. Slaves throughout the United States also mixed West African religious beliefs with Christianity. In slave quarters, spiritual leaders not only preached a Christianity of equality but also told fortunes and warned away "haunts" (spirits of the dead).

Black resistance to slavery took many forms. Slaves might work carelessly in an effort to resist a master's or mistress's demands. During the course of their workday, some slaves broke hoes and other farm implements. A cook might burn the biscuits, thus spoiling a special dinner party for her mistress. Striking out more directly, the African-influenced "conjurer"—often a woman who had a knowledge of plants and herbs—could wreak havoc on a white family by concocting poisons or encouraging disruptive behavior among slaves.

Slaves also stole goods from their masters and at times stole themselves by running away. (This practice was more common among young, unmarried men than among those who had family obligations.) Despite the extraordinary peril involved, some slaves revolted. In St. Charles and St. John the Baptist parishes in Louisiana, an 1811 revolt of 400 slaves cost two whites their lives and left several plantations in flames. The original participants, led by a free man of color, Charles Deslondes, acquired new members as they marched toward New Orleans. U.S. troops cut their advance short, killing sixty-six of them. In the Southeast in 1817 and 1818, 400 to 600 runaway slaves converged on the swamps of central Florida, uniting with Indian refugees from the Red Stick War. Together, they raided Georgia plantations until Andrew Jackson and his soldiers halted them in April 1818.

Chicago Historical Society, ICHi-22005

■ From colonial times through the abolition of slavery in 1865, runaways were a persistent problem for slaveholders. This advertisement was published in the Centerville, Maryland, *Times and Eastern-Shore Public Advertiser*. Typically, the owner describes the runaways in terms of their height, skin color, and their distinguishing characteristics.

To justify their own behavior, masters and mistresses created a number of myths about the black people they exploited. Whites had a vested interest in believing that their slaves felt gratitude toward them. Skilled in the so-called deference ritual, some slaves hid their true feelings and acted submissively in the presence of white people. Owners and overseers alike interpreted this behavior as a sign of black contentment.

Although some planters boasted of their fatherly solicitude for their slaves, most slave owners harbored deep fears about the men and women they held in bondage. These fears explain the barbaric punishments that some owners inflicted on men, women, and children. Even in "respectable" southern families, slave owners branded, mutilated, and beat enslaved workers for resisting discipline or to deliver a warning to other potentially defiant slaves. In the slave South, American cries of freedom, equality, opportunity, and the blessings of citizenship rang hollow.

Conclusion

In the first two decades of the nineteenth century, striking historical developments stirred the spirit of American nationalism. The Louisiana Purchase magnified the natural wealth of the young nation, and the federal government encouraged citizens to exploit that wealth through trade and settlement. The Embargo of 1807 and the War of 1812 freed the country from the British menace in the Northwest Territory and on the high seas. The war also bolstered the American economy by stimulating technological innovation and the growth of manufacturing. Territorial expansion combined with economic development created new jobs for a burgeoning population.

Southern cotton planters and northern factory owners derived their newfound prosperity from very different sources: staple crop agriculture on one hand and the emerging industrial system on the other. At the same time, these two groups had much in common. As they expanded their operations, whether sprawling plantations or gigantic mill complexes, they displaced smaller landowners and raised land prices. Members of both elite groups proved restless entrepreneurs, eager to move around to find the freshest lands and the cheapest labor. Their personal wealth and their political power set them apart from the people under them—the slaves and wage earners—who produced that wealth. And both the southern "lords of the lash" and the northern "lords of the loom" depended on large numbers of slaves to grow cotton. Producing and processing cotton yielded tangible benefits for a few and created a new, harsher world of work for many.

Sites to Visit

Lewis and Clark Expedition
www.cp.duluth.mn.us/~tmcs/lewsclrk1.htm
This site offers assorted materials treating the expedition that explored the Louisiana Territory.

Barbary Treaties
www.yale.edu/lawweb/avalon/diplomacy/barbary
This site includes the texts of treaties between the United States and the Barbary states, 1789–1816.

Documents from the War of 1812
www.yale.edu/lawweb/avalon/19th.htm
This site includes important documents from the War of 1812.

Whole Cloth: Discovering Science and Technology Through American Textile History
www.si.edu/lemelson/centerpieces/whole_cloth/
The Jerome and Dorothy Lemelson Center for the Study of Invention and Innovation and Society for the History of Technology assembled this site. It includes excellent activities and sources related to early American manufacturing and industry.

Indian Affairs: Laws and Treaties
http://digital.library.okstate.edu/kappler/
This digitized text at Oklahoma State University includes preremoval treaties with the Five Civilized Tribes and other groups.

For Further Reading

General

Stephen E. Ambrose, *Undaunted Courage: Meriwether Lewis, Thomas Jefferson, and the Opening of the American West* (1996).

Joanne P. Melish, *Disowning Slavery: Gradual Emancipation and "Race" in New England, 1780–1860* (1998).

Carroll Pursell, *The Machine in America: A Social History of Technology* (1995).

David J. Weber, *The Spanish Frontier in North America* (1992).

The British Menace

Robert J. Allison, *The Crescent Obscured: the United States and the Muslim World, 1776–1815* (1995).

W. Jeffrey Bolster, *Black Jacks: African-American Seamen in the Age of Sail* (1997).

Thomas J. Fleming, *Duel: Alexander Hamilton, Aaron Burr and the Future of America* (1999).

Burton Spivak, *Jefferson's English Crisis: Commerce, Embargo, and the Republican Revolution* (1974).

John Sugden, *Tecumseh: A Life* (1998).

The War of 1812

Donald R. Hickey, *The War of 1812: A Forgotten Conflict* (1989).

Robert V. Remini, *The Battle of New Orleans* (1999).

Robert Allen Rutland, *The Presidency of James Madison* (1990).

David C. Skaggs and Larry L. Nelson, eds., *The Sixty Years' War for the Great Lakes, 1754–1814* (2001).

The "Era of Good Feelings"?

Frank Lawrence Owsley, Jr. and Gene A. Smith, *Filibusters and Expansionists: Jeffersonian Manifest Destiny, 1800–1821* (1997).

Theda Perdue, *Cherokee Women: Gender and Culture Change, 1700–1835* (1998).

Kirkpatrick Sale, *The Fire of His Genius: Robert Fulton and the American Dream* (2001).

Ronald Schultz, *The Republic of Labor: Philadelphia Artisans and the Politics of Class, 1720–1830* (1993).

The Rise of the Cotton Plantation Economy

Eugene D. Genovese, *Roll, Jordan, Roll: The World the Slaves Made* (1976).

Charles W. Joyner, *Down by the Riverside: A South Carolina Slave Community* (1984).

Michael Mullin, *Africa in America: Slave Acculturation and Resistance in the American South and British Caribbean* (1992).

Jeffrey Robert Young, *Domesticating Slavery: The Master Class in Georgia and South Carolina, 1670–1837* (1999).

For quizzes and other resources on these topics, go to www.longmanamericanhistory.com.

Expanding Westward: Society and Politics in the "Age of the Common Man," 1819–1832

CAMPAIGNING FOR POLITICAL OFFICE IN TENNESSEE IN THE 1820S WAS NOT AN ACTIVITY FOR THE faint of heart. Candidates competed against each other in squirrel hunts, the loser footing the bill for the barbecue that followed. A round of speechmaking often was capped by several rounds of whiskey enjoyed by candidates and supporters alike. Into this boisterous arena stepped a man unrivaled as a campaigner. David Crockett ran successfully for several offices, including local justice of the peace in 1818, state legislator in 1821 and 1823, and U.S. congressman in 1827, 1829, and 1833. The plainspoken Crockett knew how to play to a crowd and rattle a rival. He bragged about his skill as a bear hunter and ridiculed the fancy dress of his opponents. He condemned closed-door political caucuses (small groups of party insiders who hand-picked candidates) and praised grassroots democracy. Crockett claimed he could out-shoot, out-drink, and out-debate anyone who opposed him. If his opponent lied about him, why, then, he would lie about himself: "Yes fellow citizens, I can run faster, walk longer, leap higher, speak better, and tell more and bigger lies than my competitor, and all his friends, any day of his life." Crockett's blend of political theater and folksy backwoods banter earned him the allegiance of voters like him—men who, though having little formal education, understood the challenges of carving a homestead out of the dense thickets of western Tennessee.

During the 1820s, European American settlers in the trans-Appalachian West transformed the style and substance of American politics. In 1790, 100,000 Americans (not including Indians) lived west of the Appalachians; half a century later that number had increased to 7 million, or about four out of ten Americans. Beginning with Kentucky in 1792, western states began to relax or abolish property requirements for adult male voters. Even the English that Americans spoke changed. New words introduced into the political vocabulary reflected the rough-hewn, woodsman quality of western electioneering: candidates hit the campaign trail, giving "stump" speeches along the way. They supported their party's platform with its "planks" (positions on the issues). As legislators, they voted for "pork-barrel" projects that would benefit their constituents at home. Emphasizing his modest origins,

DOCUMENT

Davy Crockett, Advice to Politicians (1833)

■ John Gadsby Chapman painted this portrait of Davy Crockett.

David Crockett became widely known as Davy Crockett. (It is hard to imagine anyone calling the Sage of Monticello Tommy Jefferson.)

Western settlers attacked what they considered centralized, eastern-based institutions of wealth and privilege. They scorned a six-person Supreme Court that could overturn the laws of Congress and the individual states. They charged that the privately owned Second Bank of the United States enriched its own board of directors at the expense of indebted farmers. Western voters rejoiced with the 1828 election of Andrew Jackson to the presidency; here, they claimed, was a man who would battle eastern financiers and at the same time support white settlers' claims to Indian lands in the West. Jackson held out the promise that ordinary people would have a political voice and access to expanding economic opportunities.

During his two terms in office (1828–1836), Andrew Jackson of Tennessee so dominated the American political landscape that historians have called him the symbol of an age and the representative man of his time. Born in humble circumstances, orphaned at age fourteen, Jackson achieved public acclaim as a lawyer, military officer, and finally president. He promoted a strong central government, and the authority of the chief executive in particular, and he had fought against foreign military forces (the British in the War of 1812) and Native Americans. He clashed with southern states' rights advocates.

Democracy had its limits during this period. While voter participation in presidential elections soared, from 25 percent of eligible voters in 1824 to 50 percent in 1828, even most free people could not vote, including Native Americans, women, and free people of color. Further complicating this age was the rise of distinct social classes. Acquiring great economic and political significance, the class system seemed to mock the idea of equality. The outlines of this system appeared in the 1820s in the Northeast, where business and factory managers received salaries, not hourly wages, and their wives were full-time homemakers and mothers. New forms of popular literature, such as the *Ladies Magazine*, published in Boston, glorified the middle-class family, especially the pious wife and mother who held moral sway over it.

The "age of the common man" was thus rife with irony. Jackson himself embodied many apparent contradictions. An Indian-fighter, he adopted a young Indian boy as his ward. A foe of privilege, he was a slave owner. A self-professed champion of farmers and artisans, he expressed contempt for their representatives in Congress. He also took steps to expand the power of the executive branch. The 1820s revealed these larger contradictions as national leaders pursued a more democratic form of politics on one hand and supported a system based on class and racial differences on the other. The resulting tensions shaped American society and politics in the third decade of the nineteenth century.

The Politics Behind Western Expansion

DOCUMENT

Expanding America and Internal Improvements

As the United States gained new territory through negotiation and conquest and people moved west, the nation felt the impact. President Monroe warned Europeans not to intervene any longer in the Western hemisphere. Americans settling west of the Appalachian mountains found a spokesman in Andrew Jackson. Once in the West, settlers faced the same kinds of conflicts that increasingly preoccupied Easterners, especially those between masters and slaves and debtors and creditors. Congressional debates over whether Missouri should be admitted to the Union as a slave or free state sent shock waves throughout the country. Of the political conflict over the fate of slavery in the territories, the elderly Thomas Jefferson wrote, "This momentous question, like a firebell in the night, awakened and filled me with terror. I considered it at once as the death knell of the Union."

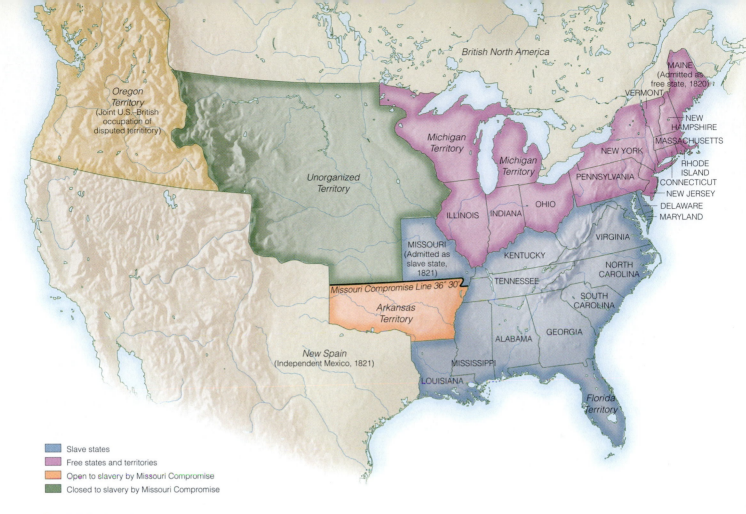

Slave states

Free states and territories

Open to slavery by Missouri Compromise

Closed to slavery by Missouri Compromise

■ **MAP 11.1**

THE MISSOURI COMPROMISE   Missouri applied for statehood in 1819, threatening the balance between eleven free and eleven slave states. According to a compromise hammered out in Congress, Missouri was admitted as a slave state, and Maine, formerly part of Massachusetts, was admitted as a free state. Slavery was banned above the 36°30′ parallel.

The Missouri Compromise

Missouri Compromise of 1820–1821

In 1819 the United States consisted of twenty-two states. Slavery was legal in half of them. Late that year, the territory of Missouri applied for statehood. This move set off panic in both the North and South because a twenty-third state was bound to upset the delicate balance of senators between slave and free states. The debate over the future of Missouri occupied Congress from December 1819 to March 1820.

In the Senate, Rufus King of New York claimed that Congress had the ultimate authority to set laws governing slavery. However, his colleague William Pinckney of Maryland retorted that new states possessed the same rights as the original thirteen; that is, they could choose whether to allow slavery. Maine's application for admission to the Union suggested a way out of the impasse. Speaker of the House of Representatives Henry Clay of Kentucky successfully proposed a plan. Missouri would join the Union as a slave state at the same time that Maine, originally part of Massachusetts, would become the twenty-fourth state and be designated a free one. In the future, slavery would be prohibited from all Louisiana Purchase lands north of latitude 36°30′, an area that included all territory north of present-day Missouri and Oklahoma.

The day Congress sealed the compromise, Secretary of State John Quincy Adams of Massachusetts walked home from the Capitol with Senator John C. Calhoun of South Carolina. The two men engaged in a muted but intense debate over slavery. Calhoun claimed that the institution "was the best guarantee to equality among the whites." Slavery, he asserted, demonstrated that all white men were equal to one another and superior to all blacks. Unnerved by Calhoun's

263

■ **MAP 11.2**

PRINCIPAL CANALS BUILT BY 1860 Many canals were expensive ventures and, in some cases, engineering nightmares. The Erie Canal had a competitive advantage because it snaked through the Mohawk Valley, the only major level pass through the mountain chain that stretched from Canada to Georgia. In contrast, the Pennsylvania Main Line Canal, which ran from Harrisburg to Pittsburgh, used a combination of inclined planes and steam engines in ten separate locations to haul boats up and down the Allegheny Mountains.

comments, Adams concluded that the debate over Missouri had "betrayed the secret of [Southerners'] souls." By reserving backbreaking toil for blacks, wealthy planters fancied themselves aristocratic lords of the manor. Adams confided in his diary that night, "They look down upon the simplicity of a Yankee's manners, because he has no habits of overbearing like theirs and cannot treat negroes like dogs." Adams feared that North-South conflicts might someday imperil the nation itself.

Ways West

Missouri was just one of the territories west of the Mississippi whose population had increased during this period. Through land grants and government financing of new methods of transportation, Congress encouraged European American migrants to push their way west and south. The Land Act of 1820 enabled westerners to buy a minimum 80 acres at a price of $1.25 an acre in cash—even in those days, a bargain homestead. Built with the help of government legal and financial aid, new roads and canals, steamboats, and, after the early 1830s, railroads facilitated migration. Between 1820 and 1860, the number of steamboats plying the

HAULING THE WHOLE WEEKS PICKING

■ The rich bottomlands of the Mississippi Delta proved ideal for growing cotton. After the forced removal of the Five Civilized Tribes from the Old Southwest, slave owners established expansive plantations in the delta. This scene, painted in 1842 by artist William Henry Brown, shows a group of slaves bringing in "the whole weeks picking" of cotton on the Vick plantation near Vicksburg, Mississippi.

William Henry Brown, *Hauling the Whole Weeks Picking*, 1842. Historic New Orleans Collection (1975.93.1 & 1975.93.2)

Mississippi River jumped from 60 to more than 1,000. Canals linked western producers to eastern consumers of grains and cattle and connected western consumers to eastern producers of manufactured goods. Shipping costs and times between Buffalo and New York shrank. Cities such as Rochester and Syracuse, New York, and Cincinnati, Ohio, flourished because of their location along key waterways.

AUDIO

"The Erie Canal"

The most important of these man-made water highways was the Erie Canal. Completed in 1825, this engineering marvel used 83 **canal locks** to link the Great Lakes directly to the East Coast by way of the Hudson River. Public acclaim was thunderous. Upstate New York's economy thrived. And New York City, at the mouth of the Hudson, emerged as the most important port and financial center in the country.

Americans took a variety of routes west. In the 1820s, desperate planters moved out of the exhausted lands of the upper South (the states of Virginia and Maryland), the Carolinas, and Georgia, westward into Alabama, Arkansas, Louisiana, and Mississippi. This migration across the Appalachian Mountains furthered the nationalist idea of the "expansion of liberty and freedom," a view held by many white men regardless of political affiliation. Yet it also spread slavery. The sight of slave coffles—groups of men, women, and children bound together in chains, hobbling down a city street or a country road— became increasingly common in this western region. In 1821 Virginia, North Carolina, South Carolina, and Georgia had produced two-thirds of the nation's cotton crop; the rest came from recently settled areas. Just a dozen years later the proportions shifted: Tennessee, Louisiana, Alabama, Mississippi, and Florida together produced two-thirds of all cotton, and the remaining one-third came from older areas.

The westward expansion of cotton farming continued the European process of clearing the land had started in the early colonial period. This, combined with hunting game with firearms, had altered the backwoods **ecology** east of the Mississippi. When farmers dammed rivers, drained ponds and swamps, and chopped down trees, they unavoidably destroyed the places where wildlife lived and the food supply they ate. European demands for beaver hats led to the near-extinction of beaver east of the Mississippi River.

■ MAP 11.3

MEXICO'S FAR NORTHERN FRONTIER IN 1822   This map shows Mexico's far northern frontier in 1822. When Moses Austin died suddenly in 1821, the task of supervising the settlement of in-migrants from the United States fell to his son Stephen. The Mexican government authorized the younger Austin to act as empresario of the settlement. He was responsible for the legal and economic regulations governing the settlements clustered at the lower reaches of the Colorado and Brazos rivers.

European Americans also migrated across the border into Mexican territory. In 1821 Spain approved the application of a U.S. citizen, Moses Austin, to settle 300 American families on 200,000 fertile acres along the Colorado and Brazos river bottoms in southeastern Texas. Austin died soon after, but his son Stephen carried on his legacy. Within two years, the younger Austin had received permission (now from the government of newly independent Mexico) to bring in another 100 families. These settlers, together with **squatters**, numbered about 1,500 people. Although the Mexican constitution prohibited slavery, some of the newcomers brought their slaves with them, and some free people of color came on their own. All these migrants from the United States called themselves **Texians** to distinguish themselves from the *Tejanos*, or Spanish-speaking residents of the region. These newly arrived Texians agreed to adopt the Roman Catholic faith and become citizens of Mexico. During the rest of the decade, 900 additional families sponsored by Austin arrived in Texas. They were followed by 3,000 more squatters. Mexican officials feared that they would lose authority over the mass of American newcomers within their borders.

The Panic of 1819 and the Plight of Western Debtors

In 1819 a financial panic swept across the nation, followed by an economic depression that hit western states and territories particularly hard. The Second Bank of the United States played a major role in triggering this economic downturn, which came to be called the Panic of 1819. Granted a twenty-year charter by Congress in 1816, the Second Bank resembled its predecessor, seeking to regulate the national economy through loans to state and local banks. In 1819 the bank clamped down on small, local **wildcat banks**, which had extended credit to many people who could not repay their loans. Many homesteaders were not self-sufficient farmers but producers of staple crops or proprietors of small enterprises. They relied on credit from banks and local private lenders. As a result, the bank's crackdown on wildcat banks had a devastating impact on western households. Debtors unable to meet their obligations had their mortgages foreclosed, their homes seized, and their crops and equipment confiscated. Ruined by the Panic of 1819, many western farmers developed an abiding hatred of the Bank of the United States and a deep resentment of eastern financiers.

Davy Crockett's own family history suggests the plight of families dependent on bank credit to create homesteads out of western territory. The son of a propertyless squatter, Crockett had an intense fear of debt. Although he campaigned as a hunter and a farmer, he had built several enterprises on land he leased or owned on Shoal Creek in south-central Tennessee: a water-powered grist mill, a gunpowder factory (worked by slaves), an iron ore mine, and a liquor distillery. For each venture, he had to borrow money from local creditors. Spending much of his time away from home, Crockett relied on his wife, Elizabeth, and his children to manage these businesses. (He had three children by his first wife, Polly, who died in 1815, and eventually would have a total of nine by Elizabeth.)

The depression of 1819 cut off Crockett's sources of credit, and in 1822 a flash flood swept away his grist mill and powder factory. Without milled grain, the distillery could no longer operate. Creditors immediately set upon the family, demanding payment of their debts. The Crocketts were fortunate enough to own land they could sell, using the proceeds to repay their debts and then moving farther west in Tennessee.

Others were not so lucky. Small farmers who lost their land through foreclosure in the Panic of 1819 could not produce crops for the eastern market, contributing to the rise in the price of food. Deprived of credit, small shopkeepers also felt the effects of the depression. With rising unemployment, consumers could not afford to buy cloth, and as the demand for cotton fell, southern plantation owners, too, felt the contraction. Within a few years Andrew Jackson would capitalize on the fears and resentments of working men, farmers, planters, and tradesmen, as he championed the "common man" in opposition to what debtors called the "eastern monied interests." In doing so he would transform the two-party system.

The Monroe Doctrine

Despite the troubled economy, James Monroe won reelection easily in 1820. On the international front, his second term opened on a tense note. Foreign nations had started claiming land or promoting their own interests near U.S. borders. The United States remained especially wary of the Spanish presence on its southern and western borders. In 1818 President Monroe had authorized General Andrew Jackson to broaden his assault on the Seminole Indians—a group composed of Native Americans and runaway slaves—in Florida. For the past two years, U.S. troops had pursued fugitive slaves into Spanish-held Florida. Now Jackson and his men seized the Spanish fort at Pensacola and claimed all of western Florida for the United

TABLE 11-1		
The Election of 1820		
Candidate	Political Party	Electoral Vote
James Monroe	Democratic-Republican	231
John Quincy Adams	Democratic-Republican	1

States. The United States demanded that Spain either suppress the Seminole population or sell all of east Florida to the United States. With the Transcontinental Treaty of 1819, Spain gave up its right to both Florida and Oregon (although Britain and Russia still claimed land in Oregon). In 1822 General Jackson became the first governor of Florida Territory.

In 1821 the czar of Russia forbade non-Russians from entering the territory north of the fifty-first parallel and the open sea 100 miles off the coast of what is now Canada and Alaska.

The Russians had established trading posts up and down that coast, some almost as far south as San Francisco Bay. Meanwhile, rumors circulated that European monarchs were planning new invasions of Latin America.

Fearful of an alliance between Russia, Prussia, Austria, Spain, and France, President Monroe and Secretary of State John Quincy Adams formulated a policy that became a landmark in American diplomatic history. Adams rejected a British proposal that Great Britain and the United States join forces to oppose a further Spanish encroachment in Latin America. He convinced Monroe that the United States must stand alone against the European powers—Spain in the south and Russia in the northwest—if it hoped to protect its own interests in the Western Hemisphere. In his annual message to Congress in December 1823, the president declared that the era of Europe's colonization of the Americas had ceased. Henceforth, he said, foreign nations would not be allowed to intervene in the Western Hemisphere.

The United States conceived the so-called Monroe Doctrine as a self-defense measure aimed specifically at Russia, Spain, and Britain. With the Russo-American Treaty of 1824, Russia agreed to pull back its claims to the area north of 54°40′, the southern tip of the present-day Alaska panhandle. However, the United States did not have the naval power to back up the Monroe Doctrine with force.

DOCUMENT

The Monroe
Doctrine (1823)

The doctrine was at first more a statement of principle than a blueprint for action, intended to discourage European powers from political or military meddling in the Western Hemisphere. The doctrine would have greater international significance in the late nineteenth century, when the United States developed the military might to enforce it.

Andrew Jackson's Rise to Power

The election of 1824 provided a striking contrast to the bland affair four years earlier in which Monroe had been elected. In 1824 the field of presidential nominees was crowded, suggesting a party system in disarray. Although all the candidates called themselves "Democratic-Republicans," the label meant little more than the fact that most politicians sought to distance themselves from the outmoded "Federalist" label, which hearkened back to the post-Revolutionary period rather than pointing forward to the nation's new challenges. Nominees included Secretary of State John Quincy Adams, Representative Henry Clay of Kentucky, and Andrew Jackson, now a senator from Tennessee. Jackson received the highest number of electoral votes (99), but no candidate achieved a majority. As a result, the election went to the House of Representatives.

Clay withdrew from the race. He had promised Jackson his support but then endorsed Adams, whom the House subsequently elected. When Adams named Clay secretary of state, Jackson's supporters cried foul. The election, they charged, amounted to nothing more than a corrupt deal between two political insiders.

Haunted by these charges, Adams served his four-year term under a cloud of public distrust. A member of a respected New England family and the son of former president John Adams, the new chief executive had served with distinction in Monroe's cabinet. Still, Adams proved ill suited to the rough-and-tumble world of what came to be called the New Democracy. Adams advocated a greater federal role in internal improvements and public education, a variation on Henry Clay's "American System," a set of policies which promoted a national bank, public funding of canals and turnpikes, and a high tariff to protect domestic manufactures.

Adams's party, which called itself the National Republicans, faced a formidable chal-

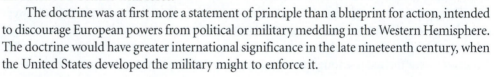

TABLE 11-2

The Election of 1824

Candidate	Political Party	Popular Vote (%)	Electoral Vote
John Quincy Adams	Democratic-Republican	30.5	84
Andrew Jackson	Democratic-Republican	43.1	99
William H. Crawford	Democratic-Republican	13.1	41
Henry Clay	Democratic-Republican	13.2	37

■ Some commentators disapproved of what they considered the excessively lively inauguration gala for President Jackson in 1829. One described the affair this way: "On their arrival at the White House, the motley crowd clamored for refreshments and soon drained the barrels of punch, which had been prepared, in drinking to the health of the new Chief Magistrate. A great deal of glassware was broken, and the East Room was filled with a noisy mob."

lenge in the election of 1828. Having seethed for four long years, Andrew Jackson's supporters (the Democratic-Republicans) now urged "the people" to reclaim the White House. The campaign was a nasty one. Jackson's opponents attacked his personal morality and that of his wife and his mother. Jackson's supporters countered with the charge that Adams himself was corrupt and that he and his cronies must be swept from office.

Jackson won a stunning victory, with his supporters hailing the well-to-do slaveholder as the president of the "common" (meaning white) man. In office, Jackson tightened his party's grip on power by introducing a national political spoils system. Through this process, successful candidates rewarded their supporters with jobs and tossed their rivals out of appointed offices. The spoils system let the Democratic-Republicans—now called the Democrats—build a nationwide political machine. Not surprisingly, it also provided fertile ground for corruption.

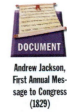

DOCUMENT

Andrew Jackson, First Annual Message to Congress (1829)

TABLE 11-3			
The Election of 1828			
Candidate	Political Party	Popular Vote (%)	Electoral Vote
Andrew Jackson	Democratic	56.0	178
John Quincy Adams	National Republican	44.0	83

Federal Authority and Its Opponents

When Americans defeated the British in the War of 1812, they ensured the physical security of the new nation. However, the war's end left a crucial question unanswered: what role would federal authority play in a republic of states? During Andrew Jackson's tenure, Congress, the chief executive, and the Supreme Court all jockeyed for influence over one another and over the states. Jackson claimed a broad popular mandate to increase the power of the presidency, and used it to end the charter of the Second Bank of the United States.

At the same time, militant southern sectionalists regarded the growth of federal executive and judicial power with alarm. If the president could impose a high tariff on the states and if the Supreme Court could deny the states the authority to govern Indians within their own borders, might not high-handed federal officials someday also threaten the South's system of slavery?

Judicial Federalism and the Limits of Law

In a series of notable cases, the Supreme Court, under the leadership of Chief Justice John Marshall, sought to limit states' power to control people and resources within their own boundaries. In *McCulloch v. Maryland* (1819), the Court supported Congress's decision to grant the Second Bank of the United States a twenty-year charter. The state of Maryland had imposed a high tax on notes issued by the bank. Declaring that "the power to tax involves the power to destroy," the Supreme Court ruled the state's action unconstitutional. The court justices held that, although the original Constitution did not mention a national bank, Congress retained the authority to create such an institution. This fact implied that Congress also had the power to preserve it. This decision relied on what came to be called a "loose construction" of the Constitution to justify "implied powers" of the government, powers not explicitly stated in the Constitution.

In 1832 a case involving the rights of the Cherokee nation brought the Court head to head with President Jackson's own brand of federal muscle-flexing. With the expansion of cotton cultivation into upland Georgia in the early nineteenth century, white residents of that state increasingly resented the presence of their Cherokee neighbors. At the same time, some Cherokee worked and worshipped in ways similar to European Americans: they cultivated farmland, converted to Christianity, and established a formal legal code. On July 4, 1827, Cherokee leaders met in convention to devise a republican constitution. In the grand tradition of the Patriots of 1776, the group proclaimed the Cherokee a sovereign nation, responsible for its own affairs and free of the dictates of individual states.

By the late 1820s, however, certain white people, including the president, were calling for the removal of the Cherokee from the Southeast. The 1829 discovery of gold in the Georgia hills brought 10,000 white miners to Cherokee territory in a gold rush that the Indians called the "Great Intrusion." President Jackson saw the very existence of the Cherokee nation as an affront to his authority and a hindrance to Georgia's economic well-being. He resented the fact that the Cherokee considered themselves a sovereign nation, independent of the U.S. president. Jackson, in fact, favored removing all Indians from the Southeast to make way for whites. He declared that Georgia should be rid of "a few thousand savages" so that "towns and prosperous farms" could develop there. In 1830, with the president's backing, Congress passed the Indian Removal Act. The act provided for "an exchange of lands with the Indians residing in any of the states or territories, and for their removal west of the river Mississippi."

Outraged by this naked land grab, the Cherokee nation refused to sign the removal treaties specified by Congress as part of the Indian Removal Act. In a petition to Congress in 1830, members of the group declared, "We wish to remain on the land of our fathers. We have a perfect and original right to claim this, without interruption or molestation." In an effort to protect their land titles, the Cherokee first tried to take their case to Georgia courts, but Georgia refused to allow them to press their claim. The Georgia legislature maintained that it had authority over all the Indians living within the state's borders, and that the Cherokee nation lacked jurisdiction over its own people. The Cherokee nation appealed to the Supreme Court.

The Cherokee hoped that the Supreme Court would support their position that they were an independent entity, not bound by the laws of Georgia. In a set of cases—*Cherokee Nation v. Georgia* (1831) and *Worcester v. Georgia* (1832)—the Court agreed that Georgia's authority did not extend to the Cherokee nation. The Court proclaimed that Indian self-

DOCUMENT

Memorial of the
Cherokee Nation
(1830)

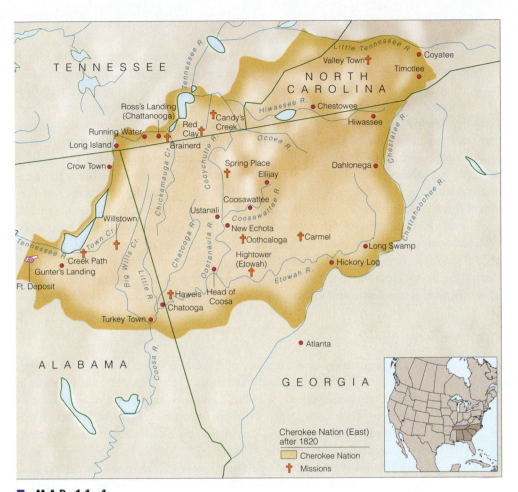

■ MAP 11.4

THE CHEROKEE NATION AFTER 1820   This map shows the Cherokee nation on the eve of removal to Indian Territory (present-day Oklahoma). The discovery of gold in the region sparked a constitutional battle over control of Cherokee land. In 1832 the Supreme Court ruled that the federal government had ultimate authority over Indian nations. The state of Georgia ignored the ruling and sought to enforce its own laws in Cherokee territory.

governing bodies were "domestic dependent nations" under the authority of the U.S. government, not the individual states. Under this ruling, Georgia lacked the authority to force Indians from their land. More generally, the states must defer to the federal government in issues related to the welfare and governance of the Indians. The governor of Georgia rejected these Supreme Court rulings, as did Jackson. Of the *Worcester* decision, Jackson declared, "John Marshall has made his decision. Now let him enforce it." In 1832 the president instead sent troops to Georgia to begin forcing the Indians out of their homeland.

The "Tariff of Abominations"

Besides engineering the removal of the Cherokee, Jacksonian Democrats continued the post–War of 1812 policy of high tariffs. In 1828 they pushed through Congress legislation that raised fees on imported manufactured products and raw materials such as wool. Facing a disastrous decline in cotton prices after the Panic of 1819, Southerners protested: to survive, they had to both sell their cotton on the open world market and buy high-priced supplies from New England or Europe. In their view, the higher the tariff on English goods, the less likely the English were to continue to purchase their cotton from southern planters. Southerners dubbed the 1828 legislation the "Tariff of Abominations."

A renewal of the tariff four years later moderated the 1828 rates. But by this time, South Carolina politicians were in no mood to sit back and accept what they saw as the arrogant wielding of federal power. They drew on past precedents in developing a theory called **nullification**—the idea that individual states had the authority to reject, or nullify, specific federal laws. The Virginia and Kentucky Resolutions of 1798 and 1799 and the Hartford Convention of New England states during the War of 1812 had previously raised this issue of state sovereignty.

DOCUMENT

Proclamation
Regarding
Nullification

Led by Senator John C. Calhoun, the nullifiers met in a convention in 1832 and declared the tariff "null and void" in South Carolina. But Jackson struck back swiftly. In his Nullification Proclamation of December 10, 1832, he argued that states' rights did not include nullification of federal laws or secession from the Union. The president then sent a token military and naval force to South Carolina to intimidate the nullifiers. Henry Clay, now senator from Kentucky, brokered a compromise agreement: a 10 percent reduction in the Tariff of 1832 over a period of eight years. This compromise finally eased tensions, and the South Carolina nullifiers retreated for the time being. However, they continued to maintain "that each state of the Union has the right, whenever it may deem such a course necessary . . . to secede peaceably from the Union."

The "Monster Bank"

A similar struggle unfolded over the power of the federal government regarding a central bank. The repository of federal funds ($10 million), the Bank of the United States in the 1830s had thirty branches and controlled the money supply by dictating how state banks should repay their loans: in paper notes or in currency. As a central (though privately held) institution, the bank also aided economic growth and development by extending loans to commercial enterprises.

In 1832 Jackson vetoed a bill that would have renewed the charter of the Second Bank of the United States, which was due to expire in 1836. Somewhat contradictorily, Jackson claimed to represent the interests of small borrowers such as farmers, but he also advocated hard money (currency in the form of gold or silver, not paper or credit extended by banks). Traditionally, small lenders objected to hard-money policies, which kept the supply of currency low and interest rates for borrowers high. Jackson also objected to the bank's work as a large commercial institution. For example, he blamed the bank for precipitating the Panic and Depression of 1819 by withholding credit from small banks, causing them to recall their loans and, in some cases, fail.

VIDEO

Jackson and the
Bank War

Jackson condemned the bank as a "monster" intent on devouring hardworking people and enriching a few eastern financiers. By vetoing the bank bill, Jackson angered members of Congress and his own cabinet. They had urged him to recharter the bank because they believed the credit system was necessary for economic progress and expansion. Convinced that Jackson had overextended his reach, his opponents seized on the issue as a sign of the chief executive's political vulnerability. However, Congress upheld Jackson's veto of the Second Bank (the bank closed when its charter expired in 1836). Nominated for president by the National Republicans in 1832, Henry Clay drew support from merchants who had benefited from Bank of the United States loans and from the sizable contingent of Jackson-haters. But Jackson won in a landslide, carrying not only his stronghold, the West, but also the South and substantial parts of New York, Pennsylvania, and New England.

TABLE 11-4

The Election of 1832

Candidate	Political Party	Popular Vote (%)	Electoral Vote
Andrew Jackson	Democratic	55.0	219
Henry Clay	National Republican	42.4	49
John Floyd	Independent	—	11
William Wirt	Anti-Masonic	2.6	7

While in office, Jackson used his veto power a total of twelve times. All his predecessors *combined* had used it just ten times. When his opponents finally formed a political party in 1834, they called themselves Whigs, after the English antimonarchist party. In choosing this name, their intention was to ridicule "King Andrew." The Whigs opposed the man who had built up the power of the presidency in defiance of Congress and the Supreme Court.

Real People in the "Age of the Common Man"

In the early 1830s, a wealthy Frenchman named Alexis de Tocqueville visited the United States and wrote about the contradictions he saw. In his book *Democracy in America* (published in 1835), Tocqueville noted that the United States lacked the rigid hierarchy of class privilege that characterized European nations. With universal white manhood suffrage, white men could vote and run for office regardless of their class or religion. However, Tocqueville also noted some sore spots in American democratic values and practices. He commented on the plight of groups deprived of the right to vote, whose lack of freedom stood out starkly in the otherwise egalitarian society of the United States. He sympathized with the southeastern Indians uprooted from their homelands. He raised the possibility that conflicts between blacks and whites might eventually lead to bloodshed. He even contrasted the situation of young unmarried white women, who seemed so free-spirited, with that of wives, who appeared cautious and dull. He concluded, "In America a woman loses her independence forever in the bonds of matrimony." Tocqueville saw America for what it was: a blend of freedom and slavery, of independence and dependence.

Wards, Workers, and Warriors: Native Americans

Population growth in the United States—and on the borderlands between the United States and Mexican territory—put pressure on Indian societies. Yet different cultural groups responded in different ways to this pressure. Some, like the Cherokee, conformed to European American ways and became sedentary farmers. Others were forced to work for whites. Still others either waged war on white settlements and military forces or retreated farther and farther from European American settlements in the hope of avoiding clashes with the intruders.

Nevertheless, prominent whites continued to denigrate the humanity of all Indians. In the 1820s, Henry Clay claimed that Indians were "essentially inferior to the Anglo-Saxon race . . . and their disappearance from the human family will be no great loss to the world." In 1828 the House of Representatives Committee on Indian Affairs surveyed the Indians of the South and concluded that "an Indian cannot work" and that all Indians were lazy and notable for their "thirst for spirituous liquors."

Richard T. Nowitz/CORBIS

■ This photo of the Fairmont Waterworks in Philadelphia shows the effects of Greek architecture on American public buildings in the early nineteenth century. Designed by Frederick C. Graff, the waterworks were completed in 1822. Numerous banks, colleges, commercial buildings, and large private homes built during this period were designed in the Greek Revival style. The United States saw itself as the embodiment of democracy, a form of government associated with Athens and other early Greek city-states.

■ Artist Charles Bird King painted this portrait of Sequoyah while the Indian leader was in Washington, D.C., in 1828. Government officials honored him for developing a written form of the Cherokee language. He is wearing a medal presented to him by the Cherokee nation in 1825. He later settled permanently in Sallisaw, in what is today Sequoyah County, Oklahoma.

Newberry Library, Chicago

MAP

**Native American
Land Cessions
to 1829**

According to the committee, when European settlers depleted reserves of wildlife, Indians as a group would cease to exist.

Members of the Cherokee nation bitterly denounced these assertions. "The Cherokees do not live upon the chase [for game]," they pointed out. Neither did the Creek, Choctaw, Chickasaw, and Seminole—the other members of the Five Civilized Tribes, so called for their varying degrees of conformity to white people's ways.

In parts of California, Spanish missionaries conquered Indian groups, converted them to Christianity, and then forced them to work in the missions. In missions up and down the California coast, Indians worked as weavers, tanners, shoemakers, bricklayers, carpenters, blacksmiths, and other artisans. Some herded cattle and raised horses. Indian women cooked for the mission, cleaned, and spun wool. They wove cloth and sewed garments.

Nevertheless, even Indians living in or near missions resisted the cultural change imposed by the intruders. Catholic missionaries complained that Indian women such as those of the Chumash refused to learn Spanish. The refusal among some Indians to completely assimilate signaled persistent, deep-seated conflicts between native groups and incoming settlers. In 1824 a revolt among hundreds of newly converted Indians at the mission *La Purisima Concepción* north of Santa Barbara revealed a rising militancy among native peoples.

After the War of 1812, the U.S. government had rewarded some military veterans with land grants in the Old Northwest. Federal agents tried to clear the way for these new settlers by ousting Indians from the area. Overwhelmed by the number of whites, some Indian groups such as the Peoria and Kaskaskia gave up their lands to the interlopers. Others took a stand against the white intrusion. In 1826 and 1827, the Winnebago attacked white families and boat pilots living near Prairie du Chien, Wisconsin. Two years later, the Sauk chief Black Hawk (known to Indians as Ma-ka-tai-me-she-kia-kiak) assembled a coalition of Fox, Winnebago, Kickapoo, and Potawatomi. Emboldened by the prospect of aid from British Canada, they clashed with federal troops and raided farmers' homesteads and miners' camps.

In August 1832 a force of 1,300 U.S. soldiers and volunteers struck back, killing 300 Indian men, women, and children encamped on the Bad Axe River in western Wisconsin. The massacre, the decisive point of what came to be called the Black Hawk War, marked the end of armed Indian resistance north of the Ohio River and east of the Mississippi.

Slaves and Free People of Color

Southern whites perceived free blacks, like Indians, as an unwelcome and dangerous presence, especially given the possibility that they would conspire with slaves to spark a rebellion. For these reasons some states began to outlaw private manumissions (the practice of individual owners freeing their slaves) and to force free blacks to leave the state altogether. In the 1820s the small proportion of free blacks within the southern population declined further.

One free black who inspired such fears was Denmark Vesey. Born on the Danish-controlled Caribbean island of St. Thomas in 1767, Vesey was a literate carpenter as well as a religious leader. In 1799 he won $1,500 in a Charleston, South Carolina, lottery and used some of the money to buy his freedom. In the summer of 1822, a Charleston court claimed to have unearthed evidence of a "diabolical plot" hatched by Vesey together with plantation slaves from the surrounding area.

Yet the historical record strongly suggests that no plot ever existed. Black "witnesses" who feared for their own lives provided inconsistent and contradictory testimony to a panel of judges. Authorities never located any material evidence of a planned uprising, such as stockpiles of weapons. Under fire from other Charleston elites for rushing to judgment, the judges redoubled their efforts to embellish vague rumors of black discontent into a tale of a well-orchestrated uprising and to implicate growing numbers of black people. As a result of the testimony of several slaves, thirty-five black men were hanged and another eighteen exiled outside the United States. Of those executed, Vesey and twenty-three other men said nothing to support even the vaguest charges of the court.

In the North, some blacks were granted the right to vote after emancipation in the late eighteenth century; however, many of those voting rights were lost in the early nineteenth century. New Jersey (in 1807), Connecticut (1818), New York (1821), and Pennsylvania (1838) all revoked the legislation that had let black men cast ballots. Free northern blacks continued to suffer under a number of legal restrictions. Most were not citizens and therefore perceived themselves as oppressed like the slaves in the South.

A new group of black leaders in the urban North began to link their fate to that of their enslaved brothers and sisters in the South. In Boston, North Carolina–born David Walker published his fiery *Walker's Appeal to the Coloured Citizens of the World* in 1829. Walker called for all blacks to integrate fully into American society, shunning racial segregation whether initiated by whites or by blacks themselves. Reminding his listeners of the horrors of the slave trade, he declared that black people were ready to die for freedom: "I give it as a fact, let twelve black men get well armed for battle, and they will kill and put to flight fifty whites."

DOCUMENT

An Account of the Late Intended Insurrection Among a Portion of Blacks of this City

Northern black leaders disagreed among themselves on the issues of integration and black separatism—for example, whether blacks should create their own schools or press for inclusion in the public educational system. A few leaders favored leaving the country altogether, believing that black people would never find peace and freedom in the United States. Founded by whites in New Jersey in 1817, the American Colonization Society (ACS) paid for a small number of black Americans to settle Monrovia, later named Liberia, on the west coast of Africa. The ACS drew support from a variety of groups, including whites in the upper South who wanted to free their slaves but believed that black and white people could not live in the same country, and some slaves and free people of color convinced that colonization would give them a fresh start. A small number of American-born blacks settled in Liberia. However, most black activists rejected colonization. They had been born on American soil, and their forebears had been buried there. Maria Stewart of Boston declared, "Before I go [to Africa] the bayonet shall pierce me through."

> *Northern black leaders disagreed among themselves on the issues of integration and black separatism.*

Northern whites sought to control black people and their movements. Outspoken black men and women such as Walker and Stewart alarmed northern whites who feared that if blacks could claim decent jobs, white people would lose their own jobs. African Americans who worked outdoors as wagon drivers, peddlers, and street sweepers were taunted and in some cases attacked by whites who demanded deference from blacks in public. In October 1824, a mob of white men invaded a black neighborhood in Providence, Rhode Island. They terrorized its residents, destroyed buildings, and left the place "almost entirely in ruins." The catalyst for the riot had come the previous day, when a group of blacks had refused to yield the inside of the sidewalk—a cleaner place to walk—to white passersby.

In the South, whites in 1831 took steps to reinforce the institution of slavery, using both violent and legal means. That year Nat Turner, an enslaved preacher and mystic, led a slave revolt in Southampton, Virginia. In the 1820s, the young Turner had looked skyward and had seen visions of "white spirits and black spirits engaged in battle . . . and blood flowed in streams." Turner believed that he had received divine instructions to lead other slaves to freedom, to "arise and prepare myself, and slay my enemies with their own weapons." In August he and a group of followers that eventually numbered eighty moved through the countryside, killing whites wherever they could find them. Ultimately, nearly sixty whites died at the

José Agustin de Escudero Describes New Mexico as a Land of Opportunity, 1827

In the early nineteenth century, many people believed that the West afforded abundant economic opportunities for those willing to work hard. However, in most areas of the trans-Appalachian West, farming was a risky venture. Farmers needed cash or credit to hire hands—or to buy slaves—to clear dense underbrush and make other improvements on the land. Floods and droughts could wipe out a year's hard work and ruin even the most industrious family.

Nevertheless, certain frontier livelihoods did not take large investments in labor or equipment. In 1827 José Agustin de Escudero, a lawyer from the Mexican state of Chihuahua, visited the northern reaches of his country and reported on the partido system of sheep raising in the colony of New Mexico. He reported that the quality and expanse of the land meant that young men of modest means could prosper after a few years without securing large loans.

Merino sheep

It can be asserted that there were no paupers in New Mexico at that time, nor could there be any. At the same time, there were no large-scale stockmen who could pay wages or make any expenditure whatever in order to preserve and increase their wealth in this branch of agriculture. A poor man, upon reaching the age when one generally starts a family, would go to a rich stockman and offer to help him take care of one or more herds of sheep. These flocks were composed of *a thousand* ewes and *ten* breeding rams, which were never separated from the herd as is the practice of stock raisers in other countries. Consequently, in each flock, not a single day would go by without the birth of two or three lambs, which the shepherd would

---

hands of Turner's rebels. Turner himself managed to evade capture for more than two months. After he was captured, he was tried, convicted, and executed.

After the Turner revolt, a wave of white hysteria swept the South. In Virginia near where the killings had occurred, whites assaulted blacks with unbridled fury. The Virginia legislature seized the occasion to defeat various antislavery proposals. Thereafter, all the slave states moved to strengthen the institution of slavery. For all practical purposes, public debate over slavery ceased.

DOCUMENT

The Confession of Nat Turner (1831)

The Legal and Economic Dependence of Women

Regardless of where they lived, enslaved women and Indian women had almost no rights under either U.S. or Spanish law. However, legal systems in the United States and the Spanish borderlands differed in their treatment of women. In the United States, most of the constraints that white married women had experienced in the colonial period still applied in the 1820s. A husband controlled the property that his wife brought to the marriage, and he had legal authority over their children. Indeed, the wife was considered her husband's possession. She had no right to make a contract, keep money she earned, vote, run for office, or serve on a jury. In contrast, in the Spanish Southwest, married women could own land and conduct business on their own. At the same time, however, husbands, fathers, and local priests continued to exert much influence over the lives of these women.

European American women's economic subordination served as a rationale for their political inferiority. The "common man" concept rested on the assumption that men had the put with the ewe and force the female to suckle without the difficulties which he would have had with a larger number of offspring. The shepherd would give the owner ten or twenty per cent of these sheep and an equal amount of wool, as a sort of interest, thus preserving the capital intact.

From the moment he received the flock, the shepherd entered into a contract in regard to the future increase, even with his own overseer. As a matter of fact, he usually contracted it at the current market price, two reales per head [an advance from the stockman], the future increase to be delivered in small numbers over a period of time. With this sum, which the shepherd had in advance, he could construct a house, and take in other persons to help him care for and shear the sheep, which was done with a knife instead of shears. The milk and sometimes the meat from the said sheep provided him sustenance; the wool was spun by his own family into blankets, stockings, etc., which could also be marketed, providing an income. Thus the wealth of the shepherd would increase until the day he became, like his overseer, the owner of a herd. He, in turn, would let out his herds to others after the manner in which he obtained his first sheep and made his fortune. Consequently, even in the homes of the poorest New Mexicans, there is never a dearth of sufficient means to satisfy the necessities of life and even to afford the comfort and luxuries of the wealthiest class in the country.

José de Escudero was a visitor to, not a resident of, New Mexico. It is possible that he oversimplified the partido shepherds' self-sufficiency in this region. Soon after winning its independence from Spain, Mexico opened New Mexico to U.S. traders. By the mid-1820s, traders were leading mule trains along the Santa Fe Trail, which ran from Franklin, Missouri, to Santa Fe, New Mexico. In his account here, Escudero indirectly highlights the roles of wives and mothers (as spinners and weavers of cloth) in preserving the economic independence of the shepherds' households.

Nevertheless, Escudero's observations suggest that a combination of factors, including the nature of the landscape (in this case suitable for sheep grazing) and the amount of initial capital necessary to the enterprise (in this case a minimal amount of cash), were crucial elements in providing young men and their families with economic opportunities on the frontier.

Questions

1. In what way does Agustin de Escudero link economic opportunity to the life cycle of rural New Mexican families?
2. What are some of the problems that a young sheep owner might encounter as he tried to build up his flock and provide for his family?
3. How might the appearance of the railroad in a few years change this sheepherding economy? ■

Source: H. Bailey Carroll and J. Villasana Haggard, trans. and ed., *Three New Mexico Chronicles* (Albuquerque, 1942), pp. 41–42.

largest stake in society because only they owned property. That stake made them responsible citizens.

Yet women contributed to the economy in myriad ways. Although few women earned cash wages in the 1820s, almost all adult women worked. In the colonial period, society had highly valued women's labor in the fields, the garden, and the kitchen. However, in the early nineteenth century, work was becoming increasingly identified as labor that earned cash wages. This attitude proved particularly common in the Northeast, where increasing numbers of workers labored under the supervision of a boss. As this belief took root, men began valuing women's contributions to the household economy less and less. If women did not earn money, many men asked, did they really work at all?

In these years, well-off women in the northeastern and mid-Atlantic states began to think of themselves as consumers and not producers of goods. They relied more and more on store-bought cloth and household supplies. Some could also afford to hire servants to perform housework for them. Privileged women gradually stopped thinking of their responsibilities as making goods or processing and preparing food. Rather, their main tasks were to manage servants and create a comfortable home for their husbands and children.

In contrast, women in other parts of the country continued to engage in the same forms of household industry that had characterized the colonial period. In Spanish settlements, women played a central role in household production. They made all of their family's clothes by carding, spinning, and weaving the wool from sheep. They tanned cowhides and ground blue corn to make tortillas, or *atole*. They produced their own candles and soap, and they

In the early nineteenth century, work was becoming increasingly identified as labor that earned cash wages.

plastered the walls of the home. In the Spanish mission of San Gabriel, California, the widow Eulalia Pérez cooked, sewed, ministered to the ill, and instructed children in reading and writing. At Mission San Diego, Apolonaria Lorenzana worked as a healer and cared for the church sacristy and priestly vestments.

Indian women also engaged in a variety of essential tasks. Sioux and Mandan women, though of a social rank inferior to men, performed a great deal of manual labor in their own villages. They dressed buffalo skins that the men later sold to traders. They collected water and wood, cooked, dried meat and fruit, and cultivated maize (corn), pumpkins, and squash with hoes made from the shoulderblades of elk. These women worked collectively within a network of households rather than individually within nuclear families.

Some women worked for cash wages during this era. New England women and children, for example, were the vanguard of factory wage-earners in the early manufacturing system. In Massachusetts in 1820, women and children constituted almost a third of all manufacturing workers. In the largest textile factories, they made up fully 80 percent of the workforce.

The business of textile manufacturing took the tasks of spinning thread and weaving cloth out of the home and relocated those tasks in factories. The famous "Lowell mill girls" are an apt example. Young, unmarried white women from New Hampshire, Vermont, and Massachusetts, these workers moved to the new company town of Lowell, Massachusetts, to take jobs as textile machine operatives. In New England, thousands of young men had migrated west, tipping the sex ratio in favor of women and creating a reserve of female laborers. But to attract young women to factory work, mill owners had to reassure them (and their parents) that they would be safe and well cared for away from home. To that end, they established boarding houses where employees could live together under the supervision of a matron—an older woman who served as their mother-away-from-home. Many young women valued the friendships they made with their coworkers and the money they made in the mills. Some of these women sent their wages back home so that their fathers could pay off the mortgage or their brothers could attend school.

Most ordinary women received little in the way of formal education. Yet elite young women had expanded educational opportunities, beginning in the early nineteenth century. Emma Willard founded a female academy in Troy, New York, in 1821, and Catharine Beecher established the Hartford (Connecticut) Female Seminary two years later. For the most part, such schools catered to the daughters of wealthy families, young women who would never have to work in a factory to survive. Hailed as a means to prepare young women to serve as wives and mothers, the schools taught geography, foreign languages, mathematics, science, and philosophy, as well as the "female" pursuits of embroidery and music.

Out of this curriculum designed especially for women emerged women's rights activists, women who keenly felt both the potential of their own intelligence and the degrading nature of their social situation. Elizabeth Cady, an 1832 graduate of the Troy Female Seminary, later went on to marry Henry B. Stanton and bear seven children. But by the 1840s, she strode onto the national stage as a tireless advocate of women's political and economic rights.

Ties That Bound a Growing Population

As the nation expanded westward, population growth and migration patterns disrupted old bonds of community. When people left their place of birth, they often severed ties with their family and original community. New forms of social cohesion arose to replace these traditional ties. New religions sought to make sense of the changing political and economic landscape. High literacy rates among the population created a new community of readers—a dispersed audience for periodicals as well as for a new, uniquely American literature. Finally, opinionmakers used the printed word to spread new ideas and values across regional boundaries. These ideas, such as glorification of male ambition, helped knit together far-flung segments of the population, men and women who began to speak of an "American character."

New Visions of Religious Faith

New forms of religious faith arose in response to turbulent times, offering one path to social cohesion. During the Indian Wars in the Old Northwest, a Winnebago prophet named White Cloud helped Black Hawk create a **coalition** of Winnebago, Potawatomi, Kickapoo, Sauk, and Fox Indians. A mystic and medicine man, White Cloud preached against white people and exhorted his followers to defend their way of life, an Indian way that knew no tribal boundaries. White Cloud, the religious leader, and Black Hawk, the military leader, surrendered together to federal troops on August 27, 1832, their alliance signifying the spiritual component in the Indians' militant resistance to whites.

VIDEO

Religious Revivalism and Reform

New religious enthusiasms took hold in other parts of the country as well. In the late 1820s and early 1830s, the Second Great Awakening swept western New York. The fervor of religious revivals so heated the region that people began to call it "the Burned-Over District." Hordes of people of various Protestant denominations attended week-long prayer meetings, sat together on the "anxious bench" for sinners, and listened, transfixed, as new converts told of their path to righteousness.

What explains this wave of religious enthusiasm? A major factor was a clergyman named Charles Grandison Finney, who managed to tap into the wellspring of hope and anxiety of the time. A former lawyer, Finney preached that people were moral free agents, fully capable of deciding between right and wrong and doing good in the world. Finney's message had great appeal during this period of rapid social, economic, and technological change. In New England and New York, for example, canals were bringing new kinds of goods to rural areas and longtime residents were departing for the Midwest. Traditional social relationships seemed threatened.

Throughout the country, religious institutions also grappled with questions about slavery. As the fear of possible black uprisings spread, white clergy in the South began to turn away from their former willingness to convert anyone. Instead, they began seeking respectability in the eyes of the well-to-do, slave-owning class. Incorporating masculine imagery into their sermons, they strove to reinforce the power of husband over wife, parent over child, and master over slave, relations that defined the typical plantation household.

Elsewhere, some church leaders sought to purge Christianity of what they saw as its too-worldly nature and to revive the early, simple church that Jesus and his disciples had established. On April 6, 1830, a young farmer named Joseph Smith founded the Church of Jesus Christ of Latter-Day Saints (also called the Mormons) in Fayette, New York. Smith said that, in a vision, an angel named Moroni presented him with the text of a holy book originally written by a Native American historian more than 1,400 years earlier. The text was called the *Book of Mormon*. Together with the Old and New Testaments, it formed the basis of a new faith. Over the next few years, the Mormon Church grew rapidly, claiming 8,000 members by the mid-1830s. However, the young church also aroused intense hostility among mainstream Protestant denominations that regarded the new group's theology and textual inspiration with suspicion.

Literate and Literary America

Around the same time, a young widow named Sarah Hale broke new ground for women. In 1821 she became the first woman to edit an American periodical when she accepted

■   **The Rev. John Atwood and family reading the Bible, 1845.**

responsibility for editing the Boston-based *Ladies Magazine*, later renamed *Godey's Lady's Book*. Once a hatmaker but now a published poet and novelist, Hale portrayed women as especially devout and thus powerful: men might claim as their domain "the government and the glory of the world," she wrote in 1832, "but nevertheless, what man shall become depends upon the secret, silent influence of women." That influence, Hale and other men and women like her believed, derived from women's roles as nurturers and caretakers. Thousands of similar magazines—most short-lived—appeared between 1825 and 1850.

Just as sentimental fiction and poetry attracted a large readership among women, a number of male writers staked their claim to emerging American literature. Washington Irving, James Fenimore Cooper, and William Cullen Bryant all explored regional histories and landscapes in their works. In *Rip Van Winkle* (1819) and the *Legend of Sleepy Hollow* (1820), Irving wrote about the legends of upstate New York. Cooper explored the western New York middle ground contested by the British, Americans, French, and Indians in the late eighteenth century in such works as *The Spy* (1821) and *The Last of the Mohicans* (1826). Bryant,

DOCUMENT

"Old Ironsides"
by Oliver Wendell
Holmes Jr.

inspired by the sight of the Illinois plains in 1832, penned "The Prairies," a praise-song to the vast plains as beautiful and "quick with life."

Along with this new American literary tradition, small towns across the nation began publishing newspapers to educate, inform, and entertain readers. News stories about national elections and legislation, about foreign monarchs and conflicts, reached log cabins in the West as well as elegant townhouses in Boston and Philadelphia. Wrote Washington Irving in 1820, "Over no nation does the press hold a more absolute control than over the people of America, for the universal education of the poorest classes makes every individual a reader."

Newspapers, books, and magazines promoted a set of values that writers claimed described an enduring American character. The ideal American supposedly was ambitious—ready to seize opportunity wherever it could be found—and at the same time devoted to home and family. In fact, these values strongly resembled those adopted by the British middle classes at the same time. Indeed, the United States spawned its own brand of middle-class sensibility called Victorianism, after the English queen who reigned from 1837 to 1901.

> *The ideal American supposedly was ambitious—ready to seize opportunity wherever it could be found—and at the same time devoted to home and family.*

Five core values defined early American Victorianism. First, the Victorians believed in the significance of the individual. People should be judged on the basis of their character, not on the circumstances of their birth. This belief, however, generally applied only to white men. Second, individuals should have the freedom to advance as far as their talents and ambition took them; no person should claim advantages over others by virtue of a noble title or aristocratic lineage. Third, work was intrinsically noble, whether performed by a canal digger wielding a pick-axe or a merchant using a quill pen. All people, regardless of their trade, deserved to reap the fruits of their labor. Fourth, everyone should exercise self-control and restraint in activities such as drinking and engaging in sexual relations. Finally, men and women occupied separate but complementary spheres. American society could be orderly and stable only if men could find a haven from the heartless world of work in their own homes. There, wives tended the hearth and infused the household with their love, self-sacrifice, and religious devotion.

Conclusion

Western settlement infused American politics with raw energy in the 1820s. Andrew Jackson was the first in a long line of presidents who boasted of their humble origins and furthered their careers by denouncing what they called the privileges enjoyed by wealthy Easterners. The challenges faced by western settlers in establishing homesteads and paying their debts emerged as national, not purely local, issues. Through the sheer force of his personality, Andrew Jackson exemplified these dramatic changes in the political landscape. Almost single-handedly, he extended the limits of executive power and remade the American party system in the process.

However, the contradictions in Jacksonian politics became glaring in the coming years. As the nation expanded its borders and diversified its economy, distinctions between social classes sharpened. The country also staked its claim to foreign territory, using violence to advance democratic values. Meanwhile, the North and South eyed each other with increasing distrust. And the contrast between those who moved from place to place voluntarily and those who were forced to move became even more dramatic.

Sites to Visit

The Second Bank of the United States, 1816–1936
odur.let.rug.nl/~usa/E/usbank/bank04.htm
> The political conflict surrounding the Second Bank of the United States contributed to the rise of the Whig party.

The Erie Canal
www.canals.state.ny.us/culture/history
> This official New York State site presents the Erie Canal as the stimulus for enormous economic and social change.

The Cherokee Nation
www.cherokee.org/culture/history.asp
> This is the official Web site of the Cherokee nation based in Talequah, Oklahoma.

Commerce of the Prairies
www.kancoll.org/books/gregg/index.html#contents
> This University of Kansas site includes information on life and commerce on the frontier between the United States and Mexico; including the Santa Fe Trail.

Pioneering the Upper Midwest: Books from Michigan, Minnesota, and Wisconsin, ca. 1820–1910
memory.loc.gov/ammem/umhtml/umhome.html
> This Library of Congress site looks at first-person accounts, biographies, promotional literature, ethnographic and antiquarian texts, colonial archival documents, and other works from the seventeenth to the early twentieth century. It covers many topics and issues related to Americans and the settlement of the upper Midwest.

The Settlement of African Americans in Liberia
www.loc.gov/exhibits/african/afam002.html
> This site contains images and text relating to the colonization movement sponsored by the American Colonization Society.

African American Women Writers from the Nineteenth Century
http://digital.nypl.org/schomburg/writers_aa19/toc.html
> The New York Public Library Schomburg Center for Research in Black Culture site contains texts of literature by African American women of the nineteenth century.

For Further Reading

General

Stuart R. Blumin, *The Emergence of the Middle Class: Social Experience in the American City, 1760–1900* (1989).

Daniel Feller, *The Jacksonian Promise: America, 1815–1840* (1995).

Melvyn Stokes and Stephen Conway, eds., *The Market Revolution in America: Social, Political, and Religious Expressions, 1800–1880* (1996).

David J. Weber, *The Spanish Frontier in North America* (1992).

The Politics Behind Western Expansion

James W. Covington, *The Seminoles of Florida* (1993).

Mark Derr, *The Frontiersman: The Real Life and Many Legends of Davy Crockett* (1993).

Timothy Matovina, *Tejano Religion and Ethnicity: San Antonio, 1821–1860* (1995).

Ronald E. Shaw, *Canals for a Nation: The Canal Era in the United States, 1790–1860* (1990).

Federal Authority and Its Opponents

William W. Freehling, *Prelude to Civil War: The Nullification Controversy in South Carolina, 1816–1836* (1966).

Michael F. Holt, *Political Parties and American Political Development from the Age of Jackson to the Age of Lincoln* (1992).

Lawrence Frederick Kohl, *The Politics of Individualism: Parties and the American Character in the Jacksonian Era* (1989).

Robert V. Remini, *Andrew Jackson and His Indian Wars* (2001).

Real People in the "Age of the Common Man"

Thomas Dublin, *Transforming Women's Work: New England Lives in the Industrial Revolution* (1994).

Albert L. Hurtado, *Intimate Frontiers: Sex, Culture and Gender in California* (1999).

Walter Licht, *Industrial America: The Nineteenth Century* (1995).

Julie Winch, *Philadelphia's Black Elite: Activism, Accommodation, and the Struggle for Autonomy, 1787–1848* (1988).

Ties That Bound a Growing Population

Jeanne Boydston, *Home and Work: Housework, Wages, and the Ideology of Labor in the Early Republic* (1990).

Richard L. Bushman, *Joseph Smith and the Beginnings of Mormonism* (1984).

Nathan O. Hatch, *The Democratization of American Christianity* (1989).

Christine L. Heyrman, *Southern Cross: The Beginnings of the Bible Belt* (1997).

For quizzes and other resources on these topics, go to www.longmanamericanhistory.com.

Peoples in Motion, 1832–1848

I N THE SPRING OF 1847, JANNICKE SAEHLE LEFT HER HOME IN BERGEN, A CITY ON THE WESTERN coast of Norway, and boarded a ship bound for New York City. From New York, the young woman traveled by steamship up the Hudson River to Albany. There she boarded a train to Milwaukee, Wisconsin. Although arduous, the journey had its pleasures. Piloted by a charming captain, the steamship resembled, in Saehle's words, "a complete house four stories high, and very elegantly furnished, with beautiful rugs everywhere." On the train, the passengers enjoyed each other's company as well as "the noteworthy sights that we rushed past." By the summer, Saehle was living with and working as a domestic servant for a Norwegian family, the Torjersens, in Koshkonong in southeastern Wisconsin. Founded in 1840, Koshkonong was a rapidly growing settlement of Norwegian immigrants farming the fertile prairie.

Jannicke Saehle was eager to make a new life for herself in the United States. For just a few months of service in the Torjersen household, she received the harvest of 3 acres of wheat for three years. In the fall, she found a job washing and ironing at a tavern in Madison. For the first five weeks, she earned a dollar a week. Then she received a raise of twenty-five cents a week, with the promise of another raise, and relief from washing, at the end of the winter. Although she could not speak English, she was pleased to "enjoy the best treatment" from the tavern owners and patrons.

In September 1847, Jannicke Saehle wrote of her good fortune in America in a letter to her family back in Norway. She described "the superabundance of food" in the Torjersen home. On his 40-acre farm, Torjersen kept swine and produced "tremendous amounts" of wheat, potatoes, beans, cabbage, cucumbers, onions, and many other kinds of vegetables. At the Madison tavern, she had "food and drink in abundance" and

■ Norwegian immigrants to the United States, 1880s.

dined on the same fare served to the guests: for breakfast, "chicken, mutton [lamb], beef or pork, warm or cold wheat bread, butter, white cheese, eggs, or small pancakes, the best coffee, tea, cream and sugar." For supper she feasted on "warm biscuits, and several kinds of cold wheat bread, cold meats, bacon, cakes, preserved apples, plums, and berries, which are eaten with cream, and tea and coffee." Saehle felt heartbroken to see excess food thrown to the chickens and pigs, for, she wrote, "I think of my dear ones in Bergen, who like so many others must at this time lack the necessaries of life."

Jannicke Saehle was just one of the more than 13,000 immigrants from Norway, Sweden, and Denmark who arrived in the United States during the 1840s. This migration continued to increase over the course of the nineteenth century. In the 1880s, more than 655,000 Scandinavians, fleeing poverty and military conflict, came to America. Many traveled to Wisconsin and Minnesota, where they farmed small homesteads and found the cold winter climate similar to that of their homeland.

In the 1830s and 1840s, patterns of settlement and employment among immigrant groups varied widely in the United States. For example, most Irish immigrants lacked the resources to move much farther west than the eastern seaboard ports where they landed. In contrast, many Germans arrived with enough money to buy farmland in the Midwest or take up a trade in eastern cities. Many immigrants relied for jobs and housing on compatriots who had already arrived. Communities of immigrants built their own religious institutions and **mutual aid societies**.

In the 1830s and 1840s, the United States was home to many peoples in motion. Groups of Indians in the Southeast and Midwest and slaves in the upper South were forced at gunpoint to move from one region of the country to another. From western Europe came poor and persecuted groups drawn to the United States by the demand for labor and the promise of religious and political freedom. Some Americans eagerly pulled up stakes and moved to nearby cities or towns in search of better jobs. Migrants with enough resources made the long journey across the Sonoran Desert in the Southwest to California or to the Oregon Territory in the Northwest.

Population movements and economic change generated new forms of community and group identity. In their native lands, many newcomers to the United States had lived and labored as peasants under the control of aristocratic landlords. Now in America these immigrants worked as wage earners or as small farmers. Urban workers founded the National Trades Union, an organization that tried to help laboring people wield political influence. Some women and men challenged basic institutions such as the **nuclear family**, slavery, and white supremacy. Some reformers established new communities based on alternative notions of marriage and child-rearing.

In politics, the so-called Second Party system had emerged by 1836, as Jacksonian Democrats squared off against the Whigs on familiar issues including tariffs and new systems of transportation. Some Americans turned to violence to advance or defend their causes. Urban mobs vented their wrath against African Americans, abolitionists, and Irish immigrants and other Roman Catholics. The government itself sponsored violence, which peaked in the late 1830s with the forced removal of southeastern Indians to the West, and again in the late 1840s, when the United States wrested a vast expanse of land from Mexico. Indeed, within the larger society, physical force seemed to be an acceptable means of resolving disputes; politicians of all persuasions followed Andrew Jackson's lead and staked their claim to national leadership on the basis of their records as soldiers, military officers, and Indian-killers.

Mass Migrations

When foreign visitors called Americans a "restless" people, they were referring to patterns of both immigration and migration within the country. Between 1830 and 1850, 2.3 million immigrants entered the United States, up from a total of

152,000 during the two previous decades. Most newcomers came from Ireland, Germany, England, Scotland, and Scandinavia. In the United States itself, individuals and families moved around the country with almost dizzying frequency in search of better jobs. They migrated from rural to urban areas, from one city to another, out west and then back to the East. In the late 1840s, almost half of all urban residents moved within a twelve-month period. For the country as a whole, an estimated one family in five moved every year, and on average every family moved once every five years. Many westward migrants had enough money to move overland and buy a homestead once they arrived in Wisconsin or Oregon. However, much of the population turnover in urban areas stemmed from landless people's relentless quest for higher wages and cheaper places to rent.

Some people moved because other people forced them to—under the crack of a whip and in manacles. Slave traders in the upper South transported thousands of slaves to the lower South for sale "on the block." U.S. soldiers forced Indians to walk from their homelands in the southeast to Indian Territory (now the state of Oklahoma). In the less settled West, however, older identities of race and ethnicity sometimes gave way to new identities forged from mixing cultures.

Newcomers from Western Europe

During this period, hardships in Western Europe led to increased immigration to the United States, especially from Ireland and the German states. For the long-suffering people of Ireland, life had become more precarious than ever by the early nineteenth century. Over the generations, small farm plots had been subdivided among heirs to the point that most holdings consisted of fewer than 15 acres each. At the same time, the population of Ireland had grown exponentially—to more than 4 million people in 1800. England treated Ireland like a colony that existed purely for the economic gain of the mother country (or, in the eyes of the Irish, an occupying power). A series of English laws and policies mandated that farmers export most of the island's grain and cattle, leaving the impoverished people to subsist mainly on a diet of potatoes. Then, beginning in 1845, a blight devastated the potato crop. In the next five years, 1 million people died and another million fled to the United States. The great Irish migration had begun.

During this period, hardships in Western Europe led to increased immigration to the United States, especially from Ireland and the German states.

Large numbers of poor Irish had settled in the United States even before the potato famine of the mid-1840s. In the 1820s, about 50,000 such immigrants arrived; the following decade saw a spike in numbers to more than 200,000. Then as the 1840s and 1850s unfolded, 1.7 million Irish men, women, and children emigrated to the United States. This exodus continued over the next century as more than 4.5 million Irish arrived.

By the 1870s, the Irish constituted fully 20 percent of the population of New York City, 14 percent of Philadelphia, and 22 percent of Boston (the "hub of Gaelic America"). The newcomers quickly formed mutual aid associations and other community organizations. In cities across America, the Sisters of Mercy, a Roman Catholic order founded in Dublin, established homes to provide lodging for single women and day nurseries for the children of working mothers.

Most Irish immigrants lacked the resources to move much farther west than the eastern seaport cities where they landed, and they soon realized that their struggle against poverty, discrimination, and religious persecution would not end in the United States. The arrival of large numbers of Irish immigrants in the 1830s threatened the jobs of native-born Protestants, who reacted with resentment and violence. Employers posted signs outside their doors reading "No Irish Need Apply." Despised for their Roman Catholicism and their supposed clannishness, the Irish competed with African Americans for the low-paying jobs at the bottom of the economic ladder. In 1834 a mob destroyed the Ursuline convent in Charlestown, near Boston, after terrifying the women and children residents and ransacking the building.

Nevertheless, by the 1850s, the Irish had gained a measure of influence. They filled many high positions in the U.S. Catholic Church and became active in the Democratic party. They

■ MAP 12.1

WESTERN TRAILS   This map shows the major trails followed by
western emigrants in the nineteenth century. Settlers endured long and
dangerous journeys. For example, beginning at Independence, Missouri, and stretching to Portland, Oregon,
the Overland Trail was 2,000 miles long. Covering the entire trail could take four to six months. Wagon
trains had to traverse rocky terrain, scale mountains, and ford rivers. Along the way, outposts such as Fort
Laramie and Fort Hall gave travelers a chance to refresh their supplies, rest their livestock, and repair their
wagons. Though resentful of such incursions, Indians rarely attacked large wagon trains.

claimed that their white skin entitled them to distance themselves from blacks and lay claim
to full American citizenship.

The hardship endured by the Irish in the early nineteenth century mirrored the political
and economic distress of many other people living in Europe at the time. The revolutions of
1848 in France, the German states, the Austrian Empire, and parts of Italy struck out against
monarchy and called for constitutional government. Rising unemployment and dramatic population increases made food scarce in both rural and urban areas, stimulating immigration
across the Atlantic.

Between 1831 and 1850, more than half a million Germans arrived in the United States.
Those numbers exploded in the next few decades. An uprising against the authoritarian Pruss-
ian state had failed in 1848, and German intellectuals, farmers, and workers alike fled across
the ocean. Wilhelm Stille came to Ohio in the mid-1830s. In letters home, he praised the
vitality of the local German immigrant community, the bountiful soil, and the "feel for freedom" that infused even the most recent newcomers.

The Slave Trade

Forced migration of enslaved workers increased during this period as the slave trade became big business. Many wealthy traders made regular trips between the upper and lower South. Traders transported men, women, and children by boat down the eastern seaboard or down the Mississippi River or chained and forced them to walk as much as 20 miles a day for seven or eight weeks at a time in the chill autumn air. Eventually, slaves stood on the block in the markets of New Orleans, Natchez, Charleston, and Savannah, where white men inspected them for health, strength, and compliance.

Between 1800 and 1860, the average price of slaves quadrupled, revealing a growing demand for bound labor. As many as one out of every ten slave children in the upper South was sold to the lower South (many to cotton planters) between 1820 and 1860. Slave households in Virginia bore the brunt of these forced separations. There, an estimated three-quarters of the people sold never saw their spouse, parents, or children again.

Between 1800 and 1860, the average price of slaves quadrupled, revealing a growing demand for bound labor.

It was sometimes worse if they did. Moses Grandy, standing on a sidewalk one day, saw his wife in chains, in a coffle passing by. He recalled the scene in his 1844 autobiography:

> Mr. Rogerson was with them on his horse, armed with pistols. I said to him. "For God's sake, have you bought my wife?" He said he had; when I asked him what she had done, he said she had done nothing, but that her master wanted money. He drew out a pistol and said that if I went near the wagon where she was, he would shoot me. I asked for leave to shake hands with her which he refused, but said I might stand at a distance and talk with her. My heart was so full that I could say very little. . . . I have never seen or heard from her from that day to this. I loved her as I love my life.

Voluntary migrations of African Americans formed the counterpoint of the slave trade as runaways and free people of color made their way out of the old slave states. An estimated 50,000 enslaved workers tried to escape each year, but few made it to the North and freedom. Some southern free people of color headed to northern cities. By 1850 more than half of all Boston blacks had been born outside Massachusetts. Of those migrants, about one-third had been born in the South, most in Virginia, Maryland, and the District of Columbia. Slave runaways who lived in fear of their safety and their lives eluded census takers, but by mid-century as many as 600 fugitives lived in Boston.

MAP
Slavery in the South

Regardless of their place of origin, many migrants took up residence with other blacks, who helped ease the newcomers' transition to city life. These boarding arrangements strengthened ties between the enslaved and the free communities. For example, when authorities arrested the runaway George Latimer in Boston in 1842, free blacks in that city took immediate action. They posted signs condemning the police as "human kidnappers." Some tried to wrench him physically from his captors. Still others sponsored protest meetings in the local African Baptist Church and made common cause with white lawyers sympathetic to abolition. Finally a group of blacks and whites raised enough money to buy Latimer from his owner and free him.

Meanwhile, throughout the urban North, whites began eyeing blacks' jobs. Irish immigrants in particular desperately sought work. Skilled black workers found it increasingly difficult to ply their trades as cooks, hotel and boat stewards, porters, brickmakers, and barbers. In 1838, 656 black artisans in Philadelphia reported that they had to abandon their work because white customers would no longer patronize them. White factory owners in Philadelphia preferred white laborers. In that same city, a bustling site of machine shops and textile factories, almost no blacks did industrial labor of any kind.

Trails of Tears

Like enslaved blacks, many Indians were forced to migrate. In 1835 President Andrew Jackson made a puzzling declaration. The removal of eastern Indian groups to Indian Territory,

■ **MAP 12.2**

INDIAN REMOVAL   This map shows the routes of forced migration of the Five Civilized Tribes in the 1830s. By the 1870s, several groups of Plains Indians, including the Cheyenne, Arapaho, Comanche, and Kiowa, had joined them in Indian Territory (present-day Oklahoma).

**Legend (map):**

Indian removal, 1829–1840
- Indian tribes' home territories
- Land granted to Indians west of the Mississippi River
- *1830* Date and route of removal

Native American Removal

he said, would ensure their "physical comfort," "political advancement," and "moral improvement." Rarely have a chief executive's words contrasted so starkly with reality.

Throughout the 1830s, the U.S. government pursued the policy of removing Indians from the Southeast by treaty or by force. The 1832 Treaty of Payne's Landing, negotiated by the Seminole Indians and James Gadsden, a representative of Secretary of War Lewis Cass, aimed to force the Seminole out of Florida and into Indian Territory (present-day Oklahoma). The federal government promised to give individual Indians cash, plus blankets for the men and dresses for the women, in exchange for their lands. Government authorities also hoped to recapture the large number of runaway slaves who had sought refuge in Seminole villages, deep in the swamps of central Florida.

Three years later, in 1835, many of the Indians had departed for the West. But a small number withdrew deeper into the Everglades and held their ground. They were led by a young man named Osceola, who with his followers waged a **guerrilla war** (based on ambush tactics rather than traditional conventions of European American warfare) against better-armed U.S. troops. Osceola's resistance, called the Second Seminole War, dragged on for seven years. Eventually, the government forced 3,000 Seminole to move west, but not until it had spent $20 million, and 1,500 U.S. soldiers had lost their lives.

The Choctaw of the southern Alabama–Mississippi region, the Chickasaw directly to the north of them, the Creek in central Georgia and Alabama, and the Cherokee of north Georgia suffered the same fate in the 1830s. The Creek remained bitterly divided among themselves on the issue of removal, as did the Cherokee. Major Ridge, his son John Ridge, and Elias Boudinot, leaders of the so-called Treaty Party of the Cherokee nation, urged their people to give up their homeland and rebuild their nation in the West. John Ross and others like him opposed the Ridges and Boudinot. The Cherokee must remain in Georgia at all costs, Ross insisted. He claimed that he spoke for a majority of Cherokee. To silence him, the U.S. government threw him in prison. Then it concluded negotiations with the Treaty Party, which agreed to sell Cherokee land to the federal government for $5 million. Elias Boudinot said, "We can die, but the great Cherokee Nation will be saved." Within a few years, the Ridges and Boudinot died at the hands of anti–Treaty Party Cherokee assassins.

In 1838 General Winfield Scott, with 7,000 troops under his command, began rounding up the citizens of the Cherokee nation. U.S. troops held men, women, and children in concentration camps before forcing them to march west. During the period from 1838 to 1839, nearly 16,000 Indians began a journey that they called the Trail on Which We Cried. Four thousand of them died of malnutrition and disease in the course of the 116-day forced march. U.S. troops confiscated or destroyed the material basis of Cherokee culture: sawmills, cotton gins, barns, homes, spinning wheels, meetinghouses, flocks, herds, and the printing press used to publish the *Cherokee Phoenix*.

Rebecca Neugin later recalled how the army troops "drove us out of our house to join other prisoners in a stockade." The soldiers let Rebecca's mother take a few cooking utensils with her; the family lost everything else. Still, Neugin's family remained intact. Many others did not. A soldier who participated in the operation saw children "separated from their parents and driven into the stockade with the sky for a blanket and the earth for a pillow."

U.S. officials claimed that troops had carried out the removal with "great judgment and humanity." However, an internal government report completed in 1841 revealed that the United States had reneged on even its most basic treaty promises. "Bribery, perjury, and forgery, short weights, issues of spoiled meat and grain, and every conceivable subterfuge was employed by designing white men." Many government agents seized goods such as blankets and food intended for Indians and sold these goods for profit. Military authorities suppressed the report, and the public never saw it.

Migrants in the West

For many native-born migrants seeking a new life west of the Mississippi, the road proved neither smooth nor easy. For example, as the Mormon community moved west from New York, they met with religious persecution. The founder of the church, Joseph Smith, aroused the anger of his neighbors in Nauvoo, Illinois. They took alarm at the Nauvoo Legion, a military company formed to defend the Mormon community. They also heard rumors (for the most part true) that Smith and other Mormon leaders engaged in plural marriage or polygamy, allowing men to marry more than one wife.

In 1844 the Nauvoo Legion destroyed the printing press owned by a group of rebellious church members who objected to what they considered Smith's authoritarian tactics. Civil authorities charged Smith and his brother Hyrum with the destruction of private property and arrested and jailed the two men in the nearby town of Carthage. In June 1844, an angry mob of non-Mormons broke into the jail and lynched the brothers.

By 1847 Brigham Young, who had inherited the mantle of leadership from Smith, determined that the Mormons could not remain in Illinois. Migrants, some of them pushing handcarts loaded with personal belongings, set out for the West. By 1852, 10,000 Mormons had settled in Salt Lake City in what is present-day Utah. With their large numbers and

Scotts Bluff National Monument, Nebraska. United States Department of the Interior, National Park Service

■ **This picture of the Whitman mission at Waiilatpu, Oregon, in 1845 shows the missionaries' house on the left, a mill in the background, a blacksmith shop in the right center, and a gathering place for worshippers on the far right. By this time the Whitmans had turned their attention from converting Indians to preaching to European American emigrants recently arrived from the East.**

church-inspired discipline, the community prospered. They created an effective irrigation system and turned the desert into a thriving agricultural community.

The Mormons had not settled an uninhabited wilderness. Around Salt Lake, Canadian trappers, Paiute Indians, and Spanish speakers from New Mexico crossed paths, some to hunt, others to gather roots and berries, herd sheep, or trade captives. A Christmas dinner celebrated near Great Salt Lake around this time revealed the multicultural mix of western life. The guests included Osborne Russell (a European American trader), a Frenchman married to a Flathead woman, and various other intermarried Cree, Snake, and Nez Perceé Indians. The group feasted on the meat of elk and deer, a flour pudding, cakes, and strong coffee. After the meal, the women cleared the table. The men smoked pipes and then went outside and conducted target practice with their guns.

European Americans also migrated to the Northwest during this period. Protestant missionaries initially settled Oregon beginning in 1834. But in contrast to the Mormons, these northwestern colonists found themselves in the midst of hostile Native Americans. One young doctor and his wife from western New York, Marcus and Narcissa Whitman, established a mission near present-day Walla Walla, Washington. More than a thousand more emigrants from the East followed the Whitmans to Oregon during the "Great Migration" of 1843.

The U.S. government aided this westward movement when it commissioned its Topographical Corps of Engineers to survey the Oregon Trail. That task fell to an expedition headed by John Charles Frémont in 1843–1844. The expedition's final report had immense practical value for the emigrants, for it mapped the way west and provided crucial information about pasture, sources of water, and climate.

The Oregon settlements founded by missionaries were fragile affairs. Discouraged and overwhelmed by homesickness, Narcissa Whitman eagerly awaited copies of the latest *Mothers'*

Magazine sent to her by female relatives in the East. After 1843 the influx of newcomers brought her some consolation but also brought outbreaks of measles, to which the Native Americans had no immunity. An ensuing epidemic among the Cayuse claimed many lives. In 1847, blaming the missionaries for the deaths of their people, several Indians attacked the Whitman mission, killing twelve whites, including Narcissa and Marcus Whitman.

New Places, New Identities

The Midwest, the West, and the borderlands between U.S. and Spanish territories were meeting places for many different cultures. Leaving established communities behind, some migrants challenged rigid definitions of who was black, Indian, Hispanic, or European American. Moving from one place to another enabled—or forced—people to adopt new individual and group identities.

People who fell into one racial category in the East sometimes acquired new identities in the West. Some people classified as "black" in the South became "white" outside the region. In 1831 George and Eliza Gilliam decided to leave their home in Virginia and make a new life for themselves in western Pennsylvania. Eliza died in 1838, and George remarried nine years later. He prospered over the course of his lifetime. He worked as a doctor and druggist and invested in and sold real estate. George and his second wife, Frances, eventually moved to Illinois, and the couple finally settled in Missouri. Several of the Gilliam children attended college in Ohio. In 1870 the census listed the value of his estate at $95,000 (the equivalent of $2 million dollars today).

George Gilliam was the son of a white father and a black mother. Although he and his first wife Eliza were very light-skinned, the commonwealth of Virginia classified them both legally as black. Beginning their married life near Petersburg, they were well aware of Virginia's tightening restrictions on free people of color and their uncertain future in Virginia, where local officials knew who they were and who their parents were. In contrast, the public records in their new home states of Pennsylvania, Illinois, and Missouri listed family members as white. Outside the slave South, the Gilliams managed to reinvent themselves and embrace opportunities sought by many other Americans in this era of migration.

> *Leaving established communities behind, some migrants challenged rigid definitions of who was black, Indian, Hispanic, or European American.*

Throughout the West, migrants forged new identities as a matter of course. For example, many people straddled more than one culture in the western borderlands. In 1828 Mexican military officer Jose Maria Sanchez described the *Tejano* settlers (Spanish-speaking natives of Mexico) he met in the province of Tejas (Texas): "Accustomed to the continued trade with the North Americans, they have adopted their customs and habits, and one may say truly that they are not Mexican except by birth, for they even speak Spanish with a marked incorrectness." In other provinces of northern Mexico, European American Protestant traders and travelers mingled with Catholic native Spanish speakers.

In parts of the West, traditional social identities yielded to new ones, based less on a single language or ethnicity than on a blend of cultures and new ways of making a living from the land. The 1830s and 1840s marked the height of the Rocky Mountain fur trade. The trade could generate huge profits for the eastern merchants who controlled it. Individual trappers fared more modestly, ranging freely across national boundaries and cultures, going wherever the bison, bear, and beaver took them. These men demonstrated a legendary ability to navigate among Spanish, French, European American, and Native American communities. Westerners coined new terms to describe the people representative of new kinds of cultural identity within trading communities. Some white men became "white Indians," and the children they had with Indian women were called "métis" (mixed bloods). William Sherley "Old Bill" Williams, a convert to the religion of the Osage Indians of the southeastern Plains, was not unusual in the ways he crossed cultural boundaries. He married an Osage woman, and when she died, he wed a New Mexican widow. His third wife was a Ute woman. Williams's life story suggests the ways that Indian and Hispanic women could serve as cultural mediators between native peoples and European American traders.

A Multitude of Voices in the National Political Arena

The increasing diversity of the American population, combined with specialized regional economies, also heightened tensions within and between different groups and sections of the country. The Second Party system, which replaced the Federalist–Anti-Federalist rivalry of the early nineteenth century, was characterized by intense competition between the Jacksonian Democrats and anti-Jackson Whigs. But this new system could not accommodate the old or new conflicts based on race, religion, ethnicity, regional loyalties, and political beliefs. Social and cultural disputes between nativists and immigrants, and between abolitionists and defenders of slavery, spilled out of the courthouse and the legislative hall and into the streets. Public demonstrations ran the gamut from noisy parades to bloody clashes. During these displays, resentments between ethnic and religious groups, arguments over political issues, and opposition to reformers often blended together.

Whigs, Workers, and the Panic of 1837

DOCUMENT

Clay, "Defense of the American System"

One polarizing force, Andrew Jackson—ill with tuberculosis—did not run for a third term in 1836. The Democrats nominated Jackson's vice president and friend Martin Van Buren of New York for president. The Jackson-haters, led by Senator Henry Clay and other congressmen, formed a political party called the Whigs. They drew their support from several groups: advocates of Clay's American System (policies that supported a national bank, public funding of canals and turnpikes, and protective tariffs), states' rights Southerners opposed to Jackson's heavy-handed use of national power, and merchants and factory owners in favor of the Second Bank of the United States. **Evangelical Protestants** from the middle classes also joined the anti-Jackson forces; they objected to his rhetoric stressing class differences because they believed that individual religious conviction, not a group's material status, should shape politics and society. Still somewhat disorganized, these allied groups fielded three candidates: Hugh White of Tennessee, Senator Daniel Webster of Massachusetts, and General William Henry Harrison of Indiana. Benefiting from the Whigs' disarray, Van Buren narrowly won the popular vote but swept the electoral college.

During this period, political candidates of all persuasions in northeastern cities began to court the allegiance of workers aligned with a new trade union movement. People worried about making a living tended to favor the Democratic party, which spoke against class privilege and the wealthy. In the late 1820s and early 1830s, a variety of trade organizations had formed to advance the interests of skilled workers (the "producing classes," they called themselves). These unions pressed for a ten-hour workday, the abolition of debtors' prisons and paper money (so that workers would receive their wages in hard currency rather than bank notes), and higher wages.

The founding of the National Trades Union (NTU) in 1834 made workers more politically visible. The union represented workers as diverse as jewelers, butchers, bookbinders, and factory work-

TABLE 12-1

The Election of 1836

Candidate	Political Party	Popular Vote (%)	Electoral Vote
Martin Van Buren	Democratic	50.9	170
William Henry Harrison	Whig		73
Hugh L. White	Whig	49.1	26
Daniel Webster	Whig		14
W.P. Magnum	Independent	—	11

ers. In Philadelphia in the early 1830s, for example, the local NTU organization, called the General Trades Union, consisted of fifty trade societies and supported a number of successful strikes. Both Whigs and Democrats professed allegiance to the union, but neither party went out of its way to represent the interests of workers over other groups, such as farmers and bookkeepers.

A major depression, the Panic of 1837, created even larger troubles for the trade union movement. Brought on by **overspeculation**—in canals, turnpikes, railroads, and slaves—the panic deepened when large grain crops failed in the West. British creditors worsened matters when they recalled loans they had made to American customers. The depression lasted until the early 1840s and devastated the NTU and its constituent organizations. Up to one-third of all Americans lost their jobs when businesses failed. Those fortunate enough to keep their jobs were in no position to press for higher wages. Not until the Civil War era did members of the laboring classes recapture political momentum at the national level.

Suppression of Antislavery Sentiment

Enslaved black workers were also at the center of contention in these years. In 1831 a Boston journalist named William Lloyd Garrison launched *The Liberator*, a newspaper dedicated to "immediate emancipation" of all slaves. Two years later, a group of sixty blacks and whites formed the American Anti-Slavery Society. That same year, Great Britain had abolished slavery in the British West Indies. This move encouraged like-minded Americans eager to cooperate with their British counterparts to abolish slavery everywhere. In the United States, the abolitionist movement enlisted the energies of a dedicated group of people who believed not only that slavery was immoral but also that the federal government must take immediate steps to destroy this "peculiar institution."

Garrison, First issue of *The Liberator*

Both northern communities of free people of color and white women and men provided moral and financial support to the society. All the supporters showed a great deal of courage within a larger American society indifferent to the issue of slavery. Well-to-do black leaders, including Henry Highland Garnet, Charles Lenox Remond, and his sister Sarah Parker Remond, spoke out on behalf of southern blacks in chains. Fugitive slaves, including Frederick Douglass, Solomon Northup, and William and Ellen Craft, electrified northern abolitionist audiences with their firsthand accounts of the brutality of slavery and of their own daring escapes from bondage.

A few white women also became active in the abolitionist cause. Sarah and Angelina Grimké, for example, left the household of their slave-owning father in Charleston, South Carolina, and moved to Philadelphia. The Grimké sisters spoke before groups composed of men and women, blacks and whites in the North, an act offensive to many other whites. They were struck by what they considered the similar legal constraints of slaves and white women. White men considered both groups to be unworthy of citizenship rights, childlike in their demeanor, well-suited for domestic service, and inherently unintelligent.

Abolitionist activities provoked outrage not only from southern slave owners but also from anti-abolitionists and their allies in Congress—in other words, most northern whites. In Washington, D.C., the House of Representatives imposed a gag rule on antislavery petitions, forbidding them to be read aloud or entered into the public record. Supporters of slavery also resorted to violence. In 1834 a mob of whites attacked a school for young women of color operated by a white teacher, Prudence Crandall, near New Haven, Connecticut. A local paper charged that the school was fostering "levelling [egalitarian] principles, and intermarriage between whites and blacks." The next year in Boston a different mob attacked the *Liberator* founder, William Lloyd Garrison, tying a rope around him and parading him through the streets of that city while onlookers jeered. In 1837 in Alton, Illinois, a group of whites murdered outspoken abolitionist Rev. Elijah

■ Born a slave in Maryland in 1818, Frederick Douglass became a leading abolitionist speaker, editor, and activist. Not content to condemn southern slaveholders exclusively, he also criticized northern employers for not hiring blacks. Trained as a ship caulker, Douglass faced job discrimination in the shipyards of New Bedford, Massachusetts, where he and his wife, Anna, settled soon after he escaped slavery and they moved north (in 1838).

■ The artist titled this print *New Method of Assorting the Mail, as Practised by Southern Slave-Holders.* In July 1835, a proslavery mob broke into the U.S. post office in Charleston, South Carolina, and burned abolitionist literature. The sign on the side of the building offers a "Reward for Tappan." The brothers Arthur and Lewis Tappan were wealthy New York City merchants who funded abolitionist activities. Southern slaveholders hoped to stem the North-South flow of abolitionist literature, which took the form of sermons, pamphlets, periodicals, and resolutions.

P. Lovejoy. Hounded out of Missouri because of his antislavery pronouncements, Lovejoy had moved directly across the river to Alton, in free-state Illinois, where he published the *Alton Observer* and organized the Illinois Anti-Slavery Society. Antiblack riots broke out in New York City, Philadelphia, and Cincinnati in 1834, and again in Philadelphia in 1842.

Still, these dramatic episodes had little noticeable impact on the two major political parties. In 1840 the Democrats renominated Van Buren, although many people blamed him for the depression. Eager to find a candidate as popular as Andrew Jackson, the Whigs selected William Henry Harrison; his supporters called him "Old Tippecanoe" in recognition of his defeat of Indians at the battle of the same name in 1811. As Harrison's running mate the Whigs chose John Tyler, who had been both governor of and a senator from Virginia. To counter their reputation as well-heeled aristocrats, which in fact they were, the Whigs promoted Harrison as a simple, humble man living in a log cabin and drinking hard cider. They rallied around the slogan "Tippecanoe and Tyler Too."

By this time, the Whigs had gained strong support among wealthy southern planters, who worried that Van Buren would not protect their interests in slavery. Harrison won the election, but he contracted pneumonia at his inauguration and died within one month of taking office. Ridiculed as "His Accidency," Tyler assumed the presidency and soon lost his core constituency, Whigs who favored a strong central government, by vetoing bills for both a national bank and higher tariffs. The new president represented members of the Whig party who were ardent supporters of states' rights. As a result, he proved a poor standard-bearer for the numerous nationalist-minded Whigs. Tyler learned a hard lesson: that members of his own party were a loose coalition of groups with varying views on a range of issues rather than a unified party bound to a single idea or principle.

Abolitionists could claim few victories, either real or symbolic, during these years. However, they did take heart from the *Amistad* case. In 1839 Spanish slave traders attempted to transport fifty-three illegally purchased Africans to Havana, Cuba, on a ship named *Amistad*. En route to Havana, the Africans, under the leadership of a young man named Cinqué, rebelled, killed the captain, and took over the ship. Soon after, U.S. authorities captured the ship off the coast of Long Island. President Van Buren wanted to send the blacks to Cuba. However, a federal district court judge in Hartford, Connecticut, ruled that because the African slave trade had been illegal since 1808, the Africans had been wrongfully enslaved. The U.S. government appealed the case to the Supreme Court.

To raise funds for the *Amistad* case, Philadelphia black leader Robert Purvis paid to have Cinqué's portrait painted; then antislavery activists sold copies for $1 each. In 1841 former president John Quincy Adams argued the Africans' case before the high court. The court ruled in their favor. Of the original fifty-three men, women, and children, thirty-five had survived the ordeal, and they returned to Africa. Slavery advocates and abolitionists alike pondered the question: Could the law be used to dismantle slavery?

TABLE 12-2			
The Election of 1840			
Candidate	Political Party	Popular Vote (%)	Electoral Vote
William Henry Harrison	Whig	53.1	234
Martin Van Buren	Democratic	46.9	60
James G. Birney	Liberty	<1	—

Nativists as a Political Force

Immigration, like slavery, aroused strong feelings. Among the active players on the political scene in the early nineteenth century were the **nativists**, who opposed immigration and immigrants. The immigrants who came to the United States were a varied group in terms of their jobs, religion, and culture. Some farmed homesteads in Michigan, and others worked in northeastern factories. But to nativists, these distinctions made little difference: all immigrants were foreigners and thus unwelcome. Some nativists were also **temperance** advocates calling for the prohibition of alcohol; they objected to the Irish drinking in taverns and the Germans drinking in their *Biergarten*. Protestants worried that large numbers of Catholic immigrants

Unknown Artist, *La Amistad*, c. 1840. New Haven Colony Historical Society, New Haven, CT (#1972.1)

■ Abolitionists hailed the eventual freeing of the *Amistad* captives as one of their few successes in the fight against slavery before the Civil War. This picture shows the Spanish slave ship, commandeered by the captives under the leadership of Cinqué, anchored off Culloden Point, Long Island, in 1839. Initially charged with the murder of the ship's captain, the Africans were held in New Haven, Connecticut, until a U.S. Supreme Court ruling led to their release and return to Africa in 1842.

would be loyal to the pope in Rome, the head of the Catholic Church, and thus undermine American democracy. Members of the working classes, black and white, feared the loss of their jobs to desperate newcomers who would accept low, "starvation" wages. But nativists objected just as much when immigrants kept to themselves—in their Catholic schools or in their German *Turnverein* (gymnastics clubs). They also complained when immigrants participated in U.S. politics as individual voters and members of influential voting blocs.

Samuel F. B. Morse, the artist and inventor, was among the most vocal nativists. In the early 1840s, he ceased painting portraits and turned his creative energies to developing a form of long-distance electric communication. Congress financed construction of the first telegraph line, which ran from Washington to Baltimore. In May 1844, Morse sent a message in code, "What hath God wrought!" and the modern telegraph was born. The precursor of all later communication innovations, the telegraph revolutionized the spread of information and tied the country together.

DOCUMENT

Morse, Foreign Immigration

Morse was convinced that Catholic immigrants in particular (mostly the Irish) were a grave threat to American democracy. In his book *Imminent Dangers to the Free Institutions of the United States* (1835), Morse charged that Catholics favored "monarchical power" over republican governments. Catholicism was like a cancer, he wrote, "We find it spreading itself into every nook and corner of the land; churches, chapels, colleges, nunneries and convents are springing up as if by magic every where." In his fears, Morse expressed nostalgia for a simpler past, even as his technical ingenuity paved the way for the modern world.

In 1844 an openly nativist political organization, the American Republican party, elected six of its candidates to Congress and dozens of others to local political offices. In 1849 nativists founded the Order of the Star-Spangled Banner. Also called the Know-Nothing party, the group got its name by cautioning its members to profess ignorance when asked about its existence.

■ Taken on May 9, 1844, this daguerreotype is one of the first American photographs to record an urban civil disturbance. A crowd gathers outside Philadelphia's Girard Bank, at the corner of Third and Dock streets. At the time, soldiers called in to quell the riot were occupying the bank. Called the Bible Riots, the clash between Protestant and Catholic workers revealed tensions arising from nativism, temperance activism, and the use of the Protestant version of the Bible in the public schools.

Library Company of Philadelphia (59541.D)

Anti-Catholic prejudices in particular helped to justify territorial expansion. Many U.S. Protestants believed the government was justified in seizing the land of Spanish-speaking Catholics in the West. They claimed religious and cultural superiority over Hispanics. As Protestant explorers, traders, and travelers reported on their experiences in the Southwest, their condemnation of Mexican Roman Catholics set the stage for the U.S. conquest of northern Mexico in the late 1840s.

Reform Impulses

I n August 1841, writer Lydia Maria Child recorded a striking scene in New York City: a march sponsored by the Washington Society, a temperance group, was snaking its way through the streets. The procession stretched for 2 miles and consisted of representatives from "all classes and trades." The marchers carried banners depicting streams and rivers (the pure water favored over liquor) and poignant scenes of the grateful wives and children of reformed drunkards. Stirred by the martial sounds of trumpets and drums, Child wrote that the music was "the voice of resistance to evil." She added, "Glory to resistance! for through its agency men become angels."

Inspired by faith in the perfectibility of human beings and heartened by the rapid pace of technological progress, many Americans set about trying to "make angels out of men," in Child's words. In the process, various reform associations targeted personal habits such as dress and diet, conventional beliefs about sexuality and the status of women, and institutions such as schools, churches, and slavery. Their efforts often brought women out of the home and into public life. Yet not all Americans shared the reformers' zeal, and even those who did rarely agreed about the appropriate means to transform society.

Public Education

In the eyes of some Americans, a growing nation needed new forms of tax-supported schooling. As families moved from one area of the country to another, public education advocates pointed out, children should be able to pick up in one school where they had left off in another. Members of a growing middle class wanted to provide their children with schooling beyond basic literacy instruction (reading and writing skills) and had the resources to do so.

Horace Mann, a Massachusetts state legislator and lawyer, was one of the most prominent educational reformers. In 1837 Mann became secretary of the first state board of education. He stressed the notion of a **common school system** available to all boys and girls regardless of class or ethnicity. In an increasingly diverse nation, schooling promoted the acquisition of basic knowledge and skills. But it also provided instruction in what Mann and others called American values: hard work, punctuality, and sobriety.

How exactly would educators teach reading and writing skills and moral values? The dictionary of Connecticut's Noah Webster (published in 1828) and the McGuffey's *Reader* series, first published in 1836, provided a way. In his books, William H. McGuffey, a college professor and Presbyterian minister, combined lessons in reading with lessons in moral behavior: "Beautiful feet are they that go / Swiftly to lighten another's woe." Over the next twenty years, the McGuffey series sold more than 7 million copies.

By the 1840s, public school systems attended by white children had cropped up across the North and the Midwest. Local school boards eagerly tapped into the energies of women as teachers. School officials claimed that women were naturally nurturing and could serve as "mothers away from home" for small children. Furthermore, schools could pay women only a fraction of what men earned. Between the 1830s and 1840s, the number of female schoolteachers in Massachusetts jumped more than 150 percent. In 1846 writer and educator Catharine Beecher created a Board of National Popular Education, which sent unmarried female New England teachers to the Midwest.

Despite the lofty goals of Mann and other reformers, public schooling did not offer a "common" experience for all American children. Almost exclusively, northern white children benefited from public school systems. Slightly more than one-third of all white children attended school in 1830; twenty years later, the ratio had increased to more than one-half. In northern cities, these proportions were considerably higher; there reformers were able to provide elementary-school instruction for relatively large numbers of white children, both immigrant and native-born.

> *Despite the lofty goals of Mann and other reformers, public schooling did not offer a "common" experience for all American children.*

By contrast, few black children had the opportunity to attend public schools. In the South, slave children were forbidden by law to learn to read and write. Recalled one former slave many years later, "dey [owners] didn't teach 'em nothin' but wuk [work]." By the 1830s, schools for even the children of free people of color had to meet in secret. In the North, many black households needed the labor of children to survive, resulting in black school-attendance rates well below those of whites. Throughout the Northeast and Midwest, black children remained at the mercy of local officials, who decided whether they could attend the schools their parents' tax dollars helped to support.

All over the country, education remained an intensely grassroots affair, belying the reformers' call for uniform systems. Local communities raised money for the teacher's salary, built the schoolhouse, and provided wood to heat the building. Southern states did not develop uniform public education systems until the late nineteenth century. Lacking local, popular support for tax-supported schooling, poor white children remained illiterate, while wealthy parents hired tutors for their own children or sent them to private academies.

Other forms of education also multiplied. The number of colleges more than doubled (46 to 119) between 1830 and 1850. Founded in 1837, Mount Holyoke, a college for women in Massachusetts, and Oberlin in Ohio, which accepted black men as well as women of both races, were unusual for their liberal admission policies. Lyceums—informal lectures offered by speak-

■ Artist Albertus Browere titled this 1844 painting *Mrs. McCormick's General Store.* These barefoot boys are getting into trouble. Reformers advocated universal, compulsory schooling as one way to rid street corners of young mischief makers. Had these youngsters lived in the country, they probably would have been working in the fields.

Albertus del Orient Browere, *Mrs. McCormick's General Store,* 1844. Fenimore Art Museum, Cooperstown, NY (N-0387.55) ers who traveled from place to place—attracted hordes of adults regardless of their formal education. By the mid-1830s, approximately 3,000 local lecture associations, mostly in New England and the Midwest, were sponsoring such series. In addition, local agricultural fairs offered informal practical instruction to rural people.

Formal training for professionals such as physicians and lawyers also changed during this period. By the 1830s, almost all states required that doctors be licensed. The only way to attain such a license was to attend medical school, and these schools still excluded women. In regions of the country where medical schools appeared, the self-taught midwife gradually yielded to the formally educated male physician. In contrast, in rural communities of black and white Southerners, Native Americans, and Hispanics, women continued to practice time-honored ways of midwifery and healing.

Alternative Visions of Social Life

As in education, the crosscurrents of reform showed up clearly in debates about sexuality, the family, and the proper role of women. For example, reformer Sylvester Graham argued that even husbands and wives must monitor their sexual activity. Sexual excess between husband and wife, he claimed, caused ills ranging from headaches, chills, and impaired vision, to loss of memory, epilepsy, insanity, and "disorders of the liver and kidneys." Graham also promoted a diet of special crackers made of wheat flour (now called Graham crackers) and fruit (in place of alcohol and meat) in addition to a regimen of plain living reinforced with cold showers.

Other reformers disagreed with Graham's notion that people must repress their sexuality to lead a good and healthy life. Defying conventional standards of morality, sponsors of a number of experimental communities discouraged marriage-based monogamy (a legal commitment between a man and a woman to engage in sexual relations only with each other) and made child-rearing the responsibility of the entire community rather than just the child's parents. These communities were **communitarian**—seeking to break down exclusive relations between husband and wife, parent and child, employer and employee—in an effort to advance the well-being of the whole group, not just individuals within it. These communities were also **utopian**, seeking to forge new kinds of social relationships that would, in the eyes of the reformers, serve as a model for the larger society.

Many of these communities explicitly challenged mainstream views related to property ownership and the system of wage labor as well as rules governing relations between the sexes. The Scottish industrialist and socialist Robert Owen founded New Harmony in Indiana in 1825, basing his experiment on principles of "cooperative labor." In 1826 Owen released his "Declaration of Mental Independence," which condemned private property, organized religion, and marriage. By this time, 900 persons had joined the New Harmony order.

Several other prominent communitarian experiments that challenged conventional marital relations were vehemently criticized, and participants were sometimes physically attacked by their neighbors. Salt Lake City Mormons, who practiced plural marriage, continued to meet intense hostility from outsiders. Another group, the Oneida Community, founded in upstate New York near Utica in 1848 by John Humphrey Noyes, went even further than the Mormons in advocating an alternative to monogamy. At its peak, Oneida consisted of 300 members who endorsed the founder's notion of "complex marriage," meaning communal sexual unions and community-regulated parent-child relations. Charges of adultery eventually forced Noyes to flee the country and seek refuge in Canada.

> *The crosscurrents of reform showed up most clearly in debates about sexuality, the family, and the proper role of women.*

MAP

Utopian Communities before the Civil War

Network of Reformers

Many moral reforms overlapped with and reinforced each other. For example, women's rights advocates often supported temperance. Husbands who drank, they pointed out, were more likely to abuse their wives and children. Sarah and Angelina Grimké gained prominence as both abolitionists and advocates for women's rights. They also followed Sylvester Graham's program, and for a short time they sported "bloomers" (loose fitting pants, popularized by dress reformer Amelia Bloomer) in place of cumbersome dresses.

Dorothea Dix spearheaded a major reform effort that gained the support of a variety of politicians and activists. As a young woman, Dix had worked as a teacher and writer. In 1836 she visited England, where she met several prominent British reformers. Five years later she volunteered to teach a Sunday school class for women at an East Cambridge jail not far from Boston. Her first day there, in March 1841, changed her life—and the face of American antebellum reform—forever.

Dix found among the inmates not only women accused of prostitution and vagrancy, but also women who were clearly mentally ill. All of them were miserable, shivering in the cold. Dix was horrified that insane persons were imprisoned with criminals. She set out on a campaign to investigate the conditions under which the mentally ill were confined. Over the next 18 months, she investigated every prison, almshouse, and asylum in Massachusetts. She kept careful notes, which later formed the basis of her petitions, or "memorials," demanding better treatment for all insane persons. At one place she found people "confined…in *cages, closets, cellars, stalls, pens! Chained, naked, beaten with rods,* and *lashed* into obedience." Dix presented her findings to the Massachusetts state legislature. Heartened by the public outcry she had inspired, she widened her investigation to include the states of Rhode Island and New York. In the late 1840s, she traveled to another dozen states in the South, Mid-Atlantic, and Midwest.

The organized women's rights movement drew its greatest inspiration from the abolitionist cause. Elizabeth Cady Stanton, for example, and other American women attended the 1840 World Anti-Slavery Convention in London. Male leaders of the British and Foreign Anti-Slavery Society relegated the women delegates to a balcony and excluded them from the formal deliberations. Eight years later, Cady Stanton worked with Lucretia Mott, a Quaker minister, Susan B. Anthony, a women's rights activist, and other similarly inclined men and women to organize a women's rights convention at Seneca Falls, New York.

DOCUMENT

Trial of
Susan B. Anthony

Women's rights advocates made some progress independent of the abolitionist movement. For instance, in 1839 Mississippi passed the nation's first Married Women's Property Law. The ruling was intended to protect the fortunes of the married daughters of wealthy planters. In 1848 both New York and Pennsylvania passed legislation giving married women control over any real property (land) or personal property they brought to marriage.

Massachusetts resident Margaret Fuller explored many reform impulses of the day during her brief life (1810–1850). Educated in the classics by her father at home in Cambridge, in the 1830s she embraced a new intellectual sensibility called Transcendentalism. Fuller cultivated friendships with two other famous Transcendentalists living in the Boston area: Ralph Waldo Emerson and Henry David Thoreau. Transcendentalists believed in the primacy of the spirit and the essential harmony between people and the natural world. They took their inspiration from European Romantics, who celebrated the beauty of nature in art, music, and literature. In 1845 Fuller published *Woman in the Nineteenth Century*, one of the first feminist essays written by an American. "I would have Woman lay aside all thought, such as she habitually cherishes, of being led and taught by men," wrote Fuller. She then embraced the role of investigative journalist, writing about the plight of slaves, Indians, and imprisoned women for the New York *Tribune*.

The United States Extends Its Reach

Efforts to reform society at home went hand-in-hand with a determination to expand the nation's borders, especially in the Southwest. In the mid-1840s, the editor of the *New York Morning News* declared that the United States had a "manifest destiny" to "overspread the continent" and claim the "desert wastes." Those inhabiting the "desert wastes"—Mexican settlers and a variety of Indian groups—apparently would have little say in the matter.

The term *manifest destiny* soon became a catchall phrase, justifying American efforts not only to conquer new territory but also to seek out new markets for its goods across the oceans.

Global Trade

International political developments and technological innovations led to expanded opportunities for trading. In 1846 Britain repealed its exclusionary Corn Laws, which had protected its own agricultural markets from foreign competition. As a result, farmers in the U.S. Midwest had fresh incentive to produce wheat for export. The invention of the swift clipper ship, which ushered in "the golden age of American shipping," also helped in the expansion of global trade. Narrow-bodied vessels topped with large sails on towering masts, the new ships "clipped off" the miles. American merchants used them to import tea from China and wool from Australia. Investors from the eastern United States financed trading companies that sold antelope skins, beaver pelts, and cured beef to markets in Cuba and Europe.

Among all American exports to foreign countries, cotton was king, accounting for half of the total goods shipped after 1840. Southern planters and northern merchants alike made huge profits from the cotton trade. In 1840 English textile manufacturers depended on the fiber, and the American South produced about three-quarters of their supply. No wonder then that southern slave owners were eager to extend their land holdings into Texas. They were joined in that hope by residents of the western states, men such as former Tennessee politician Davy Crockett, hoping to press into the fresh lands of the far West and Southwest.

The Lone Star Republic

In the early 1830s, the Mexican government became alarmed by the growing number of American emigrants to Texas. Worried that the settlers would refuse to pledge allegiance to Mexico, that country closed the Texas border to further in-migration. By 1835 only one out of every eight residents of Texas was a *Tejano* (that is, a native Spanish speaker); the rest, numbering 30,000, hailed from the United States. The U.S.-born Texians, together with some prominent *Tejanos*, had become increasingly well armed and militant. They organized volunteer patrols to attack Indian settlements. These forces became the precursor of the Texas Rangers, a statewide organization of law enforcement officers.

> *In the early 1830s, the Mexican government became alarmed by the growing number of American emigrants to Texas.*

In 1836 the Texians decided to press for independence from Mexico. Only by becoming a separate nation, they believed, could they trade freely with the United States, establish their own schools, and collect and spend their own taxes. The pro-independence Texians included Davy Crockett, who had moved there in late 1835. A few months later, Crockett and other armed Texians retreated to a Spanish mission in San Antonio called the Alamo. In March 1836, a military force led by Antonio López de Santa Anna, president of the Republic of Mexico and a general in the army, battled them for thirteen days. All 187 Texians died at the hands of Santa Anna and his men; the Mexican leader lost 600 of his own troops. Historians disagree on whether all of the Alamo defenders died fighting or if some were executed by Mexican soldiers.

In April a force of Texians and their *Tejano* allies, including military leader Juan Seguin, surprised Santa Anna and his men at the San Jacinto River and killed another 600 of them. The victors captured Santa Anna and declared themselves a new nation. Sam Houston, former U.S. congressman from Tennessee and commander in chief of the Texian army, became president of the Republic of Texas (also called the Lone Star Republic) in 1837. Some *Tejanos* who objected to Mexican high-handedness joined in supporting the new republic, including Jose Antonio Navarro, Francisco Ruiz, and Lorenzo de Zavala, who became its vice president.

In the northern territories of Mexico, many Spanish speakers had long felt abandoned by the Mexican government, which had made no provisions for their self-government and, as in the case of Texas, inhibited trade relations with the United States. Although other Mexican provinces protested the way they were treated by the government, Texas was the only Mexican state to launch a successful rebellion against Mexico.

Texas's independence raised the fears of U.S. abolitionists and imperiled blacks living in the new republic. In contrast to Mexico, which had abolished slavery in 1829, Texas approved a constitution that not only legalized slavery but also prohibited free blacks from living in the country. Greenbury Logan, a black man who owned a farm near Austin, petitioned to stay. He wrote, "Every privilege dear to a free man is taken away." But **vigilantes** forced him to leave. They also forced out many *Tejanos*. Among them was Juan Seguin, who had helped defeat Santa Anna at the Battle of San Jacinto and was now the mayor of San Antonio. Not until 1981 did another *Tejano*, Henry Cisneros, hold the office of mayor of the city of San Antonio.

TABLE 12-3			
The Election of 1844			
Candidate	Political Party	Popular Vote (%)	Electoral Vote
James K. Polk	Democratic	49.6	170
Henry Clay	Whig	48.1	105
James G. Birney	Liberty	2.3	—

The Election of 1844

As an independent republic, Texas became a hotly contested political issue in the United States. During the election of 1844, politicians began to debate whether the United States should annex Texas. Van Buren was outspoken in his opposition to the idea. As a result, the frankly expansionist Democrats spurned the former president as a candidate and nominated James K. Polk of Tennessee. They called for the "reannexation" of Texas and the "reoccupation" of Oregon. Their rallying cry became "Fifty-Four Forty or Fight," a reference to their desire to own the area (expressed in terms of its longitude and latitude coordinates) claimed by the British in present-day Canada south of Alaska and west of the Continental Divide. Kentucky congressman Henry Clay received the Whig nomination after he announced he was against the **annexation** of Texas. But under pressure from Southerners, he later changed his mind, to the disgust of party leaders.

Neither the Democrats nor the Whigs had shown an interest in addressing the issue of slavery directly in the last presidential election. Yet in 1844, the controversy over the annexation of Texas made it impossible for the two parties to ignore the growing controversy over bound labor. Under the banner of the young Liberty party, some abolitionists charged that territorial expansion would mean the continued growth and prosperity of the slave system; they pointed to the public pronouncements of southern planters, who were outspoken in their desire to expand their slaveholdings into the fertile lands of Texas.

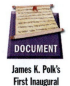

DOCUMENT

James K. Polk's
First Inaugural
Address

For their part, Democrats and Whigs believed, correctly, that most voters would ignore slavery when they cast their ballots. Thus members of both parties tried to silence both sides of the slavery debate. They turned a deaf ear to the proslavery advocates on one hand and squelched northern abolitionist opinion by ignoring petitions to Congress on the other. In the end, Polk won the election. The expansionists had elected one of their most ardent champions to the highest office in the land.

Still, Polk was not interested in going to war with Great Britain over the vast territory of Oregon. In 1846 the two countries reached a compromise. Britain would accept the 49th parallel as the border between Canada and the United States and retain the disputed islands off the coast of Vancouver. The United States settled for one-half of its original claim to Oregon. Thereafter, it was free to turn its full attention to extending its southern and western borders.

War with Mexico

VIDEO

Moving West and
the Mexican-
American War

Texian leaders wanted to become part of the United States. In 1845, as one of his last acts as president, Tyler invited Texas to become the twenty-eighth state. He also understood that annexing Texas was a way to goad Mexico into open hostilities; Mexico had warned the United States that such a move would mean war. A joint resolution of both houses of Congress confirmed Texas statehood in December 1845.

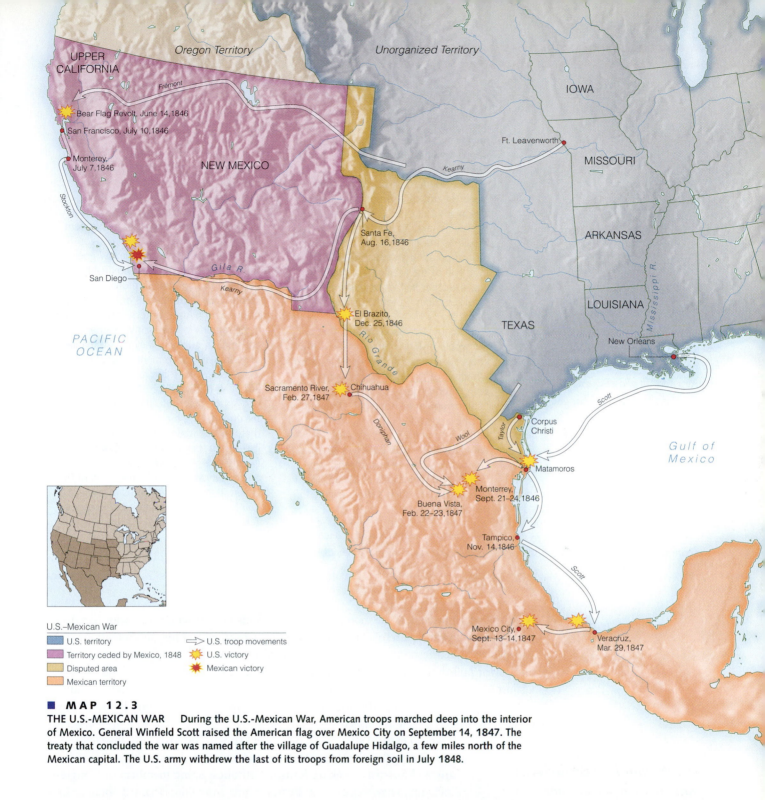

UPPER CALIFORNIA

Oregon Territory

Unorganized Territory

IOWA

Bear Flag Revolt, June 14, 1846

Frémont

San Francisco, July 10, 1846

Ft. Leavenworth

Monterey, July 7, 1846

NEW MEXICO

Kearny

MISSOURI

ARKANSAS

Stockton

Santa Fe, Aug. 16, 1846

Gila R.

Kearny

San Diego

El Brazito, Dec. 25, 1846

PACIFIC OCEAN

Rio Grande

TEXAS

LOUISIANA

Mississippi R.

New Orleans

Sacramento River, Feb. 27, 1847

Chihuahua

Doniphan

Wool

Taylor

Corpus Christi

Scott

Gulf of Mexico

Matamoros

Buena Vista, Feb. 22–23, 1847

Monterrey, Sept. 21–24, 1846

Tampico, Nov. 14, 1846

Scott

Mexico City, Sept. 13–14, 1847

Veracruz, Mar. 29, 1847

U.S.–Mexican War

- U.S. territory
- Territory ceded by Mexico, 1848
- Disputed area
- Mexican territory

⇨ U.S. troop movements
✴ U.S. victory
✴ Mexican victory

■ MAP 12.3

THE U.S.-MEXICAN WAR During the U.S.-Mexican War, American troops marched deep into the interior of Mexico. General Winfield Scott raised the American flag over Mexico City on September 14, 1847. The treaty that concluded the war was named after the village of Guadalupe Hidalgo, a few miles north of the Mexican capital. The U.S. army withdrew the last of its troops from foreign soil in July 1848.

The boundaries between Mexico and the new state of Texas remained in dispute. Mexico recognized the Nueces River as the boundary for Texas. In contrast, Texians and U.S. politicians envisioned the boundary a hundred miles to the south at the Rio Grande. Complicating matters further, the new president, James K. Polk, had sent an envoy, John Slidell, to purchase California and a disputed section of Texas from Mexico. Mexico refused the deal. Nevertheless, around this time, Polk wrote in his diary that if he could not acquire all of New Mexico and California through diplomatic negotiation, he was determined to obtain them by force. The stage was set for war.

Armed conflict broke out in January 1846. U.S. troops, under the command of General Zachary Taylor (a veteran of wars against Tecumseh, the Seminole, and Black Hawk), clashed

Senator John C. Calhoun Warns Against Incorporating Mexico into the United States

In January 1848, Senator John C. Calhoun delivered a speech, addressing his remarks to President Polk and to his fellow lawmakers. He urged them to resist calls to incorporate all of a conquered Mexico into the United States. Calhoun favored the spread of slavery into new territories. However, here he expresses the fear that residents of Mexico were incapable of becoming suitable U.S. citizens for "racial" reasons.

It is without example or precedent, either to hold Mexico as a province, or to incorporate her into our Union. No example of such a line of policy can be found. We have conquered many of the neighboring tribes of Indians, but we never thought of holding them in subjection—never of incorporating them into our Union. They have either been left as an independent people amongst us, or been driven into the forests.

I know further, sir, that we have never dreamt of incorporating into our Union any but the Caucasian race—the free white race. To incorporate Mexico, would be the first instance of the kind of incorporating an Indian race; for more than half of the Mexicans are Indians, and the other half is composed chiefly of mixed tribes. I protest such a union as that! . . .

Sir, it is a remarkable fact, that in the whole history of man, as far as my knowledge extends, there is no instance whatever of any civilized colored races being found equal to the establishment of free popular government, although by far the largest portion of the human family is composed of these races. . . . Are we to associate with ourselves as equals, companions, and fellow-citizens, the Indians and mixed race of Mexico? Sir, I should consider such a thing as fatal to our institutions.

Calhoun then moves on to another theme. He disputes the notion that Mexico can begin as a territory and then work its way up to statehood, following the standards Congress set for other western territories.

You can establish a Territorial Government for every State in Mexico, and there are some twenty of them. You can appoint governors, judges, and magistrates. You can give the people a subordinate government, allowing them to legislate for themselves, whilst you defray the cost. So far as the law goes, the thing is done. There is no analogy between this and our Territorial Governments. Our Territories are only an offset of our own people, or foreigners from the same regions from which we came. They are small in number. They are incapable of forming a government. It would be inconvenient for them to sustain a government, if it were formed; and they are very much obliged to the United States for undertaking the trouble, knowing that, on the attainment of their majority—when they come to manhood—at twenty-one—they will be introduced to an equality with all other members of the Union. It is entirely different with Mexico. You have no need of armies to keep your Territories in subjection. But when you incorporate Mexico, you must have powerful armies to keep them in subjection.

---

with a Mexican force near the mouth of the Rio Grande near Matamoros. Taylor had deliberately moved his troops across the Nueces River into disputed territory; his intention was to provoke an armed response from Mexico. A skirmish ensued, eleven Americans were killed, and Taylor pulled back. Polk used this military action as justification for a declaration of war against Mexico. The president declared, "American blood has been shed on American soil."

Not all Americans supported the war. Transcendentalists such as Henry David Thoreau objected to what they saw as a naked land grab. Refusing to pay taxes for what he considered a war to expand slavery, Thoreau went to jail. Nativists also objected to the war, fearing that the United States would have to assimilate thousands of Indians and Spanish-speaking Roman Catholics. Some members of Congress, including a newly elected U.S. Representative from Illinois named Abraham Lincoln, also condemned Polk's "act of aggression."

Predictably, opponents of slavery were among Polk's most outspoken critics. Soon after the outbreak of war, Representative David Wilmot of Pennsylvania attached an amendment to a bill appropriating money for the war. Called the Wilmot Proviso, the measure declared that "neither slavery nor involuntary servitude shall ever exist" in territories the United States acquired from Mexico. Though a member of the Democratic party, Wilmot spoke primarily as a white Northerner; he wanted to preserve the West for "the sons of toil of my own race and color." Wilmot's views show how racial prejudice and antislavery sentiment coexisted in the minds of many white Northerners. The House approved the proviso, but the Senate did not. Southern Democrats claimed that Congress had no right to deprive slaveholders of their private property anywhere in the nation.

> **The Wilmot Proviso declared that "neither slavery nor involuntary servitude shall ever exist" in territories the United States acquired from Mexico.**

DOCUMENT

Corwin, "Against the Mexican War"

Portrait of John C. Calhoun by Charles Bird King, c. 1818–1825.

You may call it annexation, but it is a forced annexation, which is a contradiction in terms, according to my conception. You will be involved, in one word, in all the evils which I attribute to holding Mexico as a province. In fact, it will be but a Provincial Government, under the name of a Territorial Government. How long will that last? How long will it be before Mexico will be capable of incorpo- ration into our Union? Why, if we judge from the examples before us, it will be a very long time. Ireland has been held in subjection by England for seven or eight hundred years, and yet still remains hostile, although her people are of kindred race with the conquerors. A few French Canadians on this continent yet maintain the attitude of hostile people; and never will the time come, in my opinion, Mr. President, that these Mexicans will be reconciled to your authority. . . . Of all nations of the earth they are the most pertinacious—have the highest sense of nationality—hold out the longest, and often even with the least prospect of effecting their object. On this subject also I have conversed with officers of the army, and they all entertain the same opinion, that these people are now hostile, and will continue so. . . .

We make a great mistake, sir, when we suppose that all people are capable of self-government. We are anxious to force free government on all; and I see that it has been urged in a very respectable quarter, that it is the mission of this country to spread civil and religious liberty over all the world, and especially this continent. It is a great mistake. None but people advanced to a very high state of moral and intellec- tual improvement are capable, in a civilized state, of maintaining free government; and amongst those who are so purified, very few, indeed, have had the good fortune of forming a constitution capable of endurance.

Calhoun also warns that "these twenty-odd Mexican States" would eventually have power in Congress. He asks his listeners whether they would want their own states "governed by" these peoples.

Questions

1. *Why does Calhoun assume that, if the United States incorporates Mexico into its territory, the federal government "must have powerful armies to keep them [Mexicans] in subjection"?*
2. *How might Calhoun's more extreme expansionist colleagues—those in favor of seizing all of Mexico—have countered his arguments against such action?* ■

Source: Clyde A. Milner, ed., *Major Problems in the History of the American West: Documents and Essays* (1989), pp. 219–221.

Meanwhile, Polk launched a three-pronged campaign against Mexico. He sent Taylor into northern Mexico and ordered General Stephen Watts Kearny into New Mexico and then into California. Following the third directive of the campaign, General in Chief of the U.S. Army Winfield Scott coordinated an **amphibious landing** of 10,000 soldiers at Vera Cruz, on the Gulf of Mexico coast. Mexican forces tried to defend their homeland using guerrilla tactics. But U.S. soldiers overcame them in part by terrorizing civilians. Scott acknowledged that the men under his command had "committed atrocities to make Heaven weep and every American of Christian morals blush for his country. . . . Murder, robbery and rape of mothers and daughters in the presence of tied-up males of the families."

In September 1847, Mexico City surrendered, and the war ended. Mexico had been in no shape to resist superior U.S. firepower. The United States paid for Scott's victory with 13,000 lives and $100 million. The Mexicans lost 20,000 lives. In the Treaty of Guadalupe Hidalgo (approved by the Senate in 1848) Mexico agreed to give up its claims to Texas. The United States gained all of Texas and half of the territory of Mexico: the area west of Texas, comprising present-day New Mexico, Arizona, Utah, Nevada, and California. Male residents of areas formerly held by Mexico were given one year to decide whether to stay in the United States and become citizens or return to Mexico. They were also entitled to retain their titles to the land, a provision that proved difficult to enforce in the face of European American land hunger.

The U.S. government paid Mexico $18,250,000. Of that amount, $15 million was designated as payment for land lost; the rest was **restitution** to U.S. citizens who might bring claims against Mexico for damaged or destroyed property during the war. Americans had conflicting views of

Mexican-American War, 1846–1848

■ This painting shows the U.S. Navy going up the Tuxpan River in Mexico during the U.S.-Mexican War. Located on the Gulf Coast halfway between Vera Cruz and Tampico, Tuxpan was the last significant Mexican port to be seized by U.S. forces by the spring of 1847. Commodore M. C. Perry assembled a formidable force of marines and infantry to take over the town on April 19, 1847.

the treaty. Abolitionists saw it as a blood-drenched gift from American taxpayers to slaveholders. Others argued that Polk had squandered a rare opportunity to seize all of Mexico.

Conclusion

In the 1830s and 1840s, mass population movements affected almost every aspect of American life. Immigrants from western Europe helped to swell the nation's labor force in midwestern farming communities and eastern cities. The arrival of the Roman Catholic Irish provoked a backlash among native-born Protestants and spawned a nativist political movement. Reformers in the United States and Europe went back and forth across the Atlantic, exchanging ideas related to women's rights, abolition, and utopian communities. As European Americans pushed the boundaries of the country west and south, they clashed with Indians and with foreign powers that claimed those lands as their own. Thus migration and immigration had profound consequences for American politics, ideas, society, and economics.

Most striking was the restlessness among land-hungry slave owners and antislavery forces alike. The war with Mexico in general and the clash over the Wilmot Proviso in particular opened a new chapter in the debate over slavery. In considering the proviso, congressmen gave up their party loyalties as Democrats or Whigs and began to think of themselves as Southerners and Northerners. When Wilmot proclaimed that he wanted to preserve the West for his "own color," he revealed that even antislavery Northerners did not necessarily embrace black people as equals. When Southerners indicated that even the vast expanse of Texas would not satisfy their desire for land, they revealed that the conflict over slavery was far from over. In fact, that conflict was about to enter a new and ominous stage.

Sites to Visit

The American Whig Party, 1834–1856
odur.let.rug.nl/~usa/E/uswhig/whigsxx.htm
> This site explores the rise and fall of the anti-Jackson Whig party.

Alexis de Tocqueville Tour: Exploring Democracy in America
www.tocqueville.org/
> Text and images are part of this companion site to C-SPAN's programming on Tocqueville.

America's First Look into the Camera: Daguerreotype Portraits and Views, 1839–1864
memory.loc.gov/ammem/daghtml/daghome.html
> The Library of Congress's daguerreotype collection consists of more than 650 photographs from the 1839–1864 period. The collection includes portraits, architectural views, and some street scenes.

Influence of Prominent Abolitionists
www.loc.gov/exhibits/african/afam006.html
> This Library of Congress exhibit includes pictures and text related to abolitionists.

Western Trails Project
http://skyways.lib.ks.us/KSL/trails/
> This site provides primary sources and images related to the Oregon Trail and other trails and European Americans' early movement westward.

Mountain Men and the Fur Trade
www.xmission.com/~drudy/amm.html
> This site includes private correspondence from early settlers in the area west of the Mississippi River.

Exploring *Amistad*
amistad.mysticseaport.org/main/welcome.html
> The Mystic Seaport Museum in Mystic, Connecticut, maintains this site, which includes collections of historical documents related to the slave revolt aboard the *Amistad* and the trial that followed.

Native Americans
www.americanwest.com/pages/nathome.htm
> A collection of links to homepages of Native American nations.

American Presidency: A Glorious Burden
americanhistory.si.edu/presidency/index.html
> The Smithsonian Institution maintains this site on American presidents.

"Been Here So Long": Selections from the WPA American Slave Narratives
newdeal.feri.org/asn/index.htm
> A site devoted to the interviews of former slaves conducted in the late 1930s.

The U.S.-Mexican War, 1846–1848
www.pbs.org/Kera/usmexicanwar/
> This bilingual site explores the causes, course, and outcome of the Mexican-American War.

For Further Reading

General

Michael Holt, *The Rise and Fall of the American Whig Party: Jacksonian Politics and the Onset of the Civil War* (1999).

Mary P. Ryan, *The Cradle of the Middle Class: The Family in Oneida County, New York, 1790–1865* (1983).

Charles G. Sellers, *The Market Revolution: Jacksonian America, 1815–1846* (1991).

David J. Weber, *The Spanish Frontier in North America* (1992).

Mass Migrations

John Ehle, *Trail of Tears: The Rise and Fall of the Cherokee Nation* (1988).

John Mack Faragher, *Women and Men on the Overland Trail* (1979).

Walter Johnson, *Soul by Soul: The Inside of the Antebellum Slave Market* (1999).

Philip J. Schwarz, *Migrants Against Slavery: Virginians and the Nation* (2001).

A Multitude of Voices in the National Political Arena

Donald B. Cole, *Martin Van Buren and the American Political System* (1984).

Paul A. Gilje, *The Road to Mobocracy: Popular Disorder in New York City, 1763–1834* (1987).

Daniel Walker Howe, *The Political Culture of the American Whigs* (1979).

David R. Roediger, *The Wages of Whiteness: Race and the Making of the American Working Class* (rev. ed., 1999).

Reform Impulses

Charles Capper, *Margaret Fuller: An American Romantic Life* (1992).

Carl Kaestle, *Pillars of the Republic: Common Schools and American Society, 1780–1860* (1983).

Henry Mayer, *All on Fire: William Lloyd Garrison and the Abolition of Slavery* (1998).

Shirley J. Yee, *Black Women Abolitionists: A Study in Activism, 1828–1860* (1992).

The United States Extends Its Reach

Arnoldo De León, *The Tejano Community, 1836–1900* (1982).

Richard Griswold Del Castillo, *The Treaty of Guadalupe Hidalgo: A Legacy of Conflict* (1990).

David Alan Johnson, *Founding the Far West: California, Oregon, and Nevada, 1840–1890* (1992).

Paul D. Lack, *The Texas Revolutionary Experience: A Political and Social History, 1835–1836* (1992).

For quizzes and other resources on these topics, go to www.longmanamericanhistory.com.

PART FIVE

Disunion
and Reunion

THE CIVIL WAR WAS THE COUNTRY'S GREATEST POLITICAL AND MORAL crisis. By 1860 the two-party system could no longer contain the dispute between proslavery and antislavery forces. That dispute centered on the fate of slavery in new western territories. Tensions accompanied large-scale migration to the west, and the 1849 Gold Rush pushed California—and the issue of slavery there—to the forefront of the nation's attention. Several dramatic developments—the secession of southern states from the Union, the formation of the Confederate States of America, and a Confederate attack on a federal fort in Charleston Harbor—precipitated all-out war. In the spring of 1861, few people could have anticipated that the conflict would drag on for four long years and claim more than 600,000 lives.

The Second Party system, based on divisions between Whigs and Democrats, unraveled in the 1850s. Both parties represented coalitions of groups that expressed cultural, not sectional, sensibilities. Yet a series of events led to a **realignment** of parties into northern and southern camps. Many Northerners chafed under the Fugitive Slave Act of 1850, which required that all citizens assist law enforcement agents in retrieving runaway slaves for their owners. The founding of the Republican party in 1854 gave a political voice to Northerners hoping to preserve the western territories for family farmers who would not have to compete for land and labor with large slaveholders. In 1857 the Supreme Court ruled that black people had no rights that any court was bound to respect. Violent conflicts between proslavery and antislavery forces in Kansas and a failed raid by abolitionists on Harpers Ferry, Virginia, in 1859 revealed that legislators' resolutions and maneuverings were insufficient to stave off bloodshed.

In pursuing a militant nationalism, Confederates hoped to compensate for their relative weakness in terms of population and industrial capacity compared with the North. They believed that they could use a large, docile black labor force to grow food and serve as a support system for the army. They anticipated that European nations, dependent on southern cotton, would extend them diplomatic recognition and that white civilians would rally to the defense of their homeland no matter what the price in money or blood. Confederates also believed that western Indians would gladly assist them in their cause against a hated U.S. army and that brilliant southern generals could indefinitely outstrategize a huge, lumbering invading army. On all these counts they miscalculated, but their miscalculations were revealed gradually.

During the war, white Southerners had to contend with two major unanticipated consequences of the conflict. First, war mobilization efforts across the South required the centralization of government and economic policymaking. Principled states' rights supporters opposed these efforts. Second, slaves and free blacks alike proved traitorous to the Confederate cause. In myriad ways—running away from their owners and spying for the enemy, slowing their work pace in the fields, and fighting for the Union army—black people served as combatants in the war. They fought for their families and their freedom and for a country that would grant them full citizenship rights. In the North, only in late 1862 did President Abraham Lincoln announce that the United States aimed to destroy slavery, but violent antidraft, antiblack riots in several cities showed that the northern population was deeply divided over emancipation.

Soon after the end of the war and Lincoln's death, in April 1865, congressional Republicans began to challenge President Andrew Johnson's plan for reconstructing the South; they considered it too lenient toward the former Confederate states. In 1867 these political leaders had enough votes to enact their own plan, calling for the enfranchisement of black men in the South, the reorganization of southern state governments under leadership loyal to the Union, and the enactment of a labor contract system between southern landowners and black laborers.

Members of the Republican party backed a strong Union, a federal system in which the central government would ensure that individual men could pursue their own self-interest in the marketplace of goods and ideas. Yet the Civil War era exposed the limits of the Republican vision. The Plains Indians sought not citizenship but freedom from federal interference. Women and working people challenged various components of the Republican ideal, with its emphasis on unbridled individualism and federal subsidies of business. African Americans aspired to own property, vote, and send their children to school, just as other nineteenth-century Americans did. They wanted to farm their own land and care for their own families free from white intrusion. Yet congressional Republicans did not enact large-scale land redistribution programs; most thought that once the rebels were subdued and slavery abolished, their duty was done.

Civil strife persisted into the postwar period. Union generals turned from quelling the southern rebellion to putting down armed resistance among the Plains Indians. Former rebels formed vigilante groups to attack black voters and their allies in the South. By the early 1870s, most Northerners had lost interest in the welfare of the former slaves and acquiesced as former Confederates reclaimed state governments. The last occupying forces withdrew from the South in 1877. In welding the country together as a single economic and political unit, the Republicans had triumphed. However, white Southerners retained control over their local social and political affairs. The revolution to secure African American civil rights was stalled for nearly 100 years.

1864	Fort Pillow massacre of African American (Union) soldiers Sand Creek (Colorado) massacre Sherman's march to the sea
1865	Freedmen's Bureau is formed Confederacy is defeated Lincoln is assassinated; Andrew Johnson becomes president Thirteenth Amendment is ratified
1866	Civil Rights Act of 1866 National Labor Union is founded Equal Rights Association is founded Ku Klux Klan is organized Congress approves Fourteenth Amendment
1867	National Grange is founded United States purchases Alaska from Russia Reconstruction Act of 1867
1868	Johnson is impeached and acquitted U.S.-China Burlingame Treaty Colored Labor Union is founded Fourteenth Amendment is ratified
1869	Congress approves Fifteenth Amendment Transcontinental Railroad is completed National Woman Suffrage Association and American Woman Suffrage Association are formed Knights of Labor is founded
1870	Fifteenth Amendment is ratified
1871	Ku Klux Klan Act
1872	Apex Mining Act of 1872 Congress creates Yellowstone National Park Susan B. Anthony attempts to vote Crédit Moblier scandal
1873	Timber Culture Act Onset of depression
1874	Freedman's Savings Bank fails
1875	Civil Rights Act Resumption Act Whiskey Ring is exposed
1876	Battle of Little Big Horn Contested presidential election between Rutherford B. Hayes and Samuel J. Tilden
1877	Compromise of 1877 California Workingmen's party is formed Great Railroad Strike

The Crisis over Slavery, 1848–1860

O N JANUARY 24, 1848, HENRY WILLIAM BIGLER TOOK A BREAK FROM BUILDING A SAWMILL FOR JOHN Sutter in California's Sacramento Valley and penned in his pocket diary, "This day some kind of mettle was found . . . that looks like goald."

GOLD! News of the discovery at Sutter's mill spread like wildfire. Immigrants from all over the world and migrants from all over the United States began to pour into the foothills of the Sierra Nevada Mountains in 1849. Dubbed "the Forty-Niners," they journeyed westward across the mountains, from the **tenements** of New York City and the great plantations of Mississippi; north from Mexico; and over the oceans, from western Europe, China, and South America. Equipping themselves with simple mining tools, the Forty-Niners began to dig for buried treasure, determined to stake a claim and make a fortune.

During the Gold Rush years of 1848 to 1859, various cultural groups were thrown in close proximity to each other. People from Belgium, France, Germany, Scotland, Chile, and Long Island learned to appreciate flour and corn tortillas (*tortillas de harina* and *tortillas de maiz*) and beef cooked in chile, staples of the Mexican diet. The disproportionate number of men permitted small numbers of women to challenge European American gender conventions. A gold miner might take a break from washing his clothes, straighten his aching back, and watch a Mexican woman and her daughter, well mounted on their horses, rounding up a herd of near-wild cattle. An-Choi, a Chinese immigrant woman, earned a tidy sum by opening a brothel that catered to gold miners. Biddy Mason, an enslaved woman, successfully sued for her freedom and became the first African American homesteader in Los Angeles.

■ Chinese and European American miners pan for gold in the Auburn Ravine in California in 1852.

California became part of the United States as a result of the U.S.-Mexican War. In the 1848 Treaty of Guadalupe Hidalgo, Mexico agreed to hand over territory stretching from Texas northwest to California. As a result, the United States obtained a vast expanse of land—almost 530,000 square miles—called the Mexican Cession. In addition to the land, the nation added to its population large numbers of men, women, and children already living in the area—13,000 Spanish speakers and 100,000 Indians (all former Mexican citizens) in California alone. After 1848 many new settlers streamed into California, and the migrants pressed for statehood. The Gold Rush exacerbated tensions over slavery, pushing the nation down the road toward the Civil War.

California became a state in 1850, but only after a bitter Congressional debate over the extension of slavery. The resulting Compromise of 1850 included several provisions bearing on the issue of slavery: California would be admitted as a free state; slave-trading would be outlawed in the District of Columbia; carved out of the Mexican Cession, the Utah and New Mexico territories could decide for themselves whether or not to legalize slavery. Finally, a new, harsh, fugitive slave law provided for the capture and return of slaves who found their way to free states in the North or West, including California. Though called a compromise, in fact these provisions inflamed the passions on both sides of the slavery debate—abolitionists in the North and slave owners in the South.

Despite California's status as a free state, the principle of free labor was often violated. In 1850 the state enacted a law that provided for the indenture or apprenticeship of Indian children to white men for indeterminate periods of time. The law also allowed for the hiring out, to the highest bidder, of adult Indians deemed guilty of **vagrancy**.

California's Fugitive Slave Law of 1852 decreed that, regardless of his or her current status, a black person who entered the state as a slave and thereafter attempted to remain on free soil was a fugitive slave. That year, three African American gold miners, Robert Perkins, Carter Perkins, and Sandy Perkins, all former slaves who had been freed by their owner, were arrested under the law and ordered re-enslaved in their native Mississippi.

Other California labor systems revealed that the principle of free labor was not carried out in practice. Chinese immigrants to California entered the country organized in companies, or district associations, indebted to merchants for their transportation and bound to work for an employer until the debt was repaid. Fearing competition from cheap labor, alarmed European Americans labeled these Asian workers "coolies" (i.e., enslaved laborers). By 1852 the Chinese in California (almost all of them men) had been pushed out of mining as a result of the discriminatory Foreign Miners Tax, a measure leveled with special force against both Chinese and Mexican miners. Although the Treaty of Guadalupe Hidalgo guaranteed U.S. citizenship rights to Mexicans, those rights were not enforced under the law. Many Mexicans found themselves vulnerable to violence and land **dispossession** perpetrated by the growing European American majority.

Continued European American migration into the Midwest, the Great Plains, and the Southwest intensified conflicts over land with Native Americans and Latinos. Rapid population growth, the coming together of many different cultures, and dramatic economic changes all fueled the conflict over slavery. All over the nation, Americans gradually united around a radical proposition: whether human beings could be held as private property was an issue on which there could be no compromise.

Regional Economies and Conflicts

It is tempting to view the decade of the 1850s with an eye toward the impending firestorm of 1861. However, in the early 1850s, few Americans could have anticipated the Civil War. At midcentury, the United States was going through a period of rapid transition. New developments such as railroads, the factory system, and more efficient farm equipment led to significant changes in regional economies and began to give shape to an emerging national economy. Migration into the Midwest accelerated. Slavery shaped life in the South, though most

MAP

United States
Territorial
Expansion in
the 1850s

white southerners were not plantation owners. Annexation of land in the Southwest and West and the conquest of Indians on the Plains produced wrenching social upheavals for Native Americans in those regions. Meanwhile, Americans continued to wrestle with the role of slavery in this rapidly changing society, while a free labor ideology grew stronger in the North.

Native American Economies Transformed

On the Plains, Indians confronted wrenching transformations in their way of life. Forced to relocate from the Southeast to Indian Territory (present-day Oklahoma), the Five Southern ("Civilized") Tribes, the Cherokee, Choctaw, Creek, Chickasaw, and Seminole, grappled with the task of rebuilding their political institutions. By the 1850s, the Cherokee had established a new capital at Talequah, along with public schools. They published a Cherokee newspaper (the *Advocate*) and created a flourishing print culture in their own language.

To the north and west of Indian Territory, Plains Indian tribes such as the Sioux, Kiowa, and Arapaho exploited the horse, which had been introduced by Europeans in the Southwest in the seventeenth century. By raiding, trading, and breeding, these groups increased their stock of horses, which they used to hunt bison and transport their lodges and food from site to site. With abundant food and the means to trade with whites, these groups prospered for a brief period in the mid-nineteenth century. Their beadwork and animal-skin painting exemplified the artistic vitality of their cultures.

In the 1850s, U.S. officials negotiated treaties with various Plains Indian groups to enable European Americans to move west without fear of attack. Most settlers were bent on heading straight for California or the Northwest, traversing the Plains, which they called the Great American Desert in the mistaken belief that the absence of trees there demonstrated the infertility of the soil. The Fort Laramie Treaty of 1851 and the Treaty of Fort Atkinson three years later provided that the government could build roads and establish forts along western trails and that, in return, Indians would be compensated with supplies and food for their loss of hunting rights in the region. A young Cheyenne woman, Iron Teeth, recalled "the government presents" to her people in these terms: "We were given beef, but we did not care for this kind of meat. Great piles of bacon were stacked upon the prairies and distributed to us, but we used it only to make fires or to grease robes for tanning." She and her family sought out other items from government trading posts: "brass kettles, coffee-pots, curve-bladed butcher knives, boxes of black and white thread."

Land Conflicts in the Southwest

To the Southwest, the United States had gained control over a vast expanse of land, provoking legal and political conflicts over the rights and labor of the people who lived there, both natives and newcomers. Under the terms of the Treaty of Guadalupe Hidalgo, Mexico **ceded** not only California but also the province of New Mexico, territory that included the present-day states of New Mexico, Arizona, Utah, Nevada, and western Colorado. In 1853 the United States bought an additional tract of land from Mexico, 55,000 acres located in the area south of the Gila River (in present-day New Mexico and Arizona). Overseen by the U.S. secretary of war, a Mississippi planter named Jefferson Davis, the agreement was called the Gadsden Purchase (after James Gadsden, a railroad promoter and one of the American negotiators).

In Texas newly arrived European Americans battled native *Tejanos* (people of Mexican origin or descent) for political and economic supremacy. White migrants from the southern United States brought their slaves with them to the region, claiming that the institution of slavery was crucial for commercial development. German immigrants came to central and east Texas, founding towns with German names such as Fredericksburg, Weimar, and Schulenburg. During the 1850s, **commercial farming** continued to replace **subsistence homesteading** as the

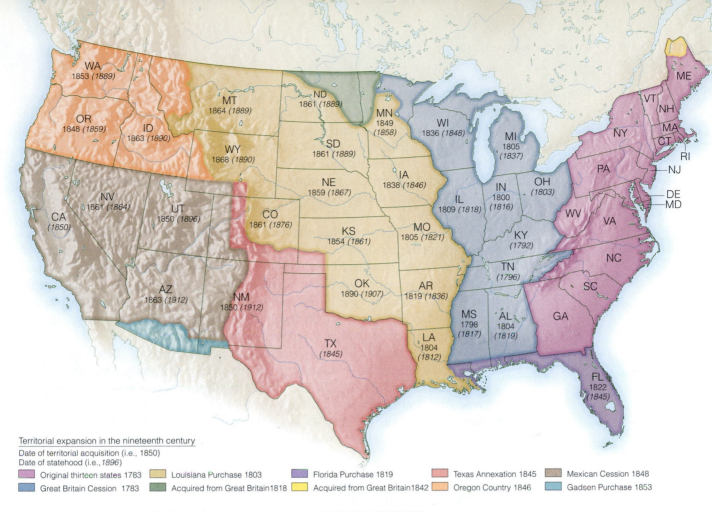

Territorial expansion in the nineteenth century

Date of territorial acquisition (i.e., 1850)
Date of statehood (i.e., 1896)

■ Original thirteen states 1783	■ Louisiana Purchase 1803	■ Florida Purchase 1819
■ Great Britain Cession 1783	■ Acquired from Great Britain 1818	■ Acquired from Great Britain 1842

■ Texas Annexation 1845	■ Mexican Cession 1848
■ Oregon Country 1846	■ Gadsden Purchase 1853

▲ **MAP 13.1 TERRITORIAL EXPANSION IN THE NINETEENTH CENTURY**
As a result of the Mexican War (1846–1848), the United States won the territory west of Texas by conquest. In 1853, James Gadsden, U.S. ambassador to Mexico, received congressional approval to pay Mexico $15 million for 55,000 square miles in present-day southern Arizona and New Mexico. That year marked the end of U.S. continental expansion.

cattle industry spread and the railroads penetrated the region. Although European Americans monopolized the courts and regional political institutions, *Tejanos* retained cultural influence throughout Texas, dominating the cuisine and styles of music and architecture.

Some Spanish-speaking residents in the Southwest reacted forcefully when U.S. courts disregarded the land titles held by *Californios* and *Tejanos*. In the early 1850s, California authorities battled Mexican social bandits such as Joaquin Murrieta, who, with his men, raided European American settlements. Murrieta and others argued that they were justified in stealing from privileged European Americans who, they claimed, disregarded the lives and property of Mexicans. In 1859 in the Rio Grande Valley of Texas, tensions between the *Tejano* majority and groups of European American law enforcement officers known as the Texas Rangers erupted into full-scale warfare. Juan Cortina, who had fought on the side of Mexico during the Mexican War, orchestrated attacks on European Americans and their property in the vicinity of Brownsville. U.S. retaliation led to Cortina's War, pitting the Mexican leader against a young U.S. colonel, Robert E. Lee. Cortina became a hero to *Tejanos*. "You have been robbed of your property, incarcerated, chased, murdered, and hunted like wild beasts," he declared, "to me is entrusted the work of breaking the chains of your slavery."

Ethnic and Economic Diversity in the Midwest

Migrants to the Midwest in these years encountered less resistance. The Yankee Strip (named for the northeasterners who migrated there) ran through northern Ohio, Indiana, and Illinois and encompassed the entire states of Michigan, Wisconsin, and Minnesota. Here migrants from New England settled and established public schools and Congregational churches. Immigrants from western Europe also made a home in this region—the Germans, Belgians, and Swiss in Wisconsin, the Scandinavians in Minnesota. At times cultural conflict wracked even the smallest rural settlements. In some Wisconsin villages, equally matched numbers of Yankees and Germans contended for control over the local public schools, with the group in power posting notices for school board elections in its own language, hoping that its rivals would not show up at the polls.

The lower Midwest, including the southern portions of Ohio, Indiana, and Illinois, retained strong cultural ties to the southern states, from which many settlers had migrated. Though residing in free states, they maintained broad support for the institution of slavery. In some cases, they outnumbered their Yankee counterparts and managed to shape the legal system in a way that reflected a distinct antiblack bias. For example, Indiana's state constitution, approved in 1851, prohibited black migrants from making contracts with whites, testifying in trials that involved whites, voting, and entering the state.

Most rural midwestern households followed the seasonal rhythms characteristic of traditional systems of agriculture. However, by the mid-nineteenth century, family farming had become dependent on expensive machinery and hostage to the national and international grain markets. John Deere's steel plow (invented in 1837) and Cyrus McCormick's horse-drawn mechanical reaper (patented in 1854) boosted levels of grain production. Improved agricultural efficiency meant that the Midwest, both upper and lower, was fast becoming the breadbasket of the nation.

Regional Economies of the South

Like the Midwest, the South at midcentury had its own diversity. The South Atlantic states encompassed a number of regional economies. Bolstered by the high price of cotton on the world market, slave plantations prospered in the Black Belt, a wide swath of fertile soil stretching west from Georgia. In many areas of the South, planters concentrated their money and energy on cotton, diverting slaves from nonagricultural labor to toil in the fields. During the 1850s, enslaved Virginia sawmill laborers, South Carolina skilled artisans, and Georgia textile mill operatives all found themselves reduced to the status of cotton hands. In some cases, white laborers took their places in mills and workshops. In other parts of the South, slaves combined field work with nonagricultural work.

Increasingly, northern critics described the South as a land of economic extremes, with wealthy planters enjoying their white-columned mansions while degraded blacks slaved obediently in the fields. The reality was more complicated. Even among whites, there were huge variations in material conditions and daily experiences. A large amount of wealth in land and slaves was concentrated among a small percentage of the white population, and many non-slaveholding whites were **tenant farmers**, leasing their land, mules, and implements from wealthy planters. In some areas, as many as one of five farms was operated by tenant farmers.

At the same time, about half the total southern white population consisted of **yeoman** farmers, families that owned an average of 50 acres and produced most of what they consumed themselves, with the occasional help of a hired hand (a leased slave or a wage-earning white person). In upcountry Georgia and South Carolina, yeoman farmers maintained local economies that were little affected by the cotton culture of the great planters in the Black Belt. These families grew what they needed: corn for themselves and their livestock and small amounts of cotton that the women spun, wove, and then sewed into clothing. Men and women alike labored in neighborhood networks of exchange, trading farm produce such as milk and eggs for services such as shoemaking and blacksmithing.

The institution of slavery discouraged immigrants from moving to the rural South in large numbers. German artisans realized that slave labor would undercut their own wages, and Scandinavian farmers understood that they could not compete with large planters in terms of landowning or slave owning. However, the ethnic diversity of southern port cities offered a striking contrast to the countryside, where native-born Protestants predominated. In 1860, 54 percent of all skilled workers and 69 percent of unskilled workers in Mobile, Alabama, were immigrants.

Throughout the slave states, black people continued to challenge the underpinnings of white supremacy. On the back roads of the plantation counties, late at night, poor workers of both races colluded to deprive the planter elite of their ill-gotten gain. Slaves swapped hams pilfered from smokehouses and bags of cotton lifted from storehouses for cash and goods offered by landless whites.

Southern blacks were a diverse group. In the cities, planters allowed highly skilled slaves to hire themselves out and keep part of the money they earned for themselves. In their pride of craft and in their relative freedom to come and go as they pleased, these people inhabited a world that was neither completely slave nor completely free. Located primarily in the upper South and in the largest towns, communities composed of free people of color supported churches and clandestine schools, mocking the white notion that all black people possessed a childlike temperament and were incapable of caring for themselves.

A Free Labor Ideology in the North

In reaction to the southern slave system, the rural areas of the Northeast and Mid-Atlantic spawned a potent **free labor ideology**, which held that workers should reap what they sow, unfettered by legal systems of slavery and indentured servitude. Free labor advocates glorified the family farmer, the sturdy landowner of modest means, the husband and father who labored according to the dictates of the season and owed his soul— and his vote and the land he tilled—to no master. Nevertheless, the reality that sustained this ideal was eroding in the North during the 1850s.

More and more Northerners were earning wages by working for bosses, rather than tilling their own land. Faced with competition from Midwestern farmers and burdened by unfavorable growing conditions imposed by rocky soil and a long winter, New Englanders were migrating to nearby towns and mill villages and to the West. By 1860 the region's textile and shoemaking industries were largely mechanized. From New Hampshire to Rhode Island, growing numbers of water-powered factories perched along the **fall line**, where rivers spilled swiftly out of the foothills and into the coastal plain. The all-white factory workforce included men and women, adults and children, Irish Catholics and native-born Protestants, failed farmers and young men and women eager to leave the uncertain, hardscrabble life of the countryside for the promise of the mill towns and the seaport cities.

Although Northerners in general contrasted themselves to the "backward slave South," their region of the country retained elements of unfree labor systems. New Jersey did not officially emancipate the last of its slaves until 1846, and throughout the North, vestiges of slavery lingered through the mid-nineteenth century. As a group of disproportionately poor people, blacks in New England, the Mid-Atlantic, and the Midwest were vulnerable to labor exploitation, including indentured servitude and a system of "apprenticeship" whereby black children were taken from their parents and forced to work for whites.

Many nonslave workers did not receive pay for their labors. As is the case today, wives and mothers throughout the country performed almost all of their work in the home without monetary compensation, although the measure of a white man was rendered

■ Maine textile workers, with their shuttles, pose for a formal portrait around 1860. Although women factory workers developed a collective identity distinct from that of middle-class wives, most young, native-born women eventually married and withdrew from the paid labor force. Many male factory workers were skeptical that women could or should play an effective role in labor organizations such as unions. Nevertheless, women workers in a number of industries, including textiles and shoes, formed labor organizations in the antebellum period.

more and more in cash terms. On farms and in textile mills such as those of Pawtucket, Rhode Island, children played a key role in the livelihood of individual households but received little or nothing in cash wages. Some members of the white working classes began to condemn "**wage slavery**," a system that deprived them of what they considered a fair reward for their labors and left them at the mercy of merchant capitalists and factory bosses. These workers charged that they were paid so little by employers that their plight was similar to that of black slaves in the South.

Different regions developed specialized economies. In turn, these regions relied on each other for the production of staple crops and manufactured goods. The result was a national economy. Southern slaves produced the cotton processed in New England textile mills. Midwestern farmers grew the grain that fed eastern consumers. California Forty-Niners discovered the gold that expanded the national currency supply. Yet these patterns of economic interdependence were insufficient to resolve the persistent political question: Which groups of people are entitled to American citizenship, with all the rights and privileges that the term implies?

Individualism vs. Group Identity

In every region of the country, discriminatory ideas and practices increasingly exerted force. People were defined ever more strongly on the basis of their nationality, language, religion, and skin color. They were more and more limited in their legal status and the

George Caleb Bingham, Raftsmen Playing Cards, 1847. Saint Louis Art Museum, Ezra H. Linley Fund

■ Just as American writers explored questions of national identity, American artists portrayed everyday scenes related to the vitality of American enterprise and democracy. This painting, *Raftsmen Playing Cards* (1847), was one from George Caleb Bingham's series of pictures of Missouri rivermen. A contemporary observer speculated that the youth on the right is "a mean and cunning scamp, probably the black sheep of a good family, and a sort of vagabond idler." Large rivers such as the Missouri and Mississippi remained powerful symbols of freedom in the American imagination.

jobs they could obtain. Degrading images of legally vulnerable groups—blacks, Chinese, Hispanos—became a part of popular culture, in the songs people sang and the pictures they saw in books and magazines. Through these means, native-born Americans of British stock sought to distance themselves from people of color and from immigrants.

Paradoxically, some writers began to highlight the idea of American individualism during this time. Such authors extolled what they considered the universal qualities embedded in American nationhood. They believed that the United States consisted not of distinctive and competing groups, but of a collection of individuals, all bent on pursuing their own self-interest, variously defined. They believed that the "representative" American was ambitious and acquisitive, eager to make more money and buy new things.

Yet not everyone could afford to embrace this optimistic form of individualism. Many who were marginalized found emotional support, and in some cases even political power, in a strong group identity. For example, on the Plains, the Sioux Indians resisted the idea that U.S. officials could carve up territory and sell land to individual farmers at the expense of a people that pursued the buffalo across artificial political boundaries. During negotiations at Fort Laramie in 1851, Black Hawk, a leader of the Oglala Sioux, condemned the whites with his understatement, "You have split my land and I don't like it." In contrast to the Plains Indians, who wanted no role in American politics, African Americans and white women strove for full citizenship rights. These groups looked forward to the day when each person was accorded the same rights and was free to pursue his or her own talents and ambitions.

Putting into Practice Ideas of Social Inferiority

By promoting ideas related to the supposed inferiority of African Americans, Hispanos, and immigrants, European American men could justify barring these groups from the rights of citizenship and landownership as well as from nonmenial kinds of employment. In California, U.S. officials justified the exclusion of blacks, Indians, Chinese, and the poorest Mexicans from citizenship rights by claiming that members of these groups were nonwhite or, in the words of one state judge writing in 1854, "not of white blood." (Of course, the concept of "white blood" has no scientific basis because the different blood types—A, B, AB, and O—are found among all peoples.)

The precarious social status of various groups was revealed in patterns of their work.

The precarious social status of various groups was revealed in patterns of their work. In California, white men pursued opportunities on farms and in factories while increasing numbers of Chinese men labored as laundrymen and domestic servants. Indians toiled as field hands under white supervision. In rural Texas, Anglos established plantations and ranches while more and more Mexicans worked as *vaqueros* (cowboys), shepherds, sidewalk vendors, and **freighters**. In Massachusetts mill towns, white men and women served as the forefront of an industrial labor force while many African Americans of both sexes and all ages were confined to work in kitchens and outdoors as sweepers, cart drivers, and hawkers of goods.

Despite the divergent regional economies that shaped them, emerging ideologies of racial inferiority were strikingly similar. European Americans stereotyped all Chinese, Mexicans, and African Americans as promiscuous, crafty, "degraded," and intellectually inferior to whites. Such prejudices, in places as diverse as Boston, San Antonio, and San Francisco, prevented many people of color from reaching the limits of their own talents in mid-nineteenth-century America.

"A Teeming Nation"—America in Literature

Ideas about ethnic and racial difference coexisted with notions of American individualism, which stressed forms of universal equality. The variety of voices that gave expression to the national ideals of personal striving and ambition suggested the growth, energy, and vitality of the United States in the 1850s. In the Northeast, writers such as Ralph Waldo

DOCUMENT

"Moby Dick" by
Herman Melville

Professor Howe on the Subordination of Women

Antebellum southern elites prized what they called "natural" hierarchical social relations: the authority of fathers and husbands over daughters and wives, parents over children, rich over poor, and whites over blacks. According to slaveholders, clergy, and scholars, these relationships provided social stability and ensured that the weak and dependent would receive care from the rich and powerful. In July 1850, George Howe, professor of biblical literature at the Theological Seminary at Columbia, South Carolina, addressed the graduating class of a private women's academy. Howe suggested that the roles of women (elite white women) were enduring and never-changing.

The Endowments, Position and Education of Woman. An Address Delivered Before the Hemans and Sigourney Societies of the Female High School at Limestone Springs

The duties of life to all human beings are arduous, its objects are noble—each stage of its progress is preparatory to some other stage, and the whole a preparation to an interminable existence, upon which, in one sense, we are hereafter to enter, and in another, have already entered. Others may slightly regard the employments, trials and joys of the school girl. I am disposed to put on them a higher value. Our wives, sisters, and our mothers were in the same position yesterday. You will occupy a like [position] with them tomorrow. Whatever of virtue, of patient endurance, of poignant suffering, of useful labor, of noble impulse, of generous endeavor, of influence exerted on society for its good, has been exhibited in their example, in a few short years we shall see exhibited also in yours.

To woman, . . . there must be ascribed . . . acuteness in her powers of perception, . . . instincts . . . and emotions. When these are powerfully excited there is a wonderful vigor and determination of will, and a ready discovery of expedients to accomplish her wishes. She has readier sympathies, her fountain of tears is nearer the surface, but her emotions may not be so constant and permanent as those of man. She has greater readiness and tact, purer and more noble and unselfish desires and impulses, and a higher degree of veneration for the virtuous and exalted, and when she has found the way of truth, a heart more constant and more susceptible to all those influences which come from above. To the gentleness and quiet of her nature, to its affection and sympathy, that religion which pronounces its benediction on the peace-makers and the merciful, which recommends to them the ornament of a meek and quiet spirit, which, in the sight of the Lord, is of a great price, addresses itself with more force and greater attraction than it addresses man. Born to lean upon others, rather than to stand independently by herself, and to confide in an arm stronger than hers, her mind turns more readily to the higher power which brought her into being. . . .

Providence, then, and her own endowments mark out the proper province of woman. In some cases she may strive for the mastery, but to rule with the hand of power was never designed for her. When she thus unsexes herself she is

---

DOCUMENT

"Walden" by Henry David Thoreau

Emerson, Henry David Thoreau, Herman Melville, and Walt Whitman promoted a robust sensibility attuned to the challenges posed by the rigors of both the external world of natural beauty and the inner world of the spirit.

Some forms of literature offered an explicit critique of American materialism. According to Emerson, people were too concerned about possessions; as he put it, things were "in the saddle," riding everyone. During the 1850s, Thoreau's work became more explicitly focused on nature, as in his book *Walden* (1854). An appreciation of the wonders of nature—wonders that could be felt and tasted, as well as seen—amounted to a powerful force of democratization; anyone and everyone could participate. In turn, Thoreau actively supported the abolition of slavery; his love of nature formed the foundation of his belief in the universal dignity of all people in general and the cause of freedom for black people in particular.

In contrast, other writers celebrated busy-ness, whether in the field or workshop. In the introduction to his book of poetry titled *Leaves of Grass* (1855), Walt Whitman captured the restlessness of a people on the move: "Here is not merely a nation but a teeming nation of nations. Here is action . . . magnificently moving in vast masses." To Whitman, the expansiveness of the American landscape mirrored the American soul, "the largeness and generosity of the spirit of the citizen." His sensuous "Song of Myself" constituted an anthem for all Americans poised, gloriously diverse in their individuality, to exploit the infinite possibilities of both body and spirit.

despised and detested by man and woman alike. England's Queen Victoria at the present moment, if not more feared, is far more beloved in the quiet of her domestic life, than Elizabeth was, the most feared of her female Sovereigns.

Howe ends his address by drawing an implicit comparison between the South and the North. Like many Southerners, he associated the North with labor radicalism, abolitionism, and challenges to the "natural" position of women.

When women go about haranguing promiscuous assemblies of men, lecturing in public, either on infidelity or religion, on slavery, on war or peace—when they meet together in conventions and pass resolutions on grave questions of State—when they set themselves up to manufacture a public opinion for their own advantage and exaltation—when they meet together in organized bodies and pass resolutions about the "rights of woman," and claim for her a voice and a vote in the appointment of civil rulers, and in the government, whether of Church or State, she is stepping forth from her rightful sphere and becomes disgusting and unlovely, just in proportion as she assumes to be a man.

Louisa McCord was a member of an elite slaveholding family in South Carolina. She was an ardent supporter of slavery. Though an accomplished essayist herself, she believed that white women should remain subordinate to their fathers and husbands. In 1856 she wrote, "The positions of women and children are in truth as essentially states of bondage as any other, the differences being in degree, not kind." She added that the "true definition of slavery" thus "applies equally to the position of women in the most civilized and enlightened countries."

Questions

1. *Does Professor Howe believe that women are naturally inferior to men? Why or why not?*
2. *Why would Howe argue against citizenship rights for women, including the right to vote and serve on juries?*
3. *What were the tensions implicit in white women's status, considering that they were neither full citizens like their husbands nor slaves like the workers who toiled on their behalf?* ■

Source: George Howe, *The Endowments, Position and Education of Woman. An Address Delivered Before the Hemans and Sigourney Societies of the Female High School at Limestone Springs*, July 23, 1850 (Columbia, SC: I. C. Morgan, 1850), pp. 5, 9, 10–11.

Challenges to Individualism

Many men and women remained skeptical of—and, in some cases, totally estranged from—the wondrous possibilities inherent in Whitman's phrase "Me, Me going in for my chances." In northern cities, individualism spawned the kind of creative genius necessary for technological innovation and dynamic economic change, but it had little meaning for Native Americans in the West, most of whom were desperately seeking a collective response to new threats in the form of cattle ranchers and the U.S. cavalry. On the Great Plains, groups such as the Mandan and Pawnee performed ceremonies and rituals that celebrated kinship and village life above the individual.

African Americans in the North forged a strong sense of group identity. Though they rejected notions of white people's "racial" superiority, blacks had little choice but to think of themselves as a group separate and distinct from whites. In northern cities, blacks took in boarders and joined mutual-aid societies in order to affirm the collective interests of the larger black community. In contrast, well-to-do whites were increasingly emphasizing the sanctity of the nuclear family, composed solely of parents and children. Charismatic black Boston preacher Maria Stewart denounced the twin evils of racial and gender prejudice for condemning all black women to a life of menial labor: "How long shall the fair daughters of Africa be compelled to bury their minds and talents beneath a load of iron pots and kettles?"

Bettmann/CORBIS

■ Isabella Baumfree was born into slavery in New York State in 1797. Thirty years later she escaped from bondage and became a preacher. In 1843 she changed her name to Sojourner Truth. A powerful orator, she spoke on behalf of abolition and urged white women's-rights activists to embrace the cause of enslaved women. Truth sold small cards, called *cartes de visite*, to support herself. On this card, a portrait taken in 1864, she notes that she must sell her image ("the Shadow") to make a living.

Some groups of women embraced a collective identity of womanhood, although the definition of that identity took several forms. In the North, writers such as Catharine Beecher articulated a vision of female self-sacrifice fueled by family obligations and emotional relationships. Beecher declared that self-sacrifice formed the "grand law of the system" by which women should live their lives. Informed by religious devotion and sustained by labors of love in the home, this female world offered an alternative to the masculine individualism necessary to profit-seeking, whether on the family farm or in the bank or textile mill. Middle-class women believed they could take pride in rearing virtuous citizens and caring for overworked husbands. Sarah Willis Parton (Fanny Fern) cautioned her readers in a series of sketches published in 1853 (*Fern Leaves from Fanny's Portfolio*) that marriage is "the hardest way on earth of getting a living. You never know when your work is done."

Other groups of women cherished different kinds of aspirations. Organizers of the country's first conference devoted to the status of women, the Seneca Falls Convention held in upstate New York in 1848, derived inspiration from the abolitionist movement and protested the efforts of white men to exclude women from formal participation in it. In their demands for women's rights, Elizabeth Cady Stanton and Lucretia Mott linked the plight of the slave with the plight of free women, arguing that white men exploited and denigrated members of both groups. Stanton, Mott, and others received crucial support from African American leaders such as Sojourner Truth and Frederick Douglass. Delegates to Seneca Falls approved a document called the "Declaration of Sentiments," modeled after the Declaration of Independence: "We hold these truths to be self-evident: that all men and women are created equal." This group of women claimed for themselves a revolutionary heritage and all the rights and privileges of citizenship: to own property in their own names, to vote, to attend schools of higher learning, and to participate "in the various trades, professions, and commerce."

Many women, including enslaved workers throughout the South and hard-pressed needle-workers toiling in cramped New York City tenements, could not devote themselves full time to the care of hearth and home, nor could they aspire to a career of public agitation. In her autobiographical novel *Our Nig; or, Sketches from the Life of a Free Black, in a Two-Story White House, North* (1859), Harriet Wilson wrote bitterly of the fate of women such as her mother, a woman "early deprived of parental guardianship, far removed from relatives . . . left to guide her tiny boat over life's surges alone and inexperienced." Like the book's main character, Alfrado, Wilson herself had suffered at the hands of tyrannical white women employers, but at the end of the story Alfrado achieves a measure of dignity and independence for herself by setting up a small business. She thus offered an explicit challenge to both the arrogance of propertied white men and the homebound sentimentality of wealthy white women.

The Paradox of Southern Political Power

Slavery in the South

At the center of debates about hierarchies and equality, the institution of slavery needed to expand to survive. Decades of intensive cultivation were exhausting the cotton fields in the South. The planter elite was counting on the admission of new territories as slave states to preserve their threatened power in Congress. To slave owners, northern-sponsored efforts to block their expansion amounted to a death sentence for all that the white South held dear. In defense of the slave system, the white South had to mount a strong offense or die.

In the early 1850s, proslavery forces maintained firm control over all branches of the federal government. This derived in large part from the "three-fifths clause" of the Constitution, which gave disproportionate representation to the slave states, where each slave was counted as three-fifths of a person. Nevertheless, southern planters felt increasingly defensive as the country expanded westward. They warned against "the abolition excitement," which would necessarily upset the delicate balance between slave and free states. Gradually, this tension between southern strength and southern fears led to the fraying and then unraveling of the Jacksonian American party system, which had relied on a truce maintained between Whigs and Democrats on the issue of slavery. A new party, the Republicans, fused the democratic idealism and economic self-interest of native-born Northerners in such a powerful way that white Southerners believed that the institution of slavery was in danger of succumbing to the Yankee onslaught. And so a clash of ideas gradually slipped out of the confines of the polling place and into the realm of armed conflict.

The Party System in Disarray

In 1848, eight years after the appearance of the antislavery Liberty party, cracks in the second two-party system of Whigs versus Democrats opened wider with the founding of the Free-Soil party. Free-Soilers challenged the prevailing notion that the Whigs and Democrats could continue to smooth over the question of slavery in the territories with a variety of patchwork policies and piecemeal compromises. The Free-Soil platform promoted a forthright no-slavery-in-the-territories policy and favored the Wilmot Proviso (introduced in Congress in 1846), which would have banned slavery from all land acquired as a result of the Mexican War. In the presidential election of 1848, the Free-Soil party nominated former President Martin Van Buren, Democrat of New York. At the same time, Free-Soilers extended their appeal to the Whig party by supporting federal aid for internal improvements, free western homesteads for settlers, and protective tariffs for northern manufacturers.

TABLE 13-1			
The Election of 1848			
Candidate	Political Party	Popular Vote (%)	Electoral Vote
Zachary Taylor	Whig	47.4	163
Lewis Cass	Democratic	42.5	127
Martin Van Buren	Free-Soil	10.1	—

Nevertheless, the two major parties persisted in avoidance politics. The Democrats nominated General Lewis Cass, the "father of **popular sovereignty**," a doctrine allowing citizens of new states to decide for themselves whether to permit slavery within their borders. The Whigs put forth General Zachary Taylor, although the Louisiana slaveholder and Mexican War veteran had never held elected office. Taylor managed to parlay his military record into a close win in the fall of 1848. But Taylor died after a year and a half as president and was replaced by his vice president, Millard Fillmore.

In 1849 white Southerners confronted a disturbing reality. Although slave owners controlled the presidency and the Supreme Court and outnumbered the North in the House of Representatives, California's application for statehood in 1849 raised the specter of an unbalanced federal system consisting of sixteen free states and fifteen slave states. The abolitionist threat appeared in other guises as well: the territories of Utah and New Mexico apparently preparing to ban slavery once they became states, abolitionists clamoring for the immediate emancipation of all slaves, and black men and women, including former slave Harriet Tubman, working with abolitionists in the upper South and the North to facilitate the escape of slaves through a network of safe stops called the Underground Railroad. The "railroad" consisted of northerners, white and black, who sheltered fugitives from southern slavery in their flight to the North or, in some instances, to Canada.

The Compromise of 1850

Against this backdrop of sectional controversy, Congress debated the terms under which California would enter the Union in 1850. A young Democratic senator from Illinois, Stephen Douglas, helped cobble together the Compromise of 1850, under which California would enter the Union as a free state that year. New Mexico and Utah would eventually submit the slavery question to voters and thus put the idea of popular sovereignty to a practical test. The federal government would abolish the slave trade in Washington, D.C. (a move that did not affect the status of slaves already living there), and shore up the Fugitive Slave law of 1793 with a new, harsher measure.

The Fugitive Slave Law of 1850 essentially did away with the notion of the North as free territory, for it required local and federal law enforcement agents to retrieve runaways no matter where they sought refuge in the United States. Blacks were denied a trial or the right to testify on their own behalf. Fugitive slave commissioners earned $10 for each runaway they returned to a claimant. By compelling ordinary citizens to aid in the capture of alleged fugitives, the law brought the issue of slavery to the doorstep of northern whites.

Despite these dramatic events, the presidential campaign of 1852 was a lackluster affair. The Democrats nominated an unknown lawyer, Franklin Pierce. Although he hailed from New Hampshire, Pierce supported slavery. The Whigs turned their back on the undistinguished President Fillmore and chose as their nominee General Winfield Scott, who had gained fame during the Mexican War. Yet the Whigs split into regional factions during the election, Northerners resenting Scott's support of the Fugitive Slave Law and Southerners doubting his devotion to slavery. This split foreshadowed the end of national political parties and the emergence of regional parties, an ominous development indeed.

TABLE 13-2

The Election of 1852

Candidate	Political Party	Popular Vote (%)	Electoral Vote
Franklin Pierce	Democratic	50.9	254
Winfield Scott	Whig	44.1	42
John P. Hale	Free-Soil	5.0	—

Expansionism and Political Upheaval

The interests of southern planters affected not only domestic politics, but debates and policies related to foreign affairs as well. Even as Congress was heatedly discussing the Compromise of 1850, Southerners were contemplating ways to extend their reach across and even beyond the continental United States. They wanted to find new, fresh, fertile lands for cotton cultivation, and they hoped to incorporate those lands into the United States. Such expansion would also help to bolster the political power of slave owners in Congress by someday adding new slave states to the Union.

In 1850 the United States and Great Britain signed the Clayton-Bulwer Treaty, agreeing that neither country would seek to control the rights to any future canal spanning the Panama-

Nicaragua isthmus. In 1848 President Polk had made a gesture to buy Cuba from Spain, an offer that was rebuffed but one that did not discourage two privately financed expeditions of proslavery Americans from making forays into Cuba in an effort to seize the island by force on behalf of the United States. In 1854 the American ambassadors to Great Britain, France, and Spain met in Ostend, Belgium, and issued a statement declaring that, if Spain would not sell Cuba, the United States would be justified in taking control of the island. According to the Americans, the Monroe Doctrine gave license to the United States to rid the Western Hemisphere of European colonial powers. Noting that two of the three ambassadors hailed from slave states, abolitionists charged that the Ostend Manifesto was just one more ploy to extend the power of slaveholders throughout the Northern Hemisphere.

In 1855 a young proslavery American adventurer, Tennessee-born William Walker, gathered a band of fifty-eight mercenaries and managed to capture Granada, Nicaragua. Declaring himself president of Nicaragua, Walker encouraged the institution of slavery and won U.S. recognition for his regime in 1856. Walker was driven out of the country a year later, but his arrogance and bold move helped set the stage for the Nicaraguan anti-American movement that would resurface in the twentieth century.

The Gadsden Purchase of 1853 marked the end of westward land acquisition on the continent, but in a commercial sense, expansion continued past the edge of the continental United States. Americans saw the Pacific Ocean as a trade route and East Asia as a trading partner. Commodore Matthew Perry commanded a fleet of U.S. Navy ships that steamed into Tokyo Harbor in 1853. The treaty Perry helped arrange with Japan in 1854 protected American whaling ships, sailors, and merchants in that part of the world and opened the door to an increase in trade later in the century.

By the mid-1850s, the uniting of the continent into what would eventually become the forty-eight contiguous states was a source of sectional tension as well as national pride. Fewer and fewer Northerners supported what they considered proslavery charades, so-called legislative compromises. And the territory of Nebraska, poised on the brink of statehood, forced national lawmakers to confront again the political problem of the expansion of slavery. Once more Senator Douglas from Illinois stepped in to fill the breach. Douglas believed that mutual accommodation between North and South demanded a constant process of negotiation and flexibility on both sides. Thus he argued that the gigantic territory be split into two new states, Kansas and Nebraska, whose respective voters would decide the issue of slavery for themselves. His proposal necessitated that part of the Missouri Compromise of 1820, the part that forbade slavery above the 36°30′ line, would have to be repealed.

> *By the mid-1850s, the uniting of the continent into what would eventually become the forty-eight contiguous states was a source of sectional tension as well as national pride.*

The Kansas-Nebraska Act became law in 1854, enraging northern Free-Soilers by dismantling the 1820 agreement. They became convinced that what they called the Slave Power Conspiracy would stop at nothing until slavery overran the entire nation. The measure also had a profound effect on the Plains Indians, for it deprived them of fully one-half the land they had been granted by treaty. Specifically, the act wrought havoc on the lives of Ponca, Pawnee, Arapaho, and Cheyenne on the southern and central plains. European American settlers poured into the region, provoking Indian attacks. In September 1855, 600 American troops staged a retaliatory raid against an Indian village, Blue Water, in Nebraska, killing eighty-five Sioux and leading to an escalation in violence between Indians and settlers in the area.

The Compromise of 1850 and the Kansas-Nebraska Act

In their impatience with the two major parties, Free-Soilers were not alone in the early 1850s. The nativist American party, or Know-Nothings, condemned the growing political influence of immigrants, especially Roman Catholics. With its ranks filled with former Whigs, the party tapped into a deep wellspring of resentment against immigrants on the part of urban, native-born workers as well as Protestant farmers anxious about retaining their influence in public affairs.

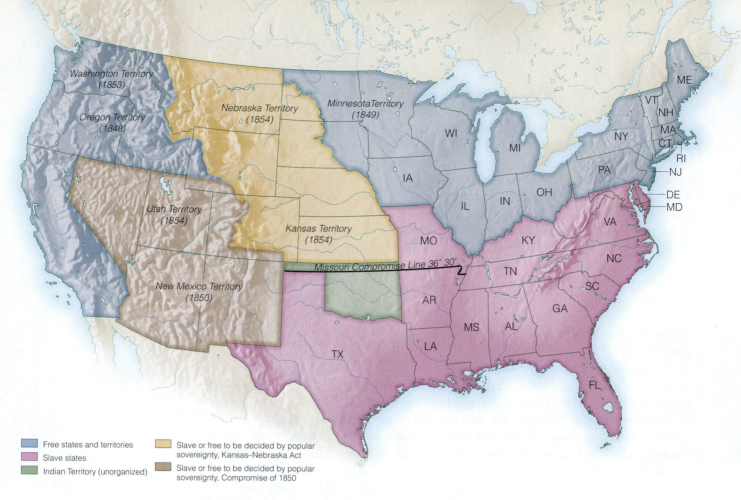

Free states and territories	Slave or free to be decided by popular sovereignty, Kansas–Nebraska Act
Slave states	
Indian Territory (unorganized)	Slave or free to be decided by popular sovereignty, Compromise of 1850

■ **MAP 13.2**

THE KANSAS-NEBRASKA ACT, 1854   Stephen A. Douglas, senator from Illinois, proposed the Kansas-Nebraska Act of 1854. Douglas hoped to ensure that any transcontinental railroad route would run through Illinois and benefit his constituents. To secure southern support for the measure, proponents of the bill repealed part of the Missouri Compromise of 1820. As a result of the act, settlers displaced many Plains Indians from their lands. In the mid-1850s, the territory of Kansas became engulfed in an internal civil war that pitted supporters of slavery against abolitionists.

The Republican Alliance

The rapid rise of the Know-Nothings further indicated that voters had grown disillusioned with the two-party system. Confirmation of that fact appeared on March 20, 1854, in the small town of Ripon, Wisconsin, when a group of disaffected Whigs created a new party called the Republicans. One core idea informed the party: that slavery must not be allowed to spread into the western territories. From this base, the Republicans built an organization so powerful that it would capture the presidency within six years.

The genius of the Republican party resided in its ability to create and maintain an alliance between groups with vastly different goals. Now forced by the Fugitive Slave Act of 1850 to serve slaveholders (by returning runaway slaves to them) and fearful of the potential of slaveholding Southerners to capture their party, some northern Democrats cast their lot with the Republicans. From the ranks of antislavery men—the long-suffering adherents of the Liberty and Free-Soil parties—came another wing of the Republicans. These party members openly proclaimed their belief in the power of the federal government to halt the relentless march of slavery and ensure that, throughout the land, free soil would be tilled by free labor, free men and women.

Yet antislavery Republicans were by no means unified on major issues apart from the extension of slavery. Many Northerners were willing to tolerate slavery as long as it could be confined to the southern states; they cared little or nothing for the rights of black people, slave or free. In fact, in the Midwest, Republicans saw no contradiction in calling for the end of slavery in one breath and for the end of black migration to the area in the next. They feared that as job competitors, blacks would force whites to work for less money than they were accustomed to, or would push whites out of jobs altogether.

From the ranks of the newly formed Illinois state Republican party emerged a formidable leader. Born in 1809 in Kentucky, Abraham Lincoln came from a modest background and followed a checkered path into Illinois Whig politics: from youthful plowhand and log-splitter, to local postmaster and county surveyor, and finally self-taught lawyer and member of the state legislature (1834–1842). Although his 6-foot 4-inch frame and humble background drew ridicule from wealthy people—a Philadelphia lawyer described him as "a tall rawly boned, ungainly back woodsman, with coarse, ill-fitting clothing"—Lincoln made good use of his oratorical gifts and political ambition in promoting the principles of free soil.

The presidential election of 1856 revealed the full dimension of the national political crisis. The Democrats nominated James Buchanan, a "dough-face" (i.e., proslavery Northerner) from Pennsylvania, with John Breckinridge of Tennessee as his running mate. In their platform, they took pains to extol the virtue of sectional compromise on the slavery issue, by this time a very unpopular position. Meanwhile, the enfeebled Whigs could do little but stand by helplessly and declare as their "fundamental article of political faith, an absolute necessity for avoiding geographical parties," another plank decidedly out of favor with a growing number of voters. The Know-Nothings cast their lot with former President Millard Fillmore, offering voters little more than an anti-immigrant platform.

TABLE 13-3

The Election of 1856

Candidate	Political Party	Popular Vote (%)	Electoral Vote
James Buchanan	Democratic	45.3	174
John C. Frémont	Republican	33.1	114
Millard Fillmore	American	21.6	8

Drawing on former members of the Free-Soil and Whig parties, the Republicans nominated John C. Frémont of California for president. Their platform stated in no uncertain terms the party's opposition to the extension of slavery, as well as Republican support for a transcontinental railroad and other federally sponsored internal improvements such as roads and harbors. The document also included the bold, noble rhetoric—in favor of "the blessings of liberty" and against "tyrannical and unconstitutional laws"—that would be the hallmark of the Republican party in the decade to come. Buchanan won the election, but Frémont's carrying eleven of the sixteen northern states boded well for the Republican party and ill for the slaveholders' union. In Illinois, Frémont had benefited from the tireless campaigning of Abraham Lincoln, who electrified ever-growing crowds of people with the declaration that "the Union must be preserved in the purity of its principles as well as in the integrity of its territorial parts."

The Deepening Conflict over Slavery

Only a small subset of Americans—adult white men—participated directly in the formation of new political parties that set the terms for congressional debates over territorial expansion and slavery. Nevertheless, during the 1850s, increasing numbers of ordinary people were drawn into the escalating conflict over the South's "peculiar institution" as some Northerners mounted concerted challenges, violent as well as peaceful, to the Fugitive Slave Law. The western territory of Kansas became a bloody battleground as abolitionists and proslavery forces fought for control of the new state government. Sites of struggle over the slavery issue also included the streets of Boston, the Supreme Court of the United States, political rallies in Illinois, and a federal arsenal in Harpers Ferry, Virginia. No longer would the opposing sides confine their disagreements to congressional debates over the admission of new states. Nor would words be the only weapons. The country was rushing headlong into nationwide armed conflict.

VIDEO

Slavery

The Rising Tide of Violence

DOCUMENT

Reminiscences of the Underground Railroad (1880)

The Fugitive Slave Law of 1850 caused fear and alarm among many Northerners. In response to the measure, some African Americans, hiding in northern cities, fled to Canada, often with the aid of conductors on the Underground Railroad. Abolitionists, white and black, made dramatic rescue attempts on behalf of men and women sought by their self-proclaimed southern owners. In Boston in 1851, a waiter named Shadrach Minkins was seized at work and charged with running away from a Virginia slaveholder. During a court hearing to determine the merits of the case, a group of blacks stormed in, disarmed the startled authorities, and, in the words of a sympathetic observer, "with a dexterity worthy of the Roman gladiators, snatched the trembling prey of the slavehunters, and conveyed him in triumph to the streets of Boston." Shadrach Minkins found safety in Montreal, Canada, and a Boston jury refused to convict his lawyers, who had been accused of masterminding his escape. The spectacular public rescue of Minkins, and other such attempts, both successful and unsuccessful, throughout the North, brought the issue of slavery into the realm of public performance in northern towns and cities.

Gradually, the war of words over slavery cascaded out of small-circulation abolitionist periodicals and into the consciousness of a nation. In particular, author Harriet Beecher Stowe managed to wed politics and sentiment in a most compelling way. Her novel *Uncle Tom's Cabin* (1852) sold more than 300,000 copies within ten months and a million copies over the next seven years. The

135,000 SETS, 270,000 VOLUMES SOLD.

UNCLE TOM'S CABIN

FOR SALE HERE.

AN EDITION FOR THE MILLION, COMPLETE IN 1 Vol., PRICE 37 1-2 CENTS.
IN GERMAN, IN 1 Vol., PRICE 50 CENTS.
IN 2 Vols., CLOTH, 6 PLATES, PRICE $1.50.
SUPERB ILLUSTRATED EDITION, IN 1 Vol. WITH 153 ENGRAVINGS.
PRICES FROM $2.50 TO $5.00.

The Greatest Book of the Age.

book, originally serialized in a magazine, *The National Era*, introduced large numbers of Northerners to the sufferings of an enslaved couple, Eliza and George. Slavery's greatest crime, in Stowe's eyes, was the forced severance of family ties between husbands and wives, parents and children.

Southern slaveholders were outraged at Stowe's attempt to portray their way of life as an unmitigated evil. A South Carolina slave-holding woman, Louisa McCord, wrote "We proclaim it [slavery], on the contrary, a Godlike dispensation, a providential caring for the weak, and a refuge for the portionless." Another Southerner, George Fitzhugh, took this argument to its logical conclusion. In his book *Cannibals All! Or, Slaves Without Masters* (1857), Fitzhugh claimed that civil society demanded the enslavement of the masses, whether white or black: "Some were born with saddles on their backs, and others booted and spurred to ride them—and the riding does them good." Fitzhugh also argued that slaves, whom he claimed were cared for by benevolent planters, were better off than northern factory workers, whom he asserted were exploited and neglected by indifferent employers.

Meanwhile, the territory of Kansas was becoming engulfed in a regional civil war. Proslavery settlers, aided and abetted by their compatriots (called Border Ruffians) from Missouri, installed their own territorial government at Shawnee Mission in 1855. Opposing these proslavery settlers were the Free-Soilers, some of whom had organized into abolitionist groups, such as the New England Emigrant Aid Company, and armed themselves with rifles.

This dangerous situation soon gave way to terrorism and insurrection on both sides. In 1855, in retaliation for a proslavery raid on the "Free-Soil" town of Lawrence, Kansas, an Ohio abolitionist named John Brown, together with his four sons and two other men, hacked to death five proslavery men at Pottowatamie Creek. The massacre only strengthened the resolve of proslavery advocates, who in the next year drew up a constitution for Kansas, which effectively nullified the principle of popular sovereignty over the issue of slavery. Called the Lecompton Constitution, the document decreed that voters might approve or reject slavery, but even if they chose to

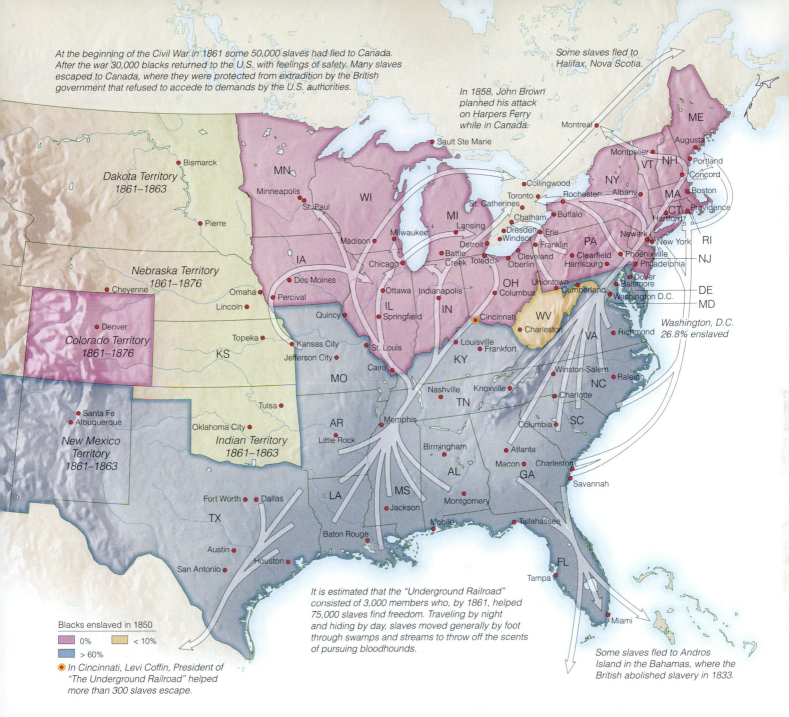

At the beginning of the Civil War in 1861 some 50,000 slaves had fled to Canada. After the war 30,000 blacks returned to the U.S. with feelings of safety. Many slaves escaped to Canada, where they were protected from extradition by the British government that refused to accede to demands by the U.S. authorities.

Some slaves fled to Halifax, Nova Scotia.

In 1858, John Brown planned his attack on Harpers Ferry while in Canada.

Washington, D.C. 26.8% enslaved

It is estimated that the "Underground Railroad" consisted of 3,000 members who, by 1861, helped 75,000 slaves find freedom. Traveling by night and hiding by day, slaves moved generally by foot through swamps and streams to throw off the scents of pursuing bloodhounds.

Blacks enslaved in 1850
- 0%
- < 10%
- > 60%

In Cincinnati, Levi Coffin, President of "The Underground Railroad" helped more than 300 slaves escape.

Some slaves fled to Andros Island in the Bahamas, where the British abolished slavery in 1833.

■ MAP 13.3

THE UNDERGROUND RAILROAD
The Underground Railroad consisted of a network of people who helped fugitives in their escape from slavery en route to the North or Canada. An escaped slave named Harriet Tubman made an estimated nineteen separate trips to the South to help an estimated 300 slaves escape to freedom. Like Tubman, most "conductors" on the Underground Railroad were blacks, many of them free men and women living in the North.

reject it, any slaves already in the state would remain slaves under the force of law. By throwing his support behind the Lecompton Constitution, President Buchanan alienated northern members of his own party, and the Democrats descended into North-South factionalism.

The spilling of blood over slavery was not confined to the Kansas frontier. In 1856 Senator Charles Sumner of Massachusetts, an outspoken abolitionist, delivered a speech on the floor of the United States Senate condemning "The Crime Against Kansas" (the Lecompton Constitution) and the men who perpetrated it, men he characterized as "hirelings picked from the drunken spew and vomit of an uneasy civilization," men who (like his own colleague Senator Butler of South Carolina) loved slavery the way that degenerates loved their prostitutes. Shortly after this speech, Congressman Preston S. Brooks of South Carolina, a relative of Senator Butler, leapt to the defense of the white South and attacked Sumner on the floor of the Senate, beating him into unconsciousness with a cane. Abolitionists contemplated the necessity of defending themselves and their interests, from the courtrooms of New England and the small towns of the West to the halls of Congress itself.

The *Dred Scott* Decision

DOCUMENT

The Supreme Court, *Dred Scott v. Sanford*

Across the street from the Capitol, proceedings in the Supreme Court were more civil but no less explosive. In 1857 a former slave named Dred Scott sued in federal court, claiming that he was a citizen of Missouri and a free man. Scott maintained that he had become free once his master had taken him onto free soil (the state of Illinois and the territory of Wisconsin). In the case of *Dred Scott v. Sanford* (1857), the court ruled that even residence on free soil did not render a slave a free person, for, regardless of their status, black people had "no rights which the white man was bound to respect." With this single decision, Chief Justice Roger B. Taney and the Court threw off the hard-won balance between slave and free states. In effect, the Court declared unconstitutional the Compromise of 1820, which had banned slavery in the region north of Missouri's southern boundary, because, the justices held, slave owners could not be deprived of their property without due process. This decision threatened the precarious freedom of the South's quarter million free people of color and extended the reach of slavery into the northern states.

Most white people residing outside the South never read the Court's ruling, but if they had, they probably would have agreed with the justices' claim that, since the earliest days of the Republic, blacks "had been regarded as beings of an inferior order, and altogether unfit to associate with the white race, either in social or political relations." At the same time, northern opinion makers warned that the decision made Northerners complicit in the slave system. Of the "slave power," the *Cincinnati Daily Commercial* thundered, "It has marched over and annihilated the boundaries of the states. We are now one great homogeneous slaveholding community." Even nonabolitionists had good reason to fear the long-term implications of the ruling, for it suggested that the institution of slavery was about to spill out of the confines of the southern states and into the rest of the country. Free white men and women feared competing with slaves in the workplace, whether in the West or East. These concerns increased with the onset of a depression in 1857 in the northeastern and midwestern states, as the mining of California gold produced inflation in the East.

The Lincoln-Douglas Debates

DOCUMENT

The Lincoln-Douglas Debates of 1858

Against this backdrop of economic turmoil and political conflict, the congressional elections of 1858 assumed great significance. In particular, the Senate contest in Illinois pitted incumbent Stephen A. Douglas against challenger Abraham Lincoln. In a series of seven public debates, the two men debated the political conflict over slavery as it had been shaped during the tumultuous decade after the Mexican War. Though no friend of the abolitionists, Douglas was quickly falling from favor within the Democratic party; the Supreme Court had nullified his proposal for popular sovereignty in the territories, and he had parted ways from his southern brethren when he denounced Kansas's Lecompton Constitution.

Lincoln ridiculed the doctrine of popular sovereignty, which he maintained was as thin as the "soup that was made by boiling the shadow of a pigeon that had starved to death." He had no desire to root out slavery in the South, but, "I have said, and I repeat, my wish is that the further spread of [slavery] may be arrested, and that it may be placed where the public mind shall rest in the belief that it is in the course of ultimate extinction." According to a reporter present, this last remark provoked great applause. And this was no minor confrontation between two candidates; it is estimated that in six of the seven debates, the two men spoke before crowds exceeding 10,000 people each. Lincoln lost the election (in which blacks were not allowed to vote as a matter of Illinois law), but, more significantly, he won the loyalty of Republicans all over the North and put the white South on notice that the days of compromise were almost over. Meanwhile, with the admission as free states of Minnesota in 1858 and Oregon in 1859, Congress began to reflect a distinct antislavery bias.

Harpers Ferry and the Presidential Election of 1860

On a Sunday night in October 1859, John Brown and nineteen other men (including at least five African Americans) launched a daring attack on the federal arsenal in Harpers Ferry, Virginia. They had received guns and moral support from some of the North's leading abolitionists, and their plan was to raid the arsenal and distribute firearms to slaves in the surrounding area, thereby inciting a general rebellion that, they hoped, would engulf the rest of

■ The election of 1858 pitted Stephen A. Douglas, Democratic senator from Illinois, against his Republican challenger, a lawyer named Abraham Lincoln. The debates between the two candidates revealed the increasing divisiveness of the slavery question. Douglas maintained that compromise on the issue was still possible; he argued that the European American men residing in territories should decide the question for themselves. Although Lincoln lost this election, he articulated a view that was rapidly gaining support throughout the North: the idea that slavery must not be allowed to spread outside the South.

■ Augustus Washington, son of a former slave, took this picture of John Brown in 1846, thirteen years before the raid on Harpers Ferry, Virginia. A pioneer daguerreotypist, Washington operated a successful studio in Hartford, Connecticut. After the passage of the Fugitive Slave Law in 1850, Washington emigrated with his family to Liberia, an African settlement for American freeborn blacks and former slaves, founded as a republic in 1847.

the South. The Virginia militia and a U.S. Marines force, commanded by Lieutenant Colonel Robert E. Lee, captured Brown and his surviving followers, but not before the insurrectionist had killed seven people and injured ten others. Brown was convicted of treason against the United States for his raid on the federal arsenal, murder, and inciting an insurrection. On December 2, 1859, before being led to the gallows, Brown handed a scrap of paper to one of his guards: "I John Brown am now quite *certain* that the crimes of this *guilty land: will* never be purged *away:* but with Blood." Brown failed as the instigator of a slave rebellion, but he succeeded as a prophet.

The raid on Harpers Ferry cast a shadow over the party conventions held in the summer of 1860. By then it was apparent that the national party system had all but disintegrated. Southerners in effect seceded from the Democratic party by walking out of their Charleston convention rather than supporting Stephen Douglas as candidate for president. Within a few weeks, representatives of both the northern and the southern wings of the party reconvened in separate conventions in Baltimore. Northerners gave the nod to Douglas and Southerners chose as their standard-bearer John C. Breckinridge, a proponent of extending slavery into the territories and annexing Cuba. Representing the discredited strategy of compromise was the candidate of the Constitutional Union party, John Bell of Tennessee.

In Chicago, the Republicans lined up behind Abraham Lincoln and agreed on a platform that had something for everybody, including measures to boost economic growth (as promoted by Henry Clay's American System earlier in the century): a proposed protective tariff, a transcontinental railroad, internal improvements, and free homesteads for western farmers. The Republicans renounced the Know-Nothings. Lincoln himself took the lead in admonishing Republicans who sought to curtail the voting rights of European immigrants, such as the Germans and Scandinavians.

Yet Republicans held out little hope for other groups demanding the rights and protection that flowed from American citizenship. Spanish-speaking residents of California, Chinese immigrants, free people of color throughout the North, Indian tribes from North Carolina to the northwestern states, the wives and daughters of men all over the country—these groups were not included in the Republicans' grand design for a country based on the principles of free labor.

Abraham Lincoln was elected president in 1860, although he received support from only 40 percent of the men who cast ballots. Lincoln won the electoral college, and he also received a plurality of the popular vote. However, ten southern states had refused to list him on the ballot; in that region of the country, he received almost no votes. Stephen Douglas won almost 30 percent of the popular vote; together, Douglas and Breckinridge outpolled Lincoln (2.2 million votes to 1.85 million). Nevertheless, the new president had swept New England, New York, Pennsylvania, and the upper Midwest. The regional interests of North and South took precedence over national political parties. By the end of 1860, South Carolina had seceded from the Union, and the nation headed toward war.

TABLE 13-4

The Election of 1860

Candidate	Political Party	Popular Vote (%)	Electoral Vote
Abraham Lincoln	Republican	39.8	180
Stephen A. Douglas	Democratic	29.5	12
John C. Breckinridge	Democratic	18.1	72
John Bell	Constitutional Union	12.6	39

Conclusion

During the 1850s, Americans on both sides of the slavery issue voiced their opinions, and their frustrations, in ever more dramatic ways. People all over the country came to feel that the debate over slavery had relevance to their lives. In the slave states, black workers remained yoked to a system that denied their humanity and mocked the integrity of their families. In the nonslave states, free people of color understood that northern racial prejudice was but a variation of the slaveholders' theme of domination. New England farm families looking to move west were convinced that western homesteads would not improve their economic security if these homesteads were surrounded by plantations cultivated by large numbers of enslaved workers. Republicans promoted a future full of hope, a future that would fulfill the long-thwarted promise of the young country as a "republic of equal rights, where the title of manhood is the title to citizenship."

In contrast, southern whites of various classes agreed on a rallying cry that stressed independence from Yankee interlopers and freedom from federal interference. Yet this unifying rhetoric carried different meanings for different groups of Southerners. The owners of large plantations were desperate to preserve their enslaved labor forces, and also hungry for fresh lands and renewed political power; these men scrambled to maintain their own privileges in the face of growing northern influence in Congress. Non-slaveholding farmers sought to produce all household necessities themselves and remain independent of the worldwide cotton market economy so crucial to the wealth of slave masters and mistresses. Yet almost all southern whites, rich and poor, stood allied, determined to take up arms to protect their households and their distinctive "southern way of life."

VIDEO
The Fitful Fifties

MAP
Slave Population Patterns, 1790 and 1860

Sites to Visit

Secession Era Editorial Project

history.furman.edu/~benson/docs/

> Furman University is digitizing editorials about the secession crisis and already includes scores of them on this site.

John Brown Trial

www.law.umkc.edu/faculty/projects/ftrials/Brown.html

> For information about the John Brown trial, this site provides a set of excellent links.

Lincoln-Douglas Debates of 1858

www.nps.gov/liho/debates.htm

> This National Park Service site includes the texts of these crucial public debates.

Compromise of 1850 and Fugitive Slave Act

www.pbs.org/wgbh/aia/part4/title.html

> From the PBS series on Africans in America, an analysis of the Compromise of 1850 and the effect of the Fugitive Slave Act on black Americans.

Words and Deeds in American History

memoryloc.gov/ammem/mcchtml/corhome.html

> A Library of Congress site containing links to sites on Frederick Douglass; the Compromise of 1850; speeches by John C. Calhoun, Daniel Webster, and Henry Clay; and other topics from the Civil War era.

Harriet Beecher Stowe and _Uncle Tom's Cabin_

xroads.virginia.edu/~HYPER/STOWE/stowe.html

> This site provides both text and descriptions of Stowe's important books and information about the author's life.

For Further Reading

General Works

Eric Foner, *Free Labor, Free Soil, Free Men: The Ideology of the Republican Party Before the Civil War* (1970).

William W. Freehling, *The Road to Disunion* (1990).

James Oliver Horton and Lois E. Horton, *In Hope of Liberty: Culture, Community and Protest Among Northern Free Blacks, 1700–1860* (1997).

Peter Kolchin, *A Sphinx on the Ameican Land: The Nineteenth-Century South in Comparative Perspective* (2003).

Nancy Isenberg, *Sex and Citizenship in Antebellum America* (1998).

Regional Economies and Conflicts

Joan Cashin, *A Family Venture: Men and Women on the Southern Frontier* (1991).

Susan Lee Johnson, *Roaring Camp: The Social World of the California Gold Rush* (2000).

John D. Majewski, *A House Dividing: Economic Development in Pennsylvania and Virginia Before the Civil War* (2000).

David Montejano, *Anglos and Mexicans in the Making of Texas, 1836–1986* (1987).

Individualism vs. Group Identity

Tomás Almaguer, *Racial Faultlines: The Historical Origins of White Supremacy in California* (1994).

Bonnie S. Anderson, *Joyous Greetings: The First International Women's Movement, 1830–1860* (2000).

Yong Chen, *Chinese San Francisco, 1850–1943: A Trans-Pacific Community* (2000).

Frances Levine, *Our Prayers Are in This Place: Pecos Pueblo Identity over the Centuries* (1999).

The Paradox of Southern Political Power

Avery O. Craven, *The Growth of Southern Nationalism, 1848–1861* (1953).

Robert E. May, *The Southern Dream of a Caribbean Empire, 1854–1861* (1973).

Leonard Richards, *The Slave Power: The Free North and Southern Domination, 1780–1860* (2000).

The Deepening Conflict over Slavery

David Herbert Donald, *Lincoln* (1995).

William E. Gienapp, *The Origins of the Republican Party, 1852–1856* (1987).

Michael F. Holt, *The Rise and Fall of the American Whig Party: Jacksonian Politics and the Onset of the Civil War* (1999).

Kate Clifford Larson, *Bound for the Promise Land: Harriet Tubman, Portrait of an American Hero* (2004).

Albert J. Von Frank, *The Trials of Anthony Burns: Freedom and Slavery in Emerson's Boston* (1998).

For quizzes and other resources on these topics, go to www.longmanamericanhistory.com.

"To Fight to Gain a Country": The Civil War

P ENSACOLA, FLORIDA, WAS THE SITE OF A DRAMATIC COURT-MARTIAL TRIAL IN APRIL 1862, WHEN five men were found guilty of treasonous acts against the Confederate States of America. "Possessed of information well calculated to aid the enemy," and thus capable of "giving intelligence" to the enemy, the defendants had endangered the security of Confederate troops stationed in the area, according to the chief prosecutor. Later, the presiding officer claimed that coastal communities were engulfed in a "general stampede" as planters tried to move slaves and livestock out of the way of the encroaching Union army. At stake in this trial was the very fate of the would-be new nation.

All of the defendants—George, Robert, Stephen, Peter, and William—were runaway slaves. The specific charges lodged against them read, "That the said slaves are intelligent beings possessing the faculties of Conveying information which would prove useful to the enemy and detrimental to the Confederate States." The charges suggest that the Confederates were forced to repudiate elements of their own proslavery beliefs, which held that black people were childlike and servile, incapable of acting on their own, and grateful for the guidance and protection of southern whites.

Prosecuting officers believed that "strong measures" were needed to prevent the nefarious activities of "spys whether white or black." These officials therefore were unprepared for the firestorm of criticism that followed the announcement of the verdict. The owner of the slaves, General Jackson Morton, expressed outrage that two of his men were marked for summary execution. In a formal complaint to Confederate authorities, Morton denounced the hearing as "vulgar and improper." By the time the controversy faded, an impressive array of Confederate military officers (from sentinels to a lieutenant, a captain, a colonel, a major general, and a general) had had to justify their actions in convening the trial. In the words of one official, "The sacrosanctity of slave property in this war has operated most injuriously to the Confederacy."

■ Sgt. F. L. Baldwin, a Union soldier, poses with an American flag as a backdrop.

Though at a distinct disadvantage compared to the North in terms of troops and materiel, the white South managed to fight on for four long, bloody years. Early on, politicians hailed slaves as a tremendous asset, an immense, easily managed labor force that would grow food and dig trenches.

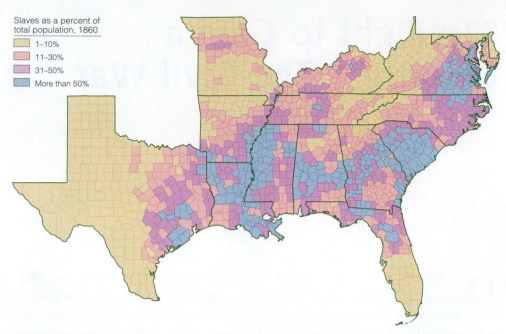

■ **MAP 14.1**
SLAVERY IN THE UNITED STATES, 1860   In the South, the areas of the greatest concentration of slaves were also the areas of greatest support for the Confederacy. During the war, the Appalachian mountain region and the upper Piedmont—the area between the mountains and the broad coastal plain—were home to people loyal to the Union and to people who became increasingly disaffected with Confederate policies as the war dragged on.

Instead, African American men and women became freedom fighters, a source of subversion in the heart of the Confederacy. In October 1862, in response to the crisis of wartime slave management, the Confederate Congress passed a measure that exempted from military service one white man for every twenty slaves on a plantation. Many slave owners used this law to shield themselves or their sons from combat duty. In turn, the Twenty-Negro Law inflamed resentment among non-slaveholding small farmers, who charged that this rich man's war was actually a poor man's fight.

As defenders of slavery, the Confederates cast themselves as rebels in an age when the principle of individual rights was gaining ground. The citizens of France, Germany, and Italy were agitating on behalf of modern, democratic nation-states, and systems of serfdom and slavery throughout Europe and the Western Hemisphere were under siege. By early 1865, desperate southern leaders were themselves considering offering slaves their liberty in return for military service.

The Republican conduct of the war revealed the party's nationalistic guiding principles. Yet several groups besides white Southerners objected to a strong federal government, one that would weld the country together geographically as well as economically. The Lincoln administration met bitter resistance from Indian tribes as diverse as the Santee Sioux of Minnesota, the Cheyenne of Colorado, and the Navajo and Apache of the Southwest. In northeastern cities, Irish immigrants battled federal draft agents and attacked black women, men, and children, their supposed competitors in the workplace. The Civil War, then, was less a "brothers' war" between the white farmers of the North and South exclusively and more a conflict that pitted diverse groups against each other over the issues of slavery, territorial expansion, federal power, and local control. Yet by the end of the war in April 1865, the Republican vision of a Union forged in blood had prevailed, at the cost of more than 600,000 lives.

Mobilization for War, 1861–1862

O n December 20, 1860, less than eight weeks after Abraham Lincoln was elected president of the United States, South Carolina seceded from the Union, determined, in the words of its own Declaration of Independence, to "resume her separate and equal place among nations." By February 1, 1861, Mississippi, Florida, Alabama, Georgia, Louisiana, and Texas (all states dependent on slave-based staple-crop agriculture) had also withdrawn from the United States of America. Three days later, representatives of the seven states met in Montgomery, Alabama, and formed the Confederate States of America. They also adopted a new constitution for their new nation. Though modeled after that of the United States, this document invoked the power of "sovereign and independent states" instead of "we, the people." Delegates to the Montgomery convention elected as their president Jefferson Davis, a wealthy Mississippi planter with an impressive record of public service. Davis was a graduate of West Point, a veteran of the Mexican War, and a former United States congressman, senator, and secretary of war.

DOCUMENT

Confederate Con-
stitution (1861)

The Secession Impulse

In some respects, the Civil War seems difficult to explain, for the two sides shared a great deal. Most of the people in the North and South were English-speaking Protestants with deep roots in the culture of the British Isles. Together they celebrated a revolutionary heritage, paying homage to George Washington and the other Founding Fathers.

VIDEO

The Union Severed

Why, then, was the white South, especially the slave South, so fearful of Abraham Lincoln? Although Lincoln enjoyed a broad electoral college victory, he won only 40% of the popular vote. Lincoln had made it clear that, as president, he would possess neither the authority nor the desire to disturb slavery as it existed in the South. However, he summed up his philosophy before the secession crisis this way: "As I would not be a *slave,* so I would not be a *master.* This expresses my idea of democracy. Whatever differs from this . . . is not democracy."

Not surprisingly, then, southern elites felt threatened by Lincoln in particular and the Republicans in general, pointing to the new president's oft-repeated promise to halt the march of slavery into the western territories. Although he was in no position to achieve this goal by executive order, Lincoln did have the power to expand the Republican base in the South by dispensing **patronage** jobs to a small group of homegrown abolitionists. He could also make appointments to the Supreme Court as openings became available. The Republican party was not a majority party; it was a sectional party of the North and the upper Midwest. But this sectional party had managed to seize control of the executive branch of government, tipping the **antebellum** balance of power between slave and free states decisively in favor of the North. Slave owners feared that John Brown's 1859 raid on the federal arsenal at Harpers Ferry, Virginia, was just the first in a series of planned attacks on the slave South.

Two last-ditch efforts at compromise failed to avert a constitutional crisis. In December 1860, as South Carolina was seceding and other states were preparing to join it, neither northern Republicans nor lower South Democrats showed any interest in a series of proposed constitutional amendments that would have severely curtailed the federal government's ability to restrict the interstate slave trade or the spread of slavery. Called the Crittenden Compromise (after its sponsor, Senator John J. Crittenden, a Whig from Kentucky), this package of proposed amendments was defeated in the Senate on January 16, 1861. A peace conference, organized by the Virginia legislature and assembled in February, revised the Crittenden Compromise, but key players were missing: the seven Confederate states and five northern states. Congress rejected the conference's recommendations at the end of February. By this time, many Americans, radicals and moderates, Northerners and Southerners, were in no mood to compromise on the issue of slavery, especially its extension into the West.

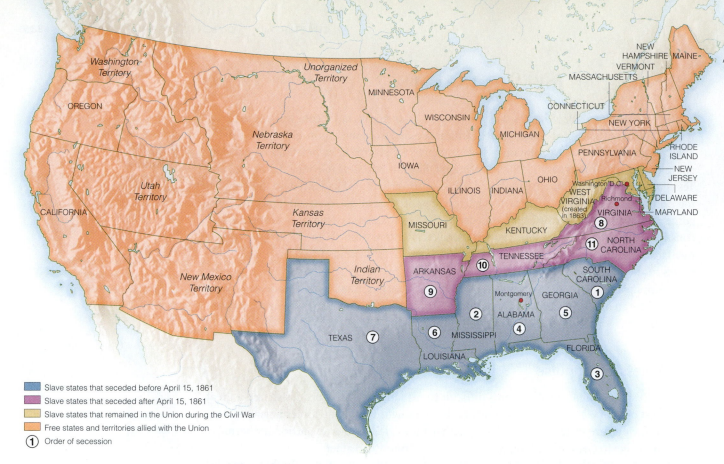

Slave states that seceded before April 15, 1861
Slave states that seceded after April 15, 1861
Slave states that remained in the Union during the Civil War
Free states and territories allied with the Union
① Order of secession

■ **MAP 14.2**

THE SECESSION OF SOUTHERN STATES, 1860–1861 The southern states seceded from the Union in stages, beginning with South Carolina in December 1860. Founded on February 4, 1861, the Confederate States of America initially consisted of only that state and six Deep South states. The four upper South states of Virginia, Arkansas, Tennessee, and North Carolina did not leave the Union until mid-April, when Lincoln called for 75,000 troops to put down the civil rebellion. The slave states of Delaware, Maryland, Kentucky, and Missouri remained in the Union, but each of those states was bitterly divided between Unionists and Confederate sympathizers.

DOCUMENT

"Lee at Fredericksburg" (1886) by J. Horace Lacy

In his inaugural address of March 4, Lincoln appealed to the South to refrain from any drastic action.

In his inaugural address of March 4, Lincoln appealed to the South to refrain from any drastic action, invoking the historic bonds of nationhood, the "mystic chords of memory, stretching from every battle-field, and patriot grave, to every living heart and hearthstone." For the most part, Lincoln's plea for unity fell on deaf ears. However, among the Southerners who initially resisted the secessionists' call to arms was the West Point graduate and Mexican War veteran Robert E. Lee of Virginia. Later, after Virginia seceded, Lee cast his lot with the Confederacy: "I cannot raise my hand against my birthplace, my home, my children," he declared. By his home, Lee meant the Commonwealth of Virginia, not the collection of disaffected states.

Indeed, in early April, the Confederacy was a rhetorical powerhouse, full of blustering firebrands. But it was also a poor excuse for an independent nation, with only one-third of the U.S. population and almost no industrial capacity. Over the next few weeks, as the seven Confederate states attempted to coax the upper South to join their revolution, Lincoln emerged as an unwitting ally in their effort.

Located in Charleston Harbor, Fort Sumter was one of two Union forts in southern territory, and in the spring of 1861 it was badly in need of supplies. On April 12, Lincoln took the high moral ground by sending provisions but not troops to the fort. The Confederates found the move provocative nonetheless and began firing on the fort. After a thirty-three-hour Confederate bombardment, the heavily damaged fort surrendered without a fight. In response, many white Southerners, such as Mary Boykin Chesnut, the wife of a high Confederate official, cheered and embraced the "pomp and circumstance of glorious war."

Three days after the capture of Fort Sumter, Lincoln (anticipating a conflict no longer than ninety days) called for 75,000 northern volunteers to quell a civil uprising "too powerful to be suppressed by the ordinary course of judicial proceedings." By the end of the month, he had ordered a blockade of southern seaports. Condemning these moves as acts of "northern aggression," the upper South, including Virginia (deprived of its western part, which now formed a new state called West Virginia), Tennessee, Arkansas, and North Carolina all seceded from the Union by May 20. Grateful for the newfound loyalty of Virginia and eager to appropriate the Tredegar Iron Works in Richmond, the Confederacy moved its capital from the down-at-the-heels Montgomery to the elegant Richmond on May 11.

Certain segments of the southern population early demonstrated that they would withhold their support from the Confederacy. Yeoman farmers in the upcountry, Louisiana sugar planters dependent on world markets for their product, and people in the hill country of east Tennessee all voted for Unionist delegates to their respective state conventions that chose secession. Enslaved black workers, of course, could hardly be counted on to defend those who kept them in bondage. The Border States of Missouri, Kentucky, Maryland, and Delaware remained within the Union, although among their residents were many outspoken people who openly sympathized with the South.

Preparing to Fight

Poised to battle each other, the South and the North faced similar challenges. Both sides had to inspire—or force—large numbers of men to fight. Both had to produce massive amounts of cannon, ammunition, and food. And both had to devise military strategies that would, they hoped, ensure victory. In early 1861, white Southerners were boasting of the stockpiles of cotton that, if needed, would serve as leverage for military support, diplomatic recognition, and financial assistance from the great European powers. Plantations brimming with hogs and corn, it was hoped, would sustain both masters and slaves, in contrast to the North, where cotton mills would lie idle and workers would soon descend to poverty and starvation.

From the beginning of the war, Confederates aimed for a strategy calculated to draw on their strengths. They would fight a purely defensive war with small units of troops deployed around the South's 6,000-mile border. Seasoned officers such as Robert E. Lee and Thomas J. Jackson would lead the charge to crush Union armies that ventured into Confederate territory. Finally, the South could command 3 million black people (a third of its total population of 9 million), all of whom, it was assumed, would do the bidding of planters and military men. Whereas the North would have to conquer the South to preserve the Union, the Confederacy would only have to survive to win its independence.

At first, the North was inclined to think little past the numbers: in 1860, it possessed 90 percent of the manufacturing capacity and three-quarters of the 30,000 railroad miles in the United States. Its population, 22 million, dwarfed that of the South. The North retained control of the (admittedly less than formidable) U.S. Navy and all other resources of the federal government, including a bureaucratic infrastructure to facilitate troop deployment and communication. Its diversified economy yielded grain as well as textiles; it could not only mobilize a large army but count on feeding it as well.

Early on, the North had a plan, but one that could hardly be dignified by the term *strategy*. It would defend its own territory from southern attack and target Confederate leaders, under the assumption that latent Union sentiment in the South would arise to smash the rebellion before it went too far. Union gunboats positioned along the East Coast and up and down the Mississippi River would seal off the Confederacy from foreign supply lines. The North would also launch a political offensive calculated to undermine Confederate sympathizers by bolstering Unionist sentiment everywhere. Lincoln, for example, continued to appeal to slaveholders loyal to the Union, whether those slaveholders lived in the Border States or deep in the heart of the Confederacy.

A Virginia Slaveholder Objects to the Impressment of Slaves

During the Civil War, some southern slave owners bitterly resisted Confederate slave impressment policies. On December 4, 1861, John B. Spiece, an Albemarle County, Virginia, slaveholder and lawyer, wrote to the Confederate attorney general and protested government policy.

Dr Sir, Although a stranger to you, yet in consequence of the excitement and distress in this section of the country, in reference to a certain matter; I am constrained to address you, not merely on my own account; but on behalf of a large number of most respectable citizens....

A practice has prevailed for some considerable time in *this* section of the country of impressing into service of the confederate army, the horses wagons and *slaves* belonging to the people.

The "Press masters" will go to their houses, and drag off their property to Just Such an extent as they choose; until it has not only created great excitement and distress; but bids fair to produce wide spread ruin. And I am told that these "Press masters" are paid by the Government the enormous price of *two dollars and fifty cents for each team which they impress*;—hence their anxiety and untiring exertions to increase the number;—thus making thirty or forty dollars pr day—

While I do not controvert the right of the Government to impress into its service *wagons and teams*; yet I do controvert the right to impress *Slaves*—It does seem to me that no one can be impress'd into military service of any kind, unless he is subject to military duty: because this whole business is relating to the Army, and is purely a military matter.—

The people in this section of the country are much attached to their slaves, and treat them in a humane manner—consequently they are exceedingly pained at having them dragged off at this inclement season of the year, and exposed to the severe weather in the mountains of north western Virginia.... Some have already died, and others have returned home afflicted with Typhoid fever, which has spread through the family to a most fatal and alarming extent.—

I am a practicing lawyer myself, but these "Press masters" will hear nothing from any one residing amongst the people.—

Therefore Sir, in consequence of the distress produced by the causes before mentioned, I am constrained to write to you; requesting you if you please, to give your opinion upon the questions involved.

To wit—If a man's wagon and team should be impress'd into Service, can his slave be impress'd to drive the said team—

Secondly—If a man has neither wagon or team can his slave be impress'd to drive some other team (*some* of the "Press masters" yield this *last* point, whilst others do not, and contend that they can impress just as many slaves as they choose from any plantation, taking all the negro men if they think proper.)—

Some few of the people have not been able to sow their grain this fall:— and there is deep dissatisfaction amongst the people—therefore I deem it proper and expedient that the authorities should know it—

Spiece goes on to cite the laws of the Commonwealth of Virginia, as amended in 1860, "by which it seems there is no power to impress Slaves." In the absence of Confederate congressional legislation to that effect, he argues, government authorities lack the legal right to take slaves from their owners. Spiece concludes his letter by suggesting that in taking slaves far from their homes, Confederate authorities were endangering the security of the would-be-new nation.

There is also a serious evil in impressing slaves for the service in North western

Northerners also invoked a Revolutionary heritage to justify their cause. However, they downplayed the issue of unjust taxation and instead stressed the glories of the Union—in Lincoln's words, "the last, best hope of mankind" in an age of kings and emperors.

Barriers to Southern Mobilization

On July 21, 1861, at Manassas Junction (Bull Run), about 30 miles southwest of Washington, D.C., Union and Confederate forces encountered each other on the field of battle for the first time. This was the fight that earned Thomas "Stonewall" Jackson his nickname and burnished his reputation, for Union troops skirmished briefly with the enemy and then turned and fled back to the capital, disgraced. In the coming weeks, Northerners gave up the idea that

These slaves are unloading ships at City Point, Virginia. Field hands impressed to work in Confederate factories, on wharves, and in mines experienced a new way of life off the plantation and out of the sight of their owners.

Library of Congress

Virginia:—whilst there they get to talking with *Union men* in disguise, and by that means learn the original cause of the difficulty between North & South: then return home and inform other negroes:—not long since one of my neighbors negro men went to his master, and desired to let him go again to the north western army—adding "I wish you to let me go further than I went before["]—I have the honor to be most respectfully your Obt Servt.

It is unknown whether Confederate officials responded to Spiece's letter.

Questions

1. *How does John Spiece demonstrate his talents as a lawyer in this letter?*

2. *In what ways does Spiece's reaction to slave impressment suggest changes in, or challenges to, southern planters' ideology of paternalism?* ■

Source: Ira Berlin, Barbara J. Fields, Thavolia Glymph, Joseph P. Reidy, and Leslie S. Rowland, eds., *Freedom: A Documentary History of Emancipation, 1861–1867,* Series 1, Vol. 1, *The Destruction of Slavery* (1985), pp. 782–783.

the effort to suppress the rebels would be an easy one, and Lincoln began to reorganize the country's officer corps and fortify its armies.

To win this initial victory, the Confederates had relied on the massing of several huge forces: those of Generals Joseph Johnston and P. G. T. Beauregard, as well as Stonewall Jackson. Consequently, southern military strategists decided they must continue to defend southern territory while going on the offensive against the Yankees (the "offensive-defensive" strategy was used for the duration of the conflict). In other matters, however, the South learned life-and-death lessons more slowly. Only gradually did the central paradox of the Confederate nation become abundantly clear: that a country founded on an agrarian ideal of "states' rights" needed to industrialize its economy and centralize its government operations to defeat the Union.

■ Farmer's cabin, Block House, New Braunfels, Texas.

The first weeks of the war revealed that the South would pursue its antebellum aims of conquering western territory for slavery. An early victory of Texas forces over Union troops in New Mexico led to the formation of what slaveholders in that region called the Confederate Territory of Arizona. Over the next year, the Confederates launched successful assaults on the cities of Albuquerque and Santa Fe, in present-day New Mexico. However, southern troops amounted to little more than a band of plunderers; in Rio Abajo, for example, farmers and ranchers switched their allegiance to the Union after the rebels raided their homesteads.

Deprived of money raised from customs duties (the U.S. Navy blockade brought a halt to established patterns of overseas trade), the Confederacy relied on floating bonds ($400 million worth), raising taxes, and a 10 percent tax on farm produce. The Confederate Treasury printed money at a furious rate ($1 billion over the course of the conflict), but its value declined precipitously; near the end of the war one Confederate dollar was worth only 1.6 cents.

Raising a volunteer army and impressing slave labor (forcing slaves to labor for the military) met with stiff resistance from various quarters of southern society. For yeoman farm families, long defensive of the independence of their own households, Confederate mobilization efforts came as a rude shock. Antebellum Southerners believed that white fathers should protect and retain control over their dependents at all times. Planters expressed a well-founded fear that slaves impressed for a wide range of tasks, whether saltmaking or chopping trees or tending brick kilns, were difficult to control now that plantation discipline had been loosened. When the Confederate call for volunteers failed to produce the number of soldiers (and menial laborers) needed to fight the Union, the Richmond government in March 1862 implemented a military conscription law (all men between ages eighteen and thirty-five—later it became forty-five—were called up for three years of service). The law exempted certain kinds of workers, such as railroad employees, schoolteachers, miners, and druggists, and allowed the buying of **substitutes** by draftees who could afford the $300 price for them. This last type of exemption allowed wealthy men to pay someone to fight in their place.

These provisions provoked anger not only among ordinary citizens but also among principled states' rights advocates such as governors Joseph Brown of Georgia and Zebulon Vance of North Carolina. Brown exempted large numbers of men from the draft, claiming that the Confederacy posed a greater threat to states' rights than did the Union. On January 1, 1862, 209,852 southern men were present for duty. Yet the northern force was more than twice as large, with 527,204.

Indians and Immigrants in the Service of the Confederacy

Just as the Confederates failed in their attempt to use fully the labor of enslaved workers, so they failed to reap much gain from the vaunted military prowess of Indians, especially those in Indian Territory (present-day Oklahoma). In 1861 southern military officials appealed to the Cherokee and the other Five Tribes for support, promising them arms and protection from Union forces in return. Only gradually and reluctantly did Cherokee leader John Ross commit his men to the Confederacy: "We are in the situation of a man standing alone upon a low naked spot of ground, with the water rising all around him." More devoted to the Confederate cause was Cherokee leader Stand Watie, who, backed by many Cherokee slaveholders, proceeded to mobilize what he called the "United Nations of Indians" as a fighting force on behalf of the Confederacy. Among those responding to the call to arms were Choctaw and Chickasaw men, who formed Company E of the 21st Mississippi Regiment, "the Indian Brigade."

Although Indian Territory was considered of great strategic value to the Confederacy, southern military officials at times expressed frustration with the traditional battle tactics of Indian warriors. They were unused to military encounters that pitted long, straight rows of men on foot against each other. At the Battle of Elkhorn Tavern (Pea Ridge) in March 1862, Indian troops abandoned the battlefield in the face of cannon fire, leading their commander, Albert Pike, to demand that in the future they be "allowed to fight in their own fashion" rather than "face artillery and steady infantry on open ground." By the summer of 1862, the Confederacy lost its advantage in Indian Territory; the Cherokee and Creek were divided in their loyalties, with some joining Union forces. By this time, the Comanche and Kiowa, resentful of the Confederacy's broken promises (guns and money diverted from them), had joined Union troops and were threatening to invade Texas.

■ **Stand Watie**

Like Native Americans, immigrants and ethnic minorities in the South were divided in their loyalties. A Jewish lawyer and slaveholder, Judah Benjamin, served as a cabinet member and trusted adviser to Jefferson Davis. Prominent southern military officers included some from Ireland, Prussia, and France. German and Irish workmen from southern cities helped fill the ranks of the Confederate army, as did an estimated 2,500 Hispanos. But ethnic loyalties could also disrupt services deemed necessary to Confederate manufacturing and transportation. The Confederate railroad director in Selma, Alabama, contended with a labor force of immigrants (most probably from Germany and Ireland), men who "do not feel identified in any great degree with the South" and who demanded high wages. They were constantly threatening to run away to Union lines, where they believed they could make more money and enjoy the luxuries denied them in war-torn Alabama.

The Course of War, 1862–1864

When the time came to marshal resources in the service of the national state, Northerners were at a distinct advantage over the states' rights men who dominated the Confederacy. Not only did the Union have more resources, but the Republicans' support for the centralization and consolidation of power also facilitated the war-mobilization process. In Congress, the Republicans took advantage of their new majority status and expanded federal programs in the realm of the economy, education, and land use. However, like Davis, Lincoln encountered vehement opposition to his wartime policies. Meanwhile, on the battlefield, Union losses were mounting. The United States confronted an uncertain fate.

The Republicans' War

Worried about disloyalty in the vicinity of the nation's capital, on April 27, 1861, Lincoln gave General Winfield Scott the power to suspend the writ of habeas corpus (a legal doctrine designed to protect the rights of people arrested) in Baltimore. By the end of the year, this policy, which allowed the incarceration of people not yet charged with a crime, was being applied in almost all of the loyal United States. Chief among those targeted were people suspected of interfering with war mobilization of men and supplies. Democrats stepped up their opposition to the president, denouncing him as a tyrant and a dictator. Meanwhile, from the other side of the political spectrum, abolitionists expressed their frustration with the administration's conciliatory policy toward the South in general and toward Unionist slaveholders in particular. Lincoln insisted that his objective was "to save the Union, and . . . neither to save or destroy slavery."

Wartime manufacturing and commerce proved to be a boon to entrepreneurs. In Cleveland a young commission-house operator named John D. Rockefeller was earning enough money to hire a substitute to serve in the army for him. In the middle of the war, he shifted his business from trading grain, fish, water, lime, plaster, and salt to refining the crude oil (used in kerosene lamps) recently discovered in western Pennsylvania. War profiteers seized their opportunities in both the North and the South. In 1862 the *Southern Cultivator*, a magazine published in Augusta, Georgia, ran an article titled "Enemies at Home," denouncing the "vile crew of speculators" who were selling everything from corn to cloth at exorbitant prices.

The Republicans' willingness to centralize wartime operations led in 1861 to the formation of the U.S. Sanitary Commission, which recruited physicians, trained nurses, raised money, solicited donations, and conducted inspections of Union camps on the front. During the war,

■ Ulysses S. Grant

■ William Sherman

■ Robert E. Lee

■ Stonewall Jackson

as many as 20,000 white and black women served as nurses, cooks, and laundresses in Union military hospitals. Black women worked primarily in the latter two categories. A long-time advocate of reform on behalf of the mentally ill during the antebellum period, Dorothea Dix, served as superintendent of nurses.

The Republicans believed that the federal government should actively promote economic growth and educational opportunity, and they enacted measures previously thwarted by Democratic presidents and Congresses. In July 1862, the Homestead Act granted 160 acres of western land to each settler who lived on and made improvements to the land for five years. Congress also passed the Morrill Act, which created a system of land grant colleges. (Many of these colleges eventually became major public universities, including Colorado State University, Kansas State University, and Utah State University.) Also approved in 1862, the Pacific Railroad Act appropriated to the Union Pacific and the Central Pacific railroads a 400-foot right-of-way along the Platte River route of the Oregon Trail and lent them $16,000 to $48,000 (depending on the terrain) per mile.

During the first year and a half of war, Union military strategy reflected a prewar Republican indifference to the rights and welfare of both northern and southern blacks. In September 1861, Lincoln revoked a directive released by General John Frémont that would have authorized the seizure of property and the emancipation of slaves owned by Confederates in the state of Missouri. The president feared that such a policy would alienate slaveholders who were considering switching their allegiance to the Union. Later that fall, the capture of Port Royal, South Carolina, allowed Union soldiers to treat blacks as "**contraband** of war," denying slaveholders their human property but failing to recognize blacks as free people with rights.

As Union forces pushed deeper into Confederate territory, U.S. officers devised their own methods for dealing with the institution of slavery. By early 1862, the North had set its sights on the Mississippi River valley, hoping to bisect the Confederacy and cut off supplies and men bound from Texas, Arkansas, and Louisiana to the eastern seaboard. In February, General Ulysses S. Grant captured Fort Henry and Fort Donelson on the Tennessee and Cumberland rivers, the Union's first major victory of the war; in April,

> *Union military strategy reflected a prewar Republican indifference to the rights and welfare of both northern and southern blacks.*

Library of Congress

■ The bodies of soldiers lie where they fell on September 17, 1862, the single day that claimed the largest number of lives in the Civil War. Like many other battles of the war, Antietam was shaped by the physical features of the battlefield itself, with soldiers on both sides seeking cover in small groves of trees and behind rocks, road ruts, and fences made of stone and wood.

New Orleans fell to Admiral David Farragut. In New Orleans, General Benjamin Butler attempted to retain the loyalty of Unionist slaveholders by returning runaway slaves to them. This policy was not always greeted with enthusiasm within Union ranks. A Massachusetts soldier, restless under the command of an officer sympathetic to "slave catching brutes," vowed, "I never will be instrumental in returning a slave to his master in any way shape or manner."

The Ravages of War: The Summer of 1862

**The Civil War
Part I: 1861–1862**

In the summer of 1862, the South suffered a hemorrhaging of its slave population as the movement of Union troops up and down the eastern seaboard opened the floodgates to runaways. Yet over the course of the summer the Confederacy persevered on the battlefield, aided by the failure of Union armies to press their advantage. In June, General George McClellan was turned back on the outskirts of Richmond, which convinced Lincoln not only of the incompetence of his chief general but also of the value of a less forgiving approach toward the South. But General John Pope, brought in from the western campaign to command the 50,000-man Army of the Potomac, did little better.

In other parts of the country, the Yankee war against the Confederates spilled over into savage campaigns against Indian tribes. An uprising among the Santee Sioux, in Minnesota killed 500 whites before the state militia quashed the rebellion at Wood Lake in the fall of 1862. General James H. Carleton routed the Texas Confederates who had been occupying New Mexico and Arizona, and then provided what he called a "wholesome lesson" to the Mescalero Apache and Navajo who had been menacing Spanish American *placitas* (communities) in the area. Carleton's Union soldiers forced the Mescaleros to accept reservation status at Bosque Redondo in the Pecos River valley. Meanwhile, Colonel Kit Carson conducted a campaign of terrorism against the Navajo, burning *hogans* and seizing crops and livestock, claiming that "wild Indians could be tamed." Many of the survivors undertook the "Long Walk" to Bosque Redondo, a forced march reminiscent of the Cherokee Trail of Tears a generation before.

On the banks of Antietam Creek in northern Virginia, on September 17, the bloodiest single day of the war claimed 20,000 lives and resulted in a Union victory, although a costly one.

To journalists and soldiers alike, battles could offer stirring sights of long rows of uniformed men arrayed against each other, their arms at the ready, regimental flags unfurled in the wind. Yet for the women of Shepardstown, Maryland, left to clean up after the Antietam slaughter, there was no talk of the glory of war, only a frantic, round-the-clock effort to feed the Confederates and bind their wounds. Surveying the battlefield wreckage, one observer, Maria Blunt, lamented the carnage: the dead but also men "without arms, with one leg, with bandaged sides and backs; men in ambulances, wagons, carts, wheelbarrows, men carried on stretchers or supported on the shoulder of some self-denying comrade." All over the South, white women established temporary hospitals in barns, private homes, and churches and mourned each human sacrifice to the cause: "A mother—a wife—a sister had loved him."

The extraordinarily high casualty rate in the war stemmed from several factors. Confederates and Federals alike fought with new kinds of weapons (rifles and sharpshooters accurate at up to 1,000 yards) while troops massed in old-style (that is, close) formation. Soft minie balls punctured and lodged in limbs, leading to high rates of amputation that in turn fostered deadly infections. One Alabama soldier observed in 1862, "I believe the Doctors kills more than they cour [cure]." In fact, twice as many Civil War soldiers died of infection and disease—diarrhea, dysentery, typhoid, pneumonia, and malaria—as were killed in combat.

The Emancipation Proclamation

Appalled by the loss of life but heartened by the immediate outcome of Antietam, Lincoln took a bold step. In September he announced that on January 1, 1863, he would proclaim all slaves in Confederate territory free. Lincoln used the Emancipation Proclamation to bolster northern morale by infusing the conflict with moral purpose and at the same time to further the Union's interests on the battleground by encouraging Southern blacks to join the U.S. army. The measure left slavery intact in the loyal Border States and in all territory conquered by the Union. Consequently, nearly 1 million black people were excluded from its provisions. Skeptical of the ability of blacks and whites to live together, Lincoln remained committed to the colonization of freed blacks outside the United States (in Central America or the West Indies).

In the congressional elections of 1862, the Democrats had picked up strength in New York, Pennsylvania, and Ohio and carried Illinois. The lower Midwest in general harbored large numbers of Democrats who opposed the war (especially now that it was an "abolition war") and called for peace with the South; these so-called Copperheads disrupted Union enlistments and encouraged military desertions. The Emancipation Proclamation electrified abolitionists, but the war effort and the growing casualties were taking their toll among the laboring classes. Especially aggrieved were the working people who paid higher taxes (relative to those paid by the wealthy) to keep the war machine running, and the dockworkers and others who lost their livelihoods when trade with foreign countries ceased. Their resentment boiled over in the summer of 1863.

Persistent Obstacles to the Confederacy's Grand Strategy

From the beginning of the war, the North's effort to blockade 3,500 miles of southern coastline met with fierce resistance on the high seas. The South made up in resourcefulness what it lacked in a navy, relying for supplies on swift steamers manned by privateers (British arms smuggled onto remote southern beaches could bring up to 700 percent in profits). Seemingly

■ Kate Cumming of Mobile, Alabama, earned the gratitude of the Confederacy for her work as a hospital matron during the war. Before and during the Civil War, many people believed that respectable women should not work in hospitals. Physicians claimed that women were likely to faint at the sight of blood and that they were not strong enough to turn patients over in their beds. Yet, as the war progressed, more and more northern and southern women defied these stereotypes and served in hospitals as nurses, administrators, and comforters of the ill and dying. Noted Cumming soon after she first entered a hospital, "The foul air from this mass of human beings at first made me giddy and sick, but I soon got over it." Still, in southern hospitals, soldiers and enslaved workers handled much of the direct patient care.

DOCUMENT

Barton, Memoirs about Medical Life at the Battlefield (1865)

invincible Confederate ships such as the ironclad *Merrimack* and the well-fortified British-built warships *Alabama* and *Florida* prowled the southeastern seaboard, sinking Union vessels and protecting the blockade runners. Nevertheless, by December 1861, Union forces had established beachheads in Confederate territory up and down the East Coast.

In November 1861, Union naval forces intercepted a British packet ship, the *Trent*, and seized two Confederate diplomats, James Mason and John Slidell, who were en route to London and Paris, where they planned to plead the South's case in a bid to gain diplomatic recognition. To avoid a rift with England, Lincoln and Secretary of State William H. Seward released the two men. In the process, Mason and Slidell lost whatever influence they might have had with European governments, and Lincoln enjoyed the praise of the British public for his moderation in handling the *Trent* affair.

More generally, Confederate hopes for diplomatic recognition foundered on the shoals of European politics and economics, in England and in the Western Hemisphere. English textile mills drew on their own immense prewar stockpiles of raw cotton and sought out new sources of fiber in Egypt and elsewhere. Also, English workers flexed their political muscle in a successful effort to forestall recognition of the slaveholders' nation. Early in the war the Confederates, who counted 2,500 Hispanics among their ranks, recognized the strategic importance of Mexico, both as a trade route for supplies and as a means of access to ports. In approaching Mexican President Benito Juarez for aid in late 1861, however, Confederate envoy John T. Pickett discovered that, although Mexicans still smarted from their defeat on their own land thirteen years before, the Juarez administration remained an ally of the United States.

By the summer of 1862, Britain and France were inclined to mediate peace in favor of Confederate independence, for the two powers assumed that the South's impressive victories in Virginia and Tennessee signaled a quick end to the war. Nevertheless, the Confederacy's autumn setbacks of Antietam and Perryville (in Kentucky), combined with ennobling rhetoric of the soon-to-be-announced Emancipation Proclamation, proved that the Union was still very much alive. The diplomatic recognition the white South so desperately craved remained elusive.

The Other War: African American Struggles for Liberation

From the onset of military hostilities, African Americans, regardless of whether they lived in the North or the South, perceived the Civil War as a fight for freedom. Although they allied themselves with Union forces, they also recognized the limitations of Union policy in ending slavery. Therefore, blacks throughout the northern and southern states were forced to take action to free themselves as individuals, families, and communities. Twenty-year-old Charlie Reason recalled his daring escape from a Maryland slave master and his decision to join the famous 54th Massachusetts Infantry composed of black soldiers: "I came to fight *not* for my country, I never had any, but to gain one." Soon after the 54th's assault on Fort Wagner (outside Charleston Harbor) in July 1863, Reason died of an infection contracted when one of his legs had to be amputated. In countless ways, black people throughout the South fought to gain a country on their own terms.

Enemies Within the Confederacy

Like the Revolutionaries of 1776, slaveholding whites were shocked when they could not always count on the loyalty of "petted" domestics. Soon after the war began, South Carolina's Mary Boykin Chesnut had expressed unease about the enigmatic behavior of one of her trusted house slaves, Laurence, asking herself of all her slaves, "Are they stolidly stupid or wiser than we

■ **All over the South, black people watched and waited for opportunities to claim their own freedom. The movement of Union troops into an area often prompted slaves to flee from the plantation. Individuals and extended families sought safety behind Union lines or in nearby towns or cities, or began the quest for long-lost loved ones.**

are, silent and strong, biding their time?" A few months later, Chesnut's cousin was murdered while sleeping, bludgeoned by a candlestick; the cousin's slaves William and Rhody were charged with the crime. Of her own mulatto servant, one of Chesnut's women friends remarked, "For the life of me, I cannot make up my mind. Does she mean to take care of me—or to murder me?" Now rising to the surface, such fears put whites on alert, guarding against enemies in their midst.

Yet no single white man or woman could halt the tide of freedom. Given the chance to steal away at night or walk away boldly in broad daylight, black men, women, and children left their masters and mistresses, seeking safety and paid labor behind Union lines. Throughout the South, black people waited and watched for an opportunity to flee from plantations, their actions depending on the movement of northern troops and the disarray of the plantations they lived on. In July 1862, the Union's Second Confiscation Act provided that the slaves of rebel masters "shall be deemed captives of war and shall be forever free," prompting Union generals to begin employing runaway male slaves as manual laborers. Consequently, military authorities often turned away women, children, older adults, and the disabled, leaving them vulnerable to spiteful masters and mistresses. For black men pressed into Union military and menial labor service, and for their families still languishing on plantations, "freedom" came at a high price indeed.

The Ongoing Fight Against Prejudice in the North and South

In the North, the Emancipation Proclamation spurred the enlistment of black men in the Union army and navy. Eventually, about 33,000 northern blacks enlisted, following the lead of their brothers-in-arms from the South. For black northern soldiers, military service opened up a wider world. Some learned to read and write in camp, and almost all felt the satisfaction of contributing to a war that they defined in stark terms of freedom versus slavery. They wore their uniforms proudly.

Union wartime policies revealed, however, that African Americans would continue to fight prejudice on many fronts. Some northern whites approved recruiting blacks, reasoning that for each black man killed in battle, one white man would be spared. Until late in the war, black soldiers were systematically denied opportunities to advance through the ranks and were paid less than whites. Although they showed loyalty to the cause in disproportionate numbers compared with white men, most blacks found themselves barred from taking up arms at all, relegated to **fatigue work** deemed dangerous and degrading to whites. They intended to labor for the Union, but, in the words of a black soldier from New York, "Instead of the musket it is the spade and the Whelbarrow and the Axe cuting in one of the horable swamps in Louisiana stinking and misery." For each white Union soldier killed or mortally wounded, two died of disease; the ratio for blacks was one to ten.

Many northern military strategists and ordinary enlisted men showed indifference at best, contempt at worst, for the desire of black fugitives to locate lost loved ones and begin to labor on their own behalf. In the course of the war, Union experiments with free black labor—on the South Carolina Sea Islands under the direction of northern missionaries, and in Louisiana, under the direction of generals Nathaniel Banks and Benjamin Butler—emphasized converting the former slaves into staple crop wage workers under the supervision of Yankees. Some of these whites, in their eagerness to establish "order" in former Confederate territory, saw blacks only as exploitable labor—if not cannon fodder, then hands to dig ditches and grow cotton.

Former slave Susie King Taylor recalled the heady, dangerous days of 1862, when she fled from Savannah and found refuge behind Union lines off the coast of Georgia. Despite little pay and poor treatment in the First South Carolina Volunteers (later known as the 33rd United States Colored Cavalry), Taylor gained a great deal of satisfaction from conducting a school for black children on St. Simon's Island and performing a whole host of tasks for the fighting men, from cleaning rifles to washing clothes and tending the ill. She understood that her own contributions to the war effort showed "what sacrifices we can make for our liberty and rights."

Battle Fronts and Home Fronts in 1863

In 1863 the North abandoned the strategy of conciliation in favor of an effort to destroy the large southern armies and deprive the Confederacy of its slave labor force. By this time, the war was causing a tremendous hardship among ordinary white folk in the South. Meanwhile, Lincoln found himself caught between African American freedom fighters who resented the poor treatment they received from many white commanders, and white Northerners who took their opposition to the war in general and the military draft in particular into the streets. Deprivation at home and the mounting casualty rates on the battlefields were reshaping the fabric of American society, North and South.

Disaffection in the Confederacy

The Civil War assaulted Southerners' senses and their land. Before the war, slave owners and their allies often contrasted the supposed tranquility of their rural society with the rude, boisterous noisiness of the North. According to this view, the South was a peaceful place of contented slaves toiling in the fields, whereas the North was the site of workers striking, women clamoring for the vote, and eccentric reformers delivering streetcorner harangues.

The war exploded on the southern landscape with ferocious force, and the rumble of huge armies on the march shook southern society to its foundations. For the first time many Southerners smelled the acrid odor of gunpowder and the stench of rotting bodies. They heard the booms of near and distant cannon and the mournful sounds of church bells tolling for the dead. They saw giant encampments of soldiers cover what used to be cotton fields. Seemingly overnight, both armies constructed gorge-spanning train trestles and huge riverside docks and warehouses, all in preparation for conflict. As soldiers withdrew from the battlefield, they left behind a scarred and blood-spattered land, cornfields mowed down, fires smoldering in their wake.

These sights and sounds were especially distressing to Southerners who objected to the war as a matter of principle or because of its disastrous effects on their households. Scattered throughout the South were communities resistant to the policies of what many ordinary whites considered the Richmond elite—the leaders of the Confederacy. In western North Carolina, a group calling themselves Heroes of America declared their loyalty to the Union. In northern Alabama, the "Free State of Jones [County]" raised troops for the Yankee army. Throughout the rural South, army deserters were welcomed home by their impoverished wives and children; it is estimated that during much of the war, as many as one-third of all Confederate soldiers were absent without leave at any particular time.

> *During much of the war, as many as one-third of all Confederate soldiers were absent without leave at any particular time.*

Groups of poor women resisted the dictates of the Davis administration, wealthy men and women who flaunted an extravagant wartime lifestyle of lavish dinners and parties. Women from Virginia to Alabama protested a Confederate 10 percent "tax-in-kind" on produce grown by farmers and the food shortages that reached crisis proportions. In April 1863, several hundred Richmond women, many of them wives of Tredegar Iron Works employees, armed themselves with knives, hatchets, and pistols and ransacked stores in search of food: "Bread! Bread! Our children are starving while the rich roll in wealth."

Whereas some white women resisted the Confederacy, others leaped to the fore to provide essential goods and services to the beleaguered new nation. Virginia's Belle Boyd kept track of Union troop movements and served as a spy for Confederate armies. Poor women took jobs as textile factory workers, and their better-educated sisters found employment as clerks for the Confederate bureaucracy. Slaveholding women busied themselves running plantations, rolling bandages, and knitting socks for soldiers. Still, many women thought their labors were in vain. Of the Confederacy's stalled progress, Georgia's Gertrude Thomas noted, "Valuable lives lost and nothing accomplished."

The Tide Turns Against the South

In the fall of 1862, Lincoln replaced General McClellan with General Ambrose E. Burnside and then General Joseph ("Fighting Joe") Hooker. In early May 1863, Lee and Jackson encountered Hooker at Chancellorsville, Virginia. The battle left Hooker reeling, but it also claimed the life of Jackson, mistakenly shot by his own men on May 2 in the early evening twilight. The South had lost one of its most ardent champions.

Lee decided to press his advantage by invading Pennsylvania and, it was hoped, encouraging northern Peace Democrats and impressing the foreign powers. The ensuing clash at Gettysburg was a turning point in the war. Drawn by reports of a cache of much-needed shoes, Confederate armies converged on the town, in the south-central part of the state and across the border from Maryland. Union forces pursued. In a three-day battle that began on July 1, the 92,000 men under the command of General George G. Meade were arrayed against the 76,000 troops of Robert E. Lee.

Gettysburg later came to represent the bloody consequences of a war fought by men with modern weapons under commanders with a premodern military sensibility. On the last day of the battle, the men under Confederate Major General George Pickett moved slowly into formation, passing hastily dug graves and the fragments of bodies blown to bits the day before. At 3 p.m., a mile-wide formation of 15,000 men gave the rebel yell and charged three-quarters of a mile across an open field to do battle with Union troops well fortified behind stone walls. Within half an hour, Pickett had lost two-thirds of his soldiers and all thirteen of his colonels. The battle's three-day toll was equally staggering: 23,000 Union and 28,000 Confederate soldiers wounded or killed. Fully one-third of Lee's army was dead or wounded.

What made men of both sides fight on under these conditions? Some remained devoted to a cause. Others cared less about the Confederacy or the Union and more about proving their manhood and upholding their family's honor. Still others sought to memorialize comrades slain in battle or to conform to standards of discipline drilled into them. Some prayed merely to survive.

The Union victory at Gettysburg on July 3 brought rejoicing in the North. The next day, General Ulysses S. Grant captured Vicksburg on the Mississippi River, a move that earned him the rank of lieutenant general (conferred by Congress). Within a year, he assumed the position of supreme commander of the Union armies.

Civil Unrest in the North

DOCUMENT

Brewster, Three Letters from the Front (1862)

Not all segments of northern society joined in the celebration. Even principled supporters of the Union war effort were growing weary of high taxes and inflated consumer prices, not to mention the sacrifices of thousands of husbands, sons, and brothers. In May, federal soldiers had arrested the defiant and outspoken Copperhead Clement Vallandigham at his home in Dayton, Ohio. Subsequently convicted of treason (he had declared the conflict "a war for the freedom of blacks and the enslavement of whites"), Vallandigham was banished to the South.

Following a military draft imposed on July 1, 1863, the northern white working classes erupted. Enraged at the wealthy who could buy substitutes, resentful of the Lincoln administration's high-handed tactics, and determined not to fight on behalf of their African American competitors in the workplace, laborers in New York City, Hartford, Troy, Newark, and Boston (many of them Irish) went on a rampage. The New York City riot of July 11–15 was especially savage as white men directed their wrath against black men, women, and children. Members of the mob burned the Colored Orphan Asylum to the ground and then mutilated their victims, before the federal government deployed 20,000 troops to New York to quell the violence and discourage other men from resisting the draft elsewhere. On August 19, the draft resumed.

The Desperate South

Meanwhile, the South had to contend not only with dissent and disaffection at home but also with the stunning battle and territorial losses it suffered at Gettysburg and Vicksburg. On August 21, Jefferson Davis proclaimed a day of "fasting, humiliation and prayer." Even as Davis was invoking the name of the Almighty, 450 rebels under the command of William Clarke Quantrill were destroying the town of Lawrence, Kansas (long a hotbed of abolitionist sentiment), and killing 150 of its inhabitants. With the exception of Quantrill and John Singleton Mosby (whose squads of men roamed northern Virginia attacking Union posts and troops in 1863), Confederate military leaders shunned guerrilla warfare, preferring to meet the enemy on a field of honor.

Before the year was out, Davis faced other setbacks as well. Grant's successes at Missionary Ridge and Lookout Mountain, in Tennessee, caused both France and England to draw back from offering overt support to the Confederacy in the form of sales of navy warships or diplomatic recognition. The Confederate president had long counted on securing the support of the great European powers; now those hopes were dashed.

Dedicating the national cemetery at Gettysburg on November 19, 1863, Lincoln delivered a short address that affirmed the nation's "new birth of freedom" and its commitment that "the government of the people, by the people, for the people, shall not perish from the earth." Lincoln's speech is one of the rhetorical masterpieces of American politics. In it he elevated the Civil War from a military conflict exclusively to a great moral struggle against slavery. Meanwhile, Grant, the hero of Vicksburg was poised at the border of northern Georgia, ready to push south to the sea and cut in half what was left of the Confederacy.

■ In September 1864, the Indian chiefs Black Kettle and White Antelope, with other Cheyenne and Arapaho leaders, met with Colonel John M. Chivington at Camp Weld, Colorado. The purpose of the meeting was to secure a truce between the Indians and European Americans in the area. Two months later, Chivington attacked an encampment of these Indians on the banks of Sand Creek, about 100 miles southeast of Denver.

The Prolonged Defeat of the Confederacy, 1864–1865

By 1864 northern generals, with Lincoln's blessing, had decided to fight a "hard war" against their tenacious enemy. Union troops were authorized to live off the land (denying southern civilians the necessities of life in the process), to seize livestock and other supplies indiscriminately, and to burn everything that the Confederates might find useful. The purposes of this strategy were twofold: to irreparably harm what was left of Confederate morale, and to facilitate the movement of northern troops through hostile territory. If northern troops could sever the area west of Georgia from the Confederacy and take Richmond and destroy its surrounding armies, the Union would be safe at last.

AUDIO

"When This Cruel War Is Over"

White Men's "Hard War" Toward African Americans and Indians

The policy of "hard war" should not be confused with total war, characterized by state-approved terrorism against civilians. However, Confederate policies toward black soldiers and Union policies toward Indian insurgents in the West did show elements of total war against particular segments of the population. In April 1864, Confederate General Nathan Bedford Forrest destroyed

Fort Pillow, a Union garrison on the Mississippi River. After surrendering, black soldiers were systematically murdered. Wounded survivors were bayoneted or burned to death. Among southern generals, conventions of war (providing for the detention and exchange of prisoners of war) did not apply to African American soldiers.

Nor were Indians accorded the minimal respect shown to most white combatants. In the early fall of 1864, a group of Cheyenne and Arapaho were camped along Sand Creek in the southeastern corner of Colorado. Black Kettle, a chief of the Cheyenne, had received promises from Union Colonel John M. Chivington and others stationed at Camp Weld in Denver that the two sides would remain at peace with each other. Therefore, on the morning of November 29, 1864, when Black Kettle saw Chivington leading a Colorado volunteer militia toward his settlement, he waved a white flag and stood his ground.

Chivington did not come in peace. That day he and his men massacred 125 to 160 Indians, mostly women, children, and old people, returning later to mutilate the bodies. In response, the Sioux, Arapaho, and Cheyenne launched their own campaigns against white migrants traveling the South and North Platte trails. Chivington declared that it was "right and honorable" to kill Indians, even children, using any means.

"Father Abraham"

The election of 1864 proceeded without major incident, although Lincoln faced some opposition within his own party. Together with his new running mate, a former slave owner from Tennessee named Andrew Johnson, Lincoln benefited from a string of preelection military victories won for him by Admiral David G. Farragut at Mobile, Alabama, and by General Philip Sheridan in Virginia's Shenandoah Valley. As a result, he defeated the Democratic nominee, his own former general, George McClellan, who managed to garner 45 percent of the popular vote. One of the keys to Lincoln's success was the "peace platform" that the Democrats had drafted at their convention the summer before. Support among Union soldiers for "Little Mac" dropped precipitously as a result, and Lincoln won three-quarters of the army's vote.

Despite his limited military experience, Lincoln possessed a strategic sense superior to that of many of his generals. He played down his own military experience, making light of his minor part in the Black Hawk War of 1832. In that conflict, he reminisced, he had engaged in "charges upon wild onions . . . [and] bloody struggles with the Musquetoes." However, he cared deeply about ordinary soldiers and talked with them whenever he had the opportunity. In return, Union troops gave "Father Abraham" their loyalty on the battlefield and, especially during the election of 1864, at the ballot box.

TABLE 14-1

The Election of 1864

Candidate	Political Party	Popular Vote (%)	Electoral Vote
Abraham Lincoln	Republican	55.0	212*
George B. McClellan	Democratic	45.0	21

*Eleven secessionist states did not participate.

The Last Days of the Confederacy

Union General William Tecumseh Sherman's forces overtook Atlanta in September 1864 and swept southeast toward the coast, living off the land and denying Confederate soldiers and civilians alike food and supplies along the way. En route to Savannah, Sherman's men liberated Andersonville Prison, a 26-square-acre Confederate camp that held 33,000 prisoners in the summer of 1864. Unable to feed their own armies and so unwilling to commit large supplies of food to the prison, the Confederate commander, Henry Wirz, stood by while 13,000 died of starvation, disease, and exposure. Wirz was the only Confederate officer to be tried, convicted, and executed for war crimes by the U.S. government.

■ **MAP 14.3**
SHERMAN'S MARCH TO THE SEA, 1864–1865   General William T. Sherman's famous march to the sea
marked the final phase of the Union effort to divide and conquer the Confederacy. Sherman's men burned
Atlanta to the ground in September 1864. In late December, they made their triumphant entry into the city
of Savannah. Sherman followed a policy of "hard war" in these final months of the war; he ordered his
troops to seize from civilians any food and livestock they could use and to destroy everything else, whether
rail lines, houses, or barns. White Southerners expressed outrage over these tactics. Still, Sherman never
systematically attacked civilians, a characteristic of the Union's "total war" against Native American peoples
in the West.

After presenting Lincoln with the "Christmas gift" of Savannah in December, Sherman
took his 60,000 troops north, slogging through swamps and rain-soaked terrain to confront
the original secessionists. Later, he recalled with satisfaction, "My aim then was to whip the
rebels, to humble their pride, to follow them to their inmost recesses, and make them fear
and dread us." By mid-February, South Carolina's state capital, Columbia, was in flames. African
American troops were among the triumphant occupiers of the charred city.

By early April 1865, Grant had overpowered Lee's army in Petersburg, Virginia. Withdrawing, Lee sent a telegram to Davis, who was attending church in Richmond, warning him
that the fall of the Confederate capital was imminent. Davis and almost all other whites fled
the city. Arriving in Richmond on April 3, only hours after the city had been abandoned, was
the commander in chief of the Union army, Abraham Lincoln. Lincoln calmly walked the streets
of the smoldering city (set afire by departing Confederates), flanked by a group of ten sailors.

**The Civil War
Part II:
1863–1865**

Throngs of black people greeted the president, exclaiming, "Glory to God! Glory! Glory! Glory!" When a black man kneeled to thank Lincoln, the president said, "Don't kneel to me. That is not right. You must kneel to God only, and thank Him for the liberty you will enjoy hereafter."

On April 9, Lee and his demoralized and depleted army of 35,000 men found themselves outnumbered by Grant and Meade, and Lee surrendered his sword at Appomattox Courthouse in northern Virginia. Union officials ensured rebel soldiers protection from future prosecution for treason, and allowed the cavalry to keep their horses for use in spring planting. When the ragtag members of the so-called Stonewall Brigade—men who had entered the war with Stonewall Jackson four years before—came forward to lay down their arm, the Union army gave them a salute of honor, acknowledging their bravery.

Watching a comedy with his wife, Mary, at Ford's Theater in Washington on the night of April 14, Lincoln was one of the last casualties of the war. Shot by John Wilkes Booth, a Confederate loyalist fearful that the president was bent on advancing "nigger citizenship," Lincoln lingered through the night but died the next morning. Booth was caught and shot within a matter of days. Of the departed president, Secretary of State Seward said, "Now he belongs to the ages."

Conclusion

Rather than asking why the South lost the Civil War, we might wonder why it took the North four years to win it. Despite all the political dissent and social conflict in the white South, despite the crumbling of the institution of slavery and the lack of support from the European powers, the Confederacy was able to mobilize huge armies under the command of brilliant tacticians such as Lee and Jackson. The war was fought on the battlefield by regiments of soldiers, not on the sea by navies or in the countryside by guerrillas. Therefore, as long as Confederate generals could deploy troops and outwit their foes during brief but monumental clashes, the Confederacy could survive to fight another day.

In terms of soldiers' lives lost—620,000—the Civil War was by far the costliest in the nation's history. (The death toll among American military personnel in the Revolution was 26,000; in World War I, 116,000; in World War II, 400,000; in Vietnam, 58,000.) At the end of the war, the Union was preserved and slavery was destroyed. Yet, in their quest for true freedom, African Americans soon learned that military hostilities were but one phase of a wider war, a war to define the nature of American citizenship and its promise of liberty and equality. Thus April 1865 marked not so much a final judgment as a transition to new battlefields.

Sites to Visit

Valley of the Shadow: Living the Civil War in Pennsylvania and Virginia
http://valley.vcdh.virginia.edu/
This project tells the histories of two communities on either side of the Mason-Dixon line during the Civil War. It includes narrative and an electronic archive of sources.

The Civil War in Charleston, South Carolina
www.awod.com/gallery/probono/cwchas/cwlayout.html
This site covers the history of the Civil War in and around Charleston.

Abraham Lincoln Association
www.alincolnassoc.com/
This site includes digital versions of Lincoln's papers.

United States Civil War Center
www.cwc.lsu.edu/
Maintained by Louisiana State University, this site aims to promote the study of the Civil War by making available "all appropriate private and public data" related to the conflict.

Civil War Women

scriptorium.lib.duke.edu/collections/civil-war-women.html

This Duke University library site includes original documents, links, and biographical information about several women and their lives during the Civil War.

Library of Congress Civil War Documents and Photographs

memory.loc.gov/ammem/

This Library of Congress site includes a wealth of texts and images related to the history of the Civil War.

Civil War Timeline

www.historyplace.com/civilwar/index.html

This site offers a comprehensive Civil War timeline that includes photographs.

National Civil War Association

www.ncwa.org/

This site documents the activities of one of the many Civil War reenactment organizations in the United States.

For Further Reading

General

David Herbert Donald, *Lincoln* (1995).

Steven Hahn, *A Nation Under Our Feet: Black Political Struggles in the Rural South from Slavery to the Great Migration* (2003).

Edward Hagerman, *The American Civil War and the Origins of Modern Warfare* (1988).

James M. McPherson, *Battle Cry of Freedom: The Civil War Era* (1988).

Reid Mitchell, *Civil War Soldiers: Their Expectations and Experiences* (1988).

Mobilization for War, 1861–1862

Gabor Borit, ed., *Lincoln's Generals* (1994).

Drew Gilpin Faust, *The Creation of Southern Nationalism: Ideology and Identity in the Civil War South* (1988).

Joseph L. Harsh, *Confederate Tide Rising: Robert E. Lee and the Making of Southern Strategy, 1861–62* (1998).

Wilfrid Knight, *Red Fox: Stand Watie and the Confederate Indian Nations During the Civil War Years in Indian Territory* (1988).

The Course of War, 1862–1864

Stephen Ash, *When the Invaders Came: Conflict and Chaos in the Occupied South, 1861–1865* (1996).

Howard Jones, *The Union in Peril: The Crisis over British Intervention in the Civil War* (1992).

Elizabeth Leonard, *All the Daring of the Soldier: Women of the Civil War Armies* (1999).

Heather Cox Richardson, *The Greatest Nation on Earth: Republican Economic Policies During the Civil War* (1997).

The Other War: African American Struggles for Liberation

Ira Berlin et al., *Freedom: A Documentary History of Emancipation*: Series 1, Vol. I: *The Destruction of Slavery*; Series 2: *The Black Military Experience* (1982).

Jacqueline Jones, *Labor of Love, Labor of Sorrow: Black Women, Work, and the Family Since Slavery* (1985).

William S. McFeely, *Frederick Douglass* (1991).

Willie Lee Rose, *Rehearsal for Reconstruction: The Port Royal Experiment* (1964).

Battle Fronts and Home Fronts in 1863

Stephen V. Ash, *Middle Tennessee Society Transformed, 1860–1870: War and Peace in the Upper South* (1988).

Iver Bernstein, *The New York City Draft Riots: Their Significance for American Society and Politics in the Age of the Civil War* (1990).

Drew Gilpin Faust, *Mothers of Invention: Women of the Slaveholding South in the American Civil War* (1996).

J. Matthew Gallman, *The North Fights the War: The Home Front* (1994).

The Prolonged Defeat of the Confederacy, 1864–1865

Michael B. Ballard, *A Long Shadow: Jefferson Davis and the Final Days of the Confederacy* (1997).

Mark Grimsley, *The Hard Hand of War: Union Military Policy Toward Southern Civilians, 1861–1865* (1995).

James M. McPherson, *For Cause and Comrades: Why Men Fought in the Civil War* (1997).

J. Tracy Power, *Lee's Miserables: Life in the Army of Northern Virginia from the Wilderness to Appomattox* (1998).

For quizzes and other resources on these topics, go to www.longmanamericanhistory.com.

Consolidating a Triumphant Union, 1865–1877

I N SAVANNAH, GEORGIA, IN MID-DECEMBER 1864, AFRICAN AMERICAN MEN, WOMEN, AND children rejoiced when the troops of Union General William Tecumseh Sherman liberated the city: the day of jubilee had come at last! The city's black community immediately formed its own school system under the sponsorship of a new group, the Savannah Education Association (SEA). The association owed its creation to the desire of freedpeople of all ages to learn to read and write. A committee of nine black clergy began by hiring fifteen black teachers and acquiring buildings (including the Old Bryan Slave Mart) for use as schools. By January 1, 1865, Savannah blacks had raised $800 to pay teachers' salaries, enabling several hundred black children to attend classes free of charge.

Following hard on the heels of the Union army, a group of northern white missionaries arrived in Savannah to seek black converts for two Protestant denominations, the Presbyterians and the Congregationalists. On the first day of school, in January 1865, these northern newcomers watched a grand procession of children wend its way through the streets of Savannah. The missionaries expressed amazement that the SEA was an entirely black-run organization. These whites had believed the former slaves incapable of creating such an impressive educational system.

In March 1865, the federal government, under the auspices of the newly formed Bureau of Refugees, Freedmen, and Abandoned Lands (Freedmen's Bureau), agreed to work with missionaries in opening schools for black children throughout the former Confederate states. In Georgia, missionaries and government officials soon became alarmed that black leaders were willing to accept financial aid from them but not willing to relinquish control of SEA schools to the whites in return. The Northerners were also distressed by the militancy of certain local black leaders. One of these leaders was Aaron Bradley, who, armed with a pistol and bowie knife, was urging other black men to vote as a bloc in all elections.

In an effort to wrest control of the SEA from Savannah blacks, northern missionaries and agents of the Freedmen's Bureau decided to withhold funds from the association. By March 1866,

■ In Savannah, African American Sunday school pupils pose for photographer William Wilson in 1890. After the Civil War, many southern black communities created, or enlarged and solidified, their own institutions, including schools and churches.

Courtesy of the Georgia Historical Society, William Wilson Collection

these efforts had paid off: the city's black community, swollen by a refugee population, was no longer able to support its own schools. Northern whites took over SEA operations, and the association ceased to exist.

Postwar political interest in the South unleashed a major conflict between supporters of African American rights and supporters of southern white privilege. Republican congressmen hoped to *reconstruct* the South by enabling African Americans to own land and to become full citizens. Southern freedpeople sought to free themselves from white employers, landlords, and clergy and to establish control over their own workplaces, families, and churches. In contrast, President Andrew Johnson appeared bent on *restoring* the antebellum power relations that made southern black people field laborers dependent on white landowners. For their part, many southern whites were determined to prevent black people from becoming truly free. Most former rebels remained embittered about the outcome of the war and vengeful toward the freedpeople.

After the war, western economic development presented new challenges for men who had fought for the Union. In order to open the West to European American miners and homesteaders, the U.S. army clashed repeatedly with Native Americans. On the Plains and in the Northwest, Indians resisted white efforts to force them to abandon their nomadic way of life and take up sedentary farming. William Tecumseh Sherman, Philip H. Sheridan, and George Custer were among the U.S. military officers who had commanded troops in the Civil War and now attempted to subdue the Plains Indians and further white settlement. Sherman declared, "We must act with vindictive earnestness against the Sioux, even to their extermination, men, women and children." The former head of the Freedmen's Bureau, General Oliver O. Howard, oversaw the expulsion of Chief Joseph and his people, the Nez Perce, from their homeland in southeast Washington's Walla Walla Valley in 1877.

The Civil War hardened the positions of the two major political parties. The Republicans remained in favor of a strong national government, one that promoted economic growth. The Democrats tended to support states' efforts to manage their own affairs, which included regulating relations between employers and employees, whites and blacks. The railroad industry represented a robust, Republican-sponsored partnership between private enterprise and the federal government. Between 1862 and 1872, the government gave the industry subsidies that included millions of dollars in cash and more than 100 million acres of land. During the postwar period, federal government officials attempted to complete the political process that the military defeat of the South had only begun: the consolidation of the Union, North and South, East and West. This process encompassed the nation as a whole.

The Struggle over the South

The Civil War had a devastating impact on the South in physical, social, and economic terms. The region had lost an estimated $2 billion in investments in slaves; modest homesteads and grand plantations alike lay in ruins; and gardens, orchards, and cotton fields were barren. More than 3 million former slaves eagerly embraced freedom, but the vast majority lacked the land, cash, and credit necessary to build family homesteads for themselves. Hoping to achieve social and economic self-determination, African American men and women traveled great distances, usually on foot, in efforts to locate loved ones and reunite families that had been separated during slavery. At the same time, landowning whites considered black people primarily as a source of agricultural labor; these whites resisted the idea that the freedpeople should be granted citizenship rights.

In the North, Republican lawmakers disagreed among themselves how best to punish the defeated but defiant rebels. President Abraham Lincoln had indicated early that after the war the government should bring the South back into the Union quickly and painlessly. His successor wanted to see members of the southern planter elite humiliated, but resisted the notion that freedpeople should become independent of white landowners. In Congress, moderate and radical Republicans argued about how far the government should go in ensuring the former slaves' freedom.

Wartime Preludes to Postwar Policies

Wartime experiments with African American free labor in Union-occupied areas foreshadowed bitter postwar debates. As early as November 1861, Union forces had occupied the Sea Islands off Port Royal Sound in South Carolina. In response, wealthy cotton planters fled to the mainland. Over the next few months, three groups of northern civilians landed on the Sea Islands with the intention of guiding blacks in the transition from slave to free labor. Teachers arrived intent on creating schools, and missionaries hoped to start churches. A third group, representing Boston investors, had also settled on the Sea Islands to assess economic opportunities; by early 1862, they decided to institute a system of wage labor that would reestablish a staple crop economy and funnel cotton directly into northern textile mills. The freed slaves, however, preferred to grow crops for their families to eat rather than cotton to sell, relying on a system of barter and trade among networks of extended families. Their goal was to break free of white landlords, suppliers, and cotton merchants.

Meanwhile, in southern Louisiana, the Union capture of New Orleans in the spring of 1862 enabled northern military officials to implement their own free (that is, nonslave) labor system. General Nathaniel Banks proclaimed that U.S. troops should forcibly relocate blacks to plantations "where they belong"; there they would continue to work for their former owners in the sugar and cotton fields, but now for wages supposedly negotiated annually. The Union army would compel blacks to work if they resisted doing so. In defiance of these orders, however, some blacks went on strike for higher wages, and others refused to work at all. Moreover, not all Union military men relished the prospect of forcing blacks to work on the plantations where they had been enslaved. Thus, federal policies returning blacks to plantations remained contested even within the ranks of the army itself.

Not all Union military men relished the prospect of forcing blacks to work on the plantations where they had been enslaved.

The Lincoln administration had no hard-and-fast **Reconstruction** policy to guide congressional lawmakers looking toward the postwar period. In December 1863, the president outlined his Ten Percent Plan. This plan would allow former Confederate states to form new state governments once 10 percent of the men who had voted in the 1860 presidential election had pledged allegiance to the Union and renounced slavery. Congress instead passed the Wade-Davis Bill, which would have required a majority of southern voters in any state to take a loyalty oath affirming their allegiance to the United States. By refusing to sign the bill before Congress adjourned, Lincoln vetoed the measure (through a **pocket veto**). However, the president approved the creation of the Freedmen's Bureau in March 1865. The bureau was responsible for coordinating relief efforts on behalf of blacks and poor whites loyal to the Union, for sponsoring schools, and for implementing a labor contract system on southern plantations. At the time of his assassination, Lincoln seemed to be leaning toward giving the right to vote to southern black men.

Presidential Reconstruction, 1865–1867

When Andrew Johnson, the seventeenth president of the United States, assumed office in April 1865 after Lincoln's death, he brought his own agenda for the defeated South. Throughout his political career, Johnson had seen himself as a champion of poor white farmers in oppo-

CORBIS

■ Freedmen's Bureau agents distributed rations to former slaves and southern whites who had remained loyal to the Union. Agents also sponsored schools, legalized marriages formed under slavery, arbitrated domestic disputes, and oversaw labor contracts between workers and landowners. This photo shows the bureau office in Petersburg, Virginia.

sition to the wealthy planter class. A man of modest background, he had been elected U.S. senator from Tennessee in 1857. He alone among southern senators remained in Congress and loyal to the Union after 1861. Lincoln first appointed Johnson military governor of Tennessee when that state was captured by the Union in 1862 and then tapped him as his running mate for the election of 1864.

Soon after he assumed the presidency, Johnson disappointed congressional Republicans who hoped that he would serve as a champion of the freedpeople. He welcomed back into the Union those states reorganized under Lincoln's Ten Percent Plan. He advocated denying the vote to wealthy Confederates, though he would allow individuals to come to the White House to beg the president for special pardons. Johnson also outlined a fairly lenient plan for readmitting the other rebel states into the Union. Poor whites would have the right to vote, but they must convene special state conventions that would renounce secession and accept the Thirteenth Amendment abolishing slavery. Further, they must repudiate all Confederate debts. The president opposed granting the vote to the former slaves; he believed that they should continue to toil as field workers for white landowners. In fact, many former rebels gradually came to see Johnson as their postwar political ally.

Johnson failed to anticipate the speed and vigor with which former Confederate leaders would move to reassert their political authority. In addition, he did not gauge accurately the resentment of congressional Republicans, who thought his policies toward the defeated South were too forgiving. The southern states that took advantage of Johnson's reunification policies passed so-called **Black Codes**. These state laws were an ill-disguised attempt to institute a system of near-slavery. They aimed to penalize "vagrant" blacks, defined as those who did not work in the fields for whites, and to deny blacks the right to vote, serve on juries, or in some cases even own land. The Black Code of Mississippi restricted the rights of a freedperson to "keep or carry fire-arms," ammunition, and knives and to "quit the service of his or her employer before the expiration of his or her term of service without good cause." The vagueness of this last provision threatened any blacks who happened not to be working under the supervision of whites at any given moment. People arrested under the Black Codes faced imprisonment or forced labor.

DOCUMENT

The Mississippi Black Code

At the end of the war, congressional Republicans were divided into two camps. Radicals wanted to use strong federal measures to advance black people's civil rights and economic independence. In contrast, moderates were more concerned with the free market and private property rights; they took a hands-off approach regarding former slaves. But members of both groups reacted with outrage to the Black Codes. Moreover, when the legislators returned to the Capitol in December 1865, they were in for a shock: among their new colleagues were four former Confederate generals, five colonels, and other high-ranking members of the Confederate elite, including former Vice President Alexander Stephens, now under indictment for treason. All of these rebels were duly elected senators and representatives from southern states. In a special session called for December 4, a joint committee of fifteen lawmakers (six senators and nine members of the House) voted to bar these men from Congress.

By January 1865, both houses of Congress had approved the Thirteenth Amendment to the Constitution, abolishing slavery. The necessary three-fourths of the states ratified the measure by the end of the year. However, President Johnson was becoming more openly defiant of his congressional foes who favored aggressive federal protection of black civil rights. He vetoed two crucial pieces of legislation: an extension and expansion of the Freedmen's Bureau and the Civil Rights Bill of 1866. This latter measure was an unprecedented piece of legislation. It called on the federal government—for the first time in history—to protect individual rights against the willful indifference of the states (as manifested, for example, in the Black Codes). Congress managed to override both vetoes by the summer of 1866.

In June of that year, Congress passed the Fourteenth Amendment. This amendment guaranteed the former slaves citizenship rights, punished states that denied citizens the right to vote, declared the former rebels ineligible for federal and state office, and voided Confederate debts. This amendment was the first to use gender-specific language, guarding against denying the vote "to any of the male inhabitants" of any state.

Even before the war ended, Northerners had moved south, and the flow increased in 1865. Black and white teachers volunteered to teach the former slaves to read and write. Some white Northerners journeyed south to invest in land and become planters in the staple crop economy. White southern critics called all these migrants **carpetbaggers**. This derisive term suggested that the Northerners hastily packed their belongings in rough bags made of carpet scraps and then rushed south to take advantage of the region's devastation and confusion. To many freedpeople, whether they worked for a carpetbagger or a Southerner, laboring in the cotton fields was but a continuation of slavery.

Some former southern (white) Whigs, who had been reluctant secessionists, now found common ground with northern Republicans who supported government subsidies for railroads, banking institutions, and public improvements. This group consisted of some members of the humbled planter class as well as men of more modest means. Southern Democrats, who sneered at any alliances with the North, scornfully labeled these whites **scalawags** (the term referred to a scrawny, useless type of horse on the Scottish island of Scalloway).

INTERPRETING HISTORY

A Southern Labor Contract

After the Civil War, many southern agricultural workers signed labor contracts. These contracts sought to control not only the output of laborers but also their lives outside the workplace.

On January 1, 1868, the planter John D. Williams assembled his workers for the coming year and presented them with a contract to sign. Williams owned a plantation in the lower Piedmont county of Laurens, South Carolina. He agreed to furnish "the said negroes" (that is, the three black men and two black women whose names were listed on the document) with mules and horses to be used for cultivating the land. The workers could receive their food, clothing, and medical care on credit. They were allowed to keep one-third of all the corn, sweet potatoes, wheat, cotton, oats, and molasses they produced. Presumably, they would pay their debts to Williams using proceeds from their share of the crop.

According to the contract, Williams's workers promised to

bind them Selves to be steady & attentive to there work at all times and to work at keeping in repair all the fences on Said plantation and assist in cuting & taking care of—all the grain crops on Said plantation and work by the direction of me [Williams] or my Agent.…

And should any of them depart from the farm or from any services at any time with out our approval they shall forfeit one dollar per day, for the first time and for the second time without good cause they shall forfeit all of their interest in the crop their to me the enjured person—they shall not be allowed to keep firearms or deadly wapons or ardent Spirits and they shall obey all lawful orders from me or my Agent and shall be honest—truthful—sober—civel—diligent in their business & for all wilful Disobedience of any lawful

After the Civil War, many rural southern blacks, such as those shown here, continued to toil in cotton fields owned by whites.

Library of Congress

orders from me or my Agent drunkenness moral or legal misconduct want of respects or civility to me or my Agent or to my Family or any elce, I am permitted to discharge them forfeiting any claims upon me for any part of the crop.…

Moses Nathan	1 full hand
Jake Chappal	" "
Milly Williams	½ " "
Easter Williams	" "
Mack Williams	" "

At the end of the contract is this addition:

We the white labores now employed by John D. Williams on his white plains plantation have lisened and heard read the foregoing Contract on this sheet of paper assign equal for the black laborers employed by him on said place and we are perfectly Satisfied with it and heare by bind our selves to abide & be Governed & Controwed by it

Wm Wyatte	1 full hand
John Wyatte	1 full hand
Packingham Wyatte	½ " "
Franklin Wyatte	½ " "
R M Hughes	1 full hand
B G Pollard	1 full hand
George Washington Pollard	1 full hand

To sign the contract, all of the blacks and two of the whites "made their marks"; that is, they signed with an "X" because they were illiterate.

Questions

1. In what ways did sharecropping differ from wage labor?

2. Do you see evidence that family or kin members worked together on Williams's plantation?

3. What is the significance of the contract addendum signed by white laborers? ■

Source: Rosser H. Taylor, "Postbellum Southern Rental Contracts" [from Furman University library, Greenville, South Carolina], *Agricultural History* 17 (1943): 122–123.

■ Residents of Edisto Island, off the coast of South Carolina, pose with a U.S. government mule cart immediately after the Civil War. U.S. troops captured the island in November 1861. The following March, the government began to distribute to blacks the lands abandoned by their former masters. In October 1865, President Andrew Johnson halted the program. A group of angry and disappointed blacks appealed to the president, claiming, "This is our home, we have made these lands what they are." After meeting with the group, General Oliver O. Howard noted, "I am convinced that something must be done to give these people and others the prospect of homesteads."

Soon after the war's end, southern white vigilantes launched a campaign of violence and intimidation against freedpeople who dared to resist the demands of white planters and other employers. Calling itself the Ku Klux Klan, a group of Tennessee war veterans soon became a white supremacist terrorist organization and spread to other states. In May 1866, violence initiated by white terrorists against blacks in Memphis, Tennessee, left forty-six freedpeople and two whites dead, and in July, a riot in New Orleans claimed the lives of thirty-four blacks and three of their white allies. These bloody encounters demonstrated the lengths to which ex-Confederates would go to reassert their authority and defy the federal government.

Back in Washington, Johnson vetoed the Fourteenth Amendment, traveling around the country and urging the states not to ratify it. He argued that policies related to black suffrage should be decided by the states. The time had come for reconciliation between the North and South, maintained the president. (The amendment would not be adopted until 1868.)

H. P. Moore/Collection of the New-York Historical Society, Neg. #37497

Congressional Republicans fought back. In the election of November 1866, they won a two-thirds majority in both houses of Congress. These numbers allowed them to claim a mandate from their constituents and to override any future vetoes by the president. Moderates and radicals together prepared to bypass Johnson to shape their own Reconstruction policies.

The Postbellum South's Labor Problem

While policymakers maneuvered in Washington, black people throughout the South aspired to labor for themselves and gain independence from white overseers and landowners. Yet white landowners persisted in regarding blacks as field hands who must be coerced into working. With the creation of the Freedmen's Bureau in 1865, Congress intended to form an agency that would mediate between these two groups. Bureau agents encouraged workers and employers to sign annual labor contracts designed to eliminate the last vestiges of the slave system. All over the South, freed men, women, and children would contract with an employer on January 1 of each year. They would agree to work for either a monthly wage, an annual share of the crop, or some combination of the two.

Most freedpeople understood they must find a way to provide for themselves first and foremost. They thought of freedom in terms of welfare for their family rather than just for themselves as individuals. Men and women embraced the opportunity to live and work together as a unit. For many couples, their first act as free people was to legalize their marriage vows. Black women shunned the advice of Freedmen's Bureau agents and planters that they continue to pick cotton. These women withdrew from field labor whenever they could afford to do so. Enslaved women had been deprived of the opportunity to attend to family life. Now freedwomen sought to devote themselves to caring for their families.

> *While policymakers maneuvered in Washington, black people throughout the South aspired to labor for themselves and gain independence from white overseers and landowners.*

Blacks along the Georgia and South Carolina coast were determined to cultivate the land on which their forebears had lived and died. They urged General Sherman to confiscate the land owned by rebels in the area. In response, in early 1865, Sherman issued Field Order Number 15, mandating that the Sea Islands and the coastal region south of Charleston be divided into parcels of 40 acres for individual freed families. He also decreed that the army might lend mules to these families to help them begin planting. Given the provisions of this order, many freed families came to expect that the federal government would grant them "40 acres and a mule."

As a result of Sherman's order, 20,000 former slaves proceeded to cultivate the property once owned by Confederates. Within a few months of the war's end, however, the War Department bowed to pressure from the white landowners and revoked the order. The War Department also provided military protection for whites to return and occupy their former lands. In response, a group of black men calling themselves Commissioners from Edisto Island (one of the Sea Islands) met in committee to protest to the Freedmen's Bureau what they considered a betrayal. Writing from the area in January 1866, one Freedmen's Bureau official noted that the new policy must be upheld but regretted that it had brought the freedpeople in "collision" with "U.S. forces."

DOCUMENT

Southern
Skepticism of
the Freedmen's
Bureau (1866)

During its brief life (1865 to 1868), the Freedmen's Bureau compiled a mixed record. The individual agents represented a broad range of backgrounds, temperaments, and political ideas. Some were former abolitionists who considered northern-style free labor to be "the noblest principle on earth." These men tried to ensure safe and fair working arrangements for black men, women, and children. In contrast, some agents had little patience with the freedpeople's drive for self-sufficiency. Some bureau offices became havens for blacks seeking redress against abusive or fraudulent labor practices, but other offices had little impact on the postwar political and economic landscape. For agents without means of transportation (a reliable horse), plantations scattered throughout the vast rural South remained outside their control. Because white landowners crafted the wording and specific provisions of labor contracts, the bureau agents who enforced such agreements often served the interests of employers rather than laborers.

DOCUMENT

A Sharecrop
Contract

The outlines of **sharecropping**, a system that defined southern cotton production until well into the twentieth century, were visible just a few years after the Civil War. Poor families, black and white, contracted annually with landlords, who advanced them supplies, such as crop seed, mules, plows, food, and clothing. Fathers directed the labor of their children in the fields. At the end of the year, many families remained indebted to their employer and, thus, entitled to nothing and obliged to work another year in the hope of repaying the debt. If a sharecropper's demeanor or work habits displeased the landlord, the family faced eviction.

Single women with small children were especially vulnerable to the whims of landlords in the postbellum period. Near Greensboro, North Carolina, for example, planter Presley George Sr. settled accounts with his field worker Polly at the end of 1865. For her year's expenses, Polly was charged a total $69 for corn, cloth, thread, and board for a child who did not work. By George's calculations, Polly had earned exactly $69 for the labor she and her three children (two sons and a daughter) performed in the course of the year, leaving her no cash of her own. Under these harsh conditions, freedpeople looked to each other for support and strength.

Building Free Communities

Soon after the war's end, southern blacks set about organizing themselves as an effective political force and as free communities devoted to the social and educational welfare of their own people. Differences among blacks based on income, jobs, culture, and skin color at times inhibited institution-building. Some black communities found themselves divided by class, with blacks who had been free before the war (including many literate and skilled light-skinned men) assuming leadership over illiterate field hands. In New Orleans, a combination of factors contributed to class divisions among people of African heritage. During the antebellum period, light-skinned free people of color, many of whom spoke French, were much more likely to possess property and a formal education than were enslaved people, who were dark-skinned English speakers. After the Civil War, the more privileged group pressed for public accommodations laws, which would open the city's theaters, opera, and expensive restaurants to all blacks for the first time. However, black churches and social organizations remained segregated according to class.

AUDIO

"Free At Last"

For the most part, postbellum black communities united around the principle that freedom from slavery should also mean full citizenship rights: the ability to vote, own land, and educate their children. These rights must be enforced by federal firepower: "a military occupation will be absolutely necessary," declared the blacks of Norfolk, "to protect the white Union men of the South, as well as ourselves." Freedpeople in some states allied themselves with white yeomen who had long resented the political power of the great planters and now saw an opportunity to use state governments as agents of democratization and economic reform.

Networks of freedpeople formed self-help organizations. Like the sponsors of the Savannah Education Association, blacks throughout the South formed committees to raise funds and

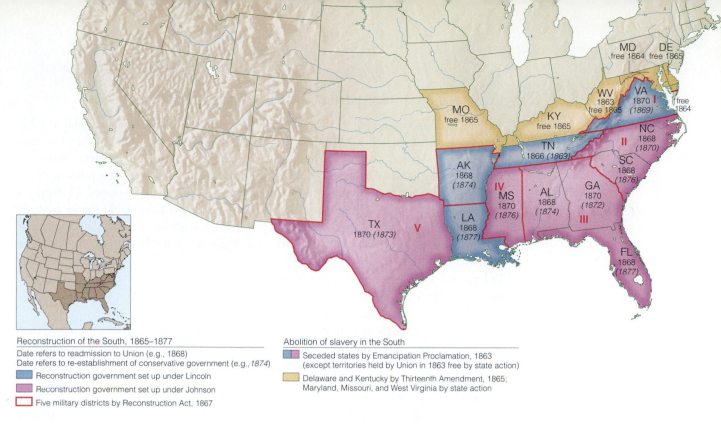

Reconstruction of the South, 1865–1877

Date refers to readmission to Union (e.g., 1868)
Date refers to re-establishment of conservative government (e.g., *1874*)

■ Reconstruction government set up under Lincoln

■ Reconstruction government set up under Johnson

□ Five military districts by Reconstruction Act, 1867

Abolition of slavery in the South

■ Seceded states by Emancipation Proclamation, 1863
(except territories held by Union in 1863 free by state action)

□ Delaware and Kentucky by Thirteenth Amendment, 1865;
Maryland, Missouri, and West Virginia by state action

■ **MAP 15.1**

RADICAL RECONSTRUCTION   Four of the former Confederate states, Louisiana, Arkansas, Tennessee, and Virginia, were reorganized under President Lincoln's Ten Percent Plan in 1864. Neither this plan nor the proposals of Lincoln's successor, Andrew Johnson, provided for the enfranchisement of the former slaves. In 1867 Congress established five military districts in the South and demanded that newly reconstituted state governments implement universal manhood suffrage. By 1870 all of the former Confederate states had rejoined the Union, and by 1877 all of those states had installed conservative (i.e., Democratic) governments.

hire teachers for neighborhood schools. Small Georgia towns, such as Cuthbert, Albany, Cave Spring, and Thomasville, with populations no greater than a few hundred, raised up to $70 per month and contributed as much as $350 each for the construction of school buildings. Funds came from the proceeds of fairs, bazaars, and bake sales; subscriptions raised by local school boards; and tuition fees. In the cash-starved postbellum South, these amounts represented a great personal and group sacrifice for the cause of education.

All over the South, black families charted their own course. They elected to take in orphans and elderly kin, pool resources with neighbors, and arrange for mothers to stay home with their children. These choices challenged the power of former slaveholders and the influence of Freedmen's Bureau agents and northern missionaries and teachers. At the same time, in seeking to attend to their families and to provide for themselves, southern blacks resembled members of other mid-nineteenth-century laboring classes who valued family ties over the demands of employers and landlords.

Tangible signs of the new emerging black communities infuriated most southern whites. A schoolhouse run by blacks proved threatening in a society where most white children had little opportunity to receive an education. Black communities were also quick to form their own churches, rather than continue to occupy an inferior place in white churches. Other sights proved equally unsettling: on a main street in Charleston, an armed black soldier marching proudly or a black woman wearing a fashionable hat and veil, the kind favored by white women of the planter class. These developments help to account for the speed with which whites organized themselves in the Klan and various other vigilante groups, aiming to preserve "the supremacy of the white race in this Republic."

MAP

Reconstruction

Congressional Reconstruction: The Radicals' Plan

The rise of armed white supremacist groups in the South helped spur congressional Republicans to action. On March 2, 1867, Congress seized the initiative. A coalition led by two radicals, Senator Charles Sumner of Massachusetts and Congressman Thaddeus Stevens of Pennsylvania, prodded Congress to pass the Reconstruction Act of 1867. The purpose of this measure was to purge the South of disloyalty once and for all. The act stripped thousands of former Confederates of voting rights. The former Confederate states would not be readmitted to the Union until they had ratified the Fourteenth Amendment and written new constitutions that guaranteed black men the right to vote. The South (with the exception of Tennessee, which had ratified the Fourteenth Amendment in 1866) was divided into five military districts. Federal troops were stationed throughout the region. These troops were charged with protecting Union personnel and supporters in the South and with restoring order in the midst of regional political and economic upheaval.

Congress passed two additional acts specifically intended to secure congressional power over the president. The intent of the Tenure of Office Act was to prevent the president from dismissing Secretary of War Edwin Stanton, a supporter of the radicals. The other measure, the Command of the Army Act, required the president to seek approval for all military orders from General Ulysses S. Grant, the army's senior officer. Grant also was a supporter of the Republicans. Both of these acts probably violated the separation of powers doctrine as put forth in the Constitution. Together, they would soon precipitate a national crisis.

During the Reconstruction period, approximately 2,000 black men of the emerging southern Republican party served as local elected officials, sheriffs, justices of the peace, tax collectors, and city councilors. Many of these leaders were of mixed ancestry, and many had been free before the war. They came in disproportionate numbers from the ranks of literate men, such as clergy, teachers, and skilled artisans. In Alabama, Florida, Louisiana,

■ This drawing by famous political cartoonist Thomas Nast depicts the first black members of Congress. Left to right, front row: Senator Hiram Revels of Mississippi (the first African American to serve in the U.S. Senate), Representatives Benjamin S. Turner of Alabama, Josiah T. Walls of Florida, Joseph H. Rainey of South Carolina, Robert B. Elliott of South Carolina. Back row: Representatives Robert G. DeLarge of South Carolina, Jefferson Long of Georgia.

Schomburg Center for Research in Black Culture, Art and Artifacts Division, The New York Public Library, Astor, Lenox and Tilden Foundations

Mississippi, and South Carolina, black men constituted a majority of the voting public. Throughout the South, 600 black men won election to state legislatures. However, nowhere did blacks control a state government, although they did predominate in South Carolina's lower House. Sixteen black Southerners were elected to the U.S. Congress during Reconstruction. Most of those elected to Congress in the years immediately after the war were free-born. However, among the nine men elected for the first time after 1872, six were former slaves. All of these politicians exemplified the desire among southern blacks to become active, engaged citizens.

Newly reconstructed southern state legislatures provided for public school systems, fairer taxation methods, bargaining rights of plantation laborers, racially integrated public transportation and accommodations, and public works projects, especially railroads. Nevertheless, the legislative coalitions forged between Northerners and Southerners, blacks and whites, were uneasy and, in many cases, less than productive. Southern Democrats (and later, historians sympathetic to them) claimed that Reconstruction governments were uniquely corrupt, with some carpetbaggers, scalawags, and freedpeople vying for **kickbacks** from railroad and construction magnates. In fact, whenever state legislatures sought to promote business interests, they opened the door to the bribery of public officials. In this respect, northern as well as southern politicians were vulnerable to charges of corruption. In the long run, southern Democrats cared less about charges of legislative corruption and more about the growing political power of local black Republican party organizations.

In Washington in early 1868, President Johnson forced a final showdown with Congress. He replaced several high military officials with more conservative men. He also fired Secretary of War Stanton, in apparent violation of the Tenure of Office Act. Shortly thereafter, in February, a newly composed House Reconstruction Committee impeached Johnson for ignoring the act, and the Senate began his trial on March 30. The president and Congress were locked in an extraordinary battle for political power.

The final vote was thirty-five senators against Johnson, one vote short of the necessary two-thirds of all senators' votes needed for conviction. Nineteen senators voted to acquit Johnson of the charges. Nevertheless, to win acquittal, he had had to promise moderates that he would not stand in the way of congressional plans for Reconstruction. Johnson essentially withdrew from policymaking in the spring of 1868. That November, Republicans urged Northerners to "vote as you shot" (that is, to cast ballots against the former Confederates) and elected Ulysses S. Grant to the presidency.

Political reunion was an uneven process, but one that gradually eroded the newly won rights of former slaves in many southern states.

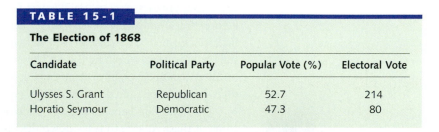

TABLE 15-1

The Election of 1868

Candidate	Political Party	Popular Vote (%)	Electoral Vote
Ulysses S. Grant	Republican	52.7	214
Horatio Seymour	Democratic	47.3	80

By the end of 1868, Arkansas, North Carolina, South Carolina, Louisiana, Tennessee, Alabama, and Florida had met congressional conditions for readmission to the Union, and two years later, Mississippi, Virginia, Georgia, and Texas followed. The Fifteenth Amendment, passed by Congress in 1869 and ratified by the necessary number of states a year later, granted all black men the right to vote. However, in some states, such as Louisiana, reunification gave Democrats license to engage in wholesale election fraud and violence toward freed men and women. In 1870–1871, a congressional inquiry into the Klan exposed pervasive and grisly assaults on Republican schoolteachers, preachers, and prospective voters, black and white. The Klan also targeted men and women who refused to work like slaves in the fields. In April 1871, Congress passed the Ku Klux Klan Act, which punished conspiracies intended to deny rights to citizens. But Klan violence and intimidation had already taken their toll on Republican voting strength.

VIDEO

Legacies of Reconstruction

Claiming Territory for the Union

While blacks and whites, northerners and southerners struggled for power in the south, poet Walt Whitman celebrated the "manly and courageous instincts" that propelled a brave, adventurous people west. Whitman hailed the march across the prairies and over the mountains as a cavalcade of progress. He and other Americans believed that the postbellum migration fulfilled a mission of national regeneration begun by the Civil War. Kansas's population grew by 240 percent in the 1860s, Nebraska's by 355 percent.

To unite the entire country together as a single economic and political unit was the Republican ideal. The railroads in particular served as vehicles of national integration. When the Central Pacific and Union Pacific Railroads met at Promontory Point, Utah, in 1869, the hammering of the spike that joined the two roads produced a telegraphic signal received simultaneously on both coasts, setting off a national celebration.

Meanwhile, regular units of United States cavalry, including two regiments of blacks, were launching attacks on Indians on the Plains, in the Northwest, and in the Southwest. Between 1865 and 1890, U.S. military forces conducted a dozen separate campaigns against western Indian peoples and met Indian warriors in battle or attacked Indian settlements in more than 1,000 engagements. In contrast to African Americans, who adamantly demanded their rights as American citizens, defiant western Indians battled a government to which they owed no allegiance.

Federal Military Campaigns Against Western Indians

In 1871 the U.S. government renounced the practice of seeking treaties with various Indian groups. This change in policy opened the way for a more aggressive effort to subdue native populations. It also hastened the expansion of the reservation system, an effort begun in the antebellum period to confine specific Indian groups to specific territories.

In the Southwest, clashes between Indians and U.S. soldiers persisted after the Civil War. In 1867 at Medicine Lodge Creek in southern Kansas, the United States signed a treaty with an alliance of Comanche, Kiowa, Cheyenne, Arapaho, and Plains Apache. This treaty could not long withstand the provocation posed by the railroad, as Indians continued to attack the surveyors, supply caravans, and military escorts that preceded the railroad work crews. The year before, the Seventh U.S. Cavalry, under the command of Lieutenant Colonel George Custer, had been formed to ward off native attacks on the Union Pacific, snaking its way across the central Plains westward from Kansas. In November 1868, Custer destroyed a Cheyenne settlement on the Washita River, in present-day Oklahoma. Custer's men murdered women and children, burned tipis, and destroyed 800 horses.

IMAGE

Geronimo and Natiche Surrender (1886)

The Apache Indians managed to elude General George Crook until 1875. Crook employed some of these Apache to track down the war chief Geronimo of the Chiricahua. Like many other Indian leaders, Geronimo offered both religious and military guidance to his people. He believed that a spirit would protect him from the white man's bullets and from the arrows of Indians in league with government troops. Yet Geronimo was tricked into a momentary surrender in 1877, and was held in irons for several months before gaining his release and challenging authorities for another nine years.

In 1874 Custer took the Seventh Cavalry into the Black Hills of the Dakotas. Supposedly, the 1868 Treaty of Fort Laramie had rendered this land off-limits to whites. Custer's mission was to offer protection for the surveyors of the Northern Pacific Railroad and to force Indians onto reservations as stipulated in the 1868 treaty. However, the officer lost no time trumpeting the fact that Indian lands were filled with gold. This report prompted a rush to the Black Hills, lands sacred to the Sioux. Within two years, 15,000 gold miners had illegally descended on Indian lands to seek their fortunes. The federal government proposed to buy the land, but leaders of the Sioux, including Red Cloud, Spotted Tail, and Sitting Bull, spurned the offer.

During the morning of June 25, 1876, Custer and his force of 264 soldiers attacked a Sun Dance gathering of 2,500 Sioux and Cheyenne on the banks of the Little Big Horn River in Montana. Custer foolishly launched his attack without adequate backup, and he and his men were easily overwhelmed and killed by Indian warriors, led by the Oglala Sioux Crazy Horse and others. Reacting to this defeat, U.S. military officials reduced the Lakota and Cheyenne to wardship status, ending their autonomy.

Indians throughout the West maintained their distinctive ways of life during these turbulent times. Horse holdings, so crucial for hunting, trading, and fighting, varied from group to group, with the Crow wealthy in relation to their Central Plains neighbors the Oglala and the Arikara. Plains peoples engaged in a lively trading system. They exchanged horses and their trappings (bridles and blankets) for eastern goods such as kettles, guns, and ammunition. Despite their differences in economy, these groups held similar religious beliefs about an all-powerful life force that governed the natural world. People, plants, and animals were all part of the same order.

The Postwar Western Labor Problem

In 1865 the owners of the Central Pacific Railroad seemed poised for one of the great engineering feats of the nineteenth century. In the race eastward from California, they would construct trestles spanning vast chasms and roadbeds traversing mountains and deserts. Government officials in Washington were eager to subsidize the railroad. What the owners lacked was a dependable labor force. The Irish workers who began the line in California struck for higher wages in compensation for brutal, dangerous work. These immigrants dropped their shovels and hammers at the first word of a gold strike nearby—or far away. As a result, in 1866 the Central Pacific had decided to tap into a vast labor source by importing thousands of Chinese men from their native Guangdong province.

Robert Benecke, photographer. DeGolyer Library, Southern Methodist University, Dallas, Texas, Ag1982.86.80

■ With this 1870 photograph, the Kansas Pacific Railroad advertised the opportunity for western travelers to shoot buffalo from the comfort and safety of their railroad car. The company's official taxidermist shows off his handiwork. Railroad expansion facilitated the exploitation of natural resources while promoting tourism.

■ Chinese construction workers labor on the Central Pacific Railroad, c. 1868. Many Chinese immigrants toiled as indentured laborers, indebted to Chinese merchant creditors who paid for their passage to California. Isolated in all-male work camps, crews of railroad workers retained their traditional dress, language, and diet. After the completion of the transcontinental railroad in 1869, some immigrants returned to China, and others dispersed to small towns and cities throughout the West.

Union Pacific Historical Collection

The Chinese toiled to extend the railroad tracks eastward from Sacramento, California, up to 10 miles a day in the desert, only a few feet a day in the rugged Sierra Nevada Mountains. In nerve-wracking feats of skill, they lowered themselves in woven baskets to implant nitro-glycerine explosives in canyon walls. Chinese laborers toiled through snowstorms and blistering heat to blast tunnels and cut passes through granite mountains. With the final linking of the railroad in Utah in 1869, many Chinese returned to California.

Signed in 1868, the Burlingame Treaty, named for Anson Burlingame, an American envoy to China, had supposedly guaranteed government protection for Chinese immigrants as visitors, traders, or permanent residents. Most immigrants were men. (Six out of ten California Chinese women were listed in the 1870 census as prostitutes, most the victims of their compatriots.) Yet the treaty did not inhibit U.S. employers, landlords, and government officials from discriminating against the Chinese.

By 1870, 40,000 Chinese lived in California and represented fully one-quarter of the state's wage earners. They found work in the cigar, woolen-goods, and boot and shoe factories of San Francisco; in the gold mining towns, now as laundry operators rather than as miners as they had before the Civil War; and in the fields as agricultural laborers. White workers began to cry unfair competition against this Asian group that was becoming increasingly integrated into the region's economy.

As a group, Chinese men differed from California Indians, who remained trapped in the traditional agricultural economy of unskilled labor. Whites appropriated Indian land and forced many men, women, and children to work as wage earners for large landowners. Deprived of their familiar hunting and gathering lands, and wracked by disease and starvation, California Indians had suffered a drastic decline in their numbers by 1870, from 100,000 to 30,000 in twenty years.

Land Use in an Expanding Nation

As with the labor force, the end of the Civil War prompted new conflicts and deepened long-standing ones over the use of the land in a rich, sprawling country. In the South, staple crop planters began to share political power with an emerging elite, men who owned railroads and textile mills. Despairing of ever achieving antebellum levels of labor efficiency, some landowners turned to mining the earth and the forests for saleable commodities. These products, obtained through extraction, included phosphate (used in producing fertilizer), timber, coal, and turpentine.

As European Americans settled in the West and Southwest, they displaced natives who had been living there for generations. For example, the U.S. court system determined who could legally claim property. Western courts also decided whether natural resources such as water, land, timber, and fish and game constituted property that could be owned by private interests. In the Southwest, European American settlers, including army soldiers who had come to fight Indians and then stayed, continued to place Hispanic land titles at risk. Citing pre-war precedents, American courts favored the claims of recent squatters over those of long-standing residents. In 1869, with the death of her husband (who had served as a general in the Union army), Maria Amparo Ruiz de Burton saw the large ranch they had worked together near San Diego slip out of her control. The first Spanish-speaking woman to be published in English in the United States, de Burton was a member of the Hispanic elite. Nevertheless, she had little political power. California judges backed the squatters who occupied the ranch.

In the 1870s, the so-called Santa Fe Ring wrested more than 80 percent of the original Spanish grants of land from Hispanic landholders in New Mexico. An alliance of European American lawyers, businesspeople, and politicians, the Santa Fe Ring defrauded families and kin groups of their land titles and speculated in property to make a profit. Whereas many ordinary Hispanic settlers saw land—with its crops, pasture, fuel, building materials, and game—as a source of livelihood, groups such as the Santa Fe Ring saw land primarily as a commodity to be bought and sold.

Seemingly overnight, boom towns sprang up wherever minerals or timber beckoned: southern Arizona and the Rocky Mountains west of Denver, Virginia City in western Nevada, the Idaho-Montana region, and the Black Hills of South Dakota. In all these places, increasing numbers of workers operated sophisticated kinds of machinery, such as rock crushers. When the vein was exhausted or the forests depleted, the towns went bust.

Railroads facilitated not only the mining of minerals but also the growth of the cattle-ranching industry. Rail connections between the Midwest and East made it profitable for Texas ranchers to pay cowboys to drive their herds of long-horned steers to Abilene, Ellsworth, Wichita, or Dodge City, Kansas, for shipment to stockyards in Chicago or St. Louis. Cattle drives were huge; an estimated 10 million animals were herded north from Texas alone between 1865 and 1890. They offered employment to all kinds of men with sufficient skills and endurance. Among the cowhands were African American horsebreakers and gunmen and Mexicans skilled in the use of the *reata* (lasso). Blacks made up about 25 percent and Hispanics about 15 percent of all cowboy outfits.

In knitting regional economies together, federal land policies were crucial to the Republican vision of a developing nation. The Mineral Act of 1866 granted title to millions of acres of mineral-rich land to mining companies, a gift from the federal government to private interests. The Timber Culture Act of 1873 allotted 160 acres to individuals in selected western states if they agreed to plant one-fourth of the acreage with trees. Four years later, the Desert Land Act provided cheap land if buyers irrigated at least part of their parcels.

The Apex Mining Act of 1872 legalized traditional mining practices in the West by validating titles approved by local courts. According to the law, a person who could locate the apex of a vein (its point closest to the surface) could lay claim to the entire vein beneath the surface.

TABLE 15-2

Estimates of Railroad Crossties Used and Acres of Forest Cleared, 1870–1910

Year	Miles of Track	Ties Renewed Annually (millions)	Ties Used on New Construction (millions)	Total Ties Annually (millions)	Acres of Forest Cleared (thousands)
1870	60,000	21	18	39	195
1880	107,000	37	21	58	290
1890	200,000	70	19	89	445
1900	259,000			91	455
1910	357,000			124	620

Source: Michael Williams, *Americans and Their Forests* (1989), 352.

The measure contributed to the wholesale destruction of certain parts of the western landscape as mining companies blasted their way through mountains and left piles of rocks in their wake. It also spurred thousands of lawsuits as claimants argued over what constituted an apex or a vein.

It was during this period that a young Scottish-born naturalist named John Muir began to explore the magnificent canyons and mountains of California. He contrasted nature's majesty with the artificial landscape created by and for humans. In the wilderness, there is nothing "truly dead or dull, or any trace of what in manufactories is called rubbish or waste," he wrote; "everything is perfectly clean and pure and full of divine lessons."

Muir was gratified by the creation of the National Park system during the postwar period. Painters and geologists were among the first Easterners to appreciate the spectacular vistas of the western landscape. In 1864 Congress set aside a small area within California's Yosemite Valley for public recreation and enjoyment. Soon after the war, railroad promoters forged an alliance with government officials in an effort to block commercial development of particularly beautiful pockets of land. Northern Pacific railroad financier Jay Cooke lobbied hard for the government to create a 2-million-acre park in what is today the northwest corner of Wyoming. As a result, in March 1872, Congress established Yellowstone National Park. Tourism would continue to serve as a key component of the western economy.

Muir and others portrayed the Yosemite and Yellowstone valleys as wildernesses, empty of human activity. In fact, both areas had long provided hunting and foraging grounds for native peoples. Yellowstone had been occupied by the people now called the Shoshone since the fifteenth century. This group, together with the Bannock, Crow, and Blackfoot, tried to retain access to Yellowstone's meadows, rivers, and forests after it became a national park. However, U.S. policymakers and military officials persisted in their efforts to mark off territory for specific commercial purposes, while Indians were confined to reservations.

Buying Territory for the Union

Before the war, Republicans had opposed any federal expansionist schemes that they feared might benefit slaveholders. However, after 1865 and the outlawing of slavery, some Republican lawmakers and administration officials advocated the acquisition of additional territory. Secretary of State William Seward led the way in 1867 by purchasing Alaska from Russia. For $7.2 million (about 2 cents an acre), the United States gained 591,004 square miles of land. Within the territory were diverse indigenous groups—Eskimo, Aleut, Tlingit, Tsimshian, Athabaskan, and Haida—and a small number of native Russians. Though derided at the time as "Seward's icebox," Alaska yielded enough fish, timber, minerals, oil, and water power in the years to come to prove that the original purchase price was a tremendous bargain.

The impulse that prompted administration support for the Alaska purchase also spawned other plans for territorial acquisitions. In 1870 some Republicans joined with Democrats in calling for the annexation of the Dominican Republic. These congressmen argued that the tiny Caribbean country would make a fine naval base, provide investment opportunities for American businesspeople, and offer a refuge for southern freedpeople.

However, influential Senator Charles Sumner warned against a takeover without considering the will of the Dominican people, who were currently involved in their own civil war. Some congressmen, in a prelude to foreign policy debates of the 1890s, suggested that the dark-skinned Dominican people were incapable of appreciating the blessings of American citizenship. In 1871 an annexation treaty failed to win Senate approval.

The Republican Vision and Its Limits

After the Civil War, victorious Republicans envisioned a nation united in the pursuit of prosperity. All citizens would be free to follow their individual economic self-interest and to enjoy the fruits of honest toil. In contrast, some increasingly vocal and well-organized groups saw the expansion of legal rights, and giving black men the right to vote in particular, as only initial, tentative steps on the path to an all-inclusive citizenship. Women, industrial workers, farmers, and African Americans made up overlapping constituencies pressing for equal political rights and economic opportunity. Together they challenged the mainstream Republican view that defeat of the rebels and destruction of slavery were sufficient to guarantee all people prosperity.

Government-business partnerships also produced unanticipated consequences for Republicans committed to what they believed was the collective good. Some politicians and business leaders saw these partnerships as opportunities for private gain. Consequently, private greed and public corruption accompanied postwar economic growth. Thus, Republican leaders faced challenges from two very different sources: people agitating for civil rights and people hoping to reap personal gain from political activities.

Postbellum Origins of the Woman Suffrage Movement

After the Civil War, the nation's middle class, which had its origins in the antebellum period, continued to grow. Dedicated to self-improvement and filled with a sense of moral authority, many middle-class Americans (especially Protestants) felt a deep cultural connection to their counterparts in England. Indeed, the United States produced its own "Victorians," so called for the self-conscious middle class that emerged in the England of Queen Victoria during her reign from 1837 to 1901.

At the heart of the Victorian sensibility was the ideal of domesticity: a harmonious family living in a well-appointed home, guided by a pious mother and supported by a father successful in business. Famous Protestant clergyman Henry Ward Beecher and his wife were outspoken proponents of this domestic ideal. According to Eunice Beecher, women had no "higher, nobler, more divine mission than in the conscientious endeavor to create a *true home*."

Yet the traumatic events of the Civil War only intensified the desire among a growing group of American women to participate fully in the nation's political life. They wanted to extend their moral influence outside the narrow and exclusive sphere of the home. Many women believed that they deserved the vote and that the time was right to demand it.

In 1866 veteran reformers Elizabeth Cady Stanton, Susan B. Anthony, and Lucy Stone founded the Equal Rights Association to link the rights of white women and African Americans. Nevertheless, in 1867, Kansas voters defeated a referendum proposing **suffrage** for both blacks and white women. This disappointment convinced some former abolitionists that the two causes should be separated—that women should wait patiently until the rights of African American men were firmly secured. Frederick Douglass declined an invitation to a women's suffrage convention in Washington, D.C., in 1868. He explained, "I am now devoting myself to a cause [if] not more sacred, certainly more urgent, because it is one of life and death to the long enslaved people of this country, and that is: negro suffrage." But African American activist and former slave Sojourner Truth warned, "There is a great stir about colored men getting their rights, but not a word about the colored women; and if colored men get their rights, and not colored women get theirs, there will be a bad time about it."

In 1869 two factions of women parted ways and formed separate organizations devoted to women's rights. The more radical wing, including Cady Stanton and Anthony, bitterly denounced the Fifteenth Amendment because it gave the vote to black men only. They helped to found the National Woman Suffrage Association (NWSA), which argued for a renewed commitment to the original Declaration of Sentiments passed in Seneca Falls, New York, two decades earlier. They favored married women's property rights, liberalization of divorce laws, opening colleges and trade schools to women, and a new federal amendment to allow women to vote. Lucy Stone and her husband, Henry Blackwell, founded the rival American Woman Suffrage Association (AWSA). This group downplayed the larger struggle for women's rights and focused on the suffrage question exclusively. Its members supported the Fifteenth Amendment and retained ties to the Republican party. The AWSA focused on state-by-state campaigns for women's suffrage.

In 1871 the NWSA welcomed the daring, flamboyant Victoria Woodhull as a vocal supporter, only to renounce her a few years later. Woodhull's political agenda ranged from free love and dietary reform to legalized prostitution, working men's rights, and women's suffrage. (In the nineteenth century, free love advocates denounced what they called a sexual double standard, one that glorified female chastity while tolerating male promiscuity.)

In 1872 one of Woodhull's critics successfully challenged her. Woodhull spent a month in jail as a result of the zealous prosecution by vice reformer Anthony Comstock, a clergyman who objected to her public discussions and writings on sexuality. Comstock assumed the role of an outspoken crusader against vice. A federal law passed in 1873, and named after him, equated information related to birth control with pornography, banning this and other "obscene material" from the mails.

Susan B. Anthony used the 1872 presidential election as a test case for women's suffrage. She attempted to vote and was arrested, tried, and convicted as a result. By this time, most women suffragists, and most members of the NWSA for that matter, had become convinced that they should focus on the vote exclusively; they therefore accepted the AWSA's policy on this issue. In the coming years, they would avoid other causes with which they might have allied themselves, including black civil rights and labor reform.

The economic developments that allowed factory managers and owners of large wheat farms to make a comfortable living for themselves did not necessarily benefit agricultural and manufacturing workers.

Workers' Organizations

Many Americans benefited from economic changes of the postwar era. Railroading, mining, and heavy industry helped fuel the national economy and in the process boosted the growth of the urban managerial class. In the Midwest, many landowning farmers prospered when they responded to an expanding demand for grain and other staple crops. In Wisconsin, wheat farmers cleared forests, drained swamps, diverted rivers, and profited from the booming world market in grain. Yet the economic developments that allowed factory managers and owners of large wheat farms to make a comfortable living for themselves did not necessarily benefit agricultural and manufacturing workers.

State Historical Society of Wisconsin, WHi (D32) 821

■ A Norwegian immigrant extended family in the town of Norway Grove, Wisconsin, poses in front of their imposing home and up-to-date carriage in this photograph taken in the mid-1870s. Linking their fortunes to the world wheat market, these newcomers to the United States prospered. Wrote one woman to her brother back home in Norway, "We all have cattle, driving oxen, and wagons. We also have children in abundance."

Indeed, during this period growing numbers of working people, in the countryside and in the cities, became caught up in a cycle of indebtedness. In the upcountry South (above the fall line, or Piedmont), formerly self-sufficient family farmers sought loans from banks to repair their war-damaged homesteads. To qualify for these loans, the farmer had to plant cotton as a staple crop, to the neglect of corn and other foodstuffs. Many sharecroppers, black and white, received payment in the form of credit only; for these families, the end-of-the-year reckoning yielded little more than rapidly accumulating debts. Midwestern farmers increasingly relied on expensive threshing and harvesting machinery and on bank loans to purchase the machinery.

Several organizations founded within five years of the war's end offered laborers an alternative vision to the Republicans' brand of individualism and nationalism. In 1867 Oliver H. Kelly, a former Minnesota farmer now working in a Washington office, organized the National Grange of the Patrons of Husbandry, popularly known as the Grange. This movement sought to address a new, complex marketplace increasingly dominated by railroads, banks, and grain elevator operators. The Grange encouraged farmers to form **cooperatives** that would market their crops and to challenge discriminatory railroad rates that favored big business.

Founded in Baltimore in 1866, the National Labor Union (NLU) consisted of a collection of craft unions and claimed as many as 600,000 members at its peak in the early 1870s. The group welcomed farmers as well as factory workers and promoted legislation for an eight-hour workday and the arbitration of industrial disputes.

In 1873 a nationwide depression threw thousands out of work and worsened the plight of debtors. Businesspeople in agriculture, mining, the railroad industry, and manufacturing had overexpanded their operations. The free-wheeling loan practices of major banks had contributed to this situation. The inability of these businesspeople to repay their loans led to the failure of major banks. With the contraction of credit, thousands of small businesses went bankrupt. The NLU did not survive the crisis.

However, by this time, a new organization had appeared to champion the cause of the laboring classes in opposition to lords of finance. Founded in 1869 by Uriah Stephens and other Philadelphia tailors, the Knights of Labor eventually aimed to unite industrial and rural workers, the self-employed and the wage earner, blacks and whites, and men and women. The Knights were committed to private property and to the independence of the farmer, the entrepreneur, and the industrial worker. The group banned from its ranks "nonproducers," such as liquor sellers, bankers, professional gamblers, stockbrokers, and lawyers.

This period of depression also laid the foundation for the Greenback Labor party, organized in 1878. Within three years after the end of the Civil War, the Treasury had withdrawn from circulation $100 million in wartime paper currency ("greenbacks"). With less money in circulation, debtors found it more difficult to repay their loans. The government also ceased coining silver dollars in 1873, despite the discovery of rich silver lodes in the West. To add insult to injury, the Resumption Act (1875) called for the government to continue to withdraw paper greenbacks. Thus, hard money became dearer, and debtors became more desperate. In 1878 the new Greenback Labor party managed to win 1 million votes and elect fourteen candidates to Congress. The party laid the foundation for the Populist party that emerged in the 1890s.

Several factors made coalition building among these American workers difficult. One was the nation's increasingly multicultural workforce. Unions, such as the typographers, were notorious for excluding women and African Americans, a fact publicized by both Frederick Douglass and Susan B. Anthony, to no avail. In 1869 shoe factory workers (members of the Knights of St. Crispin) went on strike in North Adams, Massachusetts. They were soon shocked to see seventy-five Chinese strikebreakers arrive by train from California. Their employer praised the new arrivals for their "rare industry." The shoemakers' strike collapsed quickly after the appearance of what the workers called this "Mongolian battery." Employers would continue to manipulate and divide the laboring classes through the use of ethnic, religious, and racial prejudices.

Political Corruption and the Decline of Republican Idealism

Out of the new partnership between politics and business emerged an extensive system of bribes and kickbacks. Greedy politicians of both parties challenged the Republicans' high-minded idealism.

In the early 1870s, the *New York Times* exposed the schemes of William M. "Boss" Tweed. Tweed headed Tammany Hall, a New York City political organization that courted labor unions and contributed liberally to Catholic schools and charities. Tammany Hall politicians routinely used bribery and extortion to fix elections and bilk taxpayers of millions of dollars. One plasterer employed on a city project received $138,000 in "payment" for two days' work. After the *Times* **exposé**, Tweed was prosecuted and convicted. His downfall attested to the growing influence of newspaper reporters.

Another piece of investigative journalism rocked the political world in 1872. In 1867 major stockholders of the Union Pacific Railroad had formed a new corporation, called the Crédit Mobilier, to build railroads. Heads of powerful congressional committees received shares of stock in the new company. These gifts of stock were bribes to secure the legislators' support for public land grants favorable to the new corporation. The *New York Sun* exposed a number of the chief beneficiaries in the fall of 1872, findings confirmed by congressional investigation. Among the disgraced politicians was Grant's vice president, Schuyler Colfax.

The 1872 presidential election pitted incumbent Grant against the Democratic challenger, *New York Tribune* editor Horace Greeley. Many Republicans, disillusioned with congressional corruption and eager to press forward with civil service reform, endorsed the Democratic candidate. Greeley and his Republican allies decried the patronage (or "spoils") system by which politicians rewarded their supporters with government jobs. Nevertheless, Grant won the election.

By 1872, after four bloody years of war and seven squandered years of postwar opportunity, the federal government seemed prepared to hand the South back to unrepentant rebels. The North showed what one House Republican called "a general apathy among the people concerning the war and the negro." The Civil Rights Act of 1875 guaranteed blacks equal access to public accommodations and transportation. Yet this act represented the final, half-hearted gesture of radical Republicanism. The Supreme Court declared the measure unconstitutional in 1883 on the grounds that the government could protect only political and not social rights. White Southerners reasserted their control over the region's political economy.

The presidential election of 1876 intensified public cynicism about deal making in high places. A dispute over election returns led to what came to be known as the Compromise of 1877. In the popular vote, Democrat Samuel J. Tilden outpolled Republican Rutherford B. Hayes, a former Ohio governor. However, when the electoral votes were counted, the Democrat had only 184, one short of the necessary number. Nineteen of the twenty votes in dispute came from Louisiana, South Carolina, and Florida, and these three states submitted two new sets of returns, one from each of the two main parties. A specially appointed congressional electoral commission, the Committee of Fifteen, was charged with resolving the dispute. It divided along

PLATE 17

Harper's Weekly, September 16, 1871

■ In 1871 Thomas Nast drew a series of cartoons exposing the corruption of New York City Democratic boss William M. Tweed and his political organization, Tammany Hall. In this drawing, published in *Harper's Weekly* in 1871, Nast depicts Tweed and his cronies engaging in a "wholesale" looting of the New York City treasury with the assistance of compliant police officers. Those same officers stand ready to crack down on the impoverished father who robs a bakery to feed his family. By portraying Tweed as an enemy of the poor, Nast ignored the fact that the political boss gained a large following among immigrant voters.

TABLE 15-3			
The Election of 1872			
Candidate	Political Party	Popular Vote (%)	Electoral Vote
Ulysses S. Grant	Republican	55.6	286
Horace Greeley	Democratic, Liberal Republican	43.9	66

TABLE 15-4

The Election of 1876

Candidate	Political Party	Popular Vote (%)	Electoral Vote
Rutherford B. Hayes	Republican	48.0	185
Samuel J. Tilden	Democratic	51.0	184

DOCUMENT

Samuel Tilden's Speech to the Manhattan Club Conceding the Election of 1876

partisan lines. The eight Republicans outvoted the seven Democrats to accept the Republican set of returns from Florida.

To break the logjam, the Democrats agreed that Hayes could assume office in return for the withdrawal of all remaining federal troops from the South. The Republicans tacitly agreed that their work there was finished and that blacks in the region should fend for themselves. Hayes declined to enforce the Civil Rights Act of 1875. White Southerners were free to uphold the principle of states' rights that had been traditionally invoked to deny blacks their rights in the region.

Conclusion

During the dozen or so years after the Civil War, both northern Republicans and southern Democrats registered a series of spectacular wins and crushing losses. Though humiliated by the Union victory, southern white supremacists eventually won for themselves the freedom to control their own local and state governments. As landlords, sheriffs, and merchants, these men defied the postwar federal amendments to the Constitution and deprived African Americans of basic citizenship rights. By the end of Reconstruction, northern Republicans had conceded local power to their former enemies. Even an aggressive nationalism, it turned out, could accept traditional southern hierarchies: white over nonwhite, rich over poor.

On the other hand, at the end of Reconstruction, Republicans remained in firm control of national economic policy. The white South had secured its right to conduct its own political affairs, but the Republican vision of economic growth and development had become the law of the land. This vision was a guiding principle of historic national and, increasingly, international significance. Economic innovation in particular proved to be a force of great unifying power, stronger than all the federal military forces deployed during and after the Civil War.

Sites to Visit

Impeachment of Andrew Johnson
www.impeach-andrewjohnson.com
This HarpWeek site about the impeachment includes images and text from the Reconstruction period.

Diary and Letters of Rutherford B. Hayes
www.ohiohistory.org/onlinedoc/hayes/index.cfm
The Rutherford B. Hayes Presidential Center in Fremont, Ohio, maintains this searchable database of his writings.

Freedmen and Southern Society Project (University of Maryland, College Park)
www.history.umd.edu/Freedmen/index.html
This site contains a chronology and sample documents from several collections of primary sources about emancipation and freedom in the 1860s.

History of the Suffrage Movement
www.rochester.edu/SBA/
This site includes a chronology, important texts relating to women's suffrage, and bibliographical information about Susan B. Anthony and Elizabeth Cady Stanton.

Indian Memorial at Little Big Horn Battlefield National Monument
www.nps.gov/libi/indmem.htm
The Smithsonian Institution maintains this site, providing information about the museum.

National Museum of the American Indian
www..nmai.si.edu
The Smithsonian Institution maintains this site, providing information about the museum.

Northern Great Plains, 1880–1920: Photographs from the Fred Hulstrand and F. A. Pazandak Photograph Collections
www.memory.loc.gov/ammem/award97/ndfahtml/ngphome.html
This American Memory site from the Library of Congress contains two collections from the Institute for Regional Studies at North Dakota State University with 900 photographs of rural and small-town life at the turn of the century. Included are images of sod homes and the people who built them, farms and the machinery that made them prosper, and one-room schools and the children who were educated in them.

For Further Reading

General Works

Eric Foner, *Reconstruction: America's Unfinished Revolution, 1863–1877* (1988).

David Montgomery, *Beyond Equality: Labor and the Radical Republicans, 1862–1872* (1967).

Amy Dru Stanley, *From Bondage to Contract: Wage Labor, Marriage, and the Market in the Age of Slave Emancipation* (1998).

Ronald Takaki, *A Different Mirror: A History of Multicultural America* (1993).

Richard White, "*It's Your Misfortune and None of My Own": A History of the American West* (1991).

The Struggle over the South

Peter Bardaglio, *Reconstructing the Household: Families, Sex and the Law in the Nineteenth-Century South* (1995).

Ira Berlin and Leslie S. Rowland, eds., *Families and Freedom: A Documentary History of African-American Kinship in the Civil War Era* (1997).

Dwight B. Billings, *Planters and the Making of a "New South": Class, Politics, and Development in North Carolina, 1865–1900* (1979).

Frederick Cooper, Thomas C. Holt, and Rebecca J. Scott, eds., *Beyond Slavery: Explorations of Race, Labor, and Citizenship in Post-Emancipation Societies* (2000).

Michael Golay, *A Ruined Land: The End of the Civil War* (1999).

Thomas C. Holt, *Black over White: Negro Political Leadership in South Carolina During Reconstruction* (1977).

Jacqueline Jones, *Soldiers of Light and Love: Northern Teachers and Georgia Blacks, 1865–1873* (1980).

Claiming Territory for the Union

Stephen E. Ambrose, *Nothing Like It in the World: The Men Who Built the Transcontinental Railroad, 1863–1869* (2000).

Orin G. Libby, ed., *The Arikara Narrative of the Campaign Against the Hostile Dakotas, June, 1876* (1998).

Ruth B. Moynihan, Susan Armitage, and Christiane Fischer Dichamp, eds., *So Much to Be Done: Women Settlers on the Mining and Ranching Frontier* (1990).

Larry Sklenar, *To Hell with Honor: Custer and the Little Bighorn* (2000).

Robert Wooster, *The Military and United States Indian Policy, 1865–1903* (1988).

Judy Yung, *Unbound Feet: A Social History of Chinese Women in San Francisco* (1995).

The Republican Vision and Its Limits

Leon Fink, *Workingmen's Democracy: The Knights of Labor and American Politics* (1983).

Barbara Goldsmith, *Other Powers: The Age of Suffrage, Spiritualism, and the Scandalous Victoria Woodhull* (1998).

Heather Cox Richardson, *The Death of Reconstruction: Race, Labor and Politics in the Post-Civil War North* (2001).

Lyde Cullen Sizer, *The Political Work of Northern Women Writers and the Civil War* (2000).

Irwin Unger, *The Greenback Era: A Social and Political History of American Finance, 1865–1879* (1964).

For quizzes and other resources on these topics, go to www.longmanamericanhistory.com.

Appendix

The Declaration of Independence

The Unanimous Declaration
of the Thirteen United States of America

When, in the course of human events, it becomes necessary for one people to dissolve the political bonds which have connected them with another, and to assume, among the powers of the earth, the separate and equal station to which the laws of nature and of nature's God entitle them, a decent respect to the opinions of mankind requires that they should declare the causes which impel them to the separation.

We hold these truths to be self-evident: That all men are created equal; that they are endowed by their Creator with certain unalienable rights; that among these are life, liberty, and the pursuit of happiness; that, to secure these rights, governments are instituted among men, deriving their just powers from the consent of the governed; that whenever any form of government becomes destructive of these ends, it is the right of the people to alter or to abolish it, and to institute new government, laying its foundation on such principles, and organizing its powers in such form, as to them shall seem most likely to effect their safety and happiness. Prudence, indeed, will dictate that governments long established should not be changed for light and transient causes; and accordingly all experience hath shown that mankind are more disposed to suffer, while evils are sufferable, than to right themselves by abolishing the forms to which they are accustomed. But when a long train of abuses and usurpations, pursuing invariably the same object, evinces a design to reduce them under absolute despotism, it is their right, it is their duty, to throw off such government, and to provide new guards for their future security. Such has been the patient sufferance of these colonies; and such is now the necessity which constrains them to alter their former systems of government. The history of the present King of Great Britain is a history of repeated injuries and usurpations, all having in direct object the establishment of an absolute tyranny over these states. To prove this, let facts be submitted to a candid world.

He has refused his assent to laws, the most wholesome and necessary for the public good.

He has forbidden his governors to pass laws of immediate and pressing importance, unless suspended in their operation till his assent should be obtained; and, when so suspended, he has utterly neglected to attend to them.

He has refused to pass other laws for the accommodation of large districts of people, unless those people would relinquish the right of representation in the legislature, a right inestimable to them, and formidable to tyrants only.

He has called together legislative bodies at places unusual, uncomfortable, and distant from the depository of their public records, for the sole purpose of fatiguing them into compliance with his measures.

He has dissolved representative houses repeatedly, for opposing, with manly firmness, his invasions on the rights of the people.

He has refused for a long time, after such dissolutions, to cause others to be elected; whereby the legislative powers, incapable of annihilation, have returned to the people at large for their exercise; the state remaining, in the mean time, exposed to all the dangers of invasions from without and convulsions within.

He has endeavored to prevent the population of these states; for that purpose obstructing the laws for naturalization of foreigners; refusing to pass others to encourage their migration hither, and raising the conditions of new appropriations of lands.

He has obstructed the administration of justice, by refusing his assent to laws for establishing judiciary powers.

He has made judges dependent on his will alone, for the tenure of their offices, and the amount and payment of their salaries.

He has erected a multitude of new offices, and sent hither swarms of officers to harass our people and eat out their substance.

He has kept among us, in times of peace, standing armies, without the consent of our legislatures.

He has affected to render the military independent of, and superior to, the civil power.

He has combined with others to subject us to a jurisdiction foreign to our constitution, and unacknowledged by our laws, giving his assent to their acts of pretended legislation:

For quartering large bodies of armed troops among us;

For protecting them, by a mock trial, from punishment for any murder which they should commit on the inhabitants of these states;

For cutting off our trade with all parts of the world;

For imposing taxes on us without our consent;

For depriving us, in many cases, of the benefits of trial by jury;

For transporting us beyond seas, to be tried for pretended offenses;

For abolishing the free system of English laws in a neighboring province, establishing therein an arbitrary government, and enlarging its boundaries, so as to render it at once an example and fit instrument for introducing the same absolute rule into these colonies;

For taking away our charters, abolishing our most valuable laws, and altering fundamentally the forms of our governments;

For suspending our own legislatures, and declaring themselves invested with power to legislate for us in all cases whatsoever.

He has abdicated government here, by declaring us out of his protection and waging war against us.

He has plundered our seas, ravaged our coasts, burned our towns, and destroyed the lives of our people.

He is at this time transporting large armies of foreign mercenaries to complete the works of death, desolation, and tyranny already begun with circumstances of cruelty and perfidy scarcely paralleled in the most barbarous ages, and totally unworthy the head of a civilized nation.

He has constrained our fellow-citizens, taken captive on the high seas, to bear arms against their country, to become the executioners of their friends and brethren, or to fall themselves by their hands.

He has excited domestic insurrection among us, and has endeavored to bring on the inhabitants of our frontiers the merciless Indian savages, whose known rule of warfare is an undistinguished destruction of all ages, sexes, and conditions.

In every stage of these oppressions we have petitioned for redress in the most humble terms; our repeated petitions have been answered only by repeated injury. A prince, whose character is thus marked by every act which may define a tyrant, is unfit to be the ruler of a free people.

Nor have we been wanting in our attentions to our British brethren. We have warned them, from time to time, of attempts by their legislature to extend an unwarrantable jurisdiction over us. We have reminded them of the circumstances of our emigration and settlement here. We have appealed to their native justice and magnanimity; and we have conjured them, by the ties of our common kindred, to disavow these usurpations, which would inevitably interrupt our connections and correspondence. They, too, have been deaf to the voice of justice and of consanguinity. We must, therefore, acquiesce in the necessity which denounces our separation, and hold them, as we hold the rest of mankind, enemies in war, in peace friends.

We, therefore, the representatives of the United States of America, in General Congress assembled, appealing to the Supreme Judge of the world for the rectitude of our intentions, do, in the name and by the authority of the good people of these colonies, solemnly publish and declare, that these United Colonies are, and of right ought to be, FREE AND INDEPENDENT STATES; that they are absolved from all allegiance to the British crown, and that all political connection between them and the state of Great Britain is, and ought to be, totally dissolved; and that, as free and independent states, they have full power to levy war, conclude peace, contract alliances, establish commerce, and do all other acts and things which independent states may of right do. And for the support of this declaration, with a firm reliance on the protection of Divine Providence, we mutually pledge to each other our lives, our fortunes, and our sacred honor.

JOHN HANCOCK

New Hampshire
Josiah Bartlett
William Whipple
Matthew Thornton

Massachusetts
John Adams
Samuel Adams
Robert Treat Paine
Elbridge Gerry

New York
William Floyd
Philip Livingston
Francis Lewis
Lewis Morris

Rhode Island
Stephen Hopkins
William Ellery

New Jersey
Richard Stockton
John Witherspoon
Francis Hopkinson
John Hart
Abraham Clark

Pennsylvania
Robert Morris
Benjamin Rush
Benjamin Franklin
John Morton
George Clymer
James Smith
George Taylor
James Wilson
George Ross

Delaware
Caeser Rodney
George Read
Thomas McKean

Maryland
Samuel Chase
William Paca
Thomas Stone
Charles Carroll of Carrollton

North Carolina
William Hooper
Joseph Hewes
John Penn

Virginia
George Wythe
Richard Henry Lee
Thomas Jefferson
Benjamin Harrison
Thomas Nelson Jr.
Francis Lightfoot Lee
Carter Braxton

South Carolina
Edward Rutledge
Thomas Heyward Jr.
Thomas Lynch Jr.
Arthur Middleton

Connecticut
Roger Sherman
Samuel Huntington
William Williams
Oliver Wolcott

Georgia
Button Gwinnett
Lyman Hall
George Walton

The Articles of Confederation

Between the States of New Hampshire, Massachusetts Bay, Rhode Island and Providence Plantations, Connecticut, New York, New Jersey, Pennsylvania, Delaware, Maryland, Virginia, North Carolina, South Carolina, Georgia

Article 1

The stile of this confederacy shall be "The United States of America."

Article 2

Each State retains its sovereignty, freedom and independence, and every power, jurisdiction, and right, which is not by this confederation expressly delegated to the United States, in Congress assembled.

Article 3

The said states hereby severally enter into a firm league of friendship with each other for their common defence, the security of their liberties and their mutual and general welfare; binding themselves to assist each other against all force offered to, or attacks made upon them, or any of them, on account of religion, sovereignty, trade, or any other pretence whatever.

Article 4

The better to secure and perpetuate mutual friendship and intercourse among the people of the different states in this union, the free inhabitants of each of these states, paupers, vagabonds, and fugitives from justice excepted, shall be entitled to all privileges and immunities of free citizens in the several states; and the people of each State shall have free ingress and regress to and from any other State, and shall enjoy therein all the privileges of trade and commerce, subject to the same duties, impositions, and restrictions, as the inhabitants thereof respectively; provided, that such restrictions shall not extend so far as to prevent the removal of property, imported into any State, to any other State of which the owner is an inhabitant; provided also, that no imposition, duties, or restriction, shall be laid by any State on the property of the United States, or either of them.

If any person guilty of, or charged with treason, felony, or other high misdemeanor in any State, shall flee from justice and be found in any of the United States, he shall, upon demand of the governor or executive power of the State from which he fled, be delivered up and removed to the State having jurisdiction of his offence.

Full faith and credit shall be given in each of these states to the records, acts, and judicial proceedings of the courts and magistrates of every other State.

Article 5

For the more convenient management of the general interests of the United States, delegates shall be annually appointed, in such manner as the legislature of each State shall direct, to meet in Congress, on the 1st Monday in November in every year, with a power reserved to each State to recall its delegates, or any of them, at any time within the year, and to send others in their stead for the remainder of the year.

No State shall be represented in Congress by less than two, nor by more than seven members; and no person shall be capable of being a delegate for more than three years in any term of six years; nor shall any person, being a delegate, be capable of holding any office under the United States, for which he, or any other for his benefit, receives any salary, fees, or emolument of any kind.

Each State shall maintain its own delegates in a meeting of the states, and while they act as members of the committee of the states.

In determining questions in the United States, in Congress assembled, each State shall have one vote.

Freedom of speech and debate in Congress shall not be impeached or questioned in any court or place out of Congress: and the members of Congress shall be protected in their persons from arrests and imprisonments, during the time of their going to and from, and attendance on Congress, except for treason, felony, or breach of the peace.

Article 6

No State, without the consent of the United States, in Congress assembled, shall send any embassy to, or receive any embassy from, or enter into any conference, agreement, alliance, or treaty with any king, prince, or state; nor shall any person, holding any office of profit or trust under the United States, or any of them, accept of any present, emolument, office or title, of any kind whatever, from any king, prince, or foreign state; nor shall the United States, in Congress assembled, or any of them, grant any title of nobility.

No two or more states shall enter into any treaty, confederation, or alliance, whatever, between them, without the consent of the United States, in Congress assembled, specifying accurately the purposes for which the same is to be entered into, and how long it shall continue.

No State shall lay any imposts or duties which may interfere with any stipulations in treaties entered into by the United States, in Congress assembled, with any king, prince, or state, in pursuance of any treaties already proposed by Congress to the courts of France and Spain.

No vessels of war shall be kept up in time of peace by any State, except such number only as shall be deemed necessary by the United States, in Congress assembled, for the defence of such State or its trade; nor shall any body of forces be kept up by any State, in time of peace, except such number only as, in the judgment of the United States, in Congress assembled, shall be deemed requisite to garrison the forts necessary for the defence of such State; but every State shall always keep up a well regulated and disciplined militia, sufficiently armed and accoutred, and shall provide, and constantly have ready for use, in public stores, a due number of field pieces and tents, and a proper quantity of arms, ammunition and camp equipage.

No State shall engage in any war without the consent of the United States, in Congress assembled, unless such State be actually invaded by enemies, or shall have received certain advice of a resolution being formed by some nation of Indians to invade such State, and the danger is so imminent as not to admit of a delay till the United States, in Congress assembled, can be consulted; nor shall any State grant commissions to any ships or vessels of war, nor letters of marque or reprisal, except it be after a declaration of war by the United States, in Congress assembled, and then only against the kingdom or state, and the subjects thereof, against which war has been so declared, and under such regulations as shall be established by the United States, in Congress assembled, unless such States be infested by pirates, in which case vessels of war may be fitted out for that occasion, and kept so long as the danger shall continue, or until the United States, in Congress assembled, shall determine otherwise.

Article 7

When land forces are raised by any State for the common defence, all officers of or under the rank of colonel, shall be appointed by the legislature of each State respectively, by whom such forces shall be raised, or in such manner as such State shall direct; and all vacancies shall be filled up by the State which first made the appointment.

Article 8

All charges of war and all other expences, that shall be incurred for the common defence or general welfare, and allowed by the United States, in Congress assembled, shall be defrayed out of a common treasury, which shall be supplied by the several states, in proportion to the value of all land within each State, granted to or surveyed for any person, as such land and the buildings and improvements thereon shall be estimated according to such mode as the United States, in Congress assembled, shall, from time to time, direct and appoint.

The taxes for paying that proportion shall be laid and levied by the authority and direction of the legislatures of the several states, within the time agreed upon by the United States, in Congress assembled.

Article 9

The United States, in Congress assembled, shall have the sole and exclusive right and power of determining on peace and war, except in the cases mentioned in the 6th article; of sending and receiving ambassadors; entering into treaties and alliances, provided that no treaty of commerce shall be made, whereby the legislative power of the respective states shall be restrained from imposing such imposts and duties on foreigners as their own people are subjected to, or from prohibiting the exportation or importation of any species of goods or commodities whatsoever; of establishing rules for deciding, in all cases, what captures on land or water shall be legal, and in what manner prizes, taken by land or naval forces in the service of the United States, shall be divided or appropriated; of granting letters of marque and reprisal in times of peace; appointing courts for the trial of piracies and felonies committed on the high seas, and estab-

lishing courts for receiving and determining, finally, appeals in all cases of captures; provided, that no member of Congress shall be appointed a judge of any of the said courts.

The United States, in Congress assembled, shall also be the last resort on appeal in all disputes and differences now subsisting, or that hereafter may arise between two or more states concerning boundary, jurisdiction or any other cause whatever; which authority shall always be exercised in the manner following: whenever the legislative or executive authority, or lawful agent of any State, in controversy with another, shall present a petition to Congress, stating the matter in question, and praying for a hearing, notice thereof shall be given, by order of Congress, to the legislative or executive authority of the other State in controversy, and a day assigned for the appearance of the parties by their lawful agents, who shall then be directed to appoint, by joint consent, commissioners or judges to constitute a court for hearing and determining the matter in question; but, if they cannot agree, Congress shall name three persons out of each of the United States, and from the list of such persons each party shall alternately strike out one, in the petitioners beginning, until the number shall be reduced to thirteen; and from that number not less than seven, nor more than nine names, as Congress shall direct, shall, in the presence of Congress, be drawn out by lot; and the persons whose names shall be drawn, or any five of them, shall be commissioners or judges to hear and finally determine the controversy, so always as a major part of the judges who shall hear the cause shall agree in the determination; and if either party shall neglect to attend at the day appointed, without shewing reasons which Congress shall judge sufficient, or, being present, shall refuse to strike, the Congress shall proceed to nominate three persons out of each State, and the secretary of Congress shall strike in behalf of such party absent or refusing; and the judgment and sentence of the court to be appointed, in the manner before prescribed, shall be final and conclusive; and if any of the parties shall refuse to submit to the authority of such court, or to appear or defend their claim or cause, the court shall nevertheless proceed to pronounce sentence or judgment, which shall, in like manner, be final and decisive, the judgment or sentence and other proceedings being, in either case, transmitted to Congress, and lodged among the acts of Congress for the security of the parties concerned: provided, that every commissioner, before he sits in judgment, shall take an oath, to be administered by one of the judges of the supreme or superior court of the State where the cause shall be tried, "well and truly to hear and determine the matter in question, according to the best of his judgment, without favour, affection, or hope of reward": provided, also, that no State shall be deprived of territory for the benefit of the United States.

All controversies concerning the private right of soil, claimed under different grants of two or more states, whose jurisdictions, as they may respect such lands and the states which passed such grants, are adjusted, the said grants, or either of them, being at the same time claimed to have originated antecedent to such settlement of jurisdiction, shall, on the petition of either party to the Congress of the United States, be finally determined, as near as may be, in the same manner as is before prescribed for deciding disputes respecting territorial jurisdiction between different states.

The United States, in Congress assembled, shall also have the sole and exclusive right and power of regulating the alloy and value of coin struck by their own authority, or by that of the respective states; fixing the standard of weights and measures throughout the United States; regulating the trade and managing all affairs with the Indians not members of any of the states; provided that the legislative right of any State within its own limits be not infringed or violated; establishing and regulating post offices from one State to another throughout all the United States, and exacting such postage on the papers passing through the same as may be requisite to defray the expences of the said office; appointing all officers of the land forces in the service of the United States, excepting regimental officers; appointing all the officers of the naval forces, and commissioning all officers whatever in the service of the United States; making rules for the government and regulation of the said land and naval forces, and directing their operations.

The United States, in Congress assembled, shall have authority to appoint a committee to sit in the recess of Congress, to be denominated "a Committee of the States," and to consist of one delegate from each State, and to appoint such other committees and civil officers as may be necessary for managing the general affairs of the United States, under their direction; to appoint one of their number to preside; provided that no person be allowed to serve in the office of president more than one year in any term of three years; to ascertain the necessary sums of money to be raised for the service of the United States, and to appropriate and apply the same for defraying the public expences; to borrow money or emit bills on the credit of the United States, transmitting, every half year, to the respective states, an account of the sums of money so borrowed or emitted; to build and equip a navy; to agree upon the number of land forces, and to make requisitions from each State for its quota, in proportion to the number of white inhabitants in such State; which requisitions shall be binding; and, thereupon, the legislature of each State shall appoint the regimental officers, raise the men, and cloathe, arm, and equip them in a soldier-like manner, at the expence of the United States; and the officers and men so cloathed, armed, and equipped, shall march to the place appointed and within the time agreed on by the United States, in Congress assembled; but if the United States, in Congress assembled, shall, on consideration of circumstances, judge proper that any State should not raise men, or should raise a smaller number than its quota, and that any other State should raise a greater number of men than the quota thereof, such extra number shall be raised, officered, cloathed, armed, and equipped in the same manner as the quota of such State, unless the legislature of such State shall judge that such extra number cannot be safely spared out of the same, in which case they shall raise, officer, cloathe, arm, and equip as many of such extra number as they judge can be safely spared. And the officers and men so cloathed, armed, and equipped, shall march to the place appointed and within the time agreed on by the United States, in Congress assembled.

The United States, in Congress assembled, shall never engage in a war, nor grant letters of marque and reprisal in time of peace, nor enter into any treaties or alliances, nor coin money, nor regulate the value thereof, nor ascertain the sums and expences necessary for the defence and welfare of the United States, or any of them: nor emit bills, nor borrow money on the credit of the United States, nor appropriate money, nor agree upon the number of vessels of war to be built or purchased, or the number of land or sea forces to be raised, nor appoint a commander in chief of the army or navy, unless nine states assent to the same; nor shall a question on any other point, except for adjourning from day to day, be determined, unless by the votes of a majority of the United States, in Congress assembled.

The Congress of the United States shall have power to adjourn to any time within the year, and to any place within the United States, so that no period of adjournment be for a longer duration than the space of six months, and shall publish the journal of their proceedings monthly, except such parts thereof, relating to treaties, alliances or military operations, as, in their judgment, require secrecy; and the yeas and nays of the delegates of each State on any question shall be entered on the journal, when it is desired by any delegate; and the delegates of a State, or any of them, at his, or their request, shall be furnished with a transcript of the said journal, except such parts as are above excepted, to lay before the legislatures of the several states.

Article 10

The committee of the states, or any nine of them, shall be authorized to execute, in the recess of Congress, such of the powers of Congress as the United States, in Congress assembled, by the consent of nine states, shall, from time to time, think expedient to vest them with; provided, that no power be delegated to the said committee for the exercise of which, by the articles of confederation, the voice of nine states, in the Congress of the United States assembled, is requisite.

Article 11

Canada acceding to this confederation, and joining in the measures of the United States, shall be admitted into and entitled to all the advantages of this union; but no other colony shall be admitted into the same, unless such admission be agreed to by nine states.

Article 12

All bills of credit emitted, monies borrowed and debts contracted by, or under the authority of Congress before the assembling of the United States, in pursuance of the present confederation, shall be deemed and considered as a charge against the United States, for payment and satisfaction whereof the said United States and the public faith are hereby solemnly pledged.

Article 13

Every State shall abide by the determinations of the United States, in Congress assembled, on all questions which, by this confederation, are submitted to them. And the articles of this confederation shall be inviolably observed by every State, and the union shall be perpetual; nor shall any alteration at any time hereafter be made in any of them, unless such alteration be agreed to in a Congress of the United States, and be afterwards confirmed by the legislatures of every State.

These articles shall be proposed to the legislatures of all the United States, to be considered, and if approved of by them, they are advised to authorize their delegates to ratify the same in the Congress of the United States; which being done, the same shall become conclusive.

The Constitution of the United States of America

Preamble

We the People of the United States, in Order to form a more perfect Union, establish Justice, insure domestic Tranquility, provide for the common defence, promote the general Welfare, and secure the Blessings of Liberty to ourselves and our Posterity, do ordain and establish this Constitution for the United States of America.

Article I

Section 1

All legislative Powers herein granted shall be vested in a Congress of the United States, which shall consist of a Senate and House of Representatives.

Section 2

The House of Representatives shall be composed of Members chosen every second Year by the People of the several States, and the Electors in each State shall have the Qualifications requisite for Electors of the most numerous Branch of the State Legislature.

No Person shall be a Representative who shall not have attained to the Age of twenty five Years, and been seven Years a Citizen of the United States, and who shall not, when elected, be an inhabitant of that State in which he shall be chosen.

Representatives and direct Taxes shall be apportioned among the several States which may be included within this Union, according to their respective Numbers, *which shall be determined by adding to the whole Number of free Persons, including those bound to Service for a Term of Years, and excluding Indians not taxed, three fifths of all other Persons.** The actual Enumeration shall be made within three Years after the first Meeting of the Congress of the United States, and within every subsequent Term of ten Years, in such Manner as they shall by Law direct. The Number of Representatives shall not exceed one for every thirty Thousand, but each State shall have at Least one Representative; *and until such enumeration shall be made, the State of New Hampshire shall be entitled to chuse three, Massachusetts eight, Rhode-Island and Providence Plantations one, Connecticut five, New York six, New Jersey four, Pennsylvania eight, Delaware one, Maryland six, Virginia ten, North Carolina five, South Carolina five, and Georgia three.*

When vacancies happen in the Representation from any State, the Executive Authority thereof shall issue Writs of Election to fill such Vacancies.

The House of Representatives shall chuse their Speaker and other Officers; and shall have the sole Power of Impeachment.

---

*Passages no longer in effect are printed in italic type.

Section 3

The Senate of the United States shall be composed of two Senators from each State, *chosen by the Legislature thereof,* for six Years; and each Senator shall have one Vote.

Immediately after they shall be assembled in Consequence of the first Election, they shall be divided as equally as may be into three Classes. The Seats of the Senators of the first Class shall be vacated at the Expiration of the second Year, of the second Class at the Expiration of the fourth Year, and of the third Class at the Expiration of the sixth Year so that one third may be chosen every second Year; and if Vacancies happen by Resignation, or otherwise, during the Recess of the Legislature of any state, the Executive thereof may make temporary Appointments until the next Meeting of the Legislature, which shall then fill such Vacancies.

No Person shall be a Senator who shall not have attained to the Age of thirty Years, and been nine Years a Citizen of the United States, and who shall not, when elected, be an Inhabitant of that State for which he shall be chosen.

The Vice President of the United States shall be President of the Senate, but shall have no Vote, unless they be equally divided.

The Senate shall chuse their other Officers, and also a President *pro tempore*, in the Absence of the Vice President, or when he shall exercise the Office of President of the United States.

The Senate shall have the sole Power to try all Impeachments. When sitting for that Purpose, they shall be on Oath or Affirmation. When the President of the United States is tried the Chief Justice shall preside: And no Person shall be convicted without the Concurrence of two thirds of the Members present.

Judgment in Cases of Impeachment shall not extend further than to removal from Office, and disqualification to hold and enjoy any Office of honor, Trust or Profit under the United States: but the Party convicted shall nevertheless be liable and subject to Indictment, Trial, Judgment and Punishment, according to Law.

Section 4

The Times, Places and Manner of holding Elections for Senators and Representatives, shall be prescribed in each State by the Legislature thereof; but the Congress may at any time by Law make or alter such Regulations, except as to the Places of chusing Senators.

The Congress shall assemble at least once in every Year, *and such Meeting shall be on the first Monday in December, unless they shall by Law appoint a different Day.*

Section 5

Each House shall be the Judge of the Elections, Returns and Qualifications of its own Members, and a Majority of each shall constitute a Quorum to do Business; but a smaller Number may adjourn from day to day, and may be authorized to compel the Attendance of absent Members, in such Manner, and under such Penalties as each House may provide.

Each House may determine the Rules of its Proceedings, punish its Members for disorderly Behaviour, and, with the Concurrence of two thirds, expel a Member.

Each House shall keep a Journal of its Proceedings, and from time to time publish the same, excepting such Parts as may in their Judgment require Secrecy; and the Yeas and Nays of the Members of either House on any question shall, at the Desire of one fifth of those Present, be entered on the Journal.

Neither House, during the Session of Congress, shall, without the Consent of the other, adjourn for more than three days, nor to any other Place than that in which the two Houses shall be sitting.

Section 6

The Senators and Representatives shall receive a Compensation for their Services, to be ascertained by Law, and paid out of the Treasury of the United States. They shall in all Cases, except Treason, Felony and Breach of the Peace, be privileged from Arrest during their Attendance at the Session of their respective Houses, and in going to and returning from the same; and for any Speech or Debate in either House, they shall not be questioned in any other Place.

No Senator or Representative shall, during the Time for which he was elected, be appointed to any civil Office under the Authority of the United States, which shall have been created, or the Emoluments whereof shall have been encreased during such time, and no Person holding any Office under the United States, shall be a Member of either House during his Continuance in Office.

Section 7

All Bills for raising Revenue shall originate in the House of Representatives; but the Senate may propose or concur with Amendments as on other Bills.

Every Bill which shall have passed the House of Representatives and the Senate, shall, before it become a Law, be presented to the President of the United States; If he approve he shall sign it, but if not he shall return it, with his Objections to the House in which it shall have originated, who shall enter the Objections at large on their Journal, and proceed to reconsider it. If after such Reconsideration two thirds of that House shall agree to pass the Bill, it shall be sent, together with the Objections, to the other House, by which it shall likewise be reconsidered, and if approved by two thirds of that House, it shall become a Law. But in all such Cases the Votes of both Houses shall be determined by yeas and Nays, and the Names of the Persons voting for and against the Bill shall be entered on the Journal of each House respectively. If any Bill shall not be returned by the President within ten Days (Sundays excepted) after it shall have been presented to him, the Same shall be a Law, in like Manner as if he had signed it, unless the Congress by their Adjournment prevent its Return, in which Case it shall not be a Law.

Every Order, Resolution, or Vote to which the Concurrence of the Senate and House of Representatives may be necessary (except on a question of Adjournment) shall be presented to the President of the United States; and before the Same shall take Effect, shall be approved by him, or being disapproved by him, shall be repassed by two thirds of the Senate and House of Representatives, according to the Rules and Limitations prescribed in the Case of a Bill.

Section 8

The Congress shall have Power To lay and collect Taxes, Duties, Imposts and Excises, to pay the Debts and provide for the common Defence and general Welfare of the United States; but all Duties, Imposts and Excises shall be uniform throughout the United States;

To borrow Money on the credit of the United States;

To regulate Commerce with foreign Nations, and among the several States, and with the Indian Tribes;

To establish an uniform Rule of Naturalization, and uniform Laws on the subject of Bankruptcies throughout the United States;

To coin Money, regulate the Value thereof, and of foreign Coin, and fix the Standard of Weights and Measures;

To provide for the Punishment of counterfeiting the Securities and current Coin of the United States;

To establish Post Offices and post Roads;

To promote the Progress of Science and useful Arts, by securing for limited Times to Authors and Inventors the exclusive Right to their respective Writings and Discoveries;

To constitute Tribunals inferior to the supreme Court;

To define and punish Piracies and Felonies committed on the high Seas, and Offences against the Law of Nations;

To declare War, grant Letters of Marque and Reprisal, and make Rules concerning Captures on Land and Water;

To raise and support Armies, but no Appropriation of Money to that Use shall be for a longer Term than two Years;

To provide and maintain a Navy;

To make Rules for the Government and Regulation of the land and naval Forces;

To provide for calling forth the Militia to execute the Laws of the Union, suppress Insurrections and repel Invasions;

To provide for organizing, arming, and disciplining, the Militia, and for governing such Part of them as may be employed in the Service of the United States, reserving to the States respectively, the Appointment of the Officers, and the Authority of training the Militia according to the discipline prescribed by Congress;

To exercise exclusive Legislation in all Cases whatsoever, over such District (not exceeding ten Miles square) as may, by Cession of particular States, and the Acceptance of Congress, become the Seat of the Government of the United States, and to exercise like Authority over all Places purchased by the Consent of the Legislature of the State in which the Same shall be, for the Erection of Forts, Magazines, Arsenals, dock-Yards, and other needful Buildings;—And

To make all Laws which shall be necessary and proper for carrying into Execution the foregoing Powers, and all other Powers vested by this Constitution in the Government of the United States, or in any Department of Officer thereof.

Section 9

The Migration or Importation of such Persons as any of the States now existing shall think proper to admit, shall not be prohibited by the Congress prior to the Year one thousand eight hundred and

eight, but a Tax or duty may be imposed on such Importation, not exceeding ten dollars for each Person.

The Privilege of the Writ of Habeas Corpus shall not be suspended, unless when in Cases of Rebellion or Invasion the public Safety may require it.

No Bill of Attainder or ex post facto Law shall be passed.

No Capitation, or other direct, Tax shall be laid, unless in Proportion to the Census or Enumeration herein before directed to be taken.

No Tax or Duty shall be laid on Articles exported from any State.

No Preference shall be given by any Regulation of Commerce or Revenue to the Ports of one State over those of another: nor shall Vessels bound to, or from, one State, be obliged to enter, clear, or pay Duties in another.

No Money shall be drawn from the Treasury, but in Consequence of Appropriations made by Law; and a regular Statement and Account of the Receipts and Expenditures of all public Money shall be published from time to time.

No Title of Nobility shall be granted by the United States: And no Person holding any Office of Profit or Trust under them, shall, without the Consent of the Congress, accept of any present, Emolument, Office, or Title, of any kind whatever, from any King, Prince, or foreign State.

Section 10

No State shall enter into any Treaty, Alliance, or Confederation; grant Letters of Marque and Reprisal; coin Money; emit Bills of Credit; make any Thing but gold and silver Coin a Tender in Payment of Debts; pass any Bill of Attainder, ex post facto Law, or Law impairing the obligation of Contracts, or grant any Title of Nobility.

No State shall, without the Consent of the Congress, lay any Imposts or Duties on Imports or Exports, except what may be absolutely necessary for executing its inspection Laws: and the net Produce of all Duties and Imposts, laid by any State on Imports or Exports, shall be for the Use of the Treasury of the United States; and all such Laws shall be subject to the Revision and Controul of the Congress.

No State shall, without the Consent of Congress, lay any Duty of Tonnage, keep Troops, or Ships of War in time of Peace, enter into any Agreement or Compact with another State, or with a foreign Power, or engage in War, unless actually invaded, or in such imminent Danger as will not admit of delay.

Article II

Section 1

The executive Power shall be vested in a President of the United States of America. He shall hold his Office during the Term of four Years, and, together with the Vice President, chosen for the same Term, be elected, as follows:

Each State shall appoint, in such Manner as the Legislature thereof may direct, a Number of Electors, equal to the whole Number of Senators and Representatives to which the State may be entitled in the Congress: but no Senator or Representative, or Person holding an Office of Trust or Profit under the United States, shall be appointed an Elector.

The Electors shall meet in their respective States, and vote by Ballot for two Persons, of whom one at least shall not be an Inhabitant of the same State with themselves. And they shall make a List of all the Persons voted for, and of the Number of Votes for each; which List they shall sign and certify, and transmit sealed to the Seat of the Government of the United States, directed to the President of the Senate. The President of the Senate shall, in the Presence of the Senate and House of Representatives, open all the Certificates, and the Votes shall then be counted. The Person having the greatest Number of Votes shall be the President, if such Number be a Majority of the whole number of Electors appointed; and if there be more than one who have such Majority, and have an equal Number of Votes, then the House of Representatives shall immediately chuse by Ballot one of them for President; and if no Person have a Majority, then from the five highest on the List the said House shall in like Manner chuse the President. But in chusing the President, the Votes shall be taken by States, the Representation from each State having one Vote; A quorum for this Purpose shall consist of a Member or Members from two thirds of the States, and a Majority of all the States shall be necessary to a Choice. In every Case, after the Choice of the President, the Person having the greatest Number of Votes of the Electors shall be the Vice President. But if there should remain two or more who have equal Votes, the Senate shall chuse from them by Ballot the Vice President.

The Congress may determine the time of chusing the Electors, and the Day on which they shall give their Votes; which Day shall be the same throughout the United States.

No person except a natural born Citizen, or a Citizen of the United States, at the time of the Adoption of this Constitution, shall be eligible to the Office of President; neither shall any Person be eligible to that Office who shall not have attained to the Age of thirty five Years, and been fourteen Years a Resident within the United States.

In Case of the Removal of the President from Office, or of his Death, Resignation, or Inability to discharge the Powers and Duties of the said Office, the Same shall devolve on the Vice President, and the Congress may by Law provide for the Case of Removal, Death, Resignation or Inability, both of the President and Vice President, declaring what Officer shall then act as President, and such Officer shall act accordingly, until the Disability be removed, or a President shall be elected.

The President shall, at stated Times, receive for his Services, a Compensation, which shall neither be encreased nor diminished during the Period for which he shall have been elected, and he shall not receive within that period any other Emolument from the United States, or any of them.

Before he enter on the Execution of his Office, he shall take the following Oath or Affirmation:—"I do solemnly swear (or affirm) that I will faithfully execute the Office of President of the United States, and will to the best of my Ability, preserve, protect and defend the Constitution of the United States."

Section 2

The President shall be Commander in Chief of the Army and Navy of the United States, and of the Militia of the several States, when called into the actual Service of the United States; he may require the Opinion, in writing, of the principal Officer in each of the executive Departments, upon any Subject relating to the Duties of their respective Offices, and he shall have Power to grant Reprieves and Pardons for Offences against the United States, except in Cases of Impeachment.

He shall have Power, by and with the Advice and Consent of the Senate, to make Treaties, provided two thirds of the Senators present concur; and he shall nominate, and by and with the Advice and Consent of the Senate, shall appoint Ambassadors, other public Ministers and Consuls, Judges of the supreme Court, and all other Officers of the United States, whose Appointments are not herein otherwise provided for, and which shall be established by Law: but the Congress may by Law vest the Appointment of such inferior Officers, as they think proper in the President alone, in the Courts of Law, or in the Heads of Departments.

The President shall have Power to fill up all Vacancies that may happen during the Recess of the Senate, by granting Commissions which shall expire at the End of their next Session.

Section 3

He shall from time to time give to the Congress Information of the State of the Union, and recommend to their Consideration such Measures as he shall judge necessary and expedient; he may, on extraordinary Occasions, convene both Houses, or either of them, and in Case of disagreement between them, with Respect to the Time of Adjournment, he may adjourn them to such Time as he shall think proper; he shall receive Ambassadors and other public Ministers; he shall take Care that the Laws be faithfully executed, and shall Commission all the officers of the United States.

Section 4

The President, Vice President and all civil Officers of the United States, shall be removed from Office on Impeachment for, and Conviction of, Treason, Bribery or other high Crimes and Misdemeanors.

Article III

Section 1

The judicial Power of the United States, shall be vested in one supreme Court, and in such inferior Courts as the Congress may from time to time ordain and establish. The Judges, both of the supreme and inferior Courts, shall hold their offices during good Behaviour, and shall, at stated Times, receive for their Services, a Compensation, which shall not be diminished during their Continuance in Office.

Section 2

The judicial Power shall extend to all Cases, in Law and Equity, arising under this Constitution, the Laws of the United States, and Treaties made, or which shall be made, under their Authority;—to all Cases affecting Ambassadors, other public Ministers and Consuls;—to all Cases of admiralty and maritime Jurisdiction;—to Controversies to which the United States shall be a Party;—to Controversies between two or more States;—between a State and Citizens of another State;—between Citizens of different States;—between Citizens of the same State claiming Lands under Grants of different States, and between a State, or the Citizens thereof, and foreign States, Citizens or Subjects.

In all Cases affecting Ambassadors, other public Ministers and Consuls, and those in which a State shall be Party, the supreme Court shall have original Jurisdiction. In all the other Cases before mentioned, the supreme Court shall have appellate Jurisdiction, both as to Law and Fact, with such Exceptions, and under such Regulations as the Congress shall make.

The Trial of all Crimes, except in Cases of Impeachment, shall be by Jury; and such Trial shall be held in the State where the said Crimes shall have been committed, but when not committed within any State, the Trial shall be at such Place or Places as the Congress may by Law have directed.

Section 3

Treason against the United States, shall consist only in levying War against them, or in adhering to their Enemies, giving them Aid and Comfort. No person shall be convicted of Treason unless on the Testimony of two Witnesses to the same overt Act, or on Confession in open Court.

The Congress shall have Power to declare the Punishment of Treason, but no Attainder of Treason shall work Corruption of Blood, or Forfeiture except during the Life of the Person attainted.

Article IV

Section 1

Full Faith and Credit shall be given in each State to the public Acts, Records, and judicial Proceedings of every other State. And the Congress may by general Laws prescribe the Manner in which such Acts, Records and Proceedings shall be proved, and the Effect thereof.

Section 2

The Citizens of each State shall be entitled to all Privileges and Immunities of Citizens in the several States.

A Person charged in any State with Treason, Felony, or other Crime, who shall flee from Justice, and be found in another State, shall on Demand of the executive Authority of the State from which he fled, be delivered up, to be removed to the State having Jurisdiction of the Crime.

No Person held to Service or Labour in one State, under the Laws thereof, escaping into another, shall, in Consequence of any Law or Regulation therein, be discharged from such Service or Labour, but shall be delivered up on Claim of the Party to whom such Service or Labour may be due.

Section 3

New States may be admitted by the Congress into this Union; but no new State shall be formed or erected within the Jurisdiction of any other State; nor any State be formed by the Junction of two or more States, or Parts of States, without the Consent of the Legislatures of the States concerned as well as of the Congress.

The Congress shall have Power to dispose of and make all needful Rules and Regulations respecting the Territory or other Property belonging to the United States; and nothing in this Constitution shall be so construed as to Prejudice any Claims of the United States, or of any particular States.

Section 4

The United States shall guarantee to every State in this Union a Republican Form of Government, and shall protect each of them against Invasion; and on Application of the Legislature, or of the Executive (when the Legislature cannot be convened) against domestic violence.

Article V

The Congress, whenever two thirds of both Houses shall deem it necessary, shall propose Amendments to this Constitution, or, on the Application of the Legislatures of two thirds of the several States, shall call a Convention for proposing Amendments, which, in either Case, shall be valid to all Intents and Purposes, as Part of this Constitution, when ratified by the Legislatures of three fourths of the several States, or by Conventions in three fourths thereof, as the one or the other Mode of Ratification may be proposed by the Congress; Provided *that no Amendment which may be made prior to the Year One thousand eight hundred and eight shall in any Manner affect the first and fourth Clauses in the Ninth Section of the first Article;* and that no State, without its Consent, shall be deprived of its equal Suffrage in the Senate.

Article VI

All Debts contracted and Engagements entered into, before the Adoption of this Constitution, shall be as valid against the United States under this Constitution, as under the Confederation.

This Constitution, and Laws of the United States which shall be made in Pursuance thereof; and all Treaties made, or which shall be made, under the Authority of the United States, shall be the supreme Law of the Land; and the Judges in every State shall be bound thereby, any Thing in the Constitution or Laws of any State to the Contrary notwithstanding.

The Senators and Representatives before mentioned, and the Members of the several State Legislatures, and all executive and Judicial Officers, both of the United States and of the several States, shall be bound by Oath or Affirmation, to support this Constitution; but no religious Test shall ever be required as a Qualification to any Office of public Trust under the United States.

Article VII

The Ratification of the Conventions of nine States, shall be sufficient for the Establishment of this Constitution between the States so ratifying the Same.

Done in Convention by the Unanimous Consent of the States present the Seventeenth Day of September in the Year of our Lord one thousand seven hundred and Eighty seven and of the Independence of the United States of America the Twelfth* IN WITNESS whereof We have hereunto subscribed our Names,

George Washington
President and Deputy from Virginia

Delaware
George Read
Gunning Bedford Jr.
John Dickinson
Richard Bassett
Jacob Broom

Maryland
James McHenry
Daniel of St. Thomas Jenifer
Daniel Carroll

Virginia
John Blair
James Madison Jr.

North Carolina
William Blount
Richard Dobbs Spraight
Hugh Williamson

South Carolina
John Rutledge
Charles Cotesworth Pinckney
Charles Pinckney
Pierce Butler

Georgia
William Few
Abraham Baldwin

New Hampshire
John Langdon
Nicholas Gilman

Massachusetts
Nathaniel Gorham
Rufus King

Connecticut
William Samuel Johnson
Roger Sherman

New York
Alexander Hamilton

New Jersey
William Livingston
David Brearley
William Paterson
Jonathan Dayton

Pennsylvania
Benjamin Franklin
Thomas Mifflin
Robert Morris
George Clymer
Thomas FitzSimons
Jared Ingersoll
James Wilson
Gouverneur Morris

---

*The Constitution was submitted on September 17, 1787, by the Constitutional Convention, was ratified by conventions of the several states at various dates up to May 29, 1790, and became effective on March 4, 1789.

Amendments to the Constitution

Amendment I

Congress shall make no law respecting an establishment of religion, or prohibiting the free exercise thereof; or abridging the freedom of speech, or of the press; or the right of the people peaceably to assemble, and to petition the Government for a redress of grievances.

Amendment II

A well regulated Militia being necessary to the security of a free State, the right of the people to keep and bear Arms, shall not be infringed.

Amendment III

No Soldier shall, in time of peace be quartered in any house, without the consent of the Owner, nor in time of war, but in a manner to be prescribed by law.

Amendment IV

The right of the people to be secure in their persons, houses, papers, and effects, against unreasonable searches and seizures, shall not be violated, and no Warrants shall issue, but upon probable cause, supported by Oath or affirmation, and particularly describing the place to be searched, and the persons or things to be seized.

Amendment V

No person shall be held to answer for a capital, or otherwise infamous crime, unless on a presentment or indictment of a Grand Jury, except in cases arising in the land or naval forces, or in the Militia, when in actual service in time of War or public danger; nor shall any person be subject for the same offense to be twice put in jeopardy of life or limb; nor shall be compelled in any criminal case to be a witness against himself, nor be deprived of life, liberty, or property, without due process of law; nor shall private property be taken for public use, without just compensation.

Amendment VI

In all criminal prosecutions, the accused shall enjoy the right to a speedy and public trial, by an impartial jury of the State and district wherein the crime shall have been committed, which district shall have been previously ascertained by law, and to be informed of the nature and cause of the accusation; to be confronted with the witnesses against him; to have compulsory process for obtaining witnesses in his favor, and to have the Assistance of Counsel for his defence.

Amendment VII

In Suits at common law, where the value in controversy shall exceed twenty dollars, the right of trial by jury shall be preserved, and no fact tried by a jury, shall be otherwise reexamined in any Court of the United States, than according to the rules of the common law.

Amendment VIII

Excessive bail shall not be required, nor excessive fines imposed, nor cruel and unusual punishments inflicted.

Amendment IX

The enumeration in the Constitution, of certain rights, shall not be construed to deny or disparage others retained by the people.

Amendment X*

The powers not delegated to the United States by the Constitution, nor prohibited by it to the States, are reserved to the States respectively, or to the people.

Amendment XI
[Adopted 1798]

The Judicial power of the United States shall not be construed to extend to any suit in law or equity, commenced or prosecuted against one of the United States by Citizens of another State, or by Citizens or Subjects of any Foreign State.

Amendment XII
[Adopted 1804]

The Electors shall meet in their respective states, and vote by ballot for President and Vice President, one of whom, at least, shall not be an inhabitant of the same state with themselves; they shall name in their ballots the person voted for as President, and in distinct ballots the person voted for as Vice President, and they shall make distinct lists of all persons voted for as President, and of all persons voted for as Vice President, and of the number of votes for each, which lists they shall sign and certify, and transmit sealed to the seat of the government of the United States, directed to the President of the Senate;—The President of the Senate shall, in the presence of the Senate and House of Representatives, open all the certificates and the votes shall then be counted;—The person having the greatest number of votes for President, shall be the President, if such number be a majority of the whole number of Electors appointed; and if no person have such majority, then from the persons having the highest numbers not exceeding three on the list of those voted for as President, the House of Representatives shall choose immediately, by ballot, the President. But in choosing the President, the votes shall be taken by states, the representation from each state having one vote; a quorum for this purpose shall consist of a member or members from two-thirds of the states, and a majority of all

---

*The first ten amendments (the Bill of Rights) were ratified and their adoption was certified on December 15, 1791.

the states shall be necessary to a choice. And if the House of Representatives shall not choose a President whenever the right of choice shall devolve upon them, before *the fourth day of March* next following, then the Vice President shall act as President, as in the case of the death or other constitutional disability of the President.—The person having the greatest number of votes as Vice President, shall be the Vice President, if such number be a majority of the whole number of Electors appointed, and if no person have a majority, then from the two highest numbers on the list, the Senate shall choose the Vice President; a quorum for the purpose shall consist of two-thirds of the whole number of Senators, and a majority of the whole number shall be necessary to a choice. But no person constitutionally ineligible to the office of President shall be eligible to that of Vice President of the United States.

Amendment XIII
[Adopted 1865]

Section 1

Neither slavery nor involuntary servitude, except as a punishment for crime whereof the party shall have been duly convicted, shall exist within the United States, or any place subject to their jurisdiction.

Section 2

Congress shall have power to enforce this article by appropriate legislation.

Amendment XIV
[Adopted 1868]

Section 1

All persons born or naturalized in the United States, and subject to the jurisdiction thereof, are citizens of the United States and of the State wherein they reside. No State shall make or enforce any law which shall abridge the privileges or immunities of citizens of the United States; nor shall any State deprive any person of life, liberty, or property, without due process of law; nor deny to any person within its jurisdiction the equal protection of the laws.

Section 2

Representatives shall be apportioned among the several States according to their respective numbers, counting the whole number of persons in each State, excluding Indians not taxed. But when the right to vote at any election for the choice of electors for President and Vice President of the United States, Representatives in Congress, the Executive and Judicial officers of a State, or the members of the Legislature thereof, is denied to any of the male inhabitants of such State, being twenty-one years of age, and citizens of the United States, or in any way abridged, except for participation in rebellion, or other crime, the basis of representation therein shall be reduced in the proportion which the number of such male citizens shall bear to the whole number of male citizens twenty-one years of age in such State.

Section 3

No person shall be a Senator or Representative in Congress, or elector of President and Vice President, or hold any office, civil or military, under the United States, or under any State, who, having previously taken an oath, as a member of Congress, or as an officer of the United States, or as a member of any State legislature, or as an executive or judicial officer of any State, to support the Constitution of the United States, shall have engaged in insurrection or rebellion against the same, or given aid or comfort to the enemies thereof. But Congress may by a vote of two-thirds of each House, remove such disability.

Section 4

The validity of the public debt of the United States, authorized by law, including debts incurred for payment of pensions and bounties for services in suppressing insurrection or rebellion, shall not be questioned. But neither the United States nor any State shall assume or pay any debt or obligation incurred in aid of insurrection or rebellion against the United States, or any claim for the loss or emancipation of any slave; but all such debts, obligations and claims shall be held illegal and void.

Section 5

The Congress shall have power to enforce, by appropriate legislation, the provisions of this article.

Amendment XV
[Adopted 1870]

Section 1

The right of citizens of the United States to vote shall not be denied or abridged by the United States or by any State on account of race, color, or previous condition of servitude.

Section 2

The Congress shall have power to enforce this article by appropriate legislation.

Amendment XVI
[Adopted 1913]

The Congress shall have power to lay and collect taxes on incomes, from whatever source derived, without apportionment among the several States, and without regard to any census or enumeration.

Amendment XVII
[Adopted 1913]

The Senate of the United States shall be composed of two Senators from each State, elected by the people thereof, for six years; and each Senator shall have one vote. The electors in each State shall have the qualifications requisite for electors of the most numerous branch of the State legislatures.

When vacancies happen in the representation of any State in the Senate, the executive authority of such State shall issue writs of election to fill such vacancies: *Provided*, That the legislature of any State may empower the executive thereof to make temporary appointments until the people fill the vacancies by election as the legislature may direct.

This amendment shall not be so construed as to affect the election or term of any Senator chosen before it becomes valid as part of the Constitution.

Amendment XVIII
[Adopted 1919, repealed 1933]

Section 1

After one year from the ratification of this article the manufacture, sale, or transportation of intoxicating liquors within, the importation thereof into, or the exportation thereof from the United States and all territory subject to the jurisdiction thereof for beverage purposes is hereby prohibited.

Section 2

The Congress and the several States shall have concurrent power to enforce this article by appropriate legislation.

Section 3

This article shall be inoperative unless it shall have been ratified as an amendment to the Constitution by the legislatures of the several States, as provided in the Constitution, within seven years from the date of the submission hereof to the States by the Congress.

Amendment XIX
[Adopted 1920]

The right of citizens of the United States to vote shall not be denied or abridged by the United States or by any State on account of sex.

Congress shall have power to enforce this article by appropriate legislation.

Amendment XX
[Adopted 1933]

Section 1

The terms of the President and Vice President shall end at noon on the 20th day of January, and the terms of Senators and Representatives at noon on the 3d day of January, of the years in which such terms would have ended if this article had not been ratified and the terms of their successors shall then begin.

Section 2

The Congress shall assemble at least once in every year, and such meeting shall begin at noon on the 3d day of January, unless they shall by law appoint a different day.

Section 3

If, at the time fixed for the beginning of the term of the President, the President elect shall have died, the Vice President elect shall become President. If a President shall not have been chosen before the time fixed for the beginning of his term, or if the Pres-

ident elect shall have failed to qualify, then the Vice President elect shall act as President until a President shall have qualified; and the Congress may by law provide for the case wherein neither a President elect nor a Vice President elect shall have qualified, declaring who shall then act as President, or the manner in which one who is to act shall be selected, and such person shall act accordingly until a President or Vice President shall have qualified.

Section 4

The Congress may by law provide for the case of the death of any of the persons from whom the House of Representatives may choose a President whenever the right of choice shall have devolved upon them, and for the case of the death of any of the persons from whom the Senate may choose a Vice President whenever the right of choice shall have devolved upon them.

Section 5

Sections 1 and 2 shall take effect on the 15th day of October following the ratification of this article.

Section 6

This article shall be inoperative unless it shall have been ratified as an amendment to the Constitution by the legislatures of three fourths of the several States within seven years from the date of its submission.

Amendment XXI
[Adopted 1933]

Section 1

The eighteenth article of amendment to the Constitution of the United States is hereby repealed.

Section 2

The transportation or importation into any State, Territory, or possession of the United States for delivery or use therein of intoxicating liquors in violation of the laws thereof, is hereby prohibited.

Section 3

This article shall be inoperative unless it shall have been ratified as an amendment to the Constitution by conventions in the several States, as provided in the Constitution, within seven years from the date of the submission hereof to the States by the Congress.

Amendment XXII
[Adopted 1951]

Section 1

No person shall be elected to the office of the President more than twice, and no person who has held the office of President, or acted as President, for more than two years of a term to which some other person was elected President shall be elected to the office of the President more than once. But this Article shall not apply to any person holding the office of President when this Article was proposed by the Congress, and shall not prevent any person who may be holding the office of President, or acting as President, during the term within which this Article becomes operative from holding the office of President or acting as President during the remainder of such term.

Section 2

This article shall be inoperative unless it shall have been ratified as an amendment to the Constitution by the legislatures of three-fourths of the several States within seven years from the date of its submission to the States by the Congress.

Amendment XXIII
[Adopted 1961]
Section 1

The District constituting the seat of Government of the United States shall appoint in such manner as the Congress shall direct:

A number of electors of President and Vice President equal to the whole number of Senators and Representatives in Congress to which the District would be entitled if it were a State, but in no event more than the least populous State; they shall be in addition to those appointed by the States, but they shall be considered, for the purposes of the election of President and Vice President, to be electors appointed by a State; and they shall meet in the District and perform such duties as provided by the twelfth article of amendment.

Section 2

The Congress shall have power to enforce this article by appropriate legislation.

Amendment XXIV
[Adopted 1964]
Section 1

The right of citizens of the United States to vote in any primary or other election for President or Vice President, for electors for President or Vice President, or for Senator or Representative in Congress, shall not be denied or abridged by the United States or any state by reason of failure to pay any poll tax or other tax.

Section 2

The Congress shall have the power to enforce this article by appropriate legislation.

Amendment XXV
[Adopted 1967]
Section 1

In case of the removal of the President from office or his death or resignation, the Vice President shall become President.

Section 2

Whenever there is a vacancy in the office of the Vice President, the President shall nominate a Vice President who shall take the office upon confirmation by a majority vote of both houses of Congress.

Section 3

Whenever the President transmits to the President pro tempore of the Senate and the Speaker of the House of Representatives his written declaration that he is unable to discharge the powers and duties of his office, and until he transmits to them a written declaration to the contrary, such powers and duties shall be discharged by the Vice President as Acting President.

Section 4

Whenever the Vice President and a majority of either the principal officers of the executive departments or of such other body as Congress may by law provide, transmit to the President pro tempore of the Senate and the Speaker of the House of Representatives their written declaration that the President is unable to discharge the powers and duties of his office, the Vice President shall immediately assume the powers and duties of the office as Acting President.

Thereafter, when the President transmits to the President pro tempore of the Senate and the Speaker of the House of Representatives his written declaration that no inability exists, he shall resume the powers and duties of his office unless the Vice President and a majority of either the principal officers of the executive department or of such other body as Congress may by law provide, transmit within four days to the President pro tempore of the Senate and the Speaker of the House of Representatives their written declaration that the President is unable to discharge the powers and duties of his office. Thereupon Congress shall decide the issue, assembling within 48 hours for that purpose if not in session. If the Congress, within 21 days after receipt of the latter written declaration, or, if Congress is not in session, within 21 days after Congress is required to assemble, determines by two-thirds vote of both houses that the President is unable to discharge the powers and duties of his office, the Vice President shall continue to discharge the same as Acting President; otherwise, the President shall resume the powers and duties of his office.

Amendment XXVI
[Adopted 1971]
Section 1

The right of citizens of the United States, who are 18 years of age or older, to vote shall not be denied or abridged by the United States or any state on account of age.

Section 2

The Congress shall have the power to enforce this article by appropriate legislation.

Amendment XXVII
[Adopted 1992]

No law, varying the compensation for the services of the Senators and Representatives shall take effect, until an election of Representatives shall have intervened.

Presidential Elections

Year	Candidates	Parties	Popular Vote	Electoral Vote	Voter Participation
1789	**George Washington**		a	69	
	John Adams			34	
	Others			35	
1792	**George Washington**		a	132	
	John Adams			77	
	George Clinton			50	
	Others			5	
1796	**John Adams**	Federalist	a	71	
	Thomas Jefferson	Democratic-Republican		68	
	Thomas Pinckney	Federalist		59	
	Aaron Burr	Dem.-Rep.		30	
	Others			48	
1800	**Thomas Jefferson**	Dem.-Rep.	a	73	
	Aaron Burr	Dem.-Rep.		73	
	John Adams	Federalist		65	
	C. C. Pinckney	Federalist		64	
	John Jay	Federalist		1	
1804	**Thomas Jefferson**	Dem.-Rep.	a	162	
	C. C. Pinckney	Federalist		14	
1808	**James Madison**	Dem.-Rep.	a	122	
	C. C. Pinckney	Federalist		47	
	George Clinton	Dem.-Rep.		6	
1812	**James Madison**	Dem.-Rep.	a	128	
	De Witt Clinton	Federalist		89	
1816	**James Monroe**	Dem.-Rep.	a	183	
	Rufus King	Federalist		34	
1820	**James Monroe**	Dem.-Rep.	a	231	
	John Quincy Adams	Dem.-Rep.		1	
1824	**John Quincy Adams**	Dem.-Rep.	108,740 (30.5%)	84	26.9%
	Andrew Jackson	Dem.-Rep.	153,544 (43.1%)	99	
	William H. Crawford	Dem.-Rep.	46,618 (13.1%)	41	
	Henry Clay	Dem.-Rep.	47,136 (13.2%)	37	
1828	**Andrew Jackson**	Democratic	647,286 (56.0%)	178	57.6%
	John Quincy Adams	National Republican	508,064 (44.0%)	83	
1832	**Andrew Jackson**	Democratic	687,502 (55.0%)	219	55.4%
	Henry Clay	National Republican	530,189 (42.4%)	49	
	John Floyd	Independent		11	
	William Wirt	Anti-Mason	33,108 (2.6%)	7	
1836	**Martin Van Buren**	Democratic	765,483 (50.9%)	170	57.8%
	William Henry Harrison	Whig		73	
	Hugh L. White	Whig	739,795 (49.1%)	26	
	Daniel Webster	Whig		14	
	W. P. Magnum	Independent		11	
1840	**William Henry Harrison**	Whig	1,274,624 (53.1%)	234	80.2%
	Martin Van Buren	Democratic	1,127,781 (46.9%)	60	
	J. G. Birney	Liberty	7,069	—	

aElectors selected by state legislatures.

Year	Candidates	Parties	Popular Vote	Electoral Vote	Voter Participation
1844	**James K. Polk**	Democratic	1,338,464 (49.6%)	170	78.9%
	Henry Clay	Whig	1,300,097 (48.1%)	105	
	J. G. Birney	Liberty	62,300 (2.3%)	—	
1848	**Zachary Taylor**	Whig	1,360,967 (47.4%)	163	72.7%
	Lewis Cass	Democratic	1,222,342 (42.5%)	127	
	Martin Van Buren	Free-Soil	291,263 (10.1%)	—	
1852	**Franklin Pierce**	Democratic	1,601,117 (50.9%)	254	69.6%
	Winfield Scott	Whig	1,385,453 (44.1%)	42	
	John P. Hale	Free-Soil	155,825 (5.0%)	—	
1856	**James Buchanan**	Democratic	1,832,955 (45.3%)	174	78.9%
	John C. Frémont	Republican	1,339,932 (33.1%)	114	
	Millard Fillmore	American	871,731 (21.6%)	8	
1860	**Abraham Lincoln**	Republican	1,865,593 (39.8%)	180	81.2%
	Stephen A. Douglas	Democratic	1,382,713 (29.5%)	12	
	John C. Breckinridge	Democratic	848,356 (18.1%)	72	
	John Bell	Union	592,906 (12.6%)	39	
1864	**Abraham Lincoln**	Republican	2,213,655 (55.0%)	212[b]	73.8%
	George B. McClellan	Democratic	1,805,237 (45.0%)	21	
1868	**Ulysses S. Grant**	Republican	3,012,833 (52.7%)	214	78.1%
	Horatio Seymour	Democratic	2,703,249 (47.3%)	80	
1872	**Ulysses S. Grant**	Republican	3,597,132 (55.6%)	286	71.3%
	Horace Greeley	Dem.; Liberal Republican	2,834,125 (43.9%)	66[c]	
1876	**Rutherford B. Hayes**[d]	Republican	4,036,298 (48.0%)	185	81.8%
	Samuel J. Tilden	Democratic	4,300,590 (51.0%)	184	
1880	**James A. Garfield**	Republican	4,454,416 (48.5%)	214	79.4%
	Winfield S. Hancock	Democratic	4,444,952 (48.1%)	155	
1884	**Grover Cleveland**	Democratic	4,874,986 (48.5%)	219	77.5%
	James G. Blaine	Republican	4,851,981 (48.2%)	182	
1888	**Benjamin Harrison**	Republican	5,439,853 (47.9%)	233	79.3%
	Grover Cleveland	Democratic	5,540,309 (48.6%)	168	
1892	**Grover Cleveland**	Democratic	5,556,918 (46.1%)	277	74.7%
	Benjamin Harrison	Republican	5,176,108 (43.0%)	145	
	James B. Weaver	People's	1,041,028 (8.5%)	22	
1896	**William McKinley**	Republican	7,104,779 (51.1%)	271	79.3%
	William Jennings Bryan	Democratic People's	6,502,925 (47.7%)	176	
1900	**William McKinley**	Republican	7,207,923 (51.7%)	292	73.2%
	William Jennings Bryan	Dem.-Populist	6,358,133 (45.5%)	155	
1904	**Theodore Roosevelt**	Republican	7,623,486 (57.9%)	336	65.2%
	Alton B. Parker	Democratic	5,077,911 (37.6%)	140	
	Eugene V. Debs	Socialist	402,283 (3.0%)	—	
1908	**William H. Taft**	Republican	7,678,908 (51.6%)	321	65.4%
	William Jennings Bryan	Democratic	6,409,104 (43.1%)	162	
	Eugene V. Debs	Socialist	420,793 (2.8%)	—	
1912	**Woodrow Wilson**	Democratic	6,293,454 (41.9%)	435	58.8%
	Theodore Roosevelt	Progressive	4,119,538 (27.4%)	88	
	William H. Taft	Republican	3,484,980 (23.2%)	8	
	Eugene V. Debs	Socialist	900,672 (6.0%)	—	
1916	**Woodrow Wilson**	Democratic	9,129,606 (49.4%)	277	61.6%
	Charles E. Hughes	Republican	8,538,221 (46.2%)	254	
	A. L. Benson	Socialist	585,113 (3.2%)	—	
1920	**Warren G. Harding**	Republican	16,152,200 (60.4%)	404	49.2%
	James M. Cox	Democratic	9,147,353 (34.2%)	127	
	Eugene V. Debs	Socialist	919,799 (3.4%)	—	
1924	**Calvin Coolidge**	Republican	15,725,016 (54.0%)	382	48.9%
	John W. Davis	Democratic	8,386,503 (28.8%)	136	
	Robert M. La Follette	Progressive	4,822,856 (16.6%)	13	

[b]Eleven secessionist states did not participate.
[c]Greeley died before the electoral college met. His electoral votes were divided among the four minor candidates.
[d]Contested result settled by special election.

Year	Candidates	Parties	Popular Vote	Electoral Vote	Voter Participation
1928	**Herbert Hoover**	Republican	21,391,381 (58.2%)	444	56.9%
	Alfred E. Smith	Democratic	15,016,443 (40.9%)	87	
	Norman Thomas	Socialist	267,835 (0.7%)	—	
1932	**Franklin D. Roosevelt**	Democratic	22,821,857 (57.4%)	472	56.9%
	Herbert Hoover	Republican	15,761,841 (39.7%)	59	
	Norman Thomas	Socialist	881,951 (2.2%)	—	
1936	**Franklin D. Roosevelt**	Democratic	27,751,597 (60.8%)	523	61.0%
	Alfred M. Landon	Republican	16,679,583 (36.5%)	8	
	William Lemke	Union	882,479 (1.9%)	—	
1940	**Franklin D. Roosevelt**	Democratic	27,244,160 (54.8%)	449	62.5%
	Wendell L. Willkie	Republican	22,305,198 (44.8%)	82	
1944	**Franklin D. Roosevelt**	Democratic	25,602,504 (53.5%)	432	55.9%
	Thomas E. Dewey	Republican	22,006,285 (46.0%)	99	
1948	**Harry S. Truman**	Democratic	24,105,695 (49.5%)	304	53.0%
	Thomas E. Dewey	Republican	21,969,170 (45.1%)	189	
	J. Strom Thurmond	State-Rights Democratic	1,169,021 (2.4%)	38	
	Henry A. Wallace	Progressive	1,156,103 (2.4%)	—	
1952	**Dwight D. Eisenhower**	Republican	33,936,252 (55.1%)	442	63.3%
	Adlai E. Stevenson	Democratic	27,314,992 (44.4%)	89	
1956	**Dwight D. Eisenhower**	Republican	35,575,420 (57.6%)	457	60.6%
	Adlai E. Stevenson	Democratic	26,033,066 (42.1%)	73	
	Other	—	—	1	
1960	**John F. Kennedy**	Democratic	34,227,096 (49.9%)	303	62.8%
	Richard M. Nixon	Republican	34,108,546 (49.6%)	219	
	Other	—	—	15	
1964	**Lyndon B. Johnson**	Democratic	43,126,506 (61.1%)	486	61.7%
	Barry M. Goldwater	Republican	27,176,799 (38.5%)	52	
1968	**Richard M. Nixon**	Republican	31,770,237 (43.4%)	301	60.6%
	Hubert H. Humphrey	Democratic	31,270,533 (42.7%)	191	
	George Wallace	American Indep.	9,906,141 (13.5%)	46	
1972	**Richard M. Nixon**	Republican	47,169,911 (60.7%)	520	55.2%
	George S. McGovern	Democratic	29,170,383 (37.5%)	17	
	Other	—	—	1	
1976	**Jimmy Carter**	Democratic	40,828,587 (50.0%)	297	53.5%
	Gerald R. Ford	Republican	39,147,613 (47.9%)	241	
	Other	—	1,575,459 (2.1%)	—	
1980	**Ronald Reagan**	Republican	43,901,812 (50.7%)	489	52.6%
	Jimmy Carter	Democratic	35,483,820 (41.0%)	49	
	John B. Anderson	Independent	5,719,722 (6.6%)	—	
	Ed Clark	Libertarian	921,188 (1.1%)	—	
1984	**Ronald Reagan**	Republican	54,455,075 (59.0%)	525	53.3%
	Walter Mondale	Democratic	37,577,185 (41.0%)	13	
1988	**George H. W. Bush**	Republican	48,886,000 (53.4%)	426	57.4%
	Michael S. Dukakis	Democratic	41,809,000 (45.6%)	111	
1992	**William J. Clinton**	Democratic	43,728,375 (43.0%)	370	55.0%
	George H. W. Bush	Republican	38,167,416 (38.0%)	168	
	H. Ross Perot	Independent	19,237,247 (19.0%)	—	
1996	**William J. Clinton**	Democratic	45,590,703 (50.0%)	379	48.8%
	Robert Dole	Republican	37,816,307 (41.0%)	159	
	H. Ross Perot	Reform	7,866,284		
2000	**George W. Bush**	Republican	50,456,167 (47.88%)	271	51.2%
	Al Gore	Democratic	50,996,064 (48.39%)	266[e]	
	Ralph Nader	Green	2,864,810 (2.72%)	—	
	Other	—	834,774 (<1%)	—	
2004	**George W. Bush**	Republican	61,873,000 (50.8%)	286	55.3%
	John Kerry	Democratic	58,895,000 (48.3%)	251	
	Ralph Nader	Green	463,653 (<1%)	—	

[e]One District of Columbia Gore elector abstained.

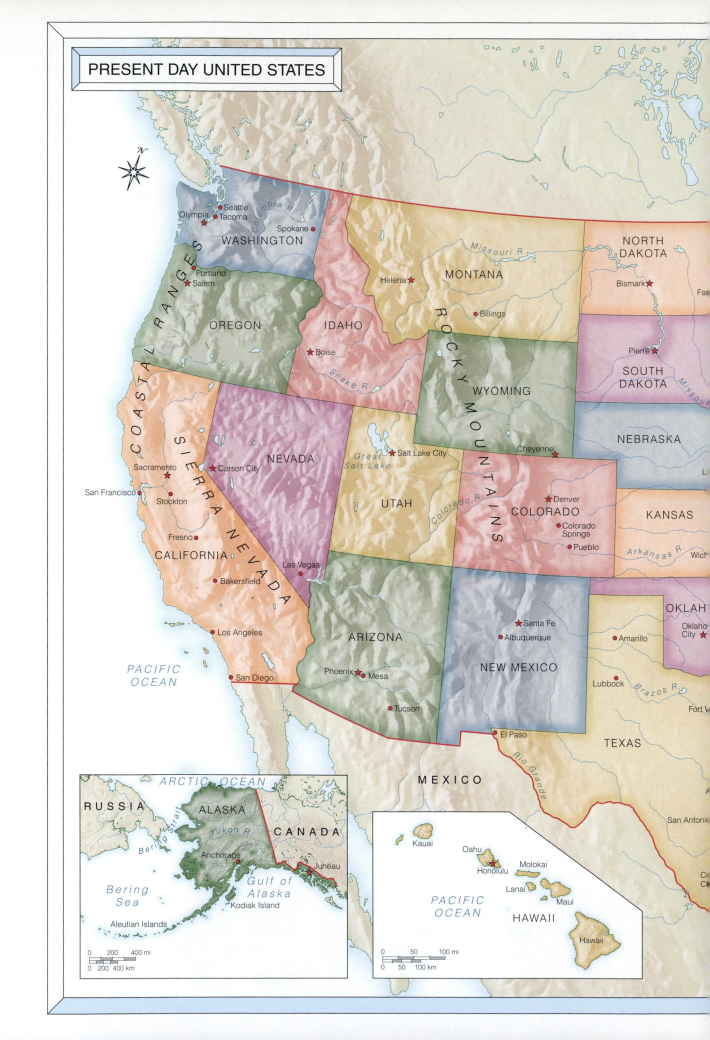

PRESENT DAY UNITED STATES

N

WASHINGTON
Seattle
Olympia ★ ● Tacoma
Spokane ●

Columbia R.

OREGON
Portland ●
★ Salem

COASTAL RANGES

IDAHO
★ Boise

Snake R.

MONTANA
Helena ★
● Billings

ROCKY MOUNTAINS

WYOMING

Cheyenne ★

NORTH DAKOTA
Bismark ★
Far

Missouri R.

Pierre ★

SOUTH DAKOTA

Missouri R.

NEBRASKA

SIERRA NEVADA

Sacramento ★
San Francisco ●
Stockton ●

Fresno ●

CALIFORNIA

NEVADA
★ Carson City

Great Salt Lake
★ Salt Lake City

UTAH

Colorado R.

Denver ★
COLORADO
Colorado Springs ●
Pueblo ●

KANSAS

Arkansas R.
Wich

Las Vegas ●
Bakersfield ●

Los Angeles ●

PACIFIC OCEAN

San Diego ●

ARIZONA
Phoenix ★ ● Mesa

Tucson ●

Santa Fe ★
Albuquerque ●

NEW MEXICO

Amarillo ●

Lubbock ●

OKLAH
Oklahoma City ★

Brazos R.
Fort W

El Paso ●

TEXAS

Rio Grande

MEXICO

San Antonio

ARCTIC OCEAN

RUSSIA

ALASKA

Yukon R.

Bering Strait

CANADA

Anchorage ●

Juneau ★

Gulf of Alaska

Bering Sea

Kodiak Island

Aleutian Islands

| 0 | 200 | 400 mi |
| 0 | 200 | 400 km |

Kauai
Oahu
Honolulu ★ Molokai
Lanai
Maui

PACIFIC OCEAN

HAWAII

Co
Ch

Hawaii

| 0 | 50 | 100 mi |
| 0 | 50 | 100 km |

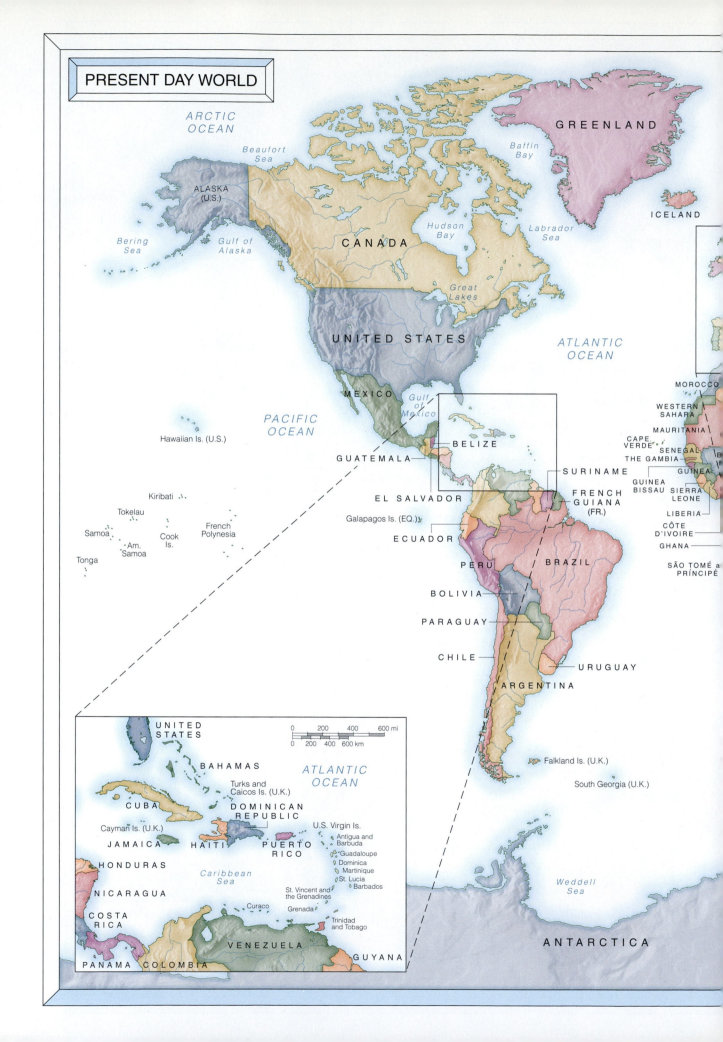

PRESENT DAY WORLD

ARCTIC
OCEAN

GREENLAND

Beaufort
Sea

Baffin
Bay

ICELAND

ALASKA
(U.S.)

Bering
Sea

Gulf of
Alaska

Hudson
Bay

Labrador
Sea

CANADA

ATLANTIC
OCEAN

Great
Lakes

UNITED STATES

MOROCCO

WESTERN
SAHARA

MAURITANIA

PACIFIC
OCEAN

MEXICO

Gulf
of
Mexico

Hawaiian Is. (U.S.)

BELIZE

CAPE
VERDE

SENEGAL

THE GAMBIA

GUATEMALA

SURINAME

GUINEA

Kiribati

EL SALVADOR

FRENCH
GUIANA
(FR.)

GUINEA
BISSAU

SIERRA
LEONE

Tokelau

French
Polynesia

Galapagos Is. (EQ.)

LIBERIA

Samoa

Cook
Is.

ECUADOR

CÔTE
D'IVOIRE

Am.
Samoa

GHANA

Tonga

PERU

BRAZIL

SÃO TOMÉ a
PRÍNCIPE

BOLIVIA

PARAGUAY

CHILE

URUGUAY

ARGENTINA

Falkland Is. (U.K.)

South Georgia (U.K.)

UNITED
STATES

0   200   400   600 mi

0   200   400 600 km

BAHAMAS

ATLANTIC
OCEAN

Turks and
Caicos Is. (U.K.)

CUBA

DOMINICAN
REPUBLIC

Cayman Is. (U.K.)

U.S. Virgin Is.

JAMAICA

HAITI

PUERTO
RICO

Antigua and
Barbuda

Guadaloupe

HONDURAS

Dominica

Martinique

St. Lucia

Caribbean
Sea

Barbados

Weddell
Sea

NICARAGUA

St. Vincent and
the Grenadines

COSTA
RICA

Curaco

Grenada

Trinidad
and Tobago

VENEZUELA

GUYANA

ANTARCTICA

PANAMA COLOMBIA

0   1000   2000   3000 mi
0   1000   2000   3000 km

ARCTIC OCEAN

Svalbard Is. (NOR.)
Novaya Zemlya
Barents Sea
Kara Sea
Laptev Sea
New Siberian Is.
East Siberian Sea

RUSSIA

Lake Baikal
Sea of Okhotsk
Sakhalin

KAZAKHSTAN
Aral Sea
Lake Balkhash
MONGOLIA

PEOPLE'S REPUBLIC OF CHINA

N. KOREA
S. KOREA
JAPAN

East China Sea

PACIFIC OCEAN

NISIA
ISRAEL
LIBYA
IRAQ
JORDAN
EGYPT
BAHRAIN
QATAR
SAUDI ARABIA
IRAN
AFGHAN.
PAKISTAN
NEPAL
BHUTAN
BANG.
U.A.E.
OMAN
INDIA
BURMA (MYANMAR)
MACAO
TAIWAN
Philippine Sea
CHAD
ERITREA
YEMEN
Arabian Sea
LAOS
VIETNAM
PHILIPPINES
Northern Mariana Is.
SUDAN
DJIBOUTI
SOMALIA
Bay of Bengal
THAILAND
South China Sea
Marshall Is.
CENT. AFRICAN REP.
ETHIOPIA
CAMBODIA
SRI LANKA
MEROON
EQUA. GUINEA
UGANDA
KENYA
MALAYSIA
BRUNEI
ON
DEM. REP. OF CONGO
RWANDA
SINGAPORE
PAPUA NEW GUINEA
Nauru
BURUNDI
TANZANIA
INDONESIA
Solomon Is.
ANGOLA
MALAWI
INDIAN OCEAN
Tuvalu
ZAMBIA
MADAGASCAR
MAURITIUS
Coral Sea
Vanuatu
Fiji
AMBIA
ZIMB.
BOTSWANA
New Caledonia (FR.)
MOZAMBIQUE
AUSTRALIA
Tasman Sea
SOUTH AFRICA
SWAZILAND
LESOTHO
NEW ZEALAND

0   200   400   600   800 mi
0   200   400   600   800 km

N

NORWAY
FINLAND
SWEDEN
North Sea
ESTONIA
IRELAND
DENMARK
LATVIA
UNITED KINGDOM
LITHUANIA
Baltic Sea
RUSSIA
ATLANTIC OCEAN
NETHERLANDS
BELGIUM
POLAND
BELARUS
GERMANY
LUX.
CZECH REPUBLIC
UKRAINE
FRANCE
LIECHT.
SLOVAKIA
SWITZ.
AUSTRIA
HUNGARY
MOLDOVA
SLOVENIA
ROMANIA
CROATIA
BOSNIA HERZ.
SERBIA
BULGARIA
GEORGIA
Black Sea
Caspian Sea
PORTUGAL
SPAIN
ITALY
MACEDONIA
ALBANIA
ARMENIA
AZERBAIJAN
Adriatic Sea
GREECE
TURKEY
MONTENEGRO
CYPRUS
SYRIA
IRAQ
Mediterranean Sea
Aegean Sea
LEBANON

Glossary

Abdicate To give up a throne or high position, to renounce sovereign power. 73

Accommodationist A person who adapts or modifies a position to ease conflict rather than holding fast to convictions in the face of opposition. 427

Acculturate To change the behavior of a group to conform to the behavior of the larger society. 434

Adage A familiar saying that embodies a common observation or a wise idea. 165

Aliens Foreign-born residents of the United States who have not been naturalized as U.S. citizens. 491

Allies Members of an alliance, such as the military coalition led by the United States, the Soviet Union, and Great Britain during World War II. 544

Almshouse A privately financed home for the poor; a poorhouse. 124

Amphibious landing A military assault that begins on the water and ends on land. 305

Anarchists Persons who reject all forms of government as inherently oppressive and undesirable. 415

Annexation Addition of territory that had belonged to one nation into another nation. 302

Annulment An official pronouncement nullifying a marriage, or declaring it invalid. 24

Antebellum The extended period before a war; usually refers to the several decades immediately before the American Civil War. 257

Anthropology The study of the origin and development of humankind. 426

Anti-Federalists A diverse and unsuccessful coalition that opposed ratification of the Constitution and feared the increased power of the proposed central government. The Anti-Federalists were named by their opponents, the Federalists. 211

Antisemitism Prejudice against Jews. 389

Aqueduct An elevated conduit or channel built to transfer water flowing from a distant source, using gravity. 000

Archaic period The second long stage of North American habitation, covering about 7,000 years, from roughly 8,000 BCE to 1000 BCE (or from 10,000 to 3,000 years ago). During this period, inhabitants adapted to diverse local environments, gathering plants and hunting smaller animals than during the previous Paleo-Indian period. 6

Archipelago A group of islands, such as the Hawaiian archipelago. 12

Ardent Passionate, devoted, zealous, fiery. 41

Armistice A truce in a military conflict; a temporary halt in hostilities by agreement between the opposing sides. 439

Asiento A contract negotiated by the Spanish crown (between 1595 and 1789) with other European powers such as Portugal, France, England, and the Netherlands to provide a fixed number of slaves annually to Spain's American colonies for a set payment. 82

Assembly line A form of industrial production popularized by the Ford Motor Company in which workers perform one task repeatedly as the products they are jointly assembling move along a conveyor. 456

Atlatl A weighted, handheld device that enabled early Native Americans to throw spears with added power and velocity. 7

Avid Eager, greedy, enthusiastic. 169

Axis A political alignment or alliance, such as the military coalition between Germany, Italy, and Japan during World War II. 532

Babel A city described in the Old Testament where constructing a tower was made impossible by the confusion of varied languages. This term from the Book of Genesis is used to describe any scene of clamor and confusion. 110

Baby boom The period of increased U.S. childbirths from roughly the early 1940s to the early 1960s. 575

Baby boomers The generation of Americans born during the era from the early 1940s to the early 1960s. 665

Barracoon An enclosure or barrack used for the confinement of slaves before their forced deportation from the African coast. 92

Bill of Rights A set of amendments assuring basic rights, proposed by James Madison to help ensure acceptance of the newly drafted Constitution, and based on suggestions from the states. Ten of the twelve items passed by Congress were ratified by the states in 1791. Taken together, these first ten amendments to the Constitution became known as the Bill of Rights. 214

Black Codes Southern state laws passed after the Civil War to limit the rights and actions of newly liberated African Americans. 360

Blacklist A (figurative or real) list of persons to be denied jobs because of their alleged loyalty to a particular cause or institution. 414

Black power The slogan used by young black nationalists in the mid- and late 1960s. 603

"Bloody shirt" A partisan rallying cry used to stir up or revive sectional or party animosity after the American Civil War; for example, post–Civil War Republicans "waved the bloody shirt," associating some Democrats with a treasonous acceptance of secession during the war, while opponents had spilled their blood for the Union. 397

Bolsheviks The Communist revolutionaries who overthrew the Russian czar in 1917 and established the Union of Soviet Socialist Republics (USSR). 480

Boston marriages Unions of two women based on long-term emotional bonds in which the women live together as if married to each other. 457

Braceros Mexican nationals working in the United States in low-wage jobs as part of a temporary work program between 1942 and 1964. (The *Bracero* program was established by an executive agreement between the presidents of Mexico and the United States, providing Mexican agricultural labor in the Southwest and the Pacific Northwest.) 578

Brunt The principal force, shock, or stress, especially of an attack. 203

Bull Moosers Supporters of Theodore Roosevelt in the 1912 presidential election when he broke from the Republican party and ran as a third-party candidate on the ticket of the Progressive (or Bull Moose) party. 464

Burgess A representative elected to the popular branch of the colonial legislature in either Virginia or Maryland. 44

Cajuns The Louisiana word for French-speaking people from Acadia (Nova Scotia) who were forced to move south in 1755 during the French and Indian War. Many of these refugees eventually moved to French Louisiana, where they have had a lasting impact on the culture. 119

Canal locks An enclosure on a canal or other waterway equipped with gates that can be closed so that boats can be raised or lowered by adjusting the water, in order to pass from one level to another. 265

Capitalism The now almost worldwide economic system of private ownership of property and profit-seeking corporations. 509

Capitulation The act of formal surrender, upon specified terms. 226

Carpetbaggers A negative term applied by Southerners to Northerners who moved to the South after the Civil War to pursue political or economic opportunities. 360

Causeway A raised roadway crossing above open water or wet ground. 10

Cede To surrender possession of. 312

Checks and balances The rules controlling interactions among the executive, legislative, and judicial branches of government, making up a novel system designed to prevent any single branch from overreaching its powers, as set forth in the Constitution in 1787. 208

Civic organizations Membership organizations that exist to further the public life and welfare of a community. 683

Coalition An alliance of parties, factions, or nations. 279

Coffle A procession or train of enslaved prisoners, bound together for travel (from the Arabic word for "caravan"). 92

Cold War The conflict and competition between the United States and the Soviet Union (and their respective allies) that emerged after 1945 and lasted until 1989. 550

Colonialism The centuries-old system of mostly European nations controlling and governing peoples and lands outside of Europe. 558

Columbian Exchange The significant two-way interchange of plants, animals, microbes, and people that occurred once Christopher Columbus established regular contact by sea between the eastern and western hemispheres. For thousands of years before 1492, despite occasional encounters, these two separate and different "worlds" had remained isolated from each other. 17

Comfort women Women, mostly Chinese and Korean, forced into sexual slavery by Japanese troops during World War II. 547

Commercial farming Agricultural system producing for markets and intended to yield a profit after crops are sold. 312

Common school system Tax-supported public education to provide elementary schooling free to young children. 297

Communism A totalitarian form of government, grounded in the theories of German philosopher Karl Marx and the practices of V. I. Lenin in Russia, that eliminated private ownership of property in supposed pursuit of complete human equality; the system of government also featured a centrally directed economy and the absolute rule of a small group of leaders. 550

Communitarian relating to communities practicing communitarianism, a form of cooperative living in small groups. 299

Conclave A private meeting, secret assembly, gathering, or convention. 211

Conservationists Advocates of conserving and protecting the natural world through the use of renewable natural resources. 462

Conspicuous consumption A term coined by the American social theorist Thorstein Veblen to describe the behavior of wealthy persons who flaunt their status through their purchase of fine clothes, large houses, fancy cars, and other highly visible material goods. 429

Consumer Economy An economic system in which most people work for wages, which they use to purchase manufactured goods and foodstuffs. 486

Containment The U.S. policy during the Cold War of trying to halt the expansion of Soviet and communist influences. 556

Contraband Goods (or, during the Civil War, slaves) seized from the enemy during war. 343

Cooperatives Organizations that produce or market goods and that are owned collectively by people who share in their profits or benefits. 376

Coverture French term for the dependent and legal status of a woman during marriage. Under English law, the male family head received legal rights, and his wife lost independent status, becoming, in legal terms, a *femme covert*. 68

Creoles People born in the United States but retaining a strong cultural identification with their forebears; especially persons of mixed Spanish or French and African descent speaking a dialect of Spanish or French. 258

Czar The monarch (king) of Russia before the 1917 revolution. 140

De facto government A government that is exercising power as if legally constituted. 156

Détente The lessening of military or diplomatic tensions, as between the United States and the Soviet Union. 617

Diaspora The dispersion of a population abroad, whether forced or voluntary. The term is often applied to Jewish settlement outside the eastern Mediterranean region, and to the spread of Africans across the Americas, due to the Atlantic slave trade. 108

Dispossession Act of taking land or other property from a group of people. 311

Don't ask, don't tell A policy established by the Clinton administration allowing gays and lesbians to serve in the military so long as they do not disclose their sexual orientation. 667

Double V The campaign by African Americans during the Second World War to fight simultaneously for victory against fascism abroad and racial discrimination at home. 543

Dust Bowl The plains regions of Oklahoma, Texas, Colorado, and New Mexico affected by severe drought in the 1930s. 512

Ecology The web of interconnections between organisms (particularly humans) and the natural environment. 265

Electoral College An intricate system in which each state appoints electors, equal in number to its representation in Congress, to elect the president and vice president. The electoral college is a provision of the Constitution (Article II, Section 1) because the framers were unwilling to approve the direct election of president and vice president. This group, or "college," of electors still makes the selection, voting according to prior party commitments rather than individual choice. 209

Emancipation National or state-sponsored program to free slaves. 345

Embargo A government order prohibiting the entry or departure of commercial ships from a port. 245

Emigrants People who leave one place and move to another. 286

Encomienda The Spanish encomienda system, imposed in Spain's American empire, requiring Indian communities to supply labor or pay tribute to a local colonial overlord (identified as an encomendero). 63

Enfranchised citizens Persons who are entitled to vote in government elections. 251

Entente The alliance of Britain, France, and Russia, later joined by the United States, during World War I. 467

Entrepreneur A person who organizes, manages, or assumes the risks in a business venture. 255

Evangelical Protestants Christians who emphasize the importance of personal faith, as well as seeking new converts. 292

Exposé A piece of investigative journalism that exposes corruption in government, business, or other institutions. 590

Extractive enterprises Businesses that harvest or extract natural products from the land or sea (fish, timber, minerals, crops). 387

Fall line The geographical division between the Piedmont and the Atlantic coastal plain where the land slopes sharply to the sea. 315

Family wage A level of income sufficient for an individual worker, usually a man, to support a spouse and family through a single salary. 524

Fascism A form of right-wing dictatorship exalting nation and race above the individual. 348

Fatigue work Unskilled manual labor. 000

Federalists A coalition of nationalist leaders who favored creating a stronger central government to replace the Articles of Confederation; they labeled their opponents as Anti-Federalists in the late 1780s. The strongest essays endorsing their proposed new Constitution were entitled *The Federalist Papers*. 211

Federation An alliance or compact between political units that agree to surrender certain powers to a central authority while still retaining other powers. 193

Feminism The belief that women and men are of equal value and that gender roles are, to a considerable degree, created by society rather than being simply natural. 608

Fireside chats The broadcasts by President Franklin Delano Roosevelt during which he spoke directly to American families, often gathered around a radio in their living room. 517

Flappers Young women in the 1910s and 1920s who rebelled against the gender conventions of the era with respect to fashion and behavior. 486

Flotilla Any sizeable fleet of ships, or, more specifically, a naval term for a unit consisting of two or more squadrons of small warships. 134

Foreclosure A legal process of seizing private property, such as a home or farm, in order to pay off a debtor's creditors. 203

Foundling home A residence for orphaned children. 449

Free trade International economic relations characterized by multinational investment and a reduction or elimination of tariffs. 534

Free labor ideology The ideas, represented most forcefully by the antebellum Republican party, that workers should profit from their own labor and that slavery is wrong. 315

Freighter Person, vehicle, or vessel that transports goods. 317

Fusion A combination, alliance. 432

Geographic mobility The phenomenon of people moving frequently from one place to another. 433

Glacier A large body of ice that endures for centuries, advancing or receding slowly as climactic conditions change. 5

Globalization The process of integration—economic, but also cultural—of different parts of the world into a more unified system of trade and communication. 13

Grassroots democracy A political system that relies on the active participation of people at the local level. 423

Great Awakening The title that was applied, in retrospect, to the interdenominational Christian revival that swept Britain's North American colonies between the 1730s and the 1750s, inspired at first by the preaching of Jonathan Edwards and George Whitefield. (A religious revival in the early nineteenth century became known as the Second Great Awakening.) 126

Great Migration The movement of African Americans out of the South to northern cities, particularly during World War I. 474

Guerrilla war A conflict fought not on the basis of conventional warfare, but rather by mobilizing small groups of fighters who attack and harass superior forces. 288

Gun control The legal regulation of firearms. 665

Hard currency Coins made of precious metals such as silver, gold, or nickel, as opposed to paper bills; also called hard money or specie. 219

Harry To torment an enemy by destructive raids or repeated small attacks. 186

Hayseeds A derogatory term applied to rural people deemed uneducated and naive (in contrast to self-proclaimed sophisticated city dwellers). 429

Headright Under the headright system, English colonial governments granted a fixed amount of land, usually 50 acres, to any head of household for every family member or hired hand that person brought into the colony. Sometimes fewer acres were granted for women and children on the grounds that they would clear and plant less land. 44

Hinterland A rural area that is linked to a nearby city through trade networks. 253

Hobo Migrant worker or poor and homeless vagrant who traveled on trains from location to location, usually in search of employment. 512

Hoovervilles Shantytowns, named for president Hoover and occupied largely by people who lost their homes and farms during the Great Depression. 452

Humanitarian intervention Warfare undertaken ostensibly in furtherance of humanitarian objectives. 670

Iberian Relating to Europe's Iberian Peninsula, the location of Spain and Portugal. 32

Impressment A policy that authorizes the seizure of persons or private property in the service of a government. 219

Indenture A document binding one person to work for another for a given period of time. Indentured servants received food, shelter, and clothing, plus "freedom dues" when their terms of service ended to help them get started independently. 86

Injunction A court order prohibiting a party from certain kinds of behavior—for example, barring a labor union from striking. 431

Internal improvements Turnpikes, canals, bridges, seaports, and other projects intended to facilitate trade and transportation within the country. 251

Iroquois League A Native American confederacy, located in central New York, originally composed of the Cayuga, Mohawk, Oneida, Onondaga, and Seneca Indians, and later including the Tuscarora as well. 38

Isthmus A narrow strip of land connecting two larger land areas (such as the isthmus of Panama). 18

Itinerant minister A preacher who travels from place to place without invitation, or who visits a circuit of churches on a regular basis. 129

Jim Crow The name given to the set of legal institutions that ensured the segregation of nonwhite people in the South. 408

Juke joint A small, inexpensive establishment where patrons could eat and drink or dance to music from a jukebox. *Juke* is a word of West African origin popularized by African Americans in the Sea Islands of South Carolina. 486

Kachina An Indian religious system, inspired by Mexican traditions, and present in the American Southwest for more than 800 years. The kachina cult used masks for group performances associated with rain, curing, fertility, warfare, and the ancestors. Among many Pueblo and Hopi Indians, this tradition was epitomized by kachina (or katsina) dolls. 64

Kayak A highly maneuverable, decked-in canoe used by Native Alaskans for travel and hunting. The light frame is covered with skins, and the paddle has a blade at each end. Popular modern versions of this traditional boat are made with canvas or fiberglass. 140

Kickbacks Money paid illegally in return for favors (for example, to a politician by a person or business that has received government contracts). 367

Laissez-Faire a belief in little or no government interference in the economy. 000

Land speculation The act of buying land in the hope of making a profit by selling it in the future. 228

Liberalism Originally a nineteenth-century belief in free-market capitalism; in the twentieth century, a belief in using the power of the federal government to increase opportunity and provisions for the least affluent citizens; by the twenty-first century, increasingly a belief in multicultural tolerance and inclusion. 644

Litigation A lawsuit or legal contest. 201

Longevity Length of life, a long duration of life. 214

Manumission A formal emancipation from slavery; the act (by an individual owner or government authority) of granting freedom to an enslaved person or persons. 101

Market Revolution The combined effects of transportation innovation, technological change, and economic growth, especially during the first half of the nineteenth century. 254

McCarthyism The political campaign led by Senator Joseph McCarthy (R-Wisconsin) to blame liberals at home for setbacks to U.S. interests abroad, due to what he considered liberals' sympathies with communism. 562

Meager Thin, sparse, scanty; lacking fullness, richness, or strength. 38

Mercantilism A commercial policy that sought to achieve economic self-sufficiency and a favorable balance of trade (often by planting colonies) in order to promote a country's prosperity, strength, and independence. Rival European imperial powers favored the strategy of mercantilism in the seventeenth and eighteenth centuries. 57

Merchant-capitalist An entrepreneur who hires workers to perform piecework in the worker's home. 255

Mesoamerica The transitional region between North and South America, composed of Mexico and Central America. 7

Mestizo A person of mixed European and American Indian ancestry. 63

Middle ground The geographical region occupied by diverse cultural groups engaged in trade. 426

Middle passage For European slave ships, the middle passage was the second of three legs in the triangular round-trip voyage from Europe to Africa to America and back to Europe. For enslaved Africans, the middle passage came to mean not only the transatlantic journey itself, but the entire process of removal from an African homeland and ultimate sale to an American master. 91

Military-industrial complex   The term given by President Dwight D. Eisenhower to the military arms industry nexus. 583

Monetary policy   Government policies designed to affect the national economy through bank lending policies, interest rates, and control of the amount of money in circulation. 218

Most-favored-nation status   A designation allowing countries to export their products to the United States with tariffs no greater than those levied against most other nations. 669

Muckrakers   The name given to a group of investigative journalists in the early twentieth century whose exposés often challenged corporate and government power. 458

Mulatto   A person of mixed European and African ancestry; the first-generation offspring of a Caucasian and a Negroid parent. 63

Muse   In Greek mythology, one of the nine sister goddesses who preside over music, poetry, and the arts. 47

Mutual aid society   An organization of people who voluntarily pool their resources in order to help members in times of illness or other personal crises. 284

NAACP   National Association for the Advancement of Colored People, founded in 1909. 564

National security state   The reorientation of the U.S. government and its budget after 1945 toward a primary focus on military and intelligence capabilities. 566

Nativists   American citizens born in the United States who oppose further immigration, especially from anywhere outside northwestern Europe. 295

New Democrats   Members of the Democratic party, many of them organized in the Democratic Leadership Council, who espouse center to center-right policies. 666

Nisei   Japanese Americans born in the United States of Japanese immigrant parents. 535

NSC-68   The 1950 directive of the National Security Council that called for rolling back, rather than merely containing, Soviet and communist influences. 566

Nuclear family   A basic family structure that has parents and their children at its center, or nucleus, but does not include grandparents, cousins, or other relatives. 284

Nullification   The doctrine that a state has the right to ignore or nullify certain federal laws with which it disagrees. 272

Okies   Migrants from Oklahoma who left the state during the Dust Bowl period in search of work. 513

Operative   A machine tender. 624

Ordnance   Cannons, artillery, and by extension general military supplies including weapons, ammunition, combat vehicles, and tools. 168

Overspeculation   Buying stocks and land that turn out to be not as valuable as the investors had originally believed. 293

Pachucos   Young Mexican American members of neighborhood gangs. 543

Paleo Indians   The earliest human inhabitants of North America, who first migrated to the continent from Siberia more than 15,000 years ago. Faced with a warming climate and the disappearance of many large game animals roughly 10,000 years ago (8000 BCE), they learned to hunt smaller animals and adapted to varied local conditions during the Archaic Period (to c. 1000 BCE). 6

Parochial schools   Schools sponsored by the Catholic Church or some other religious denomination (in contrast to public schools). 428

Patronage   System that rewards political supporters with jobs and other favors. 335

Pest house   In colonial times, a shelter to quarantine those possibly infected with contagious diseases (such as newcomers arriving in American ports from Africa or Europe) to prevent the spread of shipborne pestilence. 97

Placate   To soothe or pacify, usually by granting concessions. 10

Planned obsolescence   A concept whereby producers intend for their products to eventually become obsolete or outdated and require replacement, thus perpetuating a cycle of production and consumption. 436

Pocket veto   An indirect veto of a legislative bill made when an executive (such as a president or governor) simply leaves the bill unsigned, so that it dies after the adjournment of the legislature. 358

Political machine   A group that effectively exercises control over a political party, usually at the local level and organized around precincts and patronage. 490

Popular sovereignty   The idea that residents of a state should be able to make decisions on crucial issues, such as whether or not to legalize slavery. 321

Postbellum   Period after a war, especially after the Civil War, 1865–1877. 363

Precedent   An earlier occurrence of something similar; something done or said setting an example or pattern that can justify later actions. 18

Preemptive attack   A form of military aggression on the part of one country designed to thwart a perceived imminent attack from another. 438

Presidio   A military garrison or fortified settlement in an area under Spanish control. 111

Privateers   Ships (and their crew members) licensed to harass enemy shipping in wartime. 76

Producer economy   An economic system dominated by individuals who are self-producers of manufactured goods and foodstuffs rather than employees working for wages. 486

Progressivism   A notion of political reform central to the "Progressive Era" (the first two decades of the twentieth century), when urban reformers with a faith in progress sought to address local and national social problems through political and civic means. 458

Public domain   Lands owned by the federal government. 424

Putting out   System in which workers labor in their homes to produce goods for a merchant, who usually provides raw materials and pays them not by the hour but by each piece they finish. 255

Quitrent   A fixed rent paid annually by a tenant to a proprietor or landowner. 69

Race suicide   A fear articulated by Theodore Roosevelt and others that the low birthrate of Anglo-Saxon Americans, along with the high birthrate of immigrants from southern and eastern Europe, would result in a population in which "inferior" peoples would outnumber the "American racial stock". 454

Realignment   Change in a coalition or alliance between political parties. 308

Reconstruction   the U.S. government policies to rebuild the South after the Civil War and reintegrate it with the rest of the nation. 358

Redemption system   An eighteenth-century arrangement in which potential migrants in Europe signed up with an agent who agreed to pay for their Atlantic passage. Reaching America, the newcomer signed a pact to work for several years for an employer. In exchange for much-needed labor, the employer agreed to pay back the shipper, "redeeming" the original loan that had been made to the immigrant "redemptioner." 117

Red lining   A business practice in which lending institutions deny credit to racial or ethnic minorities who live in poor neighborhoods. 577

Redress   A remedy for a wrong; a correction or reparation. As a verb, to redress means to correct, to set right, or to remove the cause of a grievance. 149

Red Scare   Post–World War I repression of socialists, communists, and other left-wing radicals ("Reds"). 483

Regressive tax   A tax that decreases in rate as the base increases, so that someone with a large holding pays a relatively small amount. A fixed tax of $100 is regressive, since persons with $1,000 or $1 million shoulder very different relative burdens. This is the opposite of a progressive tax, where those with less pay at a lower rate. 77

Rejuvenation   To restore the youthful vigor or appearance of a thing or a person. 435

Republican mother   A wife and mother whose primary role is caring for and socializing future citizens (her children); an ideal favored by some elites after the American Revolution. 232

Requisition   To request, demand, or formally require something of someone. 36

Restitution   Giving back to the rightful owner something that has been lost or taken away. 305

Restoration   The political act of restoring monarchy to England in 1660 after the brief experiment of the Puritan Commonwealth, placing Charles II upon the throne once occupied by his Stuart father, Charles I. The following years, until the end of the Stuart family dynasty in 1688, are known in English culture and politics as the *Restoration Era*. 66

Rogue nations   A label used by the U.S. government to refer to nations it considers hostile, unpredictable, and potentially dangerous. 674

Rosie the Riveter   A heroic symbol of women workers on the homefront during World War II. 539

Sachem   Algonquin Indian term for a Native American leader or chief. 70

Scalawag   A negative term applied by southern Democrats after the Civil War to any white Southerner who allied with the Republican party. 360

Secession   Withdrawal of a state from the authority of the federal government. 250

Second New Deal   The agenda of policies and programs initiated by President Franklin Delano Roosevelt beginning in 1935 that was intended to strengthen the lot of American workers while simultaneously preserving the capitalist system. 518

Sedentary farming   Activity that requires cultivators to live in one place for extended periods of time. 228

Sedition   Acts that stir up rebellion against a government. 222

Separation of powers   The novel idea that the powers of the three branches of government—legislative, executive, and judicial—should be kept separate from one another, so that each can check and balance the powers of the other two. 208

Sharecropping   A system in which landless farmers grown crops on another person's land in exchange for a portion of the crops. 364

Sit-down strike   A strategy employed by workers agitating for better wages and working conditions in which they stop working and simply sit down, thus ceasing production and preventing strikebreakers from entering a facility to assume their jobs. 526

Sit-in   A form of civil disobedience in which activists sit down somewhere in violation of law or policy in order to challenge discriminatory practices or laws. The tactic originated during labor struggles in the 1930s and was used effectively in the civil rights movement in 1960. 581

Social Darwinism   A late-nineteenth-century variation on the theories of British naturalist Charles Darwin, promoting the idea that only the "fittest" individuals will, or deserve to, survive (i.e., the idea that society operates on principles of evolutionary biology). 397

Speakeasies   Establishments where alcohol was illegally sold during the Prohibition era. 490

Sphere of influence   An area dominated by the military, economic, and cultural power of another country. 439

Squatters   People who live on land that they do not own, without the landowner's permission. 226

Staples   Important trade items or foodstuffs. 123

Steerage   Section of a ship providing the cheapest accommodations for passengers. 000

Subsidies   Government assistance in the form of tax breaks or cash bonuses given to a person or business. 256

Subsistence homesteading   Farming to provide only for the necessities of one's family. 312

Substitute   During war, a man paid to serve in combat in another man's place. 340

Suffrage   The right to vote. 373

Sunbelt   The band of states from the Southeast to the Southwest that experienced rapid economic and population growth during and after World War II. 561

Sweatshop   A small factory where employees work long hours for low wages under poor conditions (especially in the garment industry). 659

Swords into plowshares Turning weapons of war into productive implements, such as plows, based on the biblical passage in Isaiah 2:4. 193

Tariff A government tax on imported goods. 218

Tejanos Spanish-speaking residents of the Mexican (and later, U.S.) state of Texas. 266

Temperance A social movement embracing either total opposition to alcohol consumption or support for its moderate use. 295

Tenant farmer A farmer who raises livestock and crops on land leased from wealthier owners. 150

Tenements Densely inhabited apartment buildings generally found in crowded and poor areas of cities where immigrants and ethnic minorities lived in unhealthy conditions. 310

Texians The name used by U.S.-born citizens who lived in the Mexican state of Texas. 266

Theocracy A government by officials who are regarded as divinely guided. 637

Tithe A levy or donation (generally a tenth part) given to provide support, usually for a church. 24

Total war The attacking of both military and civilian targets. 543

Townsend Plan A proposal by Dr. Francis Townsend in 1934 for a 2 percent national sales tax that would fund a guaranteed pension of $200 per month for Americans older than age 60. 521

Travois A French Canadian term for the A-frame device used by many traditional Native Americans to draw heavy loads over long distances. It consisted of two trailing poles attached to a dog or horse and supporting a platform to carry belongings. 113

Treaties Legally binding documents ratified by nations pledging them to engage or refrain from engaging in certain actions or policies. 410

Triangular trade The huge Atlantic slave trade that linked Europe, Africa, and the Americas from the sixteenth to the nineteenth century. Ships from Europe sailed to Africa to exchange trade goods for slaves. On their second leg (the infamous "middle passage"), these vessels transported the enslaved captives to ports in the Caribbean or on the American mainland. They completed their clockwise voyage by returning to Europe, usually carrying colonial staples produced by slaves, such as sugar, rice, or tobacco. 91

Trickle-down economics An economic concept whereby the government aids the wealthiest strata as well as large corporations in the belief that the benefits of this aid will "trickle down" to the middle and lower classes. 489

Truman Doctrine President Truman's March 1947 speech articulating the new policy of containment. 556

Trusts A combination of firms or corporations created for the purpose of reducing competition and controlling prices throughout an industry. 399

Tundra A cold and treeless plain typical of arctic and sub-arctic regions. 5

Two-party system A system of government characterized by two major political parties that compete against each other in "winner take all" elections. 218

Unicameral legislature A legislative body that has only one chamber, or house. 69

Utopian Relating to communities organized to strive for ideal social and political conditions. 299

Vagrancy The state of being unemployed and wandering from place to place. 311

Victorians Middle-class (chiefly Protestant) people living during the reign of Queen Victoria of England (1837–1901) who identified with British culture and who professed social values such as self-control, sexual restraint, and personal ambition. 427

Vigilantes People who seek to take the law into their own hands and punish or intimidate alleged criminals or persons who resist a certain social order (for example, white supremacy). 302

Wage slavery The idea that wage earners are exploited by employers as harshly as slaves are exploited by their owners. 316

War chest A fund accumulated to finance a war or earmarked to conduct some specific action or campaign. 195

War hawks Politicians who favor specific forms of military action as a tool of U.S. foreign policy. 245

War on drugs The global campaign spearheaded by the federal government to eliminate the production of illegal drugs and their importation into the United States, and its domestic counterpart in which drug violations are treated harshly by the legal and criminal justice system. 658

Watergate The Washington, D.C., hotel-office complex where agents of President Nixon's reelection campaign broke into Democratic Party headquarters in 1972. Nixon helped cover up the break-in, and the subsequent political scandal was called "Watergate." 617

Welfare reform The legislative campaign in the 1960s through the 1990s to abolish Aid to Families with Dependent Children in favor of a program that sets limits on the amount of time a poor family can receive government aid (culminating in the Temporary Aid to Needy Families Act of 1996). 635

Welfare state A nation in which the government provides a "safety net" of entitlements and benefits for citizens unable to economically provide for themselves. 510

Wildcat banks Small banks that make loans unsupervised by the state or other financial institutions. 267

Wobblies Members of the Industrial Workers of the World (IWW), a radical labor union formed in 1905. 460

Yellow journalism Newspaper articles, images, and editorials that exploit, distort, or exaggerate the news in order to inflame public opinion. 437

Yeoman A farmer who owns a modest amount of land (but no slaves). 123

Yiddish A language derived largely from German spoken mainly by Jews from eastern Europe. 509

Zoot suits Distinctive clothing in the 1940s worn largely by Mexican American and African American men, characterized by flared pants, long coats, and wide-brimmed hats. 543

Credits

Aldrich Rockefeller Folk Art Museum, The Colonial Williamsburg Foundation, Williamsburg, VA; **196 (Bottom):** © Natural History Museum, London.; **197:** © Natural History Museum, London.; **200:** University of Michigan, WIlliam L. Clements Library; **202:** Courtesy of Monroe County Historical Commission, Monroe, MI; **204:** George Davidson, "Attacked at Juan de Fuca Straits," c.1792. Oregon Historical Society, OrHi 85076; **210:** Susan Anne Livingston Ridley Sedgwick, "Elizabeth 'Mumbet' Freeman," 1811. Watercolor on ivory. Courtesy of the Massachusetts Historical Society (MHS image number 28); **212 (Both):** Courtesy, American Antiquarian Society; **213:** Collection of The New-York Historical Society, Accession #1903.12;

Chapter 9

Page 216: Gilbert Stuart, "Joseph Brant," 1786. Fenimore Art Museum, Cooperstown, New York. Photo by Richard Walker.; **217:** Collection of David J. and Janice L. Frent; **219:** Ralph Earl, "Elijah Boardman," 1789. The Metropolitan Museum of Art. Bequest of Susan W. Tyler, 1979. (1979.395). Photograph © The Metropolitan Museum of Art; **220:** Courtesy, American Canal and Transportation Center; **221:** Frederick Kemmelmeyer, "General George Washington Reviewing the Western Army at Fort Cumberland the 18th of October," c. 1794. Courtesy, Winterthur Museum (58.2780); **223:** Courtesy of The New Bedford Whaling Museum (#803); **225:** "The Old Plantation," c. 1795. Abby Aldrich Rockefeller Folk Art Museum, The Colonial Williamsburg Foundation, Williamsburg, VA; **228:** Courtesy of Museo de America, Madrid. Photo by Iris Engstrand; **230:** Shaker Village of Pleasant Hill, Harrodsburg, KY; **231:** Paul Rocheleau Photography; **232:** George James Warner, "Means for the Preservation of Liberty," speech delivered July 4, 1797.; **233:** Courtesy of The General Society of Mechanics and Tradesmen of the City of New York; **234:** James Peale, "The Artist and His Family," 1795. Oil on canvas, 31 1/4 x 32 3/4 in. (79.4 x 83.2 cm). Courtesy of the Pennsylvania Academy of the Fine Arts, Philadelphia (Acc. no.: 1922.1.1). Gift of John Frederick Lewis.

Part Four Opener

Page 240 (Top): William Clark, "Eulachon (T. Pacificus)," 1806, Voorhis Journal #2. William Clark Papers, Missouri Historical Society Archives; **240 (Bottom):** The American Numismatic Society; **241 (Top):** Courtesy of the Massachusetts Historical Society(MHS image number 31); **241 (Bottom):** Samuel J. Miller, "Frederick Douglass," 1847–52. Major Acquisitions Centennial Endowment, 1996.433. Photograph ©The Art Institute of Chicago

Chapter 10

Page 242: Charles Balthazar Fevret de Saint Memin, "Captain Meriwether Lewis," 1807. Collection of The New-York Historical Society, Neg. #51322; **244:** William Clark, "Eulachon (Thaleichthys Pacificus)," Entry of 25 February 1806. Voorhis Journal #2. Clark Family Collections. William Clark Papers. Missouri Historical Society, St. Louis; **245:** Courtesy, JPMorgan Chase Archives; **246:** Library of Congress; **247:** Courtesy, Dartmouth College Library; **249:** Library of Congress; **252:** Peter Turnley/CORBIS; **252:** Cherokee Women to Cherokee Council, May 2, 1817, Andrew Jackson Presidential Papers.; **253:** Unidentified Artist, "Benjamin Hawkins and the Creek Indians," ca. 1805. Oil on canvas, 35 7/8 x 49 7/8 inches. Greenville County Museum of Art, Greenville, SC, Gift of The Museum Association, Inc., with funds donated by Corporate Partners: Ernst and Young; Fluor Daniel; Director's Circle Members: Mr. and Mrs. Alester G. Furman III; Mr. and Mrs. M. Dexter Hagy; Thomas P. Hartness; Mr. and Mrs. E. Erwin Maddrey II; Mary M. Pearce; Mr. and Mrs. John Pellett, Jr.; Mr. W. Thomas Smith; Mr. and Mrs. Edward H. Stall; Eleanor and Irvine Welling; Museum Antiques Show, 1989, 1990, 1991, Elliott, Davis and Company, CPAs, sponsor; Collector's Group 1990, 1991; **254:** Museum of Spanish Colonial Art, Collections of the Spanish Colonial Arts Society, Inc., Santa Fe, NM. Bequest of Alan and Ann Vedder. Photo by Jack Parsons.; **257:** John Antrobus, "Plantation Burial," c.1860. The Historic New Orleans Collection, Accession no. 1960.46; **258:** Chicago History Museum, ICHi-22005;

Chapter 11

Page 261: John Gadsby Chapman, "Davy Crockett," date unknown. Harry Ransom Humanities Research Center, The University of Texas at Austin (neg. #65.349); **265 (Top):** William Henry Brown, "Hauling the Whole Weeks Picking," 1842. The Historic New Orleans Collection, Accession nos. 1975.93.1 & 2.; **265 (Bottom):** Collection of David J. and Janice L. Frent; **266 (Map):** Adapted from David J. Weber, *The Mexican Frontier, 1821–1846: The American Southwest Under Mexico.* Albuquerque: University of New Mexico Press, 1982. ; **269:** Library of Congress; **271 (Map):** Adapted from David J. Weber, *The Mexican Frontier, 1821-1846: The American Southwest Under Mexico.* Albuquerque: University of New Mexico Press, 1982.; **276:** From "José Agustin de Escudero Describes New Mexico as a Land of Opportunity, 1827" from *Three New Mexico Chronicles,* H. Bailey Carroll and Juan Villasana Haggard, trans. and ed. Albuquerque: Quivira Society, 1942.; **272:** Eric P. Newman Numismatic Education Society **273:** Richard T. Nowitz/CORBIS; **274 (Top):** The Newberry Library, Chicago; **274 (Bottom):** The American Numismatic Society, New York; **276:** © Kevin Fleming/CORBIS; **279:** Reproduced by permission of The Huntington Library, San Marino, California, RB 44872; **280:** Henry F. Darby, "The Reverend John Atwood and His Family," 1845. Oil on canvas, 183.2 x 244.47 cm

(72 1/8 x 96 1/4 in.). Gift of Maxim Karolik for the M. and M. Karolik Collection of American Paintings, 1815–1865, 62.269. Museum of Fine Arts, Boston. Reproduced with permission. Photograph ©2008 Museum of Fine Arts, Boston.

Chapter 12

Page 283: Minnesota Historical Society; **288 (Map):** Adapted from "Indian Removal from the Old Southwest" in Carnes and Garraty, *Mapping America's Past,* p. 86. © 1996 Arcada Editions Ltd.; **290:** Scotts Bluff National Monument, Nebraska. United States Department of the Interior, National Park Service; **293 (Top):** Courtesy of the Massachusetts Historical Society (MHS image number 31); **293 (Bottom):** Samuel J. Miller, "Frederick Douglass," 1847/52.Cased half-plate daguerreotype, plate: 14 x 10.6 cm; plate in closed case: 15.2 x 12 x 1.4 cm; plate in open case: 15.2 x 24 x 2 cm. Major Acquisitions Centennial Endowment, 1996.433. Reproduction, The Art Institute of Chicago. Photography © The Art Institute of Chicago.; **294:** The Library Company of Philadelphia; **295:** Unknown Artist, "La Amistad," c.1839. The New Haven Museum & Historical Society, New Haven, CT (1972.1); **296 (Top):** Photo courtesy of the Milwaukee County Historical Society; **296 (Bottom):** The Library Company of Philadelphia; **297:** The Newberry Library, Chicago; **298:** Albertus del Orient Browere, "Mrs. McCormick's General Store," 1844. Fenimore Art Museum, Cooperstown, New York.; **304:** John C. Calhoun, speech delivered January, 1848.; **305:** Charles Bird King (attr.), "John Caldwell Calhoun," ca. 1818–25.National Portrait Gallery, Smithsonian Institution/Art Resource, NY; **306:** Joseph Vollmering, "The U.S. Naval Expedition Under Comore. M.C. Perry, Ascending the Tuspan River," 1848. Toned lithograph (hand-colored), 15 1/4 x 22 3/8 inches. Amon Carter Museum, Fort Worth, Texas (1976.33.2)

Part Five Opener

Page 308 (Top): Michael Freeman/CORBIS; **308 (Bottom):** Harriet Beecher Stowe Center, Hartford, CT; **309 (Top):** Antique Textile Resource, Bethesda MD; **309 (Bottom):** William T. Garrell Foundry, San Francisco, "The Last Spike." The Iris & B. Gerald Cantor Center for Visual Arts at Stanford University (1998.115). Gift of David Hewes

Chapter 13

Page 310: Courtesy of the California History Room, California State Library, Sacramento, California. Mines & Mining: Gold: Scenes from Dag. #3 "Head of Auburn Ravine," 1852 (Neg. #912).; **311:** Michael Freeman/CORBIS; **312:** © DLM - Ledermuseum Offenbach ; **315:** American Textile History Museum, Lowell, Massachusetts; **316:** George Caleb Bingham, "Raftsmen Playing Cards," 1847. The Saint Louis Art Museum. Bequest of Ezra H. Linley by exchange.; **318:** George Howe, "The Endowments, Position, and Education of Woman," an address delivered July 23, 1850.;**319:** Courtesy of the Georgia Historical Society, Savannah, Georgia. D.M. Wright Papers, #1277, Box 36, Folder 286; **320:** Bettmann/CORBIS; **321:** Collection of David J. and Janice L. Frent;**326:** Harriet Beecher Stowe Center, Hartford, CT; **329 (Both):** Library of Congress; **330:** The Ohio Historical Society

Chapter 14

Page 333: Chicago History Museum, ICHi-22172; **337:** The Museum of the Confederacy, Richmond, Virginia. Photography by Katherine Wetzel; **338:** Letter from John B. Spiece to Confederate Attorney General, December 4, 1861.; **339:** Library of Congress; **341 (Top):** Carl G. von Iwonski, "Block House, New Braunfels." Yanaguana Society Collection. Daughters of the Republic of Texas Library, CT96.8; **341 (Bottom):** Western History Collections, University of Oklahoma Library; **342 (Top):** Collection of The New-York Historical Society, Accession #41526; **342 (Bottom Left):** Library of Congress; **342 (Bottom Right):** Library of Congress; **343 (Left):** Library of Congress; **343 (Right):** Courtesy National Archives; **344:** Library of Congress; **345:** The Museum of the Confederacy, Richmond Virginia; **347:** Library of Congress; **351:** Image, Courtesy Colorado Historical Society (WPA-834; 10025492) All Rights Reserved; **353 (Map):** Adapted from *The Atlas of African-American History and Politics: From Slave Trade to Modern Times* by Arwin D. Smallwood with Jeffrey M. Elliot. © McGraw-Hill, 1998. By permission of The McGraw-Hill Companies.; **354:** The National Park Service

Chapter 15

Page 356: Courtesy of the Georgia Historical Society, William Wilson Collection; **359:** CORBIS; **360:** Antique Textile Resource, Bethesda MD; **361:** Library of Congress; **362:** Photo by H.P. Moore. Collection of The New-York Historical Society, Neg. #37497; **366:** Schomburg Center for Research in Black Culture, Art and Artifacts Division, The New York Public Library/Art Resource, NY; **368:** William T. Garrell Foundry, San Francisco, "The Last Spike." The Iris & B. Gerald Cantor Center for Visual Arts at Stanford University (1998.115). Gift of David Hewes; **369:** Robert Benecke, photographer. DeGolyer Library, Southern Methodist University, Dallas, Texas, Ag1982.86.60; **370:** Union Pacific Museum; **372 (Table):** From *Americans and Their Forests: A Historical Review* by; Michael Williams. Copyright © 1989 by Cambridge University Press. Reprinted by permission of Cambridge University Press.; **375:** Wisconsin Historical Society, WHi (D32) 821; **377:** *Harpers Weekly,* Sept. 16, 1871

Index